Zimbabwe
Mozambique
Botswana
Namibia
Windhoek
Gaborone
Maputo
Limpopo
Polokwane (Pietersburg)
Mbombela (Nelspruit)
Mpumalanga
Mbabane
Eswatini
Soshanguve
Pretoria
Gauteng
Soweto
Johannesburg
Evaton
Mahikeng (Mafikeng)
North West
Kimberley
Free State
Bloemfontein
Maseru
Lesotho
KwaZulu-Natal
Pietermaritzburg
Durban
Drakensberge
Indian Ocean
Springbok
Northern Cape
South Africa
Eastern Cape
Bhisho
Gqeberha (Port Elizabeth)
Western Cape
Cape Town
Table Mountain
Cape of Good Hope
Cape Agulhas
South Atlantic Ocean
0 250 miles
0 250 km
Capital cities of South Africa
Capital cities of states and provinces
Important big cities
W0349073
6011KX © Westermann

westermann

On Track

Englisch für Gymnasien

6

von:
David Baker
Annie Cornford
Jon Hird
Claudia Maria Hugo
Fiona MacKenzie
Patricia Wedler
Story von Marcus Sedgwick mit
Illustrationen von Pete Williamson

herausgegeben von:
Helga Holtkamp

Unter Mitarbeit von: Udo Diekmann, Christine House
Beratung durch: Alexa Bradbury (Paderborn), Carolin Ihle (Stuttgart),
Janina Klösters (Essen), Jürgen Kurtz (Dortmund), Juliane Lobischer (Berlin)

Druck A[1] / Jahr 2024
Alle Drucke der Serie A sind inhaltlich unverändert.

Umschlaggestaltung: Detlef Möller, Paderborn
Coverfoto vorne: © SergeBertasiusPhotography / Shutterstock.com. Edinburgh city centre at night
Coverfoto hinten: © Molchanov, Dmitry / Shutterstock.com
Druck und Bindung: Westermann Druck GmbH, Georg-Westermann-Allee 66, 38104 Braunschweig

ISBN 978-3-14-**040326**-9

How to use this book

On Track 6 starts with a *Welcome* double-page spread. There are three regular workshops and one extra workshop on projects and skills. Each regular workshop has three parts. Parts one and two revise the grammar you have learned in previous books, and part three provides more opportunities to check your knowledge and for practice and revision.

Symbols in *On Track 6*

audio	14	Listen to a dialogue, a text, a song or a story.
video	2	Watch a video.
partner work		Work with a partner.
group work		Work with two or more partners.
whole class work		Work with the class.
bus stop	BUS	Work with a new partner.
mingling		Go around the classroom and ask questions.
placemat		Think about a topic and share your ideas in groups.
First track, On track, Fast track		Do the First track, On track and Fast track exercises.
Extra track	+	Do the extra exercise.
step 1, 2, 3, …	S1	Activities with this symbol help you with a more complex task – step by step.
grammar	→ G2	There is more information about this grammar point in the *Appendix*.

Vocabulary in *On Track 6*

In *On Track 6* you will encounter many original and authentic texts from all kinds of sources: from books, newspaper and website articles, videos and podcasts. These text types contain some specialized vocabulary that you do not have to learn to use actively, but need to know to understand the text. As in previous volumes, in *On Track 6* we have put them in grey in the *Appendix*. We have also added words in grey that are similar in German and English (but not false friends). However, all the words and phrases can be found in the two dictionaries at the end of the book.

Grammar revision in *On Track 6*

Eight main grammar topics are revised and practised in *On Track 6*. For each topic, there is an explanatory video as well as a cross reference to the Appendix.

How to use the webcodes

All the *On Track* audio and video material that you need in class or for homework is here: www.westermann.de/webcodes. You can listen and watch online or download everything. Type in the code for the workshop (for example **WES-40326-001**) without the @, click 'Aufrufen' and you will find the page for *Workshop 1*.

These are the webcodes in *On Track 6*:

Welcome:	@ WES-40326-000	Workshop 2:	@ WES-40326-002	Workshop 4:	@ WES-40326-004
Workshop 1:	@ WES-40326-001	Workshop 3:	@ WES-40326-003		

Contents

What about us?

Welcome to year 10. In *On Track 6*, we will be looking at such diverse places as India, South Africa and Canada. We will be considering contemporary issues like the effects of colonialism, political activism, conservation and cultural identity, and what all these topics mean for you today.

1 **a** Discuss which topic(s) each of the photos could be connected to. Decide on a topic that most interests your group. Brainstorm what you already know about it. Make notes and prepare and give a two-minute talk about the topic of your choice.

A

B

C

D

b Present your photo in class and give a short talk about it.

2 a Read the introduction to a podcast and watch the video that is mentioned.

Hello and welcome to *Four Corners*, a new series of podcasts which will take you around the world. We'll be looking at a range of controversial topics to see what you already know and how you feel about these issues, and, most importantly, how they impact on us, the teenagers of today. Let's start with a song by Pink which many of you know – *What about us?* Then we'll hear what some young people have to say about it. So, first watch the video, check out the lyrics and enjoy!

b Now listen to the second part of the podcast, in which three young people voice their opinions. Then do the tasks.

1 State the aspect of the video that each person talks about.
2 Explain what is meant by 'you sold us down the river'. And what does 'all the broken happy ever afters' mean?
3 Discuss which reaction to the song is most like or unlike your own and give your reasons.
4 Record your own response to *What about us?* as part of the podcast. Mention any other songs you know that deal with similar issues.

India

1 2 Do the quiz to see how much you already know about India. Then listen to the podcast and check your answers.

1 India ... in the world.
A is the biggest country
B is the largest democracy
C has the biggest population

2 India's currency is the ...
A riyal.
B rupee.
C lira.

3 India's main religion is ...
A Buddhism.
B Hinduism.
C Islam.

4 Which Indian festival is associated with colours?
A Diwali
B Holi
C Onam

5 Which Indian city is known as the Silicon Valley of India?
A Mumbai
B New Delhi
C Bengaluru

6 The Hindi film industry is known as …
A Bollywood.
B Hindiwood.
C Indiwood.

7 The most popular sport in India is …
A badminton.
B handball.
C cricket.

8 In the context of India, Partition describes …
A the division of British India into India and Pakistan.
B a system dividing people into social classes, or castes.
C splitting the country into small parts.

2 Each group chooses one of the topics covered in the podcast and does some research for a short talk. After the talks, the class will have an overview of life in India today as well as its history.

YOUR TRACK

After this workshop you will be able to:
- talk about India then and now.
- discuss the role of a key figure.
- discuss activism using arguments and counterarguments.
- understand comments on political engagement.
- write a persuasive text. (Workshop task)

India and the British

CULTURE CORNER

The British Empire

The topic of the British Empire continues to divide Britons: many are ashamed of it, but others remember it with pride.
British actions clearly benefitted the British rulers at the time, but historians disagree on the benefits to India. Its global trade was increased, though indigenous economies were ruined. Education in the English language has helped modern India's boom in technological skills, but decreased the importance of its native languages.

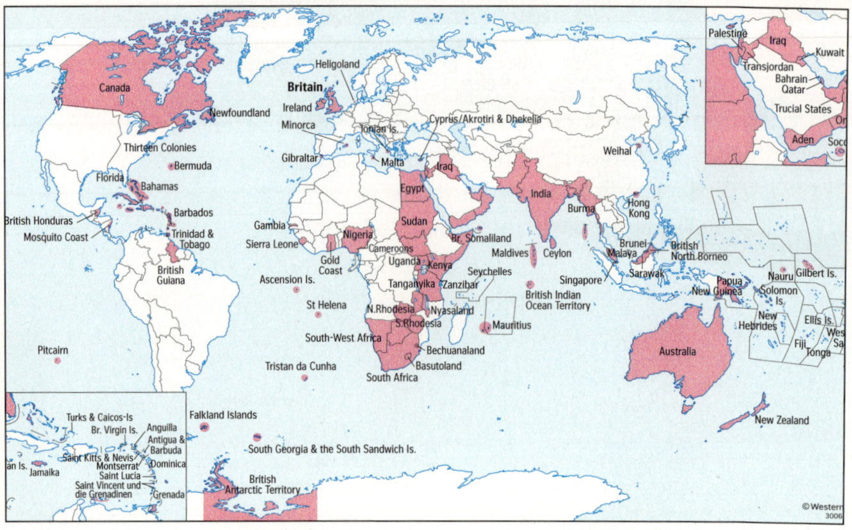

1 For good or ill?

a Read the text and answer the questions.

1. What do you understand by the expression 'the jewel in the crown'?
2. What was the reaction of the first Britons who visited India?
3. What impression did the British make on the Indian people?
4. Which phrase describes the change that happened?

2 **b** Watch the video, then answer the two questions at the end of the text in **a**.

The British Empire coloured huge areas of the world map pink. But India was the grandest, the richest and the most important territory it came to control and has often been described as 'the jewel in the crown'. In the eighteenth century, the Red Fort in Delhi was the home of India's ruling dynasty. The first British visitors were awestruck by what they found. It was clear that this was an advanced civilization. The Indians regarded the arriving British as barbarians, but by the mid-eighteenth century the balance of power had shifted decisively in favour of the British who remained in India for around two hundred years until India was finally granted independence on 15 August 1947. On that day, the first Prime Minister, Jawaharlai Nehru, raised the Indian flag at the main gate of Red Fort, a tradition which still takes place every year on Independence Day.
But how was the British Empire able to assert control over India and how did India finally succeed in gaining independence?

CULTURE CORNER

Partition of India

British rule over India finally ended at midnight on 14 – 15 August 1947 when the country was divided in two. A mainly Muslim nation, Pakistan, was created to separate the large Muslim minority from the Hindu majority.

3 Words and phrases

the 'jewel in the crown'	the most valuable, important or admired among others of its kind
to assert control	to win control over a certain area or territory
partition	the action or state of dividing or being divided into parts
refugee camp	a place which provides protection and assistance to people who had to flee their homes due to war, persecution or violence

→ Workbook, pages 6/7

2 **Memories of Partition.** Families whose lives have been shaped by Partition look back at the traumatic events of 1947 and the impact they had. With a partner, each read one text, then do the tasks below.

Text A

I was living in Amritsar, and I was nearly seven years old when Partition happened in 1947. My dad worked in the police force, and so we were definitely not poor. But it was a worrying time, as the pressures were growing, and our city had started to become unrecognizable. On that August night, our Hindu neighbour came to our door and told us to be very careful. He said that angry Hindu crowds were out to kill Muslims. Luckily, we were able to hide in his house. He risked everything when he was questioned, denying that he knew anything at all about us. After that, it was decided that we should leave Amritsar and head for Pakistan. The bus journey that followed was one of the most frightening experiences of my whole life. It was not possible to take anything with us: our house and all our belongings were left behind – all our friends, too. Over seventy years later, I am Pakistani now and proud of it, but I will never be able to return to the place of my birth. That makes me very sad.

Text B

When I was four in 1947, my family escaped to Amritsar. That night the Muslim mob tried to burn down our house. As Hindus, we had close friendships with our neighbours, many of them Muslims. We couldn't believe that overnight they had become enemies. We later heard that one man had not turned against us but had been outside, protecting our house all night. My father worked for an Englishman called Croft. On August 14, he went to work as usual, but was shocked to see the streets were strewn with dead bodies and many homes had been burnt down. Mr Croft was very upset by my father's account and sent a car to our house. We filled a chest with personal belongings but to make room for another family, we had to leave the chest behind. We had nothing, but the vehicle was packed tight with people. We drove to a refugee camp in Lahore. Later, a convoy of soldiers took us to the Indian side of the partition line – a line that had not existed twenty-four hours before.

1. Outline the memories of that night that the writer of your text has.
2. Comment on the fact that Muslim and Hindu friends helped each other.
3. Compare the writers' most significant memories of Partition.

3 **India's Independence Day**

a Watch the video or look at **G 2**. Explain the use of the active and passive in the 'Culture corner' on **page 14**.

b Complete an old man's memories with the correct form of the verbs in the box.

burn down ■ complete ■ divide ■ hear ■ take ■ tell

It was such a frightening time. While we were asleep, our school [1] by the mob. We had no idea who did it or why. We woke to find our country [2] without warning. That morning, we [3] by train from Agra to the border. The track stopped, so the rest of the journey [4] on camels. Our mother was terrified as explosions could [5] all around us. It is a story that [6] many times since that night in 1947.

»» page 36

4 **YOUR TURN: Different perspectives**

a Listen to a *Four Corners* interview with young British Indians and Pakistanis about their identity. Each choose one country and note down what 'your' teenagers say about the history of their country and life today.

b Research any points you find particularly interesting. Then share your information with your partner.

c Write a short text to present to the class.

Practice: A book about India

1 **GET STARTED!** What is a book review? Note down your ideas, then discuss them.

2 ***The White Tiger***

a What do you think *The White Tiger* is about?

> Adiga shows us a part of India that we seldom hear about: its underbelly.

> Welcome to an India where well-paid call centre workers walk the same pavements as the homeless who burn rubbish on the streets to keep warm.

> *What I've tried to do is write a novel from the point of view of someone at the bottom in India and that is an entirely different way of looking at the world from the way a middle-class person would look at the world and it tends to be a much harsher, more brutal view of life.* A. Adiga

b Complete this review with the correct form of the verbs. What does 'the Light and the Darkness' refer to?

> award ■ narrate ■ portray ■ promote ■ publish ■ reveal ■ set ■ take

The White Tiger [1] in 2008 and is Aravind Adiga's first novel. It [2] the prestigious Man Booker Prize. It [3] in India and [4] by a man named Balram Halwai, an entrepreneur in Bangalore. In the novel, his life [5] through seven letters. Balram was born in a region where the people live in extreme poverty. He [6] out of school early, nevertheless with a lot of initiative, he [7] to the job of first driver for a rich man in Delhi. It [8] that Balram has committed a terrible crime, enabling him to become wealthy enough to start his own business. In his letters, Balram describes how India got divided into two countries, the Light and the Darkness.

»» page 36

3 **READING FOCUS: A thing or two about caste**

a Read about Balram Halwai and his older brother Kishan and check any unknown words.

Halwai, my name, means "sweet-maker". That's my caste – my destiny. Everyone in the Darkness who hears that name knows all about me at once. That's why Kishan and I kept getting jobs at sweetshops wherever we went. The owner thought, *Ah, they're Halwais, making sweets and tea is in their blood.*

But if we were Halwais, then why was my father not making sweets but pulling a rickshaw? Why did I grow up breaking coals and wiping tables, instead of eating *gulab jamuns* and sweet pastries [...]? Why was I lean and dark and cunning, and not fat and creamy-skinned and smiling, like a boy raised on sweets would be?

See, this country, in its days of greatness, when it was the richest nation on earth, was like a zoo. A clean, well-kept, orderly zoo. Everyone in his place, everyone happy. Goldsmiths here. Cowherds here. Landlords there. The man called a Halwai made sweets. The man called a cowherd tended cows. The untouchable cleaned faeces. [...]

And then, thanks to all those politicians in Delhi, on the fifteenth of August 1947 – the day the British left – the cages had been let open; and the animals had attacked and ripped each other apart and jungle law replaced zoo law. Those that were the most ferocious, the hungriest, had eaten everyone else up, and grown big bellies. That was all that counted now, the size of your belly. [...] My father's father must have been a real Halwai, a sweet-maker, but when he inherited the shop, a member of some other caste must have stolen it from him with the help of the police. My father had not had the belly to fight back. That's why he had fallen all the way to the mud, to the level of a rickshaw-puller. That's why I was cheated of my destiny to be fat, and creamy-skinned, and smiling.

To sum up – in the old days there were one thousand castes and destinies in India. These days, there are just two castes: Men with Big Bellies, and Men with Small Bellies. And only two destinies: eat – or get eaten up.

from *The White Tiger* by Aravind Adiga. New York: Free Press, 2008, pp. 53 f.

Words and phrases

caste	a fixed social group or class into which individuals are born
rickshaw	a small vehicle with two wheels, pulled by one person
gulab jamuns	a sweet Indian dessert made with flour and rose water
jungle law	a situation with no laws or rules
ferocious	frightening and violent

→ Workbook, pages 8 – 10

b Read the text again and do the tasks.

1. Describe India's caste system.
2. Explain how Adiga tells this story.
3. Illustrate the use of satire in Balram's description of India as a zoo.
4. Show how the language he uses changes when he describes the law of the jungle.
5. Explain if his final conclusion is realistic, pessimistic or cynical. Give your reasons.

TIP

We can use the passive with *get* to talk about something unexpected, unwanted or negative.
India ***got divided*** *into two different countries.*

4 **Eat or get eaten.** Complete the sentences with a form of *get* and the verbs in brackets.

1. In this extract, India ___ to a 'clean, well-kept orderly zoo'. (*compare*)
2. Everyone ___ a place in the 'zoo' depending on the caste they are born into. (*give*)
3. On 15 August 1947, the animals escaped and 'zoo law' ___ by 'jungle law'. (*replace*)
4. Helped by this metaphor, the reader is quickly able to imagine just how many 'animals' ___ in the aftermath. (*kill*)
5. Halwai's grandfather's sweet shop ___ by someone from a higher caste and the protagonist ___ of his destiny. (*steal, cheat*)
6. Halwai concludes that the many castes and destinies of the old days have been reduced to just two – to eat or ___. (*eat*)

5 **How to write a fiction review**

a Read the TIP box and an online review of *The White Tiger*. Which points are covered?

TIP

When writing a review, remember these points.
- Attract your reader's attention and make clear what the aim of your review is.
- Who is the main protagonist in the story?
- When and where does it take place and what is it about (no spoilers here!)?
- What are the central themes?
- Mention what you liked and did not like.
- Who would you recommend it to?

NEWS | CALENDAR | CONTACTS | BLOG | GALLERY

If you have a weak stomach, *The White Tiger* is not a book for you! However, if like me you are fascinated by India, you should read this book to gain a deeper understanding of modern life there. The story stresses the relevance of India's past to important aspects of the country today. Balram Halwai is the narrator of the novel and it is through his eyes that we see two contrasting settings: from rural poverty to urban wealth. The main theme is the difference between the rich and the poor. Although Balram's descriptions of the conditions and injustices poor Indians suffer are very harsh, I loved the way he often makes these situations humorous. Another strong theme is corruption, and here too, despite the seriousness of the message, the writing is clever and witty enough to make you want to laugh out loud. Animals are also a significant theme and many of the characters are given animal names, which I found confusing and unhelpful, though the metaphor of the Rooster Coop was very powerful.

b Discuss with a partner if you would like to read *The White Tiger* and why / why not.

6 **YOUR CHOICE: A review.** Choose task **A** or **B**, then do a gallery walk and choose a book you would like to read.

A Find a review of an Indian book you think would interest your classmates. Add a 'Words and phrases' section to the review.

B Choose a book you enjoyed and write a review.

Passive resistance

1 Mahatma Gandhi

a The title 'Mahatma' means 'great soul' in Sanskrit. The violent death of a great soul, one of India's most loved heroes, shocked the world in 1948. Read and summarize the article.

b How would Gandhi's death be reported today? Write a breaking news flash or a social media post. Compare your ideas in class.

2 In the news

a Find examples of the passive in the article and look at the TIP box. Explain why journalists often use passive forms to report an incident.

TIP

- We can use the structure *It* … with a passive reporting verb: *It is alleged that* … .
- We can also use a subject with a passive verb + infinitive: *He was said to be* … .
- If we wish to say who was responsible for the action, we use *by*: *Gandhi is thought to have been shot by a religious fanatic.*

b Rewrite these sentences as if you were the journalist. Begin with the words given.

1. People considered that Gandhi was a highly principled lawyer. *Gandhi* …
2. Activists from other empires thought he was an inspiration. *He* …
3. Everyone knew that his values were simple, based on traditional Hindu beliefs. *It* …
4. Some believed his sympathy for Muslims was a political error. *His* …
5. Critics now think Gandhi's views were racist. *Gandhi's* …

Sat 31 Jan 1948 13.39 GMT
Assassination of Mr Gandhi

Mohandas (Mahatma) Gandhi has been assassinated at a prayer meeting in New Delhi. It is alleged that the assassin is a Hindu extremist. When news that Gandhi had been shot by a religious fanatic was announced earlier today, crowds of several thousands immediately gathered. The mood of the people appears to be one of stunned sorrow.

Mahatma Gandhi is considered by many historians to be the Father of the Nation in India. Born there in 1869 as Mohandas Gandhi, he came to Britain to study law. Once qualified, he joined an Indian law firm in South Africa, where he stayed until 1914. During his time there, he organized fellow Indians to passively resist laws that discriminated against them. He developed the principle of non-violent resistance which was described as a positive interaction between two parties with the aim of reconciliation.

In 1914, he returned to India where he began to train people in civil disobedience tactics. He is thought to have become India's strongest champion for civil rights through his belief in Satyagraha or 'Truth Force'. He organized the Freedom Movement as resistance against unpopular British laws and was repeatedly imprisoned. Gandhi also worked hard to improve the status of the caste known as the untouchables, as well as trying to create closer bonds between Hindus and Muslims. He was involved in the negotiations that led to Independence last year, but was said to be appalled at the violence that broke out.

Repercussions of the assassination are certain to be widespread and intense throughout India and Pakistan. It may produce that change of heart for which Gandhi laboured and gave his life.

6 Words and phrases

to assassinate	to murder an important or famous person, often for political reasons
extremist	a person who has extreme political or religious views
sorrow	a feeling of deep distress and sadness
non-violent resistance	a peaceful method of social and political action to challenge governments
reconciliation	the restoration of friendly relationships
to be appalled	to have a strong feeling of shock or disapproval

→ Workbook, pages 11/12

3 Still a hero?

a There are arguments for and against honouring important people from the past. Read this article and explain the final quote? How relevant is it today?

Gandhi's grandson attends statue unveiling in London [...]

In a moving ceremony attended by Gandhi's grandson, Shri Gopalkrishna Gandhi, a statue of Mahatma Gandhi has been unveiled to mark the 100th anniversary of his return to India to begin the fight for independence from British rule.

The prime minister David Cameron was joined at the ceremony by India's finance minister, Arun Jaitley. [...] Cameron described Gandhi as 'one of the most towering figures in the history of world politics'. He said that by putting Gandhi in that famous square, we were giving him an eternal home in our country. He added that the statue celebrated the incredibly special friendship between the world's oldest democracy and its largest.

After unveiling the statue opposite the Palace of Westminster, Jaitley reiterated Cameron's comments by pointing out that the statue marked an important, historic moment celebrating the strong bond between their two nations. He went on to say that India and the UK shared the same values and were a partnership of equals. He described the lasting friendship between the two countries as 'just one of many legacies left by Gandhi'. [...]

Inspiration for the sculpture was a 1931 photo of Gandhi at No 10 Downing Street. Cameron reminisced about Gandhi's visit to London saying how he had gone to see King George V bare-chested in his dhoti, carrying his symbolic stick. When later asked whether he had felt under-dressed, Gandhi had replied: 'The King is dressed for both of us'.[...] Cameron concluded by saying that many of Gandhi's teachings remained as potent today as when he had first said them, quoting his famous words: 'Be the change that you want to see in the world'.

Source [abbreviated and adapted]: Chris Johnston, "New Gandhi statue unveiled in London's Parliament Square", © Guardian News & Media Ltd 2023, 14 March 2015, https://www.theguardian.com/world/2015/mar/14/new-gandhi-statue-unveiled-in-londons-parliament-square [20.04.2023]

4

b Watch the video or look at **G 3**. Then report these statements made by the British prime minister at the ceremony.

1 I want to thank all those who have supported the Gandhi Statue Memorial Trust in making this sculpture possible.
2 The British sculptor Philip Jackson, has done an incredible job.
3 It was in London as a young man that Gandhi first learned to petition, to draft letters and to make speeches.
4 This statue celebrates the universal power of Gandhi's message.
5 I hope we can all be blessed with the wisdom of Gandhi today, tomorrow and for generations to come.

TIP

Giving arguments and counterarguments.
Opponents of this idea maintain that …
Those who disagree with these ideas may say …
They claim that … since …
Some people may (rightly) argue / disagree with …
However, to be fair …
But to be fair, …
On the one hand …, the other hand, …
They have a point, and yet …
To a certain extent they are right.
Despite the fact that …

4 YOUR TURN: We don't need another hero

a THINK: How does Germany honour its heroes? Think of statues you know of, or streets and buildings named after famous people. Who are they and where can you find them?

b PAIR: Present 'your heroes' to each other.

c SHARE: Discuss your ideas with others. Did anyone choose the same hero as you?

PART 1 PART 2 PART 3

Practice: You're not alone

1 **GET STARTED!** Like Gandhi, many activists today believe in non-violent resistance. Have you ever supported a campaign that was important to you? If so, explain what you did and why. If not, say why you would in the future, or why not.

TIP

In persuasive speech or writing, aim to:
- keep your message simple,
- use repetition to get your message across,
- show you really believe in what you're saying and
- use emotive but not hostile language.

2 Youth activism

a Read Deepak's blog about political engagement. Who is he addressing and why do you think he wrote it? Find sentences that show he has used the tips above.

Don't wait or it'll be too late!

The time for action is now. We are Gen Z and we have the most to lose from the negative effects of climate change. Greta Thunberg once told her audience that although they said they loved their children, they were stealing their future. She accused world leaders of immaturity and stated that they were leaving the crisis for young people to deal with.

How true – so we have to act! Remember, youth activism is not new. School strikes were happening over sixty years ago. We face a much tougher challenge today. Getting political action on climate change seems an impossible task.

But don't forget, we have a voice. Multinational companies know that Gen Z has an enormous spending power, and recent campaigns by young activists have already succeeded in making changes. Companies need to understand how we use social media to interact with their products and services. By hiring Gen Z advisors, companies want to connect with us. It's up to us to act or it will be too late.

b Write down Deepak's main arguments and how he supports each one. Which arguments could you use to persuade a friend to join you in a campaign?

3 Reporting

a Say how Deepak reports Greta's comments in his blog.

b Report more of Deepak's comments with the reporting verbs in the box.

believe ■ claim ■ insist ■ point out ■ say ■ warn

1 History has important examples of youth activism.
2 Companies are learning the importance of youth spending power.
3 Young people's voices have never been so clear.
4 School strikes make a massive impact.
5 Students have realized their political power.
6 Young people will never forgive the older generation.

» page 36

c Do you agree with him or not? Discuss with a partner and give your reasons.

Words and phrases

Gen Z	people born in the late 1990s and early 2000s
to be disengaged	to become emotionally separated from sth.
Islamophobia	the fear or hate of, or prejudice against the religion of Islam or Muslims
hostility	aggressive or unfriendly behaviour towards sb.

→ Workbook, pages 13 – 15

4 Britain's Greta

a Bella Lack is a young environmentalist and campaigner. Watch a news clip and answer the questions.

1. What do you think Bella wants to convey in her poem 'If Earth Could Speak'?
2. How does she use social media?
3. What is her attitude to social media?

b Now watch a video of Bella when she was 16 and a youth ambassador for Born Free. Make notes on how her passion began.

c How did Bella's words make you feel? Watch again and note down three statements she made that had the most impact on you.

d Discuss the statements you chose and explain their impact on you. Say if you share Bella's hopes and fears about the future of our planet.

5 Islamophobia

a Many young Muslims in Britain have another perspective on activism. Read the text and explain the main conclusion of the research.

b The underlined words in the text have a positive or a negative connotation and some words can have both. Add them to the diagram. Then compare with a partner.

Muslim youths are often seen as politically disengaged or potentially involved in extreme activism. […] That is why we spoke to some young Scottish Muslims about how they engage with political debates and stand up for their rights in a positive way. […] These young people are challenging the idea that they are a threat, or not interested. Instead, they are eager to engage.

However, […] some young Muslims face specific challenges that have the potential to put them off politics. Everyday experiences of Islamophobia and racism make public and political participation especially challenging. For some young Muslims, there is a fear that it could leave them open to racist hostility. Moreover, Islamophobia makes some anxious about appearing overly politicized.

Some young Muslim women felt that they had to deal with multiple prejudices, too, based not only on their religion but also their gender. Gender norms within communities and stereotypes of Muslim women – such as those associated with the hijab – were emphasized as potential barriers. But, despite this, we have found that young Muslims in Scotland, like many worldwide, are very keen to get involved in both local and global politics. […]

Source [abbreviated and adapted]: Peter Hopkins, Robin Finlay, "Young Muslims want to participate in politics – but prejudice and Islamophobia may be stoppingthem", The Conversation, 15 March 2017, https://theconversation.com/young-muslims-want-to-participate-in-politics-but-prejudice-and-islamophobia-may-be-stopping-them-73985 [16.11.2022]

6 SPEAKING FOCUS: A controversial topic

a Look at the TIP box, then choose a topic from the list and prepare a discussion.

- Animal conservation: an easy option for youth
- Youth activists: the do's and dont's of political action
- Extinction Rebellion is an important and justified movement
- Young people worldwide should get the vote at 16
- Racial prejudice is best tackled face on

TIP

- Negotiate your choice of topic with your partner: use persuasive language to decide.
- Discuss what you know and what you need to find out.
- Agree who finds arguments in favour and who against.
- Make sure you have arguments and counterarguments.

b Check you both have at least three points to make, and that you can defend them.

c Record or video your discussion for another pair. Listen to or watch each other's discussions, take notes, then give feedback.

Method coach: Recognizing text types

S1 **Identifying basic categories.** Read about four common text types and match the names in the box to the descriptions below.

Descriptive ■ Informative ■ Instructive ■ Persuasive

1 texts tell the reader how to do something: a recipe or how to install a new device. Such texts use verbs such as *must / must not* in direct language without unnecessary words. There are often diagrams or numbered points.

2 texts help the reader to picture what is being described: characters in a story or emotions in song lyrics. Such texts use adjectives, adverbs and comparisons, appealing to the reader's senses to describe how something sounds, feels, etc.

3 texts try to make the reader do something: an advert wanting to sell something or a letter from a charity asking for support. Such texts use emotive or amusing language, repetitions, exclamations, and rhetorical questions.

4 texts aim to advise or tell the reader about something: health advice on a notice board or information about an event on a website. Such texts use facts, giving information clearly and without repetition.

S2 **Communication purposes**

a Copy and complete the table below with the text types in the box. Order them according to their communicative aims.

b Discuss and explain your choices. Think of examples you've read to support them.

advert ■ blog ■ brochure ■ charity appeal ■ email ■ fictional story ■ graphic novel ■ information leaflet ■ letter ■ manual ■ newspaper or magazine article ■ recipe ■ review ■ song lyrics ■ summary ■ textbook

Inform	Instruct	Persuade	Describe
???	???	???	???

S3 **Where does it go?**

a Match each sentence to one of the four types.

1 The forest was thick with autumn leaves that crackled and spiralled away under her boots, which felt as heavy as her heart.
2 Line and grease the cake tin and pre-heat the oven to 160 degrees.
3 Don't miss this chance of a lifetime! A luxurious world cruise could be yours – why delay?
4 The figure approaching her was a tall thin man whose prominent cheek bones resembled the blades of a knife.
5 Separate the egg yolk from the white before mixing the dry ingredients.
6 Building works will continue to affect the upper school timetable.
7 Her lips moved in a silent prayer: could she dare to hope that he had come back for her?
8 Please avoid all construction areas and observe health and safety notices.
9 Relax on a sunny deck between thrilling trips to the world's most exciting cities – what's not to like?!
10 During the renovations, the science lab will be temporarily relocated to Block F.
11 One third of the flour can be replaced with ground almonds if preferred.
12 So why delay? Sign up today!

b Put the matching sentences together to make a mini-text for each text type.

c Choose two mini-texts and add a sentence to each. It can be in any position in the text.

d Read and listen to the new texts. Discuss which ones you think are the best and explain why.

→ Workbook, page 16

Workshop task: Writing different texts

S1 **The Taj Mahal.** Read the text and answer the questions.

1 What could the purpose of the text be?
2 Where might you find this text?
3 What two aspects of the Taj Mahal does the text not tell you about?

The Taj Mahal

The Taj Mahal is located on the right bank of the Yamuna River in a vast Mughal garden that encompasses nearly 17 hectares, in the Agra District in Uttar Pradesh. It was built by Mughal Emperor Shah Jahan in memory of his wife Mumtaz Mahal with construction starting in 1632 AD and completed in 1648 AD [...] the outer courtyard and its cloisters were added subsequently and completed in 1653 AD.

The tomb, mosque, guest house, main gate and the overall Taj Mahal complex have maintained the conditions of authenticity [...]. Although several important repairs and conservation work have been carried out since the British period in India, these have not compromised the original qualities of the buildings. Future conservation work will need to follow guidelines that ensure that qualities such as form and design continue to be preserved.

Source [abbreviated and adapted]: "Taj Mahal", UNESCO World Heritage Convention, https://whc.unesco.org/en/list/252/ [16.11.2022]

S2 **Jaz Hostel Agra.** Look at the layout and photo and read this text. Answer the questions.

1 What text type is it? How do you know?
2 What words are repeated most often and why?
3 How is the final paragraph different?
4 How does the last paragraph use emphasis?

Jaz Hostel Agra: your perfect location!

You will not find a better place to stay! Situated in Agra, less than 0.6 miles from the Taj Mahal, the Jaz Hostel Agra offers a restaurant, free parking, free bikes and a shared lounge. All rooms boast a kitchenette and a private bathroom.

Perfect facilities!

The accommodation provides free evening entertainment and room service. All rooms are fitted with air conditioning, a microwave, a fridge, a kettle, a shower, free toiletries and a desk. Guest rooms are equipped with a seating area.

Perfect for the whole family!

There is a children's playground. Bike hire and car hire are available. The area is popular for hiking and cycling. A business centre and vending machines with drinks and snacks are available at the hostel.

Perfect service: we speak your language!

'Great location, only a few minutes' walk to Taj. The staff were exceptionally friendly and helpful. We had a thoroughly enjoyable stay at this hotel and highly recommend it to anyone.'

S3 **A popular tourist site.** Prepare to write a short text about a popular tourist site.

- Decide on a place and think about how you might persuade someone to go there.
- Research the place you've chosen and find an appropriate photo.
- You will need a catchy title and an attractive photo.
- Swap your text with a partner and give each other feedback.

Slum life

1 The rich and the poor

A

B

C

a Match the photos of Bengaluru (formerly Bangalore) with the captions. Describe what the photos tell you about city life in India today.

1 City rubbish dumps – breed diseases
2 Bengaluru's booming IT sector
3 Slum kids provide income for families

b Choose one photo each and explain to your partner how it makes you feel.

2 A city starved of water

a Sunny, whose parents immigrated to England years ago, decided to check out his roots. Read part of his blog and answer the questions.

1 What do the residents have in common?
2 How do people get water in the city?
3 What's your reaction to the city of contrasts?

NEWS | CALENDAR | CONTACTS | BLOG | GALLERY

I decided to start my six-month stay by visiting Bengaluru. This meant adjusting to life in a very different culture. This is perhaps one of India's most globally visible cities, because of its reputation as India's Silicon Valley. Commercial buildings and malls with shining glass facades reinforce this city's image as a dynamic and booming metropolis. All that is true, but slums coexist alongside this image of prosperity, and the people who live here – rich and poor – face the problems of living in a city starved of water. Poor water supply is a legacy of colonial policies that failed to solve local problems.
In summer, it's not unusual to see public water taps on roadsides with hardly any water coming out. Everyone crowds around the tap, hoping to get some water before it runs out. People – usually women – are used to carrying enough water for several days. More privileged residents have tried to get water piped to their houses. But, even for them, interrupted water supply and rationing have always been a fact of daily life here. It's a high-tech city but there's no water – that's what amazes me.

7 **b** Watch the video or look at **G 4**. Then each read one paragraph of the blog again and find all the examples of gerunds or infinitives. Explain to each other why the forms are used.

c Complete Sunny's blog post (**page 25**) with the verbs from the box in the correct form.

be able to ■ combine ■ create ■ find ■ meet ■ plan ■ renew ■ solve

8 **Words and phrases**

slum	a very poor and crowded urban area
prosperity	the state of being successful and having a lot of money
underprivileged community	a community that has less money, education, etc. than other people in a society
cross-cultural	involving two or more different cultures

→ Workbook, pages 17/18

NEWS | CALENDAR | CONTACTS | BLOG | GALLERY

Governments have not succeeded in **1** an answer to Bengaluru's water problem. Nevertheless, some poor families today enjoy **2** access the water they need. This is thanks to local groups who managed **3** the old water tanks and wells that were closed. This was done by **4** local knowledge and innovative problem-solving. Some wells now produce about 65,000 litres of water per day, which really helps **5** residents' water demands. Big ideas have proved incapable of **6** Bengaluru's water problems since colonial times. But local, community-led plans have a good chance of **7** a strong, water-secure city: an important lesson for architects trying **8** better cities for the future.

»» page 36

3 Balaknama: 'voice of children'

a Listen to a podcast about an extraordinary newspaper in India to answer the questions.

1 Who is Lucy and what does she do?
2 What is Balaknama and why is it special?
3 Who are the 'batuni' reporters?
4 How many copies are published in total?

b What were your feelings when you heard about children living in stations?

c Discuss what current topics you would include in an article for an international newspaper.

4 Get real?

a What is a 'walking tour'? Have you ever done one – if so, where? What is your first reaction to the idea of a walking tour through the slums?

b Read about a tour to Dharavi, the biggest slum area of Mumbai. What is your opinion of slum tours after reading the brochure?

c And your hometown or city? Which places does the average tourist not usually see or visit?

Reality Tours and Travel is a responsible tour operator providing fun and authentic experiences around India. We invest 80% of our profits back into the communities we visit through our NGO Reality Gives. Our educational Dharavi Slum Tour shows visitors the industrial and residential areas of one of Asia's largest slums in the heart of Mumbai. Our tours aim to help to visitors to understand underprivileged communities better, so our guides are mostly locals. Our vision is a world where all tourism promotes cross-cultural understanding and local development.

Dharavi is an economic powerhouse in the middle of Mumbai. Through our educational walking tours, visitors experience a wide range of business activities from recycling to embroidery. As an industrial centre with many small-scale industries, Dharavi is home to over a million people from all over India. This diversity is apparent in the temples, mosques, churches and pagodas that stand side by side.

Our community centre funded through the profits from the tours is located in the residential area. Here you will learn about the programmes that our NGO Reality Gives offers the community and gain a nuanced understanding of life and work in Mumbai slums. Lunch with a local family will give them some extra income and you a further insight into life in Dharavi.

5 YOUR TURN: India: the rich and the poor

a THINK: Do some research for a talk entitled 'India: the rich and the poor'.

b PAIR: Exchange your notes, collect more information and find photos. Then prepare a talk.

c SHARE: Present your talks to the class.

Practice: Films about India

1 GET STARTED! Look at the two film posters and say which film looks more interesting.

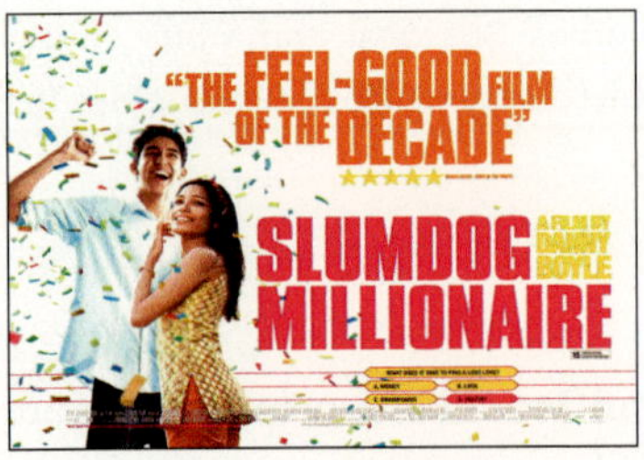

2 *Slumdog Millionaire*

a What information does the poster convey about this film? How does it attract interest without containing any spoilers?

b What do you think the film is about? If you've seen it, tell someone who hasn't.

c Read the critics' praise for the film. Discuss any new words and look them up.

"a soaring crowd-pleasing fantasy"	"a tale of eternal love"
"a cheerful hymn to life"	"explodes with narrative force"

3 A trailer

a Say what a trailer is and what it aims to do.

b Watch the trailer for *Slumdog Millionaire*. What more do you learn about the story? Would you want to watch the film? Why / Why not?

c Complete the review with the verbs from the box in the correct form. Which gave you a better insight into the film – the trailer or the review?

admit ■ answer ■ cheat ■ discover ■ enter ■ find ■ force ■ reunite ■ save ■ torture

The protagonist, Jamal, is an 18-year-old chai wallah, someone who prepares tea. Born in the slums of Mumbai, he works in a busy call centre. He decides [1] the *Who Wants To Be A Millionaire?* gameshow, which his childhood love, Latika, always watches. He is still in love with her, so he wants [2] her. Each question on the TV show mysteriously connects to his life experiences, so he manages [3] them all correctly. He becomes a national hero as people from the slums see one of their own beating the system and becoming rich and famous. The TV host suspects him of [4] in some way. The police watch a recording of the last show, hoping [5] how Jamal knows all the answers. They don't believe a chai wallah from the slums could answer such difficult questions, so they try [6] a confession of guilt out of him by [7] him. Jamal has a quiet confidence and a sense of his own destiny, which leads him to victory. He refuses [8] to doing anything wrong. Jamal and his brother Salim have a complicated relationship, but in a dramatic ending, instead of [9] himself as we might have expected, Salim helps Jamal [10] with Latika.

»» page 37

4 VIEWING FOCUS: *Lion*

a Watch the trailer for *Lion*. Have you seen the film and if so, did you enjoy it? If not, does this trailer make you want to see it? Why / Why not?

b Are the statements true or false? Correct the false statements.

1. Saroo is a child at the start of the trailer.
2. He begins to remember what happened in his early childhood.
3. As a small boy, Saroo gets separated from his big brother, Guddu.
4. The film is a true story based on a book.
5. He is determined to find the family that abandoned him.

Words and phrases

to beat a system	to achieve what one wants by breaking rules or by finding clever ways of working within them
to reassure	to make sb. feel less worried about sth.
to lower your guard	to relax and trust people
to grasp an opportunity	to take advantage of a good situation
to be astonished	to be very surprised and impressed

→ Workbook, pages 19 – 21

5 Reading between the lines

a Look at these extracts from *Lion* and read the TIP box. Then complete the mind map with information about Saroo.

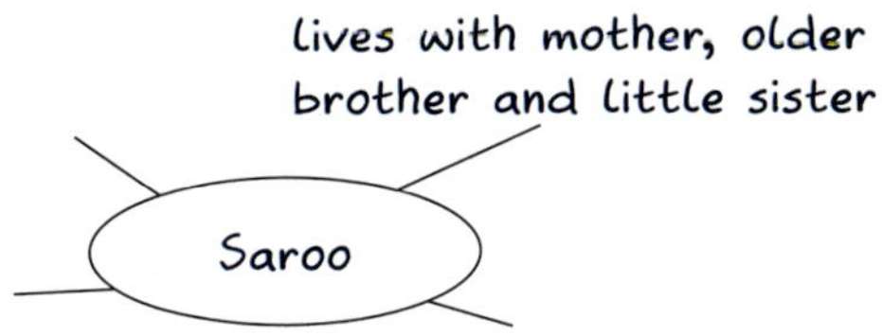

TIP

With **direct characterization**, the writer uses words to describe a character.
Indirect characterization is more subtle. The writer describes a character through their: actions, appearance, speech, thoughts and effect on others.

When I was growing up in Hobart, I had a map of India on my bedroom wall. My mother – my adoptive mother, Mum – had put it there to help me feel at home when I arrived from that country at the age of six to live with them, in 1987. She had to teach me what the map represented – I was completely uneducated and don't think I even knew what a map was, let alone the shape of India. Mum had decorated the house with Indian objects – there were some Hindu statues, brass ornaments and bells, and lots of little elephant figurines. I didn't know then that these weren't normal objects to have in an Australian house. She had also put some Indian printed fabric in my room, across the dresser, and a carved wooden puppet in a brightly coloured outfit. All these things were sort of familiar, even if I hadn't seen anything exactly like them before. Another adoptive parent might have made the decision that I was young enough to start my life in Australia with a clean slate and could be brought up without much reference to where I'd come from. But my skin colour would always have given away my origins, and anyway, she and my father chose to adopt a child from India for a reason. [...] Mum had such a dedicated belief in adoption and the authentic family that adoption created. I was worried about how my news would affect her, and I wanted to reassure her that of course they would always be my parents.

[...] I was drowning. Then I heard a splash nearby and found myself wrenched upwards, pulled to the surface and onto the steps, where I sat spluttering and coughing up murky water. I had been saved by a homeless old man who had jumped off the stone drain to reach me just in time and pluck me from the water. Then he silently made his way back up the steps and onto the riverbank, where I suppose he lived. Perhaps the kindness of that stranger lowered my guard, or perhaps I was just a five-year-old, but when I went back to swim in the river the next day, stupidly I let the rising tide and strong current surprise me again, and once more got into trouble. Amazingly, the same man rescued me – perhaps he'd kept an eye out when he saw me come back. This time, other people noticed what had happened, seeing the man helping me up onto the steps, where I hacked up more water. A crowd formed around us, and I understood enough to realise they were declaring that the gods had spared me, that it had not yet been my time to die. Maybe I felt overwhelmed by all the people pushing up close to stare at me, or just humiliated or annoyed with myself for having almost drowned a second time, but I leapt to my feet and ran away, as fast as I could. I went far along the back, until I couldn't run anymore, vowing to keep out of the river. So I don't think I ever thanked the homeless man, almost my guardian angel, for rescuing me, not once but twice.

But my experiences have undoubtedly shaped who I am today, providing me with an unshakable faith in the importance of family – however it is formed – and a belief in the goodness of people and the importance of grasping opportunities as they are presented. [...] I am astonished at the miraculous turns in my story – my mum's vision that led her to intercountry adoption, my Indian mother praying and seeing an image of me the day before we were reunited [...] It is sometimes difficult not to imagine some forces at work that are beyond my understanding.

from *Lion* by Saroo Brierley. London: Penguin, 2013, pp. 5 – 6, 48 – 49, 257

b Each write a short text about Saroo. Swap your ideas, then agree on a final version.

6 YOUR CHOICE: Reviewing a film or book.

Think about **A** a film you've watched or **B** a book you've read. Write a review of 150 – 180 words. Remember to use the present tense.

@ WES-40326-001

Traditional and modern cultures

1 *Four Corners* in Asia

12 **a** What do teenagers in India think of the tradition of arranged marriage? Listen to the *Four Corners* interview to find out.

b Now do these tasks.

1. Outline the opinion voiced in the interview which interests you most.
2. Explain what gender differences you noticed.
3. Compare the Indian teenagers' situation to your own.
4. Estimate how high the divorce rate for Indian arranged marriages is.

2 *(Un)arranged Marriage*

a Read an extract from *(Un)arranged Marriage* by Bali Rai about a teenager whose traditional Indian family believes in arranged marriages. Write down the names of the characters and say who they are.

Now, this Sunday, the old man button-holed me as I sat on the sofa, my eyes glued to the live football game on the TV. Liverpool were at home to Spurs and Liverpool had just missed a sitter. The game was really open, end-to-end stuff, but I could feel my dad and his bloodshot eyes glaring as I tried to keep my mind on the game.

'Manjit, I am talking to you.' His voice was super-calm, which was a pleasant surprise.

'Yes, Daddy-ji,' I replied, as Liverpool went past the Spurs midfield with ease. We were going to murder them. No problem.

'I have spoken to a friend of mine in India, about his daughter.' He paused for a moment. I think maybe he was waiting for me to say something. To react. But I just kept my eyes on the game and wondered what he was going to say next, about what he had agreed with his friend in India. I knew that it had to be about marriage because it had been exactly the same when he had told Harry.

[...]

Thing is, I was totally different to Harry. Totally. And there was no way I was going to say 'yes' to marrying some girl from India just by looking at a photo of her. No way. [...] I was hearing but not listening. I managed about five minutes before the old man's words started to cause my stomach to turn over. He was talking about *me*. And some *girl. From India*. He already had it all sorted out, just like it had been with Harry. All that remained was the wedding itself. She was six months older than me and coming over to England on a visitor's visa in July. Two months away!

'I have told her father that you will marry her after next summer, when you are both seventeen. If we leave it any longer, there will be too many questions from the immigration people. Once you are married, she will have the right to stay in this country and I will have my final daughter-in-law.'

from *(Un)arranged Marriage* by Bali Rai. London: Penguin, 2001, pp. 69, 70–71

b Do these tasks.

1. Discuss whose point of view the story is told from. Talk about the language used, e.g. style, choice of words, formal, colloquial, etc.
2. Outline how the writer uses characterization to describe a 'typical' sixteen-year-old. Find examples and write them down.

11 Words and phrases

to button-hole sb.	to stop sb. and make that person listen to you
daughter-in-law	the wife of a son or daughter
abusive father	a father who hurts his children physically or emotionally
to defy sb.	to refuse to obey sb.
to retaliate	to get back at sb.

TIP

Summarizing a fictional text
- Read the extract, keeping in mind the central theme.
- Take notes on the main characters and events as well as the setting.
- Use the present tense, focusing on the most important facts and ignoring any details.

3 **Manjit's story.** Complete this summary, then say what you think might happen next.

The central **idea / theme** (1) of this story is arranged marriages, written from a boy's **opinion / perspective** (2). The main **protagonist / character** (3) is Manjit, the son of a working-class Punjabi family living in Leicester. The **conflict / agreement** (4) arises because his very strict and abusive father maintains traditions and **arranges / offers** (5) for Manjit to be married to a girl from India he has never met. Manjit **agrees / rebels** (6) by defying his family in any way he can think of. To save the family **honour / fate** (7) his father retaliates by taking him on a trip to India where he is more or less kidnapped by his own family. There Manjit meets his Uncle Jag, who himself has broken with family **habit / tradition** (8). Jag helps Manjit to return to Leicester and to see other possibilities for his future. Manjit describes this as **an alternative / a choice** (9) between his family and his freedom and leaves it until the **marriage / wedding** (10) day to make his final decision.

4 **It's so unfair!** Arranged marriage is one way parents influence their children. Think of others.

5 **Rules**

a Watch the video or look at **G 5**, then complete this information about *if*-sentences.

> infinitive ■ possible ■ probable ■ simple past ■ simple present ■ unless ■ *will*-future ■ would

- We use *if*-sentences type 1 to talk about [1] future actions, often in warnings or threats. The verb in the *if*-clause is in the [2], and in the main clause the [3] or is a modal.
  *If I **don't leave** now, I'**ll be** late.*
- We can sometimes use [4] instead of *if … not.*
  ***Unless** I **leave** now, I'**ll be** late.*
- We use *if*-sentences type 2 to talk about an unreal, less [5] situation. We use the [6] in the *if*-clause and [7] / *could / might* + the [8] in the main clause.
  *If Dad **saw** me, he **would be** angry.*

b Complete these comments made by kids about the house rules they have to follow. Explain which of these situations apply to you and why.

1 If I don't finish my essay, I ___ (*not be allowed*) out next weekend.
2 I ___ (*be grounded*) for a week if I get home late again.
3 Our families are very strict. Azari and I can't meet alone ___ we get engaged.
4 If my parents ___ (*catch*) me smoking, they'd go mad.
5 My mum ___ (*kill*) me if I got my tongue pierced.
6 If I spent my money on online casino games, my dad ___ (*stop*) my allowance.

» page 37

6 **YOUR TURN: Home rules**

a Think about what rules would be suitable for people of your age.

b Make a list of rules that you both find acceptable and share it with another pair or group.

c Prepare a short talk to present to the class.

Practice: Sounds of India

1 **GET STARTED!** Add more musical genres to these. What kind of music do you like?

blues ■ country ■ jazz ■ opera ■ reggae ■ rock ■ ska ■ techno ■ world

TIP

A musician bio should include the following information about the performer:
- who they are and where they are from,
- what musical genre they represent,
- how you would describe their sound,
- what their influences are,
- why you like them.

2 **Sheila Chandra**

a A student has written a musician bio about Sheila Chandra for a project in her music class. Read it and answer the questions.

1 Why has the singer been called a pioneer of world music?
2 What happened to change the direction of her musical career?

b Match the sentence parts.

1	Chandra knows that if she talks,	a	if I manage to get a hold of it.
2	You won't be able to sing	b	if you understand them yourself?
3	I might read Chandra's book	c	will you listen to her other albums?
4	If you enjoy this song,	d	the pain will be unbearable.
5	Can you explain the lyrics to me	e	if you get this rare medical condition.

[...] Your parents or older music fans might recognize Chandra from her days in the Indian pop band Monsoon, who had a top ten hit in the 80s with their single *Ever So Lonely*. I love this song because it makes you feel what it's like to be lonely and to want to be with someone when you can't. [...] Singer-songwriter Sheila Chandra most impresses me because illness forced her to direct her creativity into writing a self-help book. She hopes this will inspire new artists in the music industry. [...]
After leaving the band, Chandra had a successful solo music career [...]. She is praised for bringing an Asian fusion sound into mainstream western music in the early days of world music as a genre. However, life has not always been so kind to the British Indian star.
In 2009, Chandra developed a rare chronic condition called burning mouth syndrome. This causes a hot or tingling feeling in the mouth [...] has an enormous impact on her everyday life. The pain never entirely goes away. She knows that if she talks or sings, the pain will get worse, so she is silent most of the time.
[...]
If she didn't have this medical problem, Chandra would still be in the music business. [...] However, she has now published a number of popular books – including one about how to organize a successful creative career [...]. Having worked in the entertainment industry since she was a teenager, Chandra arguably has the relevant skills to mentor other young upcoming musicians. [...]
In my opinion, Chandra's is a story of courage and inspiration. If you listen to *Ever So Lonely*, which was recorded long before she lost her beautiful clear voice, you might, like me, feel sad that she can no longer sing. However, in her words: 'It's only because I lost my voice that I became willing to mentor on any kind of scale – so at least my loss is another's gain.'

Source [abbreviated and adapted]: Lauren Codling, "Ex-singer Sheila Chandra: 'I found my voice again by mentoring young artists', Eastern Eye, 4 December 2019, https://www.easterneye.biz/ex-singer-sheila-chandra-i-found-my-voice-again-by-mentoring-young-artists/ [16.11.2022]

13 **Words and phrases**

to mentor sb.	to advise and guide sb.
inequality	the difference in social status, wealth or opportunity between people or groups
misogynist	showing hatred, dislike or mistrust towards women
a blessing in disguise	a bad thing that turns out to be good

3 Gully Boy Divine

a Read a bio of Gully Boy Divine. In the writer's eyes, what makes him different to other rappers?

b Add these missing sentence parts to the text.

A after his mother gave him a microphone
B and the message is clear
C because of the slang and the tempo
D Growing up in the slums of Mumbai
E and this has inspired other rappers to do the same

[1], Divine has seen a lot of inequality. He decided to create a voice for the people of his streets: the word 'gully' describes something 'from the streets or the gutters'. In 2016, he put together his band, Gully Gang, and from then, Divine's home became the headquarters of one of India's biggest hip-hop bands.

In rap circles, superstar Divine is often credited with putting Mumbai on the hip-hop map. His lyrics highlight big issues like poverty, [2].

It all started when Divine saw a mate wearing a 50 Cent T-shirt. He had never heard of the rapper, so he asked who it was. His friend told him about hip-hop and offered to lend him a CD with rap music on it. At first, Divine couldn't understand the lyrics [3], but his interest in the genre grew.

What I like about Mumbai's gully rap is that, instead of having misogynist lyrics, it's about respect for girls. Boys like Divine grow up with strong mother figures. His dad left them, and his mother had to move away to earn a living, leaving him and his brother with their grandmother. But this was a blessing in disguise, as he says. 'If I lived with mum and dad, I wouldn't be Divine now!' He got his name because he practised in church where it was peaceful.

Divine started writing music [4]. He wrote in English because he thought it was the only language that worked for hip-hop. But then as most people around him spoke Hindi, he started writing in that language. If, like me, you don't speak Hindi, you'll still enjoy a video called *City Slums*. The chorus and half the verses are in English [5], check it out and you'll see.

4 Music matters

a Complete these students' comments with the correct form of the verbs in the box.

ask ■ have ■ like ■ not like ■ meet ■ perform ■ read ■ not speak

1. If you ___ world music, you'll probably enjoy *Ever So Lonely*.
2. I ___ her book if I ever decide on a career in music.
3. If I ___ Chandra, I would tell her how much I admire her.
4. I would make my own music video if I ___ a voice like hers.
5. You will get the meaning even if you ___ the singer's language.
6. If Divine ___ here, I'll try to get tickets.
7. I ___ him if he was nasty about girls.
8. If someone ___ you to write a rap, what would it be about?

»» page 37

\+ **b** Write a rap about a topic that matters to you.

5 *City Slums*

11 **a** Watch Divine and Raja Kumari perform *City Slums*. How much more do you learn about the singers and their lifestyle from watching? How does the video make you feel? Why?

b Who do you find more interesting, Sheila Chandra or Gully Boy Divine? Give your reasons.

6 WRITING FOCUS: Writing a musician bio

a Decide who you are going to write about. Make notes on why you have chosen them and what you already know about them.

b Research online, making sure your sources are reliable. Write your bio (200–300 words) using your own words. If you have a favourite song, copy the lyrics. Illustrate your text with a photo.

c Say why you like the person or band you've chosen. If you've seen them live, describe the event. What would you ask them if you met them in real life?

d Display your bios and do a gallery walk. Give feedback on one or two.

Method coach: Preparing to write a text

S1 **Texts types.** You are going to study two texts on the same subject. Read the title and the first paragraph of each. Write down how you know which text is an informative one and which a persuasive text.

A **To celebrate National Vegetarian Week, we look at India's veggie-friendly cuisine.**
No cuisine is as closely associated with vegetarianism as Indian. The eating habits of Indians vary according to community and region. Sixty per cent of Indians are omnivore. This means only forty per cent are vegetarian.

B **Meat: to eat or not to eat?**
Would you call it a caring world in which animals suffer a horrible death to satisfy an eating preference? Reliable scientific studies show that cattle, pigs and chickens suffer. They can feel stress, they can feel pain and they can feel fear. I strongly believe that it is cruel and unethical to kill animals for food. In my opinion, vegetarianism is the best way to eat. Here are my reasons.

S2 **Analysing texts**

a The remaining three paragraphs of texts A and of B are in the wrong order. Read each paragraph and decide which text it comes from.

b Talk about the choices you made above and together put the paragraphs in the correct order to complete texts A and B.

1 In any case, animals and cows in particular are revered by Hindus because they turn this pasture into milk, produce dung for manure and fuel and pull ploughs and carts. That is why many omnivore Indians have traditionally avoided beef. Religion, too, plays a part. Hinduism, Buddhism and Jainism all advocate non-violence. The concept of 'karma' states that if a living being lives its life 'correctly' – such as by eating vegetarian food – it will be reincarnated at a higher level (i. e. as an upper caste human).

2 Not only is vegetarianism good for you, it's good for your planet. Much of the world's deforestation has happened, with catastrophic consequences, because forests have been burnt to create pasture for cattle. Gas emissions further endanger our environment. Can we really go on this way?

3 Finally, to return to the animals. I am absolutely positive that raising animals in captivity is cruel. Don't be fooled by fake statistics. Most meat comes from farming methods where animals live in filthy, overcrowded spaces. I truly think that if most compassionate people saw pigs with their tails cut off, chickens with their beaks removed or cows with horns and tails cut off with no painkillers, they would never eat meat again. Your voice matters and together we can achieve our aims.

4 One reason for this is that meat eating in India is so expensive. It is seen as aspirational and glamorous, and is associated with wealth and luxury. Many eat it only on special occasions or add it to side dishes. Vegetables, grains and beans grow well in India, so it makes sense to use the land to grow food crops, rather than use it as pasture.

5 It must be emphasized that not all Indians are vegetarian for religious reasons. Yet throughout history, figures ranging from Emperor Ashoka to Mahatma Gandhi actively promoted a vegetarian diet. In a culture where many have grown up in meat-free households, they have simply never acquired the taste or enthusiasm for meat.

6 Vegetarianism is good for you. Meat eaters argue that meat is the best source of protein. However, a vegetarian diet gives you all the nutrition you need. Non-meat sources of iron like leafy greens contain better iron than red meat, for example.

@ WES-40326-001

→ Workbook, page 27

Workshop task: Writing a persuasive text

Youth activism

Younger people are now responding with action in a political climate where many adults are inactive. Frustrated with the older generation's failure to sort out the many global problems that exist, Gen Z activists are taking matters into their own hands. 'Activism is the process of campaigning in public or working for an organization in order to bring about political or social change.' It is 'the use of direct and noticeable action to achieve a result'. These dictionary definitions describe what activism is. This article will explore some of the causes that youth activists are campaigning for and how they are doing so. It aims to explain why youth activism has increased all over the world.

While the environment, in particular climate change, is the biggest social justice issue for today's young people, they also care a lot about poverty, homelessness and hunger. Global issues such as the refugee crisis, gun control, human rights abuses and anti-war activism are all important to Generation Z. Many of these issues like gender equality involve more than one topic.

Women's rights movements aim to give females greater control of their lives. This involves tackling taboo subjects like period poverty, raising awareness of what girls and young women experience. Campaigning for gender equality also touches on education systems that discriminate against girls, and workplace situations where the so-called glass ceiling prevents women from being promoted to high level positions. Boys and young men are encouraged to respect girls and women by empowering them to support the global gender equality movements. Not only that, but gender equality can also impact on a variety of transgender issues.

Protest marches, school strikes, awareness-raising events and internet activism are the most common forms of activism with the latter being of prime significance. Using social media has evolved into digital activism, which is powerful because young people are comfortable organizing, being in a community and building their alliances online. The internet is not only where young people learn about issues but also where they can broadcast their concerns and publicize their campaigns on an international or a global level.

S1 **Youth activism.** Read an informative text about youth activism. Which of the following techniques do you find?

counterarguments ■ emotive language ■ examples ■ facts ■ repetition ■ rhetorical questions ■ statistics ■ warnings

S2 **Getting active!** Imagine you have a mutual friend who is against any form of activism – a real sceptic! Rewrite the text in **S1** to persuade your friend to become politically active.

TIP

Writing a persuasive text
- Make your opinion clear in the introduction.
- Find strong supporting evidence.
- Use emotive language but never become aggressive.
- Write in the present tense.

Useful language
- Use comparatives: *much stronger, far more beneficial, …*
- Show reasons and causes: *for that reason, so, therefore, as a result, …*
- Structure your arguments: *in the first place, next, finally, …*
- Find counterarguments: *some may argue that … but …, contrary to …, despite what some people say, …*

S3 **Over to you**

a Write a persuasive text on one of the following topics or a topic of your choice. Research your topic.
- Young people need screen time.
- Meat eating is a human right.
- All lives matter.
- Teenage volunteering is important.

b Share your texts in class and choose one to read. Give constructive feedback. Is the purpose of the text clear to the reader? Are you persuaded?

@ WES-40326-001

Mediation

1 India's youth

a You are studying the impact of the COVID-19 pandemic on young adults in different countries in your social studies class. You give a presentation in German about young adults in India, explaining how the pandemic affected young people's lives, the differences between rural and urban areas, and the situation of male and female students. Compare these aspects with your personal experiences and feelings during the pandemic. Use the information from the following text and take notes before giving your presentation.

India's youth: Hit hard by the pandemic [...]
Soaring unemployment, distance learning in conditions that are often difficult, feelings of isolation, a return to domestic work for girls from disadvantaged backgrounds. In a country where almost half the population is under 25, young people are paying a disproportionately heavy price during the health crisis. [...]

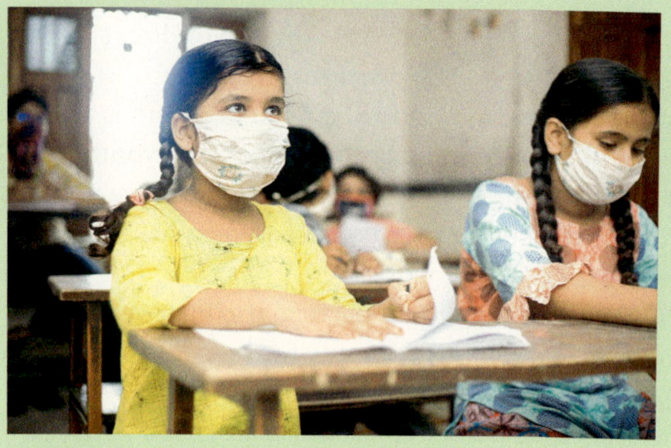

The year 2020 had started well for Gaurav – in February, he was hired as a salesman in a sports shop in the Pul Bangash area of Old Delhi. It was the first job for this 20-year-old amateur boxer who had left school early.

But the coronavirus epidemic brought all this to a brutal end. "Public transport became less frequent, and then stopped completely," Gaurav recalls. "I couldn't afford to take a taxi to work every day, so I had to quit." In any case, he would not have been able to keep his job because of the strict lockdown imposed from 25 March that year. This paralysed the Indian economy for over six months and shattered the dreams of many young people. [...]

Urban youth on the front line

The crisis caused by the pandemic is the most serious ever recorded since the country's independence in 1947. India's gross domestic product (GDP) fell by 8.5 per cent in the 2020 – 2021 fiscal year. According to a three-year survey of 170,000 households by the Centre for Monitoring Indian Economy [...], 41.2 per cent of those surveyed had lost their jobs between December 2019 and April 2020.

This figure rises to 58.5 per cent for young people aged 15 to 24. "Urban youth have been much more affected than rural youth," says Paaritosh Nath, a research fellow at the Centre for Sustainable Employment, Azim Premji University, in Bangalore. "The agricultural sector has continued to function, and the guaranteed public employment programme in rural areas has made it possible to offer work to more people there. But such a programme does not exist in the cities, except in a few states." [...]

Courses by phone

Students have also borne the full force of this crisis. For the quarter of young Indians who attend university, classes became virtual during lockdown. While the transition to distance learning has gone fairly smoothly for students at private colleges, it has been more difficult for those attending public universities, and for students who are less fortunate or live outside major urban centres.

"All our courses were delivered by voicemail on WhatsApp," says Munazza, who was completing a master's degree in English at the Jamia Millia Islamia Public University in New Delhi, at the time. "It was the only way that students who had returned to their homes in Kashmir [a northern Indian state] could continue their studies."

The pandemic has also [...] caused millions of students to interrupt their studies. In the Mysore region in the country's south, for example, 43 per cent of students in public universities were no longer following

their bachelor's degree courses in December 2020. The drop-out rate for girls has been as high as 65 per cent. "Hit by the crisis, many parents have preferred to marry off their daughters," explains sociologist and feminist writer and activist Manjima Bhattacharjya.
Students who have managed to continue their studies often suffer from a sense of isolation. When Munazza's roommates left during lockdown, the 24-year-old found herself alone in New Delhi. "After they left, I found it hard to keep studying. Even cooking was an effort," she recalls. Her hopes of finding a skilled and well-paid job have also receded. "I was offered three hours of work a day for less than what a taxi driver earns," she complained. "Why study for an extra five years if that is the case?" [...]
Finally graduating in June 2020, Munazza now plans to enrol her thesis for further studies. But universities that are still in lockdown, or have inadequate staff, could take months to release the registration forms. The year of crisis has not just been negative for her. It has helped her become more mature and get to know herself better, she admits. "I'm a person who worries by nature. I now realize that I have to learn to stay calm. If I am calm, everything will be okay."

Source [abbreviated]: Sébastien Farcis, "India's youth: Hit hard by the pandemic", The UNESCO Courier, https://en.unesco.org/courier/2021-2/indias-youth-hit-hard-pandemic [15.11.2022]

b You have also talked to your English friend about your presentation. She / he wants to know if the situation of students in Germany was similar to that of students in India. Write her / him an email in which you answer this question. Use the information from the following text and the statistics.

Corona: Kein Job, hohe Mieten – steigt jetzt auch die Zahl der Studienabbrüche? [...]
Bei einer Befragung von über 28 000 Studierenden in ganz Deutschland hat die Job-Plattform Studitemps den Jobmarkt und die finanzielle Situation von Hochschüler:innen in der Corona Pandemie erarbeitet. [...]
(D)ie Studie bringt [...] Erfreuliches ans Licht: Die Wahrscheinlichkeit, dass Studierende ihr Studium abbrechen, ist in der Corona-Krise nur wenig gestiegen – von 16,3 auf 16,6 Prozent. Ein Grund dafür könnte sein, dass Studierende trotz Krisenmodus weiterhin flexibel bleiben, und auf Jobs umschwenken, in denen Arbeitskräfte gerade händeringend gesucht werden, wie etwa in der Logistik oder im medizinischen Bereich. [...]

Source [abbreviated]: Andrea Stettner, „Corona: Kein Job, hohe Mieten – steigt jetzt auch die Zahl der Studienabbrüche?", Merkur.de, 09.03.2021, https://www.merkur.de/leben/karriere/corona-studium-abbrechen-wegen-corona-studenten-mieten-job-eltern-zr-90232769.html [15.11.2022]

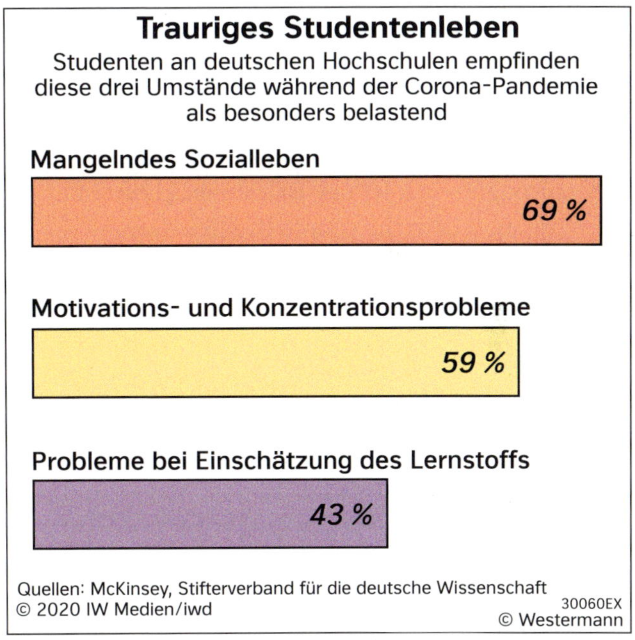

First track

3 **b** Complete an old man's memories with the correct form of the verbs in brackets.

p. 15

It was such a frightening time. While we were asleep, our school [1] (*burn down*) by the mob. We had no idea who did it or why. We woke to find our country [2] (*divide*) without warning. That morning, we [3] (*take*) by train from Agra to the border. The track stopped, so the rest of the journey [4] (*complete*) on camels. Our mother was terrified as explosions could [5] (*hear*) all around us. It is a story that [6] (*tell*) many times since that night in 1947.

2 **b** Complete this review with the correct form of the verbs in brackets. What do you think 'the Light and the Darkness' refer to?

p. 16

The White Tiger [1] (*publish*) in 2008 and is novelist Aravind Adiga's first novel. It [2] (*award*) the prestigious Man Booker Prize. It [3] (*set*) in India and [4] (*narrate*) by a man named Balram Halwai, an entrepreneur in Bangalore. In the novel, his life [5] (*portray*) through seven letters. Balram was born in a region where the people live in extreme poverty. He [6] (*take*) out of school early, nevertheless with a lot of initiative, he [7] (*promote*) to the job of first driver for a rich man in Delhi. It [8] (*reveal*) that Balram has committed a terrible crime, enabling him to become wealthy enough to start his own business. In his letters, Balram describes how India got divided into two countries, the Light and the Darkness.

3 **b** Report more of Deepak's comments starting with the words given.

p. 20

1 History has important examples of youth activism. *Deepak said that ...*

2 Companies are learning the importance of youth spending power. *He believed ...*

3 Young people's voices have never been so clear. *He pointed out ...*

4 School strikes make a massive impact. *He insisted that ...*

5 Students have realized their political power. *He claimed that ...*

6 Young people will never forgive the older generation. *He warned that ...*

2 **c** Choose the correct words to complete Sunny's blog post.

p. 24/25

NEWS | CALENDAR | CONTACTS | BLOG | GALLERY

Governments have not succeeded in **finding / to find** (1) an answer to Bengaluru's water problem. Nevertheless, some poor families today enjoy **being able to / to be able to** (2) access the water they need. This is thanks to local groups who managed **renewing / to renew** (3) the old water tanks and wells that were closed. This was done by **combining / to combine** (4) local knowledge and innovative problem-solving. Some wells now produce about 65,000 litres of water per day, which really helps **meeting / to meet** (5) residents' water demands.
Big ideas have proved incapable of **solving / to solve** (6) Bengaluru's water problems since colonial times. But local, community-led plans have a good chance of **creating / to create** (7) a strong, water-secure city: an important lesson for architects trying **planning / to plan** (8) better cities for the future.

3 **c** Choose the correct verbs to complete this film review. Then say which gave you a better insight into the film – the trailer or the film review.

p. 26

The protagonist, Jamal, is an 18-year-old chai wallah, someone who prepares tea. Born in the slums of Mumbai, he works in a busy call centre. He decides **entering / to enter** (1) the *Who Wants To Be A Millionaire?* gameshow, which his childhood love, Latika, always watches. He is still in love with her, so he wants **finding / to find** (2) her. Each question on the TV show mysteriously connects to his life experiences, so he manages **answering / to answer** (3) them all correctly. He becomes a national hero as people from the slums see one of their own beating the system and becoming rich and famous. The TV host suspects him of **cheating / to cheat** (4) in some way. The police watch a recording of the last show, hoping **discovering / to discover** (5) how Jamal knows all the answers. They don't believe a chai wallah from the slums could answer such difficult questions, so they try **forcing / to force** (6) a confession of guilt out of him by **torturing / to torture** (7) him. Jamal has a quiet confidence and a sense of his own destiny, which leads him to victory. He refuses **admitting / to admit** (8) to doing anything wrong. Jamal and his brother Salim have a complicated relationship but in a dramatic ending, instead of **saving / to save** (9) himself as we might have expected, Salim helps Jamal **reuniting / to reunite** (10) with Latika.

5 **b** Chose the correct words to complete these comments made by kids about the house rules they have to follow. Explain which of these situations apply to you and why.

p. 29

1. If I don't finish my essay, I **am not allowed / won't be allowed** out next weekend.
2. I **will be grounded / would be grounded** for a week if I get home late again.
3. Our families are very strict. Azari and I can't meet alone **if / unless** we get engaged.
4. If my parents **caught / would catch** me smoking, they'd go mad.
5. My mum **killed / would kill** me if I got my tongue pierced.
6. If I spent my money on online casino games, my dad **will stop / would stop** my allowance.

4 **a** Complete these students' comments with the correct form of the verbs in brackets.

p. 31

1. If you ___ (*like*) world music, you'll probably enjoy *Ever So Lonely*.
2. I ___ (*read*) her book if I ever decide on a career in music.
3. If I ___ (*meet*) Chandra, I would tell her how much I admire her.
4. I would make my own music video if I ___ (*have*) a voice like hers.
5. You will get the meaning even if you ___ (*not speak*) the singer's language.
6. If Divine ___ (*perform*) here, I'll try to get tickets.
7. I ___ (*not like*) him if he was nasty about girls.
8. If someone ___ (*ask*) you to write a rap, what would it be about?

Reading

1 Before you read the poem, take some time to think about the future. Close your eyes and imagine your wishes and dreams, your individual plans, as well as your fears and sorrows. Make notes. Then write down five statements about what will happen if some of them come true.

Example: *If I go to university in another city, it will be a challenge to live on my own.*

2 **a** Read the poem, preferably aloud, and summarize what it is about in one or two sentences. Talk to a partner about your first reactions. Find a variety of positive and negative adjectives to describe the tone of the poem (*surprising, appalling, magic, tragic, …*). Use references from the text to illustrate your ideas.

b Design a mind map to show the various areas of the author's personal life which are mentioned (e.g. his house, his town, people) or the topics dealt with in the poem (e.g. the weather, political affairs) and add examples.

c Discuss how the last paragraph (*his parents … carefully*) differs to the rest of the text. Then say who the 'speaker' is and what the function of this paragraph is.

3 Choose five stylistic devices and analyse their function in the poem.

TIP

Stylistic devices

- **alliteration:** repetition of a sound at the beginning of neighbouring words
- **climax:** highest point of tension in a storyline
- **irony:** saying the opposite of what you really mean
- **metaphor:** a figure of speech that directly compares one thing to another for rhetorical effect
- **parallelism:** deliberately using similar or identical words, phrases or structures in neighbouring lines, sentences or paragraphs (= repetition)
- **personification:** presenting ideas, objects or animals as human beings
- **register:** a particular type of language used in a specific situation or for a specific purpose
- **rhetorical question:** question to which no answer is expected because it is obvious
- **rhyme vs. free verse:** using words that repeat syllable sounds vs. poetry without a regular metre or rhyme
- **symbol:** an idea or image that stands for something abstract

4 Do some research about the author. Examine his personal and political background, and also consider how this has influenced his work. Write a short text about Devashish Makhija for your international school magazine (100 – 120 words).

5 As a member of the school magazine team, you take part in a literary conference on contemporary authors and meet the author. Write three questions you would like to ask him.

6 Organize a panel discussion to talk about the value of literature in the 21st century. In the discussion, students should:
- apply their prior knowledge and experiences
- use appropriate language and register, e.g. asking and answering questions, agreeing, contradicting, interrupting, …
- take account of any relevant intercultural differences

To do so follow these steps:
- Work in small groups to find pro and con arguments.
- Decide which student will be 'on stage' to represent your group.
- Choose one or two students to lead the discussion.

30586EX © Westermann

Devashish Makhija, *If I kill myself today*

If I kill myself today
Tomorrow's milk will curdle
untended at the door
Some clothes in the
washing machine will stay
unwashed forever
A hundred ants will gather in
quiet celebration around some
spilt tea in the kitchen
A desperate doorbell
will fall from favour
on deaf ears
If I kill myself today
Dust will gather where my
broom won't be
reaching anymore
Ignored, a solitary banana
will rot, surrendering itself
to flies
A stubborn pigeon will wonder why
she's not being chased out the window,
and gleefully invite some
others in
Helplessly, three bottles
of pills will age past their expiry date,
their contents intact
If I kill myself today
A cellphone will beep a reminder
at 9 a.m. tomorrow
and every ten minutes thereafter
till its battery dies
A gmail account will gather unread
emails from known ids for years
before spam slowly takes over
A Facebook profile picture will find
that it never needs to be updated
ever again
But
The elections will be held on schedule
The monsoons will come again this year
My ageing father will grow even older
The building down the road will be redeveloped
Homes will be furnished
Furniture will be bought, will age, and be replaced
The unmarried will get married
The unborn will be birthed
Newspapers will be printed
And read
And recycled
Tomatoes will be grown
Soup will be made
The kind I was prescribed for a healthier, longer life
You will have it out of a bowl
If you have it next week you will shed a tear
in my memory
it will fall in the soup
you will collect it in a spoonful
and swallow it as you
choke, and break down
If you have it next year
it will be too hot
so you will blow on it till it cools
and then you will swallow it spoonful
by spoonful
as you sit before the television
watching your favourite dinner-time soap
cursing the ad breaks
with the same intensity as today
If I kill myself today
the telecast timings will not change.

his parents gave **devashish makhijahis** name
pure chance gave him his nationality
no one asked him if he wanted the religion he got
the system gave him an education
and then proceeded to make it null and void when he
stepped out into the real world
the only thing he got to choose in his life are his
words so he likes to choose them carefully

Source: Devashish Makhija, *If I kill myself today*, Plume Poetry, https://plumepoetry.com/featured-selection-22-contemporary-indian-poets/ [25.04.2023]

PART 1

PART 2

PART 3

My review

What can I do?

Look at these sentences about Workshop 1. Are the sentences true for you? Choose the right symbol for each sentence.

1 I can talk about India then and now.
2 I can discuss the role of a key figure.
3 I can discuss activism using arguments and couterarguments.
4 I can understand comments on political engagement.

»»» = 'I'm great at this!'
»»» = 'I'm good at this.'
»»» = 'I'm OK at this.'

What do I know?

1 **About India and Pakistan.** Complete the text about the partition of India and Pakistan with the correct passive form of the verbs in brackets.

In August 1947, when independence **1** (*grant*) to the former imperial domain of British India, it **2** (*partition*) into two countries – India and Pakistan.
The demand for a separate nation for Muslims **3** (*raise*) by various Muslim leaders in the decades prior to the formation of the All-India Muslim League in 1906. Its leader, Muhammad Ali Jinnah, firmly believed that Muslims and Hindus could not live in one nation. In his opinion, Muslims' rights and demands **4** (*ignore*) in a country which **5** (*rule*) by a Hindu majority. His goal **6** (*finally + achieve*) when the British left India.
After the borders **7** (*announce*), millions of people sought to join their new country. This mass exodus **8** (*view*) today as a tragedy. As many as 14 – 16 million people **9** (*think*) to have been displaced and it **10** (*estimate*) that up to 2 million people may have died. Families **11** (*tear apart*), and the impact of the events in August 1947 **12** (*feel*) for many generations to come.
Peace for India and Pakistan, **13** (*not achieve*) yet, and the two countries' relationship **14** (*cannot + describe*) healthy. Beyond territorial disputes, Indian Muslims **15** (*frequently suspect*) of harbouring loyalties towards Pakistan, and non-Muslim minorities **16** (*consider*) vulnerable. All in all, well over a billion people still live in the shadow of Partition.

■ / 16

India then and now, pp. 14 – 15
Passive → G2 ; pp. 14 – 15

2 **About climate matters.** Young people from Pakistan and India got together in a video call to talk about issues that matter to them. Report some of their statements.

Rani	After the devastating floods we experienced, I've joined the Green Youth Movement. I intend to follow in the footsteps of Licypriya Kangujam who's been a youth activist since she was four years old.
Jai	We need to focus on issues that matter to everyone, such as education and health.
Kavi	In my view, our education system needs to change to give equal opportunities to girls.
Neel	I want to raise awareness of the extensive use of plastic.
Ajay	I joined a march demanding that CO_2 emissions are lowered as the air pollution in Delhi is too high.
Arun	Is there anything more effective than collaborating with international environmental organizations?
Vin	I've realized how important social media is in reaching like-minded activists.
Uma	I've been following Malala's story, for me she's a real inspiration.
Devi	What hope is there for our generation if young people don't act together?

1 Rani said that ...
2 She also added that ...
3 Jai pointed out ...
4 Kavi emphasized ...
5 Neel stated ...
6 Ajay mentioned ...
7 Arun wondered ...
8 Vin added ...
9 Uma told the others ...
10 Devi asked ...

■ / 10

Youth activism, pp. 20 – 21
Reported speech → G3 ; pp. 20 – 21

3 **About Indian slums.** Complete the text with the correct form of the verbs in brackets.

When you first meet Rustom, you can't help **1** (*wonder*) why this young man always seems so happy. Rustom is one of millions of young Indians who live in a slum. 'I've lived in the slum since I was young, so I refuse **2** (*let*) it get me down. For me, it's just where I live and part of who I am.' In fact, Rustom has succeeded in **3** (*make*) slum life work for him. 'When I was about six, I decided **4** (*get on with*) life. There are lots of problems in the slums, so I began **5** (*look for*) solutions rather than being negative.' Last year, Rustom managed **6** (*come up with*) two inventions. 'Clean water is a problem, so I tried **7** (*find*) a solution that was affordable and easy to put into practice. Another problem is reliable electricity. After a lot of discussions with the local authorities, they agreed **8** (*pass*) a new law that would help. I can't say I enjoy **9** (*live*) here,' Rustom says, 'but this is my home and I would miss **10** (*be*) here if I moved away.'

■ / 10

Slum life, pp. 24 – 25
Gerund or infinitive → G4 ; pp. 24 – 25

4 About traditions and cultures

a Complete the blog entry with the correct form of some of the verbs from the box.

not accept ■ ask ■ choose ■ do ■ give ■ listen ■ marry ■ need

Attitudes in India are changing when it comes to traditions and customs. In the past, it was not possible to marry someone from a different caste. The situation is changing, but it's still not easy. If you [1] someone from a different caste, it will affect all aspects of your daily life. Luckily, my father doesn't believe in arranged marriages, but if I [2] for his advice, I know he would give it to me. And he knows that if he wants to discuss something with me, I [3] to him. But my best friend's dad says that if she [4] his choice of a husband, he won't speak to her again! I really don't know what I [5] if were in her shoes. I really do feel fortunate with my parents. I know if I [6] them, they will always be there for me.
Sandra (18)

■ / 6

b Complete the dialogue between Asif and Bilal with the correct form of the verbs in brackets.

A. Hi Bilal! Can you tell me about yourself?
B. Sure, I'm seventeen and I live in Pakistan.
A. My parents are from Pakistan, so I feel like we are brothers.
B. Mmm. I'm sure if I [1] (*live*) in the UK, my life would be very different.
A. In what ways?
B. Well, as I said I'm seventeen but my parents are already talking about marriage.
A. What?
B. Yes, if I [2] (*have*) a choice, I'd wait …
A. If you [3] (*tell*) them you didn't want to get married, wouldn't they listen to you?
B. Not really. This is part of our culture. If you look at the statistics, you [4] (*find*) about half of all marriages in Pakistan are arranged. With their experience of life, your parents are often in a better position than you to choose the right partner. If that [5] (*not be*) the case, there would be more divorces in Pakistan than there are.
A. OK, but if my parents [6] (*order*) me to get married, I wouldn't be happy.
B. You also have to remember that Pakistan is generally a patriarchal society.
A. What does that mean?
B. Well, the father is the head of the household. If you [7] (*live*) there, you'd understand what I mean.
A. I think I know what you mean. If my father told me to do something and I refused, I [8] (*be*) in serious trouble.

■ / 8

Traditional and modern cultures, pp. 28 – 29

If-sentences types 1 and 2 → G5 ; pp. 28 – 29

■ / 50

What's my score?

Check your answers to the review (Workbook, p. 32) What are your scores for each section?

What was your total score?

»»» score 36 – 50
»»» score 16 – 35
»»» score 0 – 15

Do you want to change your answers to the 'What can I do?' statements on page 40?
Look at the tasks on pages 43 – 47: »»», »»» and »»». Choose the tasks to help you.

My practice pages

Talking about India then and now

1 **Indian Independence.** Choose the correct forms to complete the text about how Independence Day is celebrated.

Since independence **was granted / granted / is granted** (1), on 15 August 1947, this national holiday, **is marked / has been marked / was marked** (2) with nation-wide celebrations in India.
The main event begins when the national flag **is hoisted / hoisted / will be hoisted** (3) by the prime minister while gunshots **is fired / are fired / fired** (4) and followed by the rendition of the national anthem. The president of India addresses the nation from his or her office which **broadcast / is broadcast / broadcasts** (5) nationally.
During the day-long celebrations, there are patriotic parades, marches led by the armed forces and performances by schoolchildren.
In the northern and central cities of India, kite flying **has been considered / is considered / considered** (6) to be the main festivity. Kites of different sizes **can be seen / can see / is seen** (7) soaring high in the sky in the colours of the Indian flag. As the day is a national holiday, families tend to spend it together and enjoy fun activities that **have been done / are done / will be done** (8) for many years to come.

2 **A colourful festival.** Complete the blog about Holi with the correct passive form of the verbs in brackets.

You wanted to know more about Holi so read my personal account of my favourite holiday. Holi **1** (*observe*) on the last full moon day in the month of Falgun, the 12th month of the Hindu calendar so the date changes every year. Although it is a religious festival, known as the Festival of Colours, it **2** (*intend*) to celebrate the arrival of spring as well as fertility, love and colours.
As a young child, I **3** (*teach*) about the origins of the religious rituals behind the celebrations, but for me the highlights have always been the excitement, fun, dizzying arrays of colours and yummy food which the festive period **4** (*associate*) with. I can vividly recall how awe-struck I was as a young child every time the bonfire **5** (*light*) and the effigy **6** (*throw*) into the flames. Later, I understood the significance – if the effigy **7** (*burn*), evil will be destroyed.
The second day, the throwing of colours is even more fun. Everyone **8** (*can + see*) out in the streets or in the parks, armed with paint powder and coloured water. In my life, I **9** (*chase*) by young and old and got totally soaked. But I have always known that if you complain, you **10** (*laugh at*). And the best thing is that no social rules apply, throwing paint on older people, on strangers **11** (*regard*) as acceptable. On that day, I **12** (*never tell off*) for being mischievous!

3 **Your festival.** Write a blog entry about your favourite festive celebration. Include details about its origin, how it is celebrated and why you like it. Use the passive when appropriate.

PART 1

PART 2

PART 3

Talking about youth activism and engagement

Read this interview with Ana, a young British Muslim, then do one of the three exercises below.

Max Good afternoon, I am Max Smith and you are listening to the *Four Corners* culture podcast. Today, I'm joined by Ana, a young British Muslim and we're going to talk about what is important to young British Muslims. Welcome, Ana.

Ana Thank you for inviting me.

Max Ana, what issues are important to young British Muslims today?

Ana For the most part they are the same as for any other young person living in the UK. Top of the list is probably climate change as it affects people everywhere.

Max Are you actively supporting the issue?

Ana Yes, I am. I've raised more than £3000 for a climate change charity and created a climate change club at my school.

Max Do you see yourself as the Muslim Greta Thunberg?

Ana Haha. Not at all. I'm not quite in her league! Plus one of the problems is that young people are often concerned about how being seen as an activist might impact their future.

Max What do you mean?

Ana Well, some of my friends shy away from active participation especially when they see people on the news being arrested for protesting.

Max I understand. What are some of the other concerns young Muslims have?

Ana Education is high on our priority list. 50% of Muslims living in the UK are under 25 and a lot are unemployed …

Max … but a lot of you are at school or university.

Ana Yes, and so the quality of education is really important.

Max Are young Muslims interested in politics?

Ana Not really. I am, but it frustrates me that politicians seem disconnected from local communities.

Max Are you planning to vote when you can?

Ana Yes, I will definitely vote because the UK is my home, so I have to find meaningful ways of making my citizenship count. However, I will never vote for somebody just because I know them. For me it's their policies and track records that matter.

Max I hear that charity is important for Muslims?

Ana Yes, it is. We have something called Zakat.

Max Zakat? What's that?

Ana If a Muslim earns a certain amount of money, they have to give a percentage to a charitable cause. It's one of the pillars of our faith.

Max Ana, thank you for your time today. It was very interesting.

4 »» **A British Muslim.** Complete this summary of the interview with the verbs in the box.

affected ■ could ■ earned ■ had created ■ had raised ■ had to ■ saw ■ seemed ■ was ■ was planning ■ were ■ would vote

Max introduced Ana and explained that they were going to talk about issues that **1** important to young British Muslims. Ana said that climate change was an extremely important topic as it **2** people everywhere. She told Max how she **3** £3000 for a climate change charity and **4** a climate change club at her school. However, she mentioned that some of her friends were worried when they **5** people being arrested for protesting about climate change. Next, Ana spoke about the importance of education. She pointed out that education **6** a high priority due to the high number of young unemployed Muslims in the UK. Next they discussed politics, and Max wanted to know if Ana **7** to vote when she **8**. She replied that she **9** because the UK was her home, but she added how frustrated she was by politicians who **10** disconnected from local communities. Finally they talked about charity, and Ana described how, according to Zakat, a Muslim who **11** a certain amount of money **12** give a percentage to a charitable cause. She concluded by saying it was one of the pillars of the Islamic faith.

5 **A British Muslim.** Complete this summary of the interview with the verbs in brackets in the correct form.

Max introduced Ana and explained that they were going to talk about issues that 1 (*be*) important to young British Muslims. Ana said that climate change was an extremely important topic as it 2 (*affect*) people everywhere. She told Max how she 3 (*raise*) £3000 for a climate change charity and 4 (*create*) a climate change club at her school. However, she mentioned that some of her friends were worried when they 5 (*see*) people being arrested for protesting about climate change. Next, Ana spoke about the importance of education. She pointed out that education 6 (*be*) a high priority due to the high number of young unemployed Muslims in the UK. Next they discussed politics, and Max wanted to know if Ana 7 (*plan*) to vote when she 8 (*can*). She replied that she 9 (*vote*) because the UK was her home, but she added how frustrated she was by politicians who 10 (*seem*) disconnected from local communities. Finally they talked about charity, and Ana described how, according to Zakat, a Muslim who 11 (*earn*) a certain amount of money 12 (*have to*) give a percentage to a charitable cause. She concluded by saying it was one of the pillars of the Islamic faith.

6 **A British Muslim.** Complete this summary of the interview with the verbs in brackets in the correct form. Choose the most suitable reporting verbs from the box. Sometimes more than one is possible.

added ■ concluded by saying ■ described ■ explained ■ mentioned ■ pointed out ■ replied ■ said ■ told ■ wanted to know

Max introduced Ana and 1 that they were going to talk about issues that 2 (*be*) important to young British Muslims. Ana 3 that climate change was an extremely important topic as it 4 (*affect*) people everywhere. She 5 Max how she 6 (*raise*) £3000 for a climate change charity and 7 (*create*) a climate change club at her school. However, she 8 that some of her friends were worried when they 9 (*see*) people being arrested for protesting about climate change. Next, Ana spoke about the importance of education. She 10 that education 11 (*be*) a high priority due to the high number of young unemployed Muslims in the UK. Next they discussed politics, and Max 12 if Ana 13 (*plan*) to vote when she 14 (*can*). She 15 that she 16 (*vote*) because the UK was her home, but she 17 how frustrated she was by politicians who 18 (*seem*) disconnected from local communities. Finally they talked about charity, and Ana 19 how, according to Zakat, a Muslim who 20 (*earn*) a certain amount of money 21 (*have to*) give a percentage to a charitable cause. She 22 it was one of the pillars of the Islamic faith.

Talking about life in a slum

7 **Slum life.** Choose the correct forms to complete the blog.

My name is Rama and I'm a charity worker. I work in one of the biggest slums in India near the city of Mumbai. Nobody deserves to live / living (1) in such poor conditions. In my work, I try to help / helping (2) the women who find themselves living in the slum. When you talk to them, you can't help to feel / feeling (3) sad, their lives are so difficult. One thing that always amazes is me is how they manage to stay / staying (4) positive. When I first decided to work / working (5) for the charity, most of my friends and my family thought I was crazy. I must admit to think / thinking (6) the same on occasions. However, the work is so rewarding that I wouldn't want to do / doing (7) anything else. I'd suggest to visit / visiting (8) one of the slums to get a better idea of what I mean.

8 **Charity in the slums.** Complete the conversation with the correct form of the verbs in the box.

apply ■ be offered ■ help ■ ignore ■ make ■ pay ■ provide ■ share ■ talk ■ work

Max Last week on the programme we promised 1 more about slum life in India. On today's programme we have Rama Patel a charity worker who has worked in the slums for over twenty years. She has agreed 2 some of her experiences with us. Welcome to the programme, Ms Patel.

Rama Call me Rama and thank you for inviting me.

Max When did you first start 3 in the slums?

Rama Oh, it was just after I graduated from university. I had always wanted 4 people less fortunate than me, and one of my lecturers suggested 5 for a job with a local charity. I did and I was surprised 6 the job.

Max So, what exactly do you do in your role?

Rama My title is 'Women's outreach coordinator'. My main job is to give advice to women living in the slums to help them improve their lives.

Max Why is the charity so important for people living in the slums?

Rama The first thing to remember is that people who live there can't afford 7 anyone for advice. You also have to remember that the government has failed 8 these people with even the basic requirements.

Max So, the charity fills the gaps that are left by the government, right?

Rama Yes, they'll deny 9 these people, but the reality is that they have been forgotten.

Max They must be so happy to see you ...

Rama Yes, and if I can succeed in 10 a difference to just one person's life, that makes me happy.

Max Rama, thank you for coming in today and good luck with your work in the future.

9 **Problems and solutions.** Complete the sentences about slum life in India using the correct form of the verbs in brackets.

1 When you live in a slum, you should ___ (*avoid* + *drink*) the water if possible.
2 Since Partition, all governments in India have ___ (*fail* + *deal*) with the problem of slums.
3 Experts ___ (*recommend* + *provide*) every adult living in a slum with an opportunity of work.
4 For years, politicians have been ___ (*promise* + *sort out*) the issue of slums, but the situation only ___ (*seems* + *be*) worse than ever.
5 Many people living in slums can't ___ (*afford* + *feed*) their families properly.
6 The conditions in the slums ___ (*keep on* + *get*) worse despite all the promises from politicians.
7 Most people born in a slum don't ___ (*manage* + *move*) to a better place to live. They almost always remain in the same slum.
8 Unless solutions are found soon regarding clean water and sanitation in slums, millions of people ___ (*risk* + *become*) seriously ill.

Talking about traditions and customs

10 **A traditional view.** Here are some things Indian and Pakistani teenagers living in England said. Choose the correct options to complete their statements.

1 My mother **is / will be** very upset if she finds my new tattoo.
2 I know that if I ever **disobey / disobeyed** my father, I would be in serious trouble.
3 If I lived in Pakistan, life **is / would be** quite different.
4 Unless the caste system changes, I **won't be able to / wouldn't be able to** marry my girlfriend.
5 If someone **tells / told** me who to marry I would be shocked.
6 If you **aren't born / weren't born** into an Indian family, you will find these traditions strange.
7 If my parents ever **catch / caught** me with my boyfriend, I would be in serious trouble.
8 How do you think you **would feel / felt** if your parents were as strict as mine?

11 **If I …** Complete the sentences with your own ideas.

1 If I lived in India, …
2 Unless someone explains the tradition to me, …
3 If my parents tried to arrange my marriage, …
4 If you asked me to explain some common traditions in India and Pakistan, …
5 If the caste system existed in Germany, …
6 Unless you live in a country like India or Pakistan, …
7 In India if the caste system was abolished, …
8 I come from a very traditional family. If my mother told me what to do, …

12 **What if …?** Write six conditional sentences about the following topics: arranged marriages, the caste system, patriarchal families.

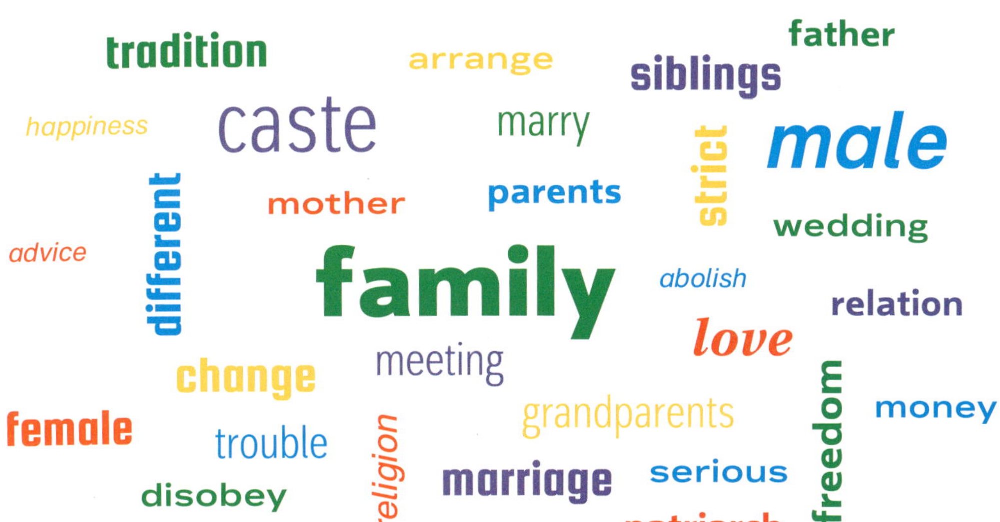

@ WES-40326-001

14 Marcus Sedgwick

Cudweed and the bagpipes

ONE

Flying upside down is something I don't do very often. When I was younger, I used to do it a lot (mostly to show off[1] to young lady ravens). But these days I find that flying upside down leads to all sorts of problems, most of which end up with me having one wing in a bandage for a few weeks.

However, as this story about Cudweed and the bagpipes starts, I was flying upside down, outside the castle. Not only that, but I was flying upside down holding a letter in my beak, also upside down, so that Cudweed could read it.

Because he was also upside down.

He was at that moment dangling from a long rope, that was wrapped around his ankle.

He was slowly revolving[2], just as you imagine a fourteen-year-old boy would slowly revolve when hanging from the battlements[3] of the castle by a single rope wrapped around his ankle.

Now, maybe I started this story in the wrong place, and I should go back a little, to the reason why Cudweed was hanging by a rope from the battlements.

It all began one morning when Valevine seemed very grumpy, during breakfast. He is often grumpy over breakfast, for example, when he hasn't slept well, but this morning there was something more seriously wrong. He was looking through his diary, counting on his fingers and, it seemed, doing some calculations.

'Blast[4]!' he said, finally. 'What is it?' asked Solstice.

(I should mention that Solstice is now away at university but had just come back for the Easter holidays. So, everything was just like old times, which is to say; total chaos.)

'Bad news, I'm afraid,' her father said.

Cudweed immediately looked worried.

'Bad news?' he asked. 'News? The bad kind? Bad?'

'I'm afraid so, my boy,' Valevine said. He looked deadly serious. 'It's time to clean the windows.'

'What windows?' asked Solstice.

'The windows of the castle, obviously,' Valevine said.

'But we don't clean the castle windows!' said Cudweed.

'Yes, we do! Every ten years, on May the 23rd. Whether they need doing or not.'

'They need doing!' said Minty, who had been silent up to now. 'Look at them! They're so dirty you can barely see out of them!'

'But I don't remember doing them before,' said Solstice.

'Well, for one thing, we used to pay someone else to do them,' Minty explained. 'But we decided to save the money. And for another thing, you would have been very young the last time. But if ten years have passed, then it's time to do them ourselves.'

'Yes, dear,' said Valevine. He looked at Solstice and Cudweed. 'So, who's going to do the outside?'

'The *what*?' asked Cudweed.

So that was how it had started, with a long argument about whether it would be Solstice or Cudweed who would abseil on a rope down the walls of the castle to do the outside of the windows that did not open.

It was a very long argument, during which I hid, and I only came out when it turned out that they had decided to toss a coin.

Cudweed lost. And so there he was, abseiling down the outside of the castle walls, with a bucket of hot water in one hand.

---

[1] **to show off** [ʃəʊ ɒf] angeben – [2] **to revolve** [rɪˈvɒlv] sich drehen – [3] **battlements** [ˈbætlmənts] Zinnen – [4] **Blast!** [blɑːst] *ugs.* So ein Mist!

I sat on the top of the East Tower and watched the whole thing.

I did not expect it to end well.

But in fact, it didn't even *start* well.

Cudweed looked nervous. Anxious. To be honest he looked terrified. He had just made it to his first window when Solstice stuck her head out of the window next to him, one that did open, and shouted, 'how's it going?'

Well, that was enough for Cudweed to drop the bucket, which fell a few hundred metres to the rocks below the castle wall and smashed[5] into tiny pieces.

He screamed, and started trying to climb back up, frantically. I have no idea how he managed it, but in his desperation[6], he somehow succeeded in letting the rope slip from his waist and get tangled around[7] his ankle. So, there he was; hanging upside down with just the rope around one ankle, way above the ground and with nothing else to save him.

At that moment, Valevine poked his head out[8] of the window next to Solstice.

'Spot of bother[9], eh?'

Cudweed screamed again, for about five minutes. Then he took a deep breath and then he shouted, 'Get me out of here!'

Now, the next thing that happened was Minty, who poked her head out of a third window, and said, 'Cudweed, stop messing around when you should be cleaning windows. Anyway, you have an important letter.'

She was waving the letter in her hand, and she clearly expected him to read it, there and then.

'Now?' cried Cudweed.

'Yes, now!' said Minty. 'It's very important.'

'I'm a bit busy,' said Cudweed.

'Stop making excuses[10]!' said Minty. 'You always make excuses.'

Now personally, I thought that Cudweed had a point, but Minty would not be stopped.

She saw that she was too far away to hand the letter to Cudweed, so she had me fly over, and take it from her. Then I had to fly upside down so Cudweed could read it.

And he did, eventually, and that involved some very clever flying from me, not only upside down, but hovering[11] in front of Cudweed's face for long enough for him to take the whole thing in[12].

Finally, when he had read it, he was not happy.

He took an even deeper breath and then he shouted 'Get me out of here!' so loud, and so crossly, that everyone did what they should have done in the first place, and rushed up to the rooftops[13] to haul[14] Cudweed back up to safety.

'What is it?' asked Solstice once Cudweed was safe again and everyone had got their breath back.

Cudweed showed the letter to everyone.

'I have to do work experience!!' he said. 'It's an official letter. It says that although I have been home-schooled, I still have to go and do work experience somewhere. Real work! In a real company!'

'Well, what's so bad about that?' asked Solstice.

'I don't want to!' cried Cudweed.

'Ah,' said Solstice. 'That is a problem. I see.'

'No, you don't see,' Cudweed said, 'it's *even worse* than that!'

At this point he glared at[15] his parents.

'I would have had a free choice of places to go, but …'

'But …?' asked Solstice, who was also looking at her parents as if she knew what Cudweed was about to say.

'Apparently, this letter is a final warning. They sent five other letters over the last four months, explaining what I needed to do. And what I needed to do was choose from a long list of the places I could go to.'

---

[5] **to smash** [smæʃ] zeschmettern; zerschlagen – [6] **desperation** [ˌdespəˈreɪʃən] Verzweiflung – [7] **to get tangled around** [get ˈtæŋgəld əˈraʊnd] sich in etw./um etw. wickeln; verwicklen – [8] **to poke out** [pəʊk aʊt] aus etw. herausschauen – [9] **spot of bother** [spɒt əv ˈbɒðə] in Schwierigkeiten – [10] **to make excuses** [meɪk ɪkˈskjuːsɪz] Ausflüchte machen; Ausreden haben – [11] **to hover** [ˈhɒvə] schweben – [12] **to take sth. in** [teɪk ˈsʌmθɪŋ ɪn] etw. aufnehmen; etw. verstehen – [13] **rooftop** [ˈruːftɒp] Dach – [14] **to haul** [hɔːl] ziehen – [15] **to glare at sb.** [gleə ət ˈsʌmbɒdi] jdn. zornig anstarren

'Do you know what happened to those letters, Father? Mother?' asked Solstice, who knew *perfectly well* what had happened to those letters.

'Well, we have to light the fires in the castle with *something*,' said Valevine, looking very uncomfortable.

'I thought so,' said Cudweed. 'So now there is just a choice of three things left.'

He did not look happy, and when he read from the letter, we saw why.

'One! I can go to a factory at the docks where they turn the insides[16] of fish into dog food.'

'Oh,' said Solstice, looking ill.

'Two! I can go to a university department where they are running ten boring experiments into the most boring jobs of all time, and study what makes them boring by doing the boring jobs.'

'Ah,' said Valevine. 'Eeee. Oh.'

'Or, three!' said Cudweed, 'I can go to a tiny place in the very far north of Scotland and learn how to make bagpipes!'

'Hmm,' said Minty, 'which one are you going to choose?'

'Well, it will have to be the bagpipes, won't it?' said Cudweed, looking very cross.

'It doesn't sound so bad, does it?' said Solstice. 'Scotland might be fun.'

'Scotland will be cold and wet,' Cudweed said. 'I know it will.'

'Making bagpipes might be fun,' Minty added.

'No it won't,' said Cudweed, firmly.

'Why not?' asked Valevine. 'It could be a useful thing to learn.'

'Useful?!' cried Cudweed, looking angrier than ever. 'Anyway, I don't want to. For one thing, bagpipes sound like someone is strangling[17] a cat. No, that's wrong, two cats. And for another thing, it's cruel!'

'Cruel?' asked Minty, 'How is it cruel?'

'You know how they make bagpipes?' Cudweed asked. Everyone shook their heads.

'Well, it's obvious, isn't it?' Cudweed said. 'You only have to look at them! Obviously, you just take a sheep, and turn it inside out. Then you drill some holes in one of its legs and blow. That's why they make such an awful sound – it's the dead sheep screaming.'

Everyone stared at Cudweed.

'I'm not sure that's how you make bagpipes,' said Solstice. 'In fact, I'm pretty sure it isn't.'

'It is,' said Cudweed, 'and it's cruel. Not only to the sheep, but to everyone who has to listen to the things afterwards.'

'I really think you might be wrong,' said Solstice.

'Well,' said Minty, 'it looks like you're going to have the chance to find out, doesn't it?'

'Unless you prefer the job at the fish factory?' asked Valevine, 'Or the boring research into boring things?'

Cudweed didn't even bother replying to this suggestion from his father, and he stomped off to his room, explaining that he was going to start packing, because he had to leave in two days' time, and that he was going to spend most of his time experimenting with putting different things in his ears to try to block out the sound of the bagpipes.

I felt really sorry for him, and I tried to cheer him up by sitting in his room with him while he put various things in his ears, like socks, pasta and the stalks[18] of large flowers, with the flowers still attached. Having

---

[16] **insides** [ɪnˈsaɪdz] Innereien – [17] **to strangle** [ˈstræŋgl] erdrosseln; ersticken – [18] **stalk** [stɔːk] Stängel – [19] **hi-fi (high fidelity)** [ˈhaɪ faɪ] Hi-Fi-Anlage; Stereoanlage

put something in his ears, he would then play music as loud as he could on his hi-fi[19], and then he'd shake his head sadly, because nothing he tried blocked the sound out completely.

But he was so unhappy, I didn't want to leave him, and I made myself comfortable on a pile of his clothes while he went on trying to find the perfect earplugs[20].

Two days later, Cudweed sat on a train, heading north to Scotland. Solstice, Minty and Valevine had taken him to the station with his two suitcases and put him on board. The train rattled[21] along at high speed, and as it went, the weather got worse. It got colder and colder, and then it started raining, and it was hard to believe it was May.

How do I know this?

Well, that is very simple.

I had spent a long time sitting with Cudweed in his room while he put things in his ears. I didn't want to leave him because he looked so miserable, but eventually, as he worked on long into the night, I had fallen asleep on the pile of clothes on his bed.

And the next thing I knew, I woke up in a small dark place that smelled of socks, and it didn't take me long to work out what had happened – Cudweed had packed me in one of his suitcases!

I'd squawked and squawked but although Cudweed heard me and quickly let me out, I already knew that it was too late, because I could feel the rocking[22] of the train and hear the noise of the wheels on the tracks[23].

'Ark!' I cried.

'Edgar!' said Cudweed, 'I'm so pleased to see you! And I'm very glad you didn't die in my suitcase.'

So was I. I mean, the lack of air was one thing, the smell of the socks was even more dangerous ...

'Are you coming with me?' asked Cudweed.

'Kaork!' I said.

'Or maybe it was just an accident[24]? Maybe you want to fly home?'

'Kraaark,' I said.

Cudweed looked out of the window, and saw the name of a small railway station flying by.

'Erm, we're a long way into Scotland already,' he said. 'Sorry. I mean, you don't have to come with me, only ...'

Now, I *could* have climbed out of the window and flown home. It wasn't that far, not for a strong raven like me.

But there were two things that stopped me.

First, it was raining, and I *really* hate flying in the rain.

And second, there was Cudweed's face.

He was looking at me with hope and sadness all mixed together, and I knew I could not leave him to face the bagpipes alone.

---

[20] **earplugs** ['ɪəplʌgz] Ohrenstöpsel – [21] **to rattle** ['rætl] rattern – [22] **to rock** [rɒk] *hier:* schaukeln – [23] **(train) tracks** [træks] Bahnschienen – [24] **accident** ['æksɪdənt] Versehen

South Africa

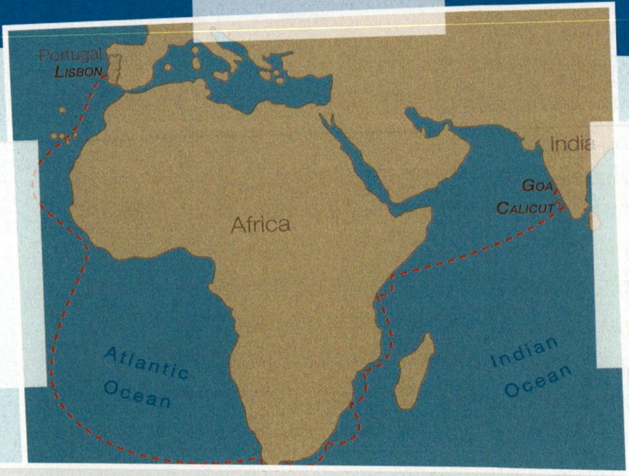

1 Kenny, a British exchange student in Johannesburg, has put together ideas for his first blog. For each section, he's found a photo and drafted a few lines. Choose the topic that you find the most interesting and research more details. Then present your topic to the class.

My classmates here in Jozi learn about the early explorers from Europe to South Africa including Bartolomeu Dias and Vasco da Gama from Portugal.

...

You notice a lot of influence from the Netherlands here. A key step in South African history was the founding of Cape Colony as a base for a Dutch trading company.

...

Most South Africans are of Black African origin. The country has eleven official languages, and this multilingual population is fluent in at least two. IsiZulu and isiXhosa are the most common. Luckily for me, English is the language of public life and the media, but it's actually spoken at home by only one in ten people. The other main language is Afrikaans, which comes from Dutch.

...

They call South Africa the Rainbow Nation because of its multicultural diversity. Its flag is a combination of colours that represents the unity and diversity of the country.

...

Of course, I'd heard of apartheid before I came, but I didn't realize it comes from the Afrikaans word for 'being apart'. It was the system of racial discrimination in South Africa between 1948 and 1993. People of colour were segregated from the minority white population by law. The system was criticized all over the world and ended when Nelson Mandela became president.

...

Jozi's a very big city! The population is nearly six million today. The Johannesburg township of Soweto, where over two million people live, is the biggest black urban settlement in Africa and is very different from the wealthy suburb where I'm staying.

...

The landscape is just awesome – I had no idea that it was so amazing. It's got everything: high, flat plateaus, a mountainous region called the Great Escarpment with the Table Mountain as well as dry sandy deserts and long white beaches.
...

From aardvarks to zebras, South Africa is full of wildlife. There are dozens of protected marine and land areas, including the Kruger National Park. But many species are in danger of extinction.
...

Sport is massive in South Africa! Rugby, cricket and soccer are the top three, with athletics and cycling super popular, too. I'm learning that sport has always been political over here.
...

2 **a** Tricia, one of Kenny's schoolmates back home, interviews him online for a school project. Look at her questions and speculate where these phrases might occur in Kenny's answers. Then listen and check.

15

badly educated ■ contradictions and extremes ■ crime and violence ■ middle classes ■ social inequalities

1 What struck you about South Africa when you first arrived?
2 Do most tourists notice the social differences in South Africa?
3 Do you think that racial discrimination is a thing of the past?
4 OK, so what is life like for the black majority of the population?
5 And finally, does it feel like a safe country to live in?

b Pool your information and summarize Kenny's impression of South Africa.

c If you could go to South Africa for a few months, where would you go and what would you be most interested in doing? Discuss and explain your choices.

YOUR TRACK

After this workshop you will be able to:

- talk about South Africa during and after apartheid.
- give a presentation about a sporting celebrity.
- express your opinion about animal conservation.
- understand issues of diversity, identity and inclusion.
- analyse a literary text and a song. (Workshop task)

Hi from Jozi!

1 It's complicated

17 **a** Kenny is staying with his Uncle Bob and cousin in Johannesburg. Listen to the first part of their conversation with Annika's classmate Elton and answer the questions.

1. How does Annika feel about her city?
2. Why does Elton describe himself as 'one of a lucky minority'?
3. What do South African teens refer to when they use the Afrikaans word 'lekker'?
4. How is Annika's experience of language learning different from Kenny's? What about your own?

18 **b** Listen to the next part of the conversation about apartheid and do the tasks.

1. Explain Elton's example of a 'pass raid' in your own words.
2. Name at least two things Annika says about apartheid.
3. Give your opinion about Bob's relationship to his colleague Amos.
4. Explain how Amos responded when Bob mentioned Mahatma Gandhi.
5. Apartheid was abolished in 1994. Comment on Bob's reference to 'the man that made it happen'.

2 Nelson Mandela

a In groups, pool what you know about Nelson Mandela.

b Read this short biography and decide where the missing phrases go.

a political group ■ and remained the symbolic leader of the anti-apartheid movement ■ closely together ■ lifted the ban on the ANC and ■ regardless of skin colour ■ throughout his 27 years in prison

Nelson Mandela was a black South African lawyer who felt everyone should be treated the same, [1]. He joined the African National Congress (ANC), [2] which campaigned for equal rights for everyone and which was later banned. Mandela, who was sentenced to life, became the world's most famous prisoner [3] – a man whose resolve remained unbroken [4]. In 1990, President FW de Klerk, who was aware that South Africa was heading towards a racial civil war, [5] released Nelson Mandela. The two men worked [6] to finally end apartheid, for which they were jointly awarded the Nobel Peace Prize in 1993. A year later, Mandela became South Africa's first black president.

16 Words and phrases

to be sentenced to life	the punishment of being sent to prison for the rest of one's life
to curtail	to reduce or limit sth.
to walk tall	to walk or behave in a way that shows one feels proud and confident
inalienable rights	a right that cannot be taken away from sb.
indignity	a situation that makes you feel embarrassed or ashamed

→ Workbook, pages 31/32

c Complete a biography from another source with words from the box in the correct form.

activist ■ campaigner ■ democratic ■ election ■ guilty ■ to imprison ■ lawyer ■ party ■ to serve ■ trial

During his early career as a [1], Mandela became a political [2] with the banned political [3], the African National Congress (ANC). In 1964, he was [4] for life for plotting violent revolution. 'I am the first accused' were the opening words of his speech in his own defence at his [5]. Mandela, who became a symbolic figurehead for anti-apartheid and anti-racist [6] throughout the world, was found [7] of organizing sabotage. He [8] 27 years in prison before being released in 1990. In 1994, the ANC won the South African [9] and Mandela became president, the first black head of state and the first person elected by a fully representative [10] election.

3 Relatively speaking

a Look at **G 6**, then find some examples of relative clauses in **2b**.

b Complete Kenny's blog with appropriate relative pronouns.

The African National Congress, [1] was formed in 1912, defended the rights of the African people. These were basic human rights [2] had been seriously curtailed. It was a political situation [3] arose after many years of oppression. Nelson Mandela was not a man [4] believed in or encouraged violence. He was a powerful speaker [5] words touched the hearts of millions. He was one of the people [6] formed an illegal organization. They found themselves in a position in [7] they had to accept the status quo or defy the law. However, they managed to break the law in a way [8] avoided violence; in other words, using passive resistance. He and others [9] started the organization were all arrested.

»» page 76

4 A rainbow nation.

Read the extracts from Mandela's speech when he became president in 1994 and do the tasks.

[...] we shall build the society in which all South Africans, both black and white, will be able to walk tall without any fear in their hearts, assured of the inalienable right to human dignity – a rainbow nation at peace with itself and the world. [...]

Let there be justice for all.

Let there be peace for all. Let there be work, bread, water and salt for all.

Let each know that for each the body, the mind and the soul have been freed to fulfil themselves. Never, never, and never again shall it be that this beautiful land will again experience the oppression of one by another and suffer the indignity of being the skunk of the world.

Let freedom reign. [...]

Source [abbreviated]: Nelson Mandela, 1994 Presidential Inauguration, South African Government, 10 May 1994, https://www.gov.za/statement-president-african-national-congress-nelson-mandela-his-inauguration-president-democratic [27.02.2023]

1 Outline the context in which Mandela makes this speech.
2 Show how the words 'rainbow nation' are so evocative.
3 Explain two possible reasons why Mandela mentions salt.
4 Comment on any of the techniques or devices below which Mandela uses.

aggression ■ contrast ■ emotion ■ example ■ humour ■ irony ■ repetition ■ rhetorical question ■ sincerity

5 YOUR TURN: *The Foreign Me*

a Discuss what aspects of life in Germany may have led a South African woman living in Berlin, to write a book entitled *The Foreign Me*.

12 **b** Watch the video about Matilda, then summarize and comment on her experiences.

c Talk about how to make a newcomer feel welcome in your community.

Practice: Accept and respect

1 **GET STARTED!** What does 'accept and respect' mean to you? Find a way to illustrate it, then present your ideas to the class.

Ask
Curious
Contrast
Each other
Partner
Tolerance

2 ***Tsotsi*, a film review**

a Combine the sentences from a review with *that, which, who, whose* or *where*. You will sometimes have to make other changes.

The movie Tsotsi is about gang violence. Tsotsi is set in a slum in Johannesburg.
*The movie Tsotsi, **which** is set in a slum in Johannesburg, is about gang violence.*

1. The main protagonist is a teenager known as Tsotsi. He has been hardened by his tough life.
2. 'Tsotsi' is South African slang. It means 'urban crook or criminal'.
3. Tsotsi runs away from home and lives with other homeless kids. His mother is dying.
4. One day during a gang hit, Tsotsi steals a car. He finds a three-month-old baby in it.
5. He abandons the car, but takes the baby back to the slum. He lives in the slum.
6. The next six days bring about a change in Tsotsi. The change couldn't be foreseen.

»» page 76

b Complete the phrases in the TIP box with your own ideas to write a review of an action film.

TIP

Writing a film review
The main protagonist is … who …
The action takes place when … and it is set in …
It has good characters, most of whom …
The film will appeal to viewers who …
Without giving any spoilers, the film has an ending that …
In my opinion, this is …

»» **c** Complete your review with more details. Check on the internet if necessary.

3 **Privilege**

a Discuss these anonymous quotes about privilege.

Privilege is invisible to those who have it.

When you are accustomed to privilege equality feels like oppression.

Privilege is like a glass shield, protecting some from life's harsh realities while leaving others exposed to the storms.

Privilege is having doors open for you that others must break down.

Privilege is the headstart in the race of life, leaving others far behind at the starting line.

b Talk about what you understand by the word 'privilege'. What privileges have you earned, for example now you are more senior at school?

19 Words and phrases

inclusivity	the policy of treating all types of people, things or ideas fairly and equally
divisive	causing disagreement between people
able-bodiedness	having a strong and healthy body
poignantly	causing a strong feeling of sadness
heteronormativity	the assumption that heterosexuality is the only mode of sexual orientation

→ Workbook, pages 33 – 35

c Read the introduction to an article about privilege in South Africa's 'rainbow nation' today. Talk about what you think a 'privilege walk' is.

How can we begin a conversation about diversity and inclusivity? The 'privilege walk' exercise helps participants develop awareness of themselves, which can improve how they relate to others. In this way, it invites people to think about ways inclusivity can create positive changes in their relationships.

4 READING FOCUS: The privilege walk

a Read the whole article. List any new words, then compare with a partner. If you can't work out the meanings, check in a dictionary.

Apartheid capitalized on differences in race, culture and gender. When it was finally abolished in 1994, South Africa introduced a new ideology in the name of nation building: 'rainbowism'. This emphasized common ground and sameness rather than a focus on difference and was meant to fight racism and discrimination. […]

This worldview is problematic on many levels. It focuses on the parts of multi-culturalism that are comfortable for a white minority. Privilege is a particularly complex, emotional and difficult topic to discuss. How can conversations around race, class and gender be allowed back into classrooms without becoming emotionally harmful and divisive? […]

A number of academics devised an activity called the 'privilege walk'. […] The walk visualizes systemic privilege in a way that mere discussions cannot. Participants are presented with statements related to race, gender, class, sexuality, age, religion, able-bodiedness and so on. Students then either step forward or back depending on whether the question reinforces privilege or oppression. Some examples of the statements are: If one or both of your parents have a university degree, take one step forward; if you rely, or have relied, primarily on public transportation, take one step back; if you are able to move through the world without fear of sexual assault, take one step forward; if you feel bad about how your identities are portrayed by the media, take one step back. This exercise almost always leaves white men at the front of the room and black women at the back – just as it is in society. Students end up positioned in a social grid that poignantly represents society's current state.

The privilege walk created space for interesting conversations about the legacy of apartheid and how South Africa still values whiteness, masculinity and heteronormativity. It was the start of something valuable. […]

Source [abbreviated and adapted]: Daniela Gachago, Asanda Ngoasheng, "South Africa's 'rainbow nation' is a myth that students need to unlearn", The Conversation, 19 October 2016, https://theconversation.com/south-africas-rainbow-nation-is-a-myth-that-students-need-to-unlearn-66872 [27.02.2023]

b Explain the process and the function of the privilege walk activity in your own words. Do you think this is a good way to develop self-awareness or not? Give reasons for your answers.

5 YOUR CHOICE: Are you one of the lucky ones?

a Choose whether you wish to write four more statements to encourage awareness of privilege or to draw attention to lack of privilege.

b Display your questions, read them all and then, as a class, choose the best for a privilege walk.

c Decide if you wish to do the walk. Then get into two groups. Group **A** does the walk and group **B** collects ideas as to how to support those less fortunate or privileged.

@ WES-40326-002

Sports and politics

PART 1

PART 2

PART 3

1 **A challenging relationship.** Discuss how sports and politics influence each other and think of examples to illustrate this.

2 **Dolly dropped**

a Read the article. Explain in your own words how D'Oliveira made history.

It was not until 1968 that the British had the problem of apartheid in cricket brought home to them in a dramatic way over the 'D'Oliveira affair'.

Basil D'Oliveira, an outstanding South African all-rounder known as Dolly, was not allowed to play cricket for his country of birth. Born of Indian and Portuguese parents, he was labelled as Cape Coloured, which disqualified him from playing in a 'whites only' team. He left South Africa in 1960 to play in England. By 1968, he was a top player and the organizers of the team, the MCC, should have chosen him for an English tour of South Africa. However, there was considerable speculation about whether the English team might not be permitted to enter South Africa with Basil D'Oliveira in it.

When Dolly was omitted from that touring team, it provoked one of the sharpest controversies in the history of English cricket. The uproar that followed their decision not to include him must have shocked the MCC. A journalist at that time suggested that a businessman might have tried to bribe Dolly not to play, but that may have been a rumour. The MCC could and should have responded differently. However, when one of the team due to play against South Africa was injured, D'Oliveira was included in the team at the eleventh hour. As a result, the South African government was furious. Prime Minister Vorster's speech in Bloemfontein, in which he announced that a team with D'Oliveira in it was unwelcome, was received by his audience with huge enthusiasm. As a consequence of this reaction, neither D'Oliveira nor the English team went to South Africa.

b With the help of a dictionary, decide which heading you would choose for an article about D'Oliveira and explain why.

WHEN RACISM STUMPS CRICKET

D'OLIVEIRA CHANGES THE COLOUR OF SPORT

DOLLY OUT: IT'S JUST NOT CRICKET!

TIP

Modals to express doubt and certainty

- We use *might / may / could* + *have* + past participle if we are unsure about something.
  *A businessman **might have tried** a bribe but it **may / could have been** a rumour.*
- We use *should / must* + *have* + past participle if we are very sure about something.
  *The MCC **should have responded differently**.*
  *The uproar **must have shocked** them.* → G7

3 **The Dolly affair: a summary**

a Complete the summary with *could / should / must / might have* + the past participle of a verb from the box. More than one modal is sometimes possible.

offer ■ never play ■ react ■ select ■ not understand

Classified as 'Cape Coloured', D'Oliveira [1] for South Africa. He was a great all-rounder so the MCC [2] him for the English team, but they did not. Someone [3] D'Oliveira money not to play, but that's not certain. People were convinced that the MCC [4] in another way. The world [5] the impact of apartheid without the Dolly affair.

»» p. 76

b How does this story make you feel? Complete these sentences.

1 A non-white sportsperson in 1968 must have ...
2 In my opinion, the UK government should have ...
3 If I'd been a teenager back then, I might have ...

20 **Words and phrases**

controversy a (public) disagreement that involves different ideas or opinions about sth.
uproar a loud and angry protest
to bribe to give sb. sth. in return for a favour

→ Workbook, pages 36/37

4 *Invictus*

13 **a** Watch the trailer for the film *Invictus*. Outline the main theme in your own words. Explain if you would like to watch it and why (not).

21 **b** Kenny watched *Invictus* with Annika and Elton. Listen to the first part of their conversation and decide if the statements are true or false.

1 Elton agrees with Kenny that *Invictus* is a feel-good movie.
2 Annika believes Mandela used rugby to calm white men's fears.
3 The importance of rugby at Elton's school tells us something about the school.
4 The name 'Springbok' was enough to ensure that the South African team won.
5 Most white South Africans thought the Springbok icon shouldn't change.

5 A lesser man would have failed

14 **a** Watch the video or look at **G 5** and decide what this sentence means.

If Mandela hadn't recognized the importance of rugby to white South African identity, he would not have achieved so much.

A Mandela understood the potential of rugby, but didn't achieve his goals.
B Mandela didn't understand the potential of rugby and so didn't achieve his goals.
C Mandela understood the potential of rugby, so he achieved his goals.

b Look at the score chart for the 1995 Rugby World Cup and complete the sentences with the correct form of the verbs in brackets.

17.06.1995	South Africa	19	15	France	F.
18.06.1995	England	29	45	New Zealand	N.Z.
3rd place play-off, 22.06.1995	France	19	9	England	E.
Final, 24.06.1995	South Africa	15	12 (after extra time)	New Zealand	N.Z.

1 If South Africa ___ (*not win*) in the semi-finals, they ___ (*not qualify*) for the final.
2 New Zealand ___ (*not be*) in the final if they ___ (*lose*) to England on 18 June.
3 If England ___ (*win*) the play off, they ___ (*be*) in third place.
4 South Africa ___ (*not win*) the final if they ___ (*not score*) in extra time.

»» **page 76**

6 The Springboks win.

22 Listen to the rest of the friends' conversation and do the tasks.

1 Explain why Elton says that Mandela made a brave gesture.
2 Comment on what Elton means by 'the icing on the cake'.
3 Discuss the significance of Siya Kolisi being captain in the 2018 World Cup.
4 In Annika's opinion, 'a lesser man would have failed'. Explain in your own words what she means and give your own opinion.

TIP

- **Expressing doubt**
  I'm not entirely sure.
  I'm not certain I understand; but I don't really get why …
- **Expressing certainty**
  certainly / obviously / unquestionably
  There's no doubt about it.
  What is undeniable is that …

7 YOUR TURN: Making a difference

a THINK: 'Sometimes sport really does make a difference in society'. Which of these two sporting stories do you think made a bigger impact.

b PAIR: Find someone who disagrees with you and discuss your opinions.

c SHARE: Share your information with another pair and ask questions to find out more.

Practice: Headline news

1 **GET STARTED!** Compile a list of top sports idols.

2 **Sensations sell**

a Zola Budd, a South African runner, competed for Britain in the 1984 Olympics. Before you read an article about her, decide if the headlines are positive or negative.

BAREFOOT ZOLA FINDS STORMY HARBOUR

TEENAGE PRODIGY UNWELCOME IN ENGLAND

ZOLA: I'LL RUN MY HEART OUT FOR BRITAIN

ZOLA GO HOME

OLYMPIC CHANCE FOR BLOEMFONTEIN GIRL

MAIL BRINGS WONDER GIRL ZOLA TO BRITAIN

b Read about Zola Budd's early life. Decide where the missing phrases go.

A and she became a celebrity
B a privileged teenager from a racist nation
C and sensations sell newspapers
D where they lived
E faster than any woman had run it before
F running without shoes
G when Zola was old enough
H and South Africa was banned from participating

Zola was skinny and terrible at team sports, but her idolized older sister Jenny liked running so [1], she ran, too. They ran at high altitude over the hills surrounding Bloemfontein, [2]. They ran barefoot like all the children in rural South Africa. They ran for fun, and Zola got fast.

When Zola was 14, her sister died. No one in the family talked about it. And Zola? She ran harder than ever. 'If Jenny hadn't died,' she said, 'I probably would have become a nurse.' A few years after Jenny's death, she ran 5,000 metres in 15:01.83, [3]. Life would never be normal for Zola again. In 1983, *Daily Mail* journalist John Bryant spotted some race results that suggested there was a white South African teenage girl, [4], who was breaking world records. The Olympics were coming up [5], and to Bryant, that made the story irresistible. *The Mail* offered the Budds £100,000 for exclusive rights to Zola's story. They also promised to fast-track her so she would receive a British passport. That allowed her to run in the Olympics [6].

There were demos when she arrived in England. People booed her and shouted insults. When interviewed, the shy teenager admitted knowing nothing about Mandela. She was a white South African, [7], using a technicality for her personal ambition. She was a sensation, [8].

c Complete Kenny's conversation with Tricia using the correct form of the verbs in brackets.

Tricia Why did Zola Budd ran barefoot?
Kenny If she [1] (*not live*) in rural South Africa, Zola [2] (*not run*) without shoes. And she probably [3] (*not become*) a runner if she [4] (*not lose*) her sister.
Tricia And Bryant came across her by chance?
Kenny Yes, Bryant [5] (*never hear*) of Zola if he [6] (*not read*) some race results.
Tricia But why was it so sensational?
Kenny If South Africa [7] (*not be banned*) from the Olympics, the story [8] (*not hit*) the headlines.
Tricia But she didn't have a British passport?
Kenny No. Zola [9] (*not be able to*) run in the Olympics if she [10] (*not receive*) a British passport so quickly.
Tricia And she hadn't heard of Mandela?
Kenny If she [11] (*be*) a black South African, I'm sure she [12] (*know*) about Mandela.

23 **Words and phrases**

to idolize sb. to admire and respect sb. very much
eligible having the necessary qualities

→ Workbook, pages 38/39

3 Sport for all

24 **a** Kenny and Tricia are giving a class presentation about sport for athletes with a disability. Listen to Tricia's part and do the tasks.

1. Explain the origin of 'Paralympics'.
2. Mention at least two ways Tricia says you should refer to people with disabilities.
3. Describe why being overly politically correct can be perceived as patronizing.

b Complete Kenny's information about South African para-athlete Charl du Toit with some of the correct phrases from the box.

had done ■ had seen ■ had understood ■ hadn't been ■ hadn't had ■ might have chosen ■ might not have chosen ■ would choose ■ would have understood ■ would never have seen ■ you'd have been

Why did Charl choose this sport? He [1] running if his father [2] an athletics coach. **What condition does he have?** Although he had had cerebral palsy from birth, Charl had always competed against able-bodied guys. If he [3] an injury in his teens, he [4] a physio, who said he was eligible to compete in para sports. **What happened next?** He took some tests and everything became much clearer. If he [5] the tests earlier, he [6] some of his difficulties, for example why he couldn't use his right hand properly. And when it came to deciding on a university, the choice was clear: if top sprinter coach Suzanne Ferreira [7] at Stellenbosch University, he [8] to study somewhere else. **Is Charl a Living Legend?** If you [9] him run in Rio, [10] in little doubt that he was a great athlete! He definitely has celebrity status in South Africa, not just for being a gold medallist.

4 SPEAKING FOCUS: Good press, bad press

25 **a** Listen to an interview about Marcus Rashford. Do research for a talk and think about the following:

- What is he famous for?
- What global event happened, with what result?
- How did he react, what did he achieve and how was he received by the media?

b Pool your information. Then compile your ideas into one talk to give to the class.

c After the talks, write an evaluation sheet to help you improve your talks in the future.

5 In the news

a On the board, list sportspeople or other celebrities who recently made headline news. Each pair chooses somebody different. Then do research and make notes.

b Take turns to talk for two or three minutes and record your talk. Check if you can make any improvements. Choose the best one to present.

c Listen to the talks and fill in the evaluation sheet from **4c**. Give each other feedback.

Method coach: Literary terms and devices

CULTURE CORNER

Trevor Noah
Trevor Noah was born to a South African mother and a Swiss father in South Africa in the 1980s, when according to the apartheid laws, he was labelled 'coloured'. He lived in Soweto with his grandmother and mother, from whom he learned several of the languages spoken in South Africa. Now in the US, he is a successful comedian, writer, and TV personality.

S1 ***Born a Crime.*** Discuss what you think the title of Trevor Noah's autobiography *Born a Crime* means.

S2 **Literary terms**

a Match the terms in the box with the definitions.

narrator ■ plot ■ point of view ■ protagonist ■ setting ■ theme

1 the main subject of a book or story
2 the character telling the story
3 when and where the story takes place
4 the perspective from which the story is told
5 one of the main characters in the story
6 the storyline and how it develops

b Now read a review of one of the stories in *Born a Crime*. Which of the points 1 – 6 does it contain?

Chameleon is an autobiographical short story in a collection called *Born a Crime* by South African author Trevor Noah. He writes in the first person about growing up as neither a black nor a white child at a time when apartheid laws separated black and white people. Kept largely secret from the white authorities, Noah stands out among nearly a million residents in the black township of Soweto as the boy with lighter skin. 'I was famous in my neighborhood just because of the color of my skin.' Whilst the themes of racism and equality he deals with are complex and serious, Noah's writing style is simplistic, and often funny. For example, one metaphor compares skin color with white, dark and milk chocolate: '... and I was the milk chocolate. But we were all just chocolate.' As a so-called 'colored boy' growing up in a black African family, he enjoys certain 'privileges' and says his family 'treated me like I was white'. An example of this and his effective use of humour is when Noah describes how his grandfather insists on being his chauffeur. Noah acknowledges this as strange but never challenges him. 'What was I going to say? "I believe your perception of race is flawed, Grandfather"? No. I was five. I sat in the back.' One of the most interesting aspects of *Chameleon* is Noah's ability to speak several African languages, and he adds spice to his story by using some of them. He finds this skill invaluable in connecting with people of different races and backgrounds, for example being accepted by black classmates when he proves he can speak their language. *Chameleon* is written from an interesting perspective and its themes are important and continue to have relevance today. It is also very enjoyable to read so I can recommend it and the other stories in this collection.

S3 **Literary devices**

a Read the TIP box, then watch the video. Say which literary devices these examples illustrate.

15

she's as strong as a bear — mother is an ocean
my TV speaks hatred — boom, boom, boom
a jar of jolly juicy jujubes

TIP

Literary devices
- Identify the literary devices used.
- Relate them to a character, the main theme or setting.
- Give examples or quotes.
- Comment on how effective each device is.

b Now read some examples from *Born a Crime*. Which literary devices do they illustrate?

1 apartheid's walls cracked and crumbled
2 [...] the benchmark is black. [...] Black is beautiful.
3 A dog is [...] like a bicycle but with emotions.
4 In my class we had all kinds of kids. Black kids, white kids, Indian kids, colored kids [...]
5 Trevor, [...] you're sitting on a gold mine.

→ Workbook, page 40

Workshop task: Analysing an extract

S1 Preparing to write an analysis

a Read an extract from *Chameleon*. Summarize in a few sentences what happens.

Then recess came. We went out on the playground, and black kids were *everywhere*. It was an ocean of black, like someone had opened a tap and all the black had come pouring out. I was like, *Where were they all hiding?* The white kids I'd met that morning, they went in one direction, the black kids went in another direction, and I was left standing in the middle, totally confused. [...]

I was eleven years old. and it was like I was seeing my country for the first time. In the townships you don't see segregation, because everyone is black. [...] Before that day, I had never seen people being together and yet not together, occupying the same space yet choosing not to associate with each other in any way. In an instant I could see, I could feel, how the boundaries were drawn. Groups moved in color patterns across the yard, up the stairs, down the hall. It was insane. I looked over at the white kids I'd met that morning. Ten minutes earlier I'd thought I was at a school where they were a majority. Now I realized how few of them there actually were compared to everyone else.

I stood there awkwardly by myself in this no-man's-land in the middle of the playground. Luckily, I was rescued by the Indian kid from my class, a guy named Theesan Pillay. Theesan was one of the few Indian kids in school, so he'd noticed me, another obvious outsider, right away. He ran over to introduce himself. "Hello, fellow anomaly! You're in my class. Who are you? What's your story?" We started talking and hit it off. [...]

Through our conversation it came up that I spoke several African languages, and Theesan thought a colored kid speaking black languages was the most amazing trick. He brought me over to a group of black kids. "Say something," he told them, "and he'll show you he understands you." One kid said something in Zulu, and I replied to him in Zulu, everyone cheered. Another kid said something in Xhosa, and I replied to him in Xhosa. Everyone cheered. [...]

The black kids were fascinated. In South Africa back then, it wasn't common to find a white person or a colored person who spoke African languages: during apartheid white people were always taught that those languages were beneath them. So the fact that I did speak African languages immediately endeared me to the black kids.

"How come you speak our languages?" they asked.

"Because I'm black," I said, "like you."

"You're not black."

"Yes, I am."

"No, you're not. Have you not seen yourself?"

They were confused at first. Because of my color, they thought I was a colored person, but speaking the same languages meant that I belonged to their tribe. It just took them a moment to figure it out. It took me a moment, too.

from *The Chameleon by* Trevor Noah. In: *Born a Crime: Stories from a South African Childhood*. New York: Spiegel & Gran International Edition, 2016, pp. 57–50.

TIP

Summarizing an extract

It is set in … / The action takes place in …
It's written from the point of view of …
It describes / illustrates / shows / explains …
The conflict arises when … / A crisis is reached as …
The resolution of the plot / problem happens when …

b Discuss what the most significant theme is and how it makes you feel. Then note down any relevant parts from the extract for a written answer.

TIP

Annotating an extract

- Read the extract to get a sense of its purpose.
- Check the task so you know exactly what you have to do.
- Read the text again and annotate relevant parts.
- Highlight key parts to quote in your answer.
- Link a feature to its effect on the reader.

S2 Writing an analysis

a Using your preparation from above, write a short analysis of this extract. Make sure you:

- explain the effect of any literary devices and
- include quotes and examples.

b Check your text, then swap with a partner and give each other constructive feedback.

Wildlife in South Africa

1 **The Big Five.** Name the animals in the photo and say what they have in common. Then read the text and do the tasks below.

A visit to the Rainbow Nation will usually combine at least one city and a safari park to create a diverse itinerary. The phrase 'the Big Five' is often used to market safari holidays, but it was first coined by big-game hunters more than 100 years ago and refers to elephants, buffalo, rhinos, lions and leopards. In other words, it was originally a hit-list rather than a safari checklist.

Four of the Big Five can still be hunted in South Africa, at a price. A lioness is typically the cheapest, costing around $9,000 to hunt, while a white rhino can cost more than $125,000, according to one report. In colonial times, big game hunting was associated with aristocracy and glamour. Today, game hunting still belongs to the elite and privileged, due to the enormous cost of doing it. Nowadays public opinion leans towards disgust rather than admiration over the killing of the Big Five.

1. Outline what the main point of the text is.
2. Analyse the difference between a hit-list and a checklist in this context.
3. Compare and contrast the attitudes to big game hunting now and in the past.

2 **Controversial conservation**

27 **a** Tricia and her parents are talking to Kenny about a possible itinerary for their upcoming trip to South Africa. Listen and note down what they hope to do. Then compare with a partner.

b Do the tasks.

1. Outline what Tricia and her parents most want to do on their trip to Cape Town.
2. Assess Tricia's reaction to visiting Robben Island compared with her mother's.
3. Explain the advantages of going to Buffelsfontein Game Reserve.
4. Discuss what you learn about ecotourism from this conversation. Add anything you know, possibly from your own holidays.

3 **We've booked!**

16 **a** Watch the video or look at **G 1** and complete the rules. There are two items you don't need. Choose examples below (A – D) to illustrate each rule.

ago ■ for ■ past ■ present ■ present perfect ■ present perfect progressive ■ since ■ when

- We use the [1] with action verbs when there is a link between the [2] and the [3]. A past time is not mentioned and we often focus on the result. Example(s) ______
- We also use it with state verbs like *be, have* and *know*. Example(s) ______
- We use the [4] with action verbs to focus on the length an action in progress. Typical signal words are [5] with a period of time and [6] with a point of time. Example(s) ___

A *We've known each other for years.*
B *We've been talking about this trip for years.*
C *We've been planning it since 2021.*
D *I've read Mandela's book.*

page 77

26 **Words and phrases**

itinerary a detailed plan of a journey
poaching the illegal hunting or capturing of wild animals

→ Workbook, pages 41 – 43

b Complete the sentences with the best form of the verbs in brackets.

1 Tricia's parents ___ (*always want*) to go to South Africa.
2 Her father's firm ___ (*work*) with a company there for 12 years now.
3 Dave's colleague, Elias, ___ (*invite*) the family to stay with them.
4 Since they booked their flights, the Hansons ___ (*discuss*) what to do there.
5 Tricia ___ (*decide*) she doesn't want to go to Robben Island prison.
6 She doesn't understand why they ___ (*make*) it into a museum.
7 Tricia and Kenny ___ (*talk about*) the pros and cons of ecotourism.
8 They ___ (*know*) each other since primary school.

»» page 77

4 Rhinos at risk

a In 2020, as the world grappled with the impact of the Covid-19 pandemic, South Africa's efforts to protect rhinos faced a tough challenge. The pandemic not only disrupted daily life but also raised concerns about the survival of rhinos. Read this report and evaluate how the crisis affected South Africa's conservation projects.

Around 70 years ago, Africa was home to more than 60,000 rhinos in Zambia alone. However, by 2019, their global population had decreased to a perilous 15,000 to 25,000, with poaching being the primary threat. In the face of this bleak scenario, the pandemic caused additional challenges.

The pandemic's most immediate impact on rhinos came with the abrupt stop of international tourism. Africa's vast national parks and private game reserves, typically bustling with travellers, were suddenly deserted. The absence of tourists, while beneficial in reducing human disturbances, created a vacuum that poachers sought to exploit. Illegal rhino horn trade, particularly in Asia, saw a disturbing increase, with some even promoting rhino horn as a Covid-19 cure on social media platforms.

Nonetheless, amidst these alarming trends, there were glimmers of hope. Rhino killings in South Africa, which currently has almost 80% of the world's rhino population, witnessed a 53% decline in the first half of the year. Movement restrictions and disrupted international flights made trade difficult for poachers.

One notable success story emerged from Marataba, north of Johannesburg. It is a privately managed section of Marakele National Park, and the vets there have succeeded in keeping a healthy rhino population despite all the challenges. Marataba's dedication to rhino conservation became a ray of hope in the midst of challenges.

As World Rhino Day approaches on September 22nd, we can conclude that the pandemic made it harder to protect rhinos, but there is hope that, by working together globally, we can save these amazing animals before it is too late.

b What do these numbers refer to in the text?

19 ■ 22 ■ 53 ■ 70 ■ 80 ■ 2019 ■ 15,000 ■ 25,000 ■ 60,000

5 YOUR TURN: The animal world

a THINK: Choose a topic from the word cloud that interests you. What do you already know about it? What else would you like to find out? Make a note of your questions.

therapy animals · the fur trade · circuses · hunting · poaching · zoos · domestic pets · animal rescue centres · intensive farming · wildlife conservation · safaris

b PAIR: Ask each other your questions, then work together to find some answers.

c SHARE: Exchange information with another pair and ask questions to find out more.

»» **d** Write a paragraph about your chosen topic outlining why it is important to you.

Practice: Making a difference

1 **GET STARTED!** Look at the photos and describe what you see. Would you like to do what these teenagers are doing?

2 **Voluntourism**

a After the holiday in Cape Town, Tricia looked into voluntourism. What does it mean?

A Helping out for free at your local tourist office
B Combining a trip abroad with volunteering
C Volunteering to clean up waste at a tourist site

b Tricia reports her findings to Kenny. Complete her email with the verbs from the box in the present perfect or present perfect progressive.

be ■ come across ■ give ■ look ■ make up ■ read ■ run ■ try ■ win

Hey Kenny
I 1 at my photos of SA all weekend and I can't wait to go back! I 2 for ages to find an ethical project for next year, but recently I 3 two or three negative reports in the press about voluntourism. I 4 several comments saying that some companies misrepresent their projects. But I 5 really impressed by projects like *People and Places* which 6 an award, because they 7 a record 80% of their profits back to the community, which is great. And someone commented that *GVI Planet* is a good all-rounder which 8 conservation projects for a while now. So, it's a choice between those two, but I think I 9 my mind. Let me know what you think.
Love for now
Tricia

page 77

3 **VIEWING FOCUS: The Black Mambas**

a Before you watch, read what Tricia said about a group of women who inspire her. Talk about what work you think these young women do.

What they do is important and amazing. People have always said it's a man's job, but they have been doing it since 2013.'

28 **Words and phrases**

to patrol	to go around an area to check that it is free from trouble or danger
reserve	a piece of land that is a protected area for animals, plants, etc.
to be empowered	to have the authority and power to do sth.
patronizing	speaking or behaving towards sb. as if they are stupid

17 **b** Watch a video clip about the Black Mambas. Summarize the young women's explanation of their work and why they love it.

c Discuss which of these reactions to the video you empathize with. Then write a comment.

Liz Hobbs • 2 months ago
The women patrolling the reserve appeared empowered and this was inspirational. It sent a good strong message. 411

Ashton Welch • 6 months ago
The soft focus and shots of half-naked women seemed exploitative and patronizing. It sent the wrong message. 50

TIP

To identify the aim of a video, consider these points:

- Who made it and who is the target audience?
- What is the mood of the video and its main message?
- How does it use evocative camera shots and music?
- Are the viewer's reactions manipulated? If so, how?

4 Volunteering in South Africa

29 **a** Listen to a radio phone-in show about volunteering holidays in South Africa. Think about which organization interests you most and note down your reasons.

b Compare your choice with a partner by doing the tasks. Then present your answers to the class.

1. Using your notes, explain to each other which volunteer holiday you would prefer and why.
2. Discuss what information or lack of information led you to your choice.
3. If none of these programmes truly appeals, talk about what type of volunteer work you would consider.

5 A helping hand

a A friend of yours is thinking of volunteering, so you share Tony's story with them. Complete your email with the verbs in brackets in the present perfect or present perfect progressive. Sometimes both are possible.

Hey!
I [1] (*mean*) to write for ages, but my school project [2] (*keep*) me busy. I know you [3] (*think*) about going on a volunteering holiday before you leave Africa. My advice is: just do it! A guy I know called Tony [4] (*just return*) from a reserve where they look after baby rhinos. He had the most amazing time there. In fact, he [5] (*talk*) about nothing else since he got home. Believe it or not, he [6] (*even be*) on a radio show to talk about it! Apparently, while he was there, he fell in love … with an orphan rhino! Seriously though, he says that he [7] (*make*) some lifelong friends, and not just among the rhinos!
I [8] (*copy*) Tony into this mail so if you need any more info, just ask him, OK?
Good luck, speak soon, …

page 77

b What effect do all the emojis have? Do you use emojis in your messages? If so, talk about how you use them and if not, explain why not.

6 Planning and recording a radio phone-in show

a Choose a topic you are all interested in for a radio phone-in show. Decide who is the interviewer / interviewees, then draft ideas for your script. Don't write the complete script as otherwise your interview will not sound natural.

b Record your interview. Then play it to the class and give each other feedback.

Music matters

1 South African sounds

a Talk about the kind of music you like. What do you know about the music of South Africa?

b Read part of an article about South African music. Each group researches one genre to find out more. Then pool your information.

South Africa's music is rich and diverse, and many genres derive their sound from the country's complex political history, especially colonialism and apartheid. By the end of the 19th century, South African cities attracted foreign musicians like American ragtime players. Enoch Sontonga was a South African composer best known for writing the Xhosa hymn *Nkosi Sikelel' iAfrika* in 1897 as a protest against colonialism. In a shortened form, this has been sung as the first half of the national anthem of South Africa since 1994.

In the early 20th century, the government imposed restrictions on blacks, including a nightly curfew. At this time, **marabi**, a style from the Johannesburg slums, became popular. Later **kwela** street music, evolved from the marabi sound, brought South African music into the international spotlight.

Christian churches spread across South Africa integrating African musical elements into their worship, resulting in South African **gospel music**, one of the most popular forms of music in the country today.

In the 1930s, the South African music scene saw the rise in importance of **Zulu a cappella**. *Mbube*, written and recorded in 1939 by a South African Zulu singer Solomon Linda, became a hit and was the first time the Zulu sound was heard worldwide.

Since then, many other musical genres such as **bubblegum**, a form of pure South African pop music, or **kwaito**, a South African style of hip hop, have influenced the music scene, many with a strong political focus. Anti-apartheid protest songs produced outside South Africa played a central role in the liberation struggle. However, such music was not without its controversies – such as *Wimoweh, The Lion Sleeps Tonight* and Paul Simon's *Graceland* album.

CULTURE CORNER

A distinguished career rewarded American singer-songwriter Paul Simon with 12 Grammy Awards as well as a Grammy Lifetime Achievement Award for his work as half of the duo Simon and Garfunkel. In 1986, Simon caused controversy by breaking the boycott of South Africa and recording his *Graceland* album there.

2 The *Graceland* controversy

31 **a** Listen to a podcast about the *Graceland* album and complete the sentences.

1 *Graceland* was …

2 *Graceland* was controversial because …

3 The cultural appropriation debate focused on …

32 **b** Read the definition, then listen to the second episode of the podcast. Each partner focuses on one person and presents their viewpoint. Discuss who you sympathize with more.

cultural appropriation UNCOUNTABLE NOUN
If a person is accused of cultural appropriation, it is thought they have taken and used elements of another culture as their own.
His latest album has been criticized for its racist cultural appropriation.

30 Words and phrases

genre a style or category of art, music or literature
ragtime a black American musical style of piano-based music from the 1980s
buzz word a word or phrase that becomes popular for a period of time

→ Workbook, pages 46/47

3 What you need to know

a Look at **G 7**, then complete the rules with the verbs in the box.

> be forced to ■ be obliged to ■ be required to ■ don't have to ■ don't need to ■ have to ■ must ■ need to ■ needn't

- To express necessity formally, we can use [1] or [2].
- We can use [3], [4] or [5] to express necessity in a neutral way.
- If an action is not necessary, we can use [6], [7] or [8].
- If the action is necessary but unwelcome, we can use [9].

b Complete the sentences with your ideas.

1 In my opinion, we **need to / don't need to** talk about cultural appropriation because …
2 I think musicians today **must / don't have to** be aware of …
3 When our parents were young, they **had to / didn't have to** …, but now …

4 Cultural appropriation

a Discuss how cultural appropriation might be relevant in the fashion industry.

33 **b** Listen and discuss the interviewer's questions:
- Is dressing up a thing of the past?
- Is cultural appropriation always wrong?
- Can it work the other way around?

5 Giving advice

a Look at **G 7**, then complete the rules with the verbs in the box. You need some more than once.

> had to ■ have to ■ must ■ should ■ will have to

- We use [1] or *ought to* to give advice. *Designers* [2] */ **ought to** be aware of cultural appropriation.*
- We use [3] to give stronger advice. *You* [4] *avoid giving offence.*
- We use a form of [5] to give stronger advice in the past or future. *They* [6] / [7] *apologize.*

b Complete these comments with verbs from **3a**. Sometimes more than one is possible.

Tonya, your interview really missed the point, in my view. Diversity is the buzz word right now: we are always being advised that we [1] to respect other cultures and enjoy the differences between us.
My skin is white, but I have big crazy hair. I always [2] braid it or it looks a real mess. In any case, we [3] never forget that imitation is the sincerest form of flattery. Surely cultural exchange is a good thing. – Kylie S.

Tonya, great to hear your interview with Sukesh. I live in London where a famous department store recently [4] apologize for using white models to advertise hair braids. The critics had a point, in my opinion. The store [5] not to have used white models. My parents are from Ghana, so I know that historically, in African culture, braids were a way of signalling your tribe and status. We [6] be more careful not to trivialize African culture and reduce it to a fashion fad. – Dakarai A.

c Compare the two arguments and write a message to the person you agree with more.

CULTURE CORNER

Fenómenos do Semba, an Angolan dance group, created dance moves to the South African hit song *Jerusalema*. The #JerusalemaDanceChallenge video went viral. Soon everyone was posting their own dance videos, all with a message of hope in the single word 'Jerusalema', amplified by an electronic beat created by Johannesburg-based musician and producer Master KG.

6 YOUR TURN: *Jerusalema*. Research some of the videos and choose your favourite to present to the class.

Practice: South African style

1 GET STARTED!

a Describe the fashions and the models in the photos. Talk about what you like or don't like.

b Choose the options in this mini quiz that best describe your attitude to fashion. Compare your choices with a partner and then with the class.

Fashionista or fashion victim ... or neither?
How true is the saying 'You are what you wear' and does it apply to you? Choose the options which best match your attitude to fashion.

1 I wear clothes that I like. / feel comfortable. / are the latest fashion.
2 Every morning I put on whatever's cleanest. / the coolest thing I've got. / jeans and a T-shirt.
3 I refuse to wear anything that is in fashion. / isn't in fashion. / my parents buy me.
4 When I'm on the internet, I always / never / sometimes look at the fashion adverts.
5 In my opinion, fashion is for girls / boys / anybody.

2 More than just makeup

a Talk about whether or not makeup is important to you. When do you wear it, if at all, and what is your favourite look for yourself or for others?

b Read the introduction to a video about wearing makeup and consider what Wenzile might be going to say about it.

'I'm Wenzile Thwala, a vlogger and activist from Johannesburg, South Africa. And today I want to share with you guys a bit about myself and my love for makeup.'

18

c Watch the video and point out the main focus of Wenzile's message. Talk about how it compares with what you expected to hear and do the tasks.

1 Describe Wenzile and the impression she made on you.
2 Explain why she used to sneak into her sister's room.
3 Talk about the significance of her changed attitude when she reached 18.
4 Summarize why Wenzile used makeup in the past and why she uses it now.
5 Compare what you like or don't like about the makeup Wenzile wears.

d Complete the sentences so that they are true for you.

1 You don't have to wear makeup ...
2 In other words, you mustn't ...
3 You shouldn't be afraid of ...
4 When I was younger, I had to ...
5 But when I'm 18, I will / won't have to ...

34

Words and phrases

fashion victim a person who follows every fashion trend
stereotype a set idea about what sb. or sth. is like
preconception an opinion formed without much information or experience
couture the designing, making and selling of expensive fashionable clothing

→ Workbook, pages 48–50

3 The Smarteez

a Read about the young men who changed the look of a new generation of South Africans. Then do the tasks.

Fashion in Africa is often reduced to stereotypes, such as batik prints and beaded necklaces. But in South Africa in the recent past, a new wave of designers challenged these preconceptions and found their place in the global fashion industry. One of the first fashion collectives to bring township street style to the catwalk started around 2010 from a small, disorganized studio in the back streets of Soweto: a group of guys calling themselves The Smarteez.

'For decades, international designers have been borrowing influences from Africa: tribal and animal prints, head wraps, safari suits, wooden jewellery, Masai blankets and so on. Now designers are doing it for themselves,' remembers Thabo from The Smarteez collective.

Since the turn of the century, South Africa has been experiencing a creative revolution, and some of the freshest ideas and most inspiring people came out of former townships like Soweto. The Smarteez created technicolour couture for the 'Rainbow Generation' and were determined to take full advantage of their freedom in the new South Africa by refusing any limits on their self-expression.

Floyd, another member of the collective, was eight when Nelson Mandela became president in 1994. For his parents' generation, Soweto is the spiritual home of the fight for black freedom the extravagant fashions of The Smarteez was hard to understand. Floyd understood past struggles but argued that it was important to push forward. His generation was in a different place. Pointing out the multi-racial staff and customers surrounding him in the smart Braamfontein coffee shop, he explained:

'We don't really have that hate or divide between us, you know? Our parents are very submissive people. They were made to feel inferior and they wanted to pass that down to our generation: this is how you have to do things, this is how you shouldn't do things. We're breaking through those barriers. We are all equal. We need to take pride in who we are and where we are, and that needs to start with supporting each other.'

1 Talk about Thabo's attitude to international designers in the past.
2 Explain the significance of the 'Rainbow Generation' in the context of young designers from Soweto.
3 Compare the attitudes of the young and old generations to new ideas from the townships.
4 Discuss what Floyd meant when he talked about breaking through barriers.

+ **b** Choose a fashion style which is popular at the moment and write a short text about it with photos.

4 WRITING FOCUS: If you like me, like me!

a Who do you admire and / or follow? Note down a few reasons for your choice.

b Agree on one of the people and research extra information. Structure your notes.

c Write a text about this person but don't name them. Display all your texts and do a gallery walk. How many people do you recognize?

5 YOUR CHOICE: I am what I am. Do one of the tasks below.

A Choose a quote from below. Explain what it means and why you can or can't identify with it.

B Find or write your own quote. Explain what it means and why you have chosen it.

Clothing & fashion are kind of my security blanket, almost. — Billie Eilish

Just be you. That's the best advice I can give. There are seven billion people in this world and there is no one like you. — Ed Sheeran

'Imitation is the highest form of flattery' all too often means 'Appropriation is the easiest form of thievery'. — Jamie Arpin-Ricci

Method coach: Preparing a song analysis

TIP

Lyrics are just another form of creative text written to be performed for an audience. Songwriters often use similar stylistic devices and language features to other writers.

S1 *Gimme Hope Jo'anna*

19

a The song *Gimme Hope Jo'anna* was released in 1988 but banned in South Africa. Based on the title and what you know about South Africa, explain what you think the song is about. Then watch the video and see if you wish to change your first ideas.

b Complete the text with words from the box.

anthem ■ artist ■ ban ■ cultures ■ lively ■ lyrics ■ personification ■ rhythm ■ stations ■ tune

The *Jo'anna* of reggae [1] Eddy Grant's song is a [2] of Johannesburg. It is not the capital of South Africa, but Joburg is the biggest city and a cultural melting pot of all South Africa's major [3].
The songwriter Eddy Grant never visited South Africa, but his song struck a chord with many people there, and despite the [4], they repeatedly played the song at private clubs or at home. After 1994, it became an unofficial national [5] and could be heard frequently on major radio [6].
Gimme Hope Jo'anna is an upbeat reggae [7] with an ethnic vibe and a punchy [8]. The pennywhistle tune is especially African-sounding. In spite of the [9] quality of this song – intended to get toes tapping – the [10] are really the most important feature.

TIP

Analysing lyrics

The purpose of this song is to convey / depict …
The songwriter uses … in order to evoke / portray …
The song appeals to the listener's emotions by …
The rhythm reflects / suggests …
The word … is a clue to …
The idea is presented / expressed / illustrated by …

S2 The role of music

a Discuss the role of the video in Eddy Grant's song. How does this compare to other music videos you know and enjoy?

b Read more about the background to *Gimme Hope Jo'anna*. Choose one of the following questions to discuss with a partner.

- Can music have an impact on global affairs?
- Should concerts be politically motivated?

The system of apartheid was introduced three years after the United Nations was established on the principle that all men are created equal. In their own countries, Africans were oppressed by the white minority. There were strong criticisms and loud demonstrations by governments and people around the world against apartheid and pressures were applied to bring an end to it. Eddy Grant used music to highlight the injustices in his famous hit song of 1988. It is believed that he wrote the song in honour of Nelson Mandela, the symbol of the apartheid struggle.
Eddy Grant performed *Gimme Hope Jo'anna* at a concert in Hyde Park, London on 27 June 2008 as a tribute to Mandela on his 90th birthday. Grant's passionate performance is a reminder of what South Africans endured and the world observed. It acknowledges and praises those who fought against and helped overthrow apartheid. It is also a reminder that such oppressive systems should never again be allowed to exist.

@ WES-40326-002

→ Workbook, page 51

Workshop task: Analysing song lyrics

S1 **Interpreting the general message.** Match each description with one of the song's four verses. Write your own description of the chorus. Then compare your ideas.

- Refers to the financing of the country's armed forces.
- Suggests that the regime cannot survive much longer.
- Mentions the oppression of one race by another.
- Hints at corruption and media influence.

Well Jo'anna she runs a country
She runs in Durban and the Transvaal
She makes a few of her people happy oh
She don't care about the rest at all
She's got a system they call apartheid
It keeps a brother in subjection
But maybe pressure will make Jo'anna see
How everybody could live as one

Gimme hope Jo'anna
Hope Jo'anna
Gimme hope Jo'anna
'Fore the morning come
Gimme hope Jo'anna
Hope Jo'anna
Hope before the morning come

I hear she make all the golden money
To buy new weapons any shape of guns
While every mother in black Soweto fears
The killing of another son
Sneakin' across all the neighbours' borders
Now and again having little fun
She doesn't care if the fun and games she play
Is dang'rous to ev'ryone

Gimme hope Jo'anna
Hope Jo'anna
Gimme hope Jo'anna
'Fore the morning come ...

She's got supporters in high up places
Who turn their heads to the city sun
Jo'anna give them the fancy money
Oh to tempt anyone who'd come
She even knows how to swing opinion
In every magazine and the journals
For every bad move that this Jo'anna makes
They got a good explanation

Gimme hope Jo'anna
Hope Jo'anna ...

Even the preacher who works for Jesus
The Archbishop who's a peaceful man
Together say that the freedom fighters
Will overcome the very strong
I wanna know if you're blind Jo'anna
If you wanna hear the sound of drums
Can't you see that the tide is turning
Oh don't make me wait till the morning come

Gimme hope Jo'anna
Hope Jo'anna
Gimme hope Jo'anna
'Fore the morning come

Gimme hope Jo'anna
Grant, Edmund (Text)

S2 **Looking closer.** Look at the lyrics in more detail, check any news words and find examples of literary devices. What does listening to the song add to your understanding of the lyrics and the situation in South Africa at that time?

S3 **Researching and presenting the lyrics**

a In four groups, research one part of the song and prepare a mini presentation. Each analysis should include stylistic devices used by the songwriter.

b Listen to the presentations. Then use the evaluation sheet you created on **page 61, 4c** to give each other constructive feedback.

Mediation

1 College of Magic

a In your English class, you are creating a wall newspaper on the topic of South Africa. You write an article about the College of Magic in Cape Town which deals with current social developments in South Africa, and why this college is therefore important. Base your text on this article from a German magazine.

„Hier komme ich sogar mit reichen weißen Kindern zusammen. Und wir werden alle gleich behandelt“

In Südafrika nimmt der Rassismus zu, im Stadtbild separieren sich die Menschen zusehends wieder nach Hautfarbe. Eine Schule für Zauberei ist Zufluchtsort für viele Kinder – aus den reichen Vierteln und den Townships.

Auf Einrädern kreisen sie auf dem Vorplatz um den versiegelten Brunnen herum, zeigen sich Kartentricks und werfen Keulen, Bälle oder Reifen in die Luft. Während die anderen Kinder und Jugendlichen Jonglieren üben, hält Khanya Ncusane einen Holzstab hoch und lässt an dessen Spitze einen Plastikteller rotieren. „Toll, schau mal, was ich kann“, ruft die Elfjährige. [...]

Khanya läuft in den hinteren Raum im Parterre, wo sich bereits acht Schülerinnen und Schüler versammelt haben. Sam, Ovayo, Unako, Shane, Lulo, Sarah, Uthandi: Mädchen und Jungen im Alter von zehn bis 15 Jahren, mit heller oder dunkler Hautfarbe.

Sie kommen aus den Townships der Vorstadt oder aus wohlhabenden Vierteln, aus armen oder reichen Verhältnissen, aus christlichen oder muslimischen Familien. Die einen werden in SUVs zur Schule chauffiert, die anderen steigen aus überladenen Minibussen.

„Wir repräsentieren die Vielfalt Südafrikas“, sagt der Lehrer Yadhir Maharaj, 24. Seine Vorfahren waren aus Indien eingewanderte Lohnsklaven. Er arbeitet als IT-Experte in einer Software-Firma, jeden Samstag unterrichtet er ehrenamtlich im College.

Auch der Close-up-Magier und Entertainer Anele Dyasi, 23, arbeitet als freiwillige Lehrkraft am College of Magic. [...]

Das Wertvollste, das er auf dem College of Magic gelernt hat? Dyasi muss nicht lange überlegen: „Gutes Englisch und Selbstvertrauen.“ Sein Zuhause war Khayelitsha, der größte Township von Kapstadt, in dem fast ausschließlich Schwarze leben.

„Ich bin dem College dankbar, dass ich da rausgekommen bin“, sagt Dyasi. „Denn es ist eine Gegenwelt, eine Insel der Toleranz und des gegenseitigen Respekts. Es gibt hier null Rassismus.“

Nach solchen Orten muss man in Südafrika lange suchen. Denn die Vision einer Regenbogen-Nation ist 27 Jahre nach dem Untergang der Apartheid verblasst: Die Volksgruppen driften zusehends auseinander, rassistische Zwischenfälle nehmen zu, das öffentliche Leben, die Wohnviertel, Strände, Parks, Kneipen oder Verkehrsmittel sind vielerorts wieder nach Hautfarben segregiert. Die Wohlstandskluft zwischen schwarzen und weißen Bürgern ist so tief wie eh und je.

An der Pforte des College steht an dem Morgen ein schlaksiger Herr, der die Nachzügler begrüßt. Dunkler Anzug, seidenes Einstecktuch, rote Krawatte, sehr britisch im Auftreten: David Gore, 60, der Direktor, gelernter Rechtsanwalt, Magier und Entertainer.

Gore hat das College of Magic vor 41 Jahren gegründet, als gemeinnützige Organisation, die ausschließlich von Spenden lebt. „Wir legen höchsten Wert auf Vielfalt und wollen ein Mikrokosmos unserer multiethnischen Nation sein“, sagt Gore. „Es geht hier um viel mehr als um ein paar Zaubertricks.“

Das College sei eine „Schule fürs Leben“, die vor allem benachteiligten Kindern zugutekomme. Sie lernen soziale und sprachliche Kompetenzen, Toleranz und Rücksichtnahme, aber auch Disziplin, Ausdauer und Teamwork, und weil all diese Fähigkeiten spielerisch vermittelt werden, haben sie dabei jede Menge Spaß. [...]

Source [abbreviated]: Bartholomäus Grill, „Hier komme ich sogar mit reichen weißen Kindern zusammen. Und wir werden alle gleich behandelt“, Spiegel Ausland, 05.06.2021; https://www.spiegel.de/ausland/suedafrika-wie-das-college-of-magic-kinder-und-jugendliche-zusammenbringt-a-15a3d66d-3235-4924-a135-1f4a7c6a2e50 [09.01.2023]

→ Workbook, pages 52/53

b After you have written your article, you take a look at the homepage of the College of Magic. Your mother knows about your article and sees the College's homepage on your tablet. Tell her how other people can support a student at this college or the college itself.

c Your mother has seen the abbreviation NPO on the homepage. You have already found out that NPO stands for non-profit organization. Explain to your mother what an NPO is and look for other examples of NPOs on the internet.

Sponsor a student in need

You could be the driving force behind South Africa's next magic star.
Being an NPO, ongoing funding is essential to keeping our doors open. To this end, we established the *Sponsor a Student* initiative, which gives you the opportunity to help transform a young person's life.
We channel this support into some of Cape Town's most deserving communities through our Magic in the Community project. This project brings hope to children who may otherwise have had little or no opportunities for success, teaching them entertainment skills, growing their confidence, building their communication ability and giving them a brighter vision for their future. [...]

Sponsor a student

Your donation could transform a child's future. By sponsoring an underprivileged student, you give them the opportunity to join the life-changing courses offered at the College of Magic.
Your donation will contribute towards their:

- Tuition fees
- Equipment for routines
- Smart clothing for live performances
- Transport expenses
- Food

[...]
$600 will sponsor ONE student for a full year
$300 will sponsor ONE student for 6 months [...]
The College of Magic depends on the generosity of individuals, corporate sponsors and other funding partners to continue the important work we do. There are many ways to assist: financial support, donations of items on our wishlist and donations of professional services. [...]

Source [abbreviated]: College of Magic, Transform a Child's Life through the Power of Magic, https://www.collegeofmagic.com [09.01.2023]

First track

3 **b** Kenny uses what he has learned about South Africa's political past for his next blog. Complete it with the correct relative pronouns.

p. 55

The African National Congress, **who / which** (1) was formed in 1912, defended the rights of the African people. These were basic human rights **which / whose** (2) had been seriously curtailed. It was a political situation **who / which** (3) arose after many years of oppression. Nelson Mandela was not a man **who / which** (4) believed in or encouraged violence. He was a powerful speaker **whose / which** (5) words touched the hearts of millions. He was one of the people [6] formed an illegal organization. They found themselves in a position in [7] they had to accept the status quo or defy the law. However, they managed to break the law in a way [8] avoided violence; in other words, using passive resistance. He and others [9] started the organization were all arrested.

2 **a** Complete the sentences from a review with *that, which, who, whose* or *where*.

p. 56

The movie Tsotsi, ***which*** *is set in a slum in Johannesburg, is about gang violence.*

1 The main protagonist is a teenager known as Tsotsi ___ has been hardened by his tough life.
2 Tsotsi, ___ is South African slang, means 'urban crook or criminal'.
3 Tsotsi, ___ mother is dying, runs away from home and lives with other homeless kids.
4 One day during a gang hit, Tsotsi steals a car in ___ he finds a three-month-old baby.
5 He abandons the car, but takes the baby back to the slum ___ he lives.
6 The next six days bring about a change in Tsotsi ___ couldn't be foreseen.

3 **a** Complete the summary with *could / should / must / might have* + past participle of the verbs in brackets. More than one modal is sometimes possible.

p. 58

Classified as 'Cape Coloured', D'Oliviera [1] (*never play*) for South Africa. He was a great all-rounder so the MCC [2] (*select*) him for the English team, but they did not. Someone [3] (*offer*) D'Oliviera money not to play, but that's not certain. People were convinced that the MCC [4] (*react*) in another way. The world [5] (*not understand*) the impact of apartheid without the Dolly affair.

5 **b** Look at the score chart for the 1995 Rugby World Cup and choose the correct form of the verbs to complete the sentences.

p. 59

17.06.1995	South Africa	19	15	France	F.
18.06.1995	England	29	45	New Zealand	N.Z.
3rd place play-off, 22.06.1995	France	19	9	England	E.
Final, 24.06.1995	South Africa	15	12 (after extra time)	New Zealand	N.Z.

1 If South Africa **hadn't won / wouldn't have won** in the semi-finals, they **hadn't qualified / wouldn't have qualified** for the final.
2 New Zealand **hadn't been / wouldn't have been** in the final if they **had lost / would have lost** to England on 18 June.
3 If England **had won / would have won** the play off, they **had been / would have been** in third place.
4 South Africa **hadn't won / wouldn't have won** the final if they **hadn't scored / wouldn't have scored** in extra time.

3 16 p. 64

a Watch the video or look at **G 1** and complete the rules with words from the box.

> for ■ past ■ present ■ present perfect ■ present perfect progressive ■ since

- We use the [1] with action verbs when there is a link between the [2] and the [3]. A past time is not mentioned and we often focus on the result.
  I've read Mandela's book.
- We also use it with state verbs like *be*, *have* and *know*.
  We've known each other for ages.
- We use the [4] with action verbs to focus on the length of an action still in progress. Typical signal words are [5] with a period of time and [6] with a point of time.
  We've been talking about a trip for years.
  We've been planning it since 2021.

3 p. 65

b Choose the best form to complete the sentences.

1 Tricia's parents **have always wanted / have always been wanting** to go to South Africa.
2 Her father's firm **has worked / has been working** with a company there for 12 years now.
3 Dave's colleague, Elias, **has invited / has been inviting** the family to stay with them.
4 Since they booked their flights, the Hansons **have discussed / have been discussing** what to do there.
5 Tricia **has decided / has been deciding** she doesn't want to go to Robben Island prison.
6 She doesn't understand why they **have made / have been making** it into a museum.
7 Tricia and Kenny **have talked about / have been talking about** the pros and cons of ecotourism.
8 They **have known / have been knowing** each other since primary school.

2 p. 66

b Tricia reports her findings to Kenny. Complete her email with the verbs in the present perfect or present perfect progressive.

> Hey Kenny
> I [1] (*look*) at my photos of SA all weekend and I can't wait to go back! I [2] (*try*) for ages to find an ethical project for next year, but recently I [3] (*read*) two or three negative reports in the press about voluntourism. I [4] (*come across*) several comments saying that some companies misrepresent their projects. But I [5] (*be*) really impressed by projects like *People and Places* which [6] (*win*) an award, because they [7] (*give*) a record 80% of their profits back to the community, which is great. And someone commented that *GVI Planet* is a good all-rounder which [8] (*run*) conservation projects for a while now. So, it's a choice between those two, but I think I [9] (*make up*) my mind. Let me know what you think.
> Love for now
> Tricia

5 p. 67

a A friend of yours is thinking of volunteering, so you share Tony's story with them. Choose the correct option to complete your email. Sometimes both are possible.

> Hey!
> I**'ve meant / 've been meaning** (1) to write for ages, but my school project **has kept / has been keeping** (2) me busy. I know you**'ve thought / 've been thinking** (3) about going on a volunteering holiday before you leave Africa. My advice is: just do it! A guy I know called Tony **has just returned / has just been returning** (4) from a reserve where they look after baby rhinos. He had the most amazing time there. In fact, he **has talked / has been talking** (5) about nothing else since he got home. Believe it or not, he**'s even been / 's even been being** (6) on a radio show to talk about it! Apparently, while he was there, he fell in love … with an orphan rhino!
> Seriously though, he says that he **has made / has been making** (7) some lifelong friends, and not just among the rhinos!
> I**'ve copied / 've been copying** (8) Tony into this mail so if you need any more info, just ask him, OK?
> Good luck, speak soon, …

Reading

Nelson Mandela, *Long Walk to Freedom*

Long Walk to Freedom is Nelson Mandela's autobiography chronicling his extraordinary life. He recounts his early years, activism against apartheid, and his imprisonment for 27 years. The book portrays his firm dedication to justice, equality, and freedom. It is an inspiring account of Mandela's lifelong struggle against oppression and his commitment to building a democratic and inclusive society.

[...] **IN JAIL**, all prisoners are classified by the authorities as one of four categories: A, B, C, or D. A is the highest classification and confers the most privileges; D is the lowest and confers the least. All political prisoners, or what the authorities called 'security prisoners', were automatically classified as D on admission. The privileges affected by these classifications included visits and letters, studies, and the opportunity to buy groceries and incidentals – all of which are the lifeblood of any prisoner. It normally took years for a political prisoner to raise his status from D to C.

We despised the classification system. It was corrupt and demeaning, another way of repressing prisoners in general and political prisoners in particular. We demanded that all political prisoners be in one category. Although we criticized it, we could not ignore it: the classification system was an inflexible feature of prison life. If you protested that, as a D group prisoner, you could receive only one letter every six months, the authorities would say, 'Improve your behavior, become a C group prisoner, and you will be able to receive two letters every six months.'

If you complained that you did not receive enough food, the authorities would remind you that if you were in A group, you would be able to receive money orders from the outside and purchase extra food at the prison tuckshop. Even a freedom fighter benefits from the ability to buy groceries and books.

The classifications generally ran parallel to the length of one's sentence. If you were sentenced to eight years, you would generally be classified as D for the first two years, C for the next two, B for the following two and A for the last two. But the prison authorities wielded the classification system as a weapon against political prisoners, threatening to lower our hard-won classifications in order to control our behavior.

Though I had been in prison for nearly two years before I was taken to Robben Island, I was still in D group when I arrived. While I desired the privileges that came with higher classifications, I refused to compromise my conduct. The fastest way to raise one's classification was to be docile and not complain. 'Ag, Mandela, you are a troublemaker,' the warders would say. 'You will be in D group for the rest of your life.' [...]

As a D group prisoner, I was entitled to have only one visitor, and write and receive only one letter every six months. I found this one of the most inhumane restrictions of the prison system. Communication with one's family is a human right; it should not be restricted by the artificial gradations of a prison system. But it was one of the facts of prison life.

Visits and letters were restricted to 'first degree' relatives. This was a restriction we not only found irksome but racist. The African sense of immediate family is very different from that of the European or Westerner. Our family structures are larger and more inclusive; anyone who claims descent from a common ancestor is deemed part of the same family.

In prison, the only thing worse than bad news about one's family is no news at all. It is always harder to cope with the disasters and tragedies one imagines than with the reality, however grim or disagreeable. A letter with ill tidings was always preferable to no letter at all.

But even this miserable restriction was abused by the authorities. The anticipation of mail was overwhelming. Mail-call took place once a month, and sometimes six months would go by without a letter. To be allowed one letter in six months and then not to receive it is a great blow. One wonders: What has happened to my wife and children, to my mother and my sisters? When I did not receive a letter I felt as dry and barren as the Great Karroo desert. Often the authorities would withhold mail out of spite. I can remember warders saying, 'Mandela, we have received a letter for you, but we cannot give it to you.' No explanation of why, or who the letter is from. It required all my self-discipline not to explode at such times. Afterward, I would protest through the proper channels, and sometimes get it.

When letters did arrive, they were cherished. A letter was like the summer rain that could make even the desert bloom. When I was handed a letter by the authorities, I would not rush forward and grab it as I felt like doing, but take it in a leisurely manner. Though I yearned to tear it open and read it on the spot, I would not give the authorities the satisfaction of seeing my eagerness, and I would return slowly to my cell as though I had many things to occupy me before opening a letter from my family.

During the first few months, I received one letter from Winnie, but it was so heavily censored that not much more than the salutation was left. The island's censors would black out the offending passages in ink, but they later changed this when they realized we could wash away the ink and see what was underneath. They began to use razors to slice out whole paragraphs. Since most letters were written on both sides of a single piece of paper, the material on the other side would also be excised. They seemed to relish delivering letters in tatters. The censorship delayed the delivery of mail because warders, some of whom were not proficient in English, might take as long as a month to censor a letter. The letters we wrote were censored as well; they were often as cut up as those we received.

[...]

from *Long Walk to Freedom* by Nelson Mandela. London: Abacus Books, 2013. Kindle Edition.

1 Talk about whether you would be willing to accept hard living conditions in order to fight for your (idealistic) aims. Give reasons and find examples.

2 Do some research about Nelson Mandela's life and draw a timeline with the most important, outstanding or even unusual facts. You can add pictures as well. Alternatively prepare a short talk or combine both.

3 Describe Nelson Mandela's situation in prison with regard to:
- his status as a prisoner and
- the way mail was dealt with.

4 Examine the consequences for the prisoners in the extract and their lives. What was allowed, what was forbidden? What amenities were granted to the prisoners. Consider 'official' organizations and structures regarding the prisoners as well as personal feelings and emotional responses from Mandela. Use your own words and quote from the text where appropriate.

5 **a** Gather information about the book the excerpt is taken from and analyse the point of view of narration.

b Choose three stylistic devices from the excerpt and explain their use.

6 **YOUR CHOICE:** Quotations. Choose task **A** or **B** and present your quote to the class, explaining why you chose it and its relevance to you and / or society today.

A Choose one of the quotes below.

B Research and choose another quote by Nelson Mandela.

Education is the most powerful weapon which you can use to change the world.

I learned that courage was not the absence of fear, but the triumph over it.

7 Find examples of resistance fighters throughout the centuries. Choose your favourite and write an obituary (*Nachruf*) for a newspaper (about 200 words).

8 As a group, organize an exhibition for a wider audience including all your chosen favourites. Design short tasks for the visitors to make them curious to find out more.

9 Discuss if a politically motivated fight against the system can be compared to today's climate / environmental activists. Include your position for or against using militant means to achieve your aims. Give reasons for your arguments.

My review

What can I do?

Look at these sentences about Workshop 2. Are the sentences true for you? Choose the right symbol for each sentence.

1. I can talk about apartheid.
2. I can discuss sports and politics.
3. I can talk about animal conservation.
4. I can talk about diversity, identity and inclusion.

»»» = 'I'm great at this!'
»»» = 'I'm good at this.'
»»» = 'I'm OK at this.'

What do I know?

1 About apartheid

a Like Mandela, Steve Biko was a South African anti-apartheid activist. Complete the text with the phrases from the box and relative pronouns.

he founded in 1969 ■ was released in 1997 ■ heard about Biko's death on the BBC news ■ included phrases in isiXhosa ■ is in the song ■ death at the hands of the police in 1977 shocked the world ■ was held in honour of Nelson Mandela's seventieth birthday

Steven Biko, [1], was a South African anti-apartheid activist. The South African Students' Organisation, [2], was very important in the anti-apartheid movement. In 1980 Peter Gabriel, [3], released a song dedicated to him. The song, [4], gained positive critical acclaim. It also brought the struggles against apartheid to a wide audience. One of the most powerful verses [5] is: *You can blow out a candle / but you can't blow out the fire / Once the flames begin to catch / The wind will blow it higher.* At the concert [6], Gabriel performed the song to a watching world. Later, *Cry Freedom*, [7], brought the story of Biko to the attention of a new generation of people worldwide.

■ / 7

b Combine the sentences from a review about the film *Cry Freedom*. Use relative pronouns. You will sometimes have to make other changes.

1. *Cry Freedom* is about Steve Biko's final days. It is set in South Africa.
2. The film stars Denzel Washington and Kevin Kline. The film was shot in Zimbabwe rather than South Africa.
3. Donald Wood became close friends with Biko. He was a South African journalist.
4. Richard Attenborough directed the film. He is other films include *Gandhi and A Bridge Too Far.*
5. A list appears at the end of the film. It contains the names of many people who died in police custody.
6. *Cry Freedom* won many awards. It was nominated for three Oscars.

■ / 6

Apartheid, pp. 54 – 55
Relative clauses → G6; pp 54 – 55

2 About sport and politics.

Look at the information about Siya Kolisi, then complete some excerpts from various interviews with the correct form of the verbs in brackets.

Siya Kolisi (born in 1991) is a black rugby player who comes from a humble background. He started to play rugby at the age of seven. His life changed when he got a rugby scholarship at Grey High School in Portland. He made history as the first black captain of the South African rugby team, the Springboks. In 2019, he led the South African team to victory in the Rugby World Cup. Siya and his wife Rachel share a passion for fighting inequality and bettering the lives of under-resourced communities. Together they co-founded the Kolisi Foundation in 2019. The aim of the Foundation is to provide food security, fight against gender-based violence as well as provide education and sports development programmes.

Q: Who do you attribute your success to?
A: Without a doubt it's my grandmother. If she **1** (*not support*) me, I **2** (*not be*) where I am today.

Q: What did training with your local junior team mean to you?
A: Everything. My life **3** (*probably turn out*) differently if the coach, Eric Sonqwiqi, **4** (*not push*) me to the limits.

Q: Who was your sporting hero when you were in high school?
A: Shalk Burger. But, if you **5** (*tell*) me then that one day Shalk would not only be my teammate but my friend, too, I **6** (*think*) you'd lost your mind.

Q: You are the first black captain of Springbok. How do you feel about it?
A: Humbled. However, my appointment sends a clear message to disadvantaged young people in South Africa: if you **7** (*work*) hard, nothing **8** (*be*) impossible.

Q: What prompted you to launch the Kolisi Foundation?
A: The pandemic. If we **9** (*not recognize*) the threat posed by the Corona virus, we **10** (*not react*) so quickly.

Q: How did you decide on the focus of the Foundation?
A: By reflecting on my personal experiences. For example, if I **11** (*not see*) violence against women in my family and in my neighbourhood, I probably **12** (*not feel*) the need to address it.

Q: What's the motto of the Foundation?
A: If we **13** (*work*) together as one, we **14** (*can + achieve*) anything.

Q: Any when you can no longer play rugby?
A: When I **15** (*be*) too old for rugby, I **16** (*put*) all my energy into bettering the lives of deprived communities.

■ / 16

If-sentences → G5; pp. 58 – 59

3 **About animal conservation.** Complete the interview with the present perfect or present perfect progressive..

Host: On today's programme I'd like to welcome Greg.
Greg: Thanks for inviting me.
Host: How long **1** (*you / be interested*) in sharks?
Greg: I **2** (*always be drawn to*) the ocean.
Host: **3** (*you / ever worry*) about being attacked?
Greg: Not really. In 2022, there were just eleven deaths worldwide from shark attacks. Most shark attacks aren't fatal. For the last twenty years or so, I **4** (*spend*) more and more time in a place called Shark Alley …
Host: I **5** (*hear*) of Shark Alley. Surely that's a dangerous place?
Greg: It can be, but I **6** (*dive*) there for quite a long time and I **7** (*only be attacked*) twice …
Host: What happened?
Greg: On both occasions the problem was connected to the tourist boats …
Host: You **8** (*lose) me* there …
Greg: In recent years, the number of boats taking tourists to Shark alley **9** (*increase*). You wouldn't believe it but I **10** (*even see*) tourists throwing meat into the water to attract more sharks. I **11** (*complain*) to the authorities about it for years, but so far they **12** (*do*) nothing about it.
Host: That does sound dangerous …
Greg: It is. Last year about ten Great Whites started circling me. I **13** (*never feel*) so scared. But you mustn't show you're frightened because they can sense your fear?
Host: Well, Greg. Our time is up, but it **14** (*be*) really interesting talking to you. I hope you'll come back again soon.
Greg: Sure. Next time I'd like to talk a bit more about how we can protect sharks …

■ / 14

Present perfect and present perfect progressive
→ G1; pp. 64 – 65

4 About diversity

a Complete the sentences with words from the workshop.

1. During apartheid people were **s**... because of their colour.
2. Apartheid, the system of **r**... discrimination in South Africa lasted almost 50 years.
3. The ideas of **i**... and diversity are very important in South Africa today.
4. People like Trevor Noah who were of mixed race were labelled **c**... under apartheid laws.
5. Under apartheid, people were often persecuted because of their race or **s**...
6. Unfortunately, there are still issues of **i**... with some people much worse off than others. Many of these problems exist in other countries.
7. Some para-athletes like Charl du Toit have competed against **a**... competitors.

■ / 7

b Complete the dialogue about the 2018 American superhero film *Black Panther* and Afrofuturism with the words from the box. You will need to use some more than once.

'll have to ■ might have been ■ must ■ must have been ■ need to ■ ought to ■ should ■ shouldn't

Olu: What are you reading? It [1] be interesting as you didn't respond when I called your name.

Sade: It's an article about the *Black Panther* film and Afrofuturism. You [2] read it. It says that the Afrofuturistic approach in education could instil a more balanced view of equality in students.

Olu: Oh, come on! It's impossible for one film to have such a huge impact.

Sade: You [3] be so dismissive. The writer here says that he conducted a study with young teachers who'd watched the film and concluded they [4] help their students question and transform society's imbalanced power relations. It [5] a revolutionary moment for them.

Olu: Okay. So, is this like the privilege walk?

Sade: No. The walk [6] an eye-opener, but did it lead to any changes? Of course, we [7] acknowledge its value in raising awareness to inequality, but it stopped there.

Olu: You've got me interested. How [8] Afrofuturism be used? Tell me more.

Sade: If you're interested, you [9] do some research and [10] watch the film, too.

■ / 10

Modals → G7; pp. 58 – 59, 60 – 61, 68 – 69

■ / 60

What's my score?

Check your answers to the review (Workbook, p. 57) What are your scores for each section?

What was your total score?

»»» score 46 – 60
»»» score 26 – 45
»»» score 0 – 25

Do you want to change your answers to the 'What can I do?' statements on page 80? Look at the tasks on pages 83 – 87: »»», »»» and »»». Choose the tasks to help you.

My practice pages

Talking about apartheid

1 **Goodbye Bafana.** Complete the text with the relative pronouns *which, who* and *that.*

The film 'Goodbye Bafana', [1] was released in 2007, has been nominated for several awards. It is based on a book [2] was written by James Gregory, the former prison officer [3] guarded a black prisoner, Nelson Mandela, for 21 years in three different locations.
Gregory, played by Joseph Finnes, is an ideal candidate for a job on Robben Island [4] requires him to monitor the correspondence and visits of Mandela and his comrades. He is selected because he knows the Xhosa language [5] Mandela spoke. The film shows how the friendship [6] is forming between the two men transforms the guard's views. Gregory, [7] is deeply racist, is impressed by Mandela's quiet leadership. As the friendship between him and Mandela grows and matures, Gregory's alliance, [8] had been with the government, gradually shifts to the struggle for a free, multiracial, democratic South Africa.

2 **Robben Island.** Complete the text about Robben Island with the phrases from the box and the correct relative pronouns.

is a UNESCO World Heritage Site ■ Mandela was kept in ■ Nelson Mandela was jailed for 18 years ■ now work as tour guides ■ prisoners went through ■ want to observe nature and wildlife ■ were either separated due to illnesses ■ were originally brought in by the Dutch

Robben Island, [1] lies approximately 7 kilometres off the coast and 12 kilometres from Cape Town harbour. From the end of the 17th century, the island was used to isolate groups of people [2] or were convicts. Today it is best known as the place in [3]. A trip to the island allows tourists to experience the life [4]. Many visitors are touched by the personal stories of the former prisoners [5]. Attractions on the island include not only the cell [6] but also the quarry where prisoners worked. Robben Island does not disappoint those visitors [7]. It is natural habitat for the African penguin. Rabbits, [8] roam freely.

3 **The Soweto Uprising.** Combine the sentences about the uprising using relative clauses.

1 The 1976 uprising profoundly changed the socio-political landscape in South Africa. It began in Soweto and spread countrywide.
2 Events can be traced back to apartheid policies. The events triggered the uprising.
3 Black students in Soweto protested against the Afrikaans Medium Decree of 1974. It forced all black schools to use Afrikaans and English as instruction languages.
4 Few people there spoke Afrikaans. It was regarded as 'the language of the oppressor'.
5 On 16 June 1976, black students walked to Orlando Stadium for a rally. It was a protest against having to learn Afrikaans.
6 On their way, the students were met by heavily armed police. The police fired tear gas and live ammunition on the protesters.
7 One of the first students to be shot dead was 12-year-old Hector Pieterson. The photo of Pieterson became the symbol of the uprising.
8 Today the protest is commemorated by a national holiday, Youth Day. Youth Day honours all the young people who died in the struggle against apartheid.

Talking about sport and politics

4 **Probability and possibility.** Choose the correct verb forms to complete the sentences.

1 If you **are / were** good enough, the colour of your skin shouldn't matter.
2 If P. W. Botha **didn't fall / hadn't fallen** ill, de Klerk wouldn't have become president of South Africa.
3 If you **like / had liked** cricket or rugby, then South Africa is a good country to live in as these are the two national sports.
4 If Mandela **died / had died** in prison, everything today would be very different in South Africa.
5 If Natalie du Toit **didn't lose / hadn't lost** her lower left leg in a car accident, her career might have turned out very differently.
6 If South African rugby players **are / had been** professional in 1995, would they still have won the World Cup?
7 If you **belong / had belonged** to the ANC under apartheid, you would have risked being arrested.
8 If you **were / had been** a young swimmer living in Cape Town, you'd want to be part of the Chad Le Clos swimming academy.

5 **Three people.** Read the information, then complete sentences using the prompts.

Francois Pienaar was a South African Rugby player. He played for the national team, the Springboks, between 1993 and 1996. He was captain of the team that won the Rugby World Cup in in South Africa in 1995. Later in the same year rugby became a professional sport. Before that, all players had been amateurs. A year later, Pienaar was controversially dropped from the team and he moved to England as a player-coach.

Natalie du Toit was born in Cape Town in 1984. She began swimming at a young age and was only 14 when she competed at the Commonwealth Games. In 2001, she was involved in a traffic accident and her lower left leg was amputated. However, she refused to give up swimming. She won many medals at the Paralympic Games but also competed against able-bodied swimmers.

Chad le Clos was born in 1992 and started swimming competitively at the age of 12. At the 2012 Olympic Games in London, he beat the legendary Michael Phelps in the men's 200m butterfly. After becoming the most successful Commonwealth Games swimmer in 2018, he decided to launch a swimming foundation to encourage youngsters.

1 If Francois Pienaar | not be captain of the Springboks | team | not win the Rugby World Cup in 1995.
2 If the South African rugby team | not drop him | then he | might never play in England.
3 If Natalie du Toit | not be such a good swimmer | she not win so many awards.
4 If young people | want a good role-model | then Natalie du Toit | be perfect candidate.
5 If Michael Phelps | beat | Chad Le Clos at the 2012 Olympics | Le Clos' career | be very different.
6 If Chad Le Clos | compete today | his main challengers | be from the USA.

6 **If …** Combine the two sentences to create a conditional sentence. You might need to make other changes to the sentences.

Example: Britain gave Zola Budd citizenship. She ran in the 1984 Olympics.
If Britain hadn't given Zola Budd citizenship, she wouldn't have run in the 1984 Olympics.

1. In 1995, Pienaar fought for the rights of his teammates in the Springboks. Consequently, he was sacked as captain the following year.
2. Du Toit lost her lower left leg in an accident. She became a Paralympic swimmer.
3. Some South African nationals live outside the country. They can only cast their vote for the National Assembly.
4. Le Clos beat Phelps at the London Olympics. That's why he became a national hero.
5. Nelson Mandela was released from prison in 1990. He became president four years later.
6. Du Toit's achievements inspired a lot of people. Now she is successful as a motivational speaker.

Talking about animal conservation

7 **It's hard to choose.** Anna wants to volunteer with ACE (African Conservation Experience) but is unsure which is the right programme. Choose the correct verb forms.

Since I made the decision to volunteer, I've tried / 've been trying (1) to finalize my trip. Initially I wanted to go for the Phinda Wildlife Research Project but I've seen / have been seeing (2) so many exciting programmes that it's hard to choose. For the past week I've read / 've been reading (3) reviews written by volunteers who worked on different projects, and each and every account sounds amazing. I've noted down / 've been noting down (4) loads of questions and have requested / have been requesting (5) a video chat with an ACE representative, but they haven't replied / haven't been replying (6) yet. My parents have bombarded / have been bombarding (7) me with different suggestions and have nagged / have been nagging (8) me all the time to make up my mind. I know they mean well, but it doesn't help.

8 **A day as a volunteer.** During his time at a wildlife resort, Lucas writes a blog post every day. Read his account of one day and put the verbs in brackets in the correct form. Use the present perfect or present perfect progressive.

Another evening here at the Rhino Sanctuary. I [1] (*have*) a busy day. It's after the evening feed, and I am preparing dinner with my friends. Since we got back to our accommodation, we [2] (*chat*) about the day. Charlie works with the 'rhino' team. They [3] (*monitor*) rhinos which were released back into the wilderness, and he says that they [4] (*extremely* + *be concerned*) about one rhino which seems to have disappeared. But they [5] (*follow*) the tracks of another one which should lead them to the lost rhino. I am quite jealous, really …
Melany [6] (*work*) alongside an experienced wildlife vet since we started. Today, for the first time, she [7] (*witness*) an injured baby rhino being delivered by helicopter to the centre. I [8] (*never see*) her so excited! She says that she [9] (*make up*) her mind – she definitely wants to be a vet.
As for me – I am still undecided. But one thing is certain: I [10] (*build up*) a connection with the animals which I had never thought possible.

9 **Your volunteering.** Choose one of the tasks.

1. Imagine that you are volunteering with ACE (African Conservation Experience. Write a blog entry using. Use the present perfect and present perfect progressive where appropriate.

OR

2. In the summer holidays you are planning to volunteer with a wildlife project in South Africa. Write about your preparation – using the present perfect and present perfect progressive where appropriate.

Talking about diversity and inclusion

10 Living together

a Match the words to the definitions.

1 able-bodied	5 inclusivity
2 appropriation	6 inequalities
3 coloured	7 multicultural
4 diversity	8 segregated

a when people are separated and treated differently because of different races, religions or sexes
b the idea that everyone should be included
c having parents who are of different races and so a darker skin
d the unfair differences between groups of people in society
e physically strong, fit and healthy in contrast to somebody who isn't
f a range of people or things that are very different from each other
g the act of taking something that belongs to somebody else, without permission
h including people of several different cultures

b Complete with the correct modal verbs.

Rick You really **might / should** (1) listen to this album *Graceland*. It's amazing!
Dave Wasn't that Michael Jackson's home?
Rick No, that was Neverland, but you **could / should** (2) be thinking of Elvis Presley whose home was called Graceland.
Dave Yes, that **must / would** (3) be it. So, who is the album by?
Rick It's by an American singer-songwriter called Paul Simon.
Dave I **might / must** (4) have heard of him. I think my gran has some of his records.
Rick She **might have / might have been** (5) – he was popular in the 1960s.
Dave And what's so special about it?
Rick Well, it was influenced by street music from South Africa and recorded there in the 1980s.
Dave Wow! That **must / should** (6) have been difficult with apartheid.
Rick Yes, many people thought he **couldn't / shouldn't** (7) have gone to South Africa, especially as there was a cultural boycott at the time. However, Simon told the press that he knew he **should / might** (8) be criticized, but he was following his musical instinct and thought he **ought to / might** (9) try to work with the artists whose music he was listening to.
Dave It sounds like it's worth listening to. **I'll / I'd** (10) try and do that soon.

11 A diverse nation

a Complete the sentences with the words from the box. There are three words you do not need.

> able-bodied ■ appropriation ■ coloured ■ diversity ■ inclusivity ■ inequalities ■ multicultural ■ racial ■ segregated ■ sexuality

1 During apartheid blacks were _____ and often lived in townships.
2 In the past, there was a lot of _____ tension between blacks and whites.
3 _____ where everyone is treated equally, is an important ideal in post-apartheid South Africa.
4 Under apartheid anyone who wasn't white was often labelled _____.
5 In most countries, it is illegal to discriminate against someone because of their age, race or _____.
6 It will take decades to overcome many of the _____ that blacks faced during apartheid.
7 He was born _____ but lost a leg in a shark attack.

b Complete the text with the correct modals.

could ■ couldn't ■ might have been ■ must have ■ must have been ■ needs to ■ ought to ■ should

South Africa is often known as the Rainbow Nation, but where does this name come from and what does it mean? Many people think it **1** Nelson Mandela who came up with the term. In fact, it was Desmond Tutu who coined the label. He **2** influenced by Mandela, but there were many factors that **3** contributed to the speech he gave when he first used the term. One important thing that everyone **4** be aware of is how restricted life was for most people during apartheid. Of course, if you were black, you faced a lot of racism, but for anyone who wasn't white life **5** be equally hard. As a non-white, there were many things you **6** do and many places that were off-limits. However, there is another aspect that you **7** know about the term 'Rainbow Nation'. When Tutu used the words, he wasn't just referring to people of different races and cultures, but also the diverse nature of the landscape and wildlife across the country. He thought that the new South Africa, post-apartheid, **8** celebrate its differences and diversity and that this is what made the country so special and unique.

12 Diversity and inclusion

»» **a** Choose five words from the list and write a sentence for each word to clearly show its meaning.

able-bodied ■ appropriation ■ coloured ■ diversity ■ inclusivity ■ inequalities ■ multicultural ■ racial ■ segregated ■ sexuality

b Complete the second sentence with a modal so it has the same meaning as the first sentence.

1. People are often surprised when they find out how many different languages are spoken in South Africa.
   If you found out how many different languages are spoken in South Africa, it ...
2. When we talk about diversity in South Africa, it's important to include the landscape and wildlife.
   When we talk about diversity in South Africa, we ...
3. After about 50 years of apartheid, it's important to understand things can't change overnight.
   After about 50 years of apartheid, people ...
4. Nelson Mandela is famous around the world. I am certain everyone has heard of him.
   Nelson Mandela is famous around the world, so you ...
5. While South African society is very liberal, some barriers to total inclusivity possibly still exist today.
   South African society is very liberal, but ...
6. It's still possible to face discrimination in South Africa, but it's less likely than in the past.
   Some people ...

35 Marcus Sedgwick

Cudweed and the bagpipes

TWO

The next morning was very different. It was bright and sunny, but still, I did not fly home to Castle Otherhand. Why? I will explain ...

We had arrived late in the evening, in the middle of a heavy thunderstorm, in a remote corner of northern Scotland. Don't ask me where, all I can say is that the train station was smaller than the train itself, and that wasn't even the end of our journey. We had to take a taxi for forty-five minutes across the rainswept[1] landscape, which was mountains and moorland[2], and all looking very bleak.

The taxi driver took us to a pub which was also the local B&B[3], where we were told Cudweed would be staying during his work experience. At the back of the pub, across a courtyard[4], were some bedrooms that had been converted[5] from stables. The pub and the B&B were run by a lady called Sheila, who seemed happy to see Cudweed but less happy to see me.

'Is that thing yours?' asked Sheila, squinting[6] at me.

'He's not a thing, he's a raven,' said Cudweed. 'And no, he's not mine. He doesn't belong to me. He's my friend.'

'Oh,' said Sheila. Then she squinted some more at me. 'Just see he doesn't, you know ... make ... a mess.'

'Kraak!' I said, because that was very rude. I am a very well-behaved raven and do not make messes of any kind, never mind[7] the kind of 'mess' she was thinking about.

After that, Cudweed ate the last of the sandwiches he'd been given for the train ride, and I ate nothing, and I sulked[8] about that a lot.

Then we went to sleep, listening to the rain get heavier and heavier. And heavier.

But when we woke up the next morning, it was bright and sunny. It was warm, in fact, almost hot, and the sun was drying the roofs and the courtyard quickly. There was steam rising from the cobblestones[9] and the last traces of a gentle mist were quickly disappearing. After our miserable arrival the night before, it all seemed a little bit better.

We realized that we had overslept, Cudweed was supposed to[10] be at the bagpipe factory by nine and it was already a quarter to nine. But he insisted[11] we had breakfast before setting out[12].

'That's funny,' said Cudweed as we walked across to the pub.

He was pointing to the sign of the pub, which showed its name – The Ugly Sheep, with a picture that showed, yes, a sheep that was indeed very ugly.

'Kork!' I said to Cudweed, ignoring the pub sign.

'Yes, Edgar,' Cudweed said, 'I will make sure you get some breakfast.'

---

[1] **rainswept** ['reɪnswept] regengepeitscht – [2] **moorland** ['mʊələnd] Moorland; Sumpfland – [3] **B&B (Bed and Breakfast)** [ˌbi: ənd 'bi:] Übernachtung mit Frühstück – [4] **courtyard** ['kɔ:tjɑ:d] Hof; Innenhof – [5] **to convert sth.** [kən'vɜ:t 'sʌmθɪŋ 'ɪntə] etw. umbauen – [6] **to squint at sb.** [skwɪnt ət 'sʌmbədi] einen Blick auf jdn. / etw. werfen – [7] **never mind** ['nevə maɪnd] geschweige denn; von … gar nicht erst zu reden – [8] **to sulk** [sʌlk] schmollen – [9] **cobblestone** ['kɒblstəʊn] Kopfstein; Pflasterstein – [10] **to be supposed to do sth.** [bi sə'pəʊzd tə du:] etw. tun sollen – [11] **to insist** [ɪn'sɪst] bestehen auf – [12] **to set out** [set aʊt] aufbrechen

After breakfast, we set out for the factory, following the instructions that Sheila had given us. It was very simple; it was just a five-minute walk along the road, with high mountains to one side of us and a loch on the other, and we were there.

Now, I had been planning on getting Cudweed to the door of the factory, and then setting off home, but when we got there … well, I'll come to that.

The first thing was that Cudweed met the owner of the factory. He came outside to meet us and, since it was such a lovely morning, we stood there enjoying the sunshine.

His name was Hamish and he appeared to be very old. In fact, I would have been surprised if he was anything less than 108, but despite being more wrinkled[13] than a walnut[14], he was very quick and very sharp[15].

He looked at Cudweed and me and then he said, 'You're late! And you didn't say you were bringing a raven with you.'

'It was an accident,' explained Cudweed.

'How do you accidentally bring a raven with you?' asked Hamish, and then he waved his hand. 'Actually, I can guess ... Is he staying?'

'Yes,' said Cudweed.

'Kraak,' I said at the same time, but I was also impressed that Hamish knew I was a raven. Most people usually just say 'bird', or 'thing', or, if I'm lucky, 'crow'.

Then we met the other two students who had come to learn how to make bagpipes.

First, there was Andrew; he was a Scottish boy with a big smile on his face almost all the time it seemed.

'Hello, birdy,' he said to me, and I said, 'rork', very crossly, but Andrew didn't notice I was cross and just kept on smiling.

Andrew explained that he had come to learn how to make bagpipes because he had found out that his great-grandfather used to make them, but the family had forgotten. So now he wanted to restore the tradition.

Then there was Wiebke. She was a German student and had come all the way from Germany to learn about Scottish bagpipes. And she was doing that because her family made German bagpipes. She explained that in Germany a bagpipe was a little different and was called a Dudelsack, and she had come to learn all about the Scottish version.

Then everyone looked at Cudweed and asked why he had come.

Cudweed shrugged and said, 'I didn't want to turn fish guts[16] into dog food.'

No one said anything to that.

After a long pause, however, Hamish looked at me and said, 'So you'll be wanting to meet Catriona?'

'Kork?' I said, because I had no idea what he was talking about.

'Of course you do,' said Hamish, 'don't be shy.'

'Rarark,' I said, and I was just thinking to myself, why does he think I want to meet anyone? And why does he think I might be shy?

And then he whistled[17] and a moment later a bird flew around the corner of the factory building and landed on Hamish's shoulder.

Not just any bird, but a raven.

A lady raven.

In fact, a very beautiful lady raven.

[13] **wrinkled** ['rɪŋkld] faltig; runzlig – [14] **walnut** ['wɔ:lnʌt] Walnuss – [15] **sharp** [ʃɑ:p] hier: scharfsinnig – [16] **guts** [gʌts] Eingeweide – [17] **to whistle** ['wɪsl] pfeifen

@ WES-40326-002

And my tiny heart gave a little extra thump and I decided there and then that it might be a good idea to stay and watch over Cudweed, for a while. Just to be sure. You know?

I opened my beak to say something to her, but a strange thing happened. I couldn't think of anything to say! And before I could think again, she looked at me strangely, and flew away …

For the rest of the day Cudweed started to learn about bagpipes. To start with, he was very nervous, and it was obvious why.

On the hill behind the factory were some fields, and in the fields, there were a lot of sheep.

Hamish took everyone into the workshop and started explaining all about the history of the bagpipe. But Cudweed wasn't listening.

All he could do was stare out of the window, at the sheep. He looked nervous and sad all at once.

'Are you listening?' asked Hamish after a while, and Cudweed turned his attention back to what Hamish was saying.

But five minutes later he was just staring out of the window at the sheep again, and Hamish had to stop and get Cudweed to listen again.

This happened three more times until finally Hamish lost his patience[18].

'Cudweed! Young man! What is so interesting about the sheep?'

Cudweed looked really upset.

He stared at the floor for a long time and finally he mumbled[19] something.

'What?' asked Hamish. 'Speak up!'

'I don't want to kill a sheep,' he said.

'What?!' cried Andrew and Wiebke.

'Why do you think you have to kill a sheep?' asked Hamish.

Cudweed stared at him and his bottom lip was wobbling, and he looked as if he might cry.

'Because that's what bagpipes are made from – you take a sheep and turn it inside out and drill[20] holes in its leg bones. Don't you?'

Hamish was staring at Cudweed.

He stared at him for about thirty seconds, and then he burst out[21] laughing.

'We don't kill sheep to make bagpipes!' he said, wiping a tear from his eye.

Now Cudweed looked very embarrassed, and he still looked like he might cry.

'Oh, now, I'm sorry for laughing,' said Hamish. 'But your face! You don't need to worry – those sheep out there are nothing to do with our bagpipes!'

Wiebke raised her head and smiled at Cudweed.

'In a way, you were right to worry,' she said, 'because in the old days we used to make the bag from animal skins. Or the bladders[22] of goats; things like that. So it wasn't such a crazy thing to think. Nowadays we use modern fabrics[23]. Isn't that right, Hamish?'

She smiled at Cudweed and Cudweed looked much happier. He smiled back.

'Is, is that true?' he asked.

'Yes,' Hamish said, 'that is true. I shouldn't have laughed at you. We used to use animal skins, but now we use artificial fabric – it's much cheaper, easier to work with, and more flexible. So that's what you'll be working with. Not the bladders of dead cows.'

---

[18] **patience** ['peɪʃns] Geduld – [19] **to mumble** ['mʌmbəl] murmeln; nuscheln – [20] **to drill** [drɪl] bohren – [21] **to burst out** [bɜːst aʊt] losplatzen; herausplatzen – [22] **bladder** ['blædə] Blase – [23] **fabric** ['fæbrɪk] Stoff

Now, all this talk about bladders was getting to me[24] and I decided I needed to go and find a nice quiet spot in the corner of the field to let nature take its course. If you know what I mean.

It was a lovely morning. So when I had finished doing what I needed to do, I decided not to hurry back inside to the workshop. I could already hear the sound of drills[25] and saws[26] from inside, so I knew they were making progress. I thought I would leave Cudweed to get on with it; I had been thinking only very recently that it's about time Cudweed started to look after himself a bit more.

I mean, I know it's hard for Cudweed. He worries about everything but he's a teenager now and very soon he won't even be a teenager anymore, he'll be an adult. And all that happens very fast, so this work experience seemed like the perfect chance for him to a) stop worrying about everything all the time and b) learn to do something by himself, without me or Solstice always nearby to help.

And all of this had absolutely nothing to do with the fact that just as I was crossing the field, I saw Catriona fly by a little way ahead of me. She hadn't seen me, or, if she had, she was pretending not to. Now, it's been a long time since I was 'romantically involved' with anyone (raven or any other creature for that matter), but I had to admit, there was something about Catriona that made me want to spend some time with her.

But the first thing was to get her attention, because so far, she hadn't even said 'krurk' to me.

So that was how, for the second time in a few days, I found myself flying upside down, in an attempt to attract Catriona's attention. I flew upside down, did some rolls, some dive bombs, and some combination tricks.

I was showing off, I know it, but I couldn't think of a better way to get her attention. Sadly, none of it seemed to be working, and I was just flying upside down again, and looking backwards to see if I had got her attention, when I flew into the wall of the bagpipe factory, with a smack[27].

And that was where I was sitting in a daze[28] when Cudweed came out of the factory.

It was lunchtime, which ought to have made him happy, but he looked upset again.

'Korork?' I asked.

'No!' said Cudweed. 'I mean, yes, I am getting on okay. I have cut a piece of wood that will be the "chanter" – that's the bit with the holes that you use to make the notes – and it is going well.'

'Ark?' I said.

'Yes, but I just found something out. Hamish said that we will spend the month making and learning how to play the bagpipes, and then at the end we will all play one simple piece we have learned. And then he told us the date that will happen. May 26th!'

'Rark!' I exclaimed.

'I know!' said Cudweed. 'My birthday! In all the fuss[29] about coming here, I wasn't thinking that far ahead. It will be my birthday while I am here! I won't be at home with everyone! It's awful!'

And with that poor Cudweed stomped off to find some lunch, and I watched as he started to work his way through a huge plate of sandwiches, very grumpily.

---

[24] **to get to sb.** [get tə 'sʌmbədi] jdn. in Mitleidenschaft ziehen – [25] **drill** [drɪl] Bohrer – [26] **saw** [sɔː] Säge – [27] **smack** [smæk] Knall – [28] **in a daze** [ɪn ə 'deɪz] benommen; betäubt – [29] **fuss** [fʌs] Aufregung

Into the future

1 You are going to think about future scenarios that are currently in the balance: for you and for your world. Before you dive deeper into this topic, choose one of the quotes below and discuss what it means for you.

2 36 The podcast *Four Corners* interviewed young people around the globe to get their input into life today and what the future holds in store. Listen to four speakers and match each one with the photos they refer to. There are two photos which you don't need.

We drive into the future using only our rearview mirror. *Marshall McLuhan, Canadian sociologist (1911 – 1980)*

Step out of the history that is holding you back. Step into the new story you are willing to create. *Oprah Winfrey, American talk show host (* 1954)*

3 Work with a partner and decide which challenge interests you most. Discuss what you already know and what else you would like to learn about this topic.

YOUR TRACK

After this workshop you will be able to:

- talk about cultural identity.
- speculate about future solutions to environmental crises.
- discuss dystopian literature.
- express your opinion about free speech and global English.
- study and analyse critical thinking. (Workshop task)

Living together

1 Cultural identity

a Before you watch a video about what it means to be Canadian today, reflect on what your own nationality means to you.

20 **b** Diversity is a core element of Canada's identity and the country offers citizenship to immigrants from all over the world. Watch a government video welcoming new citizens and do the tasks.

1. Summarize the main message of the video in your own words.
2. How is the importance of diversity to Canadian society conveyed? Mention the images that made an impression on you.
3. List the benefits of becoming part of 'our Canadian family' that the Judge describes.
4. Talk about the general impression you have of Canada and Canadians from this video.

2 *The Inconvenient Indian.* Read the extract in which the author Thomas King takes a look at 'Hollywood Indians'. Then complete the following tasks.

1. A fellow Canadian writer, Margaret Atwood, described King's writing as 'funny but not funny'. Discuss what she meant by that.
2. Find examples of satire in the descriptions of the stereotypical Hollywood Indian.
3. Summarize the conclusion King reaches in this extract in your own words.

Indians were made for film. Indians were exotic and erotic. All those feathers, all that face paint, the breast plates, the bone chokers, the skimpy loincloths, not to mention the bows and arrows and spears, the war cries, the galloping horses, the stern stares, and the threatening grunts. We hunted buffalo, fought the cavalry, circled wagon trains, fought the cavalry, captured White women, fought the cavalry, scalped homesteaders, fought the cavalry. And don't forget the drums and the wild dances where we got all sweaty and lathered up, before we rode off to fight the cavalry. The only thing film had to do was to collect such materials and cobble them into a series of functioning clichés. Film dispensed with any errant subtleties and colourings and crafted three basic Indian types. There was the bloodthirsty savage, the noble savage, and the dying savage. The bloodthirsty savage was the most common. This was the familiar character who rode around wagon trains, burned settlers' cabins to the ground, bashed babies against trees, and trapped cowboys and soldiers in box canyons. The second type was the noble savage, an Indian who assisted Whites in their struggles with bloodthirsty Indians, spoke fluent English, and understood the basic precepts of supply-side capitalism. The dying Indian, on the other hand, was just that. Dying. Not from a wound. Not from any disease. This was the Indian who was simply worn out, who was well past his "best before" date, [...]. The good news is that none of these Indians was a threat. [...] No matter what happened, the question that was asked and answered again and again on the silver screen was: Can Indians survive in a modern world? And the answer [...] was always: No.

from *The Inconvenient Indian: A Curious Account of Native People in North America* by Thomas King. Minneapolis: University of Minnesota Press, 2013, Kindle Edition

37 Words and phrases

marginalization	the act of treating sb. or sth. as if they are not important
noble savage	sb. from a so-called primitive society who is uncorrupted by greed
precept	a rule that says how people should behave
citizenship	being a member of a particular country and having rights because of it
melting pot	a place where different people and ideas exist together
to assimilate	to become part of a group, country, society, etc.

→ Workbook, pages 55 – 57

3 Talking about identity

38 **a** Listen to two indigenous teenagers and summarize their attitude to their communities' cultures.

b Complete the tasks.

1. Describe what Miyawata means when she talks about 'her insignia".
2. Explain what used to happen to her elders in the residential school.
3. List the skills that Nicholas used to share with his sisters and grandmother.
4. Summarize the attitudes of both Miyawata and Nicholas to the past.

4 Talking about the past

a Amira writes about her own background. Put the first four paragraphs in the correct order.

A Even today my parents still talk about their experiences of applying for citizenship. It surprised them that colleagues they had been working with for ages had mixed feelings about immigration. They also discovered that others wanted Canada to become a melting pot like the US, a unified culture into which newcomers could assimilate.

B Discussing Canada's relationship with its more than one million First Nations people was controversial. These indigenous people do not want to lose their histories, languages, cultural practices and spiritual beliefs. Today the more than 600 First Nations communities represent over 50 nations and indigenous languages.

C My parents, who were born in Pakistan, lived for some years in the UK. They were both working in education. Shortly after I was born, when my mother had stopped working, my father lost his job. They had always wanted to move to Canada, even though they had been living in the UK for some years they emigrated again and made their new home in Canada.

D However, becoming Canadian citizens was not easy. Even if you were working and paying taxes, you needed permanent residency and to have lived here for three of the past five years to qualify. There was a challenging test about Canada and proof of language skills was required.

21 **b** Watch the video or look at **G 1**. Then each choose two past tenses, find examples of them in Amira's text and explain them to each other.

c Complete the sentences with the correct past tense of a verb from the box. There may be more than one correct option.

apply ■ become ■ decide ■ get to know ■ live ■ lose ■ meet ■ study ■ teach

1. Amira's parents ___ each other as kids. They ___ again when they ___ in England.
2. Her mother ___ at a London college for a couple of years when she ___ pregnant.
3. After her father ___ his job in England, Amira's parents ___ to emigrate to Canada.
4. After the family ___ in Canada for five years, they ___ for Canadian citizenship.

≫ page 116

d How do you understand the metaphor 'a melting pot' to define a nation's attitudes to immigration?

5 YOUR TURN: Citizenship in Germany

a **THINK:** How do people obtain citizenship in Germany? Are the language and citizenship tests similar to those in Canada?

b **PAIR:** Exchange your ideas. Work together to find out more about obtaining citizenship and prepare to talk about it to another pair.

c **SHARE:** Discuss your ideas. Then write five multiple choice questions for a citizenship test. Try them out on another group.

d Write your own short introduction to becoming a German citizen.

Practice: Being yourself

1 **GET STARTED!** Discuss which symbol represents your attitude to reading and why. Talk about the last book you read and why you read it.

2 **Misfits.** Listen to Amira and Lin, who are discussing how young adult literature can help us understand misfits. They mention two books, *I'm Alice, (I think)* and *God Loves Hair*. Which of the two would you prefer to read and why?

40

3 ***God Loves Hair***

41

a Listen to Lin's talk about *God Loves Hair*. Use these keys words to write down the information you hear about the book. Outline Lin's reasons for choosing it.

Bildungsroman ■ drawings ■ mixed-media ■ paperback ■ self-published

b Read the extract Lin has chosen. Do the tasks.

1 Describe how the bully, Will, makes his friends laugh and explain why they laugh.
2 Analyse the boy's reaction to the physical violence he suffers.
3 Talk about why the washroom incident 'feels like a betrayal'.

c Discuss how this extract makes you feel.

Blond-haired, blue-eyed Will Johnson walks close behind me on my way to class. He is on his tippy toes as though he is wearing high heels, fluttering his hands, and talking with a lisp to his audience of jocks. Is that what I look like? *Do you have to be such a sissy?* They laugh, and I pretend I am oblivious. They have to laugh because Will is the most popular boy in school. Maybe if I laughed too, Will and I could be friends. He kicks me and I say, Sorry. He is puzzled. He kicks me again, this time timidly, like a child unsure of his own strength, and I apologize again. His friends find this funny. So he keeps kicking, they keep laughing, and I keep apologizing. I'm bound to *sorry*, as though it's my only defense, as though each sorry holds a tiny spark of dignity. The same jocks surround me by my locker later and warn me of impending dangers. *Are you sure no one has beaten you up? You are definitely going to get beat up in high school. Definitely.* One of the brown jocks, the one who laughs the loudest, follows me into the washroom. He stands wide at the stall right next to me, making his presence known, I pee as fast as I can, focusing my eyes straight down, thinking about how our matching skin doesn't protect me and how that feels like a betrayal.

from *God Loves Hair* by Vivek Shraya. Vancouver: Arsenal Pulp Press, Kindle Edition

4 ***I'm Alice, (I Think)***

a Read Amira's introduction to her book choice and put each verb into a different past tense.

I'm Alice, (I Think) is a novel in the form of the diary of a Canadian teenager trying to figure out her identity. That sounds like a very serious theme but in fact her diary entries are often very funny. Alice **1** (*not know*) she was different from her peers at first. She **2** (*read*) from an early age and while other little girls **3** (*wear*) regular young teen clothes, Alice was walking around in a fantasy costume that her mother **4** (*make*) for her. Here's an extract from the beginning of the book in which Alice describes how these facts shaped her first experience of school.

39

Words and phrases

misfit	a person who is not easily accepted by other people
genderqueer	sb. who does not follow gender norms
sissy	a derogatory term to describe a man or boy seen as weak or lacking in masculinity
oblivious	not aware of or not noticing
to accuse	to say that sb. is guilty of a crime or offence

→ Workbook, pages 58 – 60

b Find examples of comic irony in this extract. Discuss why you would (not) like to read this book. Then discuss if it is easy for you to find friends and if you ever felt like a misfit.

I blame it all on *The Hobbit*. That, and my supportive home life. I grew up on one of those loving families that fail to prepare a person for real life. When I was little, my parents, especially my mother, encouraged me to be creative. [...] They were practically sick with pride when I learned to read early and they made sure I got a full set of all the classics. My favourite, although I didn't really understand it and my dad had to read most of it to me, was *The Hobbit*. We talked a lot about the characters and somewhere along the line I became convinced that I was a hobbit. My parents loved this best of all. Not only did they encourage me in thinking I was a hobbit, my mother actually made me a hobbit outfit. [...]

My parents didn't send me to kindergarten because they said they didn't feel ready yet. But then my brother MacGregor was born, and they had to spread around their urge to overprotect. So off I went for the first day of first grade, where I quickly discovered that everyone else had bonded and figured out the rules the year before. My next discovery was that kids didn't like kids who think they are hobbits. Parenting Rule Number One: Don't send your kids to school dressed like a fantasy character unless that kid has a lot of friends who also dress up as fantasy characters. When the little girl came up to me and asked me what I was supposed to be, I told her, even though some part of me dimly sensed it was a bad idea.

"I'm a hobbit", I announced proudly.

"What's that?" she asked, her little face intent. [...]

"It's from this book called *The Hobbit*. It's really good."

"You read?" asked the girl.

I was breezy. "Oh yeah. Everyone our age does, practically."

Her face took on a look any less sheltered kid would have recognised as dangerous. But I didn't see it.

"So you're a what?" she asked.

"I'm a hobbit. We are small and ordinary but also special. We can be sort of invisible sometimes. And we laugh like this." I gave her my deepest and fruitiest laugh.

"You know what I think?" she asked. I shook my head. "I think you look like an ugly boy."

I took off my pointy hat and put my hand to my hair.

"And just so you know, ugly-boy girls like you can't have friends.," continued the little blond girl.

Behind the girl stood six or seven other girls, all staring at me too. Accusing.

from *I'm Alice, (I think)* by Susan Juby. New York: HarperCollins, 2005, Kindle Edition

5 22 **VIEWING FOCUS: *The Hate U Give.*** In Angie Thomas's bestseller, the main protagonist, Starr, feels like an outsider. Inspired by the Black Lives Matter movement, the book became a successful film. Watch the trailer and do the tasks.

1. Describe the opening scene. Speculate on the relationship between Starr and Khalil.
2. Analyse the emotions conveyed in Starr's assessment of Garden Heights.
3. Contrast Starr's local school with 'the other world' of her school in Williamson.
4. Summarize Starr's dilemma as the only witness to the shooting.
5. Discuss the impact of her father's words: 'When you ready to talk, you talk. Don't ever let nobody make you be quiet'.

6 **Write a paragraph summarizing the story of *The Hate U Give.*** Say whether or not you would like to see the movie or read the book.

7 **YOUR CHOICE: The best years of your life?** Choose a film, book, video game or song that involves one of the many ups and downs teenagers experience. Then present your work as either **A** a blog post or **B** a short talk.

@ WES-40326-003

Rethinking climate change

1 (23) **Environmental literacy.** Look at the definition, then watch the video and do the quiz.

2 **The way forward.** Read part of a 15-year-old Canadian student's blog. Then do the tasks.

Environmental literacy is the way forward
by Noah Anderson

Time is running out, and we are in real danger of losing the battle against climate change. Education is a key factor in creating a greener and healthier world. It is essential to teach young people about ongoing malpractices and how to reverse them.

Environmental literacy involves being aware of the UN's 17 Sustainable Development Goals, especially those things that each of us can do on a personal and a community level. Concepts such as greenhouse gas emissions, sustainable food, clean water, carbon footprint, green taxes, green jobs, recycling, deforestation, renewable energy, etc. should be explained to young individuals, thus enabling them to make smart, sustainable decisions.

Climate change should be high up on everyone's agenda; we have been in the slow lane for too long. It is time to speed up and focus our efforts on saving our world before it is too late.

Source [adapted]: Amamya Kamboj, "Environmental literacy is the key to combat climate change", Let me breathe, 3 October 2020, https://letmebreathe.in/2020/10/03/environmental-literacy-is-the-key-to-combat-climate-change/ [31.03.2023]

1 Noah described himself in earlier blogs as 'an ambassador of football, peace, SDGs and women empowerment'. Talk about which of those issues are most important to you.
2 Explain what he means by 'ongoing mal-practices' and what you know about them.
3 Discuss whether he is largely positive or negative, realistic or naive about the future and compare his attitude to your own.

Environmental literacy UNCOUNTABLE NOUN
Environmental literacy is the knowledge, skills and ability to cope with the environment and promote environmental sustainability.

3 **In the year 2050 ...**

a Read part of an article and say which future scenario seems more likely to you.

As world leaders gather to mark the start of 2050, they will look back on the coronavirus pandemic 30 years before as a turning point in the quest to halt global warming. Nations will have collaborated to defeat the pandemic, and that will have launched a new era of cooperation to prevent a climate disaster. Investments in green energy and new technology will have yielded rapid cuts in emissions of carbon dioxide, putting the world on track to limit global warming to around 1.5 °C above pre-industrial levels. You won't be around, but will your grandchildren be enjoying a 'normal' life? Probably not.

In 2050, the world will look back and see the pandemic as little more than a blip in a long and mostly futile effort to stave off global warming. Despite a temporary drop in carbon emissions from the 2020 outbreak, countries will have turned to cheap fossil fuels to revive their economies after the crisis, so they probably won't have reduced their carbon emissions. This will mean that temperatures will have continued to rise, setting the stage for 5°C of warming by the end of the century. How do you think your grandchildren will feel about the world you have left them? What kind of world will they be living in?

Source [adapted]: Jeff Tollefson, "How hot will Earth get by 2100?", Nature, 22 April 2020, https://www.nature.com/articles/d41586-020-01125-x [31.03.2023]

(42) **Words and phrases**

malpractice	improper or illegal professional behaviour
to reverse	to change the order of the development of events
to stave off	to prevent sth. bad from happening

b Complete the tasks.

1 Compare the reasons for your evaluation of these future scenarios with your partner, discussing any differences and similarities.
2 Choose one prediction that you strongly believe in and give your reasons.
3 Pick out one prediction that you seriously doubt and explain why.
4 Comment on the tone of this article and speculate on the writer's intention.

4 Your future

24 **a** Watch the video or look at **G 1**, then each take one paragraph of the text in **3a** and find examples of the future. Explain your examples to each other.

b Complete these sentences about what the year 2050 will mean for you.

1 By 2050, the world will be ...
2 The climate crisis will have ...
3 Young people will probably still be ...
4 I probably won't have ...
5 Technological advances will / won't have ...

5 There's no planet B.

How is this photo linked to the heading? Find another photo to present to the class explaining its link to the heading.

The lungs of the earth – the Amazon rainforest

6 Hope on the horizon?

a As part of the Canadian class's project, Amira and her classmate Jeremy research this quote. What do you think the challenges are?

A new star has exploded onto the climate scene: hydrogen. It offers possibilities to move away from fossil fuels, but with its own challenges.

25 **b** They watch a video about hydrogen. Watch it too and look at the graphic. What are the different forms of hydrogen?

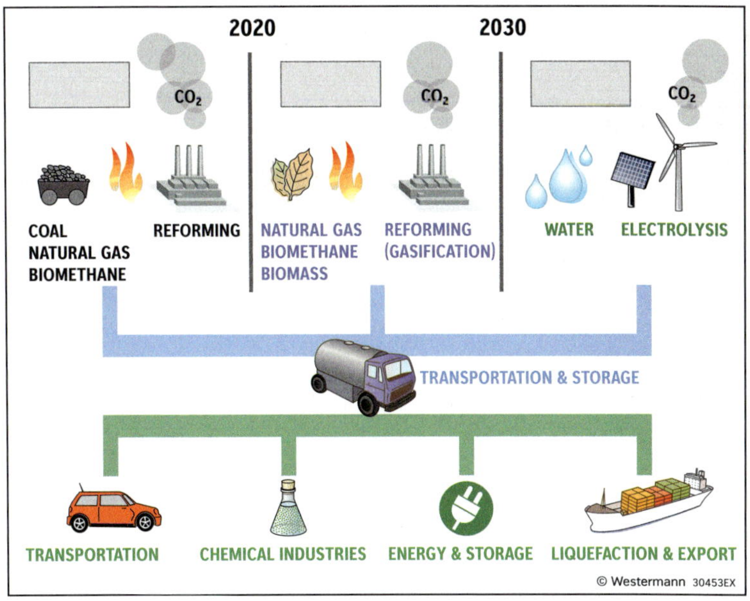

43 **c** Now listen to their presentation and put these aspects in the order mentioned.

A effects of climate change
B fossil fuel power generation
C geographical location
D harmful CO_2
E hydro dams
F power quality
G solar power electricity
H wind speed

d How has the research into green hydrogen advanced since this presentation?

7 YOUR TURN: Are you environmentally literate?

a THINK: Write a few questions for a quiz like the one you watched in **1a**.

b PAIR: Exchange your ideas. Choose the best five and swap them with another pair. How many answers did you get right?

c SHARE: Decide on the best questions for a mini quiz and make a video to show the class.

Practice: Getting our future back

1 **GET STARTED!** Think about recent podcasts you have listened to. What makes a good podcast?

2 **Teens speak out**

TIP

Conjunctions with time clauses → G8
We use the simple present after a time conjunction.
Technological advances will halt the damage ***before*** *it is too late.*

45 **a** Amira and Jeremy make a weekly podcast on climate change. Complete their conversation with the correct forms of the verbs in the box. Then listen and check.

not act ■ be (2x) ■ not be ■ become (2x) ■ do ■ live ■ reach ■ rise

J. Youth engagement in climate policy is a hot topic. I think podcasts are a great way to share views on it, and exchange information. The effects of climate change [1] more severe if countries [2] fast to reduce emissions.

A. Exactly. The temperature [3] to three degrees above pre-industrial levels unless we [4] something. Today's politicians [5] around but when they [6] all dead, it [7] a burning issue for our kids and grandchildren. Literally.

J. Yeah and higher temperatures are only part of the problem. UNICEF estimates that around 160 million children already live in regions of drought, and by 2040, one in four children [8] in areas of extreme water stress. By that time, the world [9] the tipping point that everyone's talking about now. But we can't afford to wait until it [10] too late.

»» page 116

46 **b** Listen to their first podcast about Autumn Peltier, an activist who opposes the contamination of water by the oil industry. Talk about how her background has led her to speak out for this cause.

c Listen again and complete the profile.

Autumn Peltier: international advocate for [1]; born in the year [2], a member of the Wikwemikong First Nation in [3]. Inspired by her [4], she met Canada's [5] at the age of only [6]. In her address to the [7], she stated that 'Water is the lifeblood of [8]'.

»» **d** Research another well-known environmental activist. Prepare and record your own podcast.

3 **A rich guy with an opinion**

a Many high-profile adults are also active in the campaign to halt climate change. Read and discuss what you know about Bill Gates.

CULTURE CORNER

Bill Gates, American software developer, business magnate, and philanthropist, was a co-founder of software firm Microsoft. He turned his earnings into a diversified fortune including investments in zero-carbon energy.

b Look at a chart on **page 101** from Gates' book *How to Avoid a Climate Disaster* (2021) and interpret Green Premiums in your own words.

44 **Words and phrases**

tipping point a point at which a series of small changes or incidents becomes significant enough to cause a larger, more important change
transmission lines a structure designed to carry electricity or electrical signals over large distances
intermittent not happening regularly or continuously

→ Workbook, pages 63 – 65

4 **READING FOCUS: *How to Avoid a Climate Disaster.*** Read an extract from Bill Gates' book. State your reaction to Gates' predictions. Then add the phrases and sentences below to the gaps.

A and avoid the worst effects of climate change
B 365 days a year
C The only sensible goal is zero.
D and we want to avoid major outages
E The other is zero
F the economic damage they inflict by making the planet warmer
G especially if it involves crossing national borders
H and the wind isn't blowing
I Just as we needed new tests, treatments and vaccines for the novel coronavirus,
J ideally near the equator

There are two numbers you need to know about climate change. The first is 51bn. [1]
Fifty-one billion is how many tons of greenhouse gases the world typically adds to the atmosphere every year. Zero is what we need to aim for. To stop the warming [2], humans need to stop adding greenhouse gases to the atmosphere. The climate is like a bathtub that's slowly filling up with water. Even if we slow the flow of water to a trickle, the tub will eventually overflow. Setting a goal to reduce our emissions won't do it. [3]
This sounds difficult, because it will be. [...] We cannot get to zero simply, or even mostly, by flying and driving less. [4] we need new tools for fighting climate change: zero-carbon ways to produce electricity, make things, grow food, keep our buildings cool or warm, and move people and goods around the world.
[...] One problem is that fossil fuels are so cheap. Because their prices don't factor in the true cost of climate change – [5] – it's harder for clean energy sources to compete with them. And we've spent many decades building up a system to extract fossil fuels from the ground, get energy from them, and deliver that energy, all very cheaply.
Some regions of the world simply don't have decent renewable resources. To get close to 100 percent, we'd have to move lots of energy from where it's made (sunny places, [6], and windy regions) to where it's needed (cloudy, windless ones). That would require building new transmission lines, a costly and time-consuming task – [7] – and the more power lines we install, the more the price of power goes up. In fact, transmission and distribution

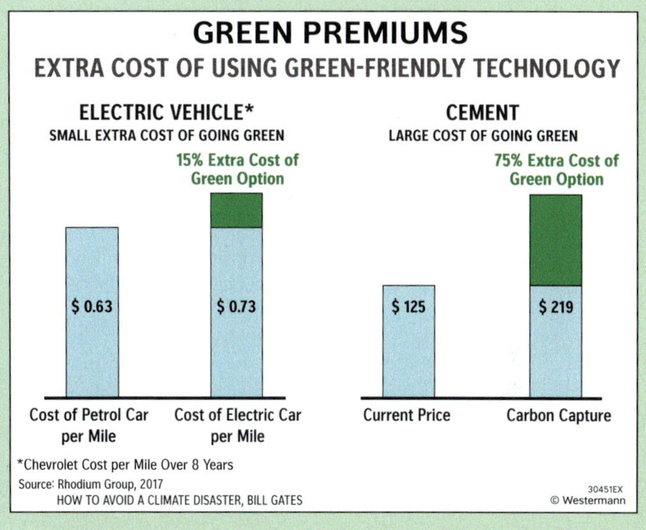

are responsible for more than a third of the final cost of electricity. And many countries don't want to rely on other countries for their electricity supplies.
But cheap oil and expensive transmission lines aren't the biggest drivers of the electricity Green Premium. The main culprits are our demand for reliability and the curse of intermittency. The sun and the wind are intermittent sources, meaning that they don't generate electricity 24 hours a day, [8]. But our need for power is not intermittent; we want it all the time. So if solar and wind represent a big part of our electricity mix, [9], we're going to need other options for when the sun isn't shining [10]. Either we need to store excess electricity in batteries or we need to add other energy sources that use fossil fuels, such as natural gas plants that run only when you need them. Either way, the economics won't work in our favor.

from *How to Avoid a Climate Disaster* by Bill Gates. New York: Penguin, 2022, Kindle Edition

5 **YOUR CHOICE: Creative solutions.** Look at some of last year's winners of *Earthshot* and choose one project to present – as **A** a podcast or **B** a text.

CULTURE CORNER

Earthshot was launched in 2020 to fund solutions for environmental challenges. It aims to award individuals and organizations in the areas of climate and energy, nature and biodiversity, oceans, air pollution, and waste.

Method coach: How to assess texts

S1 Classify a text

a Read the two texts and decide what the purpose of each one is. Here are some tips to help you:

- For text A: List the words that trigger emotions.
- For text B: Consider how the information is presented (use of tenses, choice of vocabulary, etc.).
- For each text: What is the author's intention? How does the text make you feel?

Give reasons.

A

Feel great in second-hand clothes

If you are like us, you care about the environment, you care about the future of our planet. At the same time, you are fashion conscious and passionate about new clothes. But the pleasure of purchasing a new item of clothing makes you feel guilty as you are aware of the harm the making of your brilliant new outfit caused the environment. Does this sound familiar to you?

There is a solution: make second-hand your first choice! In our shop we only sell pre-loved items, unique and vintage pieces and even designer items at affordable prices. Our motto is: fashion is eternal, fashion is affordable, fashion is sustainable, fashion is guilt-free.

Find your favourite piece and make it your own! Our staff are at hand to advise you whatever your needs.

And it gets even better. Do you need a glamorous outfit for a special occasion? Find your perfect piece, reserve it and rent it for the day. No more discarded bundle at the back of your wardrobe gathering dust and no unwanted dent in your bank balance either.

Come and see us! Join our ever-growing customer base of like-minded people. Do what is right and feel good about it!

Mark & Billie

B

Fashion is one of the largest consumer goods industries in the world and one of the most contaminating. The fashion business model that comes out with new trends every month and the idea of buying and throwing away clothes is creating a terrible impact on the planet in terms of natural resources consumption, energy and emissions. According to a 2019 report by the University of Washington, the textile industry is responsible for about one-fifth of global water pollution. And this is only one aspect of all the negative impacts manufacturing clothes from new natural or synthetic material has on our environment. Many leading textile brands are already tackling this issue. Using recycled materials, which currently stands at 65% of all production, the sector will prevent 2.8 billion tonnes of carbon dioxide being emitted by 2050. This example shows that the valuable habit of recycling clothes can be extremely beneficial in the long run. If we, consumers get into the habit of recycling our clothes instead of throwing them away, there will be real benefits to our world. To name a few, there will be savings on water consumption, our carbon footprint will be reduced, and we'll achieve a more balanced biodiversity. We must do this together, because there is no Planet B.

b Each choose one text and look up any new words. Then explain them to each other.

S2 **Questions about texts.** Look at the questions and try to answer them for your text. Are any questions not relevant to your text? If so, why not? Compare your findings.

1. What is the main point of this text?
2. Who wrote it?
3. Why was it written?
4. When was it written?
5. Has the context changed since it was written?
6. Is the evidence supported?
7. How did the author come to his or her conclusions?
8. Do you agree with the conclusions?
9. What does this add to our knowledge?
10. Why is it useful?

Workshop task: Assessing claims

S1 Looking at statistics

26 **a** Watch the animated film *When can you trust statistics?* What do you learn about the source? Do you think it is reliable?

26 **b** Choose the correct options, then compare your answers with a partner. Watch again and explain why the wrong options are false.

1 One approach to statistics is to say that
 a 98 % of them are lies.
 b they're not reliable at all.
 c you're a fool to believe them.

2 The three Cs of data wisdom are
 a be calm, check claims and be careful.
 b stay calm, get context and be careful.
 c be careful, get context and be clear.

3 When a claim has had an emotional effect on you,
 a think about your reaction before you share it.
 b analyse the data and then share it.
 c think about how others might react before you share it.

4 In the example about the NHS savings, the important question is how
 a many people are overweight in the UK.
 b much is saved by how many people.
 c significant £100 million is over five years.

5 Statistics cannot teach us anything unless
 a we use them to fight our battles.
 b they help to confirm our beliefs.
 c they inspire us to ask questions.

6 While not accepting statistical claims at face value, we should
 a not dismiss them out of hand either.
 b be cautious of those we agree with.
 c ask if the figures are increasing or decreasing.

TIP

Assessing sources for academic purposes will also help you assess real-life situations. When you have to make choices or form an opinion, you need to be well informed. An interested mindset will help you ask the right questions when looking for information.

- Is this the right source? Is it reliable? Can I check it?
- Do any of the claims make me suspicious?
- Is this information relevant for me at this moment?
- Is it possible to consider the claim from a different angle?

S2 Drawing conclusions from statistics

a Look at a statement published by a business school in Spain in 2019 relating to the performance of students in a final exam for an English language degree. In what way is the percentage of girls who took the exam presented differently and what is the effect?

> 8 % of girls who took the exam failed to receive top points. Meanwhile 58 % of boys who took the exam received grades between A and C.

b Look at the statistics reported in the UK in 2019. Explain if they are comprehensive enough.

> **The proportion of young people in England going to university has passed the symbolic 50% mark for the first time**
> Figures from the Department for Education, for 2017 – 18, show 50.2% of people going into higher education. The figures are higher for women, where 57% are going to university.
> The annual statistics on entry to higher education show the proportion of people set to go to university before the age of 30.

47 **c** Listen to an expert analysing the report. Copy the headings and make notes while listening.

The data provided in the report tells you	The data does not give information about
???	???

d Compare your notes. Discuss whether the analysis has changed your reaction to the report. Give reasons.

S3 **Writing your assessment.** Find a headline, tweet or post that offers a claim based on statistics. Do some research by checking the sources and studying the figures. Write your evaluation and share it with a partner. (See TIP box on citing sources on **page 140**.)

Back to the future

1 Tomorrow's world?

49 **a** Listen to a teacher explaining some important examples of dystopian fiction. Match the book titles with at least one of the topics they deal with.

technological control ■ environmental ruin ■ loss of personal identity ■ political oppression

1 *Brave New World* by Aldous Huxley
2 *Do Androids Dream of Electric Sheep?* by Philip K. Dick
3 *The Wall* by John Lanchester
4 *Fahrenheit 451* by Ray Bradbury
5 *Nineteen eighty-four* by George Orwell
6 *The Hunger Games* by Suzanne Collins

TIP

Question tags are often used in spoken English. → G 9
*We're all here, **aren't we**?*
*You **didn't look** at dystopian literature last year, **did you**?*

b Complete the examples from the listening.

1 It's, like, the opposite of a utopia, ___?
2 Science and technology don't help combat the climate crisis or anything, ___?
3 There won't be a problem identifying some of the dangers, ___?
4 There was a movie too, ___?
5 We seem to have a great appetite for dystopia, ___?
6 The government has complete control in *The Hunger Games*, ___?

»» page 116

c Discuss which of the developments dystopian novels describe have already come true.

2 *The Handmaid's Tale.*

50 Livvy talks about the work of a famous Canadian author, Margaret Atwood. Listen and do the tasks.

1 Outline your immediate reaction to the theme of *The Handmaid's Tale*.
2 Comment on how environmental issues impact on the future world.
3 Justify the author's status as a feminist from the summary Livvy gives.
4 Point out the characteristics of dystopian fiction that this presentation highlights.

3 Gen Z's future

a Read how young people felt about their future after the Corona crisis. Discuss which feelings are still relevant to your generation today.

b Complete the tasks.

1 Select the speakers who voice the most and the least optimistic view of their future. Compare your choices with a partner.
2 Each partner focuses on two of the speakers, pointing out the main issues that concern them. Exchange the information and talk about whether you share their concerns.
3 Explain which statement corresponds most strongly with your own feelings.

48 **Words and phrases**

celebrity culture	exposure of celebrities' personal lives on a global scale
to be thrilled to	to be pleased and excited about sth.

→ Workbook, pages 67 – 69

Rocco, 17 School student in Palermo, Italy
Before the pandemic, I had hoped to get a good job, I always thought that my future would be amazing but actually now I don't believe in an exciting future. I want to travel and see the world like my parents did, but I'm not sure that will ever be possible. During the pandemic, I realized the power of technology to keep friends together, so, although there were mental health problems, I feel as though social media helped. But we need to be aware of the risks. We'll be relying on social media for work and fun, but it's become a vehicle for fake news and the celebrity culture, which I find scary. I have an interview with a career's advisor next week. I'm hoping to get into politics, but I'm not sure how easy that will be.

Moha, 24 Business student in Geneva, from Morocco
That was my first year away from home. I was thrilled to be studying in Europe, but once the virus locked everyone down, everything just kind of fell apart. I'm pretty sure I won't finish my studies now, because I won't be able to find a job to fund them; I'll be chasing the same jobs as hundreds of other students. Young people will have to be more creative with start-up businesses and so on. I think climate change is my generation's biggest challenge. Basically, nothing makes me dread my future more than global warming. I often feel like we've already lost that battle. My partner and I decided that we're not going to bring children into this world. What's the point?

Shelley Gupta, 17 School student in, UK
School ends in June and I'll be leaving with a few bits of paper – that's all I'll have to show for seven years of studying. Frankly I have no idea what I'm going to do. The divide between black and white, rich and poor, straight and gay that got worse during the pandemic. How did it affect my life? I guess it worried a lot of us at the time because of the virus itself and the fear that this could be our 'new normal'. We'd only just started living when everything stopped, and, like, it'll never be quite the same again.

Irena Gawlak, 19 from Poznan, Poland; politics student in Utrecht, the Netherlands
The pandemic was a great shock. We were making progress with issues like gender equality and then we saw how a crisis can suddenly wreck our plans. But we also saw how most people acted responsibly – governments found money and scientists vaccines. Will we be able to capitalize on that positive energy in the future? Many people felt a sense of community, of togetherness, but that didn't last. Personally, I'm looking forward to getting a good job. I'm planning on making a difference.

4 Expressing the future

a Watch the video or look at **G 1**, then each take two of the texts and find examples of the future. Explain why each form is used.

24

b Make more sentences about the future.

Rocco — My interview | be quite soon. I | think hard about what to say.
Moha — Jobs for young people | difficult to find. They | certainly not be jobs for life.
Shelley — By the end of the term | I | take all my exams. I hope | not fail any!
Irena — My friend and I | start a podcast called 'Make a Difference'. We | meet tomorrow to discuss our ideas.

page 116

TIP

Other ways of talking about the future
We use *hope* and *want* followed by the infinitive.
*I **hope / want to travel** and see the world.*
We use *plan* and *look forward to* followed by the gerund.
*I'm **planning on making** a difference.*
*I'm **looking forward to getting** a good job.*

5 YOUR TURN: The next ten years

a THINK: Write down a question to ask a classmate about their hopes and fears for the future. Consider academic or work ambitions, global issues, family life or your own ideas.

b PAIR: Exchange your questions and write down some ideas to use in your response.

c SHARE: Now ask and answer your questions in groups using a variety of ways to talk about your future hopes and fears.

Practice: Speaking out

1 **GET STARTED!** How are these photos linked? Discuss your experiences of similar situations.

2 **MeToo**

a Read about the #MeToo Movement and discuss your reaction to the statements below.

The #MeToo Movement can be defined as a social action group that is against sexual violence and sexual assault. It encourages females who survived sexual violence to talk about their experiences. Since the early days of the #MeToo Movement, more and more people have been speaking out against sexual harassment or assault. However, some critics suggest that it ignores the rule of law and is therefore unfair to the accused.

The #MeToo Movement will continue to have influence in society.

It has changed many people's attitudes and behaviour towards women.

MeToo has had a positive impact, but it has now gone too far.

52 **b** After her talk about *The Handmaid's Tale*, Livvy talks to one of her classmates Jurek. Complete the gaps with the correct question tags. Then listen and check.

Jurek I liked your talk, Livs. I bet you got a good grade for it, [1]?

Livvy Well, Mr Ogilvie said I should've talked more about the flashback device that Margaret Atwood used, but yeah the grade was OK.

Jurek You know about the controversy over Atwood and the MeToo Movement, [2]?

Livvy To be honest, I can't remember much. It was about sexual harassment, [3]?

Jurek Yeah. The press savaged her for an open letter she signed in support of a Canadian academic, a guy who had lost his job because of sexual harassment. My point is if she questioned the whole MeToo thing, you can't call her a feminist, [4]?

Livvy That's a good point. Let me check it out ... So, she referred to the MeToo campaign as 'a witch hunt, a symptom of a broken legal system'. But people should be presumed innocent until they're proven guilty, [5]?

Jurek Well of course. And it's also true that online campaigns like #BLM and #MeToo can become irrational and aggressive. But that's not so different from the way people argue at a public meeting or in a bar, [6]?

Livvy Except that online comments are largely anonymous, [7]? That's lynch-mob mentality, if you ask me.

Jurek Hmm, well actually I think that's open to debate, Livs.

page 117

51 Words and phrases

to savage sb.	to criticize sb. cruelly
witch hunt	a campaign / investigation that targets sb. who is unfairly accused of wrongdoing
lynch mob mentality	the irrational and violent behaviour of a group of people who want to punish sb., often without regard for the facts or the law
to cancel sb.	to stop supporting sb.

→ Workbook, pages 70 – 72

3 Cancel culture

a Read a definition of the term 'cancel culture' and discuss what you know about it. Think of examples of a celebrity being 'cancelled'. Talk about who it was and what happened to them.

> ***cancel culture*** UNCOUNTABLE NOUN
> a way of behaving in a society or group, especially on social media, in which it is common to completely reject and stop supporting someone because they have said or done something that offends you

> **TIP**
>
> **Presenting arguments**
> - **Stating the issue**
>
> *The most important argument for … is …*
> *The main idea / thing is that …*
> - **Pre-empting an argument**
>
> *It's obvious / evident that … . However, / Nevertheless, …*
> *Although it is true that …, I believe that …*
> *I admit / concede that …, but we must remember that …*
> - **Sequencing a list of arguments**
>
> *For a start, …*
> *Secondly, … Thirdly, …*
> *To sum up, … / Finally, …*

b Complete some arguments for and against cancel culture with the expressions in the box. Sometimes more than one option is possible.

for a start ■ however ■ I believe ■ nevertheless ■ secondly ■ most important ■ thirdly ■ to sum up

Cancel culture: a force for good … or not?

The [1] argument for cancel culture is that nobody should be allowed to cause offense to another person, group or belief, just because they have power or prestige. Some people believe the idea that a person can be 'cancelled' – in other words, culturally blocked from having a prominent public platform – has become a toxic form of social media gang rule. I do not agree. The main idea is if a person with influence has acted badly, they can be boycotted. [2] this is legitimate for several reasons.

[3], I do not think the offender should be allowed to say anything they want, just because they are rich and famous. [4], it is true that in some cases, cancel culture has got out of control and eliminates nuance from the debate. However, I believe that even celebrities should answer for their actions. It is obvious that some public figures do not endure any long-term, career-ending effects from being cancelled, and indeed that they might even gain more public sympathy. [5], I believe that cancel culture has become an important instrument of social justice, even if it only raises awareness.

[6] I concede that the idea of 'cancelling' a person is unpleasant, and that the punishment does not always fit the crime if, for example, the reason for the cancelling is a thoughtless racist, homophobic or sexist tweet made years ago. [7], we must remember that using social media is, for many people, the most effective and sometimes the only way to express their reaction to hurtful or hateful jokes or comments. The power to ignore or 'cancel' someone whose behaviour you find unacceptable might be the only power you have.

[8], the debate around cancel culture is controversial. While some think we should be able to forgive a person and move on, for Black culture and cultures of any marginalized groups, this is an opportunity for an individual to speak out.

4 SPEAKING FOCUS: Social media

a Brainstorm ideas for a short talk entitled *Social media: free speech or a 'toxic form of gang rule'?* Follow these guidelines.
- Start by stating the issue, giving your own arguments.
- Explain your views on whether people should be allowed to say whatever they like online.
- Consider your audience and think about how you can pre-empt counterarguments.
- Use the phrases you have learned to sequence your arguments more formally.

b Write notes on cue cards, then practise by recording your talk on your phone.

c In small groups, take turns to give the talk you have prepared. Use the evaluation sheet you created on **page 61** to take notes. Give feedback, stating what you found good and what could be improved or clarified.

World English

1 The importance of English

a Read the statement by a professor of education at the University of Hong Kong. Think of some examples of World Englishes.

The term World Englishes refers to the differences in the English language that emerge as it is used in various contexts across the world. Scholars ... identify the varieties of English used in different sociolinguistic contexts, analysing their history, background, function, and influence. *Yang, 2001*

27

b Discuss your reaction to this a video about an influential model of World Englishes devised by Kachru in the 1990s.

2 The spread of world English

a Look at the TIP box, then complete the first part of Joanna Chong's presentation with the words from the box.

a little ■ a lot of ■ any ■ both ■ less ■ many ■ neither ■ some

TIP

Using quantifiers → G 10

- We use quantifiers such as ***some*** / ***hardly any*** countries before a noun to indicate amount or quantity.
- They can indicate a large proportion, e.g. ***the whole of*** the century / ***most of*** the audience / ***all*** speakers.
- They can also indicate a smaller proportion, e.g. ***less*** communication / ***a little*** English / ***no*** influence.
- Quantifiers can also compare two things, e.g. ***neither*** person / ***both*** journalist ***and*** cyclist.

There are hardly [1] corners of the world where the English language has no influence. The present-day world status of English is mainly the result of two factors: the first was the expansion of the British Empire, which resulted in the colonization of [2] parts of North America, Asia, Africa and Australasia. The second factor was the development of the USA as the world's leading economic power.

As we can see from Kachru's three concentric circles, there is an inner circle of places where English is the dominant language. This includes the UK, the United States, Canada, etc. The outer circle includes [3] countries such as India and Singapore where English became a second language. Finally, the expanding circle is made up of places where English is learned as a foreign language, such as in China and in [4] European countries.

Today the English speakers in the two outer circles outnumber the native speakers of the inner circle. In other words, there is [5] communication between speakers of English as a first language than might be expected. Why is this?

Greater mobility across the world has resulted in movement between the circles in Kachru's model with a blurring of boundaries between the outer and the expanding circles. This in turn leads to communication in English between speakers with different first languages. An example of this is a Dutch sports reporter interviewing a Spanish cyclist in English during the Italian cycling event Giro d'Italia. [6] person speaks the other's native language but [7] the journalist and the cyclist have some English. Moreover, most of the audience will have at least [8] English, no matter where they are. This method of communication, where English is the language common to all speakers, is known as English as a Lingua Franca or ELF.

Source [abbreviated and adapted]: Rui Yang, "An Obstacle or a Useful Tool? The Role of the English Language in Internationalizing Chinese Universities", Journal of Studies in International Education, Vol. 5 No. 4, pp. 341 – 358

»» page 117

53 Words and phrases

to emerge to appear
expansion the action of becoming larger
to result in to follow as a consequence of sth.

→ Workbook, pages 73/74

b Complete the tasks.

1 Summarize the growth of English as an influential language.
2 Explain the differences between the three circles in your own words.
3 Discuss the significance of the number of native speakers compared to others.
4 Think about where you speak English and complete the sentences:
- I speak *a little* / *some* English with ...
- In class, we speak *less* / *more* ... than ...
- There aren't *any* / *many* situations ...
- I have *few* / *no* opportunities to speak ...

3 Intercultural communication

54 **a** Listen to the start of the second part of Joanna Chong's presentation. Summarizes why she thinks English as a Lingua Franca (ELF) is a significant concept.

55 **b** Listen to the rest of the presentation. Then complete the sentences so they are true for you. Discuss your ideas with a partner.

I was surprised to learn from the presentation that more non-native speakers than native speakers use English to communicate.

So you mean that a conversation between, say, a Swede and a Pole is likely to be in English?

1 Most of the conversations I have in **English / my native language** are ...
2 In my opinion, we should learn **more / less** 'native-speaker correctness' and **fewer / more** communication strategies in school.
3 I **think / don't think** we have enough exposure to varieties of English from other parts of the world.
4 In the future, it's my guess that some form of English **will still / will no longer** be the global language.

4 English in Germany.

How much English are you exposed to in your everyday life? Look the signs and speculate where the pictures were taken. Why do you think English is being used here? Discuss.

5 YOUR TURN: Your English

a THINK: Make some notes about where and why you use English. Then list the situations in which you expect to use it in the future.

b PAIR: Compare your notes.

c SHARE: Team up with another pair and talk about where and why you use English and your expectations. Use paraphrasing to clarify information and ask further questions.

d Write a paragraph outlining one group member's experiences and expectations and how they compare with yours. Swap paragraphs and give each other feedback.

Practice: Broadening your horizons

1 GET STARTED! Discuss how this picture is linked to the idea of 'broadening your horizons'?

2 Why study abroad?

a Read about the Erasmus+ programme and talk about its appeal to you personally.

Enriching lives, opening minds

Erasmus+ will help participants at all stages of their lives, from school through to adulthood, to pursue stimulating opportunities for learning across Europe, both inside and outside of the classroom. You will gain valuable life-skills and international experience to help you develop personally, professionally and academically and to succeed in today's world. As well as boosting skills and employability for participants, the programme will also modernize education, training, and youth work across Europe.

b Read some of the advantages Erasmus Plus students have mentioned. Then discuss what would benefit you most and how you feel about studying abroad.

1 It helped me develop personally, professionally and academically.
2 I gained new transferable skills and boosted my employability.
3 It broadened my horizons – physically and mentally!
4 The programme increased my motivation to learn.
5 We all developed cultural awareness and open-mindedness.
6 It enhanced my self-confidence.

3 Student reviews

57 **a** Listen to a *Four corners* podcast about what some students have gained from the experience of studying abroad. Which of these topics do they all mention: *funding / language skills / comfort zones*?

b Which student says the following: Abbas Bokar, Celine Page, Mo Al Sahir, Jess Lamont?

1 You may experience a kind of culture shock.
2 Erasmus+ made it much easier to get into a Master's programme.
3 I interacted with a group of refugees.
4 It opened my mind to another culture.

4 Where in the world ...?

a India is probably not the number one destination for many students who are planning a year abroad. Or is it? Read the advert on **page 111** and evaluate how effectively it promotes study in India for international students. How would you feel about going there and why?

b Then read the advert for study in South Africa. Compare it with the advert in **a** and talk about your preferences.

c Which study programme would you and your partner choose and why?

Neither / One of us prefers ... because ...
Both of us would like to ... and our reasons are ...

56 Words and phrases

well-equipped	having the skills and resources needed to do sth.
to boost	to increase or improve sth.
proficiency test	an exam which tests a learner's level of language
tuition fee	money that a student pays to go to university
to be phased out	to gradually stop using sth.

→ Workbook, pages 75–78

With around 900 universities, India is well-equipped to handle a rise in the number of international students. The government has launched some ambitious programmes to boost the country's overseas student population from around 45,000 to 200,000.
Many programmes are taught in English – one of India's two official languages. If this isn't your native language, you may be required to sit a proficiency test.
India's warm and welcoming population will make settling in easy. If you're adventurous, you could trek the Himalayan Mountains or Rajasthan desert. You could also visit one of the nation's many cosmopolitan cities, such as Mumbai, New Delhi or Bengaluru.
Online applications are usually made directly to the university and there are plenty of scholarships available. To apply for funding, write a personal statement, explaining why you wish to study in India and what you could bring to the programme.

South Africa offers a more affordable university experience than other popular English-speaking destinations, such as the US and UK. Tuition fees are considerably lower, and the cost of living is nearly 40 % less in South Africa than in the UK.
While funding opportunities do exist for international students, they can be rare – scholarships and stipends are more likely to be offered to South African nationals. Contact your chosen university directly to find out what funding is available to you.
South Africa is home to 11 national languages, but the majority of courses are taught in English. Some more traditional universities may still offer courses in Afrikaans; however, the language is being phased out in universities to offer a more inclusive study experience. If English isn't your first language, you'll be asked for evidence of your proficiency. As part of this, you will be asked to justify your application for a scholarship in the form of an essay entitled: 'What South Africa can do for me – and what I can do for South Africa'.

5 **Studying abroad.** Listen to friends at an international school. Complete the tasks.

58

1. Outline Feline's reasons for wanting to study in the UK and explain why she might prefer another option.
2. Talk about Kai's choices and say what his final decision is likely to be.
3. Point out why Feline and Lina both like the idea of studying in New Zealand.
4. Comment on Lina's reasons for considering study in the UK and explain her preference for South Africa.
5. All three students mention diversity: state what they mean by that in your own words.
6. Lina also mentions improving her self-confidence. Describe how you feel about leaving your comfort zone.

6 **WRITING FOCUS: A personal statement.** Imagine you have chosen to do a course of study in an English-speaking country. Write a short personal statement applying to the organization of your choice. Follow the tips below.

- Identify the qualities, skills and experience the course requires and match them to your own.
- Explain why you are applying.
- Say why you think you are a suitable applicant.
- Outline your financial situation and enquire about possible funding.
- Enhance your application with knowledge about World Englishes and cultural diversity.

7 **YOUR CHOICE: What? Where? When?** Look at the *Four Corners* ad below. Then choose either to **A** record a podcast or **B** write a text for *Four Corners*.

Watch this space for our new feature *Your Choice*. Sam wants to hear your ideas. Tell us your plans for spending time abroad– as a podcast or text.

- What you want to do (study, work, volunteer ...?)
- Where you want to go (Europe, ... further away, ...?)
- When you want to go and for how long (during a summer break, after/during school or university, after you have finished school or university, ...?)

PART 1 PART 2 PART 3

Method coach: Critical thinking

S1 Reaching accurate conclusions

a Discuss and explain what you understand by the term 'critical thinking'.

b You are going to read why critical thinking is important. Skim the text below and choose the correct heading for each paragraph.

1 Make up your own mind
2 What, where, when, who, why, how?
3 Key skill in all disciplines
4 Justify your assessment

A

What does being critical mean? It does not just mean finding fault. It means assessing evidence from a variety of sources and drawing reasoned conclusions. As a result of your analysis, you may decide that a particular piece of evidence is not robust, or that you disagree with the conclusion. You should, however, be able to state why you have come to this view and incorporate this into a bigger picture.

B

Being critical goes beyond describing what you have heard in class or what you have read. It involves synthesizing, analysing and evaluating what you have learned to develop your own argument or position. Thinking about a topic in an objective and a critical way will help you to identify the different arguments.

C

Critical thinking is essential in all subjects and fields – in science and engineering, as well as the arts and humanities. The types of evidence used to develop arguments may be very different, but the processes and techniques are similar. Critical thinking is required for pre-university as well as under-graduate and postgraduate levels of study.

D

Purposeful reading can help with critical thinking because it encourages you to read actively rather than passively. When you read, ask yourself questions about what you are reading and make notes to record your views. Recognizing weaknesses or negative points in an argument will help you to evaluate its strength or validity.

c Read the article again and compare the notes you made in **a** with the ideas in the article.

S2 Acquiring data wisdom

59 **a** Read some advice about data wisdom and complete it with the words in the box. Then listen and check your answers.

agree ■ balanced ■ empathy ■ evaluate ■ indisputable ■ motives ■ original ■ prejudices ■ reject ■ reliable

Getting data savvy

We are fortunate to live in a world where there is so much information and knowledge available to us in the easiest way possible. However, not everything out there is 1, and that's where some strategies for data wisdom come in. Asking questions about a claim will help you to 2 arguments, to step back and get different perspectives. There are certain things to avoid and the first is what is called confirmation bias. This is when you automatically 3 with statements or claims because they match your own opinion. Here, the strategy is to be actively willing to change your mind. Remember, if you are not prepared to be wrong, you will never come up with anything 4. Beware of algorithms in social media platforms. These are a way of sorting preferences based on your online activities. They can be useful in matching the best content to your interests. However, they can feed into your preconceptions and 5 and confirm what you thought you already knew. Even something that seems totally true can have shades of meaning. In other words, what seems like an 6 fact can be more nuanced than you think.
Having intellectual 7 can have very successful results when you are thinking something out. Putting yourself in other people's shoes and really trying to understand their point of view can lead to a much more 8 reaction, even if, in the end, you still agree to differ.
Another key strategy in data wisdom is of course to check your sources. Critical thinking depends on being aware of ulterior 9. Does the person or organization making the claim have a vested interest? This may be as simple as trying to sell you something, but can also be used in social engineering, for example by influencing your voting choices in a government election.
And finally, avoid dismissing an argument based on the person who is making it. As a teenager, you will often have heard: 'You're too young to understand'. Equally, teenagers may 10 a claim or an argument presented by a parent or teacher with: 'You're too old to understand'. Listen to what is being said without judging it on a preconception.

b If you use any of the above strategies, say why they are useful and describe how you use them. Then consider why you use them and why you don't use others. Discuss whether you should.

→ Workbook, page 79

Workshop task: Reporting on fake news

S1 Bad influence(rs)?

a Read Amira and Lin's conversation about influencers who give their followers bad advice and summarize what they say.

Lin I watched a documentary last night about this awful person – she made a fortune by claiming she had cured herself of cancer. Pretending to be ill – I mean, who does that?

Amira That's incredible. Why did she do it?

Lin She was a wellness blogger with, would you believe, over two million followers. She was selling a diet, a diet book, an app, a lifestyle basically. And sharing photos of herself looking A-MA-ZING … beautiful, slim, gorgeous hair, really healthy …

Amira But it's easy enough to do that with photo editing software, isn't it?

Lin Yeah, but it's very convincing.

Amira Plus there are algorithms that suggest content – all you have to do is like a single post. I've done it myself: just liking a fitness programme prompted all sorts of slimming content to pop up – tips, diet pills and even body sculpting. It's insane.

Lin What's worse in this case, some genuinely sick people chose to stop traditional medical treatments because they wanted to believe they could heal their conditions naturally. And this woman was everywhere, in magazines, in the news, on people's phones.

Amira Hmm, so I guess they trusted her. How did they find out she was a fake?

Lin She lied about donating some of her book and app sales to charity. A journalist started digging and found out the truth.

Amira And the moral? Don't believe everything you read.

b Collect similar examples of influencers' harmful advice you have come across. Discuss them considering the following points:

- What made these influencers and their posts successful?
- If they had any similarities, what were they?
- What were the influencers ulterior motives?

> **TIP**
>
> **How to spot fake news online**
> - **Check the source:** Does the website look real? If you aren't sure, click on the 'About' page and look for a clear description of the organization.
> - **Spot fake photos:** Are they altered or taken from a different site? Use a tool like a reverse image search to show you if the same image is used elsewhere.
> - **Check if the story is in other places:** Look on news sites that you know and trust to confirm it's not fake.
> - **Look for other signs** such as ALL CAPS and lots of ads that pop up when you click on a link.
> - **False hopes:** If the news offers you hope for an easy solution to a problem, check it out carefully. If it sounds too good to be true, it probably isn't true.

c Discuss how you would advise a friend who you think is being influenced by a blogger.

S2 Finding a controversial report

a Find an article, a blog or report that makes a strong claim about one of the following topics. Choose a topic of your own if you prefer.

- University education makes you a better citizen
- Flying and driving less will stop global warming
- Police 'stop and search' increasing for Black youth
- Listening to classical music makes you smarter
- Young people have no interest in politics

b Copy your article and highlight anything that you feel is controversial, or which makes you doubt its accuracy. Make notes, using the tips on critical thinking and identifying fake news.

S3 An analysis

a Write an analysis of the article outlining what is good or bad about the claim. Describe how it can or cannot be verified. Write at least 200 words.

b Share your analysis in class.

Mediation

1 Generation Snowflake

a On the occasion of an anniversary with your English partner school, the next issue of your school newspaper is to be published in English. This special issue will deal with current problems faced by young people. Your task is to write an article about Generation Snowflake. Your article will include aspects that this generation is accused of, where the name Generation Snowflake comes from and why today's young people are smarter than previous generations in the eyes of the author. Use the German text for your article.

Die Generation Schneeflocke ist nicht verweichlicht – sondern einfach schlauer

[...] Pauschale Aussagen über die Jugend von heute sind bekanntlich mindestens so alt wie das Konzept „Jugend". Sicher fanden auch schon Steinzeitmenschen, dass die jungen Leute mit dem Faustkeil nicht richtig umgehen können, sich beim Zerlegen des Mammuts zu zimperlich anstellen und mit ihren neumodischen, verweichlichten Ideen [...] wirklich furchtbar nerven. [...] Aktuell sind es Headhunter, Unternehmensberater oder Personaler, die mit der Jugend von heute wirklich gar nicht zufrieden sind. Die Vorwürfe aber sind dieselben wie schon bei den alten Ägyptern: arbeitsscheu, selbstbezogen, „auf Umsturz" sinnend.

Der Headhunter Klaus Hansen etwa sagte der „Süddeutschen Zeitung" in einem 2019 erschienenen Gespräch: „Die Arbeitnehmer, die in den 1980er-Jahren und später geboren sind, leben nicht, um zu arbeiten. Sie wollen das Leben genießen." Und er meint das als Kritik: „In Firmen wie einer Unternehmensberatung hört man nicht auf zu arbeiten, wenn es dunkel wird". [...]

Dem SPIEGEL sagte Heiner Thorborg, 77, ebenfalls Personalberater, die heutigen Berufseinsteiger seien stets auf der Suche nach Selbstverwirklichung, nach Freiheit und Flexibilität. Auch das ist als Kritik gemeint: Diese Generation sei wie „Schneeflocken", die „unter Druck schmelzen". „Generation Schneeflocke" ist inzwischen tatsächlich so eine Art geflügeltes Wort in gewissen Kreisen. [...]

Es gibt aber [...] noch ein tiefer sitzendes Problem: Viele der jungen Leute, die sich einfach nicht dem Druck, den Angsthierarchien und der Selbstverleugnung unterwerfen wollen, die ihre Eltern kaputt gemacht haben, haben schlicht recht. Sie haben aus dem schlechten Beispiel ihrer Eltern gelernt, zumindest kann man das hoffen.

[...] Die Situation junger Leute heute ist, weltweit, [...] eine noch nie dagewesene. Die Generation ihrer Eltern und Großeltern – und viele der größten Arbeitgeber! – haben den Planeten nämlich in eine Situation manövriert, die ihnen selbst im Laufe ihrer Lebenszeit mit hoher Wahrscheinlichkeit katastrophale, persönlich erfahrbare Veränderungen bescheren wird.

Der „Generationenforscher" Rüdiger Maas hat über deutsche Teenager einmal gesagt, sie hätten „einen extrem hohen Kohlenstoffdioxidausstoß, zeigen aber mit dem Finger auf andere". Das passt ins Bild. Sogar an der Klimakrise ist die Jugend von heute selbst schuld.

Ein promovierter IT-Fachmann Anfang dreißig [...] sagt dagegen: „Es gibt gerade keine wichtigere Aufgabe als den Kampf gegen die Klimakrise". Er will lieber in diesem elementaren Bereich Verantwortung übernehmen, als Geld zu verdienen, „gerade auch, weil ich so privilegiert bin." Um seine Rente könne er sich später kümmern. Er ist nicht der einzige: Die BBC hat gerade lauter junge Leute porträtiert, die ihre Stellen aufgeben, um in „low carbon jobs" zu wechseln.

Diese Haltung ist in Wahrheit viel rationaler als die eines jungen BWL-Absolventen, der gern so bald wie möglich den Beraterjob, die ständigen Inlandsflüge, die 60-Stunden-Woche und das Gehalt will, das dann zur Schmerzlinderung in teure Uhren und Sportwagen investiert werden muss. [...]

Vielleicht ist die Jugend von heute ja diesmal tatsächlich anders, zumindest zum Teil: weiter nämlich.

Source [abbreviated]: Christian Stöcker, „Die Generation Schneeflocke ist nicht verweichlicht – sondern einfach schlauer, Spiegel, 30.01.2022, https://www.spiegel.de/wissenschaft/mensch/jugend-von-heute-debatte-die-generation-schneeflocke-ist-nicht-verweichlicht-sondern-einfach-schlauer-kolumne-a-df52de97-9357-4436-9bbd-8408fbb6a640 [04.04.2023]

@ WES-40326-003
→ Workbook, pages 80/81

b You want to know more about the people mentioned in the article who have moved into low carbon jobs. You read the BBC article and tell your family about the careers of the people mentioned in the article and what you think about their decision to change jobs.

The people moving from high to low-carbon careers

Watching the Red Arrows jet across the sky as a young boy, Todd Smith knew that flying was what he wanted to do when he was older. After five years' training, costing £100,000, followed by two years working as a flying instructor, he finally landed his dream job in his late twenties – working as an airline pilot.

But in 2019, the travel firm he was working for – Thomas Cook – collapsed. By this time Mr Smith had become increasingly concerned about the growing threat of climate change, and the aviation sector's carbon emissions. "I started connecting the dots, and was met with an uncomfortable conflict," he says. "I wanted to get involved in [environmental protest group] Extinction Rebellion, but knew it would be career suicide, and I had a lot of debt. It would be easier to return to the industry and pay off the debt."

Yet with the pandemic grounding aircraft, Mr Smith, who lives in the Berkshire town of Reading, decided to quit his high-flying career for good. [...]

"Of course I prefer flying and visiting exotic destinations, and earning a decent salary," says the 32-year-old. "But when confronted with the climate and ecological emergency, how could I possibly prioritise my needs, when we need to think collectively about how to tackle the biggest existential threat to humanity?"

Mr Smith is now a climate activist. He acts as a spokesperson for Extinction Rebellion and is the co-founder of Safe Landing, a movement of climate-conscious aviation sector workers.

Giving up his dream job was a tough decision, he says. "I'm doing this out of desperation, not out of choice. Financially I've been really struggling, I'm in a huge amount of debt, it's been challenging."

But he adds: "Taking action has been cathartic and eased my anxiety." [...]

Mr Smith is far from the only person to leave a previous job due to concerns about the environment.

After working in the oil and gas industry in Denmark for 10 years, Nader Beltaji has moved to a low-carbon career. He now works as a project manager at renewable energy giant RWE.

"I actually did my master's thesis on solar power and I wanted to go into that direction, but at the time there weren't many opportunities that caught my attention," says the 33-year-old who now lives in Wiltshire. "Now the landscape has completely changed."

Currently working on the construction of an offshore wind farm off north east England, Mr Beltaji says he has more job satisfaction these days.

"Climate change is certainly very much in the news, and offshore wind is part of the UK's big energy strategy, so it's good to be part of that, and know you're working on delivering the targets," he says. "Oil and gas feels like quite a dying industry." [...]

Source [abbreviated and adapted]: Suzanne Bearne, „The people moving from high to low-carbon careers", BBC, 20 January 2022, https://www.bbc.com/news/business-60036245 [04.04.2023]

PART 1
PART 2
PART 3

First track

4 p. 95 **c** Complete the sentences with the correct past tense form. There may be more than one correct option.

1 Amira's parents **got to know / were getting to know** each other as kids. They **met / were meeting** again when they **studied / were studying** in England.
2 Her mother **taught / was teaching** at a London college for a couple of years when she **became / was becoming** pregnant.
3 After her father **had lost / had been losing** his job in England, Amira's parents **decided / were deciding** to emigrate to Canada.
4 After the family **had lived / had been living** in Canada for five years, they **applied / were applying** for Canadian citizenship.

2 45 p. 100 **a** Amira and Jeremy make a weekly podcast on climate change. Complete their conversation with the correct forms of the verbs in brackets. Then listen and check.

J. Youth engagement in climate policy is a hot topic. I think podcasts are a great way to share views on it, and exchange information. The effects of climate change 1 (*become*) more severe if governments 2 (*not act*) quickly to reduce emissions.

A. Exactly. The temperature 3 (*rise*) to three degrees above pre-industrial levels unless we 4 (*do*) something. Today's politicians 5 (*not be*) around but when they 6 (*be*) all dead, it 7 (*become*) a burning issue for our children and grandchildren. Literally.

J. Yeah and higher temperatures are only part of the problem. UNICEF estimates that around 160 million children already live in regions of drought, and by 2040, one in four children 8 (*live*) in areas of extreme water stress. By that time, the world 9 (*reach*) the tipping point that everyone's talking about now. But we can't afford to wait until it 10 (*be*) too late.

1 p. 104 **b** Complete these examples from the listening with question tags in the box.

do they ■ doesn't it ■ don't we ■ isn't it ■ wasn't there ■ will there

1 It's, like, the opposite of a utopia, ▬?
2 Science and technology don't help combat the climate crisis or anything, ▬?
3 There won't be a problem identifying some of the dangers, ▬?
4 There was a movie too, ▬?
5 We seem to have a great appetite for dystopia, ▬?
6 The government has complete control in *The Hunger Games*, ▬?

4 p. 105 **b** Make more sentences about the future.

Rocco My interview | be quite soon. (*timetable*) I | think hard about what to say. (*plan*)

Moha Jobs for young people | be difficult to find. They certainly | not be jobs for life. (*prediction*)

Shelley By the end of the term | I | take all my exams. (*action finished before a future time*) I hope | not fail | any! (*prediction*)

Irena My friend and I | start a podcast called 'Make a Difference'. (*plan*) We | meet tomorrow to discuss our ideas. (*arrangement*)

2 **b** After her talk about *The Handmaid's Tale*, Livvy talks to one of her classmates Jurek. Complete the gaps with the correct question tags in the box. Then listen and check.

52

p. 106

aren't they ■ can you ■ didn't you ■ don't you ■ is it ■ shouldn't they ■ wasn't it

Jurek I liked your talk, Livs. I bet you got a good grade for it, [1]?

Livvy Well, Mr Ogilvie said I should've talked more about the flashback device that Margaret Atwood used but yeah, the grade was OK.

Jurek You know about the controversy over Atwood and the MeToo Movement, [2]?

Livvy To be honest, I can't remember much. It was about sexual harassment, [3]?

Jurek Yeah. The press savaged her for an open letter she signed in support of a Canadian academic, a guy who had lost his job because of sexual harassment. My point is if she questioned the whole MeToo thing, you can't call her a feminist, [4]?

Livvy That's a good point. Let me check it out ... So, she referred to the MeToo campaign as 'a witch hunt, a symptom of a broken legal system'. But people should be presumed innocent until they're proven guilty, [5]?

Jurek Well of course. And it's also true that online campaigns like #BLM and #MeToo can become irrational and aggressive. But that's not so different from the way people argue at a public meeting or in a bar, [6]?

Livvy Except that online comments are largely anonymous, [7]? That's lynch-mob mentality, if you ask me.

Jurek Hmm, well actually I think that's open to debate, Livs.

2 **a** Singaporean student Joanna Chong is interested in the spread of World English. Look at the TIP box, then choose the correct forms to complete the first part of her presentation.

p. 108

There are hardly **any / some** (1) corners of the world where the English language has no influence. The present-day world status of English is mainly the result of two factors: the first was the expansion of the British Empire, which resulted in the colonization of **many / much** (2) parts of North America, Asia, Africa and Australasia. The second factor was the development of the USA as the world's leading economic power.

As we can see from Kachru's three concentric circles, there is an inner circle of places where English is the dominant language. This includes the UK, the United States, Canada, etc. The outer circle includes **any / some** (3) countries such as India and Singapore where English became a second language. Finally, the expanding circle is made up of places where English is learned as a foreign language, such as in China and in **a lot of / much** (4) European countries. Here it is taught typically in schools and used for business, international trade, diplomacy and access to English language media.

Today the English speakers in the two outer circles outnumber the native speakers of the inner circle. In other words, there is **less / fewer** (5) communication between speakers of English as a first language than might be expected. Why is this?

Greater mobility across the world has resulted in movement between the circles in Kachru's model with a blurring of boundaries between the outer and the expanding circles. This in turn leads to communication in English between speakers with different first languages. An example of this is a Dutch sports reporter interviewing a Spanish cyclist in English during the Italian cycling event Giro d'Italia. **Neither / Either** (6) person speaks the other's native language but **both / neither** (7) the journalist and the cyclist have some English. Moreover, most of the audience will have at least **a little / a few** (8) English, no matter where they are. This method of communication, where English is the language common to all speakers, is known as English as a Lingua Franca or ELF.

Source [abbreviated and adapted]: Rui Yang, "An Obstacle or a Useful Tool? The Role of the English Language in Internationalizing Chinese Universities". Journal of Studies in International Education, Vol. 5 No. 4, pp. 341 – 358

Reading

Drama: Craig Taylor, *Play no. 14* (2009)

1 **a** Look at the photos and describe what you can see. What situations are the people in? Make a list of words and expressions that you associate with the police.

b Compare your lists and sort the words and expressions into positive and negative aspects.

2 Read the play on your own. Then read it out loud in class.

Craig Taylor born in Edmonton, Canada, in 1976, is a journalist who is currently living in London. He writes for several British and Canadian newspapers and magazines. His *One Million Tiny Plays about Britain* were originally published by *The Guardian*. They are a collection of everyday conversations taking place all around Britain.

(Two police officers have stopped a young man on his bicycle in Kennington, south London)

Police 1 We'd probably let you go if you hadn't lied.
Man I never lied.
Police 2 What colour was it?
Man Fine, then. Red, then.
Police 1 Why did you say it was amber?
Man Because it was amber.
Police 2 Then how did we both see you cycle through a red light?
Man You think I know that? Maybe you don't see colour so well. Maybe I look white to you.
Police 2 You don't look white to us. (*pause*)
Police 1 Nice bicycle.
Man Yeah, it is.
Police 1 A little small for you.
Police 2 You didn't want to buy a proper sized one?
Police 1 When you went to the shop?
Police 2 When did you buy that bicycle, Derek?
Man I never bought it.
Police 2 Really? You never bought it?
Police 1 That's surprising.
Man Because it's my brother's.
Police 2 He likes pink bikes, does he, Derek? Small bikes, Derek?
Man Why you calling me that? It's not my name.
Police 2 What's your name?
Man It's ... you know.

Police 1 No, we don't know.
Man It's Chilly.
Police 2 That's not what it says on your driving licence.
Police 1 Why does it say Derek?
Police 2 What's Chilly? Is that your hip hop name?
Man It's my name.
Police 1 Your gangsta name?
Man It's my name.
Police 1 Do you know what my hip hop name would be? Bizzy.
Police 2 Why's that?
Police 1 Because I get busy. I'm generally a busy person.
Police 2 See, we both like hip hop.
Police 1 Respect. (*pause*)
Police 2 So is it Chilly, Derek?
Police 1 Put on a jumper.
Police 2 If you're Chilly. (*pause*)
Man Does that mean I can go?
Police 1 You listen to 50 Cent, Derek?
Man No.
Police 1 What are you listening to? Those are some pretty nice headphones.
Police 2 They must be your brother's too?
Man They're mine.
Police 2 Like the bike.
Police 1 Now, when I ask you what colour that light was what are you going to say? Chilly?
Man Amber. Whatever. (*pause*) Red.

from *One Million Tiny Plays About Britain* by Craig Taylor. Bloomsbury Publishing: London, 2009, Kindle version

3 **a** Explain who the characters in the dialogue are and their relationship to each other.

b Describe where the scene takes place and the situation, summarizing what the three people are talking about.

4 Read the text again and do the tasks.

1. Look at lines 1 – 11 of the play and describe the structure of the sentences. Is there anything unusual?
2. Identify the stylistic devices used and explain their function in this text.
3. Examine what roles the issues of colour and hip-hop play in this microdrama.
4. Compare the structure of this microdrama with what you know about the structure of a short story and that of a classical play.

5 Using your findings from tasks **3** and **4**, write an analysis of the play (200 words).

TIP

Some key terms for analysing dramatic texts:
- **comedy:** play with a happy ending
- **tragedy:** play with a sad ending
- **act and scenes:** the formal structure of a play; each act usually consists of one or more scenes
- **playwright:** the author of a play
- **pun:** a play on words
- **props (properties):** items used by actors on stage
- **stage directions:** what the author wants the actors to do on stage
- **register:** a particular type of language used in a specific situation or for a specific purpose
- **comic relief:** including humorous elements in the plot, often to relieve tension – an amusing scene or character, a comic remark or incident

My review

What can I do?

Look at these sentences about Workshop 1. Are the sentences true for you? Choose the right symbol for each sentence.

1 I can talk about cultural identity.
2 I can speculate about future solutions to environmental crises.
3 I can discuss dystopian literature.
4 I can express my opinion about free speech.

>>> = 'I'm great at this!'
>>> = 'I'm good at this.'
>>> = 'I'm OK at this.'

What do I know?

1 About cultural identity. Complete the text with the correct past tense of the verbs in brackets.

I am a second-generation Thai living the USA. My Thai parents [1] (*emigrate*) just before I [2] (*be born*). My mother [3] (*insist*) on giving me a Thai name, but one day when I [4] (*play*) in the park, she [5] (*hear*) other kids making fun of it. A few days later, she [6] (*decide*) to have my name officially changed to a 'Western' one so I wouldn't get picked on at school. I always [7] (*know*) that I was different to the other kids, but my parents [8] (*constantly tell*) me that the US was my country, and we always [9] (*practice*) all the American traditions. At college, I [10] (*start*) to appreciate my parents' Thai culture more and I was sad that I [11] (*not learn*) the language and customs they [12] (*grow up*) with. As a young adult, I [13] (*find*) the sacrifices they [14] (*make*) for me heart breaking. I [15] (*realize*) the few difficulties we had were mostly cultural misunderstandings. At the same time, I [16] (*feel*) disconnected from my American friends because I [17] (*not completely identify*) with them either. But after I [18] (*travel*) to Thailand, it became easier to balance the two cultures and I now appreciate being multicultural.

■ / 18

Past tenses ➔ G1; pp. 94–95

2 About future solutions to environmental crises

a Complete the dialogue about environmental issues with the words from the box. There are two you don't need.

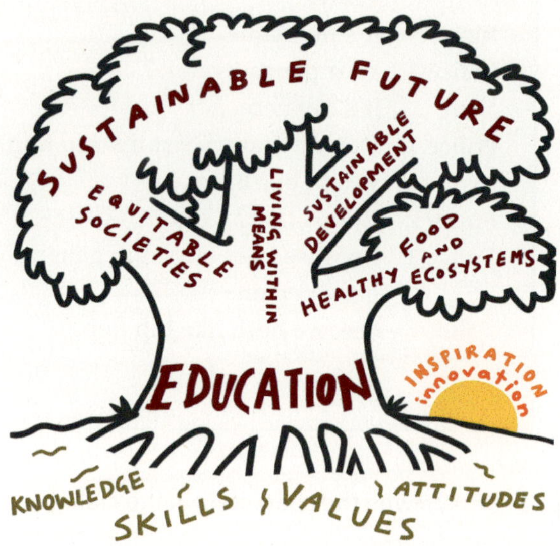

carbon ■ climate ■ emit ■ energy ■ fossil ■ green ■ greenhouse ■ levels ■ sustainable ■ zero

Abby Did you watch that programme last night about [1] change?
Bob No, I didn't. What did they say?
Abby They were talking about solutions to the current issues. Politicians say that by 2050 we will have reached net [2].
Bob What exactly does that mean?
Abby Well, I'm sure you know that when we burn [3] fuels such as coal or oil they [4] CO_2 into the atmosphere.
Bob Yes, and there are other [5] gases as well, aren't there?
Abby That's right. One of the biggest concerns is that sea [6] will continue to rise and many countries will cease to exist.
Bob I guess they were talking about how good renewable [7] is.
Abby Yes, but they were also talking about [8] jobs.

■ / 8

b Here are more sentences from the second part of the dialogue between Abby and Bob. Complete the sentences with the correct future forms of the verbs in brackets.

1 I've decided that I ▬ (*reduce*) my carbon footprint, but I'm not sure what action I ▬ (*take*). I ▬ (*take part*) in a webinar next week get some ideas.
2 My parents aren't worried about climate change – they say ▬ (*not be around*) to see the consequences. But I think that the situation ▬ (*get*) much worse before they die.
3 In thirty years' time, we ▬ (*look back*) at the actions we failed to take and ▬ (*be*) shocked.
4 Many young people say we ▬ (*not reach*) our renewable energy targets in their lifetime, which is why they ▬ (*continue*) protesting.
5 Unless we do something now, we ▬ (*not live*) in a greener world any time soon.
6 My hope is that we ▬ (*find*) some technological solutions by the end of this decade which ▬ (*ensure*) a sustainable future. ▬ / 12

The environment, pp. 98 – 99
The future → G1 ; pp. 98 – 99

3 About dystopian literature

a Match the expressions on the left with the definitions on the right.

1	authoritarian	a	to make someone lose their human qualities and make them seem like objects rather than human beings
2	to dehumanize	b	having its structure changed artificially
3	to disempower	c	to take away from someone the authority to so something
4	environmental ruin	d	believing people should follow the rules, even when these are unfair, and even if it means they lose their personal freedom
5	genetically modified	e	a time after serious damage and destruction to the world we live in
6	political oppression	f	a system of government where there is only one political party which has complete power and control over people
7	post-apocalyptic	g	the damage and destruction to the natural world and everything connected to it
8	totalitarian	h	the systematic removal of peoples' rights to their freedom and choice of who governs them

▬ / 8

b Complete the conversation about dystopian literature with question tags.

Trevor *Fahrenheit 451* was good, 1?
Mark It was okay, but it's quite old, 2?
Lucy Come on Mark, you've read older books than that, 3?
Mark Sure, it's just the style was a bit old-fashioned.
Lucy What amazes me is how many of these books with dystopian themes were written so long ago.
Trevor That's true. So, what's your favourite?
Lucy Probably *The Handmaid's Tale* by Margaret Atwood.
Trevor You like dystopian literature, 4?
Lucy I certainly prefer reading books about a dystopian future than playing silly video games based on the same ideas.
Mark Come on. Most people prefer video games, 5?
Trevor Well, I like both. Don't forget, the games probably wouldn't exist without the books first, 6?
Mark Probably not. ▬ / 6

Dystopian literature, pp. 104 – 105
Question tags → G9 ; pp. 104 – 105

4 About expressing your opinion

a Find words and phrases in the box which have a similar meaning to those listed below.

> for a start ■ however ■ I admit ■ I believe ■ it is evident ■ the main thing is ■ to sum up ■ we must remember

1 it is obvious
2 I concede
3 in conclusion
4 it is important to consider
5 nevertheless
6 the most important point is
7 first of all
8 in my opinion

■ / 8

b Choose some of the expressions from **a** to complete this presentation on the importance of free speech.

In this presentation I'm going to be talking about the importance of free speech. In recent years with movements such as MeToo and the rise of cancel culture, the topic has become a central issue again. [1] that being able to express your opinion is a fundamental right. [2], the whole issue can be rather complex. [3], where do you draw the line? [4] that a person shouldn't be allowed to say something that is racist or sexist. [5], it's quite easy for someone to take offence when other people might think there is nothing wrong with a particular comment. Another thing [6] is that with social media a comment posted in one country can be read by people living all around the world. I think [7] that people from different cultures will have different ideas about what is acceptable. [8], if somebody deliberately tries to upset someone or a group of people then that shouldn't be tolerated. [9] that just because some people say things that are unacceptable it shouldn't mean that the idea of free speech should be ditched. [10] free speech is an important principle and those who abuse it should face the consequences rather than a blanket ban.

■ / 10

Presenting arguments, pp. 106–107

■ / 70

What's my score?

Check your answers to the review (Workbook, p. 82) What are your scores for each section? What was your total score?

»»» = score 56–70
»»» = score 31–55
»»» = score 0–30

Do you want to change your answers to the 'What can I do?' statements on page 120? Look at the tasks on pages 123–127: »»», »»» and »»». Choose the tasks to help you.

My practice pages

Talking about cultural identity

1 **A question of identity.** Choose the correct options to complete the text about Mei-feu, a second generation Chinese Australian.

I am Mei-feu, a second generation Chinese Australian, commonly known as ABC. I **had been born / was born** (1) here in Perth where my parents and grandparents **had lived / were living** (2) after they **had immigrated / had been immigrating** (3) to Australia from Fiji. My grandparents found it hard to integrate because they couldn't speak English. However, both my parents **were speaking / spoke** (4) English, so they **didn't have / weren't having** (5) the same problems. As a young adult, I often wondered why my parents **hadn't sent / hadn't been sending** (6) me to a Chinese nursery or school. I remember telling my friends that I **belonged / had belonged** (7) to the 'banana generation' as I **had been / was** (8) visibly yellow on the outside and culturally 'white' on the inside. University peers were surprised that I **knew / had known** (9) so little about Chinese traditions until I **told / had told** (10) them that I **was living / had been living** (11) in Australia all of my life and **was never in / had never been to** (12) China.

2 **My identity.** Complete the text with the correct form of the verbs in brackets.

My name is Fabrice Rahim, and I am a second-generation immigrant to the US from the Ivory Coast. I **1** (*be born*) in North Riverside, Illinois, three years after my mother **2** (*emigrate*) to join her sister. She came alone as my dad **3** (*pursue*) his career in another African country. They always **4** (*keep*) in touch, but my dad never **5** (*come*) to live with us.

Mom **6** (*work*) as a medical practitioner for many years in her home country, but her qualification wasn't recognized here and she only **7** (*speak*) French. After she **8** (*learn*) some English, she **9** (*join*) my aunt and has been working as a hairdresser ever since.

As a young child, I sometimes **10** (*wonder*) why my skin colour was different, but as I **11** (*live*) in a multicultural neighborhood it never **12** (*cause*) any problems. Mom **13** (*always encourage*) me to follow my dreams, so after I **14** (*graduate*) from high school I **15** (*manage*) to get a place at a prestigious college to study architecture.

3 **British or Pakastani?** Use the notes to write a text about a second-generation Pakistani brought up in the UK.

1 parents | come over | Pakistan
2 father | be | highly respected teacher | Lahore
3 qualifications | not recognized | in UK | initially work | taxi driver
4 job | help | make new friends | British and Pakistani alike
5 before I | born | mother | work | in factory
6 we | live | area | a Pakistani community
7 young child | have | best of both worlds | enjoy | Pakistani food | have | Pakistani friends | teach | all customs | parents | practise | homeland
8 at home | parents | speak | Urdu | in nursery | I | pick up | English quickly
9 start school | fluent in English
10 have | English friends who | invite | homes | but never offer | food
11 later | find out | friends' parents | not know | I | eat | as a Muslim
12 secondary school | make new friends | actively participate | after school activities | also work in community
13 I | always feel | origin not matter | I | have | same opportunities | others | my school

Future solutions to environmental crises

4 An environmental connection

a Match the words on the left with those on the right to make collocations connected to environmental issues.

1 carbon	a change
2 sustainable	b resources
3 fossil	c contamination
4 climate	d warming
5 natural	e footprint
6 water	f fuels
7 global	g food
8 greenhouse gas	h literacy
9 environmental	i emissions

b Complete the dialogue with the correct verbs.

Amber Jake, **are you going / will you go** (1) to the protest tomorrow?

Jake I'm not sure yet. I'm not sure it **will do / will have done** (2) any good.

Amber But if we don't do something the situation certainly **isn't going to improve / won't have improved** (3).

Jake Oh, I'm not so sure. Personally, I think that within the next ten years scientists **are coming up with / will have come up with** (4) technological solutions …

Amber Oh, come on! Next you **'re going to tell / 'll be telling** (5) me that we **are going to live / will be living** (6) on the moon in the future.

Jake Sure, why not? To be honest I think by 2050 people **will be living / will have been living** (7) there for at least a decade.

Amber Wow! What an idea. So, what **are you doing / will you have been doing** (8) tomorrow instead of protesting?

Jake I haven't decided yet. I **'ll see / 'm going to see** (9) what the weather is like in the morning and make up my mind then.

5 A climate crisis

a Complete with the words from the box.

> carbon dioxide emissions ■ carbon footprint ■ climate crisis ■ climate policy ■ environmental literacy ■ fossil fuels ■ global warming ■ sustainable food ■ water contamination ■ zero carbon

1 Recently the term climate change has been replaced by _____ in the media.
2 The most imminent target is to replace _____ with renewable energy sources.
3 Unless we can halt _____, we'll suffer from more floods, droughts, fires, etc.
4 We need to prevent food shortages by implementing and practising _____ production.
5 I believe the teaching of _____ should be part of the school curriculum.
6 Unless we adhere to the _____ set out at the last COP meeting, we'll jeopardize the lives of future generations.
7 The most important goal of the developing countries should be to reach _____ use in the next 20 years.
8 According to the WHO, more than two billion people suffer from severe illnesses such as cholera caused by _____.
9 To limit the temperature rise, we need to use green energy instead of fossil fuels to reduce the _____ into the atmosphere.
10 Calculate your individual _____ to see what changes you need to make to reduce it.

b Complete the conversation between Jasmine, Tom and Charlie with the correct form of the verb in brackets.

J. So, what __1__ (*we / do*) for our school project on solutions to the environmental crisis?

T. I think the most important step is to agree on what we __2__ (*focus on*), we can't look at everything.

C. No, you're right. We __3__ (*not have*) time to present more than three ideas.

T. Let's look at technological solutions to current problems, that's what __4__ (*make*) the biggest differences.

J. That sounds good. Why don't we list the three biggest issues? I think the first is energy ...
C. You mean fossil fuels and renewables, don't you?
J. Yes, that's right. I recently saw that in 2030 the UK industries 5 (*get*) around 95% of all their energy from renewable sources ...
T. But that's just a target. I really don't think they 6 (*achieve*) that!
C. No, it's like a lot of the things governments promise. But what's the second area for us to look into?
T. How about net zero? I was thinking about technology such as carbon capture.
J. Yes, that's a good one. Of course, some scientists say that by 2030 they 7 (*invent*) technology to allow us to carry on burning fossil fuels and still reach net zero.
C. Another dream!
T. Once we've chosen a third area we 8 (*have to*) work out who ...
J. Yes, but we 9 (*not have*) a lot of time because we 10 (*give*) our presentations on Friday.

6 Solutions for our planet

a Write explanations for five of these expressions.

environmental literacy ■ carbon footprint ■ climate policy ■ zero carbon ■ sustainable food ■ climate crisis ■ fossil fuels ■ global warming

b Write sentences using the prompts.

1 in the next few years | UN | focus | food security
2 by 2035, | industries in the UK | cut | carbon emissions | by 50%
3 we | have to put in lots of effort | deal | climate crisis
4 I | measure | carbon footprint | from now on
5 climate experts | meet | Rome | next week
6 unless | everyone | do something | global warming | get worse
7 the government | look at | country | energy security | over the next few months
8 by 2100, | people | live | moon | years

About dystopian fiction

7 A dystopian world

a Choose the correct definition for each word.

1 authoritarian
a the systematic removal of people's rights to their freedom and choice of government.
b believing people should follow the rules, even when these are unfair, and even if it means they lose their personal freedom

2 to dehumanize
a to make someone lose their human qualities and make them seem like objects rather than human beings
b a system where changes are imposed on people against their will

3 to disempower
a having its structure changed artificially
b to take away from someone the authority to so something

4 environmental ruin
a a time after serious damage and destruction to the world we live in
b the damage and destruction to the natural world and everything connected to it

5 genetically modified
a having its structure changed artificially
b a system where changes are imposed on people against their will

6 political oppression
a the systematic removal of people's rights to their freedom and choice of government
b believing people should follow the rules, even when these are unfair, and even if it means they lose their personal freedom

7 post-apocalyptic
a a system of government where there is only one political party which has complete power and control over people
b a time after serious damage and destruction to the world we live in

8 totalitarian
a a system that makes someone seem like an object rather than a human being
b a system of government where there is only one political party which has complete power and control over people

b Choose the correct option to complete each sentence.

1 *The Hunger Games* and *Borne* have both been turned into films, **aren't they / haven't they**?
2 There are three different versions of the original *Blade Runner* film, **aren't there / haven't there**?
3 Jennifer Lawrence starred in the *Hunger Games* movies, **didn't she / hasn't she**?
4 *The Handmaid's Tale* wasn't Margaret Atwood's first book, **is it / was it**?
5 Many dystopian novels focus on technological control, **don't they / won't they**?
6 They won't make another version of 1984, **are they / will they**?
7 *The Road* was a fantastic movie, **wasn't it / hasn't it**?
8 All dystopian fiction is set in the future, **isn't it / will it**?

8 A dystopian world today

a Complete the text with the words from the box. There is one word you do not need.

dehumanize ■ disempower ■ environmental ruin ■ genetically modified ■ political oppression ■ post-apocalyptic ■ totalitarian

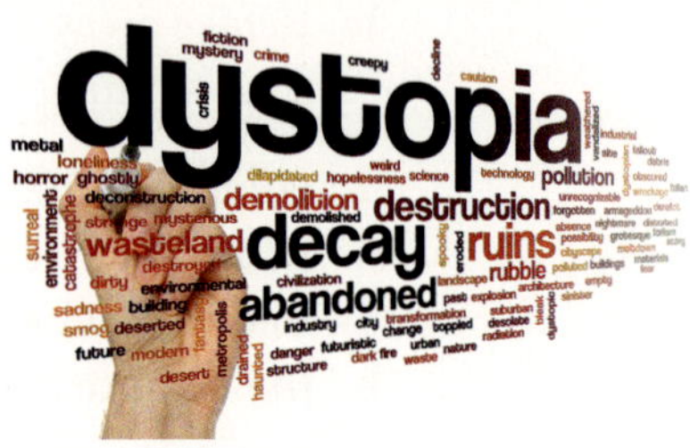

Dystopian literature has been around for over a century. Aldous Huxley's *A Brave New World* published in 1932 was an early example. The novel is about a futuristic society where embryos are [1] in order to create citizens of a certain class. In many ways, this is an attempt to [2] people turning them into robots. Just 16 years later George Orwell's classic *1984* was published. The book is about [3] where people are controlled by the [4] state of Oceania where only one party is allowed. Since the publication of these two books, there have been hundreds of others written and many of these have been made into movies or TV series. Some of the most famous are about [5] in a [6] world where society has broken down often after a man-made disaster such as a nuclear war.

b Complete the sentences with the question tags from the box. There are two you do not need.

aren't you? ■ did he? ■ didn't he? ■ don't they? ■ have you? ■ is it? ■ isn't it? ■ isn't there? ■ wasn't it? ■ were they?

1 *The Hunger Games: Catching Fire* is the second in the series of movies, ____?
2 *1984* was written in 1948 by George Orwell, ____?
3 H.G. Wells didn't write *The Road*, ____?
4 There is quite a lot of dystopian fiction for teenagers, ____?
5 Young people seem to really enjoy movies with a dystopian theme, ____?
6 You haven't read all of Margaret Atwood's book yet, ____?
7 Harrison Ford starred in *Blade Runner*, ____?
8 It's not easy to understand why dystopian fiction is so popular, ____?

9 Dystopia rules!

a Choose five words from the box and write a short text.

authoritarian ■ dehumanize ■ disempower ■ environmental ■ genetically ■ modified ■ oppression ■ political ■ post-apocalyptic ■ ruin ■ totalitarian

b Write the question tags to complete the sentences.

1 H.G. Wells wrote some of the first dystopian fiction, ___?
2 Offred is the narrator in *The Handmaid's Tale*, ___?
3 *The Road* was a post-apocalyptic novel written by American writer Cormac McCarthy, ___?
4 You don't like dystopian fiction, ___?
5 *Mad Max Fury Road* didn't win the Oscar for Best Picture in 2016, ___?
6 You've watched all *The Hunger Games* movies, ___?
7 *The Testament* by Margaret Atwood is the sequel to *The Handmaid's Tale*, ___?
8 Big Brother and Winston Smith were both characters in *1984*, ___?

Expressing opinions

10 **The good, the bad ...** Choose the correct phrases to complete the presentation about the advantages and disadvantages of social media.

Today I'm going to be talking about the advantages and disadvantages of social media. **It is evident that / The most important argument for** (1) social media has had a big impact in recent years. I **admit / believe** that (2) if we ignore this fact, it is harder to address some of the issues surrounding its use. One obvious advantage of social media is how it has helped connect like-minded people around the world. **Although, / However,** (3) while this can be seen as an advantage, it also allows people whose intentions are not always good to get in contact. **It is obvious / The main thing is** (4) that social media didn't create these people – it has just given them a useful tool. **For a start, / To sum up,** (5) these people clearly existed before the advent of social media, but their voices were seldom heard. **For a start, / Nevertheless,** (6) it is clear that the way they use social media has created problems that need to be addressed. On the other hand, as social media provides so many positive opportunities, we must find ways of dealing with the negative aspects. **Secondly, / To sum up,** (7) there are clearly advantages and disadvantages of social media *but* **we must remember / the main idea is** (8) it is not the actual social media that is the problem but the way in which some people use it. Therefore, we should be finding ways to change people's behaviour not the tool they are using.

11 **# Movements.** Put the sentences in the correct order. The first sentence is given.

A Today, I'm going to be talking about the power of # Movements. The hashtag was first suggested by Chris Messina in 2007.
B Finally, since the advent of the hashtag it has been used millions of times and has made millions of people aware of issues that they may never have heard about otherwise.
C For a start, look at how the Black Lives Matter Movement quickly spread from the US right across the world.
D However, initially the reaction of many social media platforms was negative.
E It's evident that the hashtag connected to this movement made a huge difference.
F Nevertheless, since 2007 the hashtag has been used to find supporters, arrange protests and create conversations between different users on social media platforms.
G Personally, I believe that hashtag movements have been a way of bringing like-minded people together.
H Secondly, the use of the hashtag helps people know exactly what they are going to read about and so helps them filter out topics that aren't of interest to them.
I The main idea was for it to provide a way for people to be able to easily track content related to a particular event or topic.

12 **My presentation.** Write a presentation about free speech and social media. Use the phrases below.

TIP

Presenting arguments

- **Stating the issue:** *The most important argument for … is …; The main idea / thing is that …*
- **Pre-empting an argument:** *It's obvious that …; However, / Nevertheless, …; Although it is true that …, I believe that …; I admit / concede that …, but we must remember that …*
- **Sequencing a list of arguments:** *For a start, …; Secondly, … Thirdly, …; To sum up, …; Finally, …*

60 Marcus Sedgwick

Cudweed and the bagpipes

THREE

A couple of weeks passed, and we settled into a routine. Every day Cudweed and I would leave the Ugly Sheep after breakfast and go along to the factory. It was always my favourite time, because after that first day when we arrived in the thunderstorm, the weather had been lovely; not what I was expecting from Scotland at all. And it was always really nice to fly along beside the loch on the way, while Cudweed stomped[1] along the road.

Everything was very beautiful indeed and I decided that I liked Scotland a lot.

And then there was the other reason why I enjoyed the morning journey to the factory – namely that every morning Catriona was sitting on a fence post[2] at the end of the lane that led up to the factory.

Now, usually, she flew off as soon as she saw us coming, and I wondered if she was very shy, or if she had really already decided not to talk to me for some reason or other. But one morning she didn't fly away and we actually spoke.

'Kork?' I said, and she said, 'Ark-ark.'

So naturally, I said, 'Kronk.'

She looked at me and tipped her head[3] on one side.

Then she said, 'Rork' and flew off.

So that was that, and at least it was a start, but I knew no more about her than before, really.

And Cudweed, meanwhile, was very unhappy.

The good news was that it turned out he was very good at making bagpipes. He had a natural talent for cutting and sawing and drilling things.

It was as if he was born to make bagpipes – he did everything really, really well. When Hamish explained something to the three students, Cudweed would understand it immediately and do it perfectly. In fact, he was so good that he was better than Andrew, whose ancestors had made bagpipes, and he was even better than Wiebke, who had already been helping to make the German version of bagpipes for a while. Everyone watched Cudweed with admiration[4] as he rapidly completed his first set of bagpipes and, though he couldn't play a note on them when Hamish gave them a try, he announced that he was impressed.

So you might have thought that all this would make Cudweed happy – he was getting on very well with Andrew. Andrew told us that his favourite hobby was rock climbing, and he pointed at a vertical[5] cliff that was on the other side of the valley, near the Ugly Sheep.

'I'd love to climb that!' Andrew said, and Cudweed stared at the cliff and just looked rather ill. I think he was remembering the window cleaning at the castle.

Cudweed was also getting on very well with Wiebke. It turned out that both Andrew and Wiebke were also staying at the Ugly Sheep – we just didn't meet them on that first morning because we were late to the factory. And, after a few days, I realized that Cudweed liked Wiebke in the same way that I liked Catriona. It seemed to make him happy to be making friends, and he was great at learning how to make bagpipes.

But!

But he was still worrying.

He was worrying because he wasn't going to be at home for his birthday, and the thing with Cudweed has always been that he worries SO MUCH.

I sat down with him one day.

We were back at the Ugly Sheep, after a hard day's work. Well, it had been a hard day for Cudweed – who had had to do the trickiest part of making bagpipes; putting the whole thing together. This was

[1] **to stomp** [stɒmp] stapfen; stampfen – [2] **(fence) post** [pəʊst] (Zaun-)Pfahl – [3] **to tip one's head** [tɪp wʌnz 'hed] seinen Kopf neigen – [4] **admiration** [ˌædmə'reɪʃən] Bewunderung – [5] **vertical** ['vɜːtɪkl] vertikal; senkrecht

his second set and when he had finished, Hamish had declared that it was even better than Cudweed's first attempt.

'In fact,' Hamish said, 'this is good enough to go in a shop and be sold. I am really impressed!'

But the fact that Hamish was impressed did not cheer Cudweed up. He was still upset about his birthday.

'Rerk,' I said to him.

'I know, Edgar,' he replied. 'But I just can't help it.'

'Kraaark,' I suggested. 'Konk?'

'I know. Solstice always says the same thing. She says once I worry about one thing, I start worrying about *everything*.'

'Rork-rork,' I pointed out.

'I know. I'm really good at making bagpipes. And I think Wiebke is really nice; and Andrew makes me laugh, but I can't stop worrying anyway! And then I worry that I'm worrying!'

I pecked his head in case it would help him to stop worrying. It didn't.

'And now,' said Cudweed, 'I have to play a tune on the bagpipes at a little party in two weeks' time and I can't play a single note yet. I'll be awful. Everyone will laugh.'

I thought about this and I decided that it was time for Cudweed to stop worrying about everything. I thought that maybe the best thing to do would be to leave him here alone, so he would have to just cope by himself. But every time I thought that, Catriona would fly past in the distance and I would change my mind. But at least, he could do something about learning to play the bagpipes.

'Kronk,' I told him. 'Ark, ark, awwwwwk. Rerk.'

He looked at me.

'Do you think she would?'

'Rork!' I said.

'Then okay,' he said, 'I will. I'll ask Wiebke to give me some really easy lessons and learn to play one simple tune on my bagpipes.'

'Rurk!' I said, because it was great to see him looking a bit happier.

'I'll ask her tomorrow in fact!' and he even smiled.

So there was Cudweed looking a little happier, but just at that moment, Catriona flew by, as if she was in a hurry, and my little heart jumped for a moment, and then sank sadly back down again.

The second half of Cudweed's work experience rushed by.

He had texted Solstice to tell her how upset he was that he would not be at home for his birthday, and she told him not to worry. She said they were sending his presents to him at the Ugly Sheep, and that he ought to look forward to having a birthday somewhere new for once. (And in a very special place.)

Cudweed meanwhile worked on his third set of bagpipes, which was impressive, because Andrew and Wiebke were still finishing their first ones. Hamish said that if Cudweed wanted to actually come and work for him for real when he grew up, he would be very welcome, because he had never seen anyone who was so good at making bagpipes with so little experience.

And when he wasn't working on making his bagpipes, he was learning how to play them. He had asked Wiebke if she could teach him something simple to play, because he was really not very good at playing the instrument. Andrew was there and he asked if she would help him, too, because he was also having trouble. And Wiebke had agreed, so now, every lunchtime, the three of them took their sandwiches out into the field behind the factory and Wiebke showed them the basics; blowing into the bag to keep air in it, squeezing it gently to send air down the chanter, and then she taught them a simple tune each.

So all that was going well, but still Cudweed worried.

He worried that he wasn't good enough.

He worried that he would make a fool of himself at the concert.

He worried that he worried.

There was someone else who was worried that he wasn't good enough: me.

I wondered what it was. I had tried to speak to Catriona every day, and the more I tried, the less it seemed she wanted to have to do with me.

Every day I flew upside down, or sang a raven song, or generally tried to look cute and appealing[6], but eventually I had to accept that she just wasn't interested in me. It made me very sad because I had been happy being a single raven for a very long time. And now I had suddenly seen another raven I liked and thought it would be nice to spend time with her, but she didn't want to spend time with me …

But then, one afternoon, I found out why.

I saw Catriona hurrying across the valley, with half a dead rabbit in her beak, and I thought I would try one last time to chat to her, so I followed …

She flew a long way, and I flapped along behind and did my best to keep up, but she was very fast and agile as she flew up the mountainside, to her nest, I assumed[7].

And I was right, she was flying home, and when I got there, I saw something I hadn't expected.

There was a nest and in the nest were three baby ravens, to whom she was busy feeding the mouse.

Well, I hadn't expected that.

'Kork!' I said, by way of hello, and when she turned and saw me, she said, 'kork'.

And then, finally, we had a proper chat.

I asked who the baby ravens were, and she explained that they were hers. And I asked where their father was and she explained that he had been struck by[8] lightning a few months before and now she was left to bring them up all by herself, which was why she was so busy all of the time.

'Kark,' I said, and that was just to say that I was sorry to hear about her husband, and I understood that things were difficult for her. And that I would leave her to get on with looking after the babies.

'Rark,' she said, which was her way of saying that she thought I was a nice raven and she was sorry not to have more time to spend with me, but that was how it was.

So I left her in peace feeling sorry for her, and for her husband who had been fried[9]. No raven deserves such an end. …

Then it was May 26th.

It had come around so suddenly; Cudweed's birthday and the day of the party to celebrate the end of the work experience. Just as Solstice had promised, there was a pile[10] of presents waiting for Cudweed at breakfast time, and he opened them all, and I was pleased with him, because he actually managed to enjoy himself a little. Finally, he's growing up, I thought!

But he was still worried about the concert. Hamish had said he was inviting 'one or two people', but in the end there was a group of forty or so local people who had come to hear the three students each play a tune on their new bagpipes.

Andrew went first, and he was very good.

Everyone clapped and cheered.

Then Wiebke went second, and she was incredible. She played traditional German tunes and some Scottish ones, too, and everyone clapped and cheered even more. Then it was Cudweed's turn, and he was very, very nervous, so nervous he made two attempts at starting his tune, but on the third go, he got it right, and although it was simple, everyone was really pleased and clapped and cheered for him, too.

When it was over, I flew over to him and pecked him on his head, just to congratulate him and because I wanted to point something out to him.

'Rurk,' I said, and he said, 'Edgar, what is it? You mustn't worry about me so much, I am fine.'

But he hadn't seen what I had seen, so I pecked him again, from behind, and when he turned around, he found himself face to face with the family; Solstice, and his mother and father, and even the twins.

'What are you doing here?' he asked, looking surprised.

'Oh, Cudweed!' said Minty. 'You're so clever to play that tune!'

'You heard it?' he asked.

'Yes, we sneaked in[11] at the back,' said Solstice. 'We wanted to surprise you!'

'They told us you made the bagpipes, too,' said Valevine. 'Is that true?'

'Yes, in fact I have made three sets,' said Cudweed.

---

[6] **appealing** [əˈpiːlɪŋ] attraktiv – [7] **to assume** [əˈsjuːm] annehmen – [8] **to be struck by** [biː ˈstrʌk baɪ] von etw. getroffen werden – [9] **to fry** [fraɪ] braten – [10] **pile** [paɪl] Stapel – [11] **to sneak in** [ˈsniːk ɪn] sich hineinschleichen

'Wow,' said Solstice. 'My little brother is growing up!'

'Finally,' muttered[12] Valevine, and I thought that was mean, so I pecked him, hard.

And while he was trying to fight me off and getting cross, Wiebke came over, and Cudweed said, 'Family, can I introduce you to my friend, Wiebke? She is German and she would like to come and stay with us in the castle during the summer. I assume that is fine with you all?'

And then everyone stared at Cudweed, open mouthed, because he had never sounded so mature[13] before in his whole life.

'Er, yes, of course, dear. Wiebke, how nice to meet you,' said Minty.

'Also, our friend Andrew has invited Wiebke and me to go rock climbing in a few days' time, and I would like to go.'

Everyone stared at Cudweed *again*, because we were all thinking about the fuss with the window cleaning at the castle, which had gone very badly.

'I know what you're thinking,' Cudweed said. 'But that accident with the window cleaning wasn't my fault. If you three hadn't surprised me and been shouting at me and getting me to read things, it might have gone a lot better. So, I would like to go rock climbing to find out.'

Everyone stared at Cudweed so hard that I thought their eyeballs might fall out. But they didn't.

So, a few days later, Cudweed and Wiebke went rock climbing with Andrew and, do you know what? Everything went *absolutely perfectly*.

I sat with the rest of the family as we watched them climbing up the side of a rock face in the valley near the Ugly Sheep, and I knew that Cudweed had finally started to grow up and look after himself. But the main thing that seemed to have changed was this; he was worrying about things a whole lot less.

And that would be nice for everyone. But I realized something for me, too. Cudweed had given me an idea. If he could invite Wiebke to stay with us at the castle, in the summer, there was nothing to stop me coming to Scotland from time to time to see a certain lady raven, and maybe even help her look after her baby ravens a little. From time to time.

So as Cudweed reached the top of a cliff face, I flew up to congratulate him, with a loud 'kork!', because I was very proud of him, and then I set off for the mountainside, to see what Catriona thought about my idea …

(And do you know what? She said yes.)

THE END

[12] **to mutter** ['mʌtə] murmeln – [13] **mature** [mə'tʃʊə] erwachsen

Projects and skills

1 At the end of this workshop, you will give a presentation.

- Choose one of these **topic areas:**
  Climate and sustainability
  Media and communication
  Then respond to one of the propositions below.
- For this proposition decide whether to agree, disagree or remain neutral towards it.
- Your presentation can be a talk, an article, a blog, a video or a mixture of media.
- It should show confident use of the skills you will be practising in this workshop.
- You may cover similar ground to the texts in this workshop, but you must also do independent research, and provide references for your sources.

Propositions

Climate and sustainability

1. Individuals cannot affect climate change: the responsibility lies with governments and big companies.
2. Achieving net zero carbon emissions by 2050 is impossible.

Media and communication

1. Social media does more harm than good.
2. Modern means of communicating are faster than in the past but not better.

2 Read the following extracts and note down key words you would use to summarize the topic in each extract. The first one has been **highlighted**.

1 Air **pollution** is choking our cities and causing a global health crisis. Most pollution on our roads comes from burning fossil fuels, and in the UK the main culprit is diesel-using cars and vans.

2 [This] is thought to affect around 5% of young people and has been described as more addictive than cigarettes and alcohol.

3 The rise of smartphones and tablets means children's relationships are now increasingly conducted online, and they are navigating new friendships often unchaperoned and hidden from view. In the playground or the living room at home, as adults we can observe how children are interacting with each other – and step in if we see anything concerning. In a world of 24-hour connectivity, these protections don't exist online.

4 Honey isn't the only thing bees give us. They also provide us with food by pollinating a huge range of crops, not to mention wild plants. But, like many other parts of the natural world, bees are at risk and the way we produce our food is to blame.

5 The trend over the last decade has been for increasing internet use among the older population. However, a substantial group – including the majority of those age 75 and over – are not online.

6 Soy beans are an excellent source of protein [...] [but] the agricultural industry has also become reliant on these beans for animal feed. [T]he drive to produce greater amounts of cheap meat and dairy is accelerating climate change and destroying forests.

7 New levels of connectivity + technology are further compounding + causing new exclusions. These often reflect, reproduce + amplify divides which exist between socio economic classification, ethnicity + gender to name but a few.

Sources of texts 1 – 6 (abbreviated and adapted): see text credits

3 Match the definitions with words from the texts. Which of these words could be useful in your presentation? What other vocabulary would you include and why?

1 to fill a space so as to make movement difficult or impossible
2 capable of making someone form a habit
3 not supervised
4 dependent on
5 to add detail
6 to make the negative aspects of something worse

4 Divide into two groups: each watches one video, then do the tasks.

28
29

1 Summarize the key information for the other group.
2 Explain how well the video fits with the propositions.
3 Say how well you think the presenter conveys the information.

5 In-depth

Climate and sustainability. Find out what is meant by 'the just transition' and explain whether you think it is important and why.

Media and communication. Find relevant articles or discussions in your usual news sources. Are people's current interests the same as or different from yours? Why do you think this is?

Text types (1): Text analysis

1 Text types

a Read the text about an organization called the Climate Group and do the tasks.
Decide which of the two statements characterizes the Climate Group better.

- It is a company that collects accurate information about environmental problems.
- It is an organization that campaigns to improve the environment.

b Discuss which words and expressions in the texts helped you to decide.

The Climate Group

A We're an international non-profit founded in 2003, with offices in London, New York, New Delhi, Amsterdam and Beijing.

B [Since 2003,] we've grown our network to include over 500 multinational businesses in 175 markets worldwide. [...]

C Science says that we must cap global warming at 1.5°C to avoid the disastrous effects of climate change. To be in with a fighting chance at doing this, we must halve global emissions in the next ten years – that's why the 2020s have to be the Climate Decade.

D **Our mission** is to drive climate action. Fast.

E **Our goal** is for a world of net zero carbon emissions by 2050, with greater prosperity for all.

F **We make it happen:** we convince, challenge and help organizations to make commitments, then turn them into action.
We multiply it: we build and run networks. We join up organizations to unlock the power of collective action that shares the same ambitions and creates influence.
We shout about it: we share what we achieve together to show more organizations what they could do.

G **Scale:** we power large networks and hold each organization accountable.
Speed: we focus on action now – not action tomorrow.

H **We work with** leaders and decision makers from business and government because they shape the market frameworks that can help the world achieve net zero emissions by 2050. They have the tools and influence to make it possible in the time we have left.

I **Our work is focused on systems** with the highest emissions and where our networks have the greatest opportunity to drive change. They include energy, transport, built environment and industry. [...]

Source (abbreviated and adapted): https://theclimategroup.prod.acquia-sites.com/about-us

2 **Vocabulary: Persuasive language.** Look at these phrases from the text. Would you use them in …

- a simple, factual description of a problem?
- a description to persuade people that a problem is urgent?

1 we must cap global warming (l. 7)
2 the disastrous effects of climate change (ll. 8 – 9)
3 the 2020s have to be the Climate Decade (ll. 11 – 12)
4 Our mission is to drive climate action. Fast. (l. 13)
5 We make it happen (l. 15)
6 We shout about it (l. 19)
7 Speed: we focus on action now – not action tomorrow. (l. 21)
8 to make it possible in the time we have left (ll. 26 – 27)

3 **Planning: Structuring presentations around key questions.**
Match the questions to the paragraphs in the text in **1** (A – I).

1 How big are we? Where do we work?
2 How will we know when we have succeeded?
3 In what specific areas do we work?
4 What does our organization do to help the environment?
5 What is good about the way we do our work? What makes us different?
6 What problem are we trying to solve?
7 What kind of organization are we? Where are we based?
8 What was our organization created to do?
9 Who helps us with our work?

TIP

Writing questions is often a good way to structure a text. First, think about what someone might ask you (or what you would like them to ask). Then make sure you answer those questions in your presentation.

4 **In-depth**

Look at the 17 sustainable development goals. Choose one goal and search for a campaign that deals with this goal. Find and list some expressions that are important for this campaign. Decide which ones might be useful for your presentation in relation to the proposition you have chosen (p. 132).

(The content of this publication has not been approved by the United Nations and does not reflect the views of the United Nations or its officials or Member States.)

Text types (2): Grammar and style

1 **Planning: Writing for a specific audience.**
Read texts A and B and answer these questions.

1. Who do you think wrote them and why?
2. Who are they written for?
3. What are the most important differences?
4. How does the language used in them vary?

2 **Persuasive and explanatory texts: Grammar and language features**

a Here are some ways writers and speakers use language to describe a problem and explain how to deal with it. Which of these techniques (1 – 10) are used in Text A and which in Text B?

1. Repeating the same word or phrase
2. Using contracted forms to make the tone friendly
3. Using *must* to say that something is urgent and has to happen
4. Using *people* or *you/your* to give general advice
5. Using phrases such as *A good way of* … and *It's OK to* …, to show that you are giving advice (and not telling people what to do)
6. Using short sentences for emphasis
7. Avoiding contracted forms to make the tone more serious
8. Using *we/our* to get the reader/listener to agree with the argument
9. Using modal verbs *might, can, could* to make a suggestion less strong
10. Writing a text that could easily be read aloud as part of a speech to an audience

b List examples of the language types in **a** (1 – 10) in the two texts. One example is given below.

1 Repeating the same word or phrase:

Text A: Now is the moment to … (ll. 14 + 16)

Text A

This is our darkest hour. […]

Biodiversity is being annihilated around the world. Our seas are poisoned, acidic and rising. Flooding and desertification will render vast tracts of land uninhabitable and lead to mass migration.

Our air is so toxic that the United Kingdom is breaking the law. It harms the unborn whilst causing tens of thousands to die. The breakdown of our climate has begun. There will be more wildfires, unpredictable super-storms, increasing famine and untold drought as food supplies and fresh water disappear. […]

Now is the moment to step up. To participate. To refuse to be a bystander.

Now is the moment to begin building a world where love, care and freedom are prioritized. […]

All institutions must communicate the danger we are in. We must be clear about the extreme cascading risks humanity now faces, the injustice this represents, its historic roots, and the urgent need for rapid political, social and economic change. […]

Where we need to be better, we will do what is required. We stand with people of colour, we stand with the trans community, we stand with women, we stand with disabled people, we stand with the Global Majority. We stand with all who are oppressed by our toxic system. […]

Sources (abbreviated): ll. 1 – 13: from *This Is Not a Drill: An Extinction Rebellion Handbook*, Penguin: London, 2019. Google Books; ll. 14 – 29: https://extinctionrebellion.uk/2022/01/23/xr-uk-strategy-2022/

Text B

[…] There are lots of benefits to keeping in touch with your friends on social media apps […] – it's been useful during the pandemic or other times when people can't meet up in person. There are some problems with only talking to friends online though, misunderstandings can easily happen, especially if it's just by chat and not video or voice calls. […]

A good way of not getting involved in any social media drama is to try and encourage people to meet in person, where it's safe and possible, or to at least talk in a group call or video chat. This helps people to remember that everyone there is a real person and what they say has consequences. This might not always be possible, but if people see each other in person more often, it can help stop drama before it happens.

If drama does happen, it's okay to just not get involved. One of the good things about group chats is you don't have to respond to anything you don't want to. You can also still talk to people individually if you want to, without having to reply in the main chat. By not getting involved you can let people know you're uncomfortable with drama and won't be taking any sides. […]

Source (abbreviated): https://www.childline.org.uk/get-support/ask-sam/bullying-abuse-and-safety-asksam/social-media-drama/

3 'The rule of three'

a Read the box below and find four examples of 'the rule of three' in text A. Do you think this is a good strategy? Why / Why not? Find some other examples of it online.

Text A uses a presenting strategy called 'the rule of three' (or 'triples'). This is when speakers or writers use a list of three words or expressions. The idea behind it is that a group of three items is more memorable than one item (or another number of items).

b Persuasive texts often include:
- **emotive language** (vocabulary used to make the reader / listener feel a certain emotion) and
- **hyperbole** (exaggerated language that is used to have an effect on the reader / listener).

Are there examples of these in text A?

4 In-depth

Look at the propositions again and choose the final topic of your presentation. Then decide on the format (written or spoken, for a website or podcast or for a live audience).

Propositions

Climate and sustainability

1. Individuals cannot affect climate change: the responsibility lies with governments and big companies.
2. Achieving net zero carbon emissions by 2050 is impossible.

Media and communication

1. Social media does more harm than good.
2. Modern means of communicating are faster than in the past but no better.

@ WES-40326-004

Planning your presentation

1 Research: Using your sources

a Read the texts and do the following tasks.

1 Read texts A – C about an innovation which addresses environmental problems and explain where the texts might be from:
   - a an abstract introducing an exhibitor at an exhibition for scientists
   - b a popular science website aimed at the general public
   - c a university website aimed at all university members, not just scientists

2 Evaluate whether these sources are reliable and if you can trust each of them equally. Explain why or why not.

3 Assess if there is enough information to write an article about robot bees. If not, explain what else you need to know.

b Find two more sources of information about robot bees which you trust and which give you the information you want. Explain why you have chosen them and what kind of sources provide useful information when researching online.

Text A

These Robot Bees Might Save Us From The Bee-Pocalypse

The B-Droid is coming to take real bees' jobs – and that might be exactly what we need.

Without bees, plants go un-pollinated, and eventually we starve. Usually in bleak future scenarios, it's the robots that are causing all the problems, but today the bees are dying with no machine interference. Instead, it's a robot that may save us from their demise: the B-Droid. It's a robotic bee that can buzz between flowers and pollinate plants. And the biggest winner might be the bees, because – if the robot-bees are successful – real bees won't need to be transported all over the world to pollinate commercial crops. They can stay at home and relax. [...]

Text B

B-Droid – a robot that's busy as a bee

[...] For a number of years, there have been mass deaths of bees worldwide. Environmental pollution, fungi, viruses or parasites might be to blame. Also, bees don't travel long distances well. In the United States they are transported hundreds of kilometres and, after several days of pollination, they die of fatigue. The effects of such a situation may be direr than we all think. It's estimated that a third of all agricultural crops and approximately 90% of plants growing in the wild require pollination, and bees are the main pollinators. [Our scientists] have decided to rise to the challenge and build a robot for pollinating. [...]

Text C

Could the flying B-Droid help bees with pollination?

[...] Based on the data indicated by a user, the system plans its own operation process and then executes it. This autonomous device finds flowers (recognition), locates them, (positioning system) collects their pollen and transports it to other flowers of the same species (mechanical system). It navigates itself upon the data gathered by a visual system (computer vision) and controls its own actions with a real-time computer system (control system and software). The system is made in two versions – flying and driving (on-ground mobile device). [...]

Sources of texts A – C (abbreviated and adapted): Charlie Sorrel, Fast Company, 14.12.2016, https://www.fastcompany.com/3066318/these-robot-bees-might-save-us-from-the-bee-pocalypse; Warsaw University of Technology, 02.12.2016, https://www.pw.edu.pl/engpw/Research/Business-Innovations-Technology-BIT-of-WUT/B-Droid-a-robot-that-s-busy-as-a-bee; Rafal Dalewski, "B-Droid", SciTech Poland, 2017, http://scitechpoland.com/portfolio/b-droid/ [11.04.2023]

2 Groundbreakers?

a Here are some inventions which address environmental problems in sustainable and innovative ways. Research one of them, bearing in mind these questions:

- Can you find more than one reliable source of information about this invention?
- Are there positive and negative opinions?
- Are there other similar inventions?
- Are the brand names strong and clear?

1 The Seabin
2 Groasis Waterboxx
3 Zéphyr Solar balloon
4 AirCarbon plastic
5 Eka1 and Eka2 seeds
6 Demetra

b Present your findings in a two-minute talk to the class.

3 Ways of collating ideas

a Everyone needs to find a method to bring together facts, information, ideas and opinions in a way that best helps them to shape a coherent conclusion in written or spoken form. Use mind maps if you find they work for you, but consider these other methods, too. Read the texts, then rank these four methods in your order of preference. Explain your choices.

The mind mash

Collect all your ideas on one topic on a large sheet of paper. Circle each individual point, but don't try to organize them. Then use different colours to link ideas. Soon you will have a visual representation of how to organize your ideas in your presentation. You can then give each colour a number to show the order in which you're going to present your ideas.

Variation: This method works well for a group, too: sit around a large sheet of paper to write your notes. Your first task after every point has been written down and circled is to identify and delete duplications before using colours.

Sticky notes shuffling

Use multicoloured sticky notes and an A2 or A3 piece of paper. Secure the paper to a wall. Write your ideas / opinions / information / key points onto separate sticky notes. Transfer these to your blank paper. You can then position your keynotes in groups and move them around until you are satisfied with the organization. With this method of collating ideas, it's easy to come back to your wall over a number of days as your planning crystallizes.

+ see next page!

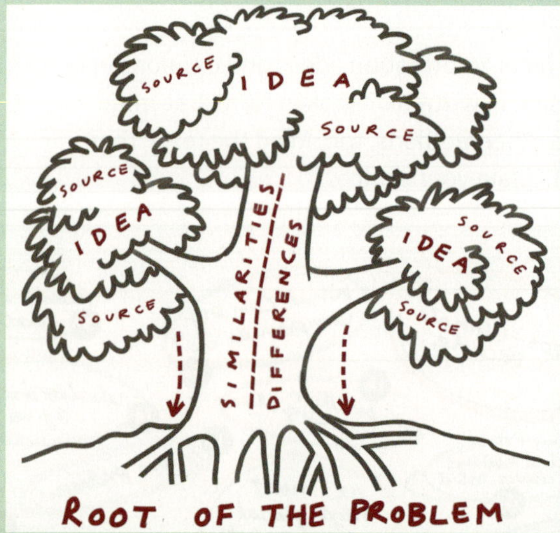

Tree to root

This method helps you to explore a problem by starting with lots of information and gradually digging down to get to the root of the problem. Start at the top of the tree by doing research and grouping together sources and information as the branches and leaves. In the trunk of the tree, explore the similarities and differences in the information you have. At ground level, consider what you know now. Then finish by reaching the root of the problem.

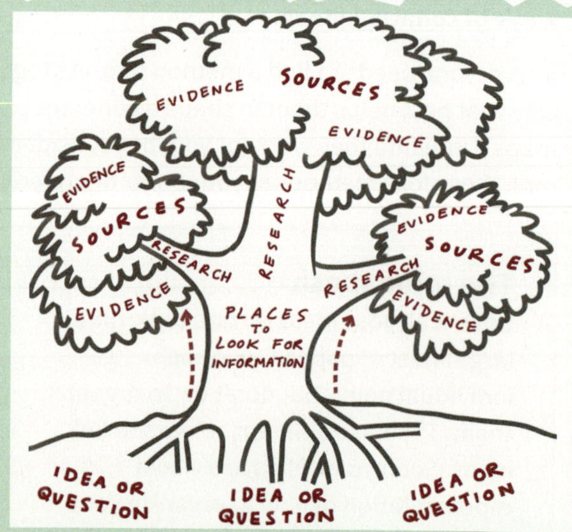

Root to tree

This method starts by exploring exactly what you want to know before doing research. Write an idea or a question at the root of your tree then work your way up, breaking your ideas down into mini-ideas or questions at ground level. Then, in the trunk of the tree identify where to look for relevant information. At the top, do targeted research to create the branches and finally make smaller branches and leaves with notes of sources and evidence to back up what you want to say.

b Research one of these innovations, collating your information and ideas using one of the methods described in **a**.

- edible cutlery
- converting fog into drinking water
- fabric created from coffee grounds
- an ethical smartphone
- a vegan water bottle

c Write a short article about your innovation showing that you have found reliable sources of information. See the TIP box on citing your sources.

4 In-depth

Investigate other methods of collating ideas, and try out any you find them interesting:

- cluster diagramming
- fishbone diagram
- Venn diagram
- rich pictures or doodles
- the five 'whys'
- causal loop diagramming

TIP

Citing print sources: Provide: the name of the author(s); the title of the work; the publisher and the year of publication; the page number (if the information can be located on a particular page or if directly quoted); for example:
Karskens, Grace, *The Rocks*, Melbourne University Press, Carlton (1997), p. 87.

Citing electronic or online sources: As a rule, provide as much information as possible concerning authorship, location and availability. These sources require similar information to print sources. However, in some cases extra information may be required: the page, paragraph or section number – what you cite will depend on the information available as many sources don't have pages – the format of the source accessed, e. g. e-book, podcast, etc.; an access date for online sources, that is, identify when a source was viewed or downloaded; and the location, such as a database or web address; for example:
UK Youth homepage: 'About us', copyright UK Youth 2020, https://www.ukyouth.org/about-us/[11.04.2023]

@ WES-40326-004

Brushing up your dictionary skills

1 A game with an aim

a Look at the different elements of the dictionary entry for 'bluff' and try to remember them.

bluff[1] / blʌf / *noun* (*no plural*) an attempt to make somebody believe you will do something or that you know something: *There was a great bit in the film when the actor said, 'I'm going to push you in the river' to the bad guy but he didn't. It was just a bluff.*
bluff[2] / blʌf / *verb* (**bluffs, bluffing, bluffed**) to try to make somebody believe you will do something or that you know something: *I don't think he's going to push him in the river – he's just bluffing.*

b Read the rules and make sure that you understand them. Clarify any questions you might have with a partner or your teacher.

The Rules

1 Your team chooses three unknown English words from a dictionary.
2 Tell the teacher your team's three words.
3 In your team, write three definitions (a, b and c) for each word – only one of which is correct.
4 Each team reads out its three words and definitions. The other teams note down which definition they think is correct.
5 For every correct definition, a team gets one point; for every incorrect definition a minus point. (So a team can have a 'minus' score!)
6 The team with the highest number of points wins.

2 **Play 'Who's bluffing?'.** Read the TIP box, write your definitions, and play the game.

TIP

Follow these instructions and make the other teams believe your definitions.

- Give the correct pronunciation(s) of the word using IPA if possible.
- Say what part of speech your word is and give the correct kind of definition.
- Include multiple meanings.
- Give plausible example sentences.

@ WES-40326-004

Presentations

1 Structuring and giving presentations

a Read the advice. Do you agree with it? Why or why not?

HOW TO PREPARE AND WRITE A PRESENTATION

Preparation for the presentation

1. Decide on whether you are going to agree or disagree with the proposition.
2. Think of personal examples from your life or your friends' lives to support your opinion.
3. Do research: find evidence to support your opinion. Also try to find evidence against your opinion.
4. Decide on what the main points of your argument are and what order to present them in.

Introduction to the presentation

5. Introduce yourself.
6. Explain why you chose the subject and why you think it is important.
7. Make your personal opinion clear – say whether you agree or disagree with the proposition.
8. Summarize what you are going to talk about and in what order.

Body of the presentation

9. Present the arguments that support your opinion one by one.
10. For each argument, give evidence that supports it.
11. Describe arguments against your opinion and then explain why you think they are wrong.
12. Use strong language when you think a problem is urgent or serious.

Conclusion to the presentation

13. Make it clear that you have come to the end of your presentation.
14. Summarize the main points of your arguments again.
15. Thank the audience for listening and ask for questions.

b The advice in **a** is for a spoken presentation. How would you change it for a written presentation? Give reasons.

2 A model presentation?

30

a Watch a presentation. In what ways has the presenter followed the advice (5 – 15) in **1a**?

TIP

Notice how the speaker asks for questions at the end. If you ask, 'Does anyone have any questions?' it's embarrassing for the speaker and the audience if there aren't any. 'I'm sure you have lots of questions for me …', sounds more confident, and should encourage the audience to ask questions.

b Match the expressions from Dr Hilton's presentation with the pieces of advice (5–15) in **1a**. Which advice has she **not** followed?

- **a** For example, we know that … ■ Here are some figures which show …
- **b** Good afternoon, my name is …
- **c** I have a professional interest in this subject, as I … ■ I also have a very personal interest, because I …
- **d** In this presentation, I'll … ■ First, I'll … ■ Then, I'll ■ After that … ■ I'll finish by …
- **e** My own view is that …
- **f** Of course, I have to accept that not everyone agrees with me. It's true that …
- **g** So, my final point is …
- **h** Thank you everyone for listening to my presentation. I'm sure you will have lots of questions for me and I'd be very happy to answer them.
- **i** The first point I want to make is … ■ My second/third point is …
- **j** … then we will see enormous problems ■ … then there will be a huge crisis

c Think about the advice when preparing your own presentation. Which pieces of advice will you follow? What language will you use?

3 **Giving a presentation.** There are a lot of things to remember and check when you prepare for, rehearse and give a presentation. Use your preferred method of collating ideas (from **pages 139/140**) to do your planning. Here is one way of doing it, using a mind map.

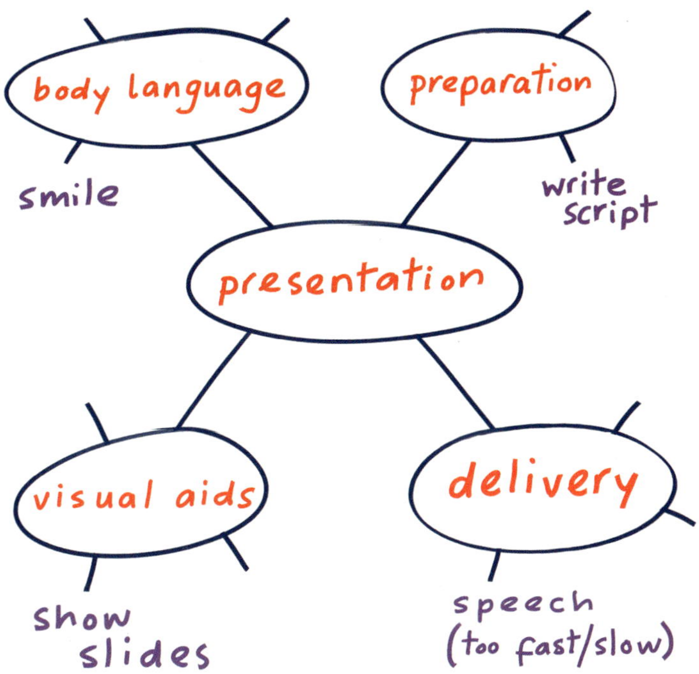

@ WES-40326-004

Giving feedback

1 **Feedback and its importance.** Use these prompts and your own ideas to write a short explanation of what feedback is and what is important when you give feedback.

2 31 **Preparing to give feedback.** Watch the video and make notes of points, both positive and negative, that you'd like to make to the presenter. Remember to think about her body language and her visual aids as well as what she says, how well she expresses it and organizes it.

3 **Giving feedback.** Write a paragraph of constructive criticism for the presenter of the video or record yourself giving oral feedback. Use your notes from **2** and choose ways of talking about positive and negative points from the box.

TIP

When you want to give **constructive criticism** clearly, don't use a positive comment followed by a negative point introduced by 'but'. People tend to hear the positive comment but not the more important negative one which follows it. You sound polite but your message is confusing. For example, the sentence 'Your body language was really good, but maybe you could gesticulate a bit less' would be more clearly expressed by 'I think your points would come across more clearly if you gesticulated a bit less. Otherwise, your body language was really good.'

Useful phrases: Talking about a presentation

Positive points
- *I thought … was very effective.*
- *… interested me / fascinated me because …*
- *I was impressed that you …*
- *Several times, I recognized that you …*
- *What I really liked / loved about your presentation / article was that …*
- *I particularly liked the way you …*
- *What I liked most was …*
- *My favourite part was … because …*

Negative points and suggestions
- *I wonder if the slide on … was clear enough.*
- *When you presented …, I noticed that …*
- *I think it would be worth mentioning / clarifying …*
- *When I listened to your introduction / conclusion, I didn't really see what you meant by …*
- *I couldn't quite understand why … / the point you were making about …*
- *Have you considered …?*
- *I suggest that you think about adding / leaving out …*
- *It might make a difference if you …*
- *It might be helpful if you …*

Appendix

Grammatical terms

Here are some of the most important **grammatical terms** in English:

active	aktiv
adjective	Adjektiv; Eigenschaftswort
adverb **adverb of frequency** **adverb of manner** **adverb of place** **adverb of time**	Adverb (Wortart); Umstandswort Adverb der Häufigkeit Adverb der Art und Weise Adverb des Ortes Adverb der Zeit
adverbial	adverbiale Bestimmung (Satzglied); Umstandsangabe
article **definite article** **indefinite article**	Artikel bestimmter Artikel unbestimmter Artikel
aspect	Aspekt
auxiliary	Hilfsverb
clause **adverbial clause** **comment clause** **contact clause** ***if*-clause** **main clause** **relative clause** **defining relative clause** **non-defining relative clause** **subordinate clause (of time)**	Teilsatz Adverbialsatz nicht notwendiger Relativsatz, der sich auf den gesamten Satz bezieht notwendiger Relativsatz ohne Relativpronomen Bedingungssatz; Konditionalis Hauptsatz Relativsatz notwendiger Relativsatz nicht notwendiger Relativsatz Temporalsatz
comparative	Komparativ; Vergleichsform
conditional / *if*-sentence **conditional / *if*-sentences type 1, 2, 3, mixed**	Konditionalis; Konditionalsatz Konditionalsatz Typ 1, 2, 3, gemischt
demonstrative determiner	Demonstrativbegleiter
future **future with *going to*** **future with *will*** **present progressive with future meaning** **simple present with future meaning** **future progressive** **future perfect**	Futur; Zukunft Futur mit *going to* Futur mit *will* Verlaufsform des Präsens mit Zukunftsbezug einfache Form des Präsens mit Zukunftsbezug Verlaufsform des Futur Futur II
gerund	Gerundium
imperative	Imperativ; Befehlsform
infinitive ***to*-infinitive**	Infinitiv; Grundform *to*-Infinitiv
modal **modal substitute**	Modalverb Ersatzform eines Modalverbs
negative	negativ; verneinend
noun **countable noun** **uncountable noun**	Substantiv; Nomen zählbares Substantiv nicht zählbares Substantiv

object **direct object** **indirect object**	Objekt direktes Objekt indirektes Objekt
participle **participle construction** **past participle** **perfect participle** **present participle**	Partizip Partizipialkonstruktion Partizip Perfekt *having* + Partizip Perfekt Partizip Präsens
passive ***by*-agent**	Passiv Handelnde(r) im Passivsatz
past **simple past** **past progressive**	Präteritum; Vergangenheit einfache Form der Vergangenheit Verlaufsform der Vergangenheit
past perfect **past perfect** **past perfect progressive**	Plusquamperfekt einfache Form des Plusquamperfekts Verlaufsform des Plusquamperfekts
plural	Plural; Mehrzahl
positive	positiv; bejaht
possessive *'s*	*s*-Genitiv
possessive determiner	Possessivbegleiter
preposition **preposition of place** **preposition of time**	Präposition Präposition des Ortes Präposition der Zeit
present **simple present** **present progressive**	Präsens; Gegenwart einfache Form des Präsens Verlaufsform des Präsens
present perfect **present perfect** **present perfect progressive**	Perfekt einfache Form des Perfekt Verlaufsform des Perfekt
pronoun **indefinite pronoun** **interrogative pronoun** **object pronoun** **personal pronoun** **possessive pronoun** **reciprocal pronoun** **reflexive pronoun** **relative pronoun** **subject pronoun**	Pronomen Indefinitpronomen; unbestimmtes Pronomen Interrogativpronomen; Fragepronomen Objektpronomen Personalpronomen Possessivpronomen; besitzanzeigendes Pronomen Reziprokpronomen Reflexivpronomen Relativpronomen Subjektpronomen
prop word *one/ones*	Stützwort *one/ones*
quantifier	Numeral; Zahlwort
question **question tag**	Frage Frageanhängsel; Bestätigungsfrage
reported speech **backshift**	indirekte Rede Rücksetzung der Zeitform um eine Stufe
singular	Singular; Einzahl
statement	Aussagesatz
subject	Subjekt
superlative	Superlativ
tense	Zeitform
verb **regular verb** **irregular verb**	Verb; Tätigkeitswort regelmäßiges Verb unregelmäßiges Verb
word order	Wortstellung

Grammar

Do you have a question about grammar?
The **grammar appendix** explains all the grammar that you have learned and revised in this book.
You can also watch the grammar videos which explain the most important grammar:
Tenses (Present and perfect tenses, Video 16; Past tenses, Video 21; Future tenses, Video 24)
The passive (Video 3)
Reported speech (Video 4)
Gerunds and infinitives (Video 7)
If-sentences (Type 1 and 2, Video 10; Type 3, Video 14)

G 1 Tenses

G 1.1 Present tenses

Workshop 2

Simple present:

- The simple present is the infinitive of the verb without *to*. For the third person singular (*he / she / it*) we add *-s*. We make negatives and questions with a form of *do*.
  *She **wants** to read the book.*
  *They **don't go** to the cinema very often.*
  *Who **does** this dog **belong** to?*
- We don't use a form of *do* when the question word is the subject of the sentence.
  *Who **helps** you if you have problems with your homework?*
- We use the simple present to talk about something that happens all the time or that is always true.
  *My mum **works** as a nurse.*
  *I **love** my dog.*
  *We normally **watch** football on Saturday afternoon.*

Present progressive:

- We form the present progressive with *am / are / is* + *-ing*. We form the negative with *am not / aren't / isn't* + *-ing*. For questions, we put the subject between *am / are / is* and the *-ing* form.
  *They**'re playing** tennis now.*
  *He **isn't working** today.*
  *What **are** you **doing**?*
- We use the present progressive to talk about what is happening now while we are speaking.
  *We **aren't eating** lunch at the moment.*
  ***Are** you **reading** that comic or can I have it?*
- Some verbs do not have a progressive form, for example *know, like, want* or *understand*.

G 1.2 Past tenses

Workshop 3

Simple past:

- With regular verbs, we add *-ed* to the infinitive of the verb to make the simple past. We form the negative with *didn't* and questions with *did*.
  *They **played** a concert in Glasgow yesterday.*
- Some verbs don't add *-ed* in the simple past. They are irregular (see the list on **pages 165 – 167**).
- We use the simple past to talk about things that happened at a time in the past. We often use expressions of time like *yesterday, last Thursday, two months ago*, etc.
  *We **stayed** in Canada for four weeks last summer.*
  *We **arrived** in the middle of a heatwave.*
  *We **didn't want** to leave – it **was** a great holiday!*
  *What similarities **did** you **find** between Canada and the USA?*

Past progressive:

- We form the past progressive with *was / were* + *-ing*. We form the negative with *wasn't / weren't* + *-ing*. For questions, we put the subject between *was / were* and the *-ing* form.
  *My parents met when they **were living** in Vancouver.*
  *Sorry, I **wasn't listening**. What did you say?*
  ***Were** the others **waiting** when you arrived?*

- We often use the past progressive together with the simple past to give background information.
  *It **was raining** when I got up.*
  *While we **were cycling** home from training last week, I had an accident and fell off my bike.*
  *Jack went home from school early yesterday because he **wasn't feeling** well.*
  *What **were** you **doing** when I saw you in town last Saturday?*

Present perfect:

- We form the present perfect with *has / have* + past participle. We form the negative with *hasn't / haven't* + past participle. For questions, we put the subject between *has / have* and the past participle.
  *She **has called** several times.*
  *I **haven't spoken** to Chloe today.*
  ***Have** you **seen** this movie before?*

- We use the present perfect in two main ways.
  - To talk about something in the past which is connected with or has consequences in the present. We often use the present perfect in this way with *yet* and *already*.
    ***I've** already **booked** the tickets.*
    *I **haven't seen** the exhibition yet.*
    ***Has** she **given** her presentation yet?*
  - To talk about something that started in the past and continues now. We often use the present perfect in this way with *for* and *since*.
    *He**'s lived** in this house for ten years.*
    *We**'ve been** friends since we were seven.*

Present perfect progressive:

- We form the present perfect progressive with *has / have* + *been* + *-ing*. We form the negative with *hasn't / haven't* + *been* + *-ing*. For questions, we put the subject between *has / have* and *been*.
  ***I've been playing** the guitar for three years / since I was 11.*
  *We **haven't been playing** very well since our trainer left.*
  *How long **have** you **been learning** English?*

- We often use the present perfect progressive to talk about an action or a situation which started in the past and continues to the present. We use it with *for, since* and *all* as well as in questions with *How long*.
  ***I've been living** here for years / since 2022.*
  *The kids **have been playing** in the garden all afternoon.*
  *Sorry, I'm late. – Don't worry. We **haven't been waiting** long.*
  *How long **have** you **been working** here?*

Past perfect:

- We form the past perfect with *had* + past participle. We form the negative with *hadn't* + past participle. For questions, we put the subject between *had* and the past participle.
  *I was late and the exam **had** already **started**.*
  *He **hadn't told** me he was Meg's friend.*
  *Which travel guide **had** they **checked** before they left home?*

- We use the past perfect to show that one event happened before another one in the past. We use the past perfect for the event that happened first and the simple past for the more recent event. We often use sequence adverbs such as *when, before, after* and *until* to link the two events.
  *After we **had spent** 15 hours on a plane, we finally **arrived**.*
  *We **had hoped** to reach this place sooner, but the bad weather **slowed** us down.*
  *The boy **had** just **had** his 8th birthday when he **had** an accident and **died**.*

- We also use the past perfect to show that something happened before a time in the past.
  *We**'d travelled** over 200 miles by 12 o'clock.*
  *I **hadn't met** him before the concert last June.*

+ see next page!

Past perfect progressive:

- We form the past perfect progressive with *had* + *been* + *-ing*. We form the negative with *hadn't* + *been* + *-ing*. For questions, we put the subject between *had* and *been*.
  *We**'d been playing** for 20 minutes when it started to rain.*
  *I **hadn't been waiting** for long when the bus came.*
  ***Had** you **been looking for** an internship for long before you got one?*

- We use the past perfect progressive to focus on the length of the earlier action and to show that it was in progress before the second action started.
  ***I'd been playing** rugby for three years when I became captain.*
  *We **hadn't been driving** for long when dad realized that he didn't have his phone.*
  *How long **had** the others **been waiting** when you finally arrived?*

G 1.3 Future tenses

Workshop 3

Will-future:

- We form the *will*-future with *will* + the infinitive of the verb without *to*. The verb form always stays the same. For negatives we use *won't*. For questions we put the subject between *will* and the infinitive of the verb without *to*.
  *I'm sure our neighbours **will help** us.*
  *They **won't be** on time.*
  ***Will** he **arrive** today?*

- We use *will* to offer or promise to do something for somebody.
  ***I'll help** you with your homework this evening.*
  *There isn't any milk in the fridge. – Don't worry. I **won't forget** to buy some this afternoon.*

- We use *will* when we decide to do something spontaneously while we are speaking.
  *You look hungry. We**'ll buy** a sandwich.*
  *I'm so tired, I **won't stay up** much longer.*

- We use *will* for predictions that are based on a personal feeling or an opinion.
  *You**'ll love** it in South Africa!*
  *It **won't take** long.*
  *It**'ll be** more expensive than you think.*

Going to-future:

- We form the *going to*-future with a form of *be* + *going to* + the infinitive of the verb without *to*. We make negatives with a negative form of *be*. For questions we put the subject between the form of *be* and *going to*.
  *I**'m going to work** during the summer holidays.*
  *She**'s not going to win** the race.*
  ***Are** you **going to start** at a new school in September?*

- We use *be* + *going to* for decisions and future plans that were made before the time of speaking.
  *I**'m going to join** the school drama club next term.*
  *We**'re going to book** our train tickets at the weekend.*

- We use *be* + *going to* for predictions that are based on present evidence. In other words, there is something in the present that indicates something in the future.
  *Look at the traffic. We**'re going to be** late.*
  *It looks like it**'s going to be** a lovely day.*

The simple present:

- We use the simple present to talk about future events when the statements are based on present facts, and when these facts are something fixed like a timetable, schedule or calendar. We use it with an expression of time.
  *The bus **leaves** at 6.30, please hurry up.*
  *The football match **starts** at three o'clock on Sunday.*

Present progressive:

- We use the present progressive to talk about future arrangements. Typically, we use it with an expression of time.
  *Next week, **I'm seeing** my cousin to discuss our holiday plans.*
  ***We're meeting** at the pizzeria this evening.*
  *When **are** Isabella and Gabriel **going** to the US?*

Future perfect:

- We form the future perfect with *will have* + past participle. We make negatives with *won't*. For questions we put the subject between *will* and *have*. We often use the future perfect with *by*.
  ***Will** you **have had** dinner by 8.30?*
- We use the future perfect to talk about something already completed by a point in the future.
  ***I'll have finished** my exams by the end of June.*
- We can use the future perfect to talk about something not completed by a point in the future.
  *I'm afraid I **won't have finished** my report by Friday.*
  *I **won't have had** time to do much research before the interview.*

Future progressive:

- We form the future progressive with *will be* + *-ing*.
  *Next year most of my friends **will be doing** an apprenticeship.*
- We use the future progressive for an action in progress at a specific time in the future.
  *Hopefully by September **I'll be working** somewhere in the US or Canada.*
  *This time tomorrow, **I'll be having** my final exam.*
  *At 3 o'clock, **we'll be driving** to the airport.*

G 2 The passive

Workshop 1

Form:

- We form the passive with the appropriate form of *be* + past participle.
  *It is a story that **is told** to many children.*
  *The meeting **has been cancelled**.*
  *The book **was published** in 1997.*
  *The year 2020 **will be remembered** for the rise of the Black Lives Matter movement.*
- We form a question by putting the subject after the auxiliary verb *be* or between the auxiliaries if there are two of them.
  ***Is** the website **updated** every day?*
  *When **will** the museum **be opened**?*
- When a verb is followed by a preposition, the preposition stays in the same position in the passive.
  *We can make sure the place **is looked after**.*
  *At the hotel, all diets **are catered for**.*

+ see next page!

- When a verb has two objects, the passive sentence can begin with either the direct or the indirect object. The direct object is usually a thing and the indirect object is usually a person. When we begin with the direct object, we use the preposition *to* or *for* before the indirect object.
  ***The land** was given back **to the original owners**.* OR ***The original owners** were given back **the land**.*
  ***Four seats** were saved **for us**.* OR ***We** were saved **four seats**.*
- Verbs that take two objects include: *ask, buy, find, get, give, lend, make, offer, pay, promise, sell, send, show, teach, tell*.

Use:

- We often use the passive when we do not mention who does an action, as we are more interested in what happens than who does it. This is usually because the person who does the action is obvious, unknown or not important. The passive also means we can avoid using vague subjects like *someone*, *people* and *they*.
  *India **was divided** into two different countries.*
  *In the book, the animals escape and 'zoo law' **is replaced** by 'jungle law'.*
- However, we can use the passive with *by* to say who does the action. This is often when we give new information about an existing topic. The passive enables us to put the existing information first and the new information second.
  *The Mini **is owned by BMW**.*
  *The film **was directed by James Cameron**.*
  *In the past, India **was ruled by the United Kingdom**.*
- We use *be* + past participle after modal verbs.
  *Explain which of the stories **can be considered** true.*
  *You **won't be contacted** unless you give us permission.*
- We use the passive infinitive *to be* + past participle after verbs that are normally followed by a *to*-infinitive (e.g. *allow, ask, expect, hope, like, need, want*).
  *Write the items in your exercise book in the order you **expect** them **to be mentioned**.*
  *Racism is a topic that **needs to be addressed**.*
- When we use the passive in a relative clause, we can sometimes omit the relative pronoun and *be*.
  *She lives in a house (that was) **built** by her grandfather.*
  *This new illness, (which was) **discovered** by a doctor in Nigeria, has not been named yet.*

The passive (all tenses) – Overview

Simple present (*am* / *is* / *are* + past participle)
*The internet **is used** by billions of people every day.*
*Today, most goods **are paid for** electronically.*

Simple past (*was* / *were* + past participle)
*The match **wasn't won** by our team.*
*The mistakes **were corrected** by the teacher.*

Present perfect (*has been* / *have been* + past participle)
*Gwen **has been hired** by a fashion company.*
*Musical genres and fashion **have been linked** to young people since the 1920s.*

***Will* (*will be* + past participle)**
*What kind of information do you think you **will be given**?*
*Many jobs **will be lost**.*

Modal verbs (*can be* / *might be* / *had to be* + past participle)
*Stories **can be used** to illustrate a point and appeal to the emotions of your audience.*
*The new website **might be launched** soon.*
*Until the early 20th century, all household chores **had to be done** by hand.*

G 3 Reported Speech

G 3.1 Reported speech in statements and questions in the present, present perfect and future

Workshop 1

Statements:

- We can use *say* and *tell* to report what someone says.
  *He **says** that he loves the area.*
  *Thomas **tells** me that you're going back to the UK.*

- We can use *that* after *say* and *tell*. There is no rule about *that* and it is usually personal choice.
  *She **says** she's not hungry. OR She **says that** she's not hungry.*

- We use an indirect object (e.g. *me, us*) after *tell*.
  *He tells **me** they are hoping to set off at about 6.30.*

- As well as *say* and *tell*, we can use reporting verbs such as *admit, agree, assure, claim, deny, inform, suggest, think*, etc.
  *He **admits** he's wrong.*
  *She **agrees** it's a good idea.*

- When we use reporting verbs in the present, the present perfect or the future, we generally keep the information we are reporting in the same tense as the original comment. This is usually to show that something is still true, relevant or important.
  *'I**'ll be** home in ten minutes.' → She says she**'ll be** home in ten minutes.*
  *'It**'s** Jenna's birthday today.' → Alice tells me it**'s** your birthday today.*
  *'I think Sam **left** about an hour ago.' → He thinks that Sam **left** about an hour ago.*
  *'We**'re going to** the beach.' → Luke says they**'re going to** the beach.*

- We sometimes need to change pronouns (*we → they*).
  *'**I**'ve lived in South India since **I** was 13.' → **He** says **he**'s lived in South India since **he** was 13.*

Questions:

- We can report a question with verbs such as *ask, want to know* and *wonder*.
  *Fred: 'Is everything OK?' → Fred**'s asking** if everything is OK.*
  *David: 'When are we leaving?' → David **wants to know** when we're leaving.*
  *Jessica: 'Where are we going next?' → She**'s wondering** where we are going next.*

- For a *yes/no*-question (without a question word) we use *if* or *whether*.
  *He **is asking** me **if** I know his brother.*
  *Olga **has asked** me **whether** I can give her a surfing lesson.*

- The word order is different from direct questions but the same as in statements.
  *'Where **does he live**?' → She wants to know where **he lives**.*
  *'When **are we leaving**?' → He keeps asking when **we're leaving**.*
  NOT ~~*She's wants to know where does he live.*~~
  ~~*He keeps asking when are we leaving.*~~

G 3.2 Reported speech in statements and questions in the past and in requests, offers, orders and advice

Workshop 1

Statements and questions:

- When reporting speech, we often use the past tense forms *said, told, asked, wanted to know, was wondering, assured, admitted, denied, explained, promised, suggested*, etc. We usually 'backshift' the tense (move the tense one step back in time) in the statement, comment or question we are reporting.

present tense →	past tense
*'I **have** no time.'*	*She said she **had** no time.*
*'What**'s** wrong with you?'*	*Keira asked Fred what **was** wrong with him.*
*'OK, I admit I**'m** wrong.'*	*He admitted he **was** wrong.*
past tense / present perfect →	past perfect
*'I **didn't want** to go.'*	*She explained she **hadn't wanted** to go.*
*'We**'ve** just **arrived**.'*	*He said they**'d** just **arrived**.*
will	*would*
*'I**'ll call** you later.'*	*She promised she**'d call** me later.*
can	*could*
*'I **can't find** it.'*	*He admitted he **couldn't find** it.*
must	*had to*
*'We **must leave** now.'*	*She said they **had to leave**.*

- We sometimes use the past tense forms of reporting verbs such as *said, told, asked, wanted to know, was wondering*, etc. and do not change the tense of the reported sentence. This is usually to show that a statement or information is still true, relevant or important.
  *'Sam **left** about an hour ago.' → He said that Sam **left** about an hour ago.*
  *'I**'ll** be home in ten minutes.' → She said she**'ll** be home in ten minutes.*
  *'Where**'s** Jamie **going**?' → She was wondering where Jamie**'s going**.*

Requests, offers, orders and advice:

- We can report a request with verbs such as *asked* and *wanted* + indirect object + *to*-infinitive.
  *'Can you wait here?' → She asked **us to wait** here.*
  *'Could you repeat the question?' → She wanted **me to repeat** the question.*

- We can report an offer with *offer* + *to*-infinitive.
  *'I can give you a lift if you like.' → Maria offered **to give** us a lift.*
  *'I'll help you if you like.' → He offered **to help** us.*

- We can report an order or advice with *told* + indirect object + (*not*) + *to*-infinitive.
  *'You should apologize to them.' → She told **me to apologize** to them.*
  *'Don't be late again.' → He told **me not to be** late again.*

- We can also use the present tense of the reporting verbs:
  *Gareth **wants** me **to help** him.*
  *She**'s asking** us **to wait** here.*
  *Petra**'s offering to give** us a lift.*
  *The life guard **is telling** us **not to swim** here.*

G 3.3 Changes to adverbs of time and place in reported speech

Workshop 1

- When we are reporting with a reporting verb in the past, we need to change adverbs of time and place.
  *'I saw Anders **yesterday.**' → She mentioned she'd seen Anders **the day before**.*
  *'I'll call you **next week**.' → She said she'd call me **the following week**.*
  *'This is the first time I've been **here**.' → He said it was the first time he'd been **there**.*

- Common changes include:
  yesterday → the day before
  tomorrow → the next day / the day after
  last weekend / week / month / year → the weekend / week / month / year before
  next weekend / week / month / year → the following weekend / week / month / year
  here → there

G 4 Gerunds and infinitives

Workshop 1

Sometimes we use two verbs together. When one verb follows another verb, the second verb is usually a gerund (*-ing*) or a *to*-infinitive.

- We use the gerund (*-ing*) after certain verbs. These include: *admit, avoid, deny, don't mind, enjoy, feel like, finish, imagine, look forward to, mention, miss, practise, prefer, recommend, risk, suggest.*
  *Many young people **enjoy travelling**.*
  *Have you **finished reading** the article?*
  *He **suggests doing** work experience at a law firm.*

- We use the *to*-infinitive after certain verbs. These include: *arrange, choose, decide, expect, hope, intend, learn, manage, need, offer, plan, promise, want, would like.*
  *She's **decided to study** music at university.*
  *Many young **want to volunteer** abroad.*
  ***I'd like to do** some kind of volunteer work.*

- Some verbs can be followed by the gerund or the *to*-infinitive with no or little difference in meaning. These include: *like, love, hate, prefer, start.*
  *I **hate getting up** early.* *I really **hate to be** late.*
  *I **prefer doing** sport.* *I **prefer to study** languages.*

Some verbs can be followed by a gerund or the *to*-infinitive, but there is a difference in meaning. These include: *try, remember, forget, stop*.

- *Try:*
  We use *try* + gerund when we do something to see what the results will be.
  I ***tried turning*** *the computer on and off, but the programme still didn't work.*

  We use *try* + *to*-infinitive when we make an effort to achieve something.
  I'm ***trying to learn*** *Russian, but it's very difficult.*

- *Remember and forget:*
  We use *remember / forget* + gerund to talk about memories.
  Do you ***remember going*** *to school for the first time?*
  I'll never ***forget visiting*** *Prague. It's so beautiful.*

  We use *remember / forget* + *to*-infinitive to say we do or don't do something.
  Did you ***remember to email*** *Julia?*
  Don't ***forget to update*** *your CV!*

- *Stop:*
  We use *stop* + gerund to talk about something ending or stopping.
  I ***stopped eating*** *meat when I was 16.*

  We use *stop* + *to*-infinitive to express the reason or purpose.
  I was working, but I ***stopped to check*** *the news for a while.*

G 5 *If*-sentences

Workshop 1/Workshop 2

There are three types of *if*-sentences, as well as mixed types (→ G5.4).

***If*-sentences type 1** → G5.1

***if*-clause: simple present**	**main clause: *will ('ll)* + infinitive**
If I ***go*** *to China,*	*I* ***will / 'll visit*** *the Great Wall.*

(= It's likely or possible that I'll visit China.)

***If*-sentences type 2** → G5.2

***if*-clause: simple past**	**main clause: *would* (*'d*) + infinitive**
If I ***went*** *to China,*	*I* ***would / I'd visit*** *the Great Wall.*

(= It's not very likely that I'll visit China.)

***If*-sentences type 3** → G5.3

***if*-clause: past perfect**	**main clause: *would* (*'d*) + *have* + past participle**
If I ***had gone*** *to China in 2019,*	*I* ***would have / I'd have visited*** *the Great Wall.*

(= I had the chance to go to China in the past, but I didn't go.)

G 5.1 *If*-sentences type 1

Workshop 1

- We use *if*-sentences type 1 to talk about things that are possible or likely to happen.
  If-sentences type 1 have the form *if* + simple present, *will / won't* + infinitive.
  If I ***think*** *something's cool, **I'll buy** it.*
  If the phone ***is*** *too expensive, I* ***won't buy*** *it.*
  If I ***need*** *some help,* ***I'll message*** *you.*
- We use *unless* to mean *if not*.
  We'll go for a walk ***unless*** *it* ***rains****. = We'll go for a walk* ***if*** *it* ***doesn't rain****.*
- We use *when* for things which will definitely happen.
  When *I get home, I'll call you.*
- We can usually put the two clauses in any order. When the *if / when / unless*-clause is first, there is a comma between the clauses.
  *If I like it****,*** *I'll buy it.*
  I'll buy it if I like it.

G 5.2 *If*-sentences type 2

Workshop 1

- We use *if*-sentences type 2 to talk about things that are impossible or hypothetical in the present or unlikely to happen in the future.
- *If*-sentences type 2 have the form *if* + simple past, *would / wouldn't* + infinitive.
  If I ***got*** *a tattoo, my parents* ***wouldn't be*** *happy.*
  If we ***drove*** *less, there* ***wouldn't be*** *so much air pollution.*
  If I ***had*** *more money,* ***I'd buy*** *a new phone.*

Note that we often use *'d* instead of *would*, especially in speaking and informal writing.

- We do not use *would* in the *if*-clause.
  If I ***had*** *more time, I'd read more books.* NOT ~~*If I would have more time, I'd read more books.*~~
- We can usually swap the order of the two clauses. When the *if*-clause is first, there is a comma between the clauses.
  *If I had more time****,*** *I'd read more books.*
  I'd read more books if I had more time.
- We can usually use *If I was …* or *If I were …* . However, we normally use *If I were you, …* .
  If I ***was / were*** *richer, I'd get a new car.*
  If I were you*, I'd work a bit harder at school.*

Note that we can use *could* or *might* in an *if*-sentence type 2.
If I had more money, I ***could buy*** *a new phone.*
If we drove less, there ***might not be*** *so much air pollution.*

G 5.3 *If*-sentences type 3

Workshop 2

- We use *if*-sentences type 3 to talk about something that didn't happen in the past. We talk about it in an imaginary or a hypothetical way.
- *If*-sentences type 3 have the form *if* + past perfect, *would / wouldn't have* + past participle.
  *If I **had seen** you, I **would have said** hello.*
  *If I **had known** about the exhibition, I **would have gone** to it.*
  *If you**'d got up** earlier, you **wouldn't have missed** the bus.*
- We often use *'d* instead of *had* and *would*, especially in speaking and informal writing. We also often use *'ve* instead of *have*.
  *If I**'d had** more money, I**'d've got** a taxi.*
- We can usually swap the order of the two clauses. When the *if*-clause is first, there is a comma between the clauses.
  *If I'd had more money**,** I would've bought it.*
  I would've bought it if I'd had more money.

Note that we can use *could have* or *might have* in an *if*-sentence type 3.
*If I hadn't been ill last week, I **could have gone** to the meeting.*
*If I'd worked harder, I **might've got** better grades in my exams.*

G 5.4 Mixed types of *if*-sentences

Workshop 1

- We use a 'mixed' *if*-sentence to talk about a past event with a present consequence. To do this we combine an *if*-sentences type 3 (to refer to the past) with an *if*-sentences type 2 (to refer to the present).
  *If you **had gone** to bed earlier, you **wouldn't be** so tired now.*
  *If I**'d had** breakfast, I **wouldn't be** so hungry now.*
  *If he **hadn't had** those lucky breaks, no one **would know** his name today.*
  *If you**'d listened**, you**'d know** what to do!*

Note that we can use *might* in a mixed *if*-sentence.
*If you'd listened to the advice, you **might not be** in this mess now.*

G 6 Relative clauses

Workshop 2

Relative pronouns:

- We use *who* for people and *which* for things. We can use *that* for both people and things. We use *whose* to show possession.

Defining relative clauses:

- A defining relative clause defines, identifies or gives necessary information about a person or thing.
- A defining relative clause comes immediately after this person or thing. The relative clause begins with a relative pronoun.
  There were basic human rights ***which had been seriously curtailed.***
  It was a political situation ***which arose after many years of oppression.***
  Nelson Mandela was not a man ***who believed in or encouraged violence.***
  He and the others ***who started the organization*** *were all arrested.*

Omission of the relative pronoun:

- A relative pronoun can be the subject or the object of a relative clause.

	relative pronoun / subject	verb	object	
There's the man	***who***	*helped*	*us*	*yesterday.*

	relative pronoun / object	subject	verb	
There's the man	***who***	*we*	*helped*	*yesterday.*

- We can omit *who*, *which* or *that* when it is the object of the relative clause.
  Is this the book (which) your parents gave you as a birthday gift?
  Mac and his family do things (that) every other family does.
  Is this the café (that) Luke mentioned the other day?
  There's the man (who) we helped yesterday.

Non-defining relative clauses:

- A non-defining relative clause gives extra non-essential information about a person or thing. The non-defining relative clause comes immediately after this person or thing and begins with *who* or *which*, but not *that*. We always separate a non-defining relative clause from the main clause with commas.
  The African National Congress, ***which was formed in 1912,*** *defended the rights of the African people.*
  Mandela, ***who was sentenced to life,*** *became the world's most famous prisoner.*
  My two older brothers, ***who I've always been very close to,*** *went to live with my dad.*
  He was born in Avalon, ***which is a small town near Los Angeles.***

Note that non-defining relative clauses are used more in writing and in more formal spoken contexts.

- We can also use a non-defining relative clause beginning with *which* to comment on the whole of the previous clause.
  I was at a party last weekend, ***which was great fun.***
  The school became mixed-sex in the 1980s, ***which was a major step forwards.***
  I missed the bus, ***which was really annoying.***

Note that non-defining relative clauses used to comment on the whole of the previous clause are quite common in spoken and more informal English.

<u>*Where* and *when*</u>:

- We can use the relative adverbs *where* and *when* in relative clauses. We use *where* to identify a place and *when* to identify a time.
  *The hotel **where we stayed** is in the city centre.*
  *I can't remember a month **when we last had so much rain**.*

G 7 Modals

Workshop 2

The modal verbs are *can, could, must, might, may, would, will, shall* and *should*.

- A modal verb always has the same form. The ending never changes.
  *She **can** speak English.*
- We use an infinitive without *to* after a modal verb.
  *I **will** help you.*
- To form a negative, we put *not* or *n't* after the modal verb.
  *You **mustn't** do that.*
- To form a question, we put the modal verb before the subject.
  ***Can** you help me?*

<u>*Can* and *could*</u>:
We use *can* to talk about ability. We use it:

- to talk about general abilities and skills.
  *My sister **can** use many computer programmes.*
  *I **can** speak French and Spanish. But I **can't** speak Italian.*
- to talk about ability at a particular time.
  *I **can't** read this. The writing is too small.*

The past tense of *can* is *could*.
*I **could** speak some English when I was four years old.*

We use *can* to talk about permission. We use it:

- to talk about rules and laws and permission given by an individual.
  *You **can't** wear trainers at work. But you **can** wear jeans.*
  *You **can** leave when you have finished the report.*
  *We **could** wear trainers at work in my last job.*

We use *can* to talk about possibility.
*We **can** have the meeting on Thursday or Friday.*
*It **could** have been a rumour.*

<u>*May* and *might*</u>:
We use *may* and *might* to say that something is possible or likely. *Might* is more common in informal contexts. The negative is *may not* and *might not*. We use them:

- to say what is possible or likely in the future.
  *I **might** start looking for a holiday job.*
  *There **may** be a slight delay with your online order.*
- to say what we think is possible or likely in the present.
  *This **might** be Nina's office. But I'm not sure.*
  *She didn't answer the phone. She **might not** be at home.*

<u>*Must*:</u>
We use *must* to talk about what is necessary or what is required. We use *must not* (or *mustn't*) to say that something is not allowed or forbidden.
*You **must** come and visit us while you are in South Africa.*
*We **mustn't** forget the tickets.*

<u>*Should*:</u>
We use *should* to make suggestions and give advice. The negative form is *shouldn't*.
*They **should** check in online.*
*It **shouldn't** be a problem.*

The past tense of *should* is *should have* + past participle.
*We're going to be late – we **should have left** earlier.*

<u>*Will* and *shall*:</u>
We use *will* in a number of ways. Note that *will* is often contracted to *'ll*. We use *will*:

- to express spontaneous decisions.
  *I'**ll** help you if you want me to.*
  *I think I'**ll** take a short break.*
- to express predictions or assumptions about the future, present or past.
  *I'm hoping I'**ll** finish my essay by Friday.*
  *Hurry up! The taxi **will** be waiting.*
  *I think the exam **will** have finished by now.*
- to talk about facts we see as inevitable or certain.
  *I'**ll** be at school all day tomorrow.*
  *She'**ll** be 21 in January.*
  *We **will** see you tomorrow.*

We mainly use *shall* in the form of a question to make offers and suggestions. We use it in this way with *I* and *we*.
***Shall** I help you?*
*What time **shall** we meet?*

G 7.1 Modal substitutes

Workshop 2

Modal substitutes include: *be able to, have to, need to, be obliged to, ought to* and *be supposed to*.

Alternatives to *can* and *could*:

- We use *be able to* as an alternative to *can* and *could*. This is usually in more formal contexts and with *will* and the present perfect.
  *Some people **are able to** speak several languages.*
  ***I'm not able to** fix the problem, I'm afraid.*
  *Unfortunately, I **wasn't able to** attend the event.*
  *He**'ll be able to** solve the problem.*
  ***I've been able to** speak English since I was four.*
- We sometimes use *be allowed to* as an alternative to *can* and *could* to talk about permission.
  ***Are** you **allowed to** use your phone for research in lessons?*
  *I **was** never **allowed to** stay up late on a school night.*

Alternatives to *must*:

- We use *need to* and *have to* as alternatives to *must*. When they are used in this way, there is usually little difference in meaning (e.g. *I **need to** prepare for my interview. / I **have to** prepare for my interview. / I **must** prepare for my interview.*).
  *They **need to** acknowledge this problem.*
  *You **need to** leave by 5.30 at the latest.*
  ***Do** you **have to** be there on Monday?*
- In more informal contexts, such as conversation, we also use *have got to*.
  ***I've got to** prepare for my exam.*
  *What time **have** we **got to** leave?*
- The past tenses are *needed to* and *had to*. We use *had to* as the past tense of *must*.
  *Sorry I'm late. I **needed to** stop at the shops on the way here.*
  *I **had to** stay at school later than usual today.*
  *He **had to** do an interview with the head teacher.*
- We use *don't need to* and *don't have to* to say that something isn't necessary.
  *We **don't need to** leave until midday.*
  *You **don't have to** drink that.*
- We use *be obliged to* as an alternative in more formal contexts. This is usually when the obligation is a rule or law.
  *You **are obliged to** report to the reception on arrival and when leaving the building.*
  *You **are not obliged to** give your private address.*

Alternatives to *should*:

- We can sometimes use *ought to* as an alternative to *should* when we are making suggestions or giving advice.
  *It **ought to** be easy now.*
  *You **ought to** wear a suit for the wedding.*
  *I think we **ought to** leave now.*
- We use *be supposed to* as an alternative to *should* when we are expressing the correct thing to do.
  *She **is supposed to** be back by lunch time.*
  ***I'm supposed to** go to New York next week.*

G 8 Conjunctions with time clauses

Workshop 3

- We often use conjunctions such as *when, while, until, before, after, as soon as* and *once* to introduce an action that is going to happen in the future.
- When we are talking about the future, we usually use the simple present after a time conjunction.
  ***When I think** of a way, I'll tell you.*
  *I'll let you know **as soon as I arrive**.*
- We can also use the present progressive after a time conjunction to express that something is in progress.
  *Let's meet **the next time** you'**re visiting** Berlin.*
- We can also use the present perfect after a time conjunction to emphasize that one action is completed before the other action.
  ***When I've finished** my presentation, I'll send it to you.*
- When we begin with the time conjunction, we put a comma between the clauses.
  When we get to the station, I'll call you.
  I'll call you when we get to the station.
- We do not use a future form with *will* after the time conjunction.
  NOT ~~*I'll call you as soon as I will arrive.*~~
  ~~*I'll email you when I will have time.*~~

G 9 Question tags

Workshop 3

We form a question tag with an auxiliary verb (*do, have, be* or a modal verb) + pronoun (*you, he, she, it, they*, etc.). We use the same auxiliary verb as in the first part of the statement. For the simple present and simple past, we use a form of *do*.

We use a negative question tag after a positive statement.
*We **seem** to have a great appetite for dystopia, **don't we**?*
*You **have** read older books than that, **haven't you**?*

We use a positive question tag after a negative statement.
*Science and technology **don't** help combat the climate crisis or anything, **do they**?*
*There **won't** be a problem identifying some of the dangers, **will there**?*

We use a question tag in two main ways:

- when we expect someone to agree with us. In this case, the intonation on the question tag falls.
  *I bet you got a good grade, **didn't you**?*
  *Online comments are largely anonymous, **aren't they**?*
- when we ask a real question, often to check something. In this case, the intonation on the question tag rises.
  *Your brother is still in the USA, **isn't he**?*
  *There was a movie too, **wasn't there**?*

G 10 Quantifiers

Workshop 3

- We use quantifiers to express the quantity of something. Quantifiers are words such as *all, a few, a little, (hardly) any, both, each, every, most (of), neither, none, no, some, the whole of.*
- To talk about things / people in general, we use *all / most / many / some / a few / no* + plural noun or uncountable noun (without *the*).
  ***All children** have the right to an education.*
  ***Most countries** have free education.*
  ***Many people** don't have a job.*
- We can also use *no* + singular noun.
  *Today, **no child** should go hungry.*
- To talk about things / people in a specific group, we use *all / most / many / some / a few / one / none* + *of* + *the / my / their* / etc. + plural noun or uncountable noun.
  ***All of my friends** were surprised.*
  ***All of my work** is interesting.*
  ***One of his ambitions** is to be a model.*
  ***None of the jobs** were interesting.*
- We can also use *all / most / many / some / a few / one / none* + *of* + pronoun.
  ***Most of them** have a summer job.*
  ***A few of us** are going to the meeting.*
- We can also use *all* + *the / my / their* / etc. + plural noun or uncountable noun (without *of*).
  ***All my friends** were surprised.*
  *I spend **all my allowance** on clothes.*
- We use *each / every* + singular noun.
  *I need to speak to **each person**.*
  ***Every child** has the right to express their opinion.*
- To talk about two things, we use *both*. We use:
  - *both* + plural noun
    *I like **both colours**.*
    ***Both jobs** were interesting.*
  - *both (of)* + *the / my / these* / etc. + plural noun
    ***Both of the jobs** were interesting.*
    ***Both my parents** speak English.*
  - *both of* + pronoun
    ***Both of them** are teachers.*
- We use a number of other expressions with *of* + plural or uncountable noun / pronoun.
  ***The majority of people** here don't have a passport.*
  ***A large percentage of them** have never travelled abroad.*
  ***A lot of people** didn't vote in the election.*
  ***Three quarters of the land** is used for farming.*
  ***A third of the population** lives in poverty.*
  ***Thirty per cent of 18-year-olds** go to university.*
  ***Half of the country** is desert.*
- We usually use these expressions without *the* to talk about things / people in general, but with *the* to talk about specific groups.
  ***Over 50% of people** don't have a passport.*
  ***Over 50% of the people** we interviewed don't have a passport.*

Irregular verbs

infinitive	simple past	past participle	German
to **arise** [əˈraɪz]	**arose** [əˈrəʊz]	**arisen** [əˈrɪzən]	entstehen
to **be**	**was / were**	**been**	sein
to **beat**	**beat**	**beaten**	schlagen
to **become**	**became**	**become**	werden
to **begin**	**began**	**begun**	beginnen, anfangen
to **bet**	**bet**	**bet**	wetten
to **bite** [baɪt]	**bit** [bɪt]	**bitten** [ˈbɪtn]	beißen
to **bleed** [bli:d]	**bled** [bled]	**bled** [bled]	bluten
to **blow**	**blew**	**blown**	blasen
to **break**	**broke**	**broken**	brechen
to **bring**	**brought**	**brought**	bringen
to **build**	**built**	**built**	bauen
to **burn**	**burnt / burned**	**burnt / burned**	(ver)brennen
to **burst**	**burst**	**burst**	platzen
to **buy**	**bought**	**bought**	kaufen
to **catch**	**caught**	**caught**	fangen
to **choose** [tʃu:z]	**chose** [tʃəʊz]	**chosen** [ˈtʃəʊzən]	auswählen
to **come**	**came**	**come**	kommen
to **cost**	**cost**	**cost**	kosten
to **cut**	**cut**	**cut**	schneiden
to **deal** [di:l]	**dealt** [delt]	**dealt** [delt]	handeln
to **dig**	**dug**	**dug**	graben
to **do** [du:]	**did** [dɪd]	**done** [dʌn]	machen, tun
to **draw**	**drew**	**drawn**	zeichnen
to **dream** [dri:m]	**dreamt** [dremt] / **dreamed** [dri:md]	**dreamt** [dremt] / **dreamed** [dri:md]	träumen

infinitive	simple past	past participle	German
to **drink**	**drank**	**drunk**	trinken
to **drive** [draɪv]	**drove** [drəʊv]	**driven** [ˈdrɪvən]	fahren
to **eat** [i:t]	**ate** [et, eɪt]	**eaten** [ˈi:tn]	essen
to **fall**	**fell**	**fallen**	fallen, stürzen
to **feed** [fi:d]	**fed** [fed]	**fed** [fed]	füttern
to **feel** [fi:l]	**felt** [felt]	**felt** [felt]	(sich) fühlen, spüren
to **fight**	**fought**	**fought**	kämpfen
to **find**	**found**	**found**	finden
to **fly**	**flew**	**flown**	fliegen
to **forget**	**forgot**	**forgotten**	vergessen
to **forgive**	**forgave**	**forgiven**	vergeben
to **freeze**	**froze**	**frozen**	frieren
to **get**	**got**	**got / gotten (AE)**	bekommen, holen
to **give**	**gave**	**given**	geben, schenken
to **go** [gəʊ]	**went** [went]	**gone** [gɒn]	gehen, fahren
to **grow** [grəʊ]	**grew** [gru:]	**grown** [grəʊn]	wachsen, anbauen
to **hang**	**hung**	**hung**	hängen
to **have (got)**	**had**	**had**	haben
to **hear** [hɪə]	**heard** [hɜ:d]	**heard** [hɜ:d]	hören
to **hide** [haɪd]	**hid** [hɪd]	**hidden** [hɪdn]	(sich) verstecken
to **hit**	**hit**	**hit**	schlagen
to **hold**	**held**	**held**	halten
to **hurt**	**hurt**	**hurt**	wehtun

infinitive	simple past	past participle	German
to **keep** [ki:p]	**kept** [kept]	**kept** [kept]	(be)halten
to **kneel** [ni:l]	**knelt** [nelt]	**knelt** [nelt]	knien
to **know** [nəʊ]	**knew** [nju:]	**known** [nəʊn]	wissen, kennen
to **lead** [li:d]	**led** [led]	**led** [led]	führen
to **learn**	**learnt / learned**	**learnt / learned**	lernen
to **leave** [li:v]	**left** [left]	**left** [left]	verlassen
to **lend**	**lent**	**lent**	leihen
to **let**	**let**	**let**	lassen
to **lie**	**lay**	**lain**	liegen
to **light** [laɪt]	**lit** [lɪt] / **lighted** ['laɪtɪd]	**lit** [lɪt] / **lighted** ['laɪtɪd]	anzünden, anmachen
to **lose** [lu:z]	**lost** [lɒst]	**lost** [lɒst]	verlieren
to **make**	**made**	**made**	machen, herstellen
to **mean** [mi:n]	**meant** [ment]	**meant** [ment]	bedeuten
to **meet** [mi:t]	**met** [met]	**met** [met]	(sich) treffen, kennen-lernen
to **mow**	**mowed**	**mown / mowed**	mähen
to **pay**	**paid**	**paid**	bezahlen
to **put**	**put**	**put**	stellen
to **quit**	**quit**	**quit**	aufhören
to **read** [ri:d]	**read** [red]	**read** [red]	lesen
to **rebuild**	**rebuilt**	**rebuilt**	wieder aufbauen
to **rewrite** [ˌri:'raɪt]	**rewrote** [ˌri:'rəʊt]	**rewritten** [ˌri:'rɪtn]	umschreiben
to **ride** [raɪd]	**rode** [rəʊd]	**ridden** ['rɪdn]	fahren, reiten
to **ring**	**rang**	**rung**	klingeln, anrufen

infinitive	simple past	past participle	German
to **rise** [raɪz]	**rose** [rəʊz]	**risen** ['rɪzən]	ansteigen, (sich) erheben
to **run**	**ran**	**run**	laufen, rennen, leiten
to **say** [seɪ]	**said** [sed]	**said** [sed]	sagen
to **see**	**saw**	**seen**	sehen
to **sell**	**sold**	**sold**	verkaufen
to **send**	**sent**	**sent**	schicken
to **set**	**set**	**set**	setzen, stellen, legen
to **shake**	**shook**	**shaken**	schütteln
to **shine** [ʃaɪn]	**shone** [ʃɒn]	**shone** [ʃɒn]	scheinen
to **shoot** [ʃu:t]	**shot** [ʃɒt]	**shot** [ʃɒt]	schießen
to **show**	**showed**	**shown / showed**	zeigen
to **shrink**	**shrank**	**shrunk**	schrumpfen
to **sing**	**sang**	**sung**	singen
to **sink**	**sank**	**sunk**	sinken
to **sit**	**sat**	**sat**	sitzen
to **slay** [sleɪ]	**slew** [slu:]	**slain** [sleɪn]	töten; schlachten
to **sleep** [sli:p]	**slept** [slept]	**slept** [slept]	schlafen
to **smell**	**smelt / smelled**	**smelt / smelled**	riechen
to **speak** [spi:k]	**spoke** [spəʊk]	**spoken** ['spəʊkən]	sprechen
to **spend**	**spent**	**spent**	verbringen, ausgeben
to **split**	**split**	**split**	sich trennen
to **spoil**	**spoilt**	**spoilt**	verderben
to **spread**	**spread**	**spread**	sich ausbreiten, etw. verteilen

infinitive	simple past	past participle	German
to **stand**	**stood**	**stood**	stehen
to **steal**	**stole**	**stolen**	stehlen
to **stick**	**stuck**	**stuck**	kleben
to **sting**	**stung**	**stung**	stechen
to **strike**	**struck**	**struck**	zuschlagen; treffen
to **strive** [straɪv]	**strove** [strəʊv]	**striven** [ˈstrɪvən]	sich bemühen
to **swim**	**swam**	**swum**	schwimmen
to **take**	**took**	**taken**	nehmen, dauern
to **teach** [tiːtʃ]	**taught** [tɔːt]	**taught** [tɔːt]	unterrichten
to **tear** [teə]	**tore** [tɔː]	**torn** [tɔːn]	reißen

infinitive	simple past	past participle	German
to **tell**	**told**	**told**	sagen, erzählen
to **think**	**thought**	**thought**	denken, glauben
to **throw**	**threw**	**thrown**	werfen
to **understand**	**understood**	**understood**	verstehen
to **wake up**	**woke up**	**woken up**	aufwachen
to **wear** [weə]	**wore** [wɔː]	**worn** [wɔːn]	tragen
to **weave**	**wove**	**woven**	weben
to **win** [wɪn]	**won** [wʌn]	**won** [wʌn]	gewinnen
to **withdraw**	**withdrew**	**withdrawn**	sich zurückziehen
to **write** [raɪt]	**wrote** [rəʊt]	**written** [ˈrɪtn]	schreiben

Vocabulary

Here are all the words from the workshops. They are in the same order as in the workshop.

There is the page number and the activity.

A ▢ at the side is for words from the listening text. A ■ is for words from videos.

Words in **grey** are important for one text. They are only in this text and you don't have to learn them.

The phonetic transcription [ ] tells you how you say a word.

Sometimes there are irregular forms (*shut*, *shut*, *shut*).

The example sentence shows you how we use a word.

= shows words with the same meaning

≠ shows words with the opposite meaning

! shows words with the same meaning in French and Latin or it gives other interesting information about the word.

When you work with the *Vocabulary*, cover the German, look at the English word and the example or picture and say the German word. You can also cover the German and the example sentences to practise the English.

Welcome Workshop

page	exercise	word	example	German
10	1a	**colonialism** [kə'ləʊniəlɪzəm]	*Colonialism is when one country takes control over another, often using it for its resources and ruling over its people.*	Kolonialismus
11	2b	**athleticism** [ˌæθ'lɛtɪsɪzm]	*I love her energy and her athleticism.*	Sportlichkeit
		bleak [bli:k]	*The settings chosen for this video shoot are bleak, quite frightening really.*	düster
		dusty ['dʌsti]	*The desert was dry and dusty.*	verstaubt
		to uplift [ʌp'lɪft]	*We provide educational opportunities to uplift young people.*	ermutigen
		to energize ['ɛnərdʒaɪz]	*The morning run really energized me for the day.*	beleben; Energie geben
		searchlight ['sɜ:rtʃlaɪt]	*The area was checked by searchlights.*	Suchscheinwerfer
		bunch [bʌntʃ]	*a bunch of spoilt kids* = *group*	Haufen
		refrain [rɪ'freɪn]	*The song has a catchy refrain.*	Refrain
		catchy ['kætʃi]	*a catchy refrain*	packend
		facial features ['feɪʃl 'fi:tʃərz]	*They had different skin colours, hair and facial features.*	Gesichtszüge

Workshop 1

page	exercise	word	example	German
12	1	**democracy** [dɪ'mɒkrəsi]	*In a democracy, people vote to choose their leaders.*	Demokratie
		currency ['kʌrənsi]	*Euro is the currency in many European countries.*	Währung
		to populate ['pɒpjuleɪt]	*India is the second most populated country in the world and the world's biggest democracy.*	bevölkern

page	exercise	Workshop 1		
		civilization [ˌsɪvəlaɪˈzeɪʃn]	*In class, we learn about ancient civilizations like the Romans and Egyptians.*	Zivilisation
		minister [ˈmɪnɪstə]	*He has been a prime minister and a foreign minister.*	Minister(in)
		wealthy [ˈwelθi]	*This large gap between the wealthy and the poor has been increasing.*	reich
		powder [ˈpaʊdər]	*Hindus celebrate spring and new life with singing, dancing and the throwing of powder paints of many different colours.*	Pulver
		metropolis [mɪˈtrɒpəlɪs]	*The largest city is Mumbai and the fastest growing metropolis is Bengaluru.*	Metropole; Großstadt
		to **stylize** [ˈstaɪlaɪz]	*Bollywood films are known for their colourful and stylized storytelling.*	stilisieren
		subcontinent [ˌsʌbkɒntɪˈnɛnt]	*India is a subcontinent of Asia.*	Subkontinent
		partition [pɑːrˈtɪʃən]	*The partition of India in 1947 led to the creation of two separate states, India and Pakistan.*	Teilung
13	1	**caste** [kæst]	*The society is divided into social classes, or castes.*	Kaste; Stand
	YT	**counterargument** [ˈkaʊntərɑːgjumənt]	*Most people agreed, there weren't many counterarguments.*	Gegenargument
		engagement [ɪnˈgeɪdʒmənt]	*Her political engagement increased as she campaigned for local environmental issues.*	Engagement; Beschäftigung
14	CC	**empire** [ˈempaɪə]	*For years, the British had a huge empire.*	Reich
		to **ruin** [ˈruːɪn]	*Indigenous economies were ruined, while big companies made money off their land.*	zerstören
		boom [buːm]	*India's boom in technological skills is impressive.*	Boom; Aufschwung
	1a	**dynasty** [ˈdaɪnəsti]	*The Red Fort in Delhi was the home of India's ruling dynasty.*	Dynastie; Herrscherhaus
		awestruck [ˈɔːstrʌk]	*We were awestruck by the stunning fireworks.*	ehrfürchtig; beeindruckt
		to **regard** [rɪˈgɑːd]	*The Indians regarded the arriving British as barbarians.*	ansehen
		barbarian [bɑːˈbɛəriən]	*The city was invaded by barbarians.*	Barbar(in); Wilde(r)
		to **shift** [ʃift]	*The balance of power had shifted from the Indians to the British.*	(sich) verschieben
		favour: in favour [ɪn ˈfeɪvə]	*The balance of power had shifted decisively in favour of the British who remained in India for around two hundred years.*	zugunsten; für
		to **assert** [əˈsɜːt]	*The British Empire couldn't assert control over India any longer.*	durchsetzen; behaupten

page	exercise	Workshop 1		
	1b	**bloody** ['blʌdi]	*The fights were bloody and horrible.*	blutig
		princely state ['prɪnsli steɪt]	*Each princely state had its own tradition and leadership.*	Fürstenstaat
		to trade [treɪd]	*They traded land for goods and money.*	handeln
		to emerge [i'mɜ:dʒ]	*As we were watching, new facts emerged in the investigation.*	ans Licht kommen
		sovereign ['sɒvrɪn]	*≠ dependent*	souverän
		to categorize ['kætəgəˌraɪz]	*= to group*	kategorisieren; einordnen
		simplification [ˌsɪmplɪfɪ'keɪʃən]	*The report's simplification made it much easier to understand the issue.*	Vereinfachung
		to sow [soʊ], **sowed, sown** [soʊd, soʊn]	*The fields are sown in spring.*	säen
		distrust [dɪs'trʌst]	*There was a deep distrust between the two rival teams.*	Misstrauen; Zweifel
		aftermath ['ɑ:ftəmæθ]	*In the aftermath of World War II, Britain lost some colonies.*	Nachwirkungen
		strain [streɪn]	*The financial strain after the war caused political changes.*	Belastung
		to cave [keɪv]	*In the end, he decided to cave and let his sister choose the movie.*	nachgeben
		to represent [ˌreprɪ'zent]	*They represented the Hindu majority and wanted one united India.*	vertreten
		rift [rɪft]	*There were rifts inside the family and they didn't speak to each other.*	Spalte; Riss
		riot ['raɪət]	*There were riots against the Brits.*	Aufstand; Protest
		to expedite ['ɛkspɪdaɪt]	*Following riots in 1946 and 1947, the British expedited their retreat, planning Indian independence behind closed doors.*	beschleunigen
		retreat [rɪ'tri:t]	*After riots in 1946 and 1947, the British made their retreat, planning Indian independence behind closed doors.*	Rückzug
		viceroy ['vaɪsrɔɪ]	*The Viceroy was the representative of the British monarch in the colonies.*	Vizekönig
		to partition [pɑ:r'tɪʃən]	*The British viceroy partitioned the territory into Hindu India and Muslim Pakistan.*	teilen; aufteilen
		minimal ['mɪnɪml]	*They only had minimal knowledge of the land and that caused great problems.*	minimal; gering
		mere [mɪə]	*In a mere five weeks, the committee drew borders with outdated maps and minimal knowledge.*	bloß; lediglich
		account [ə'kaʊnt]	*There were several accounts about what happened.*	Bericht
		sovereignty ['sɒvrɪnti]	*Unabhängigkeit*	Souveränität

page	exercise	Workshop 1		
		sexual ['sɛkʃul]	*Fearing sexual violence, parents sent females to safe areas.*	sexuel
		to flee [fli:], **fled, fled** [fled, fled]	*Muslims living in India fled villages where their families had lived for centuries.*	fliehen; flüchten
		vacuum ['vækju:m]	*The president's death created a power vacuum in the government.*	Vakuum
		to **radicalize** ['rædɪkəˌlaɪz]	*Young people were radicalized by political extremists.*	radikalisieren
		militia [mɪ'lɪʃə]	*In the power vacuum British forces left behind, radicalized militias and local groups massacred migrants.*	Miliz; Bürgerwehr
		to **occur** [ə'kɜ:r]	*= to happen*	passieren
		to **bear** [beə]	*Women had to bear the violence, suffering rape and mutilation.*	ertragen
		to **bear the brunt** [bɛə ðə brʌnt]	*The caretaker had to bear the brunt of the house falling down.*	die Hauptlast tragen
		rape [reɪp]	*Rape has often been used as a weapon of war.*	Vergewaltigung
		mutilation [ˌmju:tɪ'leɪʃən]	*In Punjab, women suffered greatly, facing rape and mutilation.*	Verstümmelung; Entstellung
		captor ['kæptə]	*= kidnapper*	Entführer(in); Geiselnehmer(in)
		temporary ['temprəri]	*The temporary decision was later taken back.*	vorübergehend
		displaced [dɪs'pleɪst]	*Many families had to flee and became permanently displaced.*	vertrieben; umgesiedelt
		to **dispute** [dɪ'spju:t]	*I have never disputed his expertise on the matter.*	bestreiten; anfechten
		to **secede** [sɪ'si:d]	*In 1971, East Pakistan seceded and became the new country of Bangladesh.*	sich abspalten
		referendum [ˌrefə'rendəm]	*There will be a referendum about the issue.*	Abstimmung; Referendum
		to **war** [wɔ:]	*= fight*	Krieg führen
		legacy ['legəsi]	*The legacies of the partition continue to influence political and social dynamics in the region.*	Vermächtnis; Erbe
		to amplify ['æmplɪfaɪ]	*Experiences have to be shared and amplified to make an impact.*	verstärken
15	2	**traumatic** [trɔ:'mætɪk]	*The earthquake was traumatic.*	traumatisch
		unrecognizable [ʌn'rɛkəgnaɪzəbl]	*After the renovation, the old building was completely unrecognizable.*	nicht wiedererkennbar
		to risk [rɪsk]	*He risked everything and denied that he knew anything.*	riskieren
		to question ['kwestʃən]	*He was questioned by the police.*	(be)fragen; in Frage stellen
		strewn [stru:n]	*The streets were strewn with dead bodies.*	übersät

page	exercise	Workshop 1		
		chest [tʃest]	*I keep my clothes in a big chest.*	Truhe; Brust
		tight [taɪt]	*The new shoes are too tight.*	eng; dicht
		convoy ['kɒnvɔɪ]	*a convoy of soldiers*	Konvoi; Geleitzug
		significant [sɪg'nɪfɪkənt]	*What are your most significant memories of the time?*	wichtig; signifikant
	3	**asleep** [ə'sli:p]	*While we were asleep, our school was attacked by the mob.*	schlafend
		explosion [ɪk'spləʊʒn]	*Our mother was terrified as explosions could be heard all around us.*	Explosion
	4	to **erupt** [ɪ'rʌpt]	*The streets of Karachi erupted in celebrations.*	ausbrechen
		to **unfold** [ʌn'fəʊld]	*Unfold the map and check were we are.*	entfalten
		to **embark** [ɪm'bɑ:k]	*About 15 million folks embarked on the largest migration ever.*	beginnen
		to **flock** [flɒk]	*Hindus and Sikhs headed to India while Muslims flocked to Pakistan.*	strömen
		to **groove** [gru:v]	*the music that gets you grooving*	grooven
		intangible [ɪn'tændʒəbl]	*The stories of our ancestors are an intangible part of our culture.*	immateriell; unfassbar
		respect [rɪ'spekt]	*Respect is important in our family.*	Respekt
		utmost ['ʌtmoʊst]	*Every guest who steps into your house is treated with the utmost respect.*	größte(r)
		vibe [vaɪb]	*The song was full of positive vibes.*	Gefühl; Flair
		fortunate ['fɔ:tʃənət]	*We are fortunate to live in a world where there is so much information and knowledge available.*	glücklich
		to **blend** ['blend]	*Blend the vegetables with the spices.*	mischen
		shebang [ʃɪ'bæŋ]	*It requires us to get rid of the whole shebang.*	Ganze; Kram
		faith [feɪθ]	*His faith gives him strength during difficult times.*	Vertrauen; Glaube
		apart [ə'pɑ:t]	*The country was torn apart brutally.*	auseinander
		scar [skɑ:r]	*You can recognize her by the scar over her right eye.*	Narbe
		gear [gɪə]	*We were dressed up in our traditional gear.*	Zeug; Kleidung
		to **bond** [bɒnd]	*We bond through our music.*	zusammenkommen
		bond [bɒnd]	*There's a strong bond between Canada and the USA.*	*hier:* Verbindung
		forward ['fɔ:rwərd]	*They stepped forward bone by one.*	vorwärts
		to **dwell** ['dwel]	*Dwelling on past horrors is not good if you want to move ahead.*	verweilen
		gene [dʒi:n]	*Her eyes are blue because of her genes.*	Gen; Erbgut

page	exercise	Workshop 1		
		thankful ['θæŋkfl]	*I'm thankful for your help.*	dankbar
		to span [spæn]	*Our ancient civilization spans thousands of years.*	umspannen
16	2a	**underbelly** ['ʌndərbɛli]	*Adiga shows us a part of India that we seldom hear about, its underbelly.*	Schattenseite
	2b	**to narrate** [nəˈreɪts]	*He narrates his parent's story.*	erzählen
		prestigious [preˈstɪdʒəs]	*He won a prestigious prize.*	renommiert
		nevertheless [ˌnɛvəðəˈlɛs]	*He got out of school early, nevertheless with a lot of initiative, he found a job.*	dennoch; trotzdem
		to enable [ɪˈneɪbl]	*That crime enabled him to become wealthy enough to start his own business.*	ermöglichen
	3a	**destiny** ['destəni]	*What was the destiny of the city after the war?*	Schicksal
		rickshaw ['rɪkʃɔ:]	*A rickshaw is a small, human-powered cart used for transportation in Asia.*	Rikscha
		to wipe [waɪp]	*Wipe your feet when you go into a flat.*	(ab)wischen
		pastry ['peɪstri]	*She liked sweet pastries with her morning coffee.*	Gebäck; Teigwaren
		cunning ['kʌnɪŋ]	*They boy was very clever and cunning.*	gerissen; schlau
		creamy-skinned ['kri:mi skɪnd]	*She is creamy-skinned.*	cremefarben; helle Haut
		orderly ['ɔ:rdərli]	*It was a clean, well-kept, orderly zoo.*	ordentlich
		goldsmith ['goʊldˌsmɪθ]	*Goldsmiths create jewelry.*	Goldschmied(in)
		cowherd ['kaʊhɜ:rd]	*Cowherds have to watch the animals all the time.*	Kuhhirt(in); Viehhirt(in)
		landlord ['lændlɔ:d]	*Who is the landlord of your flat?*	Grundbesitzer; Verpächter
		to tend [tɛnd]	*Who tends the plants when you are away?*	sich kümmern um
		untouchable [ʌnˈtʌtʃəbl]	*The untouchables are the lowest caste in India.*	Unberührbare(r)
		faeces ['fi:si:z]	*The faeces were sampled for the experiment.*	Fäkalien; Kot
		ferocious [fəˈroʊʃəs]	*Your dog is a ferocious creature!*	wild; grausam
		belly ['bɛli]	*His belly was very big.*	Bauch; Unterleib
		to inherit [ɪnˈherɪt]	*I inherited those books from my grandparents.*	erben
		mud [mʌd]	*When he fell into the mud, he got really dirty.*	Schlamm; Dreck
		to cheat [tʃi:t]	*Don't cheat during a test.*	schummeln; mogeln
17	3b	**cynical** ['sɪnɪkl]	*That was a cynical remark and hurt me a lot.*	zynisch; skeptisch
	5a	**to fascinate** ['fæsɪneɪt]	*Foreign countries fascinate me, I'd like to visit as many as possible.*	faszinieren

page	exercise	Workshop 1		
		relevance ['reləvəns]	*The story stresses the relevance of India's past.*	Bedeutung
		corruption [kə'rʌpʃn]	*Corruption is a problem in many countries, hindering economic growth.*	Korruption
		despite [dɪ'spaɪt]	*Despite the seriousness of the message, the audience liked the singer.*	obwohl; trotz
		witty ['wɪti]	*His novels are very witty, everybody loves them.* *= funny* *≠ boring*	witzig; clever
		rooster ['ru:stə]	*The rooster crowed loudly in the morning.*	Hahn
18	1a	**soul** [səʊl]	*I will put my heart and soul into the job.*	Seele; Geist
		assassination [əˌsæsɪ'neɪʃn]	*The assassination of Gandhi was a shock for the world.*	Ermordung; Attentat
		to assassinate [ə'sæsɪneɪt]	*Gandhi was assassinated at a prayer meeting in New Delhi.*	ermorden
		to allege [ə'lɛdʒ]	*= to claim*	behaupten; vorwerfen
		assassin [ə'sæsɪn]	*The assassin shot the president from a roof.*	Attentäter(in)
		extremist [ɪk'stri:mɪst]	*Extremists were responsible for the violent protest in the city.*	Extremist(in); Radikale(r)
		fanatic [fə'nætɪk]	*Gandhi was shot by a religious fanatic.*	Fanatiker(in)
		stun [stʌn]	*The mood of the people appears to be one of stunned sorrow.* *= shocked*	betäubend
		principle ['prɪnsəpl]	*He developed the principle of non-violent resistance which was described as a positive interaction between two parties.*	Prinzip
		civil ['sɪvl]	*The march was a powerful demonstration for civil rights.*	Bürger...; bürgerlich
		disobedience [ˌdɪsə'bi:diəns]	*Ghandi returned to India where he trained people in civil disobedience tactics.* *= obedience*	Ungehorsam; Widerstand
		champion ['tʃæmpiən]	*Gandhi was India's strongest champion for civil rights.*	Champion
		to imprison [ɪm'prɪzn]	*After he organized the Freedom Movement as resistance against British laws, he was repeatedly imprisoned.*	einsperren
		negotiation [nɪˌgoʊʃi'eɪʃən]	*He was involved in the negotiations that led to Independence.*	Verhandlung; Gespräch

page	exercise	Workshop 1		
		appalled [ə'pɔ:ld]	*He was appalled by the violence he saw everywhere.*	entsetzt
		repercussions [ˌri:pə'kʌʃənz]	*Repercussions were felt everywhere.*	Auswirkungen
		widespread ['waɪdspred]	*There were widespread reactions to the report.*	weitverbreitet
		to labour ['leɪbə]	*I have laboured for days to complete this complicated puzzle.*	sich quälen; arbeiten
	2b	**principled** ['prɪnsɪpəld]	*Gandhi was a highly principled lawyer.*	prinzipientreu
		sympathy ['sɪmpəθi]	*Some believed his sympathy for Muslims was a political error.*	Mitgefühl
		error ['ɛrə]	*There have been serious errors in the management of the company.*	Irrtum; Fehler
		critic ['krɪtɪk]	*Read the critics' praise for the film.*	Kritiker(in)
19	3a	**to unveil** [ʌn'veɪl]	*A statue of Ghandi was unveiled in London.*	enthüllen
		anniversary [ˌænɪ'vɜ:səri]	*My parents are celebrating their 15th wedding anniversary.*	Jahrestag
		to tower ['taʊə]	*The father towered over them demanding respect.*	überragen
		politics ['pɒlətɪks]	*Gandhi influenced world politics.*	Politik
		to reiterate [ri:'ɪtəreɪt]	*= to repeat*	wiederholen
		to reminisce [ˌrɛmɪ'nɪs]	*= to remember*	sich erinnern
		bare-chested ['bɛə'tʃɛstɪd]	*He is always bare-chested.*	mit nacktem Oberkörper
		dhoti ['dəʊti]	*He wore a white dhoti to the celebration.*	Dhoti (indisches Kleidungsstück)
		potent ['pəʊtənt]	*= powerful*	mächtig
	3b	**sculptor** ['skʌlptə]	*The stature was done by the sculptor Philip Jackson.*	Bildhauer(in)
		to bless [bles]	*The priest blessed the children.*	segnen
		wisdom ['wɪzdəm]	*Gandhi's wisdom changed the political landscape.*	Weisheit
20	TIP	**emotive** [ɪ'məʊtɪv]	*Use emotive language but never become aggressive.*	emotional; gefühlvoll
		hostile ['hɒstaɪl]	*Do not use hostile language when discussing sensitive topics, as it can lead to misunderstandings and conflict.*	feindlich; feindselig
	2a	**to address** [ə'dres]	*The president addressed the nation.*	adressieren; ansprechen
		to accuse [ə'kju:z]	*She accused world leaders of immaturity.*	beschuldigen; anklagen
		immaturity [ˌɪmə'tjʊərɪti]	*She accused world leaders of immaturity and stated that they were leaving the crisis for young people to deal with.*	Unreife; Unausgereiftheit
21	4a	**campaigner** [kæm'peɪnə]	*She is an environmentalist and campaigner against microplastics.*	Aktivist(in)
		insignificant [ˌɪnsɪg'nɪfɪkənt]	*≠ important, significant*	unbedeutend; belanglos

page	exercise	Workshop 1		
		to slither ['slɪðə]	*Snakes slithered in the jungle.*	sich schlängeln
		invincible [ɪn'vɪnsəbl]	*When you feel invincible, you think nothing can bring you down.*	unbesiegbar; unbezwingbar
		invisible [ɪn'vɪzəbl]	*The cats were invisible in the dark room.*	unsichtbar
		environmentalism [ɪnˌvaɪrən'mɛntəlɪzəm]	*Environmentalism is caring about nature and trying to protect it from harm.*	Umweltschutz; Umweltbewegung
		anthropocentric [ˌænθrəpoʊ'sɛntrɪk]	*Environmentalism is anthropocentric, we don't really look at the perspective of other animals.*	anthropozentrisch; menschenzentriert
		ape [eɪp]	*They saw a big ape at the zoo.*	Affe; Menschenaffe
		crow [krəʊ]	*Crows are big, black birds.*	Krähe
		pursuit [pə'sju:t]	*Bella Lack was in pursuit of solutions to climate change.*	Suche; Verfolgung
		epitome [ɪ'pɪtəmi]	*The quiet lake surrounded by mountains is the epitome of untouched nature.*	Inbegriff; Quintessenz
		to destruct [dɪ'strʌkt]	*= destroy*	zerstören; vernichten
		decimation [ˌdɛsɪ'meɪʃən]	*= destruction*	Dezimierung; Ausrottung
		curse [kɜ:rs]	*Technology can be a blessing and a curse.*	Fluch
		denier [dɪ'naɪə]	*The deniers of climate change are difficult to persuade otherwise.*	Leugner(in); Bestreiter(in)
	4b	**ambassador** [æm'bæsədə]	*Bella was a youth ambassador for the 'Born Free' organization.*	Botschafter(in); Gesandte(r)
		passion ['pæʃn]	*His passion for art was evident in his flat, where he had hundreds of paintings.*	Leidenschaft
		dedication [ˌdedɪ'keɪʃn]	*It took a lof of hard work and dedication.*	*hier:* Einweihung; Einsatz
		palm oil [pɑ:m 'ɔɪl]	*Palm oil production is associated with deforestation as vast areas of tropical rainforests are cleared to make way for palm oil plantations.*	Palmöl
		orang-utan [ˌɒræŋ'u:tæn]	*Orang-utans are endangered.*	Orang-Utan
		ecosystem ['i:kəʊsɪstəm]	*Pollution affects our ecosystem badly.*	Ökosystem
		wheelbarrow ['wi:lbærəʊ]	*He filled the wheelbarrow with soil to start the new garden project.*	Schubkarre
		endearing [ɪn'dɪərɪŋ]	*These apes are endearing sweet creatures, but they are endangered.*	liebenswert; reizend
		to deforest [di:'fɔ:rɪst]	*Large areas are being deforested for cattle.*	abholzen; entwalden
		destruction [dɪ'strʌkʃn]	*Humans caused a lot of nature's destruction.*	Zerstörung

page	exercise	Workshop 1		
		to undertake [ˌʌndəˈteɪk], **undertook, undertaken** [ˌʌndəˈtʊk, ˌʌndəˈteɪkən]	*What projects has he undertaken so far?*	durchführen
		plight [plaɪt]	*The charity is dedicated to easing the plight of homeless people.*	Notlage
		amusement [əˈmjuːzmənt]	*The elephants are being exploited for tourists amusement.*	Vergnügen; Unterhaltung
		barbaric [bɑːˈbærɪk]	*The treatment the elephants are getting is barbaric.*	barbarisch; unzivilisiert
		cruel [ˈkruːl]	*I think that keeping animals in cages is cruel.*	grausam
		to upset [ˈʌpset], **upset, upset**	*The loud noise upset everyone.*	verärgern; enttäuschen
		to **enlighten** [ɪnˈlaɪtən]	*Reading the book helped to enlighten her on the subject.*	aufklären; erleuchten
		footage [ˈfʊtɪdʒ]	*She used the footage in her documentary.*	Filmmaterial
		harrowing [ˈhærəʊɪŋ]	*It was a harrowing experience.*	erschütternd; quälend
		visible [ˈvɪzəbl]	*The problems were visible at the start.*	sichtbar
		distressed [dɪsˈtrɛst]	*After the accident she was very distressed.*	verzweifelt; gestresst
		alongside [əˌlɒŋˈsaɪd]	*Slums coexist alongside wealthy areas.*	neben; an der Seite von
		outraged [ˈaʊtreɪdʒd]	*She was outraged about how animals are treated in some shelters.*	entsetzt
		ignorance [ˈɪgnərəns]	*Did she act from ignorance or was it done on purpose?*	Unwissenheit; Ignoranz
		ignorant [ˈɪgnərənt]	*Many Europeans are ignorant about racism.*	unwissend; ignorant
		mahout [məˈhaʊt]	*The mahout was in charge of controlling the elephants.*	Mahout; Elefantenführer
		bull hook [bʊl hʊk]	*The bull hook was used by the elephant trainers.*	Elefantenhaken
		deflated [dɪˈfleɪtɪd]	*Do you feel more motivated or do you feel a bit deflated after those trips?*	entmutigt; entleert
		desirable [dɪˈzaɪərəbl]	*Is that a desirable outcome of the discussion?*	wünschenswert
		to **compromise** [ˈkɒmprəmaɪz]	*Our futures have been compromised and we have to save what we can.*	kompromettieren
		inspirational [ˌɪnspəˈreɪʃənl]	*Her speech was so inspirational, it motivated everyone to take action.*	begeisternd
		approach [əˈprəʊtʃ]	*Some activists take a very hard line approach to eco-activism.*	Ansatz; Kurs
		eco-activism [ˈiːkoʊˌæktɪvɪzəm]	*Some activists take a very hard line approach to eco-activism and are sometimes harming the cause.*	Öko-Aktivismus
		disruption [dɪsˈrʌpʃn]	*There was a disruption to the lecture when a mobile started ringing.*	Störung; Unterbrechung

page	exercise	Workshop 1		
		irresponsible [ˌɪrɪ'spɒnsəbl]	*Do you think it's irresponsible to carry on like before?*	unverantwortlich
		to polarize ['poʊləˌraɪz]	*The controversial topic has the potential to polarize opinions.*	polarisieren; spalten
		overall [ˌəʊvə'ɔ:l]	*I was overall impressed by the efficiency and friendliness of the service.*	allgemein
	5a	**Islamophobia** [ˌɪslæmə'foʊbiə]	*Islamophobia is the fear, hatred, or prejudice against Islam and Muslims.*	Islamophobie
		disengaged [ˌdɪsɪn'geɪdʒd]	*Muslim youths are often seen as politically disengaged.*	desinteressiert
		hostility [hɒ'stɪlɪti]	*Some young Muslims fear that they might become targets of racism and hostility.*	Feindseligkeit; Aggressivität
		to politicize [pə'lɪtɪˌsaɪz]	*The organization seemed to be very politicized.*	politisieren; auf Politik beziehen
		hijab [hɪ'dʒɑ:b]	*Muslim women often wear a hijab.*	Hijab; Kopftuch
	5b	**connotation** [ˌkɒnə'teɪʃn]	*A word can have different connotations depending on the context.*	Konnotation; Beiklang
	6a	**racial** ['reɪʃl]	*Racial discrimination can be seen everywhere.*	Rassen-
	TIP	**to negotiate** [nɪ'gəʊʃieɪt]	*Negotiate your choice of topic with your partner.*	verhandeln; aushandeln
22	S1	**to appeal** [ə'pi:l]	*The new adult fiction is appealing to the reader's senses.*	ansprechen
	S2a	**manual** ['mænjul]	*He followed the steps outlined in the manual to repair the engine.*	Handbuch
	S3a	**to crackle** ['krækl]	*The dry leaves crackled under my boots.*	knistern; prasseln
		to spiral ['spaɪrl]	*Leaves were spiralling through the air.*	wirbeln
		to grease [gri:s]	*Line and grease the cake tin and pre-heat the oven to 160 degrees.*	einfetten
		to delay [dɪ'leɪ]	*Trains are often delayed.*	verzögern
		prominent ['prɒmɪnənt]	*He had prominent cheek bones.*	hervorstehend
		cheek [tʃi:k]	*Her cheeks turned red.*	Backe
		to resemble [rɪ'zembl]	*She resembles her mother.*	aussehen wie
		blade [bleɪd]	*Careful, those blades are sharp.*	Schneide
		yolk [jəʊk]	*You use three yolks but no eggwhite.*	Eigelb; Dotter
		silent ['saɪlənt]	*Nobody spoke, everybody was silent.*	stumm
		thrilling ['θrɪlɪŋ]	*The boat trip was thrilling.*	spannend
		renovation [ˌrenə'veɪʃn]	*During the renovations, the science lab will be closed.*	Sanierung
		to relocate [ˌri:ləʊ'keɪt]	*= to move*	umziehen
		almond ['ɑ:mənd]	*We use ground almonds in many recipes.*	Mandel

page	exercise	Workshop 1		
23	S1	**cloister** ['klɔɪstə]	*The monastery had a peaceful cloister where the monks would walk and pray.*	Kloster; Kreuzgang
		subsequently ['sʌbsɪkwəntli]	*= later*	später
		authenticity [ɔːˈθɛntɪsɪti]	*His story was lacking authenticity.*	Authentizität; Echtheit
	S2	**situated** ['sɪtʃueɪtɪd]	*The government is situated in the capital.*	gelegen
		lounge [laʊndʒ]	*Jaz Hostel Agra offers a restaurant, free parking, free bikes and a shared lounge.*	Aufenthaltsraum
		to boast [bəʊst]	*All rooms boast a kitchenette and a private bathroom.*	sich rühmen
		kitchenette [ˌkɪtʃɪˈnɛt]	*It is a tiny flat, but it has a kitchenette and a private bathroom.*	Kochnische; kleine Küche
		toiletries ['tɔɪlɪtriːz]	*Shampoo, body lotion and shower gel are toiletries.*	Toilettenartikel
		to equip [ɪ'kwɪpt]	*Guest rooms are equipped with a seating area.*	ausrüsten
		exceptional [ɪk'sɛpʃənl]	*The staff were exceptionally friendly and helpful.*	außergewöhnlich; herausragend
24	1a	**to breed** [briːd] [bred, bred]	*City rubbish dumps breed diseases.*	(aus)brüten; züchten
		to boom [buːm]	*The IT sector is booming.*	boomed
		sector ['sektə]	*Bengaluru has a growing IT sector.*	Sektor
	2a	**to adjust** [ə'dʒʌst]	*You have to adjust to life in a different culture.*	(sich) anpassen
		reputation [ˌrepju'teɪʃn]	*Mumbai has a reputation as India's Silicon Valley.*	Ruf; Reputation
		facade [fə'sɑːd]	*There were new buildings with shining glass facades and interesting designs.*	Fassade
		prosperity [prɒ'sperəti]	*We want a better world with greater prosperity for all.*	Wohlstand
		roadside ['roʊdsaɪd]	*There are public water taps along the roadside but they often have very low water pressure.*	Straßenrand
		to pipe [paɪp]	*More privileged residents have tried to get water piped to their houses.*	*hier:* pumpen
		to ration ['ræʃən]	*The food was rationed.*	rationieren; einschränken
25	2c	**to renew** [rɪ'njuː]	*They renewed his contract.*	erneuern
		well [wel]	*Wells are being built to bring water to the villages.*	Brunnen
	3a	**extraordinary** [ɪk'strɔːrdɪneri]	*Kennedy had an extraordinary life that was cut short when he was shot.*	ungewöhnlich
		horrendous [hə'rendəs]	*= awful*	schrecklich
		violation [ˌvaɪə'leɪʃn]	*He acted in violation of the law.*	Verletzung
		to advocate ['ædvəkət]	*For example, the paper advocates for street children to have national identity cards.*	sich einsetzen

page	exercise	Workshop 1		
		kindness ['kaɪndnəs]	*He showed kindness by sharing his lunch with a classmate.*	Freundlichkeit; Güte
		to **humanize** ['hju:mənaɪz]	*There are stories of kindness that help humanize young people who are often ignored.*	vermenschlichen; humanisieren
		courage ['kʌrɪdʒ]	*In my opinion, this is a story of courage and inspiration.*	Mut
		to **convert** [kən'vɜ:rt]	*They've seen awful things, but their bravery has converted them into reporters who want change.*	konvertieren; umwandeln
		batuni [bə'tu:ni]	*She is a batuni, a real chatterbox.*	Schwätzer(in) (umgangssprachlich)
		to **submit** [səb'mɪt]	*You have to submit your essay tomorrow.*	abliefern
		editorial [ˌɛdɪ'tɔ:ril]	*Stories are noted down in Hindi and given to the editorial team.*	Leitartikel; redaktionell
		to **verify** ['verɪfaɪ]	*Check and verify your facts before you post.*	verifizieren
		rupee ['ru:pi]	*A rupee is a unit of currency used in several countries, including India.*	Rupie
		to **retrieve** [rɪ'tri:v]	*He reached into the drawer to retrieve his keys.*	zurückholen
		to **crush** [krʌʃ]	*They were crushed between rocks and died instantly.*	zerschlagen
		outcry ['aʊtkraɪ]	*There was a huge public outcry when the report was published.*	Aufschrei
		bravery ['breɪvəri]	*Positive reports, like acts of bravery are posted immediatly.*	Mut
		generosity [ˌdʒɛnə'rɒsɪti]	*She showed her generosity by sharing her prize with a friend.*	Großzügigkeit; Freigebigkeit
		youngster ['jʌŋstə]	*There were more youngsters than older people at the protest.*	Jugendliche(r)
		to **prioritize** [praɪ'ɒrətaɪz]	*You have to prioritize the tasks.*	priorisieren
	4b	**residential** [ˌrezɪ'denʃl]	*residential areas*	Wohn-
		powerhouse ['paʊəhaʊs]	*Dharavi is an economic powerhouse in the middle of Mumbai.*	Kraftzentrum
		embroidery [ɪm'brɔɪdəri]	*Ethnic embroidery is part of tradition.*	Stickerei
		small-scale ['smɔ:lˌskeɪl]	*This is an industrial centre with many small-scale industries.*	Klein…
		apparent [ə'pærənt]	*This diversity is apparent in the temples, mosques, churches and pagodas that stand side by side.*	offensichtlich; erkennbar
		pagoda [pə'goʊdə]	*A pagoda is a multi-tiered tower, associated with Asian religious architecture.*	Pagode
	5	**entitled** [ɪn'taɪtld]	*Do some research for a talk entitled 'India: the rich and the poor'.*	mit dem Titel

page	exercise	Workshop 1		
26	2c	**praise** [preɪz]	*There was more praise for her hard work in contrast to criticism she had received in the past.*	Lob
		hymn [hɪm]	*They were singing hymns in church.*	Hymne; Kirchenlied
		narrative ['nærətɪv]	*The text explodes with narrative force.*	Geschichte; Erzählung
	3b	**genius** ['dʒi:niəs]	*He's a genius, he knows everything.*	Genie; Begabung
		mysterious [mɪ'stɪəriəs]	*Each question on the TV show mysteriously connects to his life experiences.*	geheimnisvoll; rätselhaft
		to suspect [sə'spekt]	*I suspect he is wrong.*	vermuten
		confession [kən'feʃn]	*They didn't believe him and wanted a confession.*	Geständnis
		guilt [gɪlt]	*He didn't show guilt for his crimes when he was caught.*	Schuld; Schuldgefühl
	3c	**victory** ['vɪktəri]	*The team scored two victories in a row.*	Sieg
		to admit [əd'mɪt]	*The teenager admitted knowing nothing about Mandela.*	zugeben; eingestehen
	4a	**to whisper** ['wɪspə]	*Don't whisper, speak up.*	flüstern
27	TIP	**subtle** ['sʌtl]	*He is very direct, not very subtle.*	subtil
	5a	**brass** [bræs]	*brass ornaments*	Messing
		figurine ['fɪgjəri:n]	*Small elephant figurines decorated the shelves.*	Figur; Statuette
		fabric ['fæbrɪk]	*The dresses were made of colourful fabric.*	Stoff
		dresser ['drɛsə]	*You can put your clothes in the dresser.*	Kommode
		puppet ['pʌpɪt]	*He used puppets to entertain children at the birthday party.*	Marionette
		a clean slate [ə kli:n sleɪt]	*The matter was finished and he could start with a clean slate.*	ein unbeschriebenes Blatt
		to reassure [ˌri:ə'ʃʊr]	*I wanted to reassure her that I liked her.*	versichern
		splash [splæʃ]	*There was a splash and a fish jumped out of the water.*	Platschen
		to wrench [rɛntʃ]	*= to pull*	reissen; ziehen
		to splutter ['splʌtə]	*I spluttered out the water.*	prusten
		to pluck [plʌk]	*= to snatch*	*hier:* ziehen
		riverbank ['rɪvərbæŋk]	*The riverbank was full of discarded waste and plastic that the river had deposited.*	Ufer
		to lower ['loʊə]	*We need to lower pollution to save the environment.*	senken; herabsetzen
		guard [gɑ:d]	*The guards were constantly watching the prisoners.*	Wächter(in); Wachsamkeit
		tide [taɪd]	*Careful, the tide is rising, don't swim out.*	Strömung; Gezeiten

page	exercise	Workshop 1		
		to hack up [hæk ʌp]	*The man helped me up onto the steps, where I hacked up more water.*	heraufhusten
		to spare [speə]	*They said I lived because the Gods had spared me.*	*hier:* verschonen
		to overwhelm [ˌoʊvə'wɛlm]	*I felt overwhelmed by all the people pushing up close to stare at me.*	überwältigen
		to humiliate [hju:'mɪlieɪt]	*Don't humiliate your friends when they make mistakes; instead, offer them support and understanding.*	demütigen; erniedrigen
		to vow [vaʊ]	*I vowed never to lie to her.*	schwören
		undoubtedly [ʌn'daʊtɪdli]	*My experiences have undoubtedly shaped who I am today, providing me with an unshakable faith in the importance of family.*	zweifellos
		unshakable [ʌn'ʃeɪkəbl]	*She had an unshakable trust in her parents.*	unerschütterlich
		goodness ['gʊdnəs]	*He believed in the goodness of people.*	Güte; Wohlwollen
		to grasp [grɑ:sp]	*You should grasp opportunities as they are presented.*	greifen; festhalten
		astonished [ə'stɒnɪʃ]	*I'm astonished by how fast my little brother is learning to read.*	verblüfft; erstaunt
		miraculous [mɪ'rækjʊləs]	*I didn't expect a miraculous solution to my problems.*	wunderbar; erstaunlich
28	1a	**heel** [hi:l]	*She likes to wear shoes with high heels.*	Absatz
		head over heels [hɛd 'oʊvə hi:lz]	*It's like they're in the dark about what it's like to be head over heels for someone.*	Hals über Kopf
		matchmaking ['mætʃmeɪkɪŋ]	*The family did the matchmaking, but the young people were involved.*	Verkuppeln
		squad [skwɒd]	*= team*	Truppe
		awkwardness ['ɔ:kwədnəs]	*My first date was a mix of awkwardness and excitement.*	Unbeholfenheit; Peinlichkeit
		compatible [kəm'pætəbl]	*They look good together, they are really compatible.*	kompatibel
		lookout ['lʊkaʊt]	*He's always on the lookout for new jobs.*	Ausschau
		to hang [hæŋ]	*In the past you could be hanged for serious crimes.*	hängen
	2a	**to button-hole** ['bʌtn hoʊl]	*She button-holed me and demanded an explanation.*	sich vorknöpfen
		to glue [glu:]	*My eyes were glued to the screen.*	kleben
		to miss a sitter [mɪs ə 'sɪtə]	*In the final minutes of the game, the striker managed to miss a sitter.*	eine Chance vergeben
		bloodshot ['blʌdʃɒt]	*His eyes looked a little bloodshot.*	blutunterlaufen; gerötet
		to glare [glɛə]	*He was angry and kept glaring at her.*	starren

page	exercise	Workshop 1		
		midfield ['mɪd,fi:ld]	*Liverpool went past the Spurs midfield with ease.*	in der Mitte des Spielfeldes
		ease [i:z]	*They won the game with ease.*	Leichtigkeit
		to sort (out) [sɔ:rt]	*He helped me sort out my problems.*	(aus)sortieren
29	3	**to arise** [ə'raɪz], **arose, arisen** [ə'rəʊz, ə'rɪzn]	*The conflict arises because his father is very traditional.*	entstehen
		abusive [ə'bju:sɪv]	*She was hit by her abusive brother.*	gewalttätig
		to defy [dɪ'faɪ]	*He defied everything his parents wanted for him.*	trotzen; sich widersetzen
		fate [feɪt]	*It was my fate to look after the family.*	Schicksal
		to retaliate [rɪ'tælieɪt]	*To save the family honour his father retaliates by taking him on a trip to India, where he is kidnapped.*	sich rächen
	5a	**unreal** [,ʌn'rɪl]	*The special effects were so good, they seemed unreal.*	irreal
	5b	**to ground** [graʊnd]	*My parents grounded me for a week.*	Hausarrest geben
	5b	**to get engaged** [gɛt ɪn'geɪdʒd]	*Azari and I can't meet alone until we get engaged.*	sich verloben
		casino [kə'si:noʊ]	*They spent too much money on online casino games and lost a fortune.*	Kasino; Spielbank
30	2a	**to praise** [preɪz]	*She is praised for bringing a new sound into mainstream western music.*	loben
		fusion ['fju:ʒən]	*She is bringing an Asian fusion sound into mainstream western music.*	Fusion; Verschmelzung
		chronic ['krɒnɪk]	*He is suffering from a chronic disease.*	chronisch; anhaltend
		syndrome ['sɪndroʊm]	*She developed a rare chronic condition and had to have lifelong medication and constant medical supervision.*	Syndrom; Krankheitsbild
		to tingle ['tɪŋgl]	*She felt a tingling feeling in her hand.*	kribbeln
		arguably ['a:rgjuəbli]	*Chandra arguably has the relevant skills to mentor upcoming musicians.*	zweifellos
		upcoming [,ʌp'kʌmɪŋ]	*We are preparing for our upcoming trip to South Africa.*	aufstrebend; bevorstehend
		scale [skeɪl]	*Her artistic talent shines on any scale.*	Skala; Waage
31	3a	**inequality** [,ɪnɪ'kwɒləti]	*≠ equality*	Ungleichheit
		gutter ['gʌtə]	*They were so poor, they practically lived in the gutters.*	Gosse
		to credit ['kredɪt]	*Superstar Divine is often credited with putting Mumbai on the hip-hop map.*	zuschreiben
		misogynist [mɪ'sɒdʒɪnɪst]	*The rap, instead of having misogynist lyrics, is about respect for girls.*	Frauenfeind; Frauenhasser
		disguise [dɪs'gaɪz]	*They didn't want to be recognized and wore disguise.*	Verkleidung
		chorus ['kɔ:rəs]	*It's easy to learn the chorus lines by heart.*	Refrain; Chor

page	exercise	Workshop 1		
		to admire [əd'maɪə]	*I couldn't tell her how much I admire her.*	bewundern
32	S1	**omnivore** ['ɒmnɪvɔ:r]	*Even though they might be omnivores, many Indians don't eat beef.*	Allesesser
	S2a	**to revere** [rɪ'vɪərd]	*Cows in particular are revered by Hindus, they are sacred animals.*	verehren
		pasture ['pɑ:stʃə]	*Forests have been burnt to create pasture for cattle.*	Weide(land)
		dung [dʌŋ]	*Cows produce dung for manure and fuel.*	Dung; Mist
		plough [plaʊ]	*The plough is drawn by cows.*	Pflug
		cart [kɑ:rt]	*Cows produce dung for manure and fuel and can pull ploughs and carts.*	Wagen; Karren
		karma ['kɑ:rmə]	*He believed it was karma when he won the lottery after helping a stranger.*	Karma
		to reincarnate [ˌri:ɪn'kɑ:rneɪt]	*To be reincarnated is one of the believes of this religion.*	wiedergeboren werden
		captivity [kæp'tɪvəti]	*Raising animals in captivity is cruel.*	Gefangenschaft
		to fool [fu:l]	*Don't be fooled by fake statistics.*	täuschen
		overcrowded [ˌəʊvə'kraʊdɪd]	*Most meat comes from farming methods where animals live in filthy, overcrowded spaces.*	überfüllt
		compassionate [kəm'pæʃənət]	*Compassionate people are often vegetarians.*	mitfühlend
		beak [bi:k]	*The bird used its beak to pick up seeds from the ground.*	Schnabel
		aspirational [ˌæspɪ'reɪʃənl]	*= ambitious*	erstrebenswert; ambitioniert
		occasion [ə'keɪʒn]	*We eat it only on special occasions.*	Gelegenheit
		acquire [ə'kwaɪə]	*I never acquired a taste for meat.*	erwerben; akquirieren
		enthusiasm [ɪn'θju:ziæzəm]	*Her speech was received by his audience with huge enthusiasm and everybody applauded.*	Enthusiasmus
		iron ['aɪən]	*Non-meat sources of iron like leafy greens contain better iron than red meat.*	Eisen
		enthusiasm [ɪn'θju:ziæzəm]	*Her speech was received by his audience with huge enthusiasm and everybody applauded.*	Enthusiasmus
33	S1	**taboo** [tæ'bu:]	*What is normal in one country can be taboo in another.*	Tabu
		alliance [ə'laɪəns]	*They discussed the alliance of western states.*	Bündnis; Allianz
		to broadcast ['brɔ:dkɑ:st]	*It was broadcast on the internet first.*	senden
		to publicize ['pʌblɪˌsaɪz]	*The internet is a place where you can publicize your campaigns on an international or a global level.*	veröffentlichen

page	exercise	Workshop 1		
	S2	**mutual** ['mju:tʃul]	*John and I have a mutual friend who is a real sceptic.*	gegenseitig; gemeinsam
		sceptic ['skɛptɪk]	*She never believes politicians, she's a real sceptic.*	Skeptiker(in)
	TIP	**evidence** ['evɪdəns]	*Find strong supporting evidence.*	Beweis(e)
38	2a	**appalling** [ə'pɔ:lɪŋ]	*They lived in appalling conditions.*	entsetzlich
		tragic ['trædʒɪk]	*She was killed in a tragic accident.*	tragisch
	2b	**affair** [ə'feə]	*Can music have an impact on global affairs?*	Angelegenheit; Affäre
	TIP	**storyline** ['stɔ:ri,laɪn]	*Before you write, develop the storyline.*	Handlungsstrang
	4	**to examine** [ɪg'zæmɪn]	*Examine his personal and political background, and also consider how this has influenced his work.*	untersuchen
	6	**prior** ['praɪə]	*You have to apply prior knowledge and experiences.*	vorherige
		to contradict [,kɒntrə'dɪkt]	*The two brothers contradicted each other in the interview.*	widersprechen
39		**to curdle** ['kɜ:rdl]	*The milk curdled and became sour.*	gerinnen; koagulieren
		untended [ʌn'tɛndɪd]	*Mice were running around untended.*	unbeachtet
		ant [ænt]	*Most ants live in the ground.*	Ameise
		dust [dʌst]	*There was dust under the bed.*	Staub
		broom [bru:m]	*He cleaned the floors with a broom.*	Besen
		solitary ['sɒlətri]	*= alone*	einsam
		to surrender [sə'rendə]	*The enemy surrendered.*	sich ergeben
		stubborn ['stʌbərn]	*She was a stubborn student.*	dickköpfig
		pigeon ['pɪdʒɪn]	*Pigeons in big cities are very common, often looking for food in crowded urban areas.*	Taube
		gleeful ['gli:fʊl]	*= happy*	fröhlich; vergnügt
		to age [eɪdʒ]	*My parents are ageing but very fit.*	alt werden; altern
		expiry date [ɪk'spaɪəri deɪt]	*The expiry date on the yogurt was yesterday, but you can still eat it.*	Verfallsdatum
		intact [ɪn'tækt]	*≠ damaged*	unversehrt; intakt
		to beep [bi:p]	*Something is beeping in the kitchen.*	piepen; signalisieren
		reminder [rɪ'maɪndə]	*She wrote herself a reminder to check the mail.*	Erinnerung
		thereafter [,ðɛr'æftə]	*= after that*	danach
		monsoon [mɒn'su:n]	*The monsoons were early with heavy rains.*	Monsun
		to redevelop [,ri:dɪ'vɛləp]	*The building down the road will be redeveloped.*	sanieren
		to furnish ['fɜ:rnɪʃ]	*Homes are provided fully furnished.*	einrichten; möblieren
		unborn [,ʌn'bɔ:n]	*Smoking can harm the unborn.*	Ungeborene(r)
		to prescribe [prɪ'skraɪb]	*What did the doctor prescribe?*	verschreiben
		to choke [tʃəʊk]	*He choked on a fishbone.*	ersticken

page	exercise	Workshop 1		
		to curse [kɜːrs]	*He was cursing the ad breaks because they interrupted the program.*	(ver)fluchen
		intensity [ɪnˈtɛnsɪti]	*They are protesting with the same intensity as before.*	Intensität; Stärke
		telecast [ˈtɛlɪkæst]	*= broadcast*	Sendezeit
		pure [pjʊə]	*Pure chance made her an athlete.*	rein
		to proceed [prəˈsiːd]	*= to continue*	fortfahren
		void [vɔɪd]	*= empty* *≠ valid*	nichtig
40	1	**imperial** [ɪmˈpɪəril]	*The former imperial domain of British India was granted independence.*	kaiserlich; imperial
		domain [dəˈmeɪn]	*The lion roamed across its domain, the African savannah.* *= territory*	Domäne; Bereich
		firm [fɜːm]	*He firmly believed that Muslims and Hindus could not live in one nation.*	fest
		exodus [ˈɛksədəs]	*This mass exodus is viewed as a tragedy today.*	Flucht; Exodus
		territorial [ˈɛksədəs]	*They agreed on new territorial borders.*	Gebiets-
		dispute [dɪˈspjuːt]	*The two friends had a small dispute over who would get the last cookie.*	Disput; Streitgespräch
		loyalty [ˈlɔɪəlti]	*There is a strong sense of loyalty in their friendship group.*	Loyalität; Treue
		vulnerable [ˈvʌlnərəbl]	*Many parts of the world are ecologically vulnerable.*	verletzlich; verwundbar
41	2	**to devastate** [ˈdɛvəˌsteɪt]	*The floods devastated the village completely.*	verwüsten; zerstören
		footsteps [ˈfʊtˌstɛps]	*I intend to follow in the footsteps of other activists.*	Fußstapfen
		to collaborate [kəˈlæbəreɪt]	*Collaborating with international environmental organizations is really effective.*	zusammenarbeiten
		like-minded [ˈlaɪkˌmaɪndɪd]	*I've realized how important social media is in reaching like-minded activists.*	gleichgesinnt
42	4b	**patriarchal** [ˌpeɪtriˈɑːrkl]	*Pakistan was a patriarchal society, where woman played minor roles.*	patriarchalisch
43	1	**to hoist** [hɔɪst]	*The national flag is hoisted every morning outside the building.*	hissen
		rendition [rɪnˈdɪʃən]	*There was a rendition of the national anthem.*	Wiedergabe
		patriotic [ˌpeɪtriˈɒtɪk]	*Patriotic parades, armed forces marches, and schoolchildren's performances are highlights of the celebrations.*	patriotisch
		kite [kaɪt]	*When it's windy, you can fly kites.*	Drachen

page	exercise	Workshop 1		
		fertility [fə'tɪlɪti]	*The Festival of Colours celebrates spring, fertility, love, and colours.*	Fruchtbarkeit; Fertilität
		dizzying ['dɪziɪŋ]	*The roads dizzying turns made me feel sick.*	schwindelerregend
		array [ə'reɪ]	*= range*	Vielfalt
		festive ['fɛstɪv]	*What are your favourite festive celebrations during the year?*	festlich
		vivid ['vɪvɪd]	*We lived in a vivid neighbourhood.*	lebhaft
		bonfire ['bɒnfaɪə]	*A bonfire is a large outdoor fire used for burning wood in celebrations or events.*	Lagerfeuer
		effigy ['ɛfɪdʒi]	*The effigy was burned in the bonfire.*	Abbild; Effigie
		flame [fleɪm]	*The flames of the fire could be seen in the dark.*	Flamme
		with regard to [wɪð rɪ'gɑ:rd tu:]	*Describe his situation with regard to his status as a prisoner.*	unter Berücksichtigung
		mischievous ['mɪstʃɪvəs]	*The mischievous little boy hid his sister's toy.*	schelmisch; unartig
44		**priority** [praɪ'ɒrəti]	*Education has a high priority.*	Priorität
		to disconnect [ˌdɪskə'nekt]	*Someone has disconnected the power lines, there is no electricity. = to connect*	trennen; abschalten
		charitable ['tʃærətəbl]	*She works for a charitable cause and doesn't earn much.*	Wohltätigkeits...
		pillar ['pɪlə]	*What are the pillars of the Islamic religion?*	Säule

page	exercise	Workshop 2		
52	1	**suburb** ['sʌbɜ:rb]	*We don't live in the centre, we live in the suburbs.*	Außenbezirk
		apartheid [ə'pɑ:rteɪd]	*Apartheid comes from the Afrikaans word for being apart or seperated.*	Apartheid
		to segregate ['sɛgrɪgeɪt]	*People of colour were segregated from the minority white population by law.*	trennen (durch Gesetzt)
53		**aardvark** ['ɑ:dvɑ:k]	*The aardvark slept all day and ate insects all night.*	Erdferkel
	2a	**contradiction** [ˌkɒntrə'dɪkʃn]	*His words were a contradiction; he said he was full but kept eating more.*	Widerspruch
		upmarket ['ʌpˌmɑ:rkɪt]	*The city has some very upmarket suburbs, but just around the corner, you're in neglected slum areas.*	exklusiv; reich
		to neglect [nɪ'glekt]	*There are neglected slum areas where people live in shacks.*	vernachlässigen
		shack [ʃæk]	*People live in shacks in the slums.*	Hütte
		flashy ['flæʃi]	*You don't show off flashy phones or cameras in poor areas – that's always a bad idea.*	auffällig; schrill

page	exercise	Workshop 2		
54	1a	**decent** ['di:snt]	*Some regions of the world simply don't have decent renewable resources.*	anständig
		sporty ['spɔ:ti]	*He is a very sporty person, fit and full of energy.*	sportlich
	1b	**to abolish** [ə'bɒlɪʃ]	*Apartheid was abolished in 1994.*	abschaffen
	2b	**unbroken** [ʌn'broʊkən]	*Her determination was unbroken.*	ungebrochen
		jointly ['dʒɔɪntli]	*The two men worked to finally end apartheid, for which they were jointly awarded the Nobel Peace Prize in 1993.*	zusammen
55	2c	**figurehead** ['fɪgjərhɛd]	*Mandela became a symbolic figurehead for anti-apartheid.*	Galionsfigur; Symbolfigur
		representative [ˌreprɪ'zentətɪv]	*The paintings are representative of English art in the early 15th century.*	repräsentativ
	3b	**status quo** ['steɪtəs 'kwoʊ]	*They could not change the status quo legally.*	Status quo
	4	**to assure** [ə'ʃʊə]	*He assured us of his support.*	versichern
		inalienable [ɪn'eɪliənəbl]	*Dignity is an inalienable human right.*	unveräußerlich; unabdingbar
		dignity ['dɪgnɪti]	*He treated everyone with dignity and respect.*	Würde
		skunk [skʌŋk]	*Skunks defend themselves by spraying at their enemies.*	Stinktier
		evocative [ɪ'vɒkətɪv]	*The old photo was evocative of her childhood memories.*	evokativ; anregend
	5	**scholarship** ['skɒləʃɪp]	*I was granted a scholarship and moved to Munich to study.*	Stipendium
		socialization [ˌsəʊʃəlaɪ'zeɪʃn]	*Education plays an important role in a child's socialization.*	Sozialisation
		to profile ['prəʊfaɪl]	*Black people are often racially profiled.*	ein Profil erstellen
		to dehumanize [di:'hju:mənaɪz]	*Bullying can dehumanize people, making them feel worthless.*	entmenschlichen
		to institutionalize [ɪn'stɪtju:ʃənəlaɪz]	*The new rules were quickly institutionalized in the company, becoming part of the daily routine.*	etablieren
		maiden ['meɪdn]	*The ship sank on its maiden voyage.*	*hier:* erstes
		academical [ˌækə'dɛmɪkl]	*Her academical interests led her to study ancient languages.*	akademisch
		to long ['lɒŋg]	*She longed to see her parents again after 20 years.*	verlangen
		ancestry ['ænsestri]	*What is his ancestry, is he South African?*	Abstammung
		to brand [brænd]	*She was branded as a leftist.*	branden
		to dilute [daɪ'lu:t]	*Dilute the juice with water.*	verdünnen
		transportation [ˌtrænspɔ:r'teɪʃən]	*Transportation in cities and especially the countryside is important.*	Verkehr

page	exercise	Workshop 2		
		basics ['beɪsɪks]	*You should learn the basics when you are still young.*	Grundlagen
		to **place** [pleɪs]	*They placed me with the students from aonther course.*	plazieren; vermitteln
		to **impose** [ɪm'pəʊz]	*In the early 20th century, the government imposed restrictions on blacks, including a nightly curfew.*	verhängen; durchsetzen
		to **elaborate** [ɪ'læbərət]	*Can you elaborate on your plans for the weekend?*	weiter ausführen
56	2a	to **harden** ['hɑːrdən]	*He has been hardened by his tough life.*	(ab)härten
		crook [krʊk]	*Be careful, there are crooks who are trying to get your money.*	Gauner(in); Schwindler(in)
		to **abandon** [ə'bændən]	*She abandoned her best friend.*	im Stich lassen
		to **foresee** [fɔː'siː]	*The change came suddenly and couldn't be foreseen.*	vorhersehen
	3a	**accustomed** [ə'kʌstəmd]	*When you are accustomed to privilege, equality can seem like oppression.*	gewohnt; vertraut
		shield [ʃiːld]	*A glass shield seperates the visitors from the animals.*	Scheibe; Schild
		to **be exposed to** [bi ɪk'spoʊzd tuː]	*Privilege is like a glass shield, protecting some from life's harsh realities while leaving others exposed to the storms.*	ausgesetzt sein
		headstart ['hɛdstɑːrt]	*Privilege is the headstart in the race of life, leaving others far behind at the starting line.*	Vorsprung
57	3c	**inclusivity** [ɪn'kluːsɪvɪti]	*What barriers are there in schools regarding inclusivity?*	Inklusivität
		participant [pɑː'tɪsɪpənt]	*How many participants were there?*	Teilnehmer(in)
	4a	to **capitalize** ['kæpɪtəlaɪz]	*Apartheid capitalized on differences in race, culture and gender.*	ausnutzen; kapitalisieren
		sameness ['seɪmnəs]	*The sameness of their daily routine became boring.*	Gleichheit
		worldview ['wɜːrldˌvjuː]	*This worldview is very narrow.*	Weltsicht
		problematic [ˌprɒblə'mætɪk]	*I find your attitude problematic.*	problematisch
		divisive [dɪ'vaɪsɪv]	*The new policy was divisive, causing arguments among the community members.*	spaltend; trennend
		to **devise** [dɪ'vaɪz]	*A number of academics devised an activity called the 'privilege walk'.*	ausdenken; entwickeln
		to **visualize** ['vɪʒuəlaɪz]	*The infographic visualizes the main issues.*	darstellen; visualisieren
		systemic [sɪ'stiːmɪk]	*We are experiencing a systemic crisis.*	systembedingt
		able-bodiedness ['eɪbl'bɒdidnəs]	*Able-bodieness must be maintained at all costs.*	körperliche Fitness
		to **portray** [pɔː'treɪ]	*The book portrays a whole family.*	darstellen

page	exercise	Workshop 2		
		to position [pə'zɪʃn]	= *put*	positionieren
		grid [grɪd]	*The power from different resources is put into the grid.*	Netz
		poignant ['pɔɪnjənt]	*Her artwork is a commentary on modern life that poignantly represents society's current state.*	ergreifend; schmerzlich
		masculinity [ˌmæskjʊ'lɪnɪti]	*Masculinity is still very important in some societies.*	Männlichkeit
		heteronormativity [ˌhɛtəroʊnɔ:r'mætɪvɪti]	*He believed in the concept of heteronormativity and assumed that everyone is straight.*	Heteronormativität
58	2a	**to label** ['leɪbl]	*Born of Indian and Portuguese parents, he was labelled as Cape Coloured, which disqualified him from playing in a 'whites only' team.*	beschriften; etikettieren; auszeichnen
		to disqualify [dɪs'kwɒlɪˌfaɪ]	*The team was disqualified from the match.*	disqualifizieren; ausschließen
		considerable [kən'sɪdərəbl]	*There was considerable speculation about whether the company would show its new product at the event.*	bedeutend; erheblich
		to permit [pə'mɪt]	*He was not permitted to play with the team.*	erlauben
		to omit [oʊ'mɪt]	*He was omitted from the touring team.*	auslassen
		sharp [ʃɑ:p]	*Words can be as sharp as knives.*	scharf
		controversy ['kɒntrəvɜ:si]	*The omission of Dolly provoked one of the sharpest controversies in the history of English cricket.*	Kontroverse
		uproar ['ʌpˌrɔ:r]	*Their decision not to include him was folowed by an uproar.*	Aufruhr
		to bribe [braɪb]	*A businessman might have tried to bribe Dolly not to play.*	bestechen
		furious ['fjʊəriəs]	= *very angry*	wütend
	2b	**to stump** [stʌmp]	*Her question managed to stump everyone and nobody said anything.* ! *ein Wortspiel: „stump" heißt auch Pfosten beim Kricket*	ins Stocken bringen
	TIP	**certainty** ['sɜ:tnti]	*There was no certainly that the package would arrive in time.*	Gewissheit
		unsure [ʌn'ʃʊə]	*I am unsure of the right way back.*	unsicher
	3a	**to classify** ['klæsɪfaɪ]	*You were classified as belonging to one of four groups.*	einstufen
		sportsperson ['spɔ:rtsˌpɜ:rsən]	*He was voted sportsperson of the year.*	Sportler(in)
59	4a	**unconquerable** [ʌn'kɒŋkərəbl]	*Despite numerous challenges, her spirit remained unconquerable.*	unbesiegbar
		aspiration [ˌæspɪ'reɪʃən]	*She has big aspirations to become a doctor one day.*	Bestreben; Ambition

page	exercise	Workshop 2		
		damn [dæm]	= *terrible*	verdammt
		disgrace [dɪs'greɪs]	*Cheating in the exam was a disgrace to the school's honour.*	Schande
		calculation [ˌkælkju'leɪʃn]	*A political calculation may lead to unexpected compromises.*	Berechnung; Kalkulation
	4b	**segregation** [ˌsegrɪ'geɪʃn]	*Apartheid was built on segregation.*	Rassentrennung
		antelope ['æntɪləʊp]	*The hunter killed the antilope.*	Antilope
		emblem ['ɛmbləm]	*They have the famous antelope emblem on their sweaters.*	Emblem; Symbol
	5b	**to qualify** ['kwɒlɪˌfaɪ]	*South Africa didn't qualify for the final.*	(sich) qualifizieren
	6	**jersey** ['dʒɜːrzi]	*They played in their traditional jerseys.*	Trikot; Jersey
		bodyguard ['bɒdigaːd]	*Celebrities and politicians often have bodyguards.*	Leibwächter(in)
		icing ['aɪsɪŋ]	*This was the icing on the cake and something no one, not even Mandela, could have predicted.*	Zuckerguß
		debatable [dɪ'beɪtəbl]	*The results are debatable and can't be proved.*	umstritten
		elite [ɪ'liːt]	*Black players are becoming more and more a part of elite rugby.*	Elite; Oberschicht
		to captain ['kæptɪn]	*He captained the team for many years.*	Kapitän(in) sein
60	1	**to compile** [kəm'paɪl]	*Compile a list of top sports idols.*	zusammenstellen; kompilieren
	2a	**barefoot** ['bɛərfʊt]	*They ran barefoot like all the children in rural South Africa.*	barfuß
		stormy ['stɔːrmi]	*The weather was very stormy.*	stürmisch
	2b	**skinny** ['skɪni]	*Zola was a skinny, small girl.*	dünn
		to idolize ['aɪdəlaɪz]	*She idolized her sister and did everything she wanted.*	vergöttern; idealisieren
		altitude ['æltɪˌtud]	*Runners often train at high altitude to improve performance.*	Höhe
		to surround [sə'raʊnd]	*The city is surrounded by hills.*	umgeben
		irresistible [ˌɪrɪ'zɪstəbl]	≠ *boring*	unwiderstehlich
		to boo [buː]	*People booed her and shouted insults.*	ausbuhen
		insult ['ɪnsʌlt]	*People booed her and shouted insults.*	beleidigen; verletzen
61	3a	**para-athlete** ['pærəˌæθliːt]	*A para-athlete is a person with a disability who participates in sports and athletic competitions, in events specially designed or adapted for individuals with disabilities.*	Para-Athlet(in)
		to paralyse ['pærəlaɪz]	*He was paralyzed and used a wheelchair.*	lähmen

page	exercise	Workshop 2		
		to derive [dɪˈraɪv]	*The word derives from a Greek phrase.*	(sich) ableiten; herleiten
		disabled [dɪsˈeɪbld]	*I also looked up whether it is OK to use the word 'disabled' and it seems that it is.*	behindert
		impairment [ɪmˈpɛərmənt]	*He has a visual impairment in the right eye.*	Beeinträchtigung; Schädigung
		to confine [kənˈfaɪn]	*Don't say someone is 'confined to a wheelchair' but call that person 'a wheelchair user'.*	fesseln an; einsperren
		sensitive [ˈsensətɪv]	*In a sensitive political climate it is important to stay calm.*	empfindlich
		overtly [oʊˈvɜːrtli]	*He was overtly enthusiastic about the new project, sharing his ideas with everyone.*	offen
		patronizing [ˈpætrənaɪzɪŋ]	*You should avoid being too sensitive or politically correct to prevent appearing patronizing.*	herablassend
	3b	**cerebral palsy** [ˌserəbrl ˈpɔːlzi]	*She had cerebral palsy and was unable to walk.*	zerebrale Lähmung
		eligible [ˈelɪdʒəbl]	*Who is eligible to compete in para sports?*	berechtigt
		medallist [ˈmɛdəlɪst]	*The Olympic medallist proudly stood on the podium.*	Medaillengewinner(in)
	4a	**gorgeous** [ˈgɔːdʒəs]	*She looked gorgeous in the designer dress.*	wunderschön
		hardship [ˈhɑːdʃɪp]	*She had to fight great hardship to achieve her dream of going to college.*	Not; Elend
		virus [ˈvaɪrəs]	*The Corona virus killed millions of people worldwide.*	Virus
		sinister [ˈsɪnɪstə]	*The house looked sinister in the night.* = *evil*	bösartig
62	CC	**comedian** [kəˈmiːdiən]	*Sarah Millican is a comedian, famous for her witty humour.*	Komiker(in)
	S1	**autobiography** [ˌɔːtəbaɪˈɒgrəfi]	*She wrote her biography when she turned 80.*	Autobiografie
	S2b	**autobiographical** [ˌɔːtəbaɪˈɒgrəfɪkl]	*He wrote an autobiographical novel about his upbringing.*	autobiografisch
		whilst [waɪlst]	= *while*	während
		simplistic [sɪmˈplɪstɪk]	*Noah's writing style is simplistic, and often funny.* ≠ *complicated*	einfach
		to insist [ɪnˈsɪst]	*An example of this and his effective use of humour is when Noah describes how his grandfather insists on being his chauffeur.*	bestehen auf
		chauffeur [ˈʃoʊfə]	*Famous people don't drive themselves, they have a chauffeur.*	Chauffeur(in); Fahrer(in)

page	exercise	Workshop 2		
		perception [pəˈsepʃn]	*Her perception of the situation was different from mine.*	Wahrnehmung
		flawed [flɔːd]	*He had a flawed understanding of the project's requirements.*	fehlerhaft; mangelhaft
		invaluable [ɪnˈvæljuəbl]	*His language skills are invaluable when connecting with people of different races and backgrounds.*	unschätzbar; unbezahlbar
	S3a	**imagery** [ˈɪmɪdʒəri]	*The book's vivid imagery helped me to understand the issues.*	Bilder; Bildsprache
		simile [ˈsɪmɪli]	*A simile is a figure of speech that compares two different things in an interesting way.*	Vergleich
		brittle [ˈbrɪtl]	*≠ solid*	spröde; brüchig
		fierce [fɪərs]	*as fierce as a lion* *= strong* *≠ weak*	heftig; wild
		archer [ˈɑːtʃə]	*An archer shoots with arrows.*	Bogenschütze / -schützin
		cord [kɔːrd]	*= string*	Schnur; Kordel
		potion [ˈpoʊʃən]	*The wizzard gave him a magic potion.*	Trank
		glory [ˈglɔːri]	*The sun's glory was evident in the breathtaking sunrise.*	Ehre; Schönheit
		creation [kriˈeɪʃn]	*Her latest painting is truly a beautiful creation, full of colour and life.*	Schöpfung
		hatred [ˈheɪtrɪd]	*= hate* *≠ love*	Hass
		hyperbole [haɪˈpɜːbəli]	*Hyperbole is simply an exaggerated statement.*	Übertreibung
		swift [ˈswɪft]	*= quick*	zügig
		to correspond [ˌkɒrəˈspɒnd]	*If sound corresponds to a sound, the rhyme's working.*	übereinstimmen
		to smirk [smɜːrk]	*They were smirking behind his back.*	grinsen
		to lurk [lɜːrk]	*She was lurking in the background.*	lauern
		allusion [əˈluːʒn]	*Allusion is a reference to a past piece of writing.*	Anspielung
		to ignite [ɪgˈnaɪt]	*These ideas were igniting and inspiring a new generation of activists.*	entzünden; anzünden
		eternity [ɪˈtɜːrnɪti]	*They say eternity is symbolized by the ocean.*	Ewigkeit
		to symbolize [ˈsɪmbəlaɪz]	*What symbolizes 'life' in your culture?*	symbolisieren
	S3b	**to crack** [kræk]	*The walls began to crack and then collapsed.*	knacken
		to crumble [ˈkrʌmbl]	*Old bread gets hard and crumbles.*	zerbröckeln; zerfallen
		benchmark [ˈbɛntʃmaːrk]	*This is the benchmark we get measured against.*	Maßstab; Benchmark

page	exercise	Workshop 2		
63	S1a	**recess** ['ri:ses]	*Recess is between lessons three and four.* *= break*	Pause
		occupy ['ɒkjupaɪ]	*They occupied the same table every day.*	einnehmen
		in an instant ['ɪnstənt]	*In an instant I could see what was happening.*	sofort; Moment
		outsider ['aʊtˌsaɪdə]	*In his bestseller, the main character feels like an outsider.*	Außenseiter(in)
		anomaly [ə'nɒməli]	*She has an anomaly that makes her immune to certain diseases.*	Anomalie; Abweichung
		to endear [ɪn'dɪə]	*The fact that I spoke African languages endeared me to the black kids.*	sich beliebt machen
	TIP	**resolution** [ˌrezə'lu:ʃn]	*Have you come to a resolution?*	Beschluss
		to annotate ['ænəteɪt]	*Annotate the text with useful information.*	annotieren; kommentieren
64	1	**itinerary** [aɪ'tɪnəreri]	*What is our itinerary for tomorrow?*	Reiseroute; Itinerar
		to coin [kɔɪn]	*Who first coined the phrase 'The big five'?*	prägen
		lioness ['laɪənɛs]	*The lioness roamed through the bush.*	Löwin
		rhino ['raɪnoʊ]	*Rhinos are large, plant eating animals known for their thick skin and horn on their noses.*	Nashorn
		aristocracy [ˌærɪ'stɒkrəsi]	*The richest people in a town used to be considered aristocracy.*	Aristokratie; Adel
		glamour ['glæmə]	*In colonial times, hunting was associated with aristocracy and glamour.*	Glamour; Glanz
		admiration [ˌædmɪ'reɪʃn]	*He was full of admiration for her achievements.*	Bewunderung
	2a	**obsessed** [əb'sɛst]	*She is totally obsessed with the new online game.*	besessen
		jealous ['dʒeləs]	*I'm so pleased you won and just a little bit jealous.*	eifersüchtig
		to conserve [kən'sɜ:rv]	*The prison was conserved as a museum.*	konservieren; bewahren
		carnivore ['kɑ:rnɪvɔ:r]	*≠ vegetarian*	Fleischfresser(in)
		enclosure [ɪn'kloʊʒə]	*Animls are kept in enclosures and cannot escape.*	Gehege
		indeed [ɪn'di:d]	*It seems to me that on the whole, ecotourism can indeed help to save threatened species from extinction.*	tatsächlich
65	4a	**to grapple** ['græpl]	*In 2020, the world grappled with the impact of Covid.*	ringen; kämpfen
		to disrupt [dɪs'rʌpt]	*The pandemic disrupted daily life because people had to stay at home.*	stören; unterbrechen
		perilous ['pɛrɪləs]	*= dangerous*	gefährlich

page	exercise	Workshop 2		
		additional [ə'dɪʃənl]	*The pandemic caused additional challenges.*	zusätzlich
		abrupt [ə'brʌpt]	*There was an abrupt end to the movie.*	abrupt; plötzlich
		to bustle ['bʌsl]	*Game reserves are typically bustling with travellers.*	wuseln
		to desert ['dezət]	*After the earthquake, the streets were deserted.*	im Stich lassen
		absence ['æbsəns]	*Her absence was felt by everyone in the group.*	Abwesenheit
		disturbance [dɪs'tɜ:rbəns]	*The loud noise outside created a disturbance during the meeting.*	Störung; Unruhe
		nonetheless [ˌnʌnðə'les]	*Nonetheless, amidst these alarming trends, there remains a glimmer of hope for positive change.*	nichtsdestoweniger; trotzdem
		amidst [ə'mɪdst]	*= in the middle of*	inmitten von
		glimmer ['glɪmə]	*There were glimmers of hope in all the darkness.*	Schimmer; Glitzern
		notable ['nəʊtəbl]	*One notable success story emerged from Marataba.*	bemerkenswert
		ray [reɪ]	*The current development a ray of hope.*	Strahl
		midst [mɪdst]	*There is always hope in the midst of challenges.*	Mitte
	5a	**domestic** [də'mɛstɪk]	*We are keeping dogs as domestic pets.*	häuslich; inländisch
		circus ['sɜ:kəs]	*The circus is in town.*	Zirkus
66	2a	**voluntourism** [vɒlən'tʊərɪzəm]	*Voluntourism is a combination of volunteering and tourism, where people travel to engage in voluntary work.*	Voluntourismus
	2b	**to misrepresent** [ˌmɪsrɪ'prɛzənt]	*Some companies misrepresent their projects because they want to be seen in a better light.*	falsch darstellen; verfälschen
67	3b	**conservationist** [ˌkɒnsə'veɪʃənɪst]	*Conservationists are fighting against climate change.*	Naturschützer(in)
		to patrol [pə'troʊl]	*My job is patrolling the fence around the reservation.*	patroulieren
		snare [snɛə]	*Poachers use snares to capture rhinos.*	Falle
		suspicious [sə'spɪʃəs]	*Her behaviour was very suspicious.*	verdächtig
		bullet ['bʊlɪt]	*He was killed by a bullet to the head.*	Kugel
		to snare [snɛə]	*Rhinos are endangered by snaring.*	Fallen stellen
	3c	**to empathize** ['ɛmpəθaɪz]	*Did you empathize with the losing team?*	mitfühlen; empathisieren
		exploitative [ɪk'splɔɪtətɪv]	*The soft focus and shots of half-naked women seemed exploitative and patronizing.*	ausbeuterisch

page	exercise	Workshop 2		
		to manipulate [mə'nɪpjuleɪt]	*Can social media manipulate what we think?*	manipulieren
	4a	**spokesperson** ['spoʊks,pɜ:rsən]	*She was a spokesperson for a charity.*	Sprecher(in)
		childcare ['tʃaɪld,kɛə]	*She works in childcare, taking care of little kids during the day.*	Kinderbetreuung
		paediatrician [,pi:di'ætrɪʃən]	*The pediatrician examined the child carefully, smiling at the worried parents.*	Kinderarzt; Kinderärztin
		commitment [kə'mɪtmənt]	*The organization made a commitment to guarantee real impact with their volunteer programs in Africa.*	Verpflichtung
		to direct [də'rekt]	*Who directed the film?*	Regie führen
		orphaned ['ɔ:rfənd]	*They took care of orphaned monkeys.*	verwaist
		baboon [bə'bu:n]	*Several baboons live in the forest.*	Pavian
		encounter [ɪn'kaʊntə]	*Each year, many baby animals are found injured and orphaned after bad encounters with humans, such as car accidents and hunting.*	Begegnung
		dorm [dɔ:rm]	*The accommodation was simple, you stay in dorms and cabins.*	Schlafsaal; Studentenwohnheim
		orphan ['ɔ:fn]	*Many rhinos become orphans when their mothers are killed.*	Waise
		motto ['mɒtəʊ]	*Their motto is 'Rescue, Rehabilitate and Release'.*	Motto
		quarantine ['kwɔ:rən,ti:n]	*They put us in quarantine for two weeks.*	Quarantäne
		to treasure ['treʒə]	*I treasure my friends and my family.*	schätzen
		poo [pu:]	*My job was to shovel Rhino poo together.* = *shit, faeces*	Kot
	5a	**lifelong** ['laɪflɒŋ]	*He says that he made some lifelong friends in school.*	lebenslang
	6a	**interviewee** [,ɪntəvju'i:]	*Decide who is the interviewer and who the interviewees, then record the interviews.* ≠ *interviewer*	Interviewte(r)
68	1b	**to attract** [ə'trækt]	*The museum attracts visitors from all over the world.*	anziehen
		to integrate ['ɪntɪgreɪt]	*Christian churches spread across South Africa integrating African musical elements into their worship.*	integrieren
		to result [rɪ'zʌlt]	*Christian churches in South Africa integrated African musical elements into their worship, resulting in South African gospel music.*	zur Folge haben
		bubblegum ['bʌbəlgʌm]	*Bubblegum is a name for South African pop music.*	Kaugummi

page	exercise	Workshop 2		
		liberation [ˌlɪbəˈreɪʃn]	*Anti-apartheid protest songs produced outside South Africa played a central role in the liberation struggle.*	Befreiung
	CC	**distinguished** [dɪˈstɪŋgwɪʃt]	*A distinguished career rewarded American singer-songwriter Paul Simon with 12 Grammy Awards.*	ausgezeichnet; hervorragend
		to reward [rɪˈwɔːd]	*Shew was rewarded with a prize for her engagement.*	belohnen
		boycott [ˈbɔɪkɒt]	*Simon recorded the album in South Africa during a UN cultural boycott in opposition to apartheid.*	Boycott
	2a	**to anger** [ˈæŋgə]	*The protest angered some politicians.*	verärgern
		credit [ˈkredɪt]	*Who has the credits for this book?*	Credit; Zuschreibung
		sole [səʊl]	*He has sole writing credits, but others contributed.*	alleinig
		backing artist [ˈbækɪŋ ˈɑːrtɪst]	*I was a backing artist on a couple of albums.*	Background-Sänger(in); Unterstützungs(Künstler(in))
		royalty [ˈrɔɪəlti]	*Writers and musicians often receive royalties for their work.*	*hier:* Tantiemen
		philosophical [ˌfɪləˈsɒfɪkl]	*Graceland started a larger philosophical debate about cultural appropriation.*	philosophisch
		artistic [ɑːˈtɪstɪk]	*Her artistic talent was evident in her beautiful paintings.*	künstlerisch
		unresolved [ˌʌnrɪˈzɒlvd]	*It's an unresolved debate that still pops up now and then.*	ungelöst
		to pop up [pɒp ˈʌp]	*The debate still pops up now and then.* *= appears*	auftauchen; erscheinen
	2b	**fundamental** [ˌfʌndəˈmentl]	*The white minority rule denied many fundamental rights to non-whites.*	Grund-
		to issue [ˈɪsjuː]	*As a result, the United Nations issued sanctions on the country.*	*hier*: verhängen
		sanction [ˈsæŋkʃn]	*The United Nations issued sanctions on the country.*	Sanktion
		to boycott [ˈbɔɪkɒt]	*As a result, the United Nations issued sanctions on the country – including UN Resolution 35/206, for 'all writers, musicians and other personalities to boycott' the nation.*	boykottieren
		solidarity [ˌsɒlɪˈdærɪti]	*The resolution was a show of solidarity against apartheid.*	Solidarität
		altruistic [ˌæltruˈɪstɪk]	*≠ selfish*	altruistisch; selbstlos
69	4b	**headdress** [ˈhɛddrɛs]	*A headdress is a decorative covering worn on the head as a symbol of status.*	Kopfbedeckung
		to frown (upon) [fraʊn]	*He frowned angrily.*	die Stirn runzeln (über)

page	exercise	Workshop 2		
		catwalk ['kætwɔ:k]	*The white models on the catwalk were all wearing black.*	Laufsteg; Catwalk
		cornrow ['kɔ:nrəʊ]	*Cornrows are a hairstyle where the hair is braided very close to the head.*	Cornrow; dünner Zopf
		wig [wɪg]	*The models were wearing wigs over their own hair.*	Perücke
		to **trivialize** ['trɪvɪəˌlaɪz]	*Don't trivialize the issue, it is important.*	banalisieren
		geisha ['geɪʃə]	*As a geisha she is trained in music and dancing.*	Geisha
		turban ['tɜ:rbən]	*A turban is made by wrapping a long piece of cloth around your head.*	Turban
		offensive [ə'fensɪv]	*= insulting*	beleidigend
		to **marginalize** ['mɑ:dʒɪnəlaɪ]	*A marginalized culture will have to adopt aspects of the stronger in order to fit in.*	ausgrenzen; marginalisieren
		to **be unable** [bi ʌn'eɪbl]	*I was unable to reach him.*	nicht in der Lage sein
	5b	**buzz word** ['bʌz wɜ:rd]	*Diversity is the buzz word right now: we are always being advised that we have to respect other cultures and enjoy the differences between us.*	Schlagwort; Modewort
		to **braid** [breɪd]	*I always braid my hair or it looks a real mess.*	flechten
		imitation [ˌɪmɪ'teɪʃən]	*He did a good imitation of the president.*	Imitation; Nachahmung
		sincere [sɪn'sɪə]	*Don't be so sincere, show a little more humour.*	ernsthaft
		flattery ['flætəri]	*Flattery means praising or complimenting someone, often in a way that makes them feel good.*	Schmeichelei
		braids [breɪdz]	*She wore her hair in braids.*	Zöpfe
		to **signal** ['sɪgnl]	*Braids are a way of signalling your tribe and status.*	signalisieren
		fashion fad ['fæʃən fæd]	*We must be careful not to trivialize African culture and reduce it to a fashion fad.*	Modetrend
	CC	**viral** ['vaɪrl]	*The video went viral and everybody watched it.*	viral
70	2c	to **sneak** [sni:k]	*I would sneak into my sister's room when it was empty.*	schleichen
		eyelash ['aɪlæʃ]	*Her eyelashes were very thick.*	Wimper
		feminine ['fɛmɪnɪn]	*It made my eyelashes bigger and it made me feel feminine and girly.*	weiblich
		clumpy ['klʌmpi]	*The mascara is very clumpy.*	klumpig
		to **contour** ['kɒntʊə]	*I use darker tones to contour my cheecks.*	konturieren
		slim [slɪm]	*She was tall with a slim face.*	schlank

page	exercise	Workshop 2		
		eyeshadow ['aɪˌʃædoʊ]	*I think dark eyeshadow looks best with brown eyes.*	Lidschatten
71	3a	**batik** [bə'ti:k]	*She likes to wear batik prints.*	Batik-
		beaded necklace ['bi:dɪd 'nɛkləs]	*She wore a beaded necklace.*	Perlenkette
		necklace ['nekləs]	*Fashion in Africa is often reduced to stereotypes, such as batik prints and beaded necklaces.*	Halskette
		preconception [ˌpri:kən'sepʃn]	*We have to challenge preconceptions and show the truth.*	Vorurteil
		collective [kə'lɛktɪv]	*The young people started a fashion collective and were soon successful.*	Kollektiv
		head wrap [hɛd ræp]	*A head wrap is a piece of cloth often worn as a fashion accessory.*	Kopfbedeckung
		couture [ku:'tʊə]	*She wore an elegant dress from a famous couture designer.*	Couture
		spiritual ['spɪrɪtʃul]	*Soweto is the spiritual home of the fight for black freedom.*	geistig
		extravagant [ɪk'strævəgənt]	*The fashions they created were very extravagant and colourful.*	extravagant
		submissive [səb'mɪsɪv]	*≠ dominant*	unterwürfig
		inferior [ɪn'fɪəriə]	*They felt inferior and didn't have confidence in their abilities.*	minderwertig; unterlegen
	5	**thievery** ['θi:vəri]	*Thievery is a crime.*	Diebstahl
72	S1a	**subjection** [səb'dʒɛkʃən]	*= domination*	Unterwerfung
		to swing [swɪŋ]	*= change*	verändern
		preacher ['pri:tʃə]	*A preacher teaches and shares religious messages with people.*	Prediger(in)
		archbishop [ˌɑ:tʃ'bɪʃəp]	*The archbishop is in charge of several local churches.*	Erzbischof
		to overcome [ˌəʊvə'kʌm], **overcame, overcome** [ˌəʊvə'keɪm, ˌəʊvə'kʌm]	*It will take a long time to overcome the challenges posed by climate change.*	überwinden; bewältigen
	S1b	**melting pot** ['mɛltɪŋ pɒt]	*In the early 20th century, the USA were a melting pot as so many people from different countries came to live there.*	Schmelztiegel
		to strike a chord [straɪk ə kɔ:rd]	*Her speech struck a chord with the audience, leaving many deeply moved.*	berühren
		upbeat ['ʌpbi:t]	*= happy*	fröhlich
		punchy ['pʌntʃi]	*The song has a punchy rhythm.*	markant
		tune [tju:n]	*He kept singing that catchy tune.*	Melodie
	TIP	**to depict** [dɪ'pɪkt]	*The purpose of this song is to depict the struggle of the Black people. = to show*	darstellen; abbilden
		to evoke [ɪ'vəʊk]	*The songwriter's lyrics evoke deep emotions in the listeners.*	hervorrufen
		rhythm ['rɪðəm]	*The rhythm is very catchy.*	Rhythmus

page	exercise	Workshop 2		
	S2b	**to oppress** [ə'pres]	*Africans were oppressed by the white minority.*	unterdrücken
		tribute ['trɪbju:t]	*The concert was a tribute to the musician's long and influential career.*	Tribut
		to endure [ɪn'djʊə]	*He had to endure a hard life in prison.*	ertragen; aushalten
		to overthrow [ˌoʊvə'θroʊ], **overthrew, overthrown** [ˌoʊvə'θru, ˌoʊvə'θrəʊn]	*They helped overthrow apartheid.*	stürzen
73	S1	**regime** [reɪ'ʒi:m]	*The regime didn't survive the protests.*	Regime
		to hint [hɪnt]	*The author hinted in his article that there was corruption involved.*	andeuten
78		**to chronicle** ['krɒnɪkl]	*= to record*	aufzeichnen
		to recount [rɪ'kaʊnt]	*He recounts his early years.*	berichten von
		imprisonment [ɪm'prɪzənmənt]	*His imprisonment lasted for 27 years.*	Inhaftierung; Gefangenschaft
		classification [ˌklæsɪfɪ'keɪʃn]	*The classification system deprived some prisoners of their rights.*	Einstufung
		to confer [kən'fɜ:r]	*The company will confer the privilege of a promotion to her.*	verleihen
		automatic [ˌɔ:tə'mætɪk]	*Data can be automatically processed.*	automatisch
		incidentals [ˌɪnsɪ'dɛntəlz]	*He saved some money for incidentals like snacks and movie tickets.*	Kleinigkeiten; Zufälligkeiten
		lifeblood ['laɪfbʌd]	*Water is the lifeblood of humanity.*	Lebenssaft
		to despise [dɪ'spaɪz]	*We despised the classification system.*	verachten; missachten
		corrupt [kə'rʌpt]	*The system was corrupt and undemocratic.*	korrupt; bestechlich
		demeaning [dɪ'mi:nɪŋ]	*It was demeaning, the way the prisoners were treated.*	erniedrigend; herabsetzend
		to repress [rɪ'prɛs]	*In prison, they were repressed by the guards.*	unterdrücken
		tuckshop ['tʌkʃɒp]	*The tuckshop at school is open during breaks.*	Kiosk
		to wield [wi:ld]	*The authorities wielded the classification system as a weapon against political prisoners.* *= to use*	als Waffe einsetzen
		to desire [dɪ'zaɪə]	*While I desired the privileges that came with higher classifications, I refused to compromise my conduct.*	begehren
		docile ['dəʊsaɪl]	*Are donkeys docile animals?*	fügsam; gehorsam
		troublemaker ['trʌblˌmeɪkə]	*Hew was the biggest troublemaker in class.*	Unruhestifter(in)
		warder ['wɔ:rdə]	*= guard*	Wärter(in)
		to be entitled [bi ɪn'taɪtld]	*As a D group prisoner, I was entitled to have only one visitor.*	das Recht haben

Workshop 2

page	exercise	word	example	translation
		to restrict [rɪ'strɪkt]	*Visits and letters were restricted to close relatives.*	einschränken; beschränken
		gradation [grə'deɪʃən]	*You can use gradiation to create a smooth transition between different shades.*	Abstufung; Gradation
		irksome ['ɜ:rksəm]	*= annoying*	ärgerlich; lästig
		to be deemed [bi di:md]	*Anyone who claims descent from a common ancestor is deemed part of the family.*	gelten
		grim [grɪm]	*We have to cope with reality, however grim or disagreeable.*	grimmig; düster
		disagreeable [ˌdɪsə'gri:əbl]	*≠ agreeable*	unangenehm; unsympathisch
		preferable ['prɛfərəbl]	*= better*	vorziehbar
		tidings ['taɪdɪŋz]	*He brought bad tidings.*	Nachrichten
		to abuse [ə'bju:s]	*She abused our trust.*	missbrauchen
		anticipation [ænˌtɪsɪ'peɪʃn]	*We waited in anticipation for the email.*	Vorfreude
		barren ['bærən]	*Deserts are mostly barren land.*	karg; unfruchtbar
		to withhold [wɪð'hoʊld], **withheld, withheld** [wɪð'held, wɪð'held]	*The company decided to withhold bonus payments until the end of the project.*	zurückhalten
79		**to cherish** ['tʃɛrɪʃ]	*The film was great, I cherished every minute of it.*	schätzen; hegen
		to bloom [blu:m]	*The summer rain made the desert bloom.*	blühen
		leisurely ['leʒəli]	*He took the letter in a leisurely manner.*	gelassen
		to yearn [jɜ:rn]	*= want*	sich sehnen
		satisfaction [ˌsætɪs'fækʃən]	*I didn't give the authorities the satisfaction of seeing my eagerness.*	Genugtuung; Befriedigung
		eagerness ['i:gərnəs]	*I walked slowly because I didn't want to show them my eagerness by rushing.*	Eifer; Begeisterung
		to censor ['sɛnsə]	*The letters were censored so it was difficult to understand them.*	zensieren
		salutation [ˌsælju'teɪʃən]	*= greeting*	Grußformel
		censor ['sɛnsə]	*The censors crossed out everything they didn't like.*	zensieren; Zensor
		passage ['pæsɪdʒ]	*They blacked out whole passages of the text.*	Abschnitt; Passage
		ink [ɪŋk]	*The letter was written in ink.*	Tinte
		razor ['reɪzə]	*They used razors to slice out offending texts.*	Rasierer
		to excise ['ɛksaɪz]	*= remove*	auslöschen
		to relish ['relɪʃ]	*= to enjoy*	genießen
		tatters ['tætərz]	*They delivered letters in tatters, so they could not be read.*	Fetzen

page	exercise	Workshop 2		
		censorship ['sɛnsərʃɪp]	*The government used censorship to control what news was shown on TV.*	Zensur; Zensierung
	1	**idealistic** [aɪˌdiːə'lɪstɪk]	*His idealistic speech about changing the world seemed too unrealistic.*	idealistisch
	4	**forbidden** [fə'bɪdən]	*What was allowed, what was forbidden?*	verboten; untersagt
		amenity [ə'miːnəti]	*There weren't many amenities for the prisoners.*	Annehmlichkeit
	5	**narration** [nə'reɪʃən]	*Analyse the point of view of narration in this new novel.*	Erzählung; Narration
	6	**triumph** ['traɪʌmf]	*To overcome my fear was a great triumph.*	Triumph
	7	**obituary** [oʊ'bɪtʃuˌɛri]	*Before he died, he wrote his own obituary.*	Nachruf; Todesanzeige
	9	**militant** ['mɪlɪtənt]	*Using militant means, the group forcefully imposed their demands.*	militant
80	1a	**acclaim** [ə'kleɪm]	*The song gained positive critical acclaim.*	Beifall; Anerkennung
	2	**humble** ['hʌmbl]	*Siya Kolisi is a black rugby player who comes from a poor family and a humble background.*	bescheiden; demütig
		under-resourced ['ʌndə rɪ'sɔːrst]	*Many under-resourced communities struggle to access quality healthcare and education.*	unterversorgt
81		**to attribute** ['ætrɪˌbjut]	*Who do you attribute your success to?*	zuschreiben
		appointment [ə'pɔɪntmənt]	*The organization waited for the appointment of a new colleague.*	Anstellung
		to prompt [prɒmpt]	*What prompted you to launch the Kolisi Foundation?*	auslösen; veranlassen
		to pose [pəʊz]	*= present*	stellen; darstellen
		to deprive [dɪ'praɪv]	*The children were deprived of a good education.*	berauben; entziehen
	3	**fatal** ['feɪtl]	*Most shark attacks aren't fatal.*	tödlich
82	4a	**to persecute** ['pɜːsɪkjuːt]	*Under apartheid, people were often persecuted because of their race.*	verfolgen
	4b	**to instil** [ɪn'stɪl]	*A different approach in education could instil a more balanced view of equality in students.*	einträufeln
		balanced ['bæləns]	*They had a balanced discussion.*	Balance
		dismissive [dɪ'smɪsɪv]	*Don't be dismissive of other people's ideas; they could be really good.*	abweisend; geringschätzig
		imbalanced [ɪm'bælənst]	*The protest highlighted society's imbalanced power relations.*	unausgeglichen; nicht ausgeglichen
		eye-opener ['aɪˌoʊpənə]	*The walk was an eye-opener, but did it lead to any changes?*	Augenöffner
83	1	**to guard** [gɑːd]	*The former prison officer guarded a black prisoner, Nelson Mandela, for 21 years in three different locations.*	bewachen

page	exercise	Workshop 2		
		to monitor ['mɒnɪtə]	*He monitored the correspondence and visits of Mandela and his comrades.*	kontrollieren
		comrade ['kɒmreɪd]	*Mandela and his comrades were in the prison on Robben Island.*	Kamerad(in)
		to mature [mə'tʃʊə]	*Their relationship matured over the years and became stronger.*	reifen; erwachsen
		gradually ['grædʒul]	*As his friendship with Mandela grows, Gregory gradually starts to support the fight for a free and equal South Africa.*	allmählich; schrittweise
	2	**to isolate** ['aɪsəleɪt]	*During the pandemic, people had to isolate.*	isolieren; absondern
		convict ['kɒnvɪkt]	*Two convicts escaped from the prison.*	Sträfling
		to disappoint [ˌdɪsə'pɔɪnt]	*The book disappointed me, it was boring.*	enttäuschen
	3	**uprising** ['ʌpˌraɪzɪŋ]	*The uprising changed the political landscape in South Africa.*	Aufstand
		countrywide ['kʌntriˌwaɪd]	*The uprising began in Soweto and spread countrywide.*	landesweit; im ganzen Land
		to trace back [treɪs bæk]	*How far can you trace your family back?*	zurückführen
		to trigger ['trɪgə]	*What triggered the revolution?*	auslösen
		oppressor [ə'presə]	*English was regarded as the language of the oppressor.*	Unterdrücker(in)
		ammunition [ˌæmjʊ'nɪʃən]	*The police fired tear gas and live ammunition on the protestors.*	Munition
		to commemorate [kə'meməreɪt]	*The protest is commemorated by a national holiday, Youth Day.* = *remember*	erinnern an
84	4	**probability** [ˌprɒbə'bɪləti]	*What is the probability of another earthquake?*	Wahrscheinlichkeit
		academy [ə'kædəmi]	= *institute*	Akademie
	5	**to amputate** ['æmpjʊˌteɪt]	*She had a traffic accident and her lower left leg was amputated.*	amputieren
		legendary ['lɛdʒəndəri]	= *famous*	legendär
		challenger ['tʃælɪndʒə]	*Who are your main challengers when you compete in the race?*	Herausforderer, Herausforderin
85	6	**citizenship** ['sɪtɪzənʃɪp]	*Britain gave the Sout African Zola Budd citizenship.*	Staatsbürgerschaft
		consequently ['kɒnsɪkwəntli]	*Consequently, he was sacked as captain the following year.*	folglich; demzufolge
		to sack [sæk]	*She was sacked.* = *to fire*	entlassen
		national ['næʃnl]	*Some South African nationals live outside the country.*	Staatsbürger(in)

page	exercise	Workshop 2		
	7	to **bombard** [bɒm'bɑ:d]	*My parents have bombarded me with different suggestions.*	bombardieren
	8	**sanctuary** ['sæŋktʃuəri]	*We need sanctuaries for endangered species.*	Schutzgebiet

page	exercise	Workshop 3		
92	1	**scenario** [sə'nɑ:riəʊ]	*Think about future scenarios that are currently in the balance.*	Szenario
		rearview mirror ['rɪəvju: 'mɪrə]	*Use your rearview mirror before you overtake.*	Rückspiegel
		sociologist [ˌsoʊsi'ɒlədʒɪst]	*A sociologist is a scientist who studies human societies.*	Soziologe / Soziologin
	2	**satisfied** ['sætɪsfaɪd]	*Are you satisfied with the results?*	zufrieden
		transphobia [træns'foʊbiə]	*Transphobia refers to dislike, prejudice, or discrimination against transgender people.*	Transphobie
		ethnicity [eθ'nɪsəti]	*People were attacked because of their ethnicity and religion.*	Ethnizität
		utopia [ju:'təʊpiə]	*It's a nice place to live, but it's no utopia.*	Utopie
		cataclysm ['kætəklɪzəm]	*= catastrophe*	Katastrophe
		authoritarian [əˌθɔ:rɪ'terɪən]	*The authoritarian regime made all the big decisions for the country.*	autoritär
		dictatorship ['dɪkteɪtərʃɪp]	*Her characters live under an authoritarian dictatorship where women become slaves.*	Diktatur; Diktatorisch
		contributor [kən'trɪbjutə]	*We like to thank all the contributors who have made this a great day.*	Mitwirkende(r); Beiträger(in)
94	1b	**prosperous** ['prɒspərəs]	*Canada is a prosperous country with a strong economy and a diverse, multicultural society.*	wohlhabend
		to **preside** [prɪ'zaɪd]	*It was the first time I presided over a meeting, and I felt a mix of excitement and nervousness.*	den Vorsitz führen
		to **bind** [baɪnd]	*Shared responsibilities can bind people together.*	binden; verpflichten
	2	**inconvenient** [ˌɪnkən'vi:niənt]	*This is an inconvenient time to call me.*	unbequem; unangenehm
		breast plate ['brɛstpleɪt]	*He adjustes his breast plate before going into battle.*	Brustplatte; Brustpanzer
		bone choker [boʊn 'tʃoʊkə]	*The bone choker completed his outfit.*	Halsband aus Knochen
		skimpy ['skɪmpi]	*They were wearing skimpy dresses.*	knapp
		loincloth ['lɔɪnklɒθ]	*A loincloth is a simple piece of clothing that's worn around the hips.*	Lendenschurz; Schurz
		to **gallop** ['gæləp]	*The horses were galloping around the field.*	galoppieren; Galopp

page	exercise	Workshop 3		
		stern [stɜːrn]	*My last head teacher was very stern. = strict*	streng
		grunt [grʌnt]	*We could hear the grunts from the pigs in the farmhouse.*	Grunzen
		cavalry ['kævlri]	*The cavalry fought against Native Americans.*	Kavallerie
		to scalp [skælp]	*Native Americans scalped their enemies.*	skalpieren
		homesteader ['hoʊmˌstedə]	*= settler*	Siedler(in)
		lathered up ['læðərd ʌp]	*= worked up*	aufgeputscht
		to cobble ['kɒbl]	*= put together*	flicken
		to function ['fʌŋkʃn]	*The car needs repair to function properly again.*	funktionieren
		cliché [klɪ'ʃeɪ]	*The film was full of clichés about Native Americans.*	Klischee; Gemeinplatz
		to dispense [dɪ'spɛns]	*Film dispensed with any errant subtleties and colourings and crafted three basic Indian types.*	verteilen; ausgeben
		errant ['ɛrənt]	*Film dispensed with any errant subtleties and crafted three stereotypes.*	irrend; fehlgeleitet
		subtlety ['sʌtlti]	*They didn't bother with subtleties, they were very direct.*	Feinheit
		colouring ['kʌlərɪŋ]	*= shade*	Färbung
		to craft [krɑːft]	*He crafted these sculptures himself.*	formen; bilden
		bloodthirsty ['blʌdˌθɜːrsti]	*They were considered bloodthirsty savages.*	blutrünstig
		savage ['sævɪdʒ]	*A clichéd savage is portrayed as being wild, untamed, and lacking in civilization and refinement.*	Wilde(r)
		noble ['noʊbl]	*She had nobel intentions, but nobody believed her.*	edel
		to bash [bæʃ]	*= hit*	schlagen
		precepts ['priːsɛpts]	*= principle*	Prinzip
		capitalism ['kæpɪtəlɪzəm]	*Capitalism encourages companies to compete in the market.*	Kapitalismus
95	3a	**powwow** ['paʊwaʊ]	*The Native American community gathered for a traditional powwow, celebrating their culture through dance, music, and storytelling.*	Powwow
		advocate ['ædvəkət]	*I see myself as an advocate for my Inuit culture.*	Anwalt, Anwältin
		ribbon ['rɪbən]	*Our ribbon skirts feature colorful ribbons that are sewn onto the fabric.*	Band; Franse
		beadwork ['biːdwɜːrk]	*She spent hours working on her beadwork.*	Perlenarbeit; Perlenkunst
		insignia [ɪn'sɪgniə]	*I wear my insignia to honour the traditions of my ancestors.*	Abzeichen; Insignien

page	exercise	Workshop 3		
		boarding school ['bɔ:rdɪŋ sku:l]	*She was sent to boarding school because they lived in a remote area.*	Internat; Pensionat
		to sew [səʊ], **sewed, sewn** [səʊd, səʊn]	*We learned to sew dresses in a workshop.*	nähen
		sealskin ['si:lskɪn]	*Shoes made out of sealskin are waterproof.*	Seehundfell
		to extend [ɪk'stɛnd]	*My love for my community extends to my love of learning its language.*	(sich) ausdehnen
		missionary ['mɪʃənri]	*German missionaries from the Moravian Church went to Greenland in the 18th century.*	Missionar(in)
	4a	**to assimilate** [ə'sɪmɪˌleɪt]	*Many people assimilated into society quickly.*	assimilieren; anpassen
		residency ['rɛzɪdənsi]	*You needed permanent residency to qualify for citizenship.*	*hier:* Aufenthaltsgenehmigung
	5	**to obtain** [əb'teɪn]	*≠ lose*	erhalten; erlangen
96	2	**misfit** ['mɪsfɪt]	*I didn't know anyone at the party and felt like a misfit.*	Außenseiter(in)
	3a	**paperback** ['pæpbæk]	*The book came out as a paperback straight away.*	Taschenbuch
		novella [noʊ'vɛlə]	*A novella is a short novel.*	Novelle
		essence ['esns]	*What is the essence of this text?*	Wesen; Wesentliche
		budding ['bʌdɪŋ]	*= growing* *≠ dying*	aufkeimend; knospend
	3b	**blond-haired** [blɒnd'hɛərd]	*They were looking for a blond-haired woman for the role.*	blondhaarig; blond
		tippy toes ['tɪpi toʊz]	*= tiptoes*	Zehenspitzen
		to flutter ['flʌtə]	*He fluttered his hands and seemed nervous.*	flattern; flimmern
		lisp [lɪsp]	*She speaks with a little lisp.*	Lispeln; Sprachfehler
		jock [dʒɒk]	*The jock confidently scored the winning goal in the soccer tournament.*	Sportler(in); Athlet(in)
		sissy ['sɪsi]	*Stop being a sissy.*	Weichei
		oblivious [ə'blɪviəs]	*They laugh, and I pretend I am oblivious.*	ahnungslos; unbewusst
		timidly ['tɪmɪdli]	*= shy*	zaghaft
		to be bound to [bi baʊnd tu:]	*Everyone is bound to make mistakes at some point in their lives.*	gebunden sein
		to surround [sə'raʊnd]	*Suddenly all those children surrounded me and asked questions.*	umgeben
		impending [ɪm'pɛndɪŋ]	*= approaching*	bevorstehend; drohend
		washroom ['wɒʃru:m]	*= bathroom*	Waschraum
		presence ['prezns]	*Your presence at the event is requested.*	Anwesenheit
		to pee [pi:]	*= to urinate*	pinkeln

page	exercise	Workshop 3		
		betrayal [bɪ'treɪl]	*He felt betrayal when his best friend told his secret to others.*	Verrat; Treuebruch
97	4b	**classics** ['klæsɪks]	*I read all the classics like Oliver Twist when I was young.*	Klassiker; klassisch
		to figure out ['fɪgə]	*Can you figure out how to do it?*	herausfinden
		to sense [sens]	*= feel*	fühlen
		intent [ɪn'tɛnt]	*The tension was intent, as everyone waited nervously for her appearance.*	ernsthaft; gespannt
		breezy ['bri:zi]	*The air was fresh and breezy.*	luftig; unbekümmert
		to shelter ['ʃeltə]	*Animals shelter their young.*	beschützen
		fruity ['fru:ti]	*I gave her my deepest and fruitiest laugh.*	*hier:* herzhaft
		pointy ['pɔɪnti]	*She was wearing very pointy shoes that made it difficult to walk.*	spitz; spitz zulaufend
	5	**barbershop** ['bɑ:rbərʃɒp]		Friseursalon; Barbierladen
		junk [dʒʌŋk]	*The high school is where you go to get junk, high or pregnant.*	*hier:* Drogen
		to reel [ri:l]	*The neighbourhood is reeling after the shooting of a 17-year-old black teenager by a white police officer.*	erschüttert sein
		assessment [ə'sesmənt]	*What is your assessment of the situation?*	Einschätzung; Bewertung
98	1	**environmental literacy** [ɪn,vaɪrən'mɛntl 'lɪtərəsi]	*He wanted to test his environmental literary.*	Umweltwissen
		trade off [treɪd ɒf]	*Taking a job nearby was a trade-off between career and being close to family.*	Kompromiss
		ozone layer ['oʊzoʊn 'leɪə]	*The ozone layer is getting thinner.*	Ozonschicht
		layer ['leɪə]	*Wear several layers of clothes when it is cold.*	Schicht
		to filter ['fɪltə]	*The ozone layer filters UV radiation.*	filtern
		acid rain ['æsɪd reɪn]	*Acid rain, can kill forests.*	saurer Regen
		radiation [,reɪdi'eɪʃən]	*The ozone layer filters UV radiation.*	Strahlung
		sewage ['su:ɪdʒ]	*Sewage is filtered and reused for watering gardens.*	Abwasser
		to discard [dɪ'skɑ:d]	*She discarded her old dresses.*	ausrangieren; wegwerfen
		to purchase ['pɜ:tʃəs]	*= to buy*	kaufen; erwerben
		polar bear ['pəʊlə beə]	*Polar bears live at the North Pole, penguins at the South Pole.*	Eisbär
		to hibernate ['haɪbərneɪt]	*Hedgehogs and other small animals hibernate during the winter to survive the cold.*	überwintern; Winterschlaf halten
	2	**malpractice** ['mæl,præktɪs]	*It is essential to teach young people about ongoing malpractices and how to reverse them.*	Kunstfehler; Fehlverhalten
		to reverse [rɪ'vɜ:s]	*They worked hard to reverse the damage caused by the storm.*	umdrehen

page	exercise	Workshop 3		
		empowerment [ɪm'paʊərmənt]	*Woman empowerment is crucial for world peace.*	Ermächtigung; Befähigung
		naive [naɪ'i:v]	*He's not realistic but naive about the future and won't listen to others.*	naiv; gutgläubig
	3a	**quest** [kwɛst]	*They are on a quest for a common solution.*	Bestreben; Suche
		to defeat [dɪ'fi:t]	*How was the pandemic defeated in the end?*	besiegen
		cooperation [kəʊ,ɒpə'reɪʃn]	*We need cooperation to fight against climate change.*	Zusammenarbeit
		to yield [ji:ld]	*Investments have yielded good results.*	liefern; nach sich ziehen
		rapid ['ræpɪd]	*= fast*	schnell
		dioxide [daɪ'ɒksaɪd]	*carbon dioxide*	Dioxid
		blip [blɪp]	*In history, the pandemic will just be a blip.*	Störung; Ausschlag
		futile ['fju:taɪl]	*All our efforts were futile, we lost.*	vergeblich; sinnlos
		to stave off [steɪv ɒf]	*= to stop*	aufhalten
		outbreak ['aʊtbreɪk]	*When was the outbreak of the pandemic?*	Ausbruch
		to revive [rɪ'vaɪv]	*Countries tried to revive their economies after the crisis.*	wiederbeleben
99	3b	**intention** [ɪn'tenʃn]	*Comment on the tone of this article and speculate on the writer's intention.*	Absicht
	6	**hydrogen** ['haɪdrədʒən]	*Hydrogen is a colourless, odourless gas, which can be used as a fuel source.*	Wasserstoff
	6b	**to combat** ['kɒmbæt]	*In order to combat climate change, we need to adopt electrification as a clean and sustainable solution.*	bekämpfen
		electrification [ɪ,lɛktrɪfɪ'keɪʃən]	*Electrification of our transport and industrial needs can help combat climate change.*	Elektrifizierung
		mode [moʊd]	*Different modes of transport, like buses, trains, and bicycles, cater to the needs of commuters.*	Modus; Art
		lorry ['lɒri]	*Lorries are used to transport goods on the road.*	Lastwagen; LKW
		odourless ['oʊdərləs]	*Hydrogen is a colourless and odourless gas.*	geruchslos
		to store [stɔ:]	*Fuel is stored in tanks.*	lagern
		electrolyser [ɪ'lɛktrəʊ,laɪzə]	*The electrolyser splits water into hydrogen and oxygen gas with no carbon emissions.*	Elektrolyseur

page	exercise	Workshop 3		
		oxygen ['ɒksɪdʒən]	*Clean electricity is used to power an electrolyser, splitting water into hydrogen and oxygen with no carbon emissions.*	Sauerstoff
		to **transport** [træn'spɔ:t]	*Hydrogen can be stored and transported easily.*	transportieren
		to **accelerate** [ək'seləreɪt]	*We want to accelerate green energy goals.*	beschleunigen
	6c	**deterrent** [dɪ'tɛrənt]	*Green hydrogen costs between three and six times more to produce than grey or blue hydrogen, which is a serious deterrent.*	Abschreckung; Abschreckungsmittel
		vested ['vɛstɪd]	*vested interests*	Eigen-; persönlich
		to **retain** [rɪ'teɪn]	*= to keep*	behalten
		consistent [kən'sɪstənt]	*But these sources are not consistent, they say different things.*	konsequent
		availability [əˌveɪlə'bɪləti]	*He reassured me of his availability.*	Verfügbarkeit
		generator ['dʒenəreɪtə]	*Generators produce energy from wind or other ressources.*	Generator; Stromerzeuger
		hydro ['haɪdroʊ]	*Hydro dams are a source of energy.*	Wasser-; Hydro-
		dam [dæm]	*Power from hydro dams can be expensive.*	Damm; Staudamm
		efficiency [ɪ'fɪʃənsi]	*Consistently high power quality is needed to ensure the efficiency of the network.*	Effizienz; Wirksamkeit
		crucial ['kru:ʃl]	*Fighting climate change is crucial to help us safe the earth.*	entscheidend; wesentlich
100	2a	**literally** ['lɪtərl]	*I literally jumped out of my seat in excitement!*	buchstäblich
	2b	to **oppose** [ə'pəʊz]	*Autumn Peltier is an activist who opposes the contamination of water.*	kämpfen gegen
		contamination [kənˌtæmɪ'neɪʃən]	*Autumn Peltier opposes the contamination of water by the oil industry.*	Kontamination; Verunreinigung
		freshwater ['freʃwɔ:tə]	*She grew up on Lake Huron, one of North America's Great Lakes – the largest group of freshwater lakes on Earth.*	Süßwasser
		to **contaminate** [kən'tæmɪneɪt]	*The water was contaminated from pollution and oil pipelines breaking.*	verunreinigen; kontaminieren
		to **endorse** [ɪn'dɔ:s]	*Prime Minister Justin Trudeau had endorsed several pipeline projects, endangering First Nations communities.*	unterstützen
	CC	**magnate** ['mægneɪt]	*Bill Gates is a very rich business magnate.*	Magnat; Industrieller
		philanthropist [fɪ'lænθrəpɪst]	*Bill Gates is a philanthropist, who gives away a lot of his wealth.*	Philanthrop(in); Wohltäter(in)

page	exercise	Workshop 3		
		to diversify ['daɪvərsɪˌfaɪ]	*He made money by diversifying his investments.*	diversifizieren; erweitern
101	4	**outage** ['aʊtɪdʒ]	*They want to avoid major outages in electricity.*	Ausfall
		vaccine ['væksi:n]	*The development of a new vaccine brought hope to millions of people around the world.*	Impfstoff
		bathtub ['bæθˌtʌb]	*Fill the bathtub with water.*	Badewanne
		flow [fləʊ]	*Even if we slow the flow of water to a trickle, the tub will eventually overflow.*	Fluss; Strom
		trickle ['trɪkl]	*There was only a trickle of water left in the bottle.*	Tropfen
		tub [tʌb]	*The tub has overflown because he left the water running.*	Wanne
		to overflow [ˌəʊvə'fləʊ]	*Careful, turn off the tap so that the tub doesn't overflow.*	überfließen
		transmission [træns'mɪʃən]	*We need new transmission lines for green electricity.*	Übertragung
		costly ['kɔ:stli]	*Building new transmission lines is a costly and time-consuming task.*	kostspielig; teuer
		time-consuming ['taɪm kən'sju:mɪŋ]	*Finding new energy sources can be time-consuming.*	zeitraubend
		distribution [ˌdɪstrɪ'bju:ʃn]	*Transmission and distribution are responsible for more than a third of the final cost of electricity.*	Verteilung
		culprit ['kʌlprɪt]	*They never found the culprit who had smashed the window.*	Schuldige(r)
		intermittency [ˌɪntə'mɪtənsi]	*≠ continuity*	Unbeständigkeit; Unstetigkeit
		intermittent [ˌɪntə'mɪtənt]	*Our need for power is not intermittent; we want it all the time.*	intermittierend; periodisch
		excess [ɪk'sɛs]	*We need to store excess electricity in batteries.*	übermäßig; überschüssig
102	S1	**conscious** ['kɒnʃəs]	*Was that a conscious decision or a mistake?*	bewusst
		bundle ['bʌndl]	*He found a bundle of clothes in his closet.*	Bündel
		dent [dent]	*No more discarded bundle at the back of your wardrobe gathering dust and no unwanted dent in your bank balance either.*	Beule; Delle
		consumption [kən'sʌmpʃn]	*Airplanes still have a very high fuel consumption.*	Verbrauch
		textile ['tekstaɪl]	*She likes working with textiles.*	Textil-
		to emit [ɪ'mɪt]	*Billions of tonnes of carbon dioxide are being emitted damaging the ozone layer.*	emittieren; ausstoßen

page	exercise	Workshop 3		
103	S1a	**to animate** ['ænɪˌmeɪt]	*They were producing an animated film.*	animieren
		to mutter ['mʌtə]	*He muttered something about lies and rumours.*	murmeln
		damned [dæmd]	*This are damned lies.*	verdammt
		to reject [rɪ'dʒekt]	*You shouldn't reject all statistics.*	zurückweisen
		to exert [ɪg'zɜːt]	*We have to exert a bit of brain power to figure out what is true and what is not.*	anstrengen
		joyful ['dʒɔɪfl]	*= happy* *≠ sad*	fröhlich
		staggering ['stægərɪŋ]	*= amazing*	erschütternd
		deficit ['defɪsɪt]	*When there is a deficit in resources, societies suffer.*	Mangel
		denial [dɪ'naɪl]	*He was in denial about failing the test, even though he didn't study.*	Verweigerung
		vindication [ˌvɪndɪ'keɪʃn]	*= justification*	Rechtfertigung
		telescope ['telɪskəʊp]	*You can watch the stars through a telescope.*	Teleskop
		astronomer [ə'strɑːnəmə]	*An astronomer is a scientist who studies stars, planets, and other objects in space.*	Astronom(in)
	S1b	**cautious** ['kɔːʃəs]	*= careful*	vorsichtig
	TIP	**mindset** ['maɪndset]	*An interested mindset will help you ask the right questions when looking for information.*	Mentalität
	S2b	**comprehensive** [ˌkɒmprɪ'hensɪv]	*Do you think the arguments are comprehensive enough?*	umfassend
	S2c	**milestone** ['maɪlstəʊn]	*It's good to set milestones if you want to achieve a complex goal.*	Meilenstein
		breakdown ['breɪkdaʊn]	*What does the racial breakdown show?*	*hier:* Aufgliederung
		prospective [prə'spektɪv]	*Prospective students should consider their career goals before choosing a course.*	möglich
		to enrol [ɪn'rəʊl]	*He came from college and enrolled as a mature student.*	einschreiben; anmelden
104	1a	**dystopia** [dɪs'təʊpiə]	*In contrast to a utopia, a dystopia is an imagined world where everything is unpleasant or bad.*	Dystopie
		didactic [daɪ'dæktɪk]	*She wanted to find a didactic approach to a problem.*	didaktisch; lehrhaft
		on the contrary [ɒn ðə 'kɒntrəri]	*The evidence, on the contrary, actually supported her argument instead of contradicting it.*	im Gegenteil
		reproduction [ˌriːprə'dʌkʃən]	*In this book, the ruling World State uses powerful conditioning technologies to control reproduction.*	*hier:* Fortpflanzung

page	exercise	Workshop 3		
		genetically [dʒəˈnetɪkli]	*The state uses powerful conditioning technologies and babies are genetically modified.*	genetisch
		to modify [ˈmɒdɪfaɪ]	*In this dystopian novel babies are genetically modified.*	modifizieren; ändern
		to drug [drʌg]	*Adults are socially programmed and drugged – all in order to maintain an authoritarian regime.*	betäuben
		fascism [ˈfæʃɪzəm]	*Fascism is a type of government where there is a very strong leader and a single political party that controls everything.*	Faschismus
		android [ˈænˌdrɔɪd]	*= robot*	Android; Roboter
		post-apocalyptic [poʊst əˌpɒkəˈlɪptɪk]	*In the post-apocalyptic world, survivors struggled to rebuild civilization in the ruins.*	postapokalyptisch; nach der Apokalypse
		uninhabitable [ˌʌnɪnˈhæbɪtəbl]	*Dystopian novels are often set in places that are uninhabitable. ≠ habitable*	unbewohnbar
		obsession [əbˈseʃn]	*Horses are her obsession.*	Fixierung; Bessessenheit
		appetite [ˈæpɪˌtaɪt]	*We seem to have a great appetite for dystopia.*	Appetit; Verlangen
		distant [ˈdɪstənt]	*I didn't know them but they were distant relatives.*	weit entfernt
		dictator [ˈdɪkteɪtə]	*There are still dictators ruling over countries in the global south.*	Diktator(in)
		bureaucracy [bjʊəˈrɒkrəsi]	*To build a new playground, they had to deal with a lot of bureaucracy including forms and approvals.*	Bürokratie; Verwaltung
		CCTV [ˌsiː siː ˈtiː ˈviː]	*CCTV is common in public places.*	Überwachungskamera; CCTV
		surveillance [səˈveɪləns]	*CCTV surveillance is common in big cities.*	Überwachung
		constantly [ˈkɒnstəntli]	*CCTV is constantly surveilling us.*	ständig
	2	**novelist** [ˈnɒvəlɪst]	*Margaret Atwood is probably our most famous novelist.*	Romanautor(in)
		screenplay [ˈskriːnpleɪ]	*She writes radio scripts and screenplays.*	Drehbuch
		totalitarian [toʊˌtælɪˈtɛəriən]	*She lives in a totalitarian state, where everything is controlled.*	totalitär
		leakage [ˈliːkɪdʒ]	*There was a leakage at the chemical factory which polluted the river.*	Leckage; Austreten
		depopulation [ˌdiːˌpɒpjuˈleɪʃn]	*Pollution and damage to the environment have caused serious depopulation.*	Entvölkerung
		to disempower [ˌdɪsɪmˈpaʊə]	*≠ to empower*	entmachten; schwächen
		to obey [oʊˈbeɪ]	*An oppressive government punishes anyone who does not obey.*	gehorchen
		to terrify [ˈterɪˌfaɪ]	*= to frighten*	erschrecken

Workshop 3

page	exercise	word	example	German
		enigmatic [ˌenɪɡˈmætɪk]	*She is an enigmatic actress.*	geheimnisvoll; rätselhaft
		uncertainty [ʌnˈsɜːtnti]	*The uncertainty of tomorrow's weather made it difficult to plan the picnic.*	Ungewissheit
105	3b	**to dread** [dred]	*Basically, nothing makes me dread my future more than global warming.*	fürchten; sich scheuen
		frankly [fræŋkli]	= *honest*	ehrlich
106	2a	**harassment** [ˈhærəsmənt]	*Since the #MeToo Movement started, more people have been speaking out against sexual harassment.*	Belästigung; Schikane
	2b	**flashback** [ˈflæʃbæk]	*He had a flashback to his childhood while looking at old photos.*	Rückblende; Flashback
		symptom [ˈsɪmptəm]	*This is a symptom of a larger issue that needs to be addressed.*	Symptom; Anzeichen
		to **presume** [prɪˈzjuːm]	= *to consider*	annehmen
		irrational [ɪˈræʃənl]	*Online campaigns like #BLM and #MeToo can become irrational and aggressive.*	irrational
		lynch mob [lɪntʃ mɒb]	*A lynch mob refers to a group of people who take the law into their own hands to punish someone.*	Lynchjustiz
		mentality [menˈtæləti]	*Mob mentality refers to the way individuals in a large group can act together without planned direction.*	Geisteshaltung
107	TIP	to **pre-empt** [priːˈɛmpt]	*He pre-empted the criticism and addressed the issue in his speech.*	zuvorkommen
		to **concede** [kənˈsiːd]	= *to admit* ≠ *to deny*	zugestehen; einräumen
	3b	to **cause offense** [kɔːz əˈfɛns]	*Nobody should be allowed to cause offense to another person.*	jdn. beleidigen
		prestige [prɛˈstiːʒ]	*They have power and prestige.*	Prestige
		legitimate [lɪˈdʒɪtɪmɪt]	*There are legitimate concerns about the impact of climate change on wildlife.*	legitim; rechtmäßig
		to **eliminate** [ɪˈlɪmɪneɪt]	*The new developments eliminated the need for outdated technology in the industry.*	beseitigen
		nuance [ˈnjuːɑːns]	*Cancel culture can get out of control and eliminate nuance from the debate.*	Nuance; Feinheit
		homophobic [ˌhoʊməˈfoʊbɪk]	*He was cancelled because of his homophobic posts.*	homophob
		hurtful [ˈhɜːtfl]	*Her hurtful words made him feel really sad and upset.*	verletzend
108	1a	**scholar** [ˈskɒlə]	= *academic*	Gelehrte(r)
		sociolinguistic [ˌsoʊsioʊˈlɪŋɡwɪstɪk]	*English is used in different sociolinguistic contexts.*	soziolinguistisch

page	exercise	Workshop 3		
	1b	**influential** [ˌɪnflu'enʃl]	*Why has English been so influential in shaping global communication and culture?*	einflussreich
	2a	**concentric** [kən'sɛntrɪk]	*Here is a model that represents these three concentric circles.*	konzentrisch
		linguistics [lɪŋ'gwɪstɪks]	*Linguistics explores the structure, use, and meaning of language.*	Linguistik
		capacity [kə'pæsəti]	*His capacity for understanding the English language improved rapidly.*	Fähigkeit
		diplomacy [dɪ'pləʊməsi]	*The government used diplomacy to settle the differences.*	Diplomatie
		lingua franca ['lɪŋgwə 'fræŋkə]	*English is the lingua franca in Europe.*	Lingua Franca; Verkehrssprache
		demographics [ˌdɛmə'græfɪks]	*What are the demographics of English speakers?*	Demografie; Bevölkerungsstatistik
		hierarchy ['haɪərɑːrki]	*Is there a hierarchy of importance among the different departments?*	Hierarchie
		to **absorb** [əb'zɔːrb]	*New words get absorbed into the language.*	absorbieren; aufnehmen
		to **delegitimize** [dɪ'lɛdʒɪtɪmaɪz]	*= make worthless*	delegitimieren; entlegitimieren
		expansion [ɪk'spænʃn]	*Many scientists are interested in the expansion of outer space.*	Ausdehnung; Expansion
		to **outnumber** [aʊt'nʌmbə]	*Today non-native English speakers outnumber native speakers.*	übersteigen
		mobility [moʊ'bɪlɪti]	*Greater mobility across the world has resulted in more pollution.*	Mobilität; Beweglichkeit
		to **blur** [blɜː]	*The sunlight was blurred by the clouds.*	verschwimmen
109	3a	**dominance** ['dɒmɪnəns]	*English spreading might show 'native-speaker' dominance, but it can also be a way of communicating between cultures.*	Dominanz; Vorherrschaft
	3b	**collaboration** [kəˌlæbə'reɪʃn]	*Collaboration refers to two or more people working together to achieve the same thing.*	Zusammenarbeit; Kollaboration
		collaborative [kə'læbərətɪv]	*The students had collaborative interactions while working on their group project.*	gemeinschaftlich
		exposure [ɪk'spəʊʒə]	*I don't think we have enough exposure to varieties of English from other parts of the world.*	Sichtbarkeit; Einblick
110		to **broaden** ['brɔːdən]	*It's important to broaden your horizons.*	erweitern; verbreitern
	2a	to **enrich** [ɪn'rɪtʃ]	*Enrich your texts with personal comments.*	verbessern; bereichern
		to **stimulate** ['stɪmjʊleɪt]	*Students were stimulated to go abroad to study.*	anregen

page	exercise	Workshop 3		
	3a	**reliant** [rɪ'laɪənt]	*We have become reliant on technology.*	abhängig
		uncertain [ʌn'sɜːrtən]	*The futures of young refugees are so uncertain because they don't know whether they can stay in the country.*	ungewiss
	3b	**transferable** [træns'fɜːrəbl]	*Transferable skills are important if you want a new job.*	übertragbar
		to boost [buːst]	*The government introduced new measurements to boost the local film industry.*	ankurbeln; steigern
		employability [ɪmˌplɔɪə'bɪlɪti]	*Diverse skills can boost your employability.*	Beschäftigungsfähigkeit
		to enhance [ɪn'hɑːns]	*Learning more skills enhanced my self-confidence.*	verstärken
111	4b	**proficiency** [prə'fɪʃnsi]	*They test your proficiency in English.*	Kenntnisse
		stipend ['staɪpɛnd]	*The students were offered a stipend for two years.*	Stipendium
		to phase out [feɪz aʊt]	*= to discontinue*	abschaffen
	6	**to enquire** [ɪn'kwaɪə]	*Outline your financial situation and enquire about possible funding.* *= ask*	anfragen; sich erkundigen
112	S1b	**discipline** ['dɪsəplɪn]	*What are your favourite disciplines in sports?*	Disziplin; Fachrichtung
		reasoned ['riːzənd]	*He drew reasoned conclusions.*	begründet
		robust [rəʊ'bʌst]	*The evidence has to be robust.*	belastbar; robust
		to **incorporate** [ɪn'kɔːpəreɪt]	*In his essay, he chose to incorporate quotes from famous authors.*	einbauen; integrieren
		to **synthesize** ['sɪnθəsaɪz]	*It involves synthesizing, what you have learned to develop your own arguments.*	synthetisieren
		humanities [hjuː'mænətis]	*Critical thinking is essential in arts and humanities.*	Geisteswissenschaften
		postgraduate [ˌpəʊst'grædʒuət]	*He studies for a post-graduate degree.*	Graduierten-
		purposeful ['pɜːpəsfl]	*Purposeful reading can help with critical thinking.*	zweckgerichtet
		validity [və'lɪdəti]	*The validity of his argument was questioned by his peers.*	Glaubhaftigkeit
	S2a	**confirmation** [ˌkɒnfə'meɪʃn]	*Send a confirmation when you receive the mail.*	Bestätigung
		beware [bɪ'weə]	*Motorists have been warned to beware of icy roads.*	vorsichtig sein
		shade [ʃeɪd]	*shades of meaning*	*hier:* Schattierung
		indisputable [ˌɪndɪ'spjuːtəbl]	*What seems like an indisputable fact could be more differentiated.*	unbestritten

page	exercise	Workshop 3		
		intellectual [ˌɪntəˈlektʃul]	*Having intellectual empathy allows one to understand and respect others' viewpoints, even if they differ from one's own.*	geistig; intellektuell
		empathy [ˈempəθi]	*Empathy is the ability to understand and share the feelings of another person.*	Empathie
		ulterior [ʌlˈtɪəriə]	*I can understand that he has ulterior motives.*	verborgen
113	S1a	**sculpting** [ˈskʌlptɪŋ]	*Showing interest in a fitness program led to a flood of slimming content, including body sculpting suggestions.*	Körpermodellierung
		to heal [hiːl]	*Some sick people chose to stop traditional medical treatments because they believed they could heal naturally.*	heilen
		moral [ˈmɒrl]	*Her moral principles guided her through difficult decisions.*	Moral
	TIP	**to alter** [ˈɔːltə]	*Are fake photos altered or taken from an unrelated site?*	bearbeiten; verändern
	S2b	**accuracy** [ˈækjʊrəsi]	*Check the accuracy of the source.*	Genauigkeit
118	2	**amber** [ˈæmbə]	*Amber is the middle colour on a traffic light.*	gelb-orange
119	4	**microdrama** [ˈmaɪkrəʊˌdrɑːmə]	*A microdrama is a very short dramatic piece or performance, typically lasting only a few minutes.*	Mikrodrama
	TIP	**pun** [pʌn]	*A pun is a play on words.*	Wortspiel
120	1	**sacrifice** [ˈsækrɪfaɪs]	*The parents made many sacrifices for their children.*	Opfer
	2a	**to cease** [siːs]	*If the sea continues to rise, many countries will cease to exist.*	aufhören; einstellen
121	3a	**systematic** [ˌsɪstəˈmætɪk]	*The systematic removal of peoples' rights often leads to social unrest.*	systematisch; methodisch
122	4b	**to tolerate** [ˈtɒləˌreɪt]	*We don't tolerate rascism.*	tolerieren
		to ditch [dɪtʃ]	*= to abandon*	ablegen
123	1	**nursery** [ˈnɜːsəri]	*= Kindergarten*	Kindergarten
	2	**practitioner** [prækˈtɪʃənə]	*She worked as a medical practitioner helping patients with their health concerns.*	Fachkraft
124	5a	**imminent** [ˈɪmɪnənt]	*The most imminent target is to replace fossile fuels.*	bevorstehend; unmittelbar
		to implement [ˈɪmplɪment]	*He implemented lots of changes but they didn't make the text better.*	umsetzen; durchführen
		curriculum [kəˈrɪkjələm]	*The school curriculum for maths covers a lot of different topics.*	Curriculum; Lehrplan
		to adhere [ədˈhɪə]	*We adhere to traditions.*	haften; festhalten
		to jeopardize [ˈdʒɛpərdaɪz]	*If we don't act soon, we'll jeopardize the lives of future generations.*	gefährden; in Gefahr bringen

page	exercise	Workshop 3		
126	7b	**to calculate** ['kælkjʊleɪt]	*Please calculate an hour for the task.*	berechnen; kalkulieren
		to star [stɑ:]	*Jennifer Lawrence starred in The Hunger Games.*	eine Hauptrolle spielen
	8a	**embryo** ['ɛmbriəʊ]	*They saw the embryo during the examination.*	Embryo
127	9b	**sequel** ['si:kwl]	*The sequel to her last book is coming out now.*	Fortsetzung
	11	**to filter out** ['fɪltər aʊt]	*Filter out the important words.*	herausfiltern; aussieben

page	exercise	Workshop 4		
132	1	**proposition** [ˌprɒpə'zɪʃn]	*= suggestion*	Vorschlag
	2	**addictive** [ə'dɪktɪv]	*Heroin is more addictive than cigarettes and alcohol.*	süchtig machend
133		**unchaperoned** [ʌn'ʃæpərəʊnd]	*The teenagers were excited to attend their first unchaperoned concert together.*	unbeaufsichtigt
		concerning [kən'sɜ:n]	*The concerning news about the storm frightened people.*	bedenklich; *auch:* hinsichtlich
		connectivity [kəˌnek'tɪvəti]	*Connectivity is very important in a tech world.*	Vernetzung
		to pollinate ['pɒləneɪt]	*Bees pollinate crops and wild plants.*	bestäuben
		soy [sɔɪ]	*Soy beans are an excellent source of protein.*	Soja
		dairy ['deəri]	*The drive to produce greater amounts of cheap meat and dairy is accelerating climate change and destroying forests.*	Milchprodukte
		to **compound** ['kɒmpaʊnd]	*Ignoring the issue now will only compound the problem in the future.*	verschlimmern
		exclusion [ɪk'sklu:ʒn]	*New levels of connectivity are causing new exclusions.*	Ausschluss
		to reproduce [ˌri:prə'dju:s]	*These reflections often reproduce and amplify existing divides, such as those based on socio-economic class.*	reproduzieren
	3	**dependent** [dɪ'pendənt]	*If you are dependent on someone, you need them for support, help, or survival.* *≠ independent*	abhängig
	4	**animations** [ˌænɪ'meɪʃənz]	*Animations make pictures look like they're moving.*	Animationen
		notification [ˌnəʊtɪfɪ'keɪʃn]	*Notifications are pushed every 30 minutes.*	Nachricht; Benachrichtigung
		reward [rɪ'wɔ:d]	*Social media rewards activate the brain's dopamine system.*	Belohnung
		dopamine ['dəʊpəmi:n]	*Dopamine is a chemical in your brain that acts like a messenger.*	Dopamin
		slot-machine ['slɒt məˌʃi:n]	*You can become addicted to playing at slot-machines.*	Spielautomat

page	exercise	Workshop 4		
		periodically [ˌpɪəriˈɒdɪkli]	= *regularly*	regelmäßig
		sophisticated [səˈfɪstɪkeɪtɪd]	*He bought a new smartphone with a sophisticated camera system.*	ausgefeilt
		to dwell [dwɛl]	= *stay* ≠ *move on*	verweilen
		to backtrack [ˈbæktræk]	*He decided to backtrack on his decision after hearing everyone's opinions.*	zurückrudern
		usage [ˈjuːsɪdʒ]	*Check your daily usage of social media.*	Nutzung
		to bow [bəʊ]	*He bowed before the king.*	sich beugen
		to employ [ɪmˈplɔɪ]	*How many people does she employ?*	beschäftigen
	5	**in-depth** [dɛpθ]	*in-depth research*	tiefgreifend; gründlich
134	1a	**to characterize** [ˈkærəktəraɪz]	*Which of the two statements characterizes the Climate Group better?*	kennzeichnen; charakterisieren
		disastrous [dɪˈzɑːstrəs]	= *catastrophic*	verheerend
		to halve [hɑːv]	*We must halve global emissions in the next ten years if we want to achieve anything.*	halbieren
		to multiply [ˈmʌltɪplaɪ]	*We build and run networks, multiplying their impact and reach.*	multiplizieren; vervielfachen
		framework [ˈfreɪmwɜːk]	*The new education policy provides a framework for improving schools.*	Rahmen
135	2	**urgent** [ˈɜːdʒənt]	*How do you persuade people that a problem is urgent?*	dringend
136	2a	**explanatory** [ɪkˈsplænətri]	*There are explanatory notes at the front of the book.*	erklärend
		to contract [kɒnˈtrækt]	*Negative forms are often contracted.*	zusammenziehen
		to annihilate [əˈnaɪəleɪt]	= *kill*	vernichten
		to poison [ˌpɔɪzn]	*Our seas are poisoned, acidic and rising.*	vergiften
		desertification [dɪˌzɜːtɪfɪˈkeɪʃn]	*We need to prevent further desertification in Africa.*	Wüstenbildung
		to render [ˈrendə]	= *to make*	machen
		tract [trækt]	*Huge tracts of land were flooded.* = *area*	Gebiet
		uninhabitable [ˌʌnɪnˈhæbɪtəbl]	*Flooding and desertification will leave large areas uninhabitable.*	unbewohnbar
		untold [ˌʌnˈtəʊld]	*He put his family through untold suffering.*	*hier:* unermesslich
		bystander [ˈbaɪstændə]	*Act, don't be just a bystander.*	Zuschauer(in)
		to cascade [kæsˈkeɪd]	*Climate change can lead to extreme weather events, which can then cause social and economic problems in a cascading effect.*	kaskadieren; sich überschlagen
		humanity [hjuːˈmænəti]	*We must be clear about the extreme risks humanity now faces.*	Menschheit

page	exercise	Workshop 4		
137	3a	**triple** ['trɪpl]	*The rule of three is also called 'tripels'.*	Dreier
138	1a	**exhibitor** [ɪg'zɪbɪtə]	*How many exhibitors were showing their products?*	Aussteller(in)
		to **buzz** [bʌz]	*It's a robotic bee that can buzz between flowers and pollinate plants.*	schwirren
		fungus ['fʌŋgəs], **fungi** ['fʌŋgaɪ]	*Fungi and viruses can cause disease.*	Pilz
		parasite ['pærəsaɪt]	*Parasites can cause diseases in animals.*	Parasit
		fatigue [fə'ti:g]	*In the United States they are transported hundreds of kilometres and, after several days of pollination, they die of fatigue.* *= exhaustion*	Erschöpfung
		dire ['daɪə]	*The effects of such a situation may be direr than we all think.*	entsetzlich; furchtbar
		interference [ˌɪntə'fɪərəns]	*The radio had a lot of interference, making it hard to hear the music.*	Interferenz; Störung
		demise [dɪ'maɪz]	*A robot may save us from their demise: the B-Droid.*	Niedergang
		to **locate** [ləʊ'keɪt]	*This autonomous device finds flowers and locates them.*	finden; orten
		pollen ['pɒlən]	*Bees collect pollen and bring it to another flower.*	Pollen
	2	**groundbreaker** ['graʊndbreɪkə]	*He was a groundbeaker and the first to create social platforms.*	Wegbereiter(in)
	2a	to **bear in mind** [bɛər ɪn maɪnd]	*Bear these questions in mind when you do your research.*	beachten; im Auge behalten
139	3a	to **collate** [kə'leɪt]	*We collated our ideas on the whiteboard.*	zusammentragen; sammeln
		coherent [kəʊ'hɪərənt]	*After reviewing all the evidence, the jury reached a coherent conclusion about the case.*	schlüssig
		mash [mæʃ]	*In a 'mind mash', you combine various ideas, thoughts, and perspectives.*	Püree
		representation [ˌreprɪzen'teɪʃn]	*You will have a visual representation of how to organize your ideas in your presentation.*	*hier:* Darstellung
		duplication [ˌdju:plɪ'keɪʃn]	*Try to avoid duplication when you write a text.*	Doppelung
		to **shuffle** ['ʃʌfl]	*Shuffle the cards.*	mischen
		keynote ['ki:nəʊt]	*Organize your keynotes in groups and move them around until you are happy with the organization.*	Hauptgedanke; Leitmotiv
		to **crystallize** ['krɪstəlaɪz]	*= to become more concrete*	(sich) herausbilden
140	3b	**edible** ['edəbl]	*Which mushrooms are edible?*	essbar
		fog [fɒg]	*Fog usually occurs early in the morning.*	Nebel

page	exercise	Workshop 4		
	4	**to investigate** [ɪn'vestɪgeɪt]	*Investigate other methods of collating ideas, and try out any you find interesting.*	untersuchen
		cluster ['klʌstə]	*She saw a cluster of wild flowers on the lawn.*	Ansammlung
		fishbone [fɪʃbəʊn]	*We used a fishbone diagram to identify the causes of the project's delays.*	Gräte
		causal ['kɔ:zl]	*Causal loop diagramming is a method to visualize how different variables in a system are connected.*	ursächlich
		loop [lu:p]	*Loop diagramming aids in systems thinking by revealing the interconnectedness and dynamics of entire systems, not just individual parts.*	Schleife
	TIP	**authorship** ['ɔ:θərʃɪp]	*Provide as much information as possible concerning authorship and availability.*	Urheberschaft; Autorenschaft
141	1a	**bluff** [blʌf]	*His story was all a bluff to get money from us.*	Täuschung
		to bluff [blʌf]	*He tried to bluff his way through the test without studying.*	täuschen
	TIP	**plausible** ['plɔ:zəbl]	*Give plausible example sentences to illustrate the use of the new vocabulary.*	einleuchtend
142	2a	**economist** [ɪ'kɒnəmɪst]	*I am an economist, that's why I focus on sustainable development and green economies.*	Wirtschaftswissen-schaftler(in)
		trillion ['trɪljən]	*Because large numbers are counted differently, an American trillion is the equivalent of German billion.*	Billion
		catastrophe [kə'tæstrəfi]	*The earhquake was a catastrophe.*	Katastrophe
		everlasting [ˌevə'lɑ:stɪŋ]	*Social media have an everlasting effect on us – whether we notice it or not.*	ewig
		trait [treɪt]	*What are the skills, knowledge and traits required to build a utopia?*	Eigenschaft
		stressor ['stresə]	*There are several stressors caused by social media.*	Stressfaktor
		insecurity [ˌɪnsɪ'kjʊərəti]	*Insecurity is basically one's lack of confidence in themselves.*	Unsicherheit
		reel [ri:l]	*You can put a reel with your clips together.*	Sammlung von Videos
		toned [toʊnd]	*Exercise will give you a toned body.*	straff
		to encounter [ɪn'kaʊntə]	*One stressor we encounter while going through our social media is FOMO.*	begegnen

page	exercise	Workshop 4		
		transaction [træn'zækʃn]	*She completed the transaction by paying with her credit card.*	Transaktion
		to **quantify** ['kwɒntɪfaɪ]	*We must quantify the results to understand the project's success.*	quantifizieren
		lightly ['laɪtli]	*Don't take these issues lightly.*	leicht
		anxiety [æŋ'zaɪəti]	*FOMO can very quickly turn into a social anxiety that causes withdrawal symptoms.*	Sorge; Ängstlichkeit
		withdrawal [wɪð'drɔːl]	*She experienced withdrawal symptoms when she quit smoking.*	Entzug
		tirelessly ['taɪərləsli]	*She has been working tirelessly.*	unermüdlich
144	TIP	to **gesticulate** [dʒe'stɪkjuleɪt]	*Don't gesticulate so much; it distracts your audience during the presentation.*	gestikulieren

Dictionary: English – German

3

3D printing [ˌθriː ˈdiː prɪntɪŋ] 3D-Druck OT 1

A

a [eɪ] ein(e) OT 1
aardvark [ˈɑːdvɑːk] Erdferkel **WS 2**, 53
to **abandon** [əˈbændən] im Stich lassen **WS 2**, 56
abbreviation [əˌbriːviˈeɪʃn] Abkürzung OT 5
to **abduct** [æbˈdʌkt] entführen OT 4
ability [əˈbɪləti] Können; Fähigkeit OT 2
able: to **be able to** [biː ˈeɪbl tuː] können OT 2
able-bodiedness [ˈeɪblˈbɒdidnəs] körperliche Fitness **WS 2**, 57
aboard [əˈbɔːd] an Bord OT 4
to **abolish** [əˈbɒlɪʃ] abschaffen **WS 2**, 54
about [əˈbaʊt] über; ungefähr; um … herum OT 1
above [əˈbʌv] oben; oberhalb OT 3
abroad [əˈbrɔːd] im Ausland OT 4
abrupt [əˈbrʌpt] abrupt; plötzlich **WS 2**, 65
to **abseil** [ˈæbseɪl] (sich) abseilen OT 2
absence [ˈæbsəns] Abwesenheit **WS 2**, 65
absolute [ˈæbsəluːt] absolut OT 3
absolutely [ˈæbsəluːtli] durchaus; total; wirklich; absolut OT 2
to **absorb** [əbˈzɔːrb] absorbieren; aufnehmen **WS 3**, 108
abstract [ˈæbstrækt] abstrakt OT 5
abuse [əˈbjuːs] Missbrauch OT 4
to **abuse** [əˈbjuːs] missbrauchen **WS 2**, 78
abusive [əˈbjuːsɪv] gewalttätig **WS 1**, 29
academic [ˌækəˈdemɪk] akademisch OT 5
academical [ˌækəˈdɛmɪkl] akademisch **WS 2**, 55
academy [əˈkædəmi] Akademie **WS 2**, 84
to **accelerate** [əkˈseləreɪt] beschleunigen **WS 3**, 99
accent [ˈæksənt] Akzent OT 1
to **accept** [əkˈsept] annehmen OT 3
acceptable [əkˈseptəbl] akzeptabel OT 5
access [ˈækses] Zugriff; Zugang OT 4
to **access** [ˈækses] zugreifen auf OT 4
accessible [əkˈsesəbl] zugänglich; barrierefrei OT 2
accessory [əkˈsesəri] Zubehör OT 3
accident [ˈæksɪdənt] Unfall OT 1
Accident and Emergency [ˈæksɪdənt ənd ɪˌmɜːdʒənsi] Notaufnahme OT 1
by accident [baɪ ˈæksɪdənt] versehentlich OT 2
accidentally [ˌæksɪˈdentəli] zufällig; versehentlich OT 3
acclaim [əˈkleɪm] Beifall; Anerkennung **WS 2**, 80
accommodation [əˌkɒməˈdeɪʃn] Unterkunft OT 2
accompanied [əˈkʌmpənid] begleitet OT 3
according to [əˈkɔːdɪŋ tə] gemäß; nach OT 3
accordion [əˈkɔːdiən] Akkordeon OT 2
account [əˈkaʊnt] Bericht **WS 1**, 14
accountable: to **hold accountable** [həʊld əˈkaʊntəbl] zur Rechenschaft ziehen OT 5
accuracy [ˈækjʊrəsi] Genauigkeit **WS 3**, 113
accurate [ˈækjərət] genau; präzise OT 4
to **accuse** [əˈkjuːz] beschuldigen; anklagen **WS 1**, 20
accustomed [əˈkʌstəmd] gewohnt; vertraut **WS 2**, 56
to **ache** [eɪk] schmerzen; wehtun OT 3
to **achieve** [əˈtʃiːv] erreichen; schaffen OT 4
achievement [əˈtʃiːvmənt] Leistung OT 2
acid rain [ˈæsɪd reɪn] saurer Regen **WS 3**, 98
acidic [əˈsɪdɪk] sauer OT 5
to **acknowledge** [əkˈnɒlɪdʒ] bestätigen; anerkennen OT 5
acoustic [əˈkuːstɪk] akustisch OT 2
acquire [əˈkwaɪə] erwerben; akquirieren **WS 1**, 32
acre [ˈeɪkə] Morgen OT 4
across [əˈkrɒs] auf der anderen Seite; hinüber OT 1
acrostic [əˈkrɒstɪk] Akrostichon OT 5
act [ækt] Gesetz; Verordnung OT 5
to **act** [ækt] (sich) verhalten; Theater spielen OT 1
to **act out** [ækt aʊt] vorführen OT 1
action [ˈækʃn] Aktion OT 1
in action [ɪn ˈækʃn] im Einsatz OT 2
to **activate** [ˈæktɪveɪt] aktivieren OT 4
active [ˈæktɪv] aktiv OT 4
activism [ˈæktɪvɪzəm] Aktivismus OT 4
activist [ˈæktɪvɪst] Aktivist(in) OT 5
activity [ækˈtɪvəti] Aktivität OT 1
actor [ˈæktə] Schauspieler(in) OT 1
actual [ˈæktʃuəl] richtig; wirklich OT 5
actually [ˈæktʃuəli] eigentlich; sogar; tatsächlich OT 2
AD (Anno Domini) [ˌeɪ ˈdi] n. Chr.; unserer Zeitrechnung OT 2
ad [æd] Werbung OT 2
adaptable [əˈdæptəbl] anpassungsfähig OT 4
to **add** [æd] hinzufügen OT 1
addicted [əˈdɪktɪd] süchtig; abhängig OT 3
addictive [əˈdɪktɪv] süchtig machend **WS 4**, 132
addition: in addition to [ɪn əˈdɪʃn tə] zusätzlich zu; neben OT 4
additional [əˈdɪʃənl] zusätzlich **WS 2**, 65
address [əˈdres] Adresse OT 1
to **address** [əˈdres] adressieren; ansprechen **WS 1**, 20
adequate [ˈædɪkwət] ausreichend; angemessen OT 5
to **adhere** [ədˈhɪə] haften; festhalten **WS 3**, 124
adjective [ˈædʒɪktɪv] Adjektiv OT 1
adjoining [əˈdʒɔɪnɪŋ] angrenzend OT 3
to **adjust** [əˈdʒʌst] (sich) anpassen **WS 1**, 24
admiration [ˌædmɪˈreɪʃn] Bewunderung **WS 2**, 64
to **admire** [ədˈmaɪə] bewundern **WS 1**, 31
admission [ədˈmɪʃn] Eintritt OT 5
to **admit** [ədˈmɪt] zugeben OT 4; eingestehen **WS 1**, 26
to **adopt** [əˈdɒpt] annehmen OT 5
adrenaline rush [əˈdrenəlɪn rʌʃ] Adrenalinstoß OT 1
adult [ˈædʌlt] Erwachsene(r) OT 1
advance [ədˈvɑːns] Fortschritt OT 4
advanced [ədˈvɑːnst] fortgeschritten OT 4
advantage [ədˈvɑːntɪdʒ] Vorteil OT 3
advent [ˈædvent] Beginn; Einführung OT 5
adventure [ədˈventʃə] Abenteuer OT 1

adventurous [ədˈventʃərəs] abenteuerlustig OT 2
adverb [ˈædvɜːb] Adverb; Umstandswort OT 1
advert [ˈædvɜːt] Inserat OT 1
to **advertise** [ˈædvətaɪz] Werbung machen für OT 2
advertisement [ədˈvɜːtɪsmənt] Werbung OT 1
advertiser [ˈædvətaɪzə] Werbeagentur; Werber OT 3
advertising [ˈædvətaɪzɪŋ] Werbung OT 2
advice [ədˈvaɪs] Rat OT 1
to **advise** [ədˈvaɪz] raten OT 4
advisor [ədˈvaɪzə] Berater(in) OT 5
advocate [ˈædvəkət] Anwalt, Anwältin **WS 3**, 95
to **advocate** [ˈædvəkət] sich einsetzen **WS 1**, 25
affair [əˈfeə] Angelegenheit; Affäre **WS 1**, 38
to **affect** [əˈfekt] sich auswirken auf OT 3
affection [əˈfekʃn] Zuneigung OT 5
to **afford** [əˈfɔːd] (sich) leisten OT 2
affordable [əˈfɔːdəbl] bezahlbar OT 4
afraid [əˈfreɪd] ängstlich OT 2
African [ˈæfrɪkən] afrikanisch OT 2
after [ˈɑːftə] nach OT 1
afterlife [ˈɑːftəlaɪf] Leben nach dem Tod OT 5
aftermath [ˈɑːftəmæθ] Nachwirkungen **WS 1**, 14
afternoon [ˌɑːftəˈnuːn] Nachmittag OT 1
afterwards [ˈɑːftəwədz] danach; nachher OT 3
again [əˈgen] wieder OT 1
against [əˈgenst] gegen OT 1
age [eɪdʒ] Alter OT 1
  to **age** [eɪdʒ] alt werden; altern **WS 1**, 39
  aged [eɪdʒd] im Alter von OT 1
agency [ˈeɪdʒənsi] Agentur; Organisation OT 4
agenda [əˈdʒendə] Tagesordnung OT 3
aggressive [əˈgresɪv] aggressiv OT 3
agile [ˈædʒaɪl] beweglich OT 3
ago [əˈgəʊ] vor OT 1
agrarian [əˈgreəriən] landwirtschaftlich OT 5
to **agree** [əˈgriː] (sich) einig sein; zustimmen OT 1
agreement [əˈgriːmənt] Vereinbarung OT 3
agricultural [ˌægrɪˈkʌltʃərəl] landwirtschaftlich OT 4
agriculture [ˈægrɪkʌltʃə] Landwirtschaft OT 2
ahead [əˈhed] voraus OT 3
AI (artificial intelligence) [ˌeɪ ˈaɪ] künstliche Intelligenz OT 5
aim [eɪm] Absicht; Ziel OT 4
to **aim** [eɪm] zielen; beabsichtigen OT 4
air [eə] Luft OT 1
airplane [ˈeəpleɪn] Flugzeug OT 4
airport [ˈeəpɔːt] Flughafen OT 1
alarm [əˈlɑːm] Wecker; Alarm OT 2
alarm clock [əˈlɑːm klɒk] Wecker OT 2
alarmed [əˈlɑːmd] beunruhigt OT 3
Alaskan [əˈlæskən] alaskisch OT 2
album [ˈælbəm] Album OT 3
alcohol [ˈælkəhɒl] Alkohol OT 3
alcoholic [ˌælkəˈhɒlɪk] alkoholisch OT 3
to **alert** [əˈlɜːt] alarmieren OT 2
algorithm [ˈælgərɪðəm] Algorithmus OT 5
alien [ˈeɪliən] Außerirdische(r); Alien OT 2
alike [əˈlaɪk] ebenso OT 5
alive [əˈlaɪv] lebendig OT 4
all [ɔːl] alles; alle OT 1
  all over [ˈɔːl əʊvə] überall OT 2
  all right [ˌɔːl ˈraɪt] gut; in Ordnung OT 1
  all set [ɔːl ˈset] bereit OT 2
to **allege** [əˈledʒ] behaupten; vorwerfen **WS 1**, 18
allergic [əˈlɜːdʒɪk] allergisch OT 2
allergy [ˈælədʒi] Allergie OT 1
alliance [əˈlaɪəns] Bündnis; Allianz **WS 1**, 33
alliteration [əˌlɪtəˈreɪʃn] Alliteration OT 5
to **allow** [əˈlaʊ] erlauben OT 3
allowance [əˈlaʊəns] Taschengeld OT 3
allowed [əˈlaʊd] erlaubt OT 3
  to **be allowed to** [biː əˈlaʊd tuː] dürfen; können OT 2
allusion [əˈluːʒn] Anspielung **WS 2**, 62
almond [ˈɑːmənd] Mandel **WS 1**, 22
almost [ˈɔːlməʊst] fast OT 2
alone [əˈləʊn] allein OT 1
along [əˈlɒŋ] entlang OT 1
alongside [əˌlɒŋˈsaɪd] neben; an der Seite von **WS 1**, 21
aloud [əˈlaʊd] laut; mit lauter Stimme OT 2
alpaca [ælˈpækə] Alpaka OT 2
alphabet [ˈælfəbet] Alphabet OT 1
alphabetical [ˌælfəˈbetɪkl] alphabetisch OT 2
already [ɔːlˈredi] schon; bereits OT 2
alright [ɔːlˈraɪt] in Ordnung OT 1
also [ˈɔːlsəʊ] auch OT 1
to **alter** [ˈɔːltə] bearbeiten; verändern **WS 3**, 113
alternative [ɔːlˈtɜːnətɪv] Alternative OT 2
although [ɔːlˈðəʊ] obwohl OT 2
altitude [ˈæltɪˌtud] Höhe **WS 2**, 60
altruistic [ˌæltruˈɪstɪk] altruistisch; selbstlos **WS 2**, 68
alumnus [əˈlʌmnaɪ] Absolvent; Ehemalige OT 4
always [ˈɔːlweɪz] immer OT 1
to **amaze** [əˈmeɪz] verwundern; erstaunen OT 5
amazed [əˈmeɪzd] erstaunt; überrascht OT 3
amazing [əˈmeɪzɪŋ] erstaunlich OT 1
ambassador [æmˈbæsədə] Botschafter(in); Gesandte(r) **WS 1**, 21
amber [ˈæmbə] gelb-orange **WS 3**, 118
ambition [æmˈbɪʃn] Ziel; Ambition OT 4
ambitious [æmˈbɪʃəs] ehrgeizig OT 4
ambulance [ˈæmbjələns] Krankenwagen OT 1
amends: to make amends [meɪk əˈmendz] Wiedergutmachung leisten; entschädigen OT 5
amenity [əˈmiːnəti] Annehmlichkeit **WS 2**, 79
American [əˈmerɪkən] amerikanisch OT 1
amidst [əˈmɪdst] inmitten von **WS 2**, 65
ammunition [ˌæmjʊˈnɪʃən] Munition **WS 2**, 83
among [əˈmʌŋ] unter; zwischen OT 3
amount [əˈmaʊnt] Menge OT 2
amphitheatre [ˈæmfɪθɪətə] Arena; Amphitheater OT 3
amplifier [ˈæmplɪfaɪə] Verstärker OT 2
to **amplify** [ˈæmplɪfaɪ] verstärken **WS 1**, 14
to **amputate** [ˈæmpjʊˌteɪt] amputieren **WS 2**, 84
amused [əˈmjuːzd] amüsiert OT 3
amusement [əˈmjuːzmənt] Vergnügen; Unterhaltung **WS 1**, 21
amusing [əˈmjuːzɪŋ] amüsant; lustig OT 5
an [æn] ein(e) OT 1
to **analyse** [ˈænəlaɪz] analysieren OT 3
analysis [əˈnæləsɪs] Analyse; Untersuchung OT 5

ancestor ['ænsestə] Vorfahr(in) OT 3
ancestry ['ænsestri] Abstammung **WS 2**, 55
to **anchor** ['æŋkə] ankern OT 4
ancient ['eɪnʃənt] antik; uralt OT 2
and [ənd] und OT 1
android ['æn,drɔɪd] Android; Roboter **WS 3**, 104
anecdote ['ænɪkdəʊt] Anekdote OT 4
angel ['eɪndʒl] Engel OT 3
anger ['æŋgə] Ärger; Wut OT 3
to **anger** ['æŋgə] verärgern **WS 2**, 68
angle ['æŋgl] Blickwinkel OT 5
angry ['æŋgri] böse OT 1
angrily ['æŋgrəli] ärgerlich; böse; zornig OT 2
animal ['ænɪml] Tier OT 1
to **animate** ['ænɪ,meɪt] animieren **WS 3**, 103
animations [,ænɪ'meɪʃənz] Animationen **WS 4**, 133
ankle ['æŋkl] Fußknöchel OT 1
to **annihilate** [ə'naɪəleɪt] vernichten **WS 4**, 136
anniversary [,ænɪ'vɜ:səri] Jahrestag **WS 1**, 19
to **annotate** ['ænəteɪt] annotieren; kommentieren **WS 2**, 63
to **announce** [ə'naʊns] ansagen; bekannt geben OT 2
announcement [ə'naʊnsmənt] Bekanntgabe; Ansage OT 2
to **annoy** [ə'nɔɪ] ärgern OT 3
annoyed [ə'nɔɪd] genervt OT 2
annoying [ə'nɔɪɪŋ] ärgerlich; nervig OT 2
annual ['ænjuəl] jährlich OT 5
anomaly [ə'nɒməli] Anomalie; Abweichung **WS 2**, 63
another [ə'nʌðə] noch ein(e); ein(e) andere(r, -s) OT 1
answer ['ɑ:nsə] Antwort OT 1
to **answer** ['ɑ:nsə] antworten; beantworten OT 1
ant [ænt] Ameise **WS 1**, 39
antelope ['æntɪləʊp] Antilope **WS 2**, 59
antenna [æn'tenə] Antenne OT 2
anthem ['ænθəm] Nationalhymne; Hymne OT 5
anthropocentric [,ænθrəpoʊ'sɛntrɪk] anthropozentrisch; menschenzentriert **WS 1**, 21
antibiotic [,æntibaɪ'ɒtɪk] antibiotisch OT 5
anticipation [æn,tɪsɪ'peɪʃn] Vorfreude **WS 2**, 78
antiseptic [,ænti'septɪk] antiseptisch; keimtötend OT 2
anxiety [æŋ'zaɪəti] Sorge; Ängstlichkeit **WS 4**, 142
anxious ['æŋkʃəs] besorgt OT 2
any ['eni] irgendein(e) OT 1
anybody ['enibɒdi] irgendjemand OT 1
anymore [,eni 'mɔ:] mehr; länger; weiter OT 2
anyone ['eniwʌn] irgendjemand OT 2
anything ['eniθɪŋ] irgendetwas OT 1
anytime ['enitaɪm] jederzeit OT 3
anyway ['enɪweɪ] trotzdem; sowieso; jedenfalls OT 1
anywhere ['eniweə] irgendwo OT 2
apart [ə'pɑ:t] auseinander **WS 1**, 15
apart from [ə'pɑ:t frəm] außer OT 3
apartheid [ə'pɑ:rteɪd] Apartheid **WS 2**, 52
apartment [ə'pɑ:tmənt] Wohnung OT 1
ape [eɪp] Affe; Menschenaffe **WS 1**, 21
to **apologize** [ə'pɒlədʒaɪz] (sich) entschuldigen OT 2
apology [ə'pɒlədʒi] Entschuldigung OT 2
app [æp] App OT 4
appalled [ə'pɔ:ld] entsetzt **WS 1**, 18
appalling [ə'pɔ:lɪŋ] entsetzlich **WS 1**, 38
apparent [ə'pærənt] offensichtlich; erkennbar **WS 1**, 25
apparently [ə'pærəntli] anscheinend OT 4
appeal [ə'pi:l] Aufruf OT 2
to **appeal** [ə'pi:l] ansprechen **WS 1**, 22
to **appear** [ə'pɪə] erscheinen; scheinen; auftauchen OT 3
appearance [ə'pɪərəns] Aussehen OT 3
appetite ['æpɪ,taɪt] Appetit; Verlangen **WS 3**, 104
appetizing ['æpɪtaɪzɪŋ] appetitlich OT 3
to **applaud** [ə'plɔ:d] applaudieren OT 2
applause [ə'plɔ:z] Applaus OT 2
apple ['æpl] Apfel OT 1
appliance [ə'plaɪəns] Gerät; Haushaltsgerät OT 3
applicant ['æplɪkənt] Bewerber(in) OT 4
application [,æplɪ'keɪʃn] Bewerbung; Antrag OT 4
to **apply** [ə'plaɪ] sich bewerben OT 3
to **appoint** [ə'pɔɪnt] ernennen OT 5
appointment [ə'pɔɪntmənt] Anstellung **WS 2**, 81
to **appreciate** [ə'pri:ʃieɪt] anerkennen; schätzen OT 5
apprentice [ə'prentɪs] Auszubildende(r); Lehrling OT 5
apprenticeship [ə'prentɪʃɪp] Lehrstelle; Ausbildung OT 5
approach [ə'prəʊtʃ] Ansatz; Kurs **WS 1**, 21
to **approach** [ə'prəʊtʃ] näher kommen; sich nähern OT 4
appropriate [ə'prəʊpriət] angemessen OT 4
appropriately [ə'prəʊpriətli] passend; angemessen OT 3
appropriation [ə,prəʊpri'eɪʃn] Aneignung OT 5
to **approve** [ə'pru:v] genehmigen; zustimmen OT 3
approximately [ə'prɒksɪmətli] ungefähr; etwa OT 5
April ['eɪprəl] April OT 1
aquatic [ə'kwætɪk] aquatisch; Wasser... OT 4
aqueduct ['ækwɪdʌkt] Aquädukt OT 3
archaeologist [,ɑ:ki'ɒlədʒɪst] Archäologe / Archäologin OT 3
archbishop [,ɑ:tʃ'bɪʃəp] Erzbischof **WS 2**, 72
archer ['ɑ:tʃə] Bogenschütze / -schützin **WS 2**, 62
architect ['ɑ:kɪtekt] Architekt(in) OT 5
architecture ['ɑ:kɪtektʃə] Architektur OT 2
to **archive** ['ɑ:kaɪv] archivieren OT 4
Arctic ['ɑ:ktɪk] arktisch; Arktis OT 4
area ['eəriə] Gebiet; Gegend OT 1
arena [ə'ri:nə] Arena OT 1
aeroplane ['eərəpleɪn] Flugzeug OT 4
arguably ['ɑ:rgjuəbli] zweifellos **WS 1**, 30
to **argue** ['ɑ:gju:] streiten; argumentieren OT 2
argument ['ɑ:gjumənt] Streit; Auseinandersetzung OT 1
argumentative [,ɑ:gju'mentətɪv] argumentativ OT 5
arid ['ærɪd] dürr; trocken OT 5
to **arise** [ə'raɪz] entstehen **WS 1**, 29
aristocracy [,ærɪ'stɒkrəsi] Aristokratie; Adel **WS 2**, 64
arm [ɑ:m] Arm OT 1
armchair ['ɑ:mtʃeə] Sessel OT 1
armed [ɑ:md] bewaffnet OT 5
army ['ɑ:mi] Armee OT 3
around [ə'raʊnd] um OT 1
to **arrange** [ə'reɪndʒ] planen; vereinbaren OT 2

arrangement [ə'reɪndʒmənt] Regelung; Vereinbarung OT 3
array [ə'reɪ] Vielfalt **WS 1**, 43
to **arrest** [ə'rest] gefangen nehmen; verhaften OT 5
arrival [ə'raɪvl] Ankunft OT 2
to **arrive** [ə'raɪv] ankommen OT 1
arrow ['ærəʊ] Pfeil OT 3
art [ɑ:t] Kunst OT 1
fine art [ˌfaɪn 'ɑ:t] Kunstwissenschaft OT 2
article ['ɑ:tɪkl] Artikel; Geschlechtswort OT 1
definite article ['defɪnət ˌɑ:tɪkl] bestimmter Artikel OT 1
indefinite article [ɪnˌdefɪnət 'ɑ:tɪkl] unbestimmter Artikel OT 1
artificial [ˌɑ:tɪ'fɪʃəli] künstlich OT 3
artificial intelligence [ˌɑ:tɪfɪʃl ɪn'telɪdʒəns] künstliche Intelligenz OT 4
artist ['ɑ:tɪst] Künstler(in) OT 3
backing artist ['bækɪŋ 'ɑ:rtɪst] Background-Sänger(in); Unterstützungs(Künstler(in)) **WS 2**, 68
artistic [ɑ:'tɪstɪk] künstlerisch **WS 2**, 68
artwork ['ɑ:twɜ:k] Artwork; Kunstwerk OT 5
arty ['ɑ:ti] gewollt künstlerisch OT 5
as [æz] als; wie OT 1
as well [əz wel] auch OT 1
asexual [ˌeɪ'sekʃuəl] asexuell OT 5
ashamed [ə'ʃeɪmd] beschämt OT 3
ashore [ə'ʃɔ:r] an Land OT 4
Asian ['eɪʒn] asiatisch OT 4
to **ask** [ɑ:sk] fragen OT 1
asleep [ə'sli:p] schlafend **WS 1**, 15
aspect ['æspekt] Aspekt OT 4
aspen ['æspən] Espe OT 2
aspiration [ˌæspɪ'reɪʃən] Bestreben; Ambition **WS 2**, 59
aspirational [ˌæspɪ'reɪʃənl] erstrebenswert; ambitioniert **WS 1**, 32
assassin [ə'sæsɪn] Attentäter(in) **WS 1**, 18
to **assassinate** [ə'sæsɪneɪt] ermorden **WS 1**, 18
assassination [əˌsæsɪ'neɪʃn] Ermordung; Attentat **WS 1**, 18
assault [ə'sɔ:lt] Angriff; Überfall OT 5
aggravated assault ['ægrəveɪtɪd ə'sɔ:lt] schwere Körperverletzung OT 5
assembly [ə'sembli] Versammlung OT 1
assembly hall [ə'sembli ˌhɔ:l] Aula OT 1

to **assert** [ə'sɜ:t] durchsetzen; behaupten **WS 1**, 14
assertive [sʌlk] bestimmt OT 3
to **assess** [ə'ses] beurteilen OT 5
assessment [ə'sesmənt] Einschätzung; Bewertung **WS 3**, 97
assessor [ə'sesər] Gutacher(in) OT 5
assignment [ə'saɪnmənt] Aufgabe OT 4
to **assimilate** [ə'sɪmɪˌleɪt] assimilieren; anpassen **WS 3**, 95
assimilation [əˌsɪmə'leɪʃn] Assimilation; Anpassung OT 4
to **assist** [ə'sɪst] unterstützen OT 5
assistant [ə'sɪstənt] Assistent(in) OT 1
to **associate** [ə'səʊsieɪt] assoziieren OT 4
association [əˌsəʊʃi'eɪʃn] Verein; Verband OT 2
to **assure** [ə'ʃʊə] versichern **WS 2**, 55
asterisk ['æstərɪsk] Sternchen; Asterisk OT 4
astonished [ə'stɒnɪʃ] verblüfft; erstaunt **WS 1**, 27
astonishing [ə'stɒnɪʃɪŋ] erstaunlich OT 5
astonishingly [ə'stɒnɪʃɪŋli] erstaunlicherweise OT 3
astronaut ['æstrənɔ:t] Astronaut(in) OT 4
astronomer [ə'strɑ:nəmə] Astronom(in) **WS 3**, 103
astronomy [ə'strɒnəmi] Astronomie OT 1
asylum seeker [ə'saɪləm si:kə] Asylbewerber(in) OT 4
at [ət] an; in; bei OT 1
at ... o'clock [æt ... ə'klɒk] um ... Uhr OT 1
at the moment [ət ðə 'məʊmənt] momentan OT 2
athlete ['æθli:t] Sportler(in) OT 2
athletic [æθ'letɪk] athletisch; sportlich OT 4
athleticism [ˌæθ'lɛtɪsɪzm] Sportlichkeit **WW**, 11
athletics [æθ'letɪks] Leichtathletik; Sport OT 1
atmosphere ['ætməsfɪə] Atmosphäre OT 3
to **attach** [ə'tætʃ] befestigen OT 4
to **attack** [ə'tæk] angreifen OT 3
attacking [ə'tækɪŋ] angreifend OT 3
attempt [ə'tempt] Versuch OT 2
to **attend** [ə'tend] besuchen OT 2
attendant [ə'tendənt] Aufseher(in); Diener(in) OT 3

attention [ə'tenʃn] Aufmerksamkeit OT 2
to **pay attention** [ˌpeɪ ə'tenʃn] aufpassen OT 2
attic ['ætɪk] Dachboden OT 3
attitude ['ætɪtju:d] Haltung; Einstellung; Ansicht OT 3
to **attract** [ə'trækt] anziehen OT 4
attraction [ə'trækʃn] Sehenswürdigkeit OT 2
attractive [ə'træktɪv] anziehend; attraktiv; reizvoll OT 4
to **attribute** ['ætrɪˌbjut] zuschreiben **WS 2**, 81
audience ['ɔ:diəns] Publikum OT 2
audio diary ['ɔ:diəʊ daɪəri] Audiotagebuch OT 2
audio file ['ɔ:diəʊ faɪl] Audiodatei OT 2
August [ɔ:'gʌst] August OT 1
aunt [ɑ:nt] Tante OT 1
au pair [ˌəʊ 'peər] Au-pair OT 5
Austrian ['ɒstriən] Österreicher(in) OT 4
authentic [ɔ:'θentɪk] authentisch; echt OT 5
authenticity [ɔ:'θɛntɪsɪti] Authentizität; Echtheit **WS 1**, 23
author ['ɔ:θə] Autor(in) OT 2
authoritarian [əˌθɔ:rɪ'tɛrɪən] autoritär **WS 3**, 92
authority [ɔ:'θɒrəti] Behörde; Autorität OT 4
authorized ['ɔ:θəraɪzd] autorisiert; berechtigt OT 5
authorship ['ɔ:θərʃɪp] Urheberschaft; Autorenschaft **WS 4**, 140
autobiographical [ˌɔ:təbaɪ'ɒgrəfɪkl] autobiografisch **WS 2**, 62
autobiography [ˌɔ:təbaɪ'ɒgrəfi] Autobiografie **WS 2**, 62
to **automate** ['ɔ:təmeɪt] automatisieren OT 4
automatic [ˌɔ:tə'mætɪk] automatisch **WS 2**, 78
automobile ['ɔ:təməbi:l] Automobil OT 4
autonomous [ɔ:'tɒnəməs] unabhängig; autonom OT 4
autumn ['ɔ:təm] Herbst OT 2
availability [əˌveɪlə'bɪləti] Verfügbarkeit **WS 3**, 99
available [ə'veɪləbl] verfügbar; erhältlich OT 3
avatar ['ævətɑ:] Avatar OT 3
avenue ['ævənju:] Allee OT 1

average ['ævərɪdʒ] durchschnittlich OT 4
to **avoid** [ə'vɔɪd] vermeiden OT 4
awake [ə'weɪk] wach OT 2
award [ə'wɔ:d] Auszeichnung OT 2
award-winning [ə'wɔ:d wɪnɪŋ] preisgekrönt OT 4
to **award** [ə'wɔ:d] vergeben; verleihen OT 4
aware [ə'weər] bewusst OT 5
awareness [ə'weənəs] Bewusstsein OT 5
away [ə'weɪ] weg OT 1
awesome ['ɔ:səm] toll; großartig OT 2
awestruck ['ɔ:strʌk] ehrfürchtig; beeindruckt **WS 1**, 14
awful ['ɔ:fl] fürchterlich; schrecklich OT 1
awkward ['ɔ:kwəd] ungeschickt; unbeholfen OT 5
awkwardness ['ɔ:kwədnəs] Unbeholfenheit; Peinlichkeit **WS 1**, 28
axis ['æksɪs] Achse OT 4
aye [aɪ] ja OT 2

B

baboon [bə'bu:n] Pavian **WS 2**, 67
baby ['beɪbi] Säugling; Baby OT 1
to **babysit** ['beɪbisɪt] babysitten OT 4
babysitter ['beɪbisɪtə] Babysitter OT 4
back [bæk] Rücken OT 1
back [bæk] zurück OT 1
backbone ['bækbəʊn] Rückgrat OT 2
background ['bækgraʊnd] Hintergrund OT 3
backhand ['bækhænd] Rückhand OT 3
backpack ['bækpæk] Rucksack OT 2
to **backpack** ['bækpæk] mit dem Rucksack reisen OT 3
to **backtrack** ['bæktræk] zurückrudern **WS 4**, 133
backup ['bækʌp] Backup; Unterstützung OT 4
backwards ['bækwədz] nach hinten; rückwärts OT 3
backyard [ˌbæk'ja:d] Garten (hinterm Haus) OT 2
bacon ['beɪkən] Speck; Bacon OT 1
bacteria [bæk'tɪəriə] Bakterie OT 5
bad [bæd] schlecht OT 1
badly ['bædli] schlecht OT 2
badge [bædʒ] Abzeichen OT 1
badminton ['bædmɪntən] Badminton OT 1
bag [bæg] Tüte; Tasche OT 1
bagel ['beɪgl] Bagel OT 1
baggage ['bægɪdʒ] Gepäck OT 2
baggage claim ['bægɪdʒ kleɪm] Gepäckausgabe OT 2
bagpipe ['bægpaɪp] Dudelsack OT 3
to **bake** [beɪk] backen OT 1
baker ['beɪkə] Bäcker(in) OT 3
bakery ['beɪkəri] Bäckerei OT 4
balance ['bæləns] Gleichgewicht OT 3
balanced ['bæləns] ausgeglichen **WS 2**, 82
ball ['bɔ:l] Ball OT 1
ballpoint pen ['bɔ:lpɔɪnt pen] Kugelschreiber OT 1
ballet ['bæleɪ] Ballett OT 3
balloon [bə'lu:n] Ballon OT 3
to **ban** [bæn] verbieten OT 3
banana [bə'nɑ:nə] Banane OT 1
band [bænd] Band OT 1
bandage ['bændɪdʒ] Verband OT 2
Bangladeshi [ˌbæŋglə'deʃi] Bangladescher(in) OT 4
bank [bæŋk] Ufer; Bank OT 3
banking ['bæŋkɪŋ] Banking; Bankwesen OT 5
bank teller [bæŋk 'telə] Kassierer(in) OT 4
banner ad ['bænə æd] Werbebanner OT 5
bar [bɑ:] Riegel; Bar OT 1
barbarian [bɑ:'beəriən] Barbar(in); Wilde(r) **WS 1**, 14
barbaric [bɑ:'bærɪk] barbarisch; unzivilisiert **WS 1**, 21
barbecue ['bɑ:bɪkju:] Grillen OT 2
barbecued ['bɑ:bɪkju:d] gegrillt OT 4
barbershop ['bɑ:rbərʃɒp] Friseursalon; Barbierladen **WS 3**, 97
bare-chested ['beə'tʃestɪd] mit nacktem Oberkörper **WS 1**, 19
barefoot ['beərfʊt] barfuß **WS 2**, 60
bargain ['bɑ:gən] Schnäppchen OT 4
to **bark** [bɑ:k] bellen OT 2
barn [bɑ:n] Scheune OT 2
barren ['bærən] karg; unfruchtbar **WS 2**, 78
barrier ['bæriə] Barriere OT 3
barrister ['bærɪstər] Rechtsanwalt / -anwältin OT 5
base [beɪs] Basis OT 4
to **base on** [beɪs ɒn] auf etw. basieren OT 4
baseball ['beɪsbɔ:l] Baseball OT 1
to **bash** [bæʃ] schlagen **WS 3**, 94
basic ['beɪsɪk] Grund-; grundsätzlich; einfach OT 4
basically ['beɪsɪkli] im Grunde OT 3
basics ['beɪsɪks] Grundlagen **WS 2**, 55
basin ['beɪsn] Becken OT 3
basis ['beɪsɪs] Grundlage; Basis OT 5
basket ['bɑ:skɪt] Korb OT 3
basketball ['bɑ:skɪtbɔ:l] Basketball OT 1
bat [bæt] Fledermaus; Schläger OT 1
long-eared bat [ˌlɒŋɪəd 'bæt] Braunes Langohr OT 2
bath [bɑ:θ] Badewanne; Bad OT 2
bathroom ['bɑ:θru:m] Badezimmer OT 1
bathtub ['bæθˌtʌb] Badewanne **WS 3**, 101
batik [bə'ti:k] Batik- **WS 2**, 71
battery ['bætri] Batterie OT 2
battle ['bætl] Schlacht OT 1
batuni [bə'tu:ni] Schwätzer(in) (umgangssprachlich) **WS 1**, 25
Bavarian [bə'veəriən] bayerisch OT 2
bay [beɪ] Bucht OT 1
to **be** [bi:] sein OT 1
beach [bi:tʃ] Strand OT 1
beadwork ['bi:dwɜ:rk] Perlenarbeit; Perlenkunst **WS 3**, 95
beak [bi:k] Schnabel **WS 1**, 32
beam [bi:m] Balken OT 3
bean [bi:n] Bohne OT 1
baked beans [ˌbeɪkt 'bi:nz] weiße Bohnen in Tomatensoße OT 1
bear [beə] Bär OT 1
to **bear** [beə] ertragen **WS 1**, 14
to **bear the brunt** [beə ðə brʌnt] die Hauptlast tragen **WS 1**, 14
to **bear in mind** [beər ɪn maɪnd] beachten; im Auge behalten **WS 4**, 138
beast [bi:st] Tier; Bestie OT 5
beat [bi:t] Takt OT 1
to **beat** [bi:t] schlagen; besiegen OT 2
beautiful ['bju:tɪfl] schön OT 1
beauty ['bju:ti] Schönheit OT 3
because [bɪ'kɒz] weil OT 1
to **become** [bɪ'kʌm] werden OT 2
bed [bed] Bett; Beet OT 1
bedbug ['bedbʌg] Bettwanze OT 1
bedroom ['bedru:m] Schlafzimmer OT 1
bee [bi:] Biene OT 1
beef [bi:f] Rindfleisch OT 2
beef brisket [bi:f 'brɪskɪt] Rinderbrust OT 4
to **beep** [bi:p] piepen; signalisieren **WS 1**, 39
beer [bɪə] Bier OT 3
beetroot ['bi:tru:t] Rote Bete OT 4
before [bɪ'fɔ:] vor OT 1

beforehand [bɪˈfɔːhænd] im Voraus OT 5
to **beg** [beg] betteln OT 5
to **begin** [bɪˈgɪn] anfangen OT 1
beginning [bɪˈgɪnɪŋ] beginnend OT 1
behalf: on behalf of [ɒn bɪˈhaːf əv] im Interesse von OT 5
to **behave** [bɪˈheɪv] (sich) benehmen OT 2
behaviour [bɪˈheɪvjə] Benehmen OT 2
to **behead** [bɪˈhed] enthaupten OT 3
behind [bɪˈhaɪnd] hinter OT 1
belief [bɪˈliːf] Glaube OT 4
to **believe** [bɪˈliːv] glauben OT 2
bell [bel] Glocke OT 1
belly [ˈbɛli] Bauch; Unterleib **WS 1**, 16
to **belong** [bɪˈlɒŋ] gehören OT 2
belongings [bɪˈlɒŋɪŋz] persönliche Sachen; Habe OT 3
below [bɪˈləʊ] unter OT 2
belt [belt] Gürtel OT 2
bench [bentʃ] Bank OT 3
benchmark [ˈbɛntʃmaːrk] Maßstab; Benchmark **WS 2**, 62
beneath [bɪˈniːθ] darunter OT 5
beneficial [ˌbenɪˈfɪʃl] nützlich OT 2
benefit [ˈbenɪfɪt] Vorteil; Nutzen OT 2
to **benefit** [ˈbenɪfɪt] guttun; profitieren OT 2
berry [ˈberi] Beere OT 4
beside [bɪˈsaid] neben OT 2
besides [bɪˈsaɪdz] außerdem OT 5
best [best] beste(r, -s) OT 1
to **bet** [bet] wetten OT 1
betrayal [bɪˈtreɪl] Verrat; Treuebruch **WS 3**, 96
between [bɪˈtwiːn] zwischen OT 1
to **beware** [bɪˈweə] vorsichtig sein **WS 3**, 112
beyond [bɪˈjɒnd] jenseits OT 5
bias [ˈbaɪəs] Voreingenommenheit OT 5
biased [ˈbaɪəst] parteiisch OT 4
bicycle [ˈbaɪsɪkəl] Fahrrad OT 2
big [bɪg] groß OT 1
bike [baɪk] Fahrrad OT 1
bike lane [ˈbaɪk leɪn] Radstreifen OT 4
to **bike** [baɪk] Rad fahren OT 3
mountain biking [ˈmaʊntən baɪkɪŋ] Mountainbiken OT 2
bilingual [ˌbaɪˈlɪŋgwəl] bilingual; zweisprachig OT 2
bill [bɪl] Rechnung OT 3
billion [ˈbɪljən] Milliarde OT 2
bin [bɪn] Eimer; Behälter OT 2
to **bind** [baɪnd] binden; verpflichten **WS 3**, 94

bingo [ˈbɪŋgəʊ] Bingo OT 1
binoculars [bɪˈnɒkjələz] Fernglas OT 2
biodiversity [ˌbaɪəʊdaɪˈvɜːsəti] Artenvielfalt; Biodiversität OT 4
biographical [ˌbaɪəˈgræfɪkl] biografisch OT 5
biography [baɪˈɒgrəfi] Biografie OT 4
biological [ˌbaɪəˈlɒdʒɪkl] biologisch OT 5
biologist [baɪˈɒlədʒɪst] Biologe/ Biologin OT 4
biology [baɪˈɒlədʒi] Biologie OT 2
bird [bɜːd] Vogel OT 1
birth [bɜːθ] Geburt OT 2
date of birth [ˌdeɪt əv ˈbɜːθ] Geburtsdatum OT 2
birthday [ˈbɜːθdeɪ] Geburtstag OT 1
birthplace [ˈbɜːθpleɪs] Geburtsort OT 4
biscuit [ˈbɪskɪt] Keks OT 1
bisexual [ˌbaɪˈsekʃuəl] bisexuell OT 5
bit [bɪt] Stück OT 1
bite [baɪt] Biss OT 2
bitterly [ˈbɪtəli] bitterlich OT 5
black [blæk] schwarz OT 1
blackberry [ˈblækbəri] Brombeere OT 1
blade [bleɪd] Schneide **WS 1**, 22
to **blame** [bleɪm] jdm. Vorwürfe machen OT 5
blank [blæŋk] leer OT 4
blanket [ˈblæŋkɪt] Decke OT 2
to **blast** [ˈblaːst] absprengen OT 5
blazer [ˈbleɪzər] Blazer; Sportjacke OT 1
blazing [ˈbleɪzɪŋ] brennend OT 5
bleaching [bliːtʃ] Entfärbung OT 5
bleak [bliːk] düster **WW**, 11
blemished [ˈblemɪʃd] fehlerhaft OT 5
to **blend** [ˈblend] mischen **WS 1**, 15
blended [ˈblendɪd] gemischt OT 5
to **bless** [bles] segnen **WS 1**, 19
blind [blaɪnd] blind OT 2
blip [blɪp] Störung; Ausschlag **WS 3**, 98
blister [ˈblɪstə] Blase (Haut) OT 2
to **block** [blɒk] blockieren OT 3
blocker [blɒkər] Blocker OT 5
blog [blɒg] Blog OT 1
blogger [blɒgə] Blogger(in) OT 3
blogpost [blɒgpəʊst] Blogeintrag OT 4
blonde [blɒnd] blond OT 1
blond-haired [blɒndˈhɛərd] blondhaarig; blond **WS 3**, 96
blood [blʌd] Blut OT 2
bloodshed [ˈblʌdʃed] Blutvergießen OT 5
bloodshot [ˈblʌdʃɒt] blutunterlaufen; gerötet **WS 1**, 28

bloodthirsty [ˈblʌdˌθɜːrsti] blutrünstig **WS 3**, 94
bloody [ˈblʌdi] blutig **WS 1**, 14
to **bloom** [bluːm] blühen **WS 2**, 79
to **blow** [bləʊ] blasen; pfeifen; wehen OT 2
blubber [ˈblʌbə] Walspeck OT 2
blue [bluː] blau OT 1
bluebird [ˈbluːbɜːd] Hüttensänger OT 3
blues [bluːz] Blues OT 1
bluff [blʌf] Täuschung **WS 4**, 141
to **bluff** [blʌf] täuschen **WS 4**, 141
to **blur** [blɜːr] verschwimmen OT 5
BMXing [ˌbiː em ˈeksɪŋ] BMX-Rad fahren OT 5
board [bɔːd] Brett; Tafel OT 1
to **board** [bɔːd] an Bord gehen OT 4
boarding school [ˈbɔːrdɪŋ skuːl] Internat; Pensionat **WS 3**, 95
to **boast** [bəʊst] sich rühmen **WS 1**, 23
boat [bəʊt] Boot OT 1
body [ˈbɒdi] Körper OT 1
bodyguard [ˈbɒdigaːd] Leibwächter(in) **WS 2**, 59
to **boil** [bɔɪl] kochen OT 2
boiled [bɔɪld] gekocht OT 1
boiling [ˈbɔɪlɪŋ] kochend heiß OT 1
bold [bəʊld] mutig; fettgedruckt OT 1
bomb [bɒm] Bombe OT 3
to **bombard** [bɒmˈbaːd] bombardieren **WS 2**, 85
bond [bɒnd] Verbindung **WS 1**, 15
to **bond** [bɒnd] zusammenkommen **WS 1**, 15
bonded laborer [ˌbɒndɪd ˈleɪbərə] Schuldknecht; Zwangsarbeiter(in) OT 4
bone [bəʊn] Knochen OT 1
bonfire [ˈbɒnfaɪə] Lagerfeuer **WS 1**, 43
bong [bɒŋ] Klang (einer Glocke) OT 1
bonus [ˈbəʊnəs] Bonus OT 5
to **boo** [buː] ausbuhen **WS 2**, 60
book [bʊk] Buch OT 1
to **book** [bʊk] buchen OT 2
bookcase [ˈbʊkkeɪs] Bücherregal OT 1
booking [ˈbʊkɪŋ] Buchung OT 2
booking office [ˈbʊkɪŋ ˌɒfɪs] Fahrkartenschalter OT 2
booklet [ˈbʊklət] Broschüre OT 2
to **bookmark** [ˈbʊkmaːk] markieren OT 4
boom [buːm] Boom; Aufschwung **WS 1**, 14
to **boom** [buːm] boomed **WS 1**, 24
to **boost** [buːst] ankurbeln; steigern **WS 3**, 110

boot [buːt] Stiefel OT 1
booth [buːð] Zelle OT 4
border ['bɔːdə] Grenze OT 3
bored [bɔːd] gelangweilt OT 1
boring ['bɔːrɪŋ] langweilig OT 1
born: to **be born** [bi 'bɔːn] geboren sein OT 2
to **borrow** ['bɒrəʊ] leihen OT 2
boss [bɒs] Chef(in) OT 2
bossy ['bɒsi] herrisch OT 2
both [bəʊθ] beide OT 1
to **bother** ['bɒðə] stören OT 4
bottle ['bɒtl] Flasche OT 1
bottled ['bɒtld] abgefüllt OT 3
bottom ['bɒtəm] unterster Teil; Boden OT 1
to **bounce back** [baʊns] wieder auf die Beine kommen OT 5
bound: to **be bound to** [bi baʊnd tuː] gebunden sein **WS 3**, 96
boundary ['baʊndri] Grenze OT 5
bouquet [bu'keɪ] Strauß; Bouquet OT 3
bow [bəʊ] Bogen OT 2
to **bow** [bəʊ] sich beugen **WS 4**, 133
bowl [bəʊl] Schüssel OT 1
bow-tie [ˌbəʊ 'taɪ] Fliege OT 2
box [bɒks] Kiste; Kästchen OT 1
boy [bɔɪ] Junge OT 1
boyband ['bɔɪbænd] Boygroup OT 2
boycott ['bɔɪkɒt] Boycott **WS 2**, 68
to **boycott** ['bɔɪkɒt] boykottieren **WS 2**, 68
bracket ['brækɪt] Klammer OT 2
to **braid** [breɪd] flechten **WS 2**, 69
braids [breɪdz] Zöpfe **WS 2**, 69
brain [breɪn] Gehirn OT 2
to **brainstorm** ['breɪnstɔːm] brainstormen OT 2
to **brainwash** ['breɪnwɒʃ] einer Gehirnwäsche unterziehen OT 5
branch [brɑːntʃ] Ast OT 2
brand [brænd] Marke OT 4
to **brand** [brænd] branden **WS 2**, 55
brand-new [ˌbrænd 'njuː] brandneu OT 2
brass [bræs] Messing **WS 1**, 27
brave [breɪv] tapfer OT 1
bravery ['breɪvəri] Mut **WS 1**, 25
Brazilian [brə'zɪliən] brasilianisch OT 2
bread [bred] Brot OT 1
breadcrumbs ['bredkrʌmz] Brotkrumen; Paniermehl OT 3
breadwinner ['bredwɪnə] Ernährer(in); Brotverdiener(in) OT 5
break [breɪk] Pause OT 1
to **break** [breɪk] brechen OT 1
breakdown ['breɪkdaʊn] Aufgliederung **WS 3**, 103
breakfast ['brekfəst] Frühstück OT 1
breakout area ['breɪkaʊt 'eəriə] Aufenthaltsraum OT 5
breast plate ['brɛstpleɪt] Brustplatte; Brustpanzer **WS 3**, 94
breath [breθ] Atem(zug) OT 2
out of breath [ˌaʊt əv' breθ] außer Atem OT 2
to **breathe** [briːð] atmen OT 2
breathless ['breθləs] atemlos OT 3
breathtaking ['breθteɪkɪŋ] atemberaubend OT 3
to **breed** [briːd] (aus)brüten; züchten **WS 1**, 24
breeze [briːz] Brise OT 3
breezy ['briːzi] luftig; unbekümmert **WS 3**, 97
to **bribe** [braɪb] bestechen **WS 2**, 58
bridge [brɪdʒ] Brücke OT 1
brief [briːf] kurz OT 5
bright [braɪt] leuchtend OT 1
brill [brɪl] sehr gut OT 1
brilliant ['brɪliənt] genial OT 1
to **bring** [brɪŋ] bringen OT 1
British ['brɪtɪʃ] britisch OT 1
brittle ['brɪtl] spröde; brüchig **WS 2**, 62
to **broadcast** ['brɔːdkɑːst] senden **WS 1**, 33
to **broaden** ['brɔːdən] erweitern; verbreitern **WS 3**, 110
broccoli ['brɒkəli] Broccoli OT 1
brochure ['brəʊʃə] Broschüre OT 1
broken ['brəʊkən] gebrochen OT 1
broom [bruːm] Besen **WS 1**, 39
brother ['brʌðə] Bruder OT 1
brown [braʊn] braun OT 1
browser ['braʊzər] Browser OT 4
brush [brʌʃ] Bürste; Pinsel OT 2
to **brush** [brʌʃ] bürsten; putzen OT 4
brutal ['bruːtl] brutal OT 5
brutality [bruː'tæləti] Brutalität OT 5
bubble ['bʌbl] Blase OT 1
bubblegum ['bʌbəlgʌm] Kaugummi **WS 2**, 68
budding ['bʌdɪŋ] aufkeimend; knospend **WS 3**, 96
buddy ['bʌdi] Kumpel OT 2
budgie ['bʌdʒi] Wellensittich OT 1
buffalo ['bʌfələʊ] Büffel OT 4
buffet ['bʌfeɪ] Buffet OT 3
buggy ['bʌgi] Pferdewagen; Kutsche OT 4
bughouse ['bʌghaʊs] Insektenhaus OT 1
to **build** [bɪld] bauen OT 1
builder ['bɪldə] Bauarbeiter(in) OT 2
building ['bɪldɪŋ] Gebäude OT 1
bulb: LED bulb [ˌel iː 'diː bʌlb] LED Birne OT 3
to **bulk up** [bʌlk ʌp] Masse zusetzen; Muskeln aufbauen OT 5
bull hook [bʊl hʊk] Elefantenhaken **WS 1**, 21
to **bulldoze** ['bʊldəʊz] planieren OT 5
bullet ['bʊlɪt] Kugel **WS 2**, 67
bulletin board ['bʊlətɪn bɔːd] Anschlagtafel; Pinwand OT 4
to **bully** ['bʊli] mobben OT 5
bully ['bʊli] Mobbingtäter(in) OT 2
bullying ['bʊliɪŋ] Mobbing OT 2
to **bump** [bʌmp] stoßen OT 2
to **bump into** ['bʌmp ˌɪntə] anstoßen; mit jdm. zusammenstoßen OT 2
bumpy ['bʌmpi] holprig; uneben OT 4
bunch [bʌntʃ] Haufen **WW**, 11
bundle ['bʌndl] Bündel **WS 3**, 102
bungee jumping ['bʌndʒi dʒʌmpɪŋ] Bungee-Jumping OT 3
bunk bed [bʌŋk bed] Etagenbett; Stockbett OT 3
bureaucracy [bjʊə'rɒkrəsi] Bürokratie; Verwaltung **WS 3**, 104
burger ['bɜːgə] Hamburger OT 1
to **burn** [bɜːn] brennen OT 2
burrito [bʊ'riːtəʊ] Burrito OT 4
bus [bʌs] Bus OT 1
bus stop ['bʌs stɒp] Bushaltestelle OT 1
bush [bʊʃ] Busch OT 2
bushfire ['bʊʃfaɪər] Buschfeuer OT 5
bushland ['bʊʃlænd] Buschland OT 5
business ['bɪznəs] Geschäft(e) OT 3
businessman ['bɪznəsmæn] Unternehmer; Geschäftsmann OT 4
businesswoman ['bɪznəswʊmən] Unternehmerin; Geschäftsfrau OT 4
busker ['bʌskər] Straßenmusiker(in) OT 5
busload ['bʌsləʊd] Busladung OT 5
to **bustle** ['bʌsl] wuseln **WS 2**, 65
busy ['bɪzi] beschäftigt OT 1
but [bʌt] aber OT 1
butcher ['bʊtʃə] Fleischer(in); Metzger(in) OT 4
butterfly ['bʌtəflaɪ] Schmetterling OT 2
button ['bʌtn] Knopf OT 1
to **button-hole** ['bʌtn həʊl] sich vorknöpfen **WS 1**, 28
to **buy** [baɪ] kaufen OT 1

to buzz [bʌz] schwirren **WS 4**, 138
buzzard ['bʌzəd] Bussard OT 2
buzz word ['bʌz wɜ:rd] Schlagwort; Modewort **WS 2**, 69
by [faɪv] bei; neben; von OT 1
bye [baɪ] Tschüss! OT 1
bystander ['baɪstændə] Zuschauer(in) **WS 4**, 136

C
cab [kæb] Taxi; Fahrerkabine; Führerhaus OT 4
cabbage ['kæbɪdʒ] Kohl OT 1
caber ['keɪbə] Baumstamm OT 3
cabin ['kæbɪn] Kabine OT 2
cabinet ['kæbɪnət] Schrank; Kabinett OT 5
cable ['keɪbl] Kabel OT 5
café ['kæfeɪ] Café OT 1
cafeteria [ˌkæfə'tɪəriə] Cafeteria OT 2
caffeine ['kæfi:n] Koffein OT 5
cage [keɪdʒ] Käfig OT 4
cake [keɪk] Kuchen OT 1
to calculate ['kælkjʊleɪt] berechnen; kalkulieren **WS 3**, 124
calculation [ˌkælkju'leɪʃn] Berechnung; Kalkulation **WS 2**, 59
calendar ['kælɪndə] Kalender OT 1
call [kɔ:l] Anruf OT 1
to call [kɔ:l] anrufen; nennen OT 1
called [kɔ:ld] namens; mit dem Namen OT 1
caller ['kɔ:lə] Anrufer(in) OT 2
calm [kɑ:m] ruhig OT 2
calmly ['kɑ:mli] ruhig OT 3
calorie ['kæləri] Kalorie OT 5
camel ['kæml] Kamel OT 5
camera ['kæmərə] Fotoapparat; Kamera OT 1
cameraman ['kæmrəmæn] Kameramann OT 5
camp [kæmp] Camp; Ferienlager OT 1
summer camp ['sʌmə kæmp] Ferienlager OT 2
to camp [kæmp] zelten OT 1
campaign [kæm'peɪn] Kampagne; Aktion OT 3
to campaign [kæm'peɪn] Kampagne OT 3
campaigner [kæm'peɪnə] Aktivist(in) **WS 1**, 21
camper ['kæmpə] Camper(in) OT 2
camper van ['kæmpə væn] Wohnmobil OT 4
campfire ['kæmpfaɪə] Lagerfeuer OT 2
campground ['kæmpgraʊnd] Zeltplatz OT 2
camping ['kæmpɪŋ] Camping; Zelten OT 1
campsite ['kæmpsaɪt] Zeltplatz; Campingplatz OT 1
campus ['kæmpəs] Campus OT 2
can [kæn] Dose OT 2
can [kæn] können OT 1
canal [kə'næl] Kanal OT 3
to cancel ['kænsl] absagen OT 4
cancer ['kænsə] Krebs OT 4
candidate ['kændɪdət] Kandidat(in) OT 4
candle ['kændl] Kerze OT 2
candlelight ['kændllaɪt] Kerzenlicht OT 4
candy ['kændi] Süßigkeit OT 4
cane toad [keɪn təʊd] Agakröte OT 5
canned [kænd] Dosen... OT 2
canoe [kə'nu:] Kanu OT 1
canoeing [kə'nu:ɪŋ] Kanufahren OT 1
canteen [kæn'ti:n] Kantine OT 1
canyon ['kænjən] Schlucht; Canyon OT 3
canyoning ['kænjənɪŋ] Canyoning OT 3
cap [kæp] Mütze OT 1
capable ['keɪpəbl] fähig OT 4
capacity [kə'pæsəti] Fähigkeit **WS 3**, 108
capital ['kæpɪtl] Hauptstadt OT 1
capitalism ['kæpɪtəlɪzəm] Kapitalismus **WS 3**, 94
to capitalize ['kæpɪtəlaɪz] ausnutzen; kapitalisieren **WS 2**, 57
capital letter [ˌkæpɪtl 'letə] Großbuchstabe OT 1
capsule ['kæpsju:l] Kapsel; Raumkapsel OT 4
captain ['kæptɪn] Spielführer(in); Kommandant(in) OT 4
to captain ['kæptɪn] Kapitän(in) sein **WS 2**, 59
caption ['kæpʃn] Bildunterschrift; Bildtext; Untertitel OT 1
captivity [kæp'tɪvəti] Gefangenschaft **WS 1**, 32
captor ['kæptə] Entführer(in); Geiselnehmer(in) **WS 1**, 14
to capture ['kæptʃə] einfangen; festnehmen OT 4
car [kɑ:] Auto OT 1
caramel ['kærəmel] Karamelle OT 3
caravan ['kærəvæn] Wohnwagen OT 1
carb [kɑ:b] Kohlenhydrat OT 5
carbohydrate [ˌkɑ:bəʊ'haɪdreɪt] Kohlenhydrat OT 5
carbon ['kɑ:bən] Karbon OT 3
carbon dioxide [ˌkɑ:bəndaɪ'ɒksaɪd] Kohlendioxid OT 5
card [kɑ:d] Karte OT 1
to care [keə] besorgt sein OT 1
to care about ['keə əˌbaʊt] (sich) interessieren; gern haben OT 2
career [kə'rɪə] Karriere OT 3
careful ['keəfl] vorsichtig; sorgfältig OT 1
careless ['keələs] sorglos; unvorsichtig OT 2
carelessly ['keələsli] leichtsinnig OT 2
carer ['keərər] Betreuer(in) OT 5
caretaker ['keəteɪkə] Hausmeister(in) OT 1
cargo ['kɑ:gəʊ] Ladung OT 4
carnivore ['kɑ:rnɪvɔ:r] Fleischfresser(in) **WS 2**, 64
car park ['kɑ: pɑ:k] Parkplatz OT 1
carpet ['kɑ:pɪt] Teppich OT 4
carriage ['kærɪdʒ] Wagen OT 1
carriage driving ['kærɪdʒ 'draɪvɪŋ] Kutschfahrten OT 2
carrier bag ['kæriə bæg] Tragetasche OT 2
carrot ['kærət] Karotte OT 1
to carry ['kæri] tragen OT 1
carsick ['kɑ:sɪk] autokrank OT 2
cart [kɑ:rt] Wagen; Karren **WS 1**, 32
carton ['kɑ:tn] Karton OT 2
cartoon [kɑ:'tu:n] Zeichentrickfilm; Cartoon OT 4
to carve [kɑ:v] schnitzen OT 2
to cascade [kæs'keɪd] kaskadieren; sich überschlagen **WS 4**, 136
case [keɪs] Tasche; Koffer OT 1
cash [kæʃ] Kleingeld; Bargeld OT 1
cash register ['kæʃ redʒɪstə] Kasse OT 2
cashier [kæ'ʃɪə] Kassierer(in) OT 4
casino [kə'si:nəʊ] Kasino; Spielbank **WS 1**, 29
to cast a spell [kɑ:st ə 'spel] einen Zauber bewirken OT 1
caste [kæst] Kaste; Stand **WS 1**, 13
castle ['kɑ:sl] Burg OT 1
casual ['kæʒuəl] locker; lässig OT 5
cat [kæt] Katze OT 1
cataclysm ['kætəklɪzəm] Katastrophe **WS 3**, 92
catastrophe [kə'tæstrəfi] Katastrophe **WS 4**, 142

catastrophic [ˌkætəˈstrɒfɪk] katastrophal OT 4
to **catch** [kætʃ] fangen OT 1
catchphrase [ˈkætʃfreɪz] Schlagwort OT 5
catchy [ˈkætʃi] packend **WW**, 11
to **categorize** [ˈkætəgəˌraɪz] kategorisieren; einordnen **WS 1**, 14
category [ˈkætəgəri] Kategorie OT 3
catering service [ˈkeɪtərɪŋ ˈsɜːvɪs] Verpflegungsservice OT 4
cathedral [kəˈθiːdrəl] Kathedrale OT 1
Catholic [ˈkæθlɪk] Katholik(in); katholisch OT 3
cattle [ˈkætl] Rinder OT 5
cattle ranching [ˈkætl ˈrɑːntʃɪŋ] Viehhaltung OT 5
catwalk [ˈkætwɔːk] Laufsteg; Catwalk **WS 2**, 69
causal [ˈkɔːzl] ursächlich **WS 4**, 140
cause [kɔːz] Grund; Anliegen OT 2
to **cause** [kɔːz] verursachen OT 2
to **cause offense** [kɔːz əˈfɛns] jdn. beleidigen **WS 3**, 107
cautious [ˈkɔːʃəs] vorsichtig **WS 3**, 103
cavalry [ˈkævlri] Kavallerie **WS 3**, 94
cave [keɪv] Höhle OT 1
to **cave** [keɪv] nachgeben **WS 1**, 14
cctv [ˌsiː siː ˈtiː ˈviː] Überwachungskamera; CCTV **WS 3**, 104
to **cease** [siːs] aufhören; einstellen **WS 3**, 120
ceiling [ˈsiːlɪŋ] Decke OT 4
to **celebrate** [ˈselɪbreɪt] feiern OT 1
celebration [ˌselɪˈbreɪʃn] Feier OT 2
celebrity [səˈlebrəti] Prominente(r) OT 3
cell [sel] Zelle OT 1
cellar [ˈselə] Keller OT 4
cellist [ˈtʃelɪst] Cellist(in) OT 2
cello [ˈtʃeləʊ] Cello OT 2
cell phone [ˈsel fəʊn] Handy OT 2
censor [ˈsɛnsə] zensieren; Zensor **WS 2**, 79
to **censor** [ˈsɛnsə] zensieren **WS 2**, 79
censorship [ˈsɛnsərʃɪp] Zensur; Zensierung **WS 2**, 79
census [ˈsensəs] Bevölkerungszählung; Befragung OT 5
cent [sent] Cent OT 1
center [ˈsentə] Mitte; Zentrum OT 1
centigrade [ˈsentɪgreɪd] Celsius OT 4
centimetre (cm) [ˈsentɪmiːtə] Zentimeter OT 2
central [ˈsentrəl] Zentral- OT 1

centre [ˈsentə] Mitte; Zentrum OT 1
to **centre around** [ˈsentər əˈraʊnd] sich auf etw. beziehen; sich auf etw. konzentrieren OT 5
century [ˈsentʃəri] Jahrhundert OT 2
cereal [ˈsɪəriəl] Cornflakes; Frühstücksflocken OT 1
cerebral palsy [ˌserəbrl ˈpɔːlzi] zerebrale Lähmung **WS 2**, 61
ceremonial [ˌserɪˈməʊniəl] zeremoniell; feierlich OT 3
ceremony [ˈserəməni] Feier OT 2
certain [ˈsɜːtn] sicher OT 3
certainly [ˈsɜːtnli] sicher; sicherlich OT 1
certainty [ˈsɜːtnti] Gewissheit **WS 2**, 58
certificate [səˈtɪfɪkət] Zeugnis; Zertifikat OT 1
certified [ˈsɜːtɪfaɪd] beglaubigt; anerkannt OT 5
chain [tʃeɪn] Kette OT 2
chair [tʃeə] Stuhl OT 1
to **challenge** [ˈtʃælɪndʒ] herausfordern OT 5
challenge [ˈtʃælɪndʒ] Herausforderung OT 2
challenger [ˈtʃælɪndʒə] Herausforderer / -forderin **WS 2**, 84
challenging [ˈtʃælɪndʒɪŋ] schwierig OT 4
chamber [ˈtʃeɪmbə] Kammer OT 2
champion [ˈtʃæmpiən] Champion **WS 1**, 18
chance [tʃɑːns] Zufall; Möglichkeit OT 2
change [tʃeɪndʒ] Wechselgeld; Änderung OT 1
to **change** [tʃeɪndʒ] ändern; wechseln OT 1
changing room [ˈtʃeɪndʒɪŋ ˌruːm] Umkleide OT 1
channel [ˈtʃænl] Programm OT 2
chaotic [keɪˈɒtɪk] chaotisch OT 5
chapter [ˈtʃæptə] Kapitel OT 1
character [ˈkærəktə] Charakter OT 1
characteristic [ˌkærəktəˈrɪstɪk] charakteristisches Merkmal OT 2
characterization [ˌkærəktəraɪˈzeɪʃn] Charakterisierung OT 5
to **characterize** [ˈkærəktəraɪz] kennzeichnen; charakterisieren **WS 4**, 134
charge: in charge [ɪn ˈtʃɑːdʒ] zuständig OT 1
to **be in charge of** [tʃɑːdʒ] für etw. verantwortlich sein OT 3

to **charge** [tʃɑːdʒ] aufladen OT 4; anklagen OT 5
charitable [ˈtʃærətəbl] Wohltätigkeits... **WS 1**, 44
charity [ˈtʃærəti] Wohlfahrtsorganisation OT 2
charming [ˈtʃɑːmɪŋ] charmant OT 3
chart [tʃɑːt] Diagramm; Chart OT 4
bar chart [ˈbɑː tʃɑːt] Balkendiagramm OT 4
pie chart [ˈpaɪ tʃɑːt] Tortendiagramm; Kreisdiagramm OT 4
to **chase** [tʃeɪs] jagen OT 1
chat [tʃæt] Unterhaltung OT 1
to **chatter** [ˈtʃætə] plaudern OT 2
chatty [ˈtʃæti] gesprächig OT 3
chauffeur [ˈʃəʊfə] Chauffeur(in); Fahrer(in) **WS 2**, 62
cheap [tʃiːp] billig OT 2
to **cheat** [tʃiːt] schummeln; mogeln **WS 1**, 16
to **check** [tʃek] überprüfen OT 1
checker [ˈtʃekə] Prüfer(in) OT 3
checkers [ˈtʃekəz] Damespiel OT 1
check-in desk [ˈtʃek ɪn desk] Abflugschalter OT 2
checklist [ˈtʃeklɪst] Checkliste OT 4
check-out [ˈtʃekaʊt] Kasse OT 4
cheek [tʃiːk] Backe **WS 1**, 22
cheeky [ˈtʃiːki] frech OT 1
to **cheer** [tʃɪə] jubeln OT 2
cheer up [tʃɪə ʌp] Kopf hoch! OT 1
cheerful [ˈtʃɪəfl] fröhlich OT 5
cheerleader [ˈtʃɪəliːdə] Cheerleader(in) OT 3
cheese [tʃiːz] Käse OT 1
chef [ʃef] Küchenchef(in); Koch / Köchin OT 1
chemical [ˈkemɪkl] Chemikalie OT 3
chemist [ˈkemɪst] Apotheker(in); Chemiker(in) OT 2
chemist's shop [ˈkemɪsts ʃɒp] Apotheke OT 2
to **cherish** [ˈtʃɛrɪʃ] schätzen; hegen **WS 2**, 79
chess [tʃes] Schach OT 1
chessboard [ˈtʃesbɔːd] Schachbrett OT 1
chest [tʃest] Truhe; Brust **WS 1**, 15
chicken [ˈtʃɪkɪn] Huhn; Hähnchen OT 1
child [tʃaɪld] Kind OT 1
childcare [ˈtʃaɪldˌkɛə] Kinderbetreuung **WS 2**, 67
childhood [ˈtʃaɪldhʊd] Kindheit OT 3
chili [ˈtʃɪli] Chili OT 2
to **chill** [tʃɪl] chillen; sich entspannen OT 5

to chill out [tʃɪl aʊt] sich entspannen OT 4
Chinese [ˌtʃaɪˈniːz] chinesisch OT 1
chip [tʃɪp] Fritte OT 1
chocoholic [ˌtʃɒkəˈhɒlɪk] Schokoladensüchtige(r) OT 3
chocolate [ˈtʃɒklət] Schokolade OT 1
choice [tʃɔɪs] Wahl OT 1
choir [ˈkwaɪə] Chor OT 1
to choke [tʃəʊk] ersticken **WS 1**, 39
choker: bone choker [boʊn ˈtʃoʊkə] Halsband aus Knochen **WS 3**, 94
cholera [ˈkɒlərə] Cholera OT 4
to choose [tʃuːz] auswählen OT 1
to chop [tʃɒp] schneiden OT 3
chopped [tʃɒpt] gehackt OT 2
chopstick [ˈtʃɒpstɪk] Essstäbchen OT 1
chore [tʃɔːr] Hausarbeit OT 4; Routinearbeit OT 5
chorizo [tʃəˈriːzəʊ] Chorizo OT 2
chorus [ˈkɔːrəs] Refrain; Chor **WS 1**, 31
chowder [ˈtʃaʊdə] dickflüssige Fischsuppe OT 3
Christmas [ˈkrɪsməs] Weihnachten OT 1
Christmas market [ˈkrɪsməs ˈmɑːkɪt] Weihnachtsmarkt OT 2
chronic [ˈkrɒnɪk] chronisch; anhaltend **WS 1**, 30
to chronicle [ˈkrɒnɪkl] aufzeichnen **WS 2**, 78
church [tʃɜːtʃ] Kirche OT 1
cinema [sɪnəmə] Kino OT 1
circle [ˈsɜːkl] Kreis OT 1
circuit [ˈsɜːkɪt] Schaltkreis OT 4
to circulate [ˈsɜːkjəleɪt] kursieren; zirkulieren OT 4
circumstance [ˈsɜːkəmstəns] Umstand; Lage OT 5
circus [ˈsɜːkəs] Zirkus **WS 2**, 65
citation [saɪˈteɪʃn] Anführung (einer Quelle) OT 2
to cite [saɪt] anführen; zitieren OT 2
citizen [ˈsɪtɪzn] Einwohner(in) OT 3
citizenship [ˈsɪtɪzənʃɪp] Staatsbürgerschaft **WS 2**, 85
city [ˈsɪti] Stadt OT 1
inner city [ˌɪnə ˈsɪti] Innenstadt OT 4
civil [ˈsɪvl] Bürger...; bürgerlich **WS 1**, 18
civilization [ˌsɪvəlaɪˈzeɪʃn] Zivilisation **WS 1**, 12
to claim [kleɪm] behaupten; beanspruchen OT 5
clan [klæn] Klan OT 3
to clap [klæp] klatschen OT 1
clarification [ˌklærəfɪˈkeɪʃn] Abklärung OT 4
to clarify [ˈklærəfaɪ] etw. klären OT 4
clarinet [ˌklærəˈnet] Klarinette OT 2
to clash [klæʃ] klirren; nicht zusammenpassen OT 2
class [klɑːs] Unterricht; Klasse OT 1
classic [ˈklæsɪk] klassisch OT 2
classical [ˈklæsɪkl] klassisch OT 2
classics [ˈklæsɪks] Klassik **WS 3**, 97
classification [ˌklæsɪfɪˈkeɪʃn] Einstufung **WS 2**, 78
to classify [ˈklæsɪfaɪ] einstufen **WS 2**, 58
classmate [ˈklɑːsmeɪt] Klassenkamerad(in) OT 3
classroom [ˈklɑːsruːm] Klassenzimmer OT 1
clause [klɔːz] Satzteil OT 2
relative clause [relətɪv ˈklɔːz] Relativsatz OT 2
clay [kleɪ] Ton OT 4
clean [kliːn] sauber OT 1
to clean [kliːn] putzen; reinigen OT 5
cleaner [ˈkliːnə] Reinigungsmittel OT 3
cleaning wipe [ˈkliːnɪŋ waɪp] Reinigungstuch OT 2
to clear [klɪə] räumen OT 4
clear [klɪə] klar OT 2
clearly [ˈklɪəli] deutlich OT 3
clever [ˈklevə] intelligent OT 1
cliché [klɪˈʃeɪ] Klischee; Gemeinplatz **WS 3**, 94
to click [klɪk] klicken OT 5
to click on [klɪk] anklicken OT 3
client [ˈklaɪənt] Mandant(in); Kunde / Kundin OT 5
cliff [klɪf] Klippe; Felsen OT 5
climate [ˈklaɪmət] Klima OT 2
climax [ˈklaɪmæks] Höhepunkt OT 5
to climb [klaɪm] klettern; steigen OT 1
climber [ˈklaɪmə] Kletterer(in) OT 2
climbing [ˈklaɪmɪŋ] Klettern; Bergsteigen OT 1
to cling [klɪŋ] (sich) an etw. klammern; an etw. festhalten OT 2
clinic [ˈklɪnɪk] Klinik OT 5
clinical [ˈklɪnɪkl] klinisch OT 5
clip [klɪp] Ausschnitt; Clip; Klammer; Klipp OT 1
cloak [kləʊk] Umhang OT 1
clock [klɒk] Uhr OT 1
cloister [ˈklɔɪstə] Kloster; Kreuzgang **WS 1**, 23
to close [kləʊz] schließen OT 1
closed [kləʊzd] geschlossen OT 1
close [kləʊz] nah OT 4
closely [ˈkləʊsli] eng OT 3
closeness [ˈkləʊsnəs] Nähe; Dichte OT 5
closet [ˈklɒzɪt] kleine Kammer; Wandschrank OT 2
close-up [ˈkləʊsʌp] Großaufnahme OT 4
cloth [klɒθ] Lappen OT 2
clothes [kləʊðz] Kleidung; Kleider OT 1
clothing [ˈkləʊðɪŋ] Kleidung OT 3
cloud [klaʊd] Wolke OT 1
cloudy [ˈklaʊdi] wolkig; bewölkt; trüb OT 4
clout [klaʊt] Einfluss OT 4
club [klʌb] Klub; Verein OT 1
clue [kluː] Hinweis OT 1
clumpy [ˈklʌmpi] klumpig **WS 2**, 70
clumsy [ˈklʌmzi] ungeschickt OT 2
cluster [ˈklʌstə] Ansammlung **WS 4**, 140
co-ed [ˌkəʊˈed] gemischtgeschlechtlich OT 2
co-educational [ˌkəʊedjəˈkeɪʃənl] gemischtgeschlechtlich OT 2
to co-found [kəʊfaʊnd] mitbegründen OT 4
coach [kəʊtʃ] Reisebus; Trainer(in) OT 1
coaching [ˈkəʊtʃɪŋ] Coaching OT 4
coal [kəʊl] Kohle OT 2
coast [kəʊst] Küste OT 1
coastal [ˈkəʊstl] Küsten... OT 1
coastguard [ˈkəʊstgɑːd] Küstenwache OT 2
coastline [ˈkəʊstlaɪn] Küstenlinie; Küste OT 5
coat [kəʊt] Mantel OT 1
to cobble [ˈkɒbl] flicken **WS 3**, 94
code [kəʊd] Verschlüsselung OT 1
code of conduct [kəʊd əv kənˈdʌkt] Verhaltensregeln OT 5
coffee [ˈkɒfi] Kaffee OT 1
coherent [kəʊˈhɪərənt] schlüssig **WS 4**, 139
coin [kɔɪn] Münze OT 1
to coin [kɔɪn] prägen **WS 2**, 64
cola [ˈkəʊlə] Cola OT 1
cold [kəʊld] Erkältung OT 5
cold [kəʊld] kalt OT 1
to collaborate [kəˈlæbəreɪt] zusammenarbeiten **WS 1**, 41
collaboration [kəˌlæbəˈreɪʃn] Zusammenarbeit; Kollaboration **WS 3**, 109
collaborative [kəˈlæbərətɪv] gemeinschaftlich **WS 3**, 109
collar [ˈkɒlə] Halsband OT 2
to collate [kəˈleɪt] zusammentragen; sammeln **WS 4**, 139
colleague [ˈkɒliːg] Kollege / Kollegin; Mitarbeiter(in) OT 4

to collect [kə'lekt] sammeln OT 1
collection [kə'lekʃn] Sammlung OT 2
collective [kə'lɛktɪv] Kollektiv **WS 2**, 71
college ['kɒlɪdʒ] Hochschule OT 2
colonial [kə'ləʊniəl] kolonial OT 4
colonialism [kə'ləʊniəlɪzəm] Kolonialismus **WW**, 10
colonist ['kɒlənɪst] Kolonist(in) OT 3
colonization [ˌkɒlənaɪ'zeɪʃn] Kolonialisierung OT 5
to colonize ['kɒlənaɪz] kolonisieren OT 5
colonizer ['kɒlənaɪzər] Ansiedler(in) OT 5
colony ['kɒləni] Kolonie OT 4
colour ['kʌlə] Farbe OT 1
coloured ['kʌləd] farbig; bunt OT 1
colourful ['kʌləfl] farbenfroh OT 3
colouring ['kʌlərɪŋ] Färbung **WS 3**, 94
column ['kɒləm] Säule; Spalte OT 1
comb [kəʊm] Kamm OT 2
to combat ['kɒmbæt] bekämpfen **WS 3**, 99
combination [ˌkɒmbɪ'neɪʃn] Kombination; Verbindung OT 3
to combine [kəm'baɪn] kombinieren; mischen OT 4
to come [kʌm] kommen OT 1
to come first / second / third [kʌm 'fɜ:st / sekənd / θɜ:d] den ersten / zweiten / dritten Platz belegen OT 2
Come in! [kʌm 'ɪn] Herein! OT 2
comedian [kə'mi:diən] Komiker(in) **WS 2**, 62
comedy ['kɒmədi] Komödie OT 5
to comfort ['kʌmfət] trösten OT 5
comfortable ['kʌmftəbl] bequem OT 1
comfy ['kʌmfi] gemütlich OT 4
comic ['kɒmɪk] Comicheft OT 1
comma ['kɒmə] Komma OT 3
commander [kə'mɑ:ndə] Kommandant(in) OT 4
commanding [kə'mɑ:ndɪŋ] befehlshabend OT 2
to commemorate [kə'meməreɪt] erinnern an **WS 2**, 83
commence [kə'mens] anfangen OT 4
comment ['kɒment] Kommentar OT 1
to comment ['kɒment] kommentieren OT 3
commerce ['kɒmɜ:s] Handel; Kommerz OT 5
commercial [kə'mɜ:ʃl] kommerziell OT 4
to commit [kə'mɪt] begehen OT 4
commitment [kə'mɪtmənt] Verpflichtung **WS 2**, 67
committee [kə'mɪti] Ausschuss; Komitee OT 2
common ['kɒmən] normal; gewöhnlich OT 4
commonwealth ['kɒmənwelθ] Commonwealth OT 5
to communicate [kə'mju:nɪkeɪt] kommunizieren; etw. vermitteln OT 4
community [kə'mju:nəti] Gemeinschaft OT 2
to commute [kə'mju:t] pendeln OT 5
commuter [kə'mju:tə] Pendler(in) OT 2
commuter rail [kəˌmju:tə 'reɪl] Pendlerbahn OT 2
company ['kʌmpəni] Unternehmen OT 4
comparative [kəm'pærətɪv] Komparativ OT 2
to compare [kəm'peə] vergleichen OT 1
comparison [kəm'pærɪsn] Vergleich OT 2
compass ['kʌmpəs] Kompass OT 2
compassionate [kəm'pæʃənət] mitfühlend **WS 1**, 32
compatible [kəm'pætəbl] kompatibel **WS 1**, 28
compensation [ˌkɒmpen'seɪʃn] Entschädigung OT 5
to compete [kəm'pi:t] mit jdm. / etw. konkurrieren OT 2
competence ['kɒmpɪtəns] Kompetenz OT 5
competent ['kɒmpɪtənt] fähig; kompetent OT 5
competition [ˌkɒmpə'tɪʃn] Konkurrenz; Wettbewerb OT 1
competitive [kəm'petətɪv] konkurrenzorientiert OT 4
competitively [kəm'petətɪvli] konkurrierend; wetteifernd OT 4
competitor [kəm'petɪtə] Konkurrent(in); Mitbewerber(in) OT 4
to compile [kəm'paɪl] zusammenstellen; kompilieren **WS 2**, 60
to complain [kəm'pleɪn] sich beschweren OT 3
complaint [kəm'pleɪnt] Beschwerde OT 2
to complete [kəm'pli:t] vervollständigen OT 1
completely [kəm'pli:tli] ganz OT 2
complex ['kɒmpleks] komplex OT 5
complicated ['kɒmplɪkeɪtɪd] kompliziert OT 2
compliment ['kɒmplɪmənt] Kompliment OT 5
to compose [kəm'pəʊz] komponieren OT 3
composer [kəm'pəʊzə] Komponist(in) OT 2
compost ['kɒmpɒst] Kompost OT 3
composting ['kɒmpɒstɪŋ] Kompostierungs- OT 4
to compound ['kɒmpaʊnd] verschlimmern **WS 4**, 133
comprehensive [ˌkɒmprɪ'hensɪv] umfassend **WS 3**, 103
compromise ['kɒmprəmaɪz] Kompromiss OT 5
to compromise ['kɒmprəmaɪz] kompromettieren **WS 1**, 21
computer [kəm'pju:tə] Computer; Rechner OT 1
computerized [kəm'pju:təraɪzd] computerbasiert; computergesteuert OT 4
computer lab [kəm'pju:tə ˌlæb] Computerraum OT 2
computing [kəm'pju:tɪŋ] Computing OT 5
comrade ['kɒmreɪd] Kamerad(in) **WS 2**, 83
con [kɒn] Nachteil OT 2
to conceal [kən'si:l] verbergen OT 5
to concede [kən'si:d] zugestehen; einräumen **WS 3**, 107
to concentrate ['kɒnsntreɪt] konzentrieren OT 3
concentration [ˌkɒnsn'treɪʃn] Konzentration OT 4
concentric [kən'sɛntrɪk] konzentrisch **WS 3**, 108
concept ['kɒnsept] Konzept; Begriff OT 4
concern [kən'sɜ:n] Sorge; Bedenken OT 5
concerning [kən'sɜ:n] bedenklich; auch: hinsichtlich **WS 4**, 133
concerned [kən'sɜ:nd] besorgt OT 5
concert ['kɒnsət] Konzert OT 1
to conclude [kən'klu:d] schließen (aus etw.); beenden OT 4
conclusion [kən'klu:ʒn] Schluss OT 3
condition [kən'dɪʃn] Bedingung OT 3
condor ['kɒndɔ:] Kondor OT 3
to conduct [kən'dʌkt] durchführen OT 3
conference ['kɒnfərəns] Konferenz OT 4

video conferencing ['vɪdiəʊ 'kɒnfərənsɪŋ] Videokonferenztechnik OT 4
web conference [web 'kɒnfərəns] Webkonferenz OT 4
to **confer** [kən'fɜ:r] verleihen **WS 2**, 78
confession [kən'feʃn] Geständnis **WS 1**, 26
confidence ['kɒnfɪdəns] Selbstvertrauen OT 5
confident ['kɒnfɪdənt] selbstbewusst; zuversichtlich OT 2
confidently ['kɒnfɪdəntli] selbstbewusst; zuversichtlich OT 2
to **confine** [kən'faɪn] fesseln an; einsperren **WS 2**, 61
to **confirm** [kən'fɜ:m] bestätigen OT 4
confirmation [ˌkɒnfə'meɪʃn] Bestätigung **WS 3**, 112
conflict ['kɒnflɪkt] Konflikt OT 2
to **conform** [kən'fɔ:m] anpassen OT 5
confused [kən'fju:zd] verwirrt OT 2
confusing [kən'fju:zɪŋ] verwirrend OT 2
to **congratulate** [kən'grætʃuleɪt] gratulieren OT 2
congratulations [kənˌgrætʃu'leɪʃnz] Glückwünsche OT 2
to **connect** [kə'nekt] verbinden OT 2
connected [kə'nektɪd] verbunden OT 1
connection [kə'nekʃn] Verbindung OT 2
connectivity [kəˌnek'tɪvəti] Vernetzung **WS 4**, 133
connotation [ˌkɒnə'teɪʃn] Konnotation; Beiklang **WS 1**, 21
conscious ['kɒnʃəs] bewusst **WS 3**, 102
consequence ['kɒnsɪkwəns] Folge; Konsequenz OT 4
consequently ['kɒnsɪkwəntli] folglich; demzufolge **WS 2**, 85
conservation [ˌkɒnsə'veɪʃn] Schutz; Erhaltung OT 2
conservationist [ˌkɒnsə'veɪʃənɪst] Naturschützer(in) **WS 2**, 67
to **conserve** [kən'sɜ:rv] konservieren; bewahren **WS 2**, 64
to **consider** [kən'sɪdə] nachdenken über OT 5
considerable [kən'sɪdərəbl] bedeutend; erheblich **WS 2**, 58
considerably [kən'sɪdərəbli] deutlich; umfangreich OT 5
consideration [kənˌsɪdə'reɪʃn] Rücksicht OT 5
to **consist of** [kən'sɪst əv] aus etw. bestehen OT 5
consistent [kən'sɪstənt] konsequent **WS 3**, 99
constant ['kɒnstənt] ständig **WS 3**, 104
constellation [ˌkɒnstə'leɪʃn] Konstellation OT 5
constitution [ˌkɒnstɪ'tju:ʃn] Verfassung OT 5
construction [kən'strʌkʃn] Bau OT 4
constructive [kən'strʌktɪv] konstruktiv OT 5
consultant [kən'sʌltənt] Berater(in) OT 5
consumer [kən'sju:mər] Verbraucher(in) OT 5
consumption [kən'sʌmpʃn] Verbrauch **WS 3**, 102
contact ['kɒntækt] Kontakt OT 1
to **be in contact with** [bi ɪn 'kɒntækt wɪð] in Kontakt mit jdm. sein OT 2
to **contain** [kən'teɪn] beinhalten; enthalten OT 3
container [kən'teɪnə] Behälter; Container OT 2
to **contaminate** [kən'tæmɪneɪt] verunreinigen; kontaminieren **WS 3**, 100
contamination [kənˌtæmɪ'neɪʃən] Kontamination; Verunreinigung **WS 3**, 100
contemporary [kən'temprəri] zeitgenössisch OT 3
content ['kɒntents] Inhalt OT 2
context ['kɒntekst] Kontext; Zusammenhang OT 4
continent ['kɒntɪnənt] Kontinent OT 3
to **continue** [kən'tɪnju:] andauern; weitermachen OT 1
to **contour** ['kɒntʊə] konturieren **WS 2**, 70
to **contract** [kɒn'trækt] zusammenziehen **WS 4**, 136
contractor [kən'træktə] Auftragnehmer(in) OT 5
to **contradict** [ˌkɒntrə'dɪkt] widersprechen **WS 1**, 38
contradiction [ˌkɒntrə'dɪkʃn] Widerspruch **WS 2**, 53
contrary: on the contrary [ɒn ðə 'kɒntrəri] im Gegenteil **WS 3**, 104
contrast ['kɒntrɑ:st] Gegenteil; Kontrast OT 3
contrasting [kən'trɑ:stɪŋ] gegensätzlich OT 4
to **contribute** [kən'trɪbju:t] mitwirken OT 4
contribution [ˌkɒntrɪ'bju:ʃn] Beitrag; Mitwirkung OT 4
contributor [kən'trɪbjutə] Mitwirkende(r); Beiträger(in) **WS 3**, 92
control [kən'trəʊl] Kontrolle OT 3
to **control** [kən'trəʊl] kontrollieren OT 4
controversial [ˌkɒntrə'vɜ:ʃl] umstritten OT 5
controversy ['kɒntrəvɜ:si] Kontroverse **WS 2**, 58
convenience [kən'vi:niəns] Bequemlichkeit; zweckmäßiges Gerät OT 4
convenient [kən'vi:niənt] günstig; praktisch OT 4
convention [kən'venʃn] Kongress; Konvention OT 4
conversation [ˌkɒnvə'seɪʃn] Gespräch OT 1
conversational [ˌkɒnvə'seɪʃənl] Gesprächs... OT 5
to **convert** [kən'vɜ:rt] konvertieren; umwandeln **WS 1**, 25
to **convey** [kən'veɪ] vermitteln OT 5
convict ['kɒnvɪkt] Verurteilte(r) OT 5
to **convict** [kən'vɪkt] verurteilen OT 5
to **convince** [kən'vɪns] überzeugen; überreden OT 4
convoy ['kɒnvɔɪ] Konvoi; Geleitzug **WS 1**, 15
to **cook** [kʊk] kochen OT 1
cooker ['kʊkə] Herd OT 3
cookie ['kʊki] Keks OT 3
cooking ['kʊkɪŋ] Kochen OT 1
to **cool** [ku:l] kühlen OT 3
cool [ku:l] kühl; cool OT 1
cooling [ku:lɪŋ] Kühl... OT 3
coop [ku:p] Hühnerstall OT 4
cooperation [kəʊˌɒpə'reɪʃn] Zusammenarbeit **WS 3**, 98
to **cope** [kəʊp] zurechtkommen OT 5
copper ['kɒpə] Kupfer OT 1
to **copy** ['kɒpi] kopieren OT 1
coral ['kɒrəl] Koralle OT 5
cord [kɔ:rd] Schnur; Kordel **WS 2**, 62
core [kɔ:] Kern; Haupt... OT 4
corn [kɔ:n] Mais OT 3
cornbread ['kɔ:nbred] Maisbrot OT 4
corner ['kɔ:nə] Ecke OT 1
cornrow ['kɔ:nrəʊ] Cornrow; dünner Zopf **WS 2**, 69
corporate ['kɔ:pərət] Korporations...; unternehmensweit OT 5
corporation [ˌkɔ:pə'reɪʃn] Unternehmen OT 4
corpse [kɔ:ps] Leiche OT 5

to correct [kə'rekt] korrigieren OT 1
correct [kə'rekt] richtig OT 1
correction [kə'rekʃn] Korrektur OT 4
to correspond [ˌkɒrə'spɒnd] übereinstimmen **WS 2**, 62
correspondence [ˌkɒrə'spɒndəns] Schriftverkehr OT 4
corresponding [ˌkɒrə'spɒndɪŋ] entsprechend OT 5
corridor ['kɒrɪdɔː] Korridor OT 2
corrupt [kə'rʌpt] korrupt; bestechlich **WS 2**, 78
corruption [kə'rʌpʃn] Korruption **WS 1**, 17
cosmopolitan [ˌkɒzmə'pɒlɪtən] kosmopolitisch; weltoffen OT 5
cost [kɒst] Kosten OT 1
to cost [kɒst] kosten OT 1
costly ['kɔːstli] kostspielig; teuer **WS 3**, 101
costume ['kɒstjuːm] Kostüm OT 2
cottage ['kɒtɪdʒ] Häuschen OT 3
cotton ['kɒtn] Baumwolle OT 4
to cough [kɒf] husten OT 2
council ['kaʊnsl] Rat OT 3
counsel ['kaʊnsl] Anwalt / Anwältin OT 5
counselling ['kaʊnsəlɪŋ] Beratung OT 5
counsellor ['kaʊnsələ] Jugendbetreuer(in); Berater(in); psychologischer Betreuer OT 2
to count [kaʊnt] zählen OT 1
countable ['kaʊntəbl] zählbar OT 1
countdown ['kaʊntdaʊn] Countdown OT 4
counter ['kaʊntə] Theke OT 3
counterargument ['kaʊntərɑːgjumənt] Gegenargument **WS 1**, 13
country ['kʌntri] Land OT 1
country dancing [ˌkʌntri 'dɑːnsɪŋ] Volkstanz OT 1
countryside ['kʌntrisaɪd] Land OT 1
countrywide ['kʌntriˌwaɪd] landesweit; im ganzen Land **WS 2**, 83
couple ['kʌpl] Paar OT 2
coupon ['kuːpɒn] Gutschein OT 2
courage ['kʌrɪdʒ] Mut **WS 1**, 25
course [kɔːs] Kurs; Gang OT 1
of course [əv 'kɔːs] natürlich OT 1
court [kɔːt] Hof; Platz OT 3; Gericht OT 5
courtyard ['kɔːtjɑːd] Hof; Innenhof OT 3
cousin ['kʌzn] Cousin(e) OT 1
couture [kuː'tʊə] Couture **WS 2**, 71
cover ['kʌvə] Abdeckung; Hülle OT 1
to cover ['kʌvə] abdecken OT 2
cow [kaʊ] Kuh OT 1
cowboy word ['kaʊbɔɪ wɜːd] Wort, das im Englischen und Deutschen gleich ist OT 2
cowherd ['kaʊhɜːrd] Kuhhirt(in); Viehhirt(in) **WS 1**, 16
coyote [kaɪ'əʊti] Kojote; Schlepper(in) OT 5
cozy ['kəʊzi] gemütlich OT 3
to crack [kræk] knacken **WS 2**, 62
cracker ['krækə] Cracker OT 3
to crackle ['krækl] knistern; prasseln **WS 1**, 22
to craft [krɑːft] formen; bilden **WS 3**, 94
cramp [kræmp] Krampf OT 2
cramped [kræmpt] beengt OT 3
cranberry ['krænbəri] Cranberry; Moosbeere OT 4
crane [kreɪn] Kran OT 4
to crash [kræʃ] krachen OT 3
crate [kreɪt] Kiste OT 4
to crawl [krɔːl] krabbeln; kriechen OT 5
crazy ['kreɪzi] verrückt OT 2
cream [kriːm] Sahne OT 1
creamy-skinned ['kriːmi skɪnd] cremefarben; helle Haut **WS 1**, 16
to create [kri'eɪt] schaffen; kreieren OT 2
creation [kri'eɪʃn] Schöpfung **WS 2**, 62
creative [kri'eɪtɪv] kreativ OT 2
creativity [ˌkriːeɪ'tɪvəti] Kreativität OT 4
creature ['kriːtʃə] Lebewesen; Wesen OT 4
credit ['kredɪt] Credit; Zuschreibung **WS 2**, 68
credit card ['kredɪt kɑːd] Kreditkarte OT 1
to credit ['kredɪt] zuschreiben **WS 1**, 31
creek [kriːk] Bach OT 3
creepy ['kriːpi] gruselig OT 5
creepy-crawly [ˌkriːpi'krɔːli] Krabbeltier OT 2
crescent ['kresnt] Sichel; sichelförmige Bauform OT 2
crew [kruː] Mannschaft; Personal OT 2
crewed [kruːd] bemannt OT 4
cricket ['krɪkɪt] Kricket OT 1
crime [kraɪm] Verbrechen OT 4
criminal ['krɪmɪnl] Kriminelle(r) OT 3
crisis ['kraɪsɪs] Krise OT 3
crisp [krɪsp] Chip OT 1
critic ['krɪtɪk] Kritiker(in) **WS 1**, 18
critical ['krɪtɪkl] kritisch; wichtig OT 5
criticism ['krɪtɪsɪzəm] Kritik OT 5
to criticize ['krɪtɪsaɪz] kritisieren OT 3
crocodile ['krɒkədaɪl] Krokodil OT 5
crook [krʊk] Gauner(in); Schwindler(in) **WS 2**, 56
crop [krɒp] Ernte; Getreide OT 4
to cross [krɒs] überqueren; kreuzen OT 1
to cross out [krɒs aʊt] ausstreichen OT 1
cross-country [ˌkrɒs 'kʌntri] querfeldein OT 2
crossly ['krɒsli] mürrisch OT 3
crossroads ['krɒsrəʊdz] Kreuzung OT 1
crow [krəʊ] Krähe **WS 1**, 21
crowd [kraʊd] Menge; Menschenmenge OT 1
crowded ['kraʊdɪd] überfüllt OT 2
crown [kraʊn] Krone OT 1
to crown [kraʊn] krönen OT 1
crucial ['kruːʃl] entscheidend; wesentlich **WS 3**, 99
cruel ['kruːl] grausam **WS 1**, 21
cruelty ['kruːəlti] Quälerei; Grausamkeit OT 5
cruise [kruːz] Kreuzfahrt OT 2
to cruise [kruːz] mit dem Boot fahren; herumfahren OT 3
to crumble ['krʌmbl] zerbröckeln; zerfallen **WS 2**, 62
to crush [krʌʃ] zerschlagen **WS 1**, 25
crush: to have a crush on sb. [həv ə krʌʃ ɒn] in jdn. verknallt sein OT 4
crutch [krʌtʃ] Krücke OT 2
to cry [kraɪ] weinen OT 1
to crystallize ['krɪstəlaɪz] sich herausbilden **WS 4**, 139
cuddly [kʌdli] kuschelig; knuddelig OT 1
cue card ['kjuː kɑːd] Karteikarte OT 4
cuisine [kwɪ'ziːn] Küche OT 3
cull [kʌl] Schlachten; Keulen OT 5
to cull [kʌl] keulen; selektiv schlachten OT 5
culprit ['kʌlprɪt] Schuldige(r) **WS 3**, 101
to cultivate ['kʌltɪveɪt] anbauen; bebauen OT 4
cultural ['kʌltʃərəl] kulturell OT 3
culture ['kʌltʃə] Kultur OT 1
cultured ['kʌltʃəd] gebildet; kultiviert OT 4
Cumbrian ['kʌmbriən] von / aus Cumbria OT 2
cunning ['kʌnɪŋ] gerissen; schlau **WS 1**, 16
cup [kʌp] Tasse OT 1
cupboard ['kʌbəd] Schrank OT 1
cupola ['kjuːpələ] Kuppel OT 4
curb [kɜːb] Bordstein OT 5

to curdle ['kɜːrdl] gerinnen; koagulieren **WS 1**, 39
to cure [kjʊə] heilen OT 4
curfew ['kɜːfjuː] Ausgangssperre OT 3
curiosity [ˌkjʊəri'ɒsəti] Neugier OT 4
curious ['kjʊəriəs] neugierig; gespannt OT 4
curly ['kɜːli] gelockt OT 3
currency ['kʌrənsi] Währung **WS 1**, 12
current ['kʌrənt] aktuell OT 4
currently ['kʌrəntli] derzeit; gerade OT 5
curriculum [kə'rɪkjələm] Curriculum; Lehrplan **WS 3**, 124
Curriculum Vitae [kəˌrɪkjələm 'viːtaɪ] Lebenslauf; Vita OT 5
curry ['kʌri] Currygericht OT 1
curried ['kʌrid] mit Curry gewürzt OT 1
curse [kɜːrs] Fluch **WS 1**, 21
to curse [kɜːrs] (ver)fluchen **WS 1**, 39
cursor ['kɜːsə] Mauszeiger OT 3
curtain ['kɜːtn] Vorhang OT 2
cushion ['kʊʃn] Kissen OT 1
custard ['kʌstəd] Vanillesoße OT 1
custodial [kʌ'stəʊdiəl] vormundschaftlich OT 5
custody ['kʌstədi] Verwahrung; Schutz OT 5
customer ['kʌstəmə] Kunde(-in) OT 3
customs ['kʌstəmz] Zoll OT 2
to cut [kʌt] schneiden OT 2
cute [kjuːt] niedlich OT 1
cutlery ['kʌtləri] Besteck OT 3
to cyberbully ['saɪbəbʊli] cybermobben OT 5
cyberbullying ['saɪbəbʊliɪŋ] Cybermobbing OT 4
cyber security ['saɪbə sɪ'kjʊərəti] Cybersicherheit; Netzsicherheit OT 4
to cycle ['saɪkl] mit dem Fahrrad fahren OT 1
cyclist ['saɪklɪst] Radfahrer(in) OT 3
cynical ['sɪnɪkl] zynisch; skeptisch **WS 1**, 17

D

dad [dæd] Papa OT 1
daily ['deɪli] täglich OT 2
dairy ['deəri] Milchprodukte **WS 4**, 133
dam [dæm] Damm; Staudamm **WS 3**, 99
to damage ['dæmɪdʒ] beschädigen; schaden OT 2
damn [dæm] verdammt **WS 2**, 59
damned [dæmd] verdammt **WS 3**, 103
dance [dɑːns] Tanz OT 1
to dance [dɑːns] tanzen OT 1
dancer ['dɑːnsə] Tänzer(in) OT 3
dancing ['dɑːnsɪŋ] Tanzen OT 1
danger ['deɪndʒə] Gefahr OT 2
dangerous ['deɪndʒərəs] gefährlich OT 1
to dare [deə] wagen; sich trauen OT 2
dark [dɑːk] dunkel OT 1
darkness ['dɑːknəs] Dunkelheit OT 5
data ['deɪtə] Daten OT 3
date [deɪt] Datum OT 2
to date [deɪt] mit jdm. ausgehen OT 5
daughter ['dɔːtə] Tochter OT 1
dawn [dɔːn] Morgendämmerung OT 4
day [deɪ] Tag OT 1
day out [deɪ 'aʊt] Tagesausflug OT 2
daytime ['deɪtaɪm] Tageszeit OT 1
day trip ['deɪ trɪp] Tagesausflug OT 2
dead [ded] tot OT 1
deaf [def] Gehörlose OT 5
deal [diːl] Geschäft; Deal OT 4
to deal with [diːl wɪð] umgehen OT 2
dear [dɪə] liebe(r, -s) OT 1
death [deθ] Tod OT 2
date of death [ˌdeɪt əv 'deθ] Todesdatum OT 2
debatable [dɪ'beɪtəbl] umstritten **WS 2**, 59
debate [dɪ'beɪt] Debatte OT 3
debating club [dɪ'beɪtɪŋ klʌb] Debattierklub OT 4
debt [det] Schuld OT 4
decade ['dekeɪd] Dekade; Jahrzehnt OT 5
December [dɪ'sembə] Dezember OT 1
decent ['diːsnt] anständig **WS 2**, 54
to decide [dɪ'saɪd] entscheiden OT 1
decimation [ˌdɛsɪ'meɪʃən] Dezimierung; Ausrottung **WS 1**, 21
decision [dɪ'sɪʒn] Entscheidung OT 1
decisive [dɪ'saɪsɪv] entscheidend OT 5
declaration [ˌdeklə'reɪʃn] Erklärung OT 4
to declare [dɪ'kleə] ausrufen; verkünden OT 4
decline [dɪ'klaɪn] Rückgang OT 5
to decline [dɪ'klaɪn] verfallen OT 5
to decorate ['dekəreɪt] dekorieren; schmücken OT 4
decorator ['dekəreɪtə] Dekorateur(in) OT 3
to decrease [dɪ'kriːs] fallen; zurückgehen OT 5
dedicated ['dedɪkeɪtɪd] engagiert OT 5
dedication [ˌdedɪ'keɪʃn] Einweihung; Einsatz **WS 1**, 21
deed [diːd] Tat OT 5
to be deemed [bi diːmd] gelten **WS 2**, 78
deep [diːp] tief OT 1
default [dɪ'fɔːlt] Standard OT 3
to defeat [dɪ'fiːt] besiegen **WS 3**, 98
defence [dɪ'fens] Verteidigung OT 5
to defend [dɪ'fend] verteidigen OT 3
defender [dɪ'fendə] Verteidiger(in) OT 3
deficit ['defɪsɪt] Mangel **WS 3**, 103
to define [dɪ'faɪn] definieren; bestimmen OT 4
definite ['defɪnət] eindeutig; bestimmt OT 1
definitely ['defɪnətli] eindeutig; bestimmt; definitiv OT 1
definition [ˌdefɪ'nɪʃn] Definition OT 1
deflated [dɪ'fleɪtɪd] entmutigt; entleert **WS 1**, 21
to deforest [diː'fɔːrɪst] abholzen; entwalden **WS 1**, 21
deforestation [ˌdiːˌfɒrɪ'steɪʃn] Abholzung OT 5
to defy [dɪ'faɪ] trotzen; sich widersetzen **WS 1**, 29
degradation [ˌdegrə'deɪʃn] Degradierung OT 5
degree [dɪ'griː] Grad; Abschluss OT 4
to dehumanize [diː'hjuːmənaɪz] entmenschlichen **WS 2**, 55
dehydrated [ˌdiːhaɪ'dreɪtɪd] dehydriert OT 2
to delay [dɪ'leɪ] verzögern **WS 1**, 22
to delegate ['delɪgət] delegieren; beauftragen OT 4
to delegitimize [dɪ'lɛdʒɪtɪmaɪz] delegitimieren; entlegitimieren **WS 3**, 108
to delete [dɪ'liːt] löschen OT 4
deli ['deli] Feinkostladen OT 5
deliberately [dɪ'lɪbərətli] absichtlich; bewusst OT 5
delicacy ['delɪkəsi] Delikatesse OT 3
delicious [dɪ'lɪʃəs] lecker OT 1
delighted [dɪ'laɪtɪd] entzückt; erfreut OT 3
to deliver [dɪ'lɪvə] liefern OT 4
delivery [dɪ'lɪvəri] Ausführung; Lieferung OT 3
demand [dɪ'mɑːnd] Nachfrage OT 4
to demand [dɪ'mɑːnd] fordern; verlangen OT 4
demeaning [dɪ'miːnɪŋ] erniedrigend; herabsetzend **WS 2**, 78
demise [dɪ'maɪz] Niedergang **WS 4**, 138

democracy [dɪˈmɒkrəsi] Demokratie **WS 1**, 12
democratic [ˌdeməˈkrætɪk] demokratisch OT 4
demographics [ˌdɛməˈgræfɪks] Demografie; Bevölkerungsstatistik **WS 3**, 108
to **demolish** [dɪˈmɒlɪʃ] abreißen OT 5
demon [ˈdi:mən] Dämon OT 5
to **demonstrate** [ˈdemənstreɪt] vorführen; zeigen OT 4
demonstration [ˌdemənˈstreɪʃn] Demonstration OT 4
demonstrative [dɪˈmɒnstrətɪv] Demonstrativbegleiter OT 1
denial [dɪˈnaɪl] Verweigerung **WS 3**, 103
denier [dɪˈnaɪə] Leugner(in); Bestreiter(in) **WS 1**, 21
denim [ˈdenɪm] Denim; Jeansstoff OT 4
to **denote** [dɪˈnəʊt] auf etw. hindeuten OT 5
density [ˈdensəti] Dichte OT 4
dent [dent] Beule; Delle **WS 3**, 102
dentist [ˈdentɪst] Zahnarzt / -ärztin OT 5
to **deny** [dɪˈnaɪ] leugnen OT 5
department [dɪˈpɑ:tmənt] Abteilung OT 5
departure [dɪˈpɑ:tʃə] Abfahrt; Abflug OT 2
departure gate [dɪˈpɑ:tʃə ˌgeɪt] Abfluggate OT 2
to **depend** [dɪˈpend] (sich) verlassen (auf); abhängen (von) OT 2
dependent [dɪˈpendənt] abhängig **WS 4**, 133
to **depict** [dɪˈpɪkt] darstellen; abbilden **WS 2**, 72
depopulation [ˌdi:ˌpɒpjuˈleɪʃn] Entvölkerung **WS 3**, 104
to **deport** [dɪˈpɔ:t] ausweisen; deportieren OT 4
depressed [dɪˈprest] deprimiert OT 4
depressing [dɪˈpresɪŋ] deprimierend OT 4
depression [dɪˈpreʃn] Depression OT 4
to **deprive** [dɪˈpraɪv] berauben; entziehen **WS 2**, 81
depth: in-depth [dɛpθ] tiefgreifend; gründlich **WS 4**, 133
deputy [ˈdepjuti] stellvertretend OT 5
to **derive** [dɪˈraɪv] (sich) ableiten; herleiten **WS 2**, 61
to **descend from** [dɪˈsend frəm] von jdm. abstammen OT 5
descendant [dɪˈsendənt] Nachkomme OT 4
descent [dɪˈsent] Abstammung OT 5
to **describe** [dɪˈskraɪb] beschreiben OT 1
description [dɪˈskrɪpʃn] Beschreibung OT 2
descriptive [dɪˈskrɪptɪv] beschreibend OT 5
desert [ˈdezət] Wüste OT 3
to **desert** [ˈdezət] im Stich lassen **WS 2**, 65
desertification [dɪˌzɜ:tɪfɪˈkeɪʃn] Wüstenbildung **WS 4**, 136
to **deserve** [dɪˈzɜ:v] verdienen OT 2
design [dɪˈzaɪn] Entwurf; Design OT 1
to **design** [dɪˈzaɪn] entwerfen OT 3
to **designate** [ˈdezɪgneɪt] ernennen; designieren OT 5
designer [dɪˈzaɪnə] Designer(in) OT 3
desirable [dɪˈzaɪərəbl] wünschenswert **WS 1**, 21
to **desire** [dɪˈzaɪə] begehren **WS 2**, 78
desk [desk] Schreibtisch OT 1
desktop [ˈdesktɒp] Desktop; Benutzeroberfläche OT 4
desperate [ˈdespərət] verzweifelt OT 5
desperately [ˈdespərətli] verzweifelt OT 3
to **despise** [dɪˈspaɪz] verachten; missachten **WS 2**, 78
despite [dɪˈspaɪt] obwohl; trotz **WS 1**, 17
dessert [dɪˈzɜ:t] Nachtisch OT 1
destination [ˌdestɪˈneɪʃn] Reiseziel OT 4
destiny [ˈdestəni] Schicksal **WS 1**, 16
to **destroy** [dɪˈstrɔɪ] zerstören OT 2
to **destruct** [dɪˈstrʌkt] zerstören; vernichten **WS 1**, 21
destruction [dɪˈstrʌkʃn] Zerstörung **WS 1**, 21
destructive [dɪˈstrʌktɪv] zerstörend; schädlich OT 5
detail [ˈdi:teɪl] Detail OT 2
detailed [ˈdi:teɪld] detailliert; genau OT 3
determination [dɪˌtɜ:mɪˈneɪʃn] Entschlossenheit OT 5
to **determine** [dɪˈtɜ:mɪn] ausmachen; bestimmen OT 5
determined [dɪˈtɜ:mɪnd] entschlossen OT 3
determiner [dɪˈtɜ:mɪnə] Bestimmungswort OT 1
deterrent [dɪˈtɛrənt] Abschreckung; Abschreckungsmittel **WS 3**, 99
detox [ˈdi:tɒks] Entzugsprogramm OT 2
deuce [dju:s] Einstand OT 3
to **devastate** [ˈdɛvəˌsteɪt] verwüsten; zerstören **WS 1**, 41
devastated [ˈdevəsteɪtɪd] am Boden zerstört; erschüttert OT 5
to **develop** [dɪˈveləp] entwickeln OT 2
developer [dɪˈveləpə] Entwickler(in) OT 5
development [dɪˈveləpmənt] Entwicklung OT 4
device [dɪˈvaɪs] Gerät OT 3
devil [ˈdevl] Teufel OT 5
to **devise** [dɪˈvaɪz] ausdenken; entwickeln **WS 2**, 57
dhoti [ˈdoʊti] Dhoti (indisches Kleidungsstück) **WS 1**, 19
diabetes [ˌdaɪəˈbi:ti:z] Diabetes OT 5
to **diagnose** [ˈdaɪəgnəʊz] diagnostizieren OT 4
diagram [ˈdaɪəgræm] Schaubild; Diagramm OT 3
to **dial** [ˈdaɪəl] wählen OT 2
dialect [ˈdaɪəlekt] Dialekt OT 5
dialogue [ˈdaɪəlɒg] Dialog OT 1
diary [ˈdaɪəri] Terminkalender; Tagebuch OT 1
to **dictate** [dɪkˈteɪt] bestimmen OT 5
dictator [ˈdɪkteɪtə] Diktator(in) **WS 3**, 104
dictatorship [ˈdɪkteɪtərʃɪp] Diktatur; Diktatorisch **WS 3**, 92
dictionary [ˈdɪkʃənri] Wörterbuch OT 1
didactic [daɪˈdæktɪk] didaktisch; lehrhaft **WS 3**, 104
to **die** [daɪ] sterben OT 1
diesel [ˈdi:zl] Diesel OT 3
diet [ˈdaɪət] Diät OT 3
dietary [ˈdaɪətəri] diätetisch OT 5
dieting [ˈdaɪətɪŋ] Schlankheitskuren; Diäten OT 5
to **differ** [ˈdɪfər] abweichen OT 5
difference [ˈdɪfrəns] Unterschied OT 1
different [ˈdɪfrənt] unterschiedlich OT 1
to **differentiate** [ˌdɪfəˈrenʃieɪt] unterscheiden OT 5
difficult [ˈdɪfɪkəlt] schwer; schwierig OT 1
difficulty [ˈdɪfɪkəlti] Schwierigkeit OT 4
to **dig** [dɪg] graben OT 1
digit [ˈdɪdʒɪt] Ziffer OT 2
digital [ˈdɪdʒɪtl] digital OT 3
digitalization [ˌdɪdʒɪtəlaɪˈzeɪʃn] Digitalisierung OT 5
digital native [ˈdɪdʒɪtl ˈneɪtɪv] Digital Native OT 5
dignity [ˈdɪgnɪti] Würde **WS 2**, 55
dilemma [dɪˈlemə] Dilemma OT 4

to dilute [daɪ'lu:t] verdünnen **WS 2**, 55
dim [dɪm] trüb; schwach OT 4
dimension [daɪ'menʃn] Abmessung OT 2
dingo ['dɪŋgəʊ] Dingo OT 5
dining room ['daɪnɪŋ ru:m] Esszimmer OT 1
dinner ['dɪnə] Abendessen OT 1
dinosaur ['daɪnəsɔ:] Dinosaurier OT 1
dioxide [daɪ'ɒksaɪd] Dioxid **WS 3**, 98
to dip [dɪp] tauchen OT 4
diploma [dɪ'pləʊmə] Diplom; Urkunde OT 5
diplomacy [dɪ'pləʊməsi] Diplomatie **WS 3**, 108
dire ['daɪə] entsetzlich; furchtbar **WS 4**, 138
to direct [də'rekt] Regie führen **WS 2**, 67
direct [də'rekt] direkt OT 3
direction [də'rekʃn] Anweisung; Richtung OT 3
director [də'rektə] Leiter(in) OT 4
dirt [dɜ:t] Dreck; Schmutz OT 4
dirty ['dɜ:ti] schmutzig OT 1
disability [ˌdɪsə'bɪləti] Behinderung OT 2
disabled [dɪs'eɪbld] behindert **WS 2**, 61
disadvantage [ˌdɪsəd'vɑ:ntɪdʒ] Nachteil OT 3
disadvantaged [ˌdɪsəd'vɑ:ntɪdʒd] benachteiligt OT 5
to disagree [ˌdɪsə'gri:] anderer Meinung sein OT 2
disagreeable [ˌdɪsə'gri:əbl] unangenehm; unsympathisch **WS 2**, 78
disagreement [ˌdɪsə'gri:mənt] Meinungsverschiedenheit OT 2
to disappear [ˌdɪsə'pɪə] verschwinden OT 3
to disappoint [ˌdɪsə'pɔɪnt] enttäuschen **WS 2**, 83
disappointed [ˌdɪsə'pɔɪntɪd] enttäuscht OT 2
disappointingly [ˌdɪsə'pɔɪntɪŋli] enttäuschend OT 3
disappointment [ˌdɪsə'pɔɪntmənt] Enttäuschung OT 5
disaster [dɪ'zɑ:stə] Katastrophe OT 2
disaster area [dɪ'zɑ:stər eəriə] Katastrophengebiet OT 2
disastrous [dɪ'zɑ:strəs] verheerend **WS 4**, 134
to discard [dɪ'skɑ:d] ausrangieren; wegwerfen **WS 3**, 98
discipline ['dɪsəplɪn] Disziplin; Fachrichtung **WS 3**, 112
to disconnect [ˌdɪskə'nekt] trennen; abschalten **WS 1**, 44
to discourage [dɪs'kʌrɪdʒ] entmutigen OT 5
to discover [dɪ'skʌvə] entdecken OT 3
discovery [dɪ'skʌvəri] Entdeckung OT 4
to discriminate [dɪ'skrɪmɪneɪt] unterschiedlich behandeln; diskriminieren OT 5
discriminated [dɪ'skrɪmɪneɪt] benachteiligt OT 5
discrimination [dɪˌskrɪmɪ'neɪʃn] Diskriminierung; Ausgrenzung OT 5
to discuss [dɪ'skʌs] besprechen OT 1
discussion [dɪ'skʌʃn] Besprechung; Diskussion OT 1
disease [dɪ'zi:z] Krankheit OT 2
to disempower [ˌdɪsɪm'paʊə] entmachten; schwächen **WS 3**, 104
disengaged [ˌdɪsɪn'geɪdʒd] desinteressiert **WS 1**, 21
disgrace [dɪs'greɪs] Schande **WS 2**, 59
disguise [dɪs'gaɪz] Verkleidung **WS 1**, 31
to disgust [dɪs'gʌst] ekeln; empören OT 5
disgusting [dɪs'gʌstɪŋ] ekelhaft OT 3
dish [dɪʃ] Gericht; Schale OT 2
dishes ['dɪʃɪz] Geschirr OT 2
to do the dishes [ˌdu: ðə 'dɪʃɪz] den Abwasch machen OT 2
dishwasher ['dɪʃwɔ:ʃər] Geschirrspülmaschine OT 4
to dislike [dɪs'laɪk] nicht mögen OT 3
to dismiss [dɪs'mɪs] entlassen; wegschicken OT 5
dismissive [dɪ'smɪsɪv] abweisend; geringschätzig **WS 2**, 82
disobedience [ˌdɪsə'bi:diəns] Ungehorsam; Widerstand **WS 1**, 18
to disobey [ˌdɪsə'beɪ] nicht gehorchen OT 5
disorganized [dɪs'ɔ:gənaɪzd] chaotisch OT 2
to dispense [dɪ'spens] verteilen; ausgeben **WS 3**, 94
dispenser [dɪ'spensə] Spender OT 5
displaced [dɪs'pleɪst] vertrieben; umgesiedelt **WS 1**, 14
display [dɪ'spleɪ] Ausstellung OT 3
dispute [dɪ'spju:t] Disput; Streitgespräch **WS 1**, 40
to dispute [dɪ'spju:t] bestreiten; anfechten **WS 1**, 14
to disqualify [dɪs'kwɒlɪˌfaɪ] disqualifizieren; ausschließen **WS 2**, 58
disrespectful [ˌdɪsrɪ'spektfl] respektlos OT 3
to disrupt [dɪs'rʌpt] stören; unterbrechen **WS 2**, 65
disruption [dɪs'rʌpʃn] Störung; Unterbrechung **WS 1**, 21
distance ['dɪstəns] Entfernung OT 2
distant ['dɪstənt] weit entfernt **WS 3**, 104
distinct [dɪ'stɪŋkt] eindeutig; eigenständig OT 5
distinctive [dɪ'stɪŋktɪv] unverwechselbar; ausgeprägt OT 5
to distinguish between [dɪ'stɪŋgwɪʃ bɪ'twi:n] zwischen etw. unterscheiden OT 5
distinguished [dɪ'stɪŋgwɪʃt] ausgezeichnet; hervorragend **WS 2**, 68
distressed [dɪs'trest] verzweifelt; gestresst **WS 1**, 21
to distribute [dɪ'strɪbju:t] verteilen OT 4
distribution [ˌdɪstrɪ'bju:ʃn] Verteilung **WS 3**, 101
district ['dɪstrɪkt] Bezirk; Gegend OT 1
distrust [dɪs'trʌst] Misstrauen; Zweifel **WS 1**, 14
to disturb [dɪ'stɜ:b] stören OT 5
disturbance [dɪs'tɜ:rbəns] Störung; Unruhe **WS 2**, 65
to ditch [dɪtʃ] ablegen **WS 3**, 122
ditto ['dɪtəʊ] ditto; ebenfalls OT 4
to dive [daɪv] tauchen OT 1
diving ['daɪvɪŋ] Tauchen OT 1
diverse [daɪ'vɜ:s] vielfältig; verschieden OT 4
to diversify ['daɪvərsɪˌfaɪ] diversifizieren; erweitern **WS 3**, 100
diversity [daɪ'vɜ:səti] Vielfältigkeit OT 4
to divide [dɪ'vaɪd] teilen OT 2
divided [dɪ'vaɪdɪd] getrennt; unterteilt OT 2
division [dɪ'vɪʒn] Trennung; Teilung OT 5
divisive [dɪ'vaɪsɪv] spaltend; trennend **WS 2**, 57
divorce [dɪ'vɔ:s] Scheidung OT 3
to divorce [dɪ'vɔ:s] sich scheiden (lassen) OT 3
dizzying ['dɪziɪŋ] schwindelerregend **WS 1**, 43
to do [du:] tun; machen OT 1

to do sth. about sth. [ˌdu: sʌm'θɪŋ ˌəbaʊt sʌm'θɪŋ] etw. gegen etw. tun OT 2
docile ['dəʊsaɪl] fügsam; gehorsam **WS 2**, 78
dockyard ['dɒkjɑ:d] Werft OT 3
doctor ['dɒktə] Arzt / Ärztin OT 1
document ['dɒkjumənt] Dokument OT 4
documentary [ˌdɒkju'mentri] Dokumentation OT 2
dog [dɔ:g] Hund OT 1
guide dog ['gaɪd dɒg] Blindenführhund OT 2
hot dog ['hɒt dɒg] Hotdog OT 2
service dog ['sɜ:vɪs dɒg] Assistenzhund OT 2
dog mess ['dɒg mes] Hundedreck OT 2
doll [dɒl] Puppe OT 3
dollar ['dɒlə] Dollar OT 1
dolphin ['dɒlfɪn] Delfin OT 1
domain [də'meɪn] Domäne; Bereich **WS 1**, 40
domestic [də'mɛstɪk] häuslich; inländisch **WS 2**, 65
dominance ['dɒmɪnəns] Dominanz; Vorherrschaft **WS 3**, 109
dominant ['dɒmɪnənt] wichtig; überwiegend OT 5
to donate [dəʊ'neɪt] spenden OT 2
donation [dəʊ'neɪʃn] Spende OT 2
to make a donation [ˌmeɪk ə dəʊ'neɪʃn] spenden OT 2
door [dɔ:] Tür OT 1
doorbell ['dɔ:bel] Klingel OT 2
doorstep ['dɔ:step] direkt vor Ort; quasi vor der Haustür OT 4
dopamine ['dəʊpəmi:n] Dopamin **WS 4**, 133
dorm [dɔ:rm] Schlafsaal; Studentenwohnheim **WS 2**, 67
double ['dʌbl] doppelt; Doppel... OT 1
double bass [ˌdʌbl 'beɪs] Kontrabass OT 2
doubles ['dʌblz] Doppel OT 3
doubt [daʊt] Zweifel OT 4
dough [dəʊ] Knete; Teig OT 2
doughnut ['dəʊnʌt] Krapfen OT 2
down [daʊn] hinunter OT 1
downhill [ˌdaʊn'hɪl] bergab OT 5
downside ['daʊnsaɪd] Nachteil OT 3
to downsize ['daʊnsaɪz] reduzieren; sich einschränken OT 3
downstairs ['daʊnsteəz] unten; im unteren Stockwerk OT 1
downtown [ˌdaʊn'taʊn] Innenstadt OT 4
downward ['daʊnwəd] abwärts; absteigend OT 5
dozen ['dʌzn] Dutzend OT 4
draft [drɑ:ft] Entwurf OT 2
to draft [drɑ:ft] entwerfen OT 5
dragon ['drægən] Drache OT 1
to drain [dreɪn] abgießen OT 2
drained [dreɪnd] abgetropft OT 2
drama ['drɑ:mə] Drama OT 1
dramatic [drə'mætɪk] dramatisch OT 5
drastic ['dræstɪk] drastisch; extrem OT 5
draughts [drɑ:fts] Damespiel OT 1
to draw [drɔ:] ziehen; zeichnen OT 1
drawback ['drɔ:bæk] Nachteil OT 5
drawer [drɔ:] Schublade OT 3
drawing ['drɔ:ɪŋ] Zeichen; Zeichnung OT 1
to dread [dred] fürchten; sich scheuen **WS 3**, 105
dream [dri:m] Traum OT 1
to dream [dri:m] träumen OT 4
dreamer ['dri:mə] Träumer(in) OT 2
dreamtime ['dri:mtaɪm] Traumzeit OT 5
dress [dres] Kleid OT 3
dress code ['dres kəʊd] Kleiderordnung; Dresscode OT 4
to dress up [dres ʌp] (sich) verkleiden OT 2
dresser ['drɛsə] Kommode **WS 1**, 27
to drill [drɪl] bohren OT 4
drink [drɪŋk] Getränk OT 1
to drink [drɪŋk] trinken OT 1
to drip [drɪp] tropfen OT 3
to drive [draɪv] fahren OT 1
driver ['draɪvə] Fahrer(in) OT 1
driverless ['draɪvələs] führerlos OT 4
driver's license ['draɪvəz laɪsns] Führerschein; Fahrerlaubnis OT 4
driving licence ['draɪvɪŋ laɪsns] Führerschein OT 2
drone [drəʊn] Drohne OT 3
to drop [drɒp] fallen lassen OT 1
drought [draʊt] Dürre OT 5
to drown [draʊn] ertrinken OT 3
drug [drʌg] Droge OT 3
to drug [drʌg] betäuben **WS 3**, 104
drugstore ['drʌgstɔ:] Apotheke; Drogerie OT 2
drums [drʌmz] Schlagzeug OT 1
dry [draɪ] trocken OT 2
duck [dʌk] Ente OT 2
due to [dju: tə] wegen; aufgrund von OT 5
dull [dʌl] uninteressant; langweilig OT 5
dumb [dʌm] blöd; dumm OT 5
to dump [dʌmp] kippen OT 5
dumpling ['dʌmplɪŋ] Kloß; Knödel OT 4
dung [dʌŋ] Dung; Mist **WS 1**, 32
duplication [ˌdju:plɪ'keɪʃn] Doppelung **WS 4**, 139
during ['djʊərɪŋ] während OT 2
dust [dʌst] Staub **WS 1**, 39
to dust off [dʌst ɒf] abwischen; abstauben OT 5
dusty ['dʌsti] verstaubt **WW**, 11
duty ['dju:ti] Pflicht OT 5
duty free [ˌdju:ti 'fri:] zollfrei OT 2
to dwell [dwel] verweilen **WS 1**, 15
dweller ['dwelə] Bewohner OT 4
dye [daɪ] Färbemittel; Farbe OT 4
dynamic [daɪ'næmɪk] Dynamik OT 5
dynasty ['daɪnəsti] Dynastie; Herrscherhaus **WS 1**, 14
dystopia [dɪs'təʊpiə] Dystopie **WS 3**, 104
dystopian [dɪs'təʊpiən] dystopisch OT 5

E

each [i:tʃ] jede(r, -s) OT 1
eager ['i:gə] eifrig OT 2
eagerness ['i:gərnəs] Eifer; Begeisterung **WS 2**, 79
eagle ['i:gl] Adler OT 2
ear [ɪə] Ohr OT 1
early ['ɜ:li] früh OT 1
to earn [ɜ:n] verdienen OT 3
earth [ɜ:θ] Erde OT 2
earthquake ['ɜ:θkweɪk] Erdbeben OT 2
ease [i:z] Leichtigkeit **WS 1**, 28
east [i:st] Ost- OT 1
Easter ['i:stər] Ostern OT 1
eastern ['i:stən] östlich OT 2
easy ['i:zi] einfach OT 1
easily ['i:zəli] leicht OT 2
to eat [i:t] essen OT 1
to echo ['ekəʊ] nachhallen; nachklingen OT 5
eco-activism ['i:koʊˌæktɪvɪzəm] Öko-Aktivismus **WS 1**, 21
eco-friendly [ˌi:kəʊ 'frendli] ökologisch OT 3
ecological [ˌi:kə'lɒdʒɪkl] ökologisch OT 5
e-commerce ['i: kɒmɜ:s] E-Commerce; Internethandel OT 4
economic [ˌi:kə'nɒmɪk] wirtschaftlich OT 4

economics [ˌiːkəˈnɒmɪks] Wirtschaftswissenschaften OT 5
economist [ɪˈkɒnəmɪst] Wirtschaftswiss enschaftler(in) **WS 4**, 142
economy [ɪˈkɒnəmi] Wirtschaft; Ökonomie OT 3
ecosystem [ˈiːkəʊsɪstəm] Ökosystem **WS 1**, 21
ecotourism [ˈikəʊtʊərɪzəm] Ökotourismus OT 3
edge [edʒ] Rand OT 3
edible [ˈedəbl] essbar **WS 4**, 140
to **edit** [ˈedɪt] überarbeiten; redigieren OT 3
editor [ˈedɪtə] Redakteur(in); Herausgeber(in) OT 2
editorial [ˌɛdɪˈtɔːril] Leitartikel; redaktionell **WS 1**, 25
to **educate** [ˈedʒukeɪt] erziehen OT 5
education [ˌedjʊˈkeɪʃən] Ausbildung OT 3
educational [ˌedʒuˈkeɪʃənl] Bildungs… OT 3
educator [ˈedʒukeɪtə] Pädagoge / Pädagogin OT 4
eel [iːl] Aal OT 4
effect [ɪˈfekt] Wirkung OT 3
effective [ɪˈfektɪv] wirksam OT 5
effectively [ɪˈfektɪvli] wirksam OT 4
effectiveness [ɪˈfektɪvnəs] Wirksamkeit OT 5
efficiency [ɪˈfɪʃənsi] Effizienz; Wirksamkeit **WS 3**, 99
efficient [ɪˈfɪʃnt] effizient OT 4
efficiently [ɪˈfɪʃntli] effizient OT 3
effigy [ˈɛfɪdʒi] Abbild; Effigie **WS 1**, 43
effort [ˈefət] Anstrengung; Mühe OT 5
egg [eg] Ei OT 1
eggplant [ˈegplɑːnt] Aubergine OT 2
eight [eɪt] acht OT 1
eighteen [ˌeɪˈtiːn] achtzehn OT 1
eighty [ˈeɪti] achtzig OT 1
either [ˈaɪðə] auch nicht OT 1
to **elaborate** [ɪˈlæbərət] weiter ausführen **WS 2**, 55
elbow [ˈelbəʊ] Ellbogen OT 1
elder [ˈeldə] Älteste(r) OT 5
elderly [ˈeldəli] älter OT 4
to **elect** [ɪˈlekt] wählen; auswählen OT 4
election [ɪˈlekʃn] Wahl OT 3
elective [ɪˈlektɪv] Auswahlfach OT 4
electric [ɪˈlektrɪk] elektrisch OT 1
electrical [ɪˈlektrɪkl] elektrisch OT 4
electricity [ɪˌlekˈtrɪsəti] Strom OT 2
electrification [ɪˌlɛktrɪfɪˈkeɪʃən] Elektrifizierung **WS 3**, 99
electrolyser [ɪˈlɛktrəʊˌlaɪzə] Elektrolyseur **WS 3**, 99
electronic [ɪˌlekˈtrɒnɪk] elektronisch OT 5
electronical [ɪˌlekˈtrɒnɪkl] elektronisch OT 5
electronically [ɪˌlekˈtrɒnɪkli] elektronisch OT 4
electronics [ɪˌlekˈtrɒnɪks] Elektronik OT 2
element [ˈelɪmənt] Bestandteil OT 2
elementary [ˌelɪˈmentri] Grund-; elementar OT 2
elementary school [ˌelɪˈmentri skuːl] Grundschule OT 2
elephant [ˈelɪfənt] Elefant OT 1
eleven [ɪˈlevn] elf OT 1
eligible [ˈelɪdʒəbl] berechtigt **WS 2**, 61
to **eliminate** [ɪˈlɪmɪneɪt] beseitigen **WS 3**, 107
elite [ɪˈliːt] Elite; Oberschicht **WS 2**, 59
elite sports [eɪˈliːt spɔːts] Spitzensport OT 3
else [els] sonst noch OT 1
elsewhere [ˌelsˈweər] woanders OT 5
email [ˈiːmeɪl] E-Mail OT 1
to **email** [ˈiːmeɪl] eine E-Mail schreiben OT 2
to **embark** [ɪmˈbɑːk] beginnen **WS 1**, 15
embarrassed [ɪmˈbærəst] verlegen; peinlich berührt OT 3
embarrassing [ɪmˈbærəsɪŋ] peinlich OT 2
ember [ˈembər] glühende Kohle OT 5
emblem [ˈɛmbləm] Emblem; Symbol **WS 2**, 59
to **embrace** [ɪmˈbreɪs] umarmen OT 5
embroidery [ɪmˈbrɔɪdəri] Stickerei **WS 1**, 25
embryo [ˈɛmbriəʊ] Embryo **WS 3**, 126
to **emerge** [iˈmɜːdʒ] ans Licht kommen **WS 1**, 14
emergency [iˈmɜːdʒənsi] Notfall OT 1
emergency services [iˈmɜːdʒənsi ˌsɜːvɪsɪz] Rettungsdienste OT 2
emigrant [ˈemɪgrənt] Auswanderer / Auswanderin OT 3
to **emigrate** [ˈemɪgreɪt] auswandern OT 4
emission [ɪˈmɪʃn] Ausstoss; Emission OT 3
to **emit** [ɪˈmɪt] emittieren; ausstoßen **WS 3**, 102
emoji [ɪˈməʊdʒi] Emoji OT 3
emoticon [ɪˈməʊtɪkɒn] Emoticon OT 5
emotion [ɪˈməʊʃn] Gefühl OT 3
emotional [ɪˈməʊʃənl] emotional OT 5
emotive [ɪˈməʊtɪv] emotional; gefühlvoll **WS 1**, 20
to **empathize** [ˈɛmpəθaɪz] mitfühlen; empathisieren **WS 2**, 67
empathy [ˈempəθi] Empathie **WS 3**, 112
emphasis [ˈemfəsɪs] Betonung OT 5
to **emphasize** [ˈemfəsaɪz] betonen OT 5
empire [ˈempaɪə] Reich **WS 1**, 14
to **employ** [ɪmˈplɔɪ] beschäftigen **WS 4**, 133
employability [ɪmˌplɔɪəˈbɪlɪti] Beschäftigungsfähigkeit **WS 3**, 110
employee [ɪmˈplɔɪiː] Angestellte(r) OT 4
employer [ɪmˈplɔɪə] Arbeitgeber(in) OT 3
employment [ɪmˈplɔɪmənt] Beschäftigung; Arbeit OT 5
to **empower** [ɪmˈpaʊə] stärken; ermächtigen OT 5
empowerment [ɪmˈpaʊərmənt] Ermächtigung; Befähigung **WS 3**, 98
to **empty** [ˈempti] entleeren; leeren OT 4
empty [ˈempti] leer OT 1
to **enable** [ɪˈneɪbl] ermöglichen **WS 1**, 16
enclosure [ɪnˈkloʊʒə] Gehege **WS 2**, 64
encounter [ɪnˈkaʊntə] Begegnung **WS 2**, 67
to **encounter** [ɪnˈkaʊntə] begegnen **WS 4**, 142
to **encourage** [ɪnˈkʌrɪdʒ] ermutigen OT 2
encouragement [ɪnˈkʌrɪdʒmənt] Aufmunterung OT 5
end [end] Ende OT 1
to **end** [end] enden OT 1
to **endanger** [ɪnˈdeɪndʒər] gefährden OT 5
endangered [ɪnˈdeɪndʒəd] gefährdet OT 2
to **endear** [ɪnˈdɪə] sich beliebt machen **WS 2**, 63
endearing [ɪnˈdɪərɪŋ] liebenswert; reizend **WS 1**, 21
ending [ˈendɪŋ] Ende; Endung OT 2
endless [ˈendləs] endlos; unendlich OT 4
to **endorse** [ɪnˈdɔːs] unterstützen **WS 3**, 100
to **endure** [ɪnˈdjʊə] ertragen; aushalten **WS 2**, 72
endzone [ˈendzəʊn] Endzone OT 3
enemy [ˈenəmi] Feind(in) OT 1

energetic [ˌenəˈdʒetɪk] aktiv; energisch OT 2
to **energize** [ˈɛnərdʒaɪz] beleben; Energie geben **WW**, 11
energy [ˈenədʒi] Energie OT 2
to **enforce** [ɪnˈfɔːs] durchsetzen OT 4
enforcement [ɪnˈfɔːsmənt] Vollstreckung OT 5
to **engage** [ɪnˈɡeɪdʒ] (sich) beschäftigen OT 4
to **get engaged** [ɡet ɪnˈɡeɪdʒd] sich verloben **WS 1**, 29
engagement [ɪnˈɡeɪdʒmənt] Engagement; Beschäftigung **WS 1**, 13
engine [ˈendʒɪn] Motor; Lokomotive OT 2
engineer [ˌendʒɪˈnɪə] Ingenieur(in); Lokführer(in) OT 3
engineering [ˌendʒɪˈnɪərɪŋ] Ingenieurwesen OT 1
to **engrave** [ɪnˈɡreɪv] gravieren; eingravieren OT 4
to **enhance** [ɪnˈhɑːns] verstärken **WS 3**, 110
enigmatic [ˌenɪɡˈmætɪk] geheimnisvoll; rätselhaft **WS 3**, 104
to **enjoy** [ɪnˈdʒɔɪ] genießen OT 1
enjoyable [ɪnˈdʒɔɪəbl] angenehm OT 2
to **enlighten** [ɪnˈlaɪtən] aufklären; erleuchten **WS 1**, 21
enormous [ɪˈnɔːməs] riesig OT 1
enough [ɪˈnʌf] genug OT 1
to **enquire** [ɪnˈkwaɪə] anfragen; sich erkundigen **WS 3**, 111
to **enrich** [ɪnˈrɪtʃ] verbessern; bereichern **WS 3**, 110
to **enrol** [ɪnˈroʊl] einschreiben; anmelden **WS 3**, 103
to **ensure** [ɪnˈʃʊə] sicherstellen OT 4
to **enter** [ˈentə] eintreten; eintragen OT 2
to **entertain** [ˌentəˈteɪn] unterhalten OT 4
entertainer [ˌentəˈteɪnə] Künstler(in); Unterhalter(in) OT 3
entertaining [ˌentəˈteɪnɪŋ] unterhaltsam; amüsant OT 3
entertainment [ˌentəˈteɪnmənt] Unterhaltung OT 3
enthusiasm [ɪnˈθjuːziæzəm] Enthusiasmus **WS 1**, 32
enthusiastic [ɪnˌθjuːziˈæstɪk] begeistert OT 3
entire [ɪnˈtaɪə] ganze(r, -s) OT 3
entitled [ɪnˈtaɪtld] mit dem Titel **WS 1**, 25
to **be entitled** [bi ɪnˈtaɪtld] das Recht haben **WS 2**, 78
entrance [ˈentrəns] Eingang OT 1
entrance hall [ˈentrəns ˌhɔːl] Eingangsbereich; Eingangshalle OT 1
entrepreneur [ˌɒntrəprəˈnɜː] Unternehmer(in) OT 5
entry [ˈentri] Eintrag; Einsendung OT 2
envelope [ˈenvələʊp] Briefumschlag OT 2
environment [ɪnˈvaɪrənmənt] Umfeld; Umwelt OT 2
environmental [ɪnˌvaɪrənˈmentl] Umwelt-; ökologisch OT 2
environmentally [ɪnˌvaɪrənˈmentəli] umwelt... OT 3
environmentalism [ɪnˌvaɪrənˈmɛntəlɪzəm] Umweltschutz; Umweltbewegung **WS 1**, 21
environmentalist [ɪnˌvaɪrənˈmentəlɪst] Umweltschützer(in) OT 3
to **envy** [ˈenvi] beneiden OT 5
epidemic [ˌepɪˈdemɪk] Epidemie OT 4
episode [ˈepɪsəʊd] Folge OT 5
epitome [ɪˈpɪtəmi] Inbegriff; Quintessenz **WS 1**, 21
equal [ˈiːkwəl] gleich; gleichberechtigt OT 4
equality [iˈkwɒləti] Gleichberechtigung OT 5
equator [ɪˈkweɪtər] Äquator OT 5
to **equip** [ɪˈkwɪpt] ausrüsten **WS 1**, 23
equipment [ɪˈkwɪpmənt] Ausrüstung OT 2
equivalent [ɪˈkwɪvələnt] entsprechend OT 4
era [ˈɪərə] Ära OT 4
to **eradicate** [ɪˈrædɪkeɪt] ausmerzen; ausrotten OT 4
errant [ˈɛrənt] irrend; fehlgeleitet **WS 3**, 94
error [ˈɛrə] Irrtum; Fehler **WS 1**, 18
to **erupt** [ɪˈrʌpt] ausbrechen **WS 1**, 15
to **escape** [ɪˈskeɪp] entkommen OT 2
e-scooter [ˈiːskuːtə] E-Roller OT 5
escort [ˈeskɔːt] Begleiter(in) OT 3
especially [ɪˈspeʃəli] besonders OT 2
essay [ˈeseɪ] Aufsatz OT 2
essence [ˈesns] Wesen; Wesentliche **WS 3**, 96
essential [ɪˈsenʃl] wichtig; wesentlich OT 4
to **establish** [ɪˈstæblɪʃ] begründen OT 4
to **estimate** [ˈestɪmeɪt] schätzen OT 5
ETA (estimated time of arrival) [ˈestɪmeɪtɪd taɪm əv əˈraɪvl] geschätzte Ankunftszeit OT 2
etc. (et cetera) [ˌet ˈsetərə] und so weiter; usw. OT 1
eternal [ɪˈtɜːnl] ewig OT 4
eternity [ɪˈtɜːrnɪti] Ewigkeit **WS 2**, 62
ethical [ˈeθɪkl] ethisch; moralisch vertretbar OT 3
ethnic [ˈeθnɪk] ethnisch OT 5
ethnically [ˈeθnɪkli] ethnisch OT 5
ethnicity [eθˈnɪsəti] Ethnizität **WS 3**, 92
etiquette [ˈetɪkət] Etikette OT 3
eureka moment [juˈriːkə ˈməʊmənt] Heureka-Erlebnis OT 4
European [ˌjʊərəˈpiːən] Europäer(in) OT 3
to **evaluate** [ɪˈvæljueɪt] bewerten OT 4
evaluation [ɪˌvæljuˈeɪʃn] Bewertung OT 5
even [ˈiːvn] sogar OT 1
evening [ˈiːvnɪŋ] Abend OT 1
evenly [ˈiːvnli] ausgeglichen OT 4
event [ɪˈvent] Ereignis OT 1
eventually [ɪˈventʃuəli] schließlich OT 3
ever [ˈevə] je OT 1
everlasting [ˌevəˈlɑːstɪŋ] ewig **WS 4**, 142
every [ˈevri] jede(r, -s) OT 1
everybody [ˈevribɒdi] jeder; alle OT 1
everyday [ˈevrideɪ] alltäglich OT 3
everyone [ˈevriwʌn] jeder OT 1
everything [ˈevriθɪŋ] alles OT 1
everywhere [ˈevriweə] überall OT 1
evidence [ˈevɪdəns] Beweis(e) **WS 1**, 33
evident [ˈevɪdənt] offensichtlich; klar OT 5
evil [ˈiːvl] Übel; Böse OT 5
evocative [ɪˈvɒkətɪv] evokativ; anregend **WS 2**, 55
to **evoke** [ɪˈvəʊk] hervorrufen **WS 2**, 72
evolution [ˌiːvəˈluːʃn] Evolution; Entwicklung OT 5
to **evolve** [ɪˈvɒlv] (sich) entwickeln OT 4
exact [ɪɡˈzækt] genau OT 2
to **exaggerate** [ɪɡˈzædʒəreɪt] übertreiben OT 4
exam [ɪɡˈzæm] Prüfung OT 1
to **examine** [ɪɡˈzæmɪn] untersuchen **WS 1**, 38
example [ɪɡˈzɑːmpl] Beispiel OT 1
excellent [ˈeksələnt] ausgezeichnet OT 3
except [ɪkˈsept] außer OT 2
exceptional [ɪkˈsɛpʃənl] außergewöhnlich; herausragend **WS 1**, 23

excerpt [ek'sɜ:pt] Ausschnitt; Auszug OT 5
excess [ɪk'sɛs] übermäßig; überschüssig **WS 3**, 101
exchange [ɪks'tʃeɪndʒ] Austausch OT 1
to **excise** ['ɛksaɪz] auslöschen **WS 2**, 79
excited [ɪk'saɪtɪd] begeistert; aufgeregt OT 1
excitement [ɪk'saɪtmənt] Aufregung OT 3
exciting [ɪk'saɪtɪŋ] aufregend OT 1
to **exclude** [ɪk'sklu:d] ausschließen OT 5
exclusion [ɪk'sklu:ʒn] Ausschluss **WS 4**, 133
exclusively [ɪk'sklu:sɪvli] ausschließlich OT 5
to **excuse** [ɪk'skju:z] entschuldigen OT 1
to **execute** ['eksɪkju:t] töten lassen; exekutieren OT 3
executive [ɪg'zekjətɪv] Führungskraft OT 5
exercise ['eksəsaɪz] körperliche Bewegung; Übung OT 1
exercise book ['eksəsaɪz bʊk] Übungsheft OT 1
to **exert** [ɪg'zɜ:t] anstrengen **WS 3**, 103
exhausted [ɪg'zɔ:stɪd] erschöpft OT 2
exhibit [ɪg'zɪbɪt] Ausstellung OT 2
to **exhibit** [ɪg'zɪbɪt] ausstellen OT 2
exhibition [ˌeksɪ'bɪʃn] Ausstellung OT 1
exhibitor [ɪg'zɪbɪtə] Aussteller(in) **WS 4**, 138
to **exist** [ɪg'zɪst] existieren OT 3
existence [ɪg'zɪstəns] Existenz OT 5
exit ['eksɪt] Ausgang; Abfahrt OT 2
exodus ['ɛksədəs] Flucht; Exodus **WS 1**, 40
exotic [ɪg'zɒtɪk] exotisch OT 2
to **expand** [ɪk'spænd] erweitern; expandieren OT 4
expanding [ɪk'spænd] erweiternd OT 2
expansion [ɪk'spænʃn] Ausdehnung; Expansion **WS 3**, 108
to **expect** [ɪk'spekt] erwarten OT 2
expectation [ˌekspek'teɪʃn] Erwartung OT 5
to **expedite** ['ɛkspɪdaɪt] beschleunigen **WS 1**, 14
expedition [ˌekspə'dɪʃn] Expedition OT 2
expensive [ɪk'spensɪv] teuer OT 1
experience [ɪk'spɪəriəns] Erfahrung OT 2
experienced [ɪk'spɪəriənst] erfahren OT 3
experiment [ɪk'sperɪmənt] Experiment OT 1
to **experiment** [ɪk'sperɪmənt] experimentieren OT 4
expert ['ekspɜ:t] Experte / Expertin OT 3
expiry date [ɪk'spaɪəri deɪt] Verfallsdatum **WS 1**, 39
to **explain** [ɪk'spleɪn] erklären OT 1
explanation [ˌeksplə'neɪʃn] Erklärung OT 1
explanatory [ɪk'splænətri] erklärend **WS 4**, 136
explicitly [ɪk'splɪsɪtli] explizit OT 5
to **explode** [ɪk'spləʊd] explodieren OT 5
to **exploit** [ɪk'splɔɪt] ausbeuten OT 3
exploitation [ˌeksplɔɪ'teɪʃn] Ausbeutung OT 4
exploitative [ɪk'splɔɪtətɪv] ausbeuterisch **WS 2**, 67
to **explore** [ɪk'splɔ:] erforschen; erkunden OT 1
explorer [ɪk'splɔ:rə] Forscher(in) OT 3
explosion [ɪk'spləʊʒn] Explosion **WS 1**, 15
export [ɪk'splɪsɪtli] exportieren OT 5
exporter [ek'spɔ:tər] Exporteur(in) OT 5
to **expose** [bi ɪk'spoʊzd tu:] aussetzen **WS 2**, 56
exposure [ɪk'spəʊʒə] Sichtbarkeit; Einblick **WS 3**, 109
to **express** [ɪk'spres] ausdrücken OT 3
expression [ɪk'spreʃn] Ausdruck OT 1
to **extend** [ɪk'stɛnd] (sich) ausdehnen **WS 3**, 95
extended [ɪk'stendɪd] erweitert OT 5
extent [ɪk'stent] Ausmaß OT 5
extinct [ɪk'stɪŋkt] ausgestorben OT 2
extinction [ɪk'stɪŋkʃn] Aussterben OT 5
extinguisher [ɪk'stɪŋgwɪʃər] Löscher OT 5
extra ['ekstrə] Extra... OT 1
extract ['ekstrækt] Auszug OT 4
extraordinary [ɪk'strɔ:rdɪneri] ungewöhnlich **WS 1**, 25
extravagant [ɪk'strævəgənt] extravagant **WS 2**, 71
extreme [ɪk'stri:m] extrem OT 3; Extrem OT 5
extremely [ɪk'stri:mli] extrem OT 3
extremist [ɪk'stri:mɪst] Extremist(in); Radikale(r) **WS 1**, 18
extroverted ['ekstrəvɜ:tɪd] extrovertiert OT 5
eye [aɪ] Auge OT 1
eye-opener ['aɪˌoʊpənə] Augenöffner **WS 2**, 82
eyebrow ['aɪbraʊ] Augenbraue OT 4
eyelash ['aɪlæʃ] Wimper **WS 2**, 70
eyelid ['aɪlɪd] Augenlid OT 2
eyeshadow ['aɪˌʃædoʊ] Lidschatten **WS 2**, 70

F

fabric ['fæbrɪk] Stoff **WS 1**, 27
fabulous ['fæbjələs] fabelhaft OT 2
facade [fə'sɑ:d] Fassade **WS 1**, 24
face [feɪs] Gesicht OT 1
to **face** [feɪs] begegnen OT 4
face paint ['feɪs peɪnt] Schminke OT 2
facial features ['feɪʃl 'fi:tʃərz] Gesichtszüge **WW**, 11
facial expression ['feɪʃl ɪkspreʃn] Gesichtsausdruck OT 4
facility [fə'sɪləti] Anlage OT 4
fact [fækt] Tatsache; Fakt OT 1
factor ['fæktə] Faktor OT 5
factory ['fæktri] Fabrik OT 4
factory-farmed ['fæktri fɑ:md] in Farmen gezüchtet; in Massen gezüchtet OT 5
factual ['fæktʃuəl] sachlich OT 4
to **fade** [feɪd] verwelken; verblassen OT 2
faeces ['fi:si:z] Fäkalien; Kot **WS 1**, 16
to **fail** [feɪl] scheitern OT 2
failure ['feɪljə] Misserfolg OT 4
faint [feɪnt] schwindlig OT 2
to **faint** [feɪnt] ohnmächtig werden OT 2
fair [feə] gerecht OT 2; Jahrmarkt OT 4
fairground ['feəgraʊnd] Jahrmarkt OT 2
fairy ['feəri] Fee OT 2
fairy tale ['feəri ˌteɪl] Märchen OT 1
faith [feɪθ] Vertrauen; Glaube **WS 1**, 15
fake [feɪk] falsch; unecht OT 5
to **fall** [fɔ:l] fallen; stürzen OT 1
to **fall apart** [fɔ:l ə'pɑ:t] auseinanderfallen OT 4
to **fall asleep** [fɔ:l ə'sli:p] einschlafen OT 2
to **fall over** [fɔ:l 'əʊvə] hinfallen; umfallen OT 2
falls [fɔ:ls] Wasserfall OT 1
false [fɔ:ls] falsch OT 1
false friend [ˌfɔ:ls 'frend] falscher Freund; Übersetzungsfalle OT 2
fame [feɪm] Ruhm; Ruf OT 3
familiar [fə'mɪliə] vertraut; bekannt OT 2
family ['fæməli] Familie OT 1

famine ['fæmɪn] Hungersnot OT 4
famous ['feɪməs] berühmt OT 1
fan [fæn] Fan OT 1
fanatic [fə'nætɪk] Fanatiker(in) **WS 1**, 18
fancy ['fænsi] schick; einfallsreich OT 2
fancy dress [ˌfænsi 'dres] Kostüm- OT 2
fantastic [fæn'tæstɪk] fantastisch OT 1
fantasy ['fæntəsi] Fantasy; Fantasie OT 2
FAQ (frequently asked questions) [ˌef eɪ 'kju:] häufig gestellte Fragen OT 1
far [fɑ:] weit OT 1
far-off ['fɑ: ɒf] fern OT 2
so far [səʊ 'fɑ:] bisher OT 2
faraway ['fɑ:rəweɪ] fern OT 4
fare [feɪk] Fahrpreis OT 5
farm [fɑ:m] Bauernhof OT 1
farmer ['fɑ:mə] Bauer / Bäuerin OT 2
farmhand ['fɑ:mhænd] Erntehelfer(in); Landarbeiter(in) OT 4
farmhouse ['fɑ:mhaʊs] Bauernhaus OT 3
farming ['fɑ:mɪŋ] Landwirtschaft OT 2
farmland ['fɑ:mlænd] Ackerland OT 4
farmworker [fɑ:mwɜ:kə] Landarbeiter(in); Farmarbeiter(in) OT 4
to fascinate ['fæsɪneɪt] faszinieren **WS 1**, 17
fascinating ['fæsɪneɪtɪŋ] faszinierend OT 3
fascination [ˌfæsɪ'neɪʃn] Faszination OT 4
fascism ['fæʃɪzəm] Faschismus **WS 3**, 104
fashion ['fæʃn] Trend; Mode OT 1
fashion fad ['fæʃən fæd] Modetrend **WS 2**, 69
fast [fɑ:st] schnell OT 1
to fasten ['fɑ:sn] anschließen; festmachen OT 1
fat [fæt] Fett OT 2
fatal ['feɪtl] tödlich **WS 2**, 81
fate [feɪt] Schicksal **WS 1**, 29
father ['fɑ:ðə] Vater OT 1
fatigue [fə'ti:g] Erschöpfung **WS 4**, 138
faucet ['fɔ:sɪt] Wasserhahn OT 4
fault [fɔ:lt] Fehler OT 2
faulty ['fɔ:lti] defekt OT 2
favour: in favour of [ɪn 'feɪvə] zugunsten; für **WS 1**, 14
favourite ['feɪvərɪt] Lieblings... OT 1
fear [fɪə] Angst; Furcht OT 3
feast [fi:st] Fest; Festmahl OT 4
to feast [fi:st] feiern; schlemmen OT 4
feather ['feðə] Feder OT 2
feature ['fi:tʃə] Sonderbeitrag; Eigenschaft; Merkmal OT 1
to feature ['fi:tʃə] aufweisen; präsentieren OT 4
February ['februəri] Februar OT 1
federal government ['fedərəl 'gʌvənmənt] Bundesregierung OT 5
federation [ˌfedə'reɪʃn] Bund OT 5
fee [fi:] Gebühr OT 3
to feed [fi:d] füttern OT 2
feedback ['fi:dbæk] Feedback OT 1
feeding ['fi:dɪŋ] Füttern OT 2
to feel [fi:l] (sich) fühlen; anfassen OT 1
feeling ['fi:lɪŋ] Gefühl OT 2
fell [fel] Berg (in Nordengland) OT 2
fellow ['feləʊ] zur gleichen Gruppe gehörend; gleichartig OT 5
female ['fi:meɪl] weiblich OT 2
feminine ['fɛmɪnɪn] weiblich **WS 2**, 70
fence [fens] Zaun OT 5
feral ['ferəl] wild OT 5
ferocious [fə'rəʊʃəs] wild; grausam **WS 1**, 16
ferris wheel ['ferɪs wi:l] Riesenrad OT 4
ferry ['feri] Fähre OT 2
fertility [fə'tɪlɪti] Fruchtbarkeit; Fertilität **WS 1**, 43
fertilizer ['fɜ:təlaɪzə] Dünger OT 3
festival ['festɪvl] Festival; Festspiele; Fest OT 1
festive ['fɛstɪv] festlich **WS 1**, 43
festivity [fe'stɪvəti] Festlichkeit OT 4
to fetch [fetʃ] holen; abholen OT 4
few [fju:] wenige OT 1
fiction ['fɪkʃn] Fiktion; Romanliteratur OT 2
fictional ['fɪkʃənl] erfunden OT 2
field [fi:ld] Feld OT 1
fieldwork ['fi:ldwɜ:k] Geländearbeit OT 4
fierce [fɪərs] heftig; wild **WS 2**, 62
fifteen [ˌfɪf'ti:n] fünfzehn OT 1
fifth [fɪfθ] fünfte(r, -s) OT 1
fifty ['fɪfti] fünfzig OT 1
fight [faɪt] Kampf OT 1
to fight [faɪt] kämpfen OT 1
figurative ['fɪgərətɪv] figurativ OT 5
figure ['fɪgə] Zahl; Figur OT 3
to figure (out) [fɪgə 'aʊt] herausfinden **WS 3**, 97
figurehead ['fɪgjərhɛd] Galionsfigur; Symbolfigur **WS 2**, 55
figurine ['fɪgjəri:n] Figur; Statuette **WS 1**, 27
file [faɪl] Datei OT 3
to fill [fɪl] füllen OT 2
film [fɪlm] Film OT 1
film director [fɪlm də'rektə] Regisseur(in) OT 2
filmmaker ['fɪlm meɪkə] Filmemacher(in) OT 5
to filter ['fɪltə] filtern **WS 3**, 98
to filter out ['fɪltər aʊt] herausfiltern; aussieben **WS 3**, 127
filthy ['fɪlθi] dreckig OT 4
final ['faɪnl] endgültig OT 1
finalist ['faɪnəlɪst] Finalist(in) OT 5
to finalize ['faɪnəlaɪz] fertigstellen; abschließen OT 5
finally ['faɪnəli] schließlich OT 1
finance ['faɪnæns] Finanzwirtschaft OT 5
financial [faɪ'nænʃl] finanziell OT 5
to find [faɪnd] finden OT 1
to find out ['faɪnd aʊt] herausfinden OT 1
finding ['faɪndɪŋ] Ergebnis; Befund OT 4
fine [faɪn] gut; prima OT 1
finger ['fɪŋgə] Finger OT 1
fingers crossed ['fɪŋgəz krɒst] Daumen gedrückt OT 1
fingernail ['fɪŋgəneɪl] Fingernagel OT 2
to finish ['fɪnɪʃ] abschließen; aufhören OT 1
fire ['faɪə] Feuer OT 2
to fire ['faɪə] entlassen OT 5
firefighter ['faɪəfaɪtə] Feuerwehrmann / -frau OT 2
firefighting [ˌfaɪə'faɪtɪŋ] Brandbekämpfung OT 2
fireplace ['faɪəpleɪs] Kamin OT 1
fire station ['faɪə steɪʃn] Feuerwache OT 2
firewood ['faɪəwʊd] Brennholz OT 4
fireworks ['faɪəwɜ:ks] Feuerwerk OT 3
firework display ['faɪəwɜ:k dɪ'spleɪ] Feuerwerk OT 4
firm [fɜ:m] Firma; Kanzlei OT 5; fest **WS 1**, 40
first [fɜ:st] erste(r, -s) OT 1
first aid [ˌfɜ:st 'eɪd] Erste Hilfe OT 2
first aid kit [ˌfɜ:st 'eɪd kɪt] Verbandkasten; Erstehilfekasten OT 2
fish [fɪʃ] Fisch OT 1
fishbone [fɪʃbəʊn] Gräte **WS 4**, 140
fish finger [ˌfɪʃ 'fɪŋgə] Fischstäbchen OT 1
fishing ['fɪʃɪŋ] Angeln OT 2
fist [fɪst] Faust OT 5
to fit [fɪt] passen OT 1
fit [fɪt] in Form; geeignet OT 2

fitness ['fɪtnəs] Fitness OT 2
five [faɪv] fünf OT 1
to **fix** [fɪks] korrigieren OT 2
fizzy ['fɪzi] kohlensäurehaltig OT 2
flag [flæg] Fahne OT 1
flagship ['flægʃɪp] Flaggschiff OT 3
flame [fleɪm] Flamme **WS 1**, 43
flamingo [flə'mɪŋgəʊ] Flamingo OT 2
flammable ['flæməbl] brennbar OT 2
flashback ['flæʃbæk] Rückblende; Flashback **WS 3**, 106
flashlight ['flæʃlaɪt] Taschenlampe OT 2
flashy ['flæʃi] auffällig; schrill **WS 2**, 53
flask [flɑːsk] Thermosflasche OT 3
flat [flæt] Wohnung OT 1
flattery ['flætəri] Schmeichelei **WS 2**, 69
flavour ['fleɪvə] Geschmack OT 2
flawed [flɔːd] fehlerhaft; mangelhaft **WS 2**, 62
flea market [fliː 'mɑːkɪt] Flohmarkt; Trödelmarkt OT 5
to **flee** [fliː] fliehen; flüchten **WS 1**, 14
flesh [fleʃ] Fleisch OT 2
flexibility [ˌfleksə'bɪləti] Flexibilität OT 5
flexible ['fleksəbl] anpassungsfähig; flexibel OT 4
flight [flaɪt] Flug OT 2
flight crew ['flaɪt kruː] Flugpersonal OT 2
to **flip** [flɪp] umdrehen OT 4
float [fləʊt] Umzugswagen; Parade-Wagen OT 4
to **float** [fləʊt] treiben; schweben OT 3
to **flock** [flɒk] strömen **WS 1**, 15
flood [flʌd] Hochwasser; Flut OT 2
flooding ['flʌdɪŋ] Fluten; Überflutung OT 4
floor [flɔː] Boden; Stockwerk OT 1
flour ['flaʊə] Mehl OT 3
flow [fləʊ] Fluss; Strom **WS 3**, 101
flower ['flaʊə] Blume OT 1
flowing ['fləʊɪŋ] fließend OT 5
fluency ['fluːənsi] Sprachbeherrschung OT 5
fluent ['fluːənt] fließend OT 3
fluffy ['flʌfi] flauschig OT 2
flute [fluːt] Querflöte OT 2
to **flutter** ['flʌtə] flattern; flimmern **WS 3**, 96
to **fly** [flaɪ] fliegen OT 1
flyer ['flaɪə] Flyer OT 4
flying ['flaɪɪŋ] Fliegen OT 1
focus ['fəʊkəs] Fokus OT 1
to **focus** ['fəʊkəs] fokussieren OT 4
focused ['fəʊkəst] fokussiert OT 4
fog [fɒg] Nebel **WS 4**, 140
to **fold** [fəʊld] falten OT 2
folk [fəʊk] Volks... OT 2
folk hero ['fəʊk hɪərəʊ] Volksheld OT 4
folklore ['fəʊklɔːr] Folklore OT 5
folks [fəʊks] Leute OT 2
to **follow** ['fɒləʊ] folgen OT 2
to **follow a journey** ['fɒləʊ ə ˌdʒɜːni] eine Reise verfolgen OT 2
follower ['fɒləʊə] Anhänger(in) OT 3
fond: to **be fond of** [bi fɒnd] etw. mögen OT 4
food [fuːd] Essen OT 1
food poisoning ['fuːd ˌpɔɪzənɪŋ] Lebensmittelvergiftung OT 2
to **fool** [fuːl] täuschen **WS 1**, 32
foolish ['fuːlɪʃ] unklug; blöd OT 5
foot [fʊt] Fuß OT 1
square foot [skweə fʊt] Quadratfuß OT 2
footage ['fʊtɪdʒ] Filmmaterial **WS 1**, 21
football ['fʊtbɔːl] Fußball OT 1
footpath ['fʊtpɑːθ] Fußpfad OT 1
footprint ['fʊtprɪnt] Fußabdruck OT 3
footsteps ['fʊtˌsteps] Fußstapfen **WS 1**, 41
for [fər] für OT 1
forbidden [fə'bɪdən] verboten; untersagt **WS 2**, 79
force [fɔːs] Kraft OT 1
to **force** [fɔːs] zwingen OT 2
forecast ['fɔːkɑːst] Prognose OT 3
foreground ['fɔːgraʊnd] Vordergrund OT 3
forehand ['fɔːhænd] Vorhand OT 3
foreign ['fɒrən] ausländisch; fremd OT 1
foreigner ['fɒrənə] Fremde(r) OT 3
foremost ['fɔːməʊst] zuvorderst OT 5
to **foresee** [fɔː'siː] vorhersehen **WS 2**, 56
forest ['fɒrɪst] Wald OT 1
forever [fər'evə] für immer OT 2
to **forget** [fə'get] vergessen OT 1
to **forgive** [fə'gɪv] vergeben OT 2
fork [fɔːk] Gabel OT 2
forklift [ˌfɔːklɪft] Gabelstapler OT 5
form [fɔːm] Form OT 1
to **form** [fɔːm] gründen; bilden OT 4
formal ['fɔːml] förmlich; formell OT 5
formally ['fɔːməli] formell OT 5
format ['fɔːmæt] Format OT 5
formation [fɔː'meɪʃn] Formation OT 5
former ['fɔːmə] ehemalig OT 4
to **formulate** ['fɔːmjuleɪt] formulieren OT 4
fort [fɔːt] Festung OT 2
fortnight ['fɔːtnaɪt] zwei Wochen OT 2
fortress ['fɔːtrəs] Zitadelle; Festung OT 3
fortunate ['fɔːtʃənət] glücklich **WS 1**, 15
fortunately ['fɔːtʃənətli] glücklicherweise OT 5
fortune ['fɔːtʃuːn] Glück; Reichtum OT 3
forty ['fɔːti] vierzig OT 1
forum ['fɔːrəm] Forum OT 5
forward ['fɔːrwərd] vorwärts **WS 1**, 15
fossil ['fɒsl] fossil OT 3
to **foul** [faʊl] foulen OT 3
to **found** [faʊnd] begründen; gründen OT 4
foundation [faʊn'deɪʃn] Grundlage; Fundament OT 5
founder ['faʊndər] Gründer(in) OT 5
fountain ['faʊntən] Springbrunnen OT 1
four [fɔː] vier OT 1
fourteen [ˌfɔː'tiːn] vierzehn OT 1
fox [fɒks] Fuchs OT 1
to **frack** [fræk] fracken OT 5
fracking ['frækɪŋ] Fracking OT 5
frame [freɪm] Rahmen OT 4
framework ['freɪmwɜːk] Rahmen **WS 4**, 134
frank [fræŋk] ehrlich **WS 3**, 105
frantic ['fræntɪk] hektisch; aufgeregt OT 3
freak [friːk] Begeisterte(r); Freak OT 4
freckle ['frekl] Sommersprose OT 2
free [friː] frei; kostenlos OT 1
freed [friːd] befreit OT 4
freedom ['friːdəm] Freiheit OT 3
freelance ['friːlɑːns] freiberuflich OT 5
freelancer ['friːlɑːnsə] Freiberufler(in) OT 5
freeze-dried ['friːz draɪd] gefriergetrocknet OT 4
freezer ['friːzə] Gefrierschrank OT 3
freezing ['friːzɪŋ] kalt OT 2
French [frentʃ] französisch; Französisch OT 1
French fries [ˌfrentʃ'fraɪz] Pommes frites OT 2
French horn [ˌfrentʃ'hɔːn] Waldhorn OT 1
frequency ['friːkwənsi] Häufigkeit OT 1
to **frequent** [friː'kwənt] aufsuchen OT 5
frequent ['friːkwənt] häufig OT 5
frequently ['friːkwəntli] häufig OT 3
fresh [freʃ] frisch OT 2

freshman ['freʃmən] Student im ersten Jahr; Studienanfänger(in) OT 4
freshwater ['freʃwɔːtə] Süßwasser **WS 3**, 100
Friday ['fraɪdeɪ] Freitag OT 1
fridge [frɪdʒ] Kühlschrank OT 1
friend [frend] Freund(in) OT 1
  to **make friends** [meɪk 'frendz] (sich) anfreunden OT 2
friendly ['frendli] freundlich OT 1
friendship ['frendʃɪp] Freundschaft OT 3
fries [fraɪz] Pommes frites OT 2
to **frighten** ['fraɪtn] erschrecken OT 3
frightened ['fraɪtnd] verängstigt OT 1
frightening ['fraɪtnɪŋ] erschreckend OT 1
frisbee ['frɪzbi] Frisbee OT 1
frizzy ['frɪzi] kraus OT 3
frog [frɒg] Frosch OT 5
from [frəm] von; aus OT 1
  from around the world [frəm əˌraʊnd ði 'wɜːld] aus aller Welt OT 1
front [frʌnt] Vorderseite; Vorderteil OT 1
  in front of [ɪn frʌnt əv] vor OT 1
frontier ['frʌntɪə] Grenzland OT 4
to **frown (upon)** [fraʊn] die Stirn runzeln (über) **WS 2**, 69
frozen ['frəʊzn] gefroren OT 4
fruit [fruːt] Obst OT 1
fruity ['fruːti] herzhaft **WS 3**, 97
frustrated [frʌ'streɪtɪd] frustriert OT 3
frustrating [frʌ'streɪtɪŋ] frustrierend OT 5
to **fry** [fraɪ] braten; frittieren OT 2
fuel ['fjuːəl] Brennstoff OT 2
to **fulfil** [fʊl'fɪl] verwirklichen; erfüllen OT 4
full [fʊl] voll OT 1
fun [fʌn] Spaß OT 1
  good fun [gʊd' fʌn] ziemlich spaßig OT 2
function ['fʌŋkʃn] Funktion OT 4
to **function** ['fʌŋkʃn] funktionieren **WS 3**, 94
to **fund** [fʌnd] finanzieren OT 3
fundamental [ˌfʌndə'mentl] Grund- **WS 2**, 68
fundraiser ['fʌndreɪzə] Spendensammler(in) OT 2
fundraising ['fʌndreɪzɪŋ] Spendensammlung OT 2
funeral ['fjuːnərəl] Beerdigung OT 5
fungus ['fʌŋgəs] Pilz **WS 4**, 138
funny ['fʌni] lustig; merkwürdig OT 1
furious ['fjʊəriəs] wütend **WS 2**, 58
to **furnish** ['fɜːnɪʃ] einrichten; möblieren **WS 1**, 39
furniture ['fɜːnɪtʃə] Möbel OT 1
further ['fɜːðə] weiter OT 4
furthermore [ˌfɜːðə'mɔːr] außerdem; weiterhin OT 5
fusion ['fjuːʒən] Fusion; Verschmelzung **WS 1**, 30
fuss [fʌs] Aufregung OT 4
fussy ['fʌsi] pingelig; wählerisch OT 2
futile ['fjuːtaɪl] vergeblich; sinnlos **WS 3**, 98
future ['fjuːtʃə] Zukunft OT 2
fuzz [fʌz] Fussel; Belag OT 4

G

gadget ['gædʒɪt] Gerät; technische Spielerei OT 4
to **gain** [geɪn] erlangen OT 1
galaxy ['gæləksi] Galaxie OT 1
gallery ['gæləri] Galerie OT 1
gallon ['gælən] Gallone OT 3
to **gallop** ['gæləp] galoppieren; Galopp **WS 3**, 94
game [geɪm] Spiel OT 1
game console ['geɪm kənsəʊl] Spielekonsole OT 4
gaming ['geɪmɪŋ] Spielen OT 4
gamer ['geɪmə] Gamer(in); Spieler(in) OT 4
gang [gæŋ] Bande; Gang OT 5
gap [gæp] Lücke OT 3
garage ['gærɑːʒ] Garage; Werkstatt OT 4
garbage ['gɑːbɪdʒ] Abfall OT 2
garbage collector ['gɑːbɪdʒ kə'lektə] Müllarbeiter(in) OT 4
garden ['gɑːdn] Garten OT 1
gardener ['gɑːdnə] Gärtner(in) OT 4
gardening ['gɑːdnɪŋ] Gartenarbeit OT 1
gas [gæs] Gas; Benzin OT 3
to **gasp** [gɑːsp] keuchen OT 2
gate [geɪt] Tor OT 1
to **gather** ['gæðə] sammeln OT 4
gatherer ['gæðərər] Sammler(in) OT 5
gay [geɪ] schwul; früher: fröhlich OT 5
gear [gɪə] Zeug; Kleidung **WS 1**, 15
geek [giːk] Geek; Spezialist(in) OT 5
geisha ['geɪʃə] Geisha **WS 2**, 69
gel [dʒel] Gel OT 1
gelateria ['dʒelə'tɪəriə] italienisches Eiscafé OT 5
gender ['dʒendə] Geschlecht; Gender OT 4
gendered ['dʒendəd] geschlechtsspezifisch OT 5
genderless ['dʒendələs] geschlechtslos OT 5
general ['dʒenrəl] allgemein OT 3
  generally ['dʒenrəli] im Allgemeinen; hauptsächlich OT 4
to **generate** ['dʒenəreɪt] erzeugen OT 4
generation [ˌdʒenə'reɪʃn] Generation OT 4
generator ['dʒenəreɪtə] Generator; Stromerzeuger **WS 3**, 99
generosity [ˌdʒɛnə'rɒsɪti] Großzügigkeit; Freigebigkeit **WS 1**, 25
generous ['dʒenərəs] großzügig OT 3
gene [dʒiːn] Gen; Erbgut **WS 1**, 15
genetically [dʒə'netɪkli] genetisch **WS 3**, 104
genius ['dʒiːniəs] Genie; Begabung **WS 1**, 26
genre ['ʒɒ̃rə] Genre OT 4
gentleman ['dʒentlmən] Herr; Gentleman OT 3
gently ['dʒentli] sanft OT 3
genuinely ['dʒenjuɪnli] echt OT 5
geocache ['dʒiːəʊkæʃ] Geocache OT 2
geocaching ['dʒiːəʊkæʃɪŋ] Geocaching OT 2
geographical [ˌdʒiːə'græfɪkl] geografisch OT 4
geography [dʒi'ɒgrəfi] Erdkunde; Geografie OT 1
geology [dʒi'ɒlədʒi] Geologie OT 2
German ['dʒɜːmən] deutsch OT 1
to **gesticulate** [dʒe'stɪkjuleɪt] gestikulieren **WS 4**, 144
gesture ['dʒestʃə] Geste OT 4
to **get** [get] bekommen OT 1
  to **get down** [get daʊn] hinunterkommen OT 2
  to **get hit** [get hɪt] getroffen sein; geschlagen sein OT 4
  to **get off** [get' ɒf] aussteigen OT 2
  to **get on** [get' ɒn] zusteigen OT 2
  to **get ready** [get 'redi] vorbereiten OT 1
  to **get rid of** [get rɪd əv] loswerden OT 3
  to **get up** [get ʌp] aufstehen OT 1
ghost [gəʊst] Geist OT 2
giant ['dʒaɪənt] riesig OT 2
gift [gɪft] Geschenk OT 1
gift voucher ['gɪft vaʊtʃə] Geschenkgutschein OT 1
gig [gɪg] Gig; Auftritt OT 5

ginormous [dʒaɪ'nɔ:məs] gigantisch OT 2
giraffe [dʒə'rɑ:f] Giraffe OT 1
girl [gɜ:l] Mädchen OT 1
to **give** [gɪv] geben OT 1
to **give a talk** [gɪv ə' tɔ:k] einen Vortrag / Referat halten OT 2
to **give up** [gɪv' ʌp] aufgeben OT 2
glad [glæd] froh OT 1
gladiator ['glædieɪtə] Gladiator(in) OT 3
glamorous ['glæmərəs] glamourös OT 4
glamour ['glæmə] Glamour; Glanz **WS 2**, 64
gland [glænd] Drüse OT 5
to **glare** [glɛə] starren **WS 1**, 28
glass [glɑ:s] Glas OT 1
glasses ['glɑ:sɪz] Brille OT 1
gleeful ['gli:fʊl] fröhlich; vergnügt **WS 1**, 39
glimmer ['glɪmə] Schimmer; Glitzern **WS 2**, 65
glimpse [glɪmps] flüchtiger Blick OT 5
to **glitter** ['glɪtə] glitzern OT 2
global ['gləʊbl] global; weltweit OT 4
global warming [ˌgləʊbl 'wɔ:mɪŋ] Klimaerwärmung; Erderwärmung OT 3
globe [gləʊb] Globus; Erdkugel OT 5
glory ['glɔ:ri] Ehre; Schönheit **WS 2**, 62
glove [glʌv] Handschuh OT 1
glue [glu:] Klebstoff OT 1
to **glue** [glu:] kleben **WS 1**, 28
to **gnaw** [nɔ:] abnagen OT 2
go: a go [ə gəʊ] ein Versuch OT 2
to **go** [gəʊ] gehen; fahren OT 1
to **go ahead** [ˌgəʊ ə'hed] weitermachen OT 4
to **go to sleep** [ˌgəʊ tə 'sli:p] einschlafen OT 1
to **go out** [gəʊ aʊt] ausgehen OT 1
goal [gəʊl] Tor OT 1
goalkeeper ['gəʊlki:pə] Torwart(in) OT 3
goat [gəʊt] Ziege OT 4
God [gɒd] Gott OT 4
godmother ['gɒdmʌðər] Patentante OT 5
gold [gəʊld] Gold OT 2
golden ['gəʊldən] golden OT 3
gold rush ['gəʊld rʌʃ] Goldrausch OT 4
goldsmith ['gəʊldˌsmɪθ] Goldschmied(in) **WS 1**, 16
to **gongoozle** [gɒŋ'gu:zl] gaffen OT 3
gongoozler [gɒŋ'gu:zlə] Gaffer OT 3
good [gʊd] gut OT 1
goodbye [gʊd'baɪ] Auf Wiedersehen! OT 1
goodies ['gʊdiz] tolle Kleinigkeiten OT 2
goodness ['gʊdnəs] Güte; Wohlwollen **WS 1**, 27
goods [gʊdz] Güter OT 4
goose [gu:s] Gans OT 4
gorgeous ['gɔ:dʒəs] wunderschön **WS 2**, 61
gospel ['gɒspl] Gospel OT 2
to **govern** ['gʌvn] regieren OT 3
government ['gʌvənmənt] Regierung OT 3
GPS (global positioning system) [ˌdʒi: pi: 'es] Navigationssystem; Globales Positionsbestimmungssystem OT 2
to **grab** [græb] greifen OT 3
gradation [grə'deɪʃən] Abstufung; Gradation **WS 2**, 78
grade [greɪd] Klassenstufe OT 2
gradualy ['grædʒuli] allmählich; schrittweise **WS 2**, 83
to **graduate** ['grædʒuət] einen akademischen Grad erlangen OT 3
graffiti [grə'fi:ti] Graffiti OT 5
grain [greɪn] Korn OT 5
gram [græm] Gramm OT 2
grammar ['græmə] Grammatik OT 1
gramophone ['græməfəʊn] Grammofon OT 4
grand [grænd] grandios; großartig OT 5
grandchild ['græntʃaɪld] Enkel(in); Enkelkind OT 3
granddad ['grændæd] Opa OT 1
grandfather ['grænfɑ:ðə] Großvater OT 2
grandma ['grænmɑ:] Oma OT 1
grandmother ['grænmʌðə] Großmutter OT 1
grandpa ['grænpɑ:] Opa OT 1
grandparents ['grænpeərənts] Großeltern OT 1
grandson ['grænsʌn] Enkel OT 1
grant [grɑ:nt] Förderung; Zuschuss OT 5
graph [grɑ:f] Graph; Diagramm OT 5
graphic ['græfɪk] Grafik OT 3
to **grapple** ['græpl] ringen; kämpfen **WS 2**, 65
to **grasp** [grɑ:sp] greifen; festhalten **WS 1**, 27
grass [grɑ:s] Gras OT 1
grateful ['greɪtfl] dankbar OT 5
grave [greɪv] Grab OT 5
gravity ['grævəti] Erdanziehungskraft; Schwerkraft OT 4
gravy ['greɪvi] Bratensoße OT 1
to **grease** [gri:s] einfetten **WS 1**, 22
great [greɪt] groß; toll OT 1
Greek [gri:k] griechisch OT 2
green [gri:n] grün OT 1
greenhouse ['gri:nhaʊs] Treibhaus OT 1
to **greet** [gri:t] grüßen OT 5
greeting ['gri:tɪŋ] Gruß OT 5
grey [greɪ] grau OT 1
grid [grɪd] Netz **WS 2**, 57
off the grid [ɒf ðə grɪd] vom Netz OT 4
grief [gri:f] Trauer OT 5
grill [grɪl] Grill OT 5
grim [grɪm] grimmig; düster **WS 2**, 78
to **grin** [grɪn] grinsen OT 2
groceries ['grəʊsəriz] Lebensmittel OT 4
grocery ['grəʊsəri] Lebensmittel OT 5
grocery store ['grəʊsəri stɔ:] Lebensmittelladen OT 4
to **groove** [gru:v] grooven **WS 1**, 15
gross [grəʊs] ätzend; ekelhaft OT 3
ground [graʊnd] Boden; Erde; Platz OT 1
to **ground** [graʊnd] Hausarrest erteilen OT 5
groundbreaker ['graʊndbreɪkə] Wegbereiter(in) **WS 4**, 138
ground control ['graʊnd kəntrəʊl] Bodenstation OT 4
group [gru:p] Gruppe OT 1
to **grow** [grəʊ] wachsen; anbauen OT 1
growth [grəʊθ] Wachstum OT 5
grubby ['grʌbi] dreckig OT 2
to **grumble** ['grʌmbl] mosern; murren; schimpfen OT 2
grunt [grʌnt] Grunzen **WS 3**, 94
to **guarantee** [ˌgærən'ti:] garantieren OT 5
guard [gɑ:d] Wächter(in); Wachsamkeit **WS 1**, 27
to **guard** [gɑ:d] bewachen **WS 2**, 83
guardian ['gɑ:diən] Betreuer(in) OT 2
to **guess** [ges] raten; schätzen OT 1
guessing game ['gesɪŋ geɪm] Rätselraten OT 1
guest [gest] Gast OT 2
guide [gaɪd] Führer(in) OT 1
guidebook ['gaɪdbʊk] Reiseführer OT 1
guideline ['gaɪdlaɪn] Richtlinie; Regel OT 3
guilt [gɪlt] Schuld; Schuldgefühl **WS 1**, 26

guilty [ˈgɪlti] schuldig OT 5
guitar [gɪˈtɑː] Gitarre OT 1
guitarist [gɪˈtɑːrɪst] Gitarrist(in) OT 1
gun [gʌn] Schusswaffe OT 4
gunman [ˈgʌnmən] Schütze OT 4
gurning [ˈgɜːnɪŋ] Grimassieren OT 2
gutter [ˈgʌtə] Gosse **WS 1**, 31
guy [gaɪ] Kerl; Typ OT 2
  guys [gaɪz] Leute OT 2
gym [dʒɪm] Fitnesscenter; Turnhalle OT 3
gymnasium [dʒɪmˈneɪziəm] Sporthalle; Turnhalle OT 4
gymnastics [dʒɪmˈnæstɪks] Gymnastik OT 1

H

habit [ˈhæbɪt] Gewohnheit OT 4
habitat [ˈhæbɪtæt] Habitat; Lebensraum OT 4
habitation [ˌhæbɪˈteɪʃn] Bewohnbarkeit OT 4
to **hack up** [hæk ʌp] heraufhusten **WS 1**, 27
hair [heə] Haare OT 1
haircut [ˈheəkʌt] Haarschnitt OT 2
hairstyle [ˈheəstaɪl] Frisur OT 5
halal [həˈlæl] halal OT 3
half [hɑːf] halbe(r, -s); halb OT 1
  half past [ˈhɑːf pɑːst] eine halbe Stunde nach OT 1
half-time [ˈhɑːf ˌtaɪm] Halbzeit OT 2
halfway [ˌhɑːfˈweɪ] halb; halbwegs OT 3
hall [hɔːl] Diele; Halle OT 1
Halloween [ˌhæləʊˈiːn] Halloween OT 2
halt [hɔːlt] Haltestelle OT 2
to **halve** [hɑːv] halbieren **WS 4**, 134
ham [hæm] Schinken OT 3
hamburger [ˈhæmbɜːgə] Hamburger OT 2
hamster [ˈhæmstə] Hamster OT 1
hand [hænd] Hand OT 1
to **hand** [hænd] reichen OT 5
  to **hand in** [hændˈ ɪn] einreichen OT 2
handbag [ˈhændbæg] Handtasche OT 3
handbook [ˈhændbʊk] Handbuch OT 3
handle [ˈhændl] Griff OT 2
handout [ˈhændaʊt] Handout; Flugblatt OT 4
handset [ˈhændset] Mobilteil OT 2
handsome [ˈhænsəm] gut aussehend OT 1
to **handwrite** [ˈhændraɪt] mit der Hand schreiben OT 5
handwriting [ˈhændraɪtɪŋ] Handschrift OT 2
handwritten [ˌhændˈrɪtn] handschriftlich OT 5
handy [ˈhændi] praktisch; nützlich OT 2
to **hang** [hæŋ] hängen **WS 1**, 28
  to **hang on** [ˌhæŋˈɒn] warten OT 2
  to **hang out** [hæŋ aʊt] abhängen; rumhängen; herumhängen OT 1
to **happen** [ˈhæpən] geschehen; passieren OT 1
  to **happen upon** [ˈhæpən əˈpɒn] zufällig entdecken OT 4
happy [ˈhæpi] glücklich OT 1
  happily [ˈhæpɪli] glücklich; glücklicherweise OT 2
harassment [ˈhærəsmənt] Belästigung; Schikane **WS 3**, 106
harbour [ˈhɑːbə] Hafen OT 2
hard [hɑːd] hart OT 1
to **harden** [ˈhɑːrdən] (ab)härten **WS 2**, 56
hardly [ˈhɑːdli] kaum OT 3
hardship [ˈhɑːdʃɪp] Not; Elend **WS 2**, 61
to **harm** [hɑːm] verletzen; schaden OT 2
harmful [ˈhɑːmfl] schädlich OT 3
harmless [ˈhɑːmləs] harmlos; unbedenklich OT 5
harness [ˈhɑːnɪs] Sicherheitsgurt; Gurt OT 1
harp [hɑːp] Harfe OT 1
harpist [ˈhɑːpɪst] Harfenist(in) OT 3
harrowing [ˈhærəʊɪŋ] erschütternd; quälend **WS 1**, 21
harsh [hɑːʃ] rau OT 5
harvest [ˈhɑːvɪst] Ernte OT 4
to **harvest** [ˈhɑːvɪst] ernten OT 4
hash browns [ˌhæʃˈbraʊnz] kleine gebratene Kartoffelwürfel, wie Rösti OT 3
hashtag [ˈhæʃtæg] Hashtag OT 5
hat [hæt] Hut; Mütze OT 1
to **hate** [heɪt] hassen OT 1
hatred [ˈheɪtrɪd] Hass **WS 2**, 62
to **have** [həv] haben OT 1
  to **have a son** [həv ə ˈsʌn] einen Sohn bekommen OT 1
  to **have got** [ˈhæv gɒt] haben OT 1
  to **have to** [ˈhæv tə] müssen OT 1
hazard [ˈhæzəd] Gefahr; Risiko OT 2
he [hiː] er OT 1
head [hed] Kopf OT 1
to **head out** [hed aʊt] aufbrechen; losfahren OT 4
to **head back** [hed bæk] gehen zurück; zurückkehren OT 5
headache [ˈhedeɪk] Kopfschmerzen OT 1
headband [ˈhedbænd] Stirnband; Kopfband OT 3
headdress [ˈhɛddrɛs] Kopfbedeckung **WS 2**, 69
heading [ˈhedɪŋ] Überschrift OT 1
headline [ˈhedlaɪn] Schlagzeile OT 2
headquarter [ˌhedˈkwɔːtə] Headquarter; Hauptsitz OT 4
headset [ˈhedset] Headset OT 4
headshot [ˈhedʃɒt] Portraitfoto OT 5
headstart [ˈhɛdstaːrt] Vorsprung **WS 2**, 56
head teacher [ˌhed ˈtiːtʃə] Schulleiter(in) OT 1
headword [ˈhedwɜːd] Stichwort OT 2
head wrap [hɛd ræp] Kopfbedeckung **WS 2**, 71
to **heal** [hiːl] heilen **WS 3**, 113
healing [ˈhiːlɪŋ] Heilung OT 5
health [helθ] Gesundheit OT 2
healthcare [ˈhelθkeə] Gesundheitswesen OT 4
healthy [ˈhelθi] gesund OT 2
heap [hiːp] Haufen OT 4
to **hear** [hɪə] hören OT 1
heart [hɑːt] Herz OT 2
  by heart [baɪ hɑːt] auswendig OT 2
heartland [ˈhɑːtlænd] Kernland; Herzland OT 4
hearty [ˈhɑːti] herzhaft OT 2
to **heat** [hiːt] heizen OT 3
heater [ˈhiːtə] Heizung OT 2
heating [ˈhiːtɪŋ] Heizung OT 3
heatwave [ˈhiːtweɪv] Hitzewelle OT 5
heaven [ˈhevn] Himmel OT 5
heavy [ˈhevi] schwer OT 1
hectare [ˈhekteər] Hektar OT 5
hectic [ˈhektɪk] hektisch OT 4
hedge [hedʒ] Hecke OT 5
hedgehog [ˈhedʒhɒg] Igel OT 1
heel [hiːl] Absatz **WS 1**, 28
  head over heels [hɛd ˈoʊvə hiːlz] Hals über Kopf **WS 1**, 28
height [haɪt] Höhe OT 1
heir [eər] Erbe / Erbin OT 5
helicopter [ˈhelɪkɒptə] Hubschrauber OT 2
hell [hel] Hölle OT 5
hello [həˈləʊ] hallo OT 1
helmet [ˈhelmɪt] Helm OT 1
to **help** [help] helfen OT 1
helper [ˈhelpə] Helfer(in) OT 3
helpful [ˈhelpfl] hilfreich OT 1
helpless [ˈhelpləs] hilflos OT 4

helpline ['helplaın] Hotline OT 2
hemisphere ['hemısfıər] Hemisphäre OT 5
hen [hen] Henne OT 2
heptathlon [hep'tæθlən] Siebenkampf OT 2
her [hə] sie; ihr OT 1
herb [hɜ:b] Kraut OT 3
herd [hɜ:d] Herd OT 4
to **herd** [hɜ:d] treiben OT 2
here [hıə] hier OT 1
heritage ['herıtıdʒ] Erbe; Tradition OT 5
hero ['hıərəʊ] Held(in) OT 3
hers [hɜ:z] ihre(r, -s) OT 2
herself [hɜ:'self] sich (selbst) OT 3
to **hesitate** ['hezıteıt] zögern OT 3
hesitation [,hezı'teıʃn] Zögern OT 3
heteronormativity [,hɛtərounə:r'mætıvıti] Heteronormativität **WS 2**, 57
heterosexual [,hetərə'sekʃuəl] heterosexuell OT 5
Hey! [heı] He! OT 1
hi [haı] hallo OT 1
to **hibernate** ['haıbərneıt] überwintern; Winterschlaf halten **WS 3**, 98
hiccup ['hıkʌp] Schluckauf OT 2
to **hide** [haıd] sich verstecken OT 3
hierarchy ['haıəra:rki] Hierarchie **WS 3**, 108
high [haı] hoch OT 1
to **highlight** ['haılaıt] hervorheben OT 3
highway ['haıweı] Highway; Landstrasse OT 3
hijab [hı'dʒa:b] Hijab; Kopftuch **WS 1**, 21
hike [haık] Wanderung OT 2
to **hike** [haık] wandern OT 1
hiker ['haıkə] Wanderer / Wanderin OT 2
hiking ['haıkıŋ] Wandern OT 1
hiking boot ['haıkıŋ bu:t] Wanderstiefel OT 2
hill [hıl] Hügel OT 1
hilly ['hıli] hügelig OT 2
him [hım] ihn; ihm OT 1
himself [hım'self] (sich) selbst OT 1
Hindu ['hındu:] hinduistisch OT 1
to **hint** [hınt] andeuten **WS 2**, 73
hip [hıp] Hüfte OT 3
hip hop ['hıp hɒp] Hip-Hop OT 1
hippopotamus [,hıpə'pɒtəməs] Nilpferd OT 2
to **hire** ['haıə] mieten OT 3
his [hız] seine(r, -s) OT 1
Hispanic [hı'spænık] hispanisch OT 3

historian [hı'stɔ:riən] Historiker(in) OT 3
historic [hı'stɒrık] historisch OT 3
historical [hı'stɒrıkl] geschichtlich OT 2
history ['hıstri] Geschichte OT 1
to **hit** [hıt] schlagen OT 1
hob [hɒb] Kochfeld OT 3
hobby ['hɒbi] Hobby OT 1
hockey ['hɒki] Hockey OT 1
to **hoist** [hɔıst] hissen **WS 1**, 43
to **hold** [həʊld] halten OT 1
holder ['həʊldər] Halter OT 5
hole [həʊl] Loch OT 1
hole punch [həʊl pʌntʃ] Locher OT 5
holiday ['hɒlədeı] Urlaub OT 1
holidaymaker ['hɒlədeımeıkə] Urlauber(in) OT 3
home [həʊm] Zuhause OT 1
homecoming ['həʊmkʌmıŋ] Absolvententreffen an Schulen oder Universitäten OT 4
homeland ['həʊmlænd] Heimat OT 4
homeless ['həʊmləs] heimatlos; obdachlos OT 3
homelessness ['həʊmləsnəs] Obdachlosigkeit OT 4
homemade ['həʊmmeıd] selbst gemacht; selbst zubereitet OT 3
homepage ['həʊmpeıdʒ] Startseite OT 1
homeschooled [,həʊm'sku:ld] zu Hause unterrichtet OT 4
homesick ['həʊmsık] voll Heimweh OT 2
homesickness ['həʊmsıknəs] Heimweh OT 4
homesteader ['hoʊm,stedə] Siedler(in) **WS 3**, 94
hometown ['həʊmtaʊn] Heimatstadt OT 4
homework ['həʊmwɜ:k] Hausaufgaben OT 1
homophobic [,hoʊmə'foʊbık] homophob **WS 3**, 107
honest ['ɒnıst] ehrlich OT 3
honey ['hʌni] Honig; Schatz (als Kosename) OT 2
to **honour** ['ɒnə] ehren OT 5
hoodie ['hʊdi] Kapuzenpullover OT 1
to **hook** [hʊk] haken OT 4
to **hope** [həʊp] hoffen OT 1
hopeful ['həʊpfl] hoffnungsvoll OT 5
hopefully ['həʊpfəli] hoffentlich OT 4
hopeless ['həʊpləs] hoffnungslos; hilflos OT 4
horizon [hə'raızn] Horizont OT 5
horizontal [,hɒrı'zɒntl] horizontal OT 4

hormone ['hɔ:məʊn] Hormon OT 5
horn [hɔ:n] Horn OT 2
horrendous [hə'rendəs] schrecklich **WS 1**, 25
horrible ['hɒrəbl] furchtbar OT 2
horror ['hɒrə] Horror; Grauen OT 2
horse [hɔ:s] Pferd OT 1
horse-drawn ['hɔ:s drɔ:n] pferdebespannt OT 1
horse riding ['raıdıŋ] Reiten OT 1
hospital ['hɒspıtl] Krankenhaus OT 1
hospitality [,hɒspı'tæləti] Gastfreundschaft OT 2
to **host** [həʊst] ausrichten OT 3
hostel ['hɒstl] Hostel OT 2
hostile ['hɒstaıl] feindlich; feindselig **WS 1**, 20
hostility [hɒ'stıləti] Feindseligkeit; Aggressivität **WS 1**, 21
hot [hɒt] heiß; scharf OT 1
hotel [həʊ'tel] Hotel OT 1
hound [haʊnd] Spürhund OT 2
hour ['aʊə] Stunde OT 1
hourly ['aʊəli] stündlich; Stunden- OT 5
house [haʊs] Haus OT 1
houseboat ['haʊsbəʊt] Hausboot OT 3
household ['haʊshəʊld] häuslich; Haushalts- OT 4
housekeeper ['haʊski:pə] Haushälter(in) OT 3
housewife ['haʊswaıf] Hausfrau OT 5
housework ['haʊswɜ:k] Hausarbeit OT 1
housing ['haʊzıŋ] Wohnraum; Unterkunft OT 3
how [haʊ] wie OT 1
however [haʊ'evə] jedoch OT 2
howl [haʊl] Geheul OT 5
hug [hʌg] Umarmung OT 1
to **hug** [hʌg] sich umarmen OT 4
huge [hju:dʒ] riesig OT 2
human ['hju:mən] menschlich OT 3; Mensch OT 5
humanitarian [hju:,mænı'teəriən] humanitär OT 5
humanity [hju:'mænəti] Menschheit **WS 4**, 136
humanities [hju:'mænətis] Geisteswissenschaften **WS 3**, 112
to **humanize** ['hju:mənaız] vermenschlichen; humanisieren **WS 1**, 25
humble ['hʌmbl] bescheiden; demütig **WS 2**, 80
to **humiliate** [hju:'mılieıt] demütigen; erniedrigen **WS 1**, 27
humorous ['hju:mərəs] humorvoll OT 5

humour ['hju:mə] Humor OT 3
hundred ['hʌndrəd] hundert OT 1
Hungarian [hʌŋ'geəriən] ungarisch OT 2
hunger ['hʌŋgə] Hunger OT 4
hungry ['hʌŋgri] hungrig OT 1
to **hunt** [hʌnt] jagen OT 2
hunter ['hʌntə] Jäger(in) OT 5
hurricane ['hʌrɪkən] Hurrikan; Orkan OT 5
to **hurry** ['hʌri] (sich) beeilen OT 1
to **hurt** [hɜ:t] schmerzen; wehtun OT 1
hurt [hɜ:t] verletzt OT 1
hurtful ['hɜ:tfl] verletzend **WS 3**, 107
husband ['hʌzbənd] Ehemann; Mann OT 2
to **hydrate** [haɪ'dreɪt] hydratisieren OT 4
hydro ['haɪdroʊ] Wasser-; Hydro- **WS 3**, 99
hydrogen ['haɪdrədʒən] Wasserstoff **WS 3**, 99
hygiene ['haɪdʒi:n] Hygiene OT 4
hymn [hɪm] Hymne; Kirchenlied **WS 1**, 26
hype [haɪp] Hype OT 5
hyperbole [haɪ'pɜ:bəli] Übertreibung **WS 2**, 62
hyper-connected ['haɪpə kə'nektɪd] angeschlossen OT 4
hyperlink ['haɪpəlɪŋk] Hyperlink OT 3
hypothermia [ˌhaɪpə'θɜ:miə] Unterkühlung OT 2

I

I [aɪ] ich OT 1
ice [aɪs] Eis OT 1
iceberg ['aɪsbɜ:g] Eisberg OT 3
ice cream [ˌaɪs'kri:m] Eis; Eiscreme OT 1
ice lolly [aɪs 'lɒli] Eis am Stiel OT 1
icing ['aɪsɪŋ] Zuckerguß **WS 2**, 59
icon ['aɪkɒn] Symbol; Ikone OT 5
iconic [aɪ'kɒnɪk] ikonisch; Kult... OT 3
ICT (information and communications technology) [ˌaɪ si:'ti:] Informations- und Kommunikationstechnologie OT 1
icy ['aɪsi] eisig OT 5
idea [aɪ'dɪə] Idee OT 1
ideal [aɪ'di:əl] ideal OT 2
ideally [aɪ'di:əli] idealerweise OT 5
idealistic [aɪˌdi:ə'lɪstɪk] idealistisch **WS 2**, 79
identical [aɪ'dentɪkl] identisch OT 5
to **identify** [aɪ'dentɪfaɪ] identifizieren OT 3
identity [aɪ'dentəti] Identität OT 3
idol ['aɪdl] Idol OT 5
to **idolize** ['aɪdəlaɪz] vergöttern; idealisieren **WS 2**, 60
if [ɪf] falls OT 1
to **ignite** [ɪg'naɪt] entzünden; anzünden **WS 2**, 62
ignition [ɪg'nɪʃn] Zündung OT 4
ignorance ['ɪgnərəns] Unwissenheit; Ignoranz **WS 1**, 21
ignorant ['ɪgnərənt] unwissend; ignorant **WS 1**, 21
to **ignore** [ɪg'nɔ:] ignorieren OT 4
ill [ɪl] krank OT 2
illegal [ɪ'li:gl] illegal OT 3
illiterate [ɪ'lɪtərət] analphabetisch OT 4
illness ['ɪlnəs] Krankheit OT 2
to **illustrate** ['ɪrɪtəbl] darstellen; illustrieren OT 3
illustration [ˌɪlə'streɪʃn] Illustration OT 2
image ['ɪmɪdʒ] Bild OT 1
imagery ['ɪmɪdʒəri] Bilder; Bildsprache **WS 2**, 62
imaginary [ɪ'mædʒɪnəri] imaginär; fiktiv OT 4
imagination [ɪˌmædʒɪ'neɪʃn] Vorstellung; Fantasie OT 4
imaginative [ɪ'mædʒɪnətɪv] fantasievoll OT 4
to **imagine** [ɪ'mædʒɪn] sich etw. vorstellen; sich einbilden; glauben OT 1
imbalanced [ɪm'bælənst] unausgeglichen; nicht ausgeglichen **WS 2**, 82
imitation [ˌɪmɪ'teɪʃən] Imitation; Nachahmung **WS 2**, 69
immaturity [ˌɪmə'tjʊərɪti] Unreife; Unausgereiftheit **WS 1**, 20
immediate [ɪ'mi:diət] unmittelbar; umgehend OT 5
immediately [ɪ'mi:diətli] sofort OT 1
immigrant ['ɪmɪgrənt] Einwanderer; Einwanderin OT 3
to **immigrate** ['ɪmɪgreɪt] einwandern OT 5
immigration [ˌɪmɪ'greɪʃn] Einwanderungskontrolle OT 2
imminent ['ɪmɪnənt] bevorstehend; unmittelbar **WS 3**, 124
impact ['ɪmpækt] Auswirkung OT 3
impairment [ɪm'pεərmənt] Beeinträchtigung; Schädigung **WS 2**, 61
to **impart** [ɪm'pɑ:t] vermitteln OT 4
impatient [ɪm'peɪʃnt] ungeduldig OT 3
impending [ɪm'pεndɪŋ] bevorstehend; drohend **WS 3**, 96
imperative [ɪm'perətɪv] Imperativ; Befehlsform OT 1
imperial [ɪm'pɪəril] kaiserlich; imperial **WS 1**, 40
to **implement** ['ɪmplɪment] umsetzen; durchführen **WS 3**, 124
to **import** ['ɪmpɔ:t] importieren; einführen OT 3
importance [ɪm'pɔ:tɔns] Bedeutung; Wichtigkeit OT 2
important [ɪm'pɔ:tnt] wichtig OT 1
to **impose** [ɪm'pəʊz] verhängen; durchsetzen **WS 2**, 55
impossible [ɪm'pɒsəbl] unmöglich OT 2
impractical [ɪm'præktɪkl] unpraktisch OT 4
to **impress** [ɪm'pres] beeindrucken OT 5
impressed [ɪm'prest] beindruckt OT 4
impression [ɪm'preʃn] Eindruck OT 5
to **imprison** [ɪm'prɪzn] einsperren **WS 1**, 18
imprisonment [ɪm'prɪzənmənt] Inhaftierung; Gefangenschaft **WS 2**, 78
to **improve** [ɪm'pru:v] verbessern OT 2
improvement [ɪm'pru:vmənt] Verbesserung OT 3
improvisation [ˌɪmprəvaɪ'zeɪʃn] Improvisation OT 2
to **improvise** ['ɪmprəvaɪz] improvisieren OT 2
in [ɪn] im OT 1
inaccessible [ˌɪnæk'sesəbl] unzugänglich OT 3
inalienable [ɪn'eɪliənəbl] unveräußerlich; unabdingbar **WS 2**, 55
inappropriate [ˌɪnə'prəʊpriət] unpassend OT 5
inch [ɪntʃ] Zoll (2,54 cm) OT 2
incident ['ɪnsɪdənt] Vorfall; Ereignis OT 5
incidentals [ˌɪnsɪ'dεntəlz] Kleinigkeiten; Zufälligkeiten **WS 2**, 78
to **include** [ɪn'klu:d] einschließen OT 1
included [ɪn'klu:dɪd] inklusive OT 1
including [ɪn'klu:dɪŋ] inklusive OT 1
inclusion [ɪn'klu:ʒn] Inklusion OT 5
inclusive [ɪn'klu:sɪv] integrativ OT 4
inclusivity [ɪn'klu:sɪvɪti] Inklusivität **WS 2**, 57
income ['ɪnkʌm] Einkommen OT 4
inconvenient [ˌɪnkən'vi:niənt] unbequem; unangenehm **WS 3**, 94
to **incorporate** [ɪn'kɔ:pəreɪt] einbauen; integrieren **WS 3**, 112

incorrectly [ˌɪnkə'rektli] falsch; fehlerhaft OT 5
increase ['ɪnkri:s] Zunahme OT 3
to **increase** [ɪn'kri:s] anwachsen; erhöhen OT 3
increasingly [ɪn'kri:sɪŋli] zunehmend OT 5
incredible [ɪn'kredəbl] unglaublich OT 2
incredibly [ɪn'kredəbli] unglaublich OT 3
incubator ['ɪŋkjubeɪtər] Inkubator; Unterstützer von Start-ups OT 5
indecision [ˌɪndɪ'sɪʒn] Unentschlossenheit OT 5
indeed [ɪn'di:d] tatsächlich **WS 2**, 64
indefinite [ɪn'defɪnət] unbestimmt OT 1
independence [ˌɪndɪ'pendəns] Unabhängigkeit OT 2
independent [ˌɪndɪ'pendənt] selbstständig OT 3
independently [ˌɪndɪ'pendəntli] selbstständig; unabhängig OT 5
index ['ɪndeks] Index; Register OT 4
indexer ['ɪndeksə] Indexer OT 4
Indian ['ɪndiən] indisch OT 2
to **indicate** ['ɪndɪkeɪt] angeben; zeigen OT 5
indigenous [ɪn'dɪdʒənəs] einheimisch OT 5
indignity [ɪn'dɪgnəti] Demütigung OT 5
indisputable [ˌɪndɪ'spju:təbl] unbestritten **WS 3**, 112
individual [ˌɪndɪ'vɪdʒuəl] Einzelne(r) OT 4
individual [ˌɪndɪ'vɪdʒuəl] individuell OT 3
individually [ˌɪndɪ'vɪdʒuəli] einzeln OT 4
indoor ['ɪndɔ:] Innen... OT 2
indoors [ˌɪn'dɔ:z] drinnen OT 3
induction [ɪn'dʌkʃn] Einführung OT 5
industrial [ɪn'dʌstriəl] Industrie... OT 2
industry ['ɪndəstri] Industrie OT 2
inequality [ˌɪnɪ'kwɒləti] Ungleichheit **WS 1**, 31
inexpensive [ˌɪnɪk'spensɪv] billig; preiswert OT 4
inexperienced [ˌɪnɪk'spɪəriənst] unerfahren OT 5
infection [ɪn'fekʃn] Entzündung OT 2
inferior [ɪn'fɪəriə] minderwertig; unterlegen **WS 2**, 71
infinite ['ɪnfɪnət] unendlich OT 4
infinitive [ɪn'fɪnətɪv] Infinitiv OT 2
to **inflict** [ɪn'flɪkt] aufdrängen OT 5
influence ['ɪnfluəns] Einfluss OT 4
to **influence** ['ɪnfluəns] beeinflussen OT 4
influencer ['ɪnfluənsə] Influencer(in) OT 5
influential [ˌɪnflu'enʃl] einflussreich **WS 3**, 108
influenza [ˌɪnflu'enzə] Grippe; Influenza OT 5
infographic [ˌɪnfəʊ'græfɪk] Infografik OT 3
informal [ɪn'fɔ:ml] informell OT 5
information [ˌɪnfə'meɪʃn] Information OT 1
informative [ɪn'fɔ:mətɪv] informativ; instruktiv OT 3
to **inform** [ɪn'fɔ:m] informieren OT 4
ingredient [ɪn'gri:diənt] Zutat OT 2
to **inhabit** [ɪn'hæbɪt] bewohnen OT 5
to **inherit** [ɪn'herɪt] erben **WS 1**, 16
inhumane [ˌɪnhju:'meɪn] inhuman; menschenunwürdig OT 4
initially [ɪ'nɪʃəli] zunächst; anfangs OT 5
initiative [ɪ'nɪʃətɪv] Initiative; Kampagne OT 4
to **injure** ['ɪndʒə] verletzen OT 2
injury ['ɪndʒəri] Verletzung OT 2
injustice [ɪn'dʒʌstɪs] Ungerechtigkeit OT 4
ink [ɪŋk] Tinte **WS 2**, 79
inn [ɪn] Gasthaus OT 2
inner ['ɪnər] innerer OT 5
innocent ['ɪnəsnt] unschuldig OT 5
innovation [ˌɪnə'veɪʃn] Innovation; Neuheit OT 4
innovative ['ɪnəveɪtɪv] innovativ OT 4
innovator ['ɪnəveɪtə] Innovator(in) OT 4
input ['ɪnpʊt] Beitrag OT 4
insane [ɪn'seɪn] verrückt; wahnsinnig OT 5
insect ['ɪnsekt] Insekt OT 1
insecurity [ˌɪnsɪ'kjʊərəti] Unsicherheit **WS 4**, 142
inside [ˌɪn'saɪd] in; innerhalb OT 1
insides [ˌɪn'saɪdz] Innereien OT 3
insight ['ɪnsaɪt] Einsicht OT 5
insignia [ɪn'sɪgniə] Abzeichen; Insignien **WS 3**, 95
insignificant [ˌɪnsɪg'nɪfɪkənt] unbedeutend; belanglos **WS 1**, 21
to **insist** [ɪn'sɪst] bestehen auf **WS 2**, 62
inspiration [ˌɪnspə'reɪʃn] Inspiration; Eingebung OT 4
inspirational [ˌɪnspə'reɪʃənl] begeisternd **WS 1**, 21
to **inspire** [ɪn'spaɪə] inspirieren; anregen OT 3
to **get inspired** [get ɪn'spaɪəd] inspiriert sein OT 4
to **install** [ɪn'stɔ:l] installieren OT 4
instance: for instance [fə'ɪnstəns] beispielsweise; zum Beispiel OT 5
instant: in an instant ['ɪnstənt] sofort; Moment **WS 2**, 63
instead [ɪn'sted] stattdessen OT 2
to **instil** [ɪn'stɪl] einträufeln **WS 2**, 82
institution [ˌɪnstɪ'tju:ʃn] Einrichtung OT 4
to **institutionalize** [ɪn'stɪtju:ʃənəlaɪz] etablieren **WS 2**, 55
to **instruct** [ɪn'strʌkt] einweisen OT 5
instruction [ɪn'strʌkʃn] Anweisung OT 1
instructive [ɪn'strʌktɪv] instruktiv; lehrreich OT 5
instructor [ɪn'strʌktə] Lehrer(in) OT 3
instrument ['ɪnstrəmənt] Instrument OT 1
insult ['ɪnsʌlt] beleidigen; verletzen **WS 2**, 60
insulted ['ɪnsʌltd] beleidigt OT 5
intact [ɪn'tækt] unversehrt; intakt **WS 1**, 39
intangible [ɪn'tændʒəbl] immateriell; unfassbar **WS 1**, 15
to **integrate** ['ɪntɪgreɪt] integrieren **WS 2**, 68
integrated ['ɪntɪgreɪtɪd] integriert OT 5
intellectual [ˌɪntə'lektʃul] geistig; intellektuell **WS 3**, 112
intelligent [ɪn'telɪdʒənt] intelligent OT 2
to **intend** [ɪn'tend] beabsichtigen OT 5
intense [ɪn'tens] stark; ernsthaft OT 5
intensity [ɪn'tensɪti] Intensität; Stärke **WS 1**, 39
intent [ɪn'tent] ernsthaft; gespannt **WS 3**, 97
intention [ɪn'tenʃn] Absicht **WS 3**, 99
to **interact** [ˌɪntər'ækt] interagieren OT 4
interaction [ˌɪntər'ækʃn] Interaktion OT 4
interactive [ˌɪntər'æktɪv] interaktiv OT 5
intercultural [ˌɪntə'kʌltʃərəl] interkulturell OT 5
interest ['ɪntrəst] Interesse OT 1
interested ['ɪntrəstɪd] interessiert OT 1
interesting ['ɪntrəstɪŋ] interessant OT 1
interference [ˌɪntə'fɪərəns] Interferenz; Störung **WS 4**, 138

interior [ɪnˈtɪəriər] Binnenland; das Innere OT 5
intermittency [ˌɪntəˈmɪtənsi] Unbeständigkeit; Unstetigkeit **WS 3**, 101
intermittent [ˌɪntəˈmɪtənt] intermittierend; periodisch **WS 3**, 101
intern [ɪnˈtɜːn] Praktikant(in); Volontär(in) OT 4
internal [ɪnˈtɜːnl] intern OT 5
internal combustion [ɪnˈtɜːnl kəmˈbʌstʃən] Verbrennungs- OT 4
international [ˌɪntəˈnæʃnəl] international OT 1
internet [ˈɪntənet] Internet OT 1
internship [ˈɪntɜːnʃɪp] Praktikum OT 4
to **interpret** [ɪnˈtɜːprət] interpretieren OT 4
interpretation [ɪnˌtɜːprəˈteɪʃn] Interpretation OT 5
interpreter [ɪnˈtɜːprɪtə] Dolmetscher(in) OT 4
to **interrupt** [ˌɪntəˈrʌpt] unterbrechen OT 2
intersex [ˈɪntəseks] Intersex OT 5
interview [ˈɪntəvjuː] Vorstellungsgespräch; Interview OT 1
to **interview** [ˈɪntəvjuː] ein Vorstellungsgespräch führen mit; interviewen OT 1
interviewee [ˌɪntəvjuˈiː] Interviewte(r) **WS 2**, 67
interviewer [ˈɪntəvjuːə] Interviewer(in) OT 1
into [ˈɪntuː] in OT 1
intonation [ˌɪntəˈneɪʃn] Intonation OT 4
to **introduce** [ˌɪntrəˈdjuːs] vorstellen OT 2
introduction [ˌɪntrəˈdʌkʃn] Vorstellung; Einführung OT 2
introductory [ˌɪntrəˈdʌktəri] Anfangs.-; Einführungs- OT 5
to **invade** [ɪnˈveɪd] einmarschieren OT 3
invaluable [ɪnˈvæljuəbl] unschätzbar; unbezahlbar **WS 2**, 62
invasion [ɪnˈveɪʒn] Invasion; Eingriff OT 5
invasive [ɪnˈveɪsɪv] invasiv OT 5
to **invent** [ɪnˈvent] erfinden OT 2
invention [ɪnˈvenʃn] Erfindung OT 4
inventor [ɪnˈventə] Erfinder(in) OT 2
inversion [ɪnˈvɜːʃn] Inversion OT 5
to **invert** [ɪnˈvɜːt] umkehren; umstellen OT 5
to **invest** [ɪnˈvest] investieren OT 3
to **investigate** [ɪnˈvestɪgeɪt] untersuchen **WS 4**, 140
investigator [ɪnˈvestɪgeɪtə] Ermittler(in) OT 4
investment [ɪnˈvestmənt] Investition OT 3
investor [ɪnˈvestə] Investor(in); Geldgeber(in) OT 4
invincible [ɪnˈvɪnsəbl] unbesiegbar; unbezwingbar **WS 1**, 21
invisible [ɪnˈvɪzəbl] unsichtbar **WS 1**, 21
invitation [ˌɪnvɪˈteɪʃn] Einladung; Aufforderung OT 1
to **invite** [ɪnˈvaɪt] einladen OT 2
to **invite along** [ɪnˈvaɪt əˈlɒŋ] mit einladen OT 2
to **involve** [ɪnˈvɒlv] einbeziehen; umfassen OT 4
involved [ɪnˈvɒlvd] involviert; teilnehmend OT 3
Iranian [ɪˈreɪniən] iranisch OT 4
Irish [ˈaɪrɪʃ] irisch OT 1
irksome [ˈɜːrksəm] ärgerlich; lästig **WS 2**, 78
iron [ˈaɪən] Eisen **WS 1**, 32
irony [ˈaɪrəni] Ironie OT 5
irrational [ɪˈræʃənl] irrational **WS 3**, 106
irregular [ɪˈregjələ] unregelmäßig OT 1
irresistible [ˌɪrɪˈzɪstəbl] unwiderstehlich **WS 2**, 60
irresponsible [ˌɪrɪˈspɒnsəbl] unverantwortlich **WS 1**, 21
irritable [ˈɪrɪtəbl] reizbar OT 3
irritated [ˈɪrɪteɪtɪd] verärgert OT 2
Islamic [ɪzˈlæmɪk] islamisch OT 5
Islamophobia [ˌɪslæməˈfoʊbiə] Islamophobie **WS 1**, 21
island [ˈaɪlənd] Insel OT 2
islander [ˈaɪləndə] Insulaner(in) OT 5
isle [aɪl] Eiland; kleine Insel OT 5
to **isolate** [ˈaɪsəleɪt] isolieren; absondern **WS 2**, 83
Israeli [ɪzˈreɪli] israelisch OT 2
issue [ˈɪsjuː] Thema; Angelegenheit; Ausgabe OT 2
to **issue** [ˈɪsjuː] verhängen **WS 2**, 68
it [ɪt] es / ihm OT 1
Italian [ɪˈtæliən] italienisch OT 2
itchy [ˈɪtʃi] juckend OT 2
item [ˈaɪtəm] Gegenstand OT 2
itinerary [aɪˈtɪnərəri] Reiseroute; Itinerar **WS 2**, 64
its [ɪts] sein; ihr OT 1
itself [ɪtˈself] sich (selbst) OT 3
ivory [ˈaɪvəri] Elfenbein OT 3

J
jacket [ˈdʒækɪt] Jacke OT 1
jack-o-lantern [ˌdʒæk ə ˈlæntən] Kürbislaterne OT 2
jail [dʒeɪl] Gefängnis OT 5
jam [dʒæm] Marmelade OT 2
Jamaican [dʒəˈmeɪkən] jamaikanisch OT 1
January [ˈdʒænjuəri] Januar OT 1
Japanese [ˌdʒæpəˈniːz] japanisch OT 1
jar [dʒɑː] Einweckglas OT 2
jazz [dʒæz] Jazz OT 2
jealous [ˈdʒeləs] eifersüchtig **WS 2**, 64
jeans [dʒiːnz] Jeans(hose) OT 1
to **jeopardize** [ˈdʒepərdaɪz] gefährden; in Gefahr bringen **WS 3**, 124
jersey [ˈdʒɜːrzi] Trikot; Jersey **WS 2**, 59
jewelry [ˈdʒuːəlri] Schmuck OT 2
jewel [ˈdʒuːəl] Juwel OT 1
job [dʒɒb] Stelle; Job; Aufgabe OT 1
to **do a good / great job** [duː ə gʊd / greɪtˈ dʒɒb] gute Arbeit leisten OT 2
job hopping [dʒɒb ˈhɒpɪŋ] wiederholter Stellenwechsel OT 5
jobless [ˈdʒɒbləs] arbeitslos OT 5
jock [dʒɒk] Sportler; Athlet **WS 3**, 96
to **jog** [dʒɒg] traben; joggen OT 2
to **join** [dʒɔɪn] Mitglied werden in; eintreten in OT 1
jointly [ˈdʒɔɪntli] zusammen **WS 2**, 54
joke [dʒəʊk] Witz OT 2
to **joke** [dʒəʊk] Witze machen OT 2
journal [ˈdʒɜːnl] Journal; Fachzeitschrift OT 5
journalism [ˈdʒɜːnəlɪzəm] Journalismus OT 5
journalist [ˈdʒɜːnəlɪst] Journalist(in) OT 2
journey [ˈdʒɜːni] Reise; Fahrt OT 1
joyful [ˈdʒɔɪfl] fröhlich **WS 3**, 103
joyride [ˈdʒɔɪraɪd] Spritztour (mit einem gestohlenen Auto) OT 5
joyriding [ˈdʒɔɪraɪdɪŋ] Spritztour (mit einem gestohlenen Auto) OT 5
judge [dʒʌdʒ] Richter(in); Preisrichter(in) OT 2
to **judge** [dʒʌdʒ] einschätzen; beurteilen OT 2
Judgement Day [ˈdʒʌdʒmənt deɪ] jüngste Gericht OT 4
judging [ˈdʒʌdʒɪŋ] Beurteilung OT 2
judo [ˈdʒuːdəʊ] Judo OT 1
juice [dʒuːs] Saft OT 1
July [dʒuˈlaɪ] Juli OT 1
jumbled [ˈdʒʌmbld] durcheinander OT 2

to jump [dʒʌmp] springen OT 2
jumper ['dʒʌmpə] Pullover OT 1
June [dʒu:n] Juni OT 1
jungle ['dʒʌŋgl] Dschungel OT 4
junior ['dʒu:niə] Junior(in) OT 2
junk [dʒʌŋk] Drogen **WS 3**, 97
junk food ['dʒʌŋk fu:d] ungesundes Essen OT 5
junky ['dʒʌŋki] schlecht; mangelhaft OT 4
just [dʒʌst] genau; nur OT 1
justice ['dʒʌstɪs] Gerechtigkeit OT 4
to justify ['dʒʌstɪfaɪ] rechtfertigen OT 5

K

kangaroo [ˌkæŋgə'ru:] Känguru OT 5
karate [kə'rɑ:ti] Karate OT 1
karma ['kɑ:rmə] Karma **WS 1**, 32
kart racing [kɑ:t reɪsɪŋ] Kartrennen OT 3
kayaking ['kaɪækɪŋ] Kajakfahren OT 2
keen: to be keen [tə bi ki:] auf etw. scharf sein; auf etw. Lust haben OT 4
to keep [ki:p] bleiben; behalten; aufbewahren OT 2
to keep away [ki:p ə'weɪ] fernbleiben; fernhalten OT 2
to keep in touch [ˌki:p ɪn 'tʌtʃ] in Kontakt bleiben OT 2
keeper ['ki:pə] Hüter(in) OT 4
ketchup ['ketʃəp] Ketchup OT 1
kettle ['ketl] Kessel; Wasserkocher OT 2
key [ki:] Schlüssel OT 1
to key (in) [ki: ɪn] tippen; eintippen OT 2
keyboard ['ki:bɔ:d] Tastatur; Keyboard OT 1
keynote ['ki:noʊt] Hauptgedanke; Leitmotiv **WS 4**, 139
keyword ['ki:wɜ:d] Stichwort OT 4
to kick [kɪk] treten OT 1
kickball ['kɪkbɔ:l] Kickball OT 4
kid [kɪd] Kind OT 1
kidnapper ['kɪdnæpə] Entführer(in) OT 2
kidney bean ['kɪdni bi:n] Kidneybohne OT 2
to kill [kɪl] töten OT 1
kilometre ['kɪləmi:tə] Kilometer OT 1
kimchi ['kɪmtʃi] Kimchi OT 1
kin [kɪn] Verwandtschaft; Familie OT 5
kind [kaɪnd] Art; freundlich; nett OT 1
kindly ['kaɪndli] netterweise OT 2
kindness ['kaɪndnəs] Freundlichkeit; Güte **WS 1**, 25
king [kɪŋ] König OT 1
kingdom ['kɪŋdəm] Königreich OT 4
kiss [kɪs] Kuss OT 3
kit [kɪt] Ausrüstung OT 2
kitchen ['kɪtʃɪn] Küche OT 1
kitchenette [ˌkɪtʃɪ'nɛt] Kochnische; kleine Küche **WS 1**, 23
kite [kaɪt] Drachen **WS 1**, 43
kite-surfing [kaɪt 'sɜ:fɪŋ] Kitesurfen OT 5
kiwi ['ki:wi:] Kiwi OT 1
knee [ni:] Knie OT 1
to kneel [ni:l] knien OT 1
knife [naɪf] Messer OT 2
to knight [naɪt] zum Ritter schlagen OT 3
knock [nɒk] Klopfen OT 2
to knock over [nɒk' əʊvə] umstoßen OT 2
to know [nəʊ] wissen OT 1
well known [ˌwel 'nəʊn] bekannt OT 2
knowledge ['nɒlɪdʒ] Wissen OT 4
knowledgeable ['nɒlɪdʒəbl] kenntnisreich OT 3
koala [kəʊ'ɑ:lə] Koala OT 5
kookaburra ['kʊkəbʌrə] Kookaburra; Lachender Hans OT 5
Korean [kə'riən] koreanisch OT 1

L

lab [læb] Labor OT 2
label ['leɪbl] Etikett OT 1
to label ['leɪbl] beschriften; etikettieren; auszeichnen **WS 2**, 58
laboratory [lə'bɒrətri] Labor OT 4
labour ['leɪbə] Arbeitskraft; Arbeit OT 4
to labour ['leɪbə] sich quälen; arbeiten **WS 1**, 18
lack [læk] Mangel OT 3
ladder ['lædə] Leiter OT 2
lady ['leɪdi] Dame OT 1
laid-back [ˌleɪd 'bæk] locker; entspannt OT 4
lake [leɪk] See OT 1
lakefront ['leɪkfrʌnt] Seeufer OT 4
lakeside ['leɪksaɪd] Seeufer OT 4
lamb [læm] Lamm OT 1
lamp [læmp] Lampe OT 1
to land [lænd] landen OT 1
landfill ['lændfɪl] Mülldeponie OT 3
landline ['lændlaɪn] Festnetz OT 4
landlord ['lændlɔ:d] Grundbesitzer; Verpächter **WS 1**, 16
landmark ['lændmɑ:k] Wahrzeichen OT 4
landscape ['lændskeɪp] Landschaft OT 2
lane [leɪn] Fahrspur; Gasse OT 2
laneway [leɪnweɪ] Sträßchen OT 5
language ['læŋgwɪdʒ] Sprache OT 1
lantern ['læntən] Laterne OT 2
lanyard ['lænjɑ:d] Umhängeband; Kordel OT 5
laptop ['læptɒp] Laptop OT 1
large [lɑ:dʒ] groß OT 2
lasagna [lə'zænjə] Lasagne OT 1
laser ['leɪzə] Laser OT 3
to last [lɑ:st] andauern OT 2
last [lɑ:st] letzte(r, -s) OT 1
late [leɪt] spät OT 1
later ['leɪtə] später OT 1
lathered up ['læðərd ʌp] aufgeputscht **WS 3**, 94
Latin ['lætɪn] Latein OT 1
Latino [læ'ti:nəʊ] lateinamerikanisch OT 2
to laugh [lɑ:f] lachen OT 1
to launch [lɔ:ntʃ] starten; auf den Markt bringen OT 4
laundry ['lɔ:ndri] Wäsche OT 4
lava ['lɑ:və] Lava OT 5
law [lɔ:] Gesetz OT 3
lawn [lɔ:n] Rasen OT 5
lawyer ['lɔɪə] Rechtsanwalt / -anwältin OT 4
layer ['leɪə] Schicht **WS 3**, 98
to lead [li:d] führen OT 3
leading ['li:dɪŋ] führend OT 2
leader ['li:də] Leiter(in) OT 1
leadership ['li:dəʃɪp] Führung OT 4
leaf [li:f] Blatt OT 4
leaflet ['li:flət] Reklamezettel OT 2
league [li:g] Liga OT 2
leakage ['li:kɪdʒ] Leckage; Austreten **WS 3**, 104
to lean [li:n] lehnen OT 3
leap [li:p] Sprung OT 5
to learn [lɜ:n] lernen OT 1
learner ['lɜ:nə] Lernende(r); Fahranfänger(in) OT 3
to lease [li:s] leasen; mieten OT 4
least [li:st] wenigste(r, -s) OT 2
leather ['leðə] Leder OT 3
to leave [li:v] verlassen OT 1
to leave behind [ˌli:v bɪ'haɪnd] hinterlassen OT 2
left [left] linke(r, -s) OT 1
leg [leg] Bein OT 1
legacy ['legəsi] Vermächtnis; Erbe **WS 1**, 14
legal ['li:gl] rechtlich; legal OT 4

legal aid [ˌliːgl ˈeɪd] Rechtshilfe OT 5
to **legalize** [ˈliːgəlaɪz] legalisieren OT 5
legend [ˈledʒənd] Legende OT 2
legendary [ˈlɛdʒəndəri] legendär **WS 2**, 84
legislation [ˌledʒɪsˈleɪʃn] Rechtsvorschriften OT 5
legitimate [lɪˈdʒɪtɪmɪt] legitim; rechtmäßig **WS 3**, 107
leisure [ˈleʒə] Freizeit OT 3
leisurely [ˈleʒəli] gelassen **WS 2**, 79
lemonade [ˌleməˈneɪd] Zitronenlimonade OT 1
to **lend** [lend] leihen OT 2
length [leŋθ] Länge OT 2
lens [lenz] Linse OT 4
leopard [ˈlepəd] Leopard OT 2
lesbian [ˈlezbiən] lesbisch OT 5
less [les] weniger OT 2
lesson [ˈlesn] Unterricht OT 1
to **let** [let] lassen OT 1
  let's [lets] lass / lasst uns OT 4
letter [ˈletə] Brief; Buchstabe OT 1
  introductory letter [ˌɪntrəˈdʌktəri ˈletə] Einführungsbrief OT 4
lettuce [ˈletɪs] Kopfsalat OT 2
level [ˈlevl] Niveau; Stufe; Standard OT 2
to **level off** [ˈlevl ɒf] einpendeln OT 5
liberation [ˌlɪbəˈreɪʃn] Befreiung **WS 2**, 68
liberty [ˈlɪbəti] Freiheit OT 1
librarian [laɪˈbreəriən] Bibliothekar(in) OT 4
library [ˈlaɪbrəri] Bibliothek OT 1
licence [ˈlaɪsns] Erlaubnis OT 3
to **lick** [lɪk] lecken OT 3
lid [lɪd] Deckel OT 2
to **lie** [laɪ] liegen OT 1
life [laɪf] Leben OT 1
lifeblood [ˈlaɪfbʌd] Lebenssaft **WS 2**, 78
lifeguard [ˈlaɪfgɑːd] Rettungsschwimmer(in) OT 4
lifelong [ˈlaɪflɒŋ] lebenslang **WS 2**, 67
lifestyle [ˈlaɪfstaɪl] Lebensstil; Lifestyle OT 4
life-threatening [ˈlaɪf ˌθretnɪŋ] lebensbedrohlich OT 2
lifetime [ˈlaɪftaɪm] Lebenszeit; Leben OT 2
to **lift** [lɪft] anheben; hochheben; heben OT 3
light [laɪt] Licht OT 1
light [laɪt] leicht OT 3
to **light** [laɪt] anzünden OT 5
lightbulb [ˈlaɪtbʌlb] Glühbirne OT 3
lighting [ˈlaɪtɪŋ] Beleuchtung OT 4
lightly [ˈlaɪtli] leicht **WS 4**, 142
like-minded [ˈlaɪkˌmaɪndɪd] gleichgesinnt **WS 1**, 41
like [laɪk] irgendwie; also; wie; als ob OT 1
to **like** [laɪk] gernhaben; mögen OT 1
  would like / love [wʊd laɪk / lʌv] hätte(n) gern; möchte(n) OT 1
likely [ˈlaɪkli] wahrscheinlich OT 3
to **limit** [ˈlɪmɪt] einschränken; begrenzen OT 3
limp [lɪmp] schlaff OT 4
line [laɪn] Linie; Text (eines Schauspielers); Seil OT 1
lingua franca [ˈlɪŋgwə ˈfræŋkə] Lingua Franca; Verkehrssprache **WS 3**, 108
linguist [ˈlɪŋgwɪst] Sprachwissenschaftler(in); Linguist(in) OT 5
linguistics [lɪŋˈgwɪstɪks] Linguistik **WS 3**, 108
link [lɪŋk] Verbindung OT 2
  linking verb [ˈlɪŋkɪŋ vɜːb] Kopula OT 2
  linking word [ˈlɪŋkɪŋ wɜːd] Verbindungswort OT 4
linked [lɪŋkt] verbunden OT 2
lion [ˈlaɪən] Löwe OT 1
lioness [ˈlaɪənɛs] Löwin **WS 2**, 64
lip [lɪp] Lippe OT 2
liquid [ˈlɪkwɪd] flüssig OT 2
lisp [lɪsp] Lispeln; Sprachfehler **WS 3**, 96
list [lɪst] Liste OT 1
to **list** [lɪst] auflisten OT 3
to **listen** [ˈlɪsn] hören; zuhören OT 1
listener [ˈlɪsnə] Hörer(in); Zuhörer(in) OT 4
liter [ˈliːtə] Liter OT 4
literacy: environmental literacy [ɪnˌvaɪrənˈmɛntl ˈlɪtərəsi] Umweltwissen **WS 3**, 98
literal [ˈlɪtərəl] wörtlich OT 5
literally [ˈlɪtərl] buchstäblich **WS 3**, 100
literary [ˈlɪtərəri] literarisch OT 5
literature [ˈlɪtrətʃə] Literatur OT 4
litre [ˈliːtə] Liter OT 5
litter [ˈlɪtə] herumliegende Abfälle OT 2
little [ˈlɪtl] klein OT 1
livable [ˈlɪvəbl] bewohnbar OT 5
to **live** [lɪv] leben; wohnen OT 1
liveable [ˈlɪvəbl] bewohnbar OT 4
lively [ˈlaɪvli] lebhaft OT 5
liver [ˈlɪvər] Leber OT 5
livestock [ˈlaɪvstɒk] Vieh; Viehbestand OT 5
living room [ˈlɪvɪŋ ruːm] Wohnzimmer OT 1
to **load up** [ləʊd ʌp] aufladen OT 5
load [ləʊd] Ladung OT 5
  loads of [ləʊdz əv] eine Menge OT 3
loan [ləʊn] Darlehen; Leihgabe OT 5
to **loathe** [ləʊð] nicht ausstehen können; hassen OT 5
local [ˈləʊkl] Einheimische(r) OT 2
local [ˈləʊkl] einheimisch OT 2
  locally [ˈləʊkəli] hier; am Ort OT 3
to **locate** [ləʊˈkeɪt] finden; orten **WS 4**, 138
located [ləʊˈkeɪtid] gelegen OT 5
location [ləʊˈkeɪʃn] Standort OT 2
loch [lɒx] See OT 1
lock [lɒk] Schloss OT 2
to **lock** [lɒk] abschließen OT 2
locker [ˈlɒkə] Spind; Schließfach OT 2
lodge [lɒdʒ] Gasthaus OT 2
log [lɒg] Holzscheit OT 3
to **log on** [ˈlɒgɒn] sich einloggen OT 3
logical [ˈlɒdʒɪkl] logisch; folgerichtig OT 5
logo [ˈləʊgəʊ] Logo OT 1
loincloth [ˈlɔɪnklɒθ] Lendenschurz; Schurz **WS 3**, 94
lonely [ˈləʊnli] einsam OT 3
long [lɒŋ] lang OT 1
to **long** [ˈlɒŋg] verlangen **WS 2**, 55
loo [luː] Klo OT 2
loo break [ˈluː breɪk] Klopause OT 2
to **look** [lʊk] sehen OT 1
  to **look after** [lʊk ɑːftə] aufpassen auf OT 1
  to **look at** [lʊk æt] anschauen; ansehen OT 1
  to **look forward to** [ˌlʊk ˈfɔːwəd tə] (sich) auf etw. freuen OT 1
  to **look lost** [lʊk lɒst] verloren aussehen OT 4
lookout [ˈlʊkaʊt] Ausschau **WS 1**, 28
loop [luːp] Schleife **WS 4**, 140
lorry [ˈlɒri] Lastwagen; LKW **WS 3**, 99
to **lose** [luːz] verlieren OT 1
loser [ˈluːzər] Verlierer(in) OT 5
loss [lɒs] Verlust OT 5
lot: a lot [ə lɒt] viel; sehr OT 1
  lots [lɒts] viel OT 1
lottery [ˈlɒtəri] Lotterie OT 3
loud [laʊd] laut OT 1
loudspeaker [ˈlaʊd ˌspiːkə] Lautsprecher OT 2

lounge [laʊndʒ] Aufenthaltsraum **WS 1**, 23
to **love** [lʌv] lieben OT 1
lovely ['lʌvli] hübsch; schön OT 1
lover ['lʌvə] Liebhaber(in) OT 3
low [ləʊ] tief OT 1
low-income [ləʊ 'ɪnkʌm] einkommensschwach OT 4
to **lower** ['ləʊə] senken; herabsetzen **WS 1**, 27
loyal ['lɔɪəl] treu OT 5
loyalty ['lɔɪəlti] Loyalität; Treue **WS 1**, 40
luck [lʌk] Glück OT 1
good luck [gʊd 'lʌk] Alles Gute! OT 2
lucky ['lʌki] glücklich; glückbringend OT 2
luckily ['lʌkɪli] glücklicherweise OT 4
luggage ['lʌgɪdʒ] Gepäck OT 4
lunch [lʌntʃ] Mittagessen OT 1
lunch break ['lʌntʃ breɪk] Mittagspause OT 1
lunchtime ['lʌntʃtaɪm] Mittagszeit OT 1
lung [lʌŋ] Lunge OT 3
to **lurk** [lɜ:rk] lauern **WS 2**, 62
lust [lʌst] Lust OT 5
luxurious [lʌg'ʒʊəriəs] luxuriös OT 2
luxury ['lʌkʃəri] Luxus OT 5
lynch mob [lɪntʃ mɒb] Lynchjustiz **WS 3**, 106
lynx [lɪŋks] Luchs OT 2
lyrics ['lɪrɪks] Songtext; Liedtext OT 2

M

ma'am [mæm] gnädige Frau OT 2
machine [mə'ʃi:n] Maschine OT 1
machinery [mə'ʃi:nəri] Maschinen OT 2
mad [mæd] verrückt; böse OT 2
madam ['mædəm] gnädige Frau OT 1
made of [meɪd əv] gemacht aus OT 2
madman ['mædmən] Irrer; Verrückter OT 4
magazine [ˌmægə'zi:n] Zeitschrift OT 1
magic ['mædʒɪk] Zauber OT 1
magical ['mædʒɪkl] magisch OT 2
magician [mə'dʒɪʃn] Zauberer / Zauberin OT 1
magnate ['mægneɪt] Magnat; Industrieller **WS 3**, 100
magnetic [mæg'netɪk] magnetisch OT 2
magnet ['mægnət] Magnet OT 1
mahout [mə'haʊt] Mahout; Elefantenführer **WS 1**, 21
maiden ['meɪdn] erstes **WS 2**, 55
mail [meɪl] Post OT 1
snail mail ['sneɪl meɪl] Schneckenpost; traditioneller Brief OT 4
mailbox ['meɪlbɒks] Briefkasten; Mailbox OT 4
mail carrier ['meɪl kæriə] Postbote / -botin OT 4
main [meɪn] Haupt... OT 1
main course ['meɪn kɔ:s] Hauptgang OT 1
mainland ['meɪnlænd] Festland OT 3
mainly ['meɪnli] hauptsächlich OT 2
to **maintain** [meɪn'teɪn] warten; pflegen OT 4
maintenance ['meɪntənəns] Wartung OT 3
major ['meɪdʒə] bedeutend OT 2
majority [mə'dʒɒrəti] Mehrheit OT 4
to **make** [meɪk] kochen; machen OT 1
to **make a mess** [meɪk ə 'mes] ein Chaos anrichten OT 2
maker ['meɪkə] Macher(in) OT 3
malamute ['mælə͵mju:t] Malamut OT 2
male [meɪl] männlich OT 2
mall [mɔ:l] Einkaufszentrum OT 3
malpractice ['mæl͵præktɪs] Kunstfehler; Fehlverhalten **WS 3**, 98
malware ['mælweə] Malware OT 3
mammal ['mæml] Säugetier OT 2
man [mæn] Mann OT 1
to **manage** ['mænɪdʒ] leiten; managen OT 1
management ['mænɪdʒmənt] Management; Geschäftsführung OT 5
manager ['mænɪdʒə] Geschäftsführer(in); Manager(in); Leiter(in) OT 1
to **mandate** ['mændeɪt] anordnen OT 5
to **manipulate** [mə'nɪpjuleɪt] manipulieren **WS 2**, 67
man-made [ˌmæn 'meɪd] menschengemacht; künstlich OT 1
manner ['mænə] Weise OT 2
manual ['mænjul] Handbuch **WS 1**, 22
manufacture [ˌmænju'fæktʃə] Herstellung; Produktion OT 4
manufacturer [ˌmænju'fæktʃərə] Hersteller(in) OT 4
manufacturing [ˌmænju'fæktʃərɪŋ] Produktion; Herstellung OT 5
manure [mə'njʊə] Dung OT 3
many ['meni] viele OT 1
many times ['meni taɪmz] häufig; oftmals OT 4
Maori ['maʊri] Maori OT 1
map [mæp] Landkarte OT 1
maple ['meɪpl] Ahorn OT 3
marathon ['mærəθən] Marathon OT 2
half marathon ['hɑ:f ˌmærəθən] Halbmarathon OT 2
marbles ['mɑ:blz] Murmelspiel OT 4
March [mɑ:tʃ] März OT 1
march [mɑ:tʃ] Marsch OT 3
marching band ['mɑ:tʃɪŋ bænd] Blaskapelle OT 4
margin ['mɑ:dʒɪn] Rand OT 5
to **marginalize** ['mɑ:dʒɪnəlaɪ] ausgrenzen; marginalisieren **WS 2**, 69
marine [mə'ri:n] Meeres... OT 4
maritime ['mærɪtaɪm] Marine... OT 3
to **mark** [mɑ:k] korrigieren OT 2
marker ['mɑ:kə] Markierung; Filzstift OT 1
market ['mɑ:kɪt] Markt OT 1
marketable ['mɑ:kɪtəbl] vermarktbar OT 4
marketing ['mɑ:kɪtɪŋ] Marketing; Vermarktung OT 4
marketplace ['mɑ:kɪtpleɪs] Markt OT 5
market segment [ˌmɑ:kɪt ˌsegment] Marktsegment OT 5
marquee [mɑ:'ki:] Markise; Zelt OT 2
marriage ['mærɪdʒ] Ehe OT 5
to **marry** ['mæri] heiraten OT 1
masculinity [ˌmæskjʊ'lɪnɪti] Männlichkeit **WS 2**, 57
mash [mæʃ] Püree **WS 4**, 139
mask [mɑ:sk] Maske OT 3
mass [mæs] Massen- OT 4
mass sport [mæs spɔ:t] Massensport OT 3
massacre ['mæsəkə] Massaker OT 3
massive ['mæsɪv] riesig OT 3
master ['mɑ:stə] Meister(in) OT 4
match [mætʃ] Spiel; Wettkampf OT 1
matchmaking ['mætʃmeɪkɪŋ] Verkuppeln **WS 1**, 28
mate [meɪt] Kumpel OT 5
material [mə'tɪəriəl] Material; Stoff OT 3
math [mæθ] Mathe OT 1
mathematician [ˌmæθəmə'tɪʃn] Mathematiker(in) OT 3
mathematics [ˌmæθə'mætɪks] Mathematik OT 1
maths [mæθs] Mathematik OT 1
matter ['mætə] Angelegenheit; Problem OT 2
What's the matter? [wɒts ðə 'mætə] Was ist los? OT 2
mature [mə'tʃʊər] reif; mündig OT 5

to mature [mə'tʃʊə] reifen; erwachsen **WS 2**, 83
maximum ['mæksɪməm] Maximum OT 2
May [meɪ] Mai OT 1
may [meɪ] könnte(n) OT 1
maybe ['meɪbi] vielleicht OT 1
mayonnaise [ˌmeɪə'neɪz] Mayonnaise OT 1
mayor [meə] Bürgermeister(in) OT 3
me [mi:] mich; mir OT 1
meadow ['medəʊ] Wiese OT 2
meal [mi:l] Mahlzeit OT 1
to mean [mi:n] bedeuten OT 1
mean [mi:n] gemein OT 2
meaning ['mi:nɪŋ] Sinn; Bedeutung OT 1
meaningful ['mi:nɪŋfl] sinnvoll OT 5
meanwhile ['mi:nwaɪl] inzwischen; mittlerweile OT 5
measles ['mi:zlz] Masern OT 5
to measure ['meʒə] messen; ausmessen; abschätzen OT 4
measurement ['meʒəmənt] Maß; Maßeinheit OT 2
meat [mi:t] Fleisch OT 1
meatball ['mi:tbɔ:l] Fleischklößchen; Hackfleischbällchen OT 1
meatloaf ['mi:t ləʊf] Hackbraten OT 3
meaty ['mi:ti] Fleisch... OT 3
mechanical [mə'kænɪkl] mechanisch OT 5
medal ['medl] Medaille OT 2
medallist ['mɛdəlɪst] Medaillengewinner(in) **WS 2**, 61
media ['mi:diə] Medien OT 2
social media [ˌsəʊʃl 'mi:diə] soziale Medien OT 2
mediation [ˌmi:di'eɪʃn] Mediation; Vermittlung OT 1
medical ['medɪkl] ärztliche Untersuchung; medizinisch OT 1
medical science ['medɪkl 'saɪəns] Heilkunde; Medizin OT 4
medication [ˌmedɪ'keɪʃn] Medikation OT 5
medicine ['medsn] Medikament; Medizin OT 2
medium ['mi:diəm] mittelgroß OT 1
medium-sized ['mi:diəm saɪzd] mittelgroß OT 2
to meet [mi:t] treffen OT 1
meeting ['mi:tɪŋ] Besprechung; Treffen OT 1
meetinghouse ['mi:tɪŋhaʊs] Andachtshaus; Gebetshaus OT 4
melody ['melədi] Melodie OT 2
to melt [melt] schmelzen OT 4
melting pot ['meltɪŋ pɒt] Schmelztiegel **WS 2**, 72
member ['membə] Mitglied OT 1
memoir ['memwɑ:] Memoiren; Erinnerung OT 5
memorable ['memərəbl] unvergesslich OT 3
to memorize ['meməraɪz] auswendig lernen; merken OT 4
memory ['meməri] Gedächtnis OT 1
mental ['mentl] geistig; mental OT 4
mentality [men'tæləti] Geisteshaltung **WS 3**, 106
to mention ['menʃn] erwähnen OT 3
mentor ['mentɔ:] Lehrmeister(in); Mentor(in) OT 4
menu ['menju:] Speisekarte OT 1
mere [mɪə] bloß; lediglich **WS 1**, 14
mess [mes] Unordnung OT 3
to mess up [ˌmes'ʌp] in Unordnung bringen; vergeigen OT 2
message ['mesɪdʒ] Nachricht OT 1
to message ['mesɪdʒɪŋ] texten OT 3
messy ['mesi] unordentlich; chaotisch OT 2
metal ['metl] Metall OT 1
metaphor ['metəfər] Metapher OT 5
method ['meθəd] Methode OT 1
metre ['mi:tə] Meter OT 1
metro ['metrəʊ] U-Bahn OT 1
metropolis [mɪ'trɒpəlɪs] Metropole; Großstadt **WS 1**, 12
Mexican ['meksɪkən] mexikanisch OT 4
microbe ['maɪkrəʊb] Mikrobe OT 4
microdrama ['maɪkrəʊˌdrɑ:mə] Mikrodrama **WS 3**, 119
microphone ['maɪkrəfəʊn] Mikrofon OT 4
microscope ['maɪkrəskəʊp] Mikroskop OT 4
microwave ['maɪkrəweɪv] Mikrowelle OT 5
mid [mɪd] in der Mitte; mittel OT 4
midday [ˌmɪd'deɪ] Mittag OT 4
middle ['mɪdl] Mitte OT 1
middle school ['mɪdl sku:l] Mittelschule OT 2
midfield ['mɪdˌfi:ld] in der Mitte des Spielfeldes **WS 1**, 28
midfielder [ˌmɪd'fi:ldə] Mittelfeldspieler(in) OT 3
midge [mɪdʒ] Mücke OT 3
midnight ['mɪdnaɪt] Mitternacht OT 1
midst [mɪdst] Mitte **WS 2**, 65
midwest [ˌmɪd'west] mittlerer Westen OT 4
midwestern [ˌmɪd'westən] mittlerer Westen OT 4
might [maɪt] könnte(n) OT 1
mighty ['maɪti] sehr; mächtig OT 3
migrant ['maɪgrənt] Migrant(in); herumziehend OT 4
to migrate [maɪ'greɪt] migrieren OT 3
migration [maɪ'greɪʃn] Migration OT 3
mile [maɪl] Meile OT 1
milestone ['maɪlstəʊn] Meilenstein **WS 3**, 103
militant ['mɪlɪtənt] militant **WS 2**, 79
military ['mɪlətri] Militär OT 4
militia [mɪ'lɪʃə] Miliz; Bürgerwehr **WS 1**, 14
milk [mɪlk] Milch OT 1
millennial [mɪ'leniəl] die Generation der Jahrtausendwende OT 4
million ['mɪljən] Million OT 1
to mime [maɪm] pantomimisch darstellen OT 2
mind [maɪnd] Verstand OT 1
to mind [maɪnd] etw. macht jdm. etw. aus OT 4
mind-expanding [maɪnd ɪk'spænd] sinneserweiternd OT 2
mind map ['maɪnd mæp] Gedankenkarte; Mindmap OT 1
mindset ['maɪndset] Mentalität **WS 3**, 103
mine [maɪn] Bergwerk; Mine OT 2
mine [maɪn] meine(r, -s) OT 2
miner ['maɪnə] Bergarbeiter OT 4
mini ['mɪni] klein OT 2
miniature ['mɪnətʃə] sehr klein OT 3
minibus ['mɪnibʌs] Kleinbus OT 2
minimal ['mɪnɪml] minimal; gering **WS 1**, 14
minimum ['mɪnɪməm] Mindest... OT 1
mining ['maɪnɪŋ] Bergbau... OT 3
minister ['mɪnɪstə] Minister(in) **WS 1**, 12
minor ['maɪnər] gering; klein OT 5
minority [maɪ'nɒrəti] Minderheit OT 5
mint [mɪnt] Minze OT 2
minute ['mɪnɪt] Minute OT 1
miraculous [mɪ'rækjʊləs] wunderbar; erstaunlich **WS 1**, 27
mirror ['mɪrə] Spiegel OT 1
rearview mirror ['rɪəvju: 'mɪrə] Rückspiegel **WS 3**, 92
mischievous ['mɪstʃɪvəs] schelmisch; unartig **WS 1**, 43
miserable ['mɪzrəbl] unglücklich OT 2
misfit ['mɪsfɪt] Außenseiter(in) OT 4

misfit [ˈmɪsfɪt] Außenseiter(in) **WS 3**, 96
misleading [ˌmɪsˈliːdɪŋ] irreführend OT 3
mismatched [ˌmɪsˈmætʃ] nicht zusammenpassend OT 4
misogynist [mɪˈsɒdʒɪnɪst] Frauenfeind; Frauenhasser **WS 1**, 31
to **misrepresent** [ˌmɪsrɪˈprɛzənt] falsch darstellen; verfälschen **WS 2**, 66
to **miss** [mɪs] vermissen OT 2
missing [ˈmɪsɪŋ] fehlend OT 1
mission [ˈmɪʃn] Mission OT 4
missionary [ˈmɪʃənri] Missionar(in) **WS 3**, 95
mistake [mɪˈsteɪk] Fehler OT 2
by mistake [baɪ mɪˈsteɪk] versehentlich OT 2
mistakenly [mɪˈsteɪkənli] fälschlich; irrtümlicherweise OT 5
mistreatment [ˌmɪsˈtriːtmənt] Misshandlung OT 5
to **misunderstand** [ˌmɪsʌndəˈstænd] missverstehen OT 5
misunderstanding [ˌmɪsʌndəˈstændɪŋ] Missverständnis OT 4
misunderstood [ˌmɪsʌndəˈstʊd] verkannt; missverstanden OT 4
to **mix** [mɪks] mischen OT 2
to **mix up** [mɪks ʌp] vermischen; durcheinanderbringen OT 2
mixed up [ˌmɪkst ˈʌp] durcheinander OT 2
mixture [ˈmɪkstʃə] Mischung OT 3
mob [mɒb] Meute OT 5
mobile [ˈməʊbaɪl] mobil OT 1
mobile phone [ˈməʊbaɪl] Handy OT 1
mobility [moʊˈbɪlɪti] Mobilität; Beweglichkeit **WS 3**, 108
modal [ˈməʊdl] Modalverb OT 2
mode [moʊd] Modus; Art **WS 3**, 99
model [ˈmɒdl] Modell OT 1
modern [ˈmɒdn] modern OT 1
to **modify** [ˈmɒdɪfaɪ] modifizieren; ändern **WS 3**, 104
module [ˈmɒdjuːl] Modul OT 4
mom [mɒm] Mama OT 1
moment [ˈməʊmənt] Moment OT 1
monarch [ˈmɒnək] Monarch(in); Herrscher(in) OT 5
monastery [ˈmɒnəstri] Kloster OT 3
Monday [ˈmʌndeɪ] Montag OT 1
money [ˈmʌni] Geld OT 1
to **monitor** [ˈmɒnɪtə] kontrollieren **WS 2**, 83
monk [mʌŋk] Mönch OT 3
monkey [ˈmʌŋki] Affe OT 2
monolingual [ˌmɒnəˈlɪŋgwəl] einsprachig OT 5
monologue [ˈmɒnəlɒg] Monolog OT 5
monotone [ˈmɒnətəʊn] monoton OT 4
monsoon [mɒnˈsuːn] Monsun **WS 1**, 39
monster [ˈmɒnstə] Monster OT 1
month [mʌnθ] Monat OT 1
monument [ˈmɒnjumənt] Denkmal OT 1
mood [muːd] Stimmung OT 5
moon [muːn] Mond OT 4
to **moor** [mɔː] vertäuen; anlegen OT 3
mooring [ˈmɔːrɪŋ] Anlegeplatz OT 3
moral [ˈmɒrl] Moral **WS 3**, 113
more [mɔː] mehr OT 1
moreover [mɔːrˈəʊvə] außerdem OT 5
morning [ˈmɔːnɪŋ] Morgen OT 1
mosque [mɒsk] Moschee OT 1
mosquito [məˈskiːtəʊ] Stechmücke OT 2
most [məʊst] der / die / das meiste; die meisten OT 1
motel [məʊˈtel] Motel OT 3
mother [ˈmʌðə] Mutter OT 1
motif [məʊˈtiːf] Motiv OT 5
motion picture [ˌməʊʃn ˈpɪktʃə] Film; Spielfilm OT 4
to **motivate** [ˈməʊtɪveɪt] motivieren OT 4
motivated [ˈməʊtɪveɪtɪd] motiviert OT 5
motivating [ˈməʊtɪveɪtɪŋ] motivierend; anregend OT 5
motivation [ˌməʊtɪˈveɪʃn] Motivation; Begründung OT 5
to **motor** [ˈməʊtə] fahren OT 3
motto [ˈmɒtəʊ] Motto **WS 2**, 67
mountain [ˈmaʊntən] Berg OT 1
mountain range [ˈmaʊntən reɪndʒ] Bergkette; Gebirgszug OT 4
mouse [maʊs] Maus OT 2
mouth [maʊθ] Mund OT 1
mouthguard [maʊθgɑːd] Mundschutz OT 2
mouthwash [ˈmaʊθwɒʃ] Mundwasser OT 4
to **move** [muːv] bewegen; umziehen OT 1
to **move on** [muːv ɒn] weitergehen OT 4
movement [ˈmuːvmənt] Bewegung OT 5
movie [ˈmuːvi] Film OT 1
moving van [ˈmuːvɪŋ ˌvæn] Umzugswagen OT 2
to **mow** [məʊ] mähen OT 5
MP (Members of Parliament) [ˌem ˈpiː] Abgeordnete OT 5
Mr [ˈmɪstə] Herr OT 1
Mrs [ˈmɪsɪz] Frau OT 1
much [mʌtʃ] viel OT 1
to **muck around** [mʌk əˈraʊnd] Herumblödeln OT 5
mud [mʌd] Schlamm; Dreck **WS 1**, 16
muffin [ˈmʌfɪn] Muffin OT 1
mug [mʌg] Becher; Tasse OT 3
mule [mjuːl] Maultier OT 3
multi [mʌlti] multi... OT 3
multicultural [ˌmʌltiˈkʌltʃərəl] multikulturell OT 5
multilogue [ˈmʌltilɒg] Multilog OT 5
multiple choice [ˌmʌltɪpl ˈtʃɔɪs] Multiple-Choice OT 2
to **multiply** [ˈmʌltɪplaɪ] multiplizieren; vervielfachen **WS 4**, 134
mum [mʌm] Mutti OT 1
mummy [ˈmʌmi] Mumie OT 2
mural [ˈmjʊərəl] Wandgemälde OT 2
to **murder** [ˈmɜːdə] ermorden OT 4
murky [ˈmɜːki] trübe OT 4
muscle [ˈmʌsl] Muskel OT 4
museum [mjuːˈziːəm] Museum OT 1
mushroom [ˈmʌʃrʊm] Pilz; Champignon OT 1
music [ˈmjuːzɪk] Musik OT 1
musical [ˈmjuːzɪkl] Musik…; musikalisch OT 2
musical instrument [ˌmjuːzɪkl ˈɪnstrəmənt] Musikinstrument OT 2
musician [mjuˈzɪʃn] Musiker(in) OT 2
Muslim [ˈmʊzlɪm] Muslim(in) OT 3
mussel [ˈmʌsl] Muschel OT 4
must [mʌst] müssen OT 1
mustard [ˈmʌstəd] Senf OT 2
mutilation [ˌmjuːtɪˈleɪʃən] Verstümmelung; Entstellung **WS 1**, 14
to **mutter** [ˈmʌtə] murmeln **WS 3**, 103
mutual [ˈmjuːtʃul] gegenseitig; gemeinsam **WS 1**, 33
my [maɪ] mein OT 1
myself [maɪˈself] ich (selbst) OT 3
mysterious [mɪˈstɪəriəs] geheimnisvoll; rätselhaft **WS 1**, 26
mystery [ˈmɪstri] Rätsel; Mysterium OT 2
myth [mɪθ] Mythos; Legende OT 5

N

to **nag** [næg] meckern; nörgeln OT 5
nail [neɪl] Nagel; Fingernagel OT 5
naive [naɪˈiːv] naiv; gutgläubig **WS 3**, 98
name [neɪm] Name OT 1

first name ['fɜ:st neɪm] Vorname OT 2
last name ['lɑ:st neɪm] Nachname OT 2
to **name** [neɪm] benennen OT 4
nap [næp] Nickerchen OT 5
nappy ['næpi] Windel OT 3
to **narrate** [nəˈreɪts] erzählen **WS 1**, 16
narration [nəˈreɪʃən] Erzählung; Narration **WS 2**, 79
narrative ['nærətɪv] Geschichte; Erzählung **WS 1**, 26
narrator [nəˈreɪtə] Erzähler(in) OT 5
narrow ['nærəʊ] eng OT 2
narrowboat ['nærəʊbəʊt] schmales Kanalboot; Hausboot OT 3
nasty ['nɑ:sti] unangenehm OT 2
nation ['neɪʃn] Nation OT 2
national ['næʃnl] national OT 1; Staatsbürger(in) **WS 2**, 85
nationality [ˌnæʃəˈnæləti] Staatsangehörigkeit OT 2
native ['neɪtɪv] einheimisch; Einheimische OT 3
natural ['nætʃrəl] natürlich OT 1
nature ['neɪtʃə] Natur OT 2
navigating ['nævɪgeɪt] Navigation OT 4
navy ['neɪvi] Marine OT 3
near [nɪə] nahe; in der Nähe von OT 1
nearby [ˌnɪəˈbaɪ] in der Nähe OT 3
nearly ['nɪəli] fast OT 1
neat [ni:t] ordentlich OT 4
necessary ['nesəsəri] notwendig OT 3
necessity [nəˈsesəti] Notwendigkeit OT 5
neck [nek] Hals OT 1
necklace ['nekləs] Halskette **WS 2**, 71
beaded necklace ['bi:dɪd ˈnɛkləs] Perlenkette **WS 2**, 71
to **need** [ni:d] brauchen OT 1
negative ['negətɪv] Verneinung; Negativ OT 1
to **neglect** [nɪˈglekt] vernachlässigen **WS 2**, 53
to **negotiate** [nɪˈgəʊʃieɪt] verhandeln; aushandeln **WS 1**, 21
negotiation [nɪˌgoʊʃiˈeɪʃən] Verhandlung; Gespräch **WS 1**, 18
neighbourhood ['neɪbəhʊd] Nachbarschaft OT 4
neighbour ['neɪbə] Nachbar(in) OT 2
neither ['naɪðə] auch nicht; weder OT 2
nerve [nɜ:v] Nerv OT 3
nervous ['nɜ:vəs] nervös OT 2
nervously ['nɜ:vəsli] nervös OT 2
nest [nest] Nest OT 3
net [net] Netz OT 3
netball ['netbɔ:l] Netzball OT 1
netbook ['netbʊk] Netbook OT 4
network ['netwɜ:k] Netzwerk OT 5
neutral ['nju:trəl] neutral OT 3
never ['nevə] nie OT 1
nevertheless [ˌnevəðəˈlɛs] dennoch; trotzdem **WS 1**, 16
new [nju:] neu OT 1
news [nju:z] Neuigkeit(en) OT 1
newsletter ['nju:zletə] Mitteilungsblatt; Newsletter OT 4
newspaper ['nju:zpeɪpə] Zeitung OT 1
next [nekst] nächste(r, -s) OT 1
next to ['nekst tu:] neben OT 1
nice [naɪs] schön; nett OT 1
to **nickname** ['nɪkneɪm] Spitzname geben OT 5
nickname ['nɪkneɪm] Spitzname OT 4
night [naɪt] Nacht OT 1
nightmare ['naɪtmeə] Albtraum OT 4
nine [naɪn] neun OT 1
nineteen [ˌnaɪnˈti:n] neunzehn OT 1
ninety ['naɪnti] neunzig OT 1
no [nəʊ] nein OT 1
noble ['noʊbl] edel **WS 3**, 94
nobody ['nəʊbədi] niemand OT 1
to **nod** [nɒd] nicken OT 2
noise [nɔɪz] Geräusch; Lärm OT 1
noisy ['nɔɪzi] laut OT 1
nomadic [nəʊˈmædɪk] nomadisch OT 5
to **nominate** ['nɒmɪneɪt] nominieren OT 4
nomination [ˌnɒmɪˈneɪʃn] Nominierung; Ernennung OT 4
none [nʌn] keine(r, -s) OT 2
nonetheless [ˌnʌnðəˈles] nichtsdestoweniger; trotzdem **WS 2**, 65
non-profit [ˌnɒnˈprɒfɪt] gemeinnützig OT 4
non-verbal [ˌnɒn ˈvɜ:bl] nonverbal OT 4
noon [nu:n] Mittag OT 4
nor [nɔ:] noch; weder noch OT 4
norm [nɔ:m] Regel; Standard OT 5
normal ['nɔ:ml] normal OT 1
normally ['nɔ:məli] gewöhnlich; normalerweise OT 1
north [nɔ:θ] Nord- OT 1
northern [nɔ:ðən] nördlich OT 2
nose [nəʊz] Nase OT 2
nosebleed ['nəʊzbli:d] Nasenbluten OT 5
not [nɒt] nicht OT 1
notable ['nəʊtəbl] bemerkenswert **WS 2**, 65
note [nəʊt] Notiz; Schein OT 1
notebook ['nəʊtbʊk] Notizbuch OT 2
nothing ['nʌθɪŋ] nichts OT 1
to **notice** ['nəʊtɪs] bemerken OT 1
noticeboard ['nəʊtɪsbɔ:d] Anschlagbrett OT 1
notification [ˌnəʊtɪfɪˈkeɪʃn] Nachricht; Benachrichtigung **WS 4**, 133
noun [naʊn] Substantiv; Nomen; Hauptwort OT 1
novel ['nɒvl] Roman OT 2
novelist ['nɒvəlɪst] Romanautor(in) **WS 3**, 104
novella [noʊˈvɛlə] Novelle **WS 3**, 96
November [nəʊˈvembə] November OT 1
now [naʊ] jetzt OT 1
nowadays ['naʊədeɪz] heutzutage OT 3
nowhere ['nəʊweə] nirgendwo OT 2
nuance ['nju:ɑ:ns] Nuance; Feinheit **WS 3**, 107
nuclear ['nju:kliə] Atom...; Nuklear... OT 3
number ['nʌmbə] Zahl; Nummer OT 1
numerous ['nju:mərəs] zahlreich; viele OT 5
nun [nʌn] Nonne OT 4
nurse [nɜ:s] Krankenschwester / -pfleger OT 1
nursery ['nɜ:səri] Kindergarten **WS 3**, 123
nut [nʌt] Nuss OT 4
nutrition [njuˈtrɪʃn] Ernährung OT 5
nutritious [njuˈtrɪʃəs] nahrhaft OT 4
NVQs (national vocational qualifications) [en vi: kju:] nationale berufliche Abschlüsse OT 5

O

oats [əʊts] Haferflocken OT 3
to **obey** [oʊˈbeɪ] gehorchen **WS 3**, 104
obituary [oʊˈbɪtʃuˌɛri] Nachruf; Todesanzeige **WS 2**, 79
object ['ɒbdʒɪkt] Gegenstand; Objekt OT 1
objection [əbˈdʒekʃn] Einwand OT 3
objective [əbˈdʒektɪv] Ziel OT 4
object pronoun [ˌɒbdʒekt ˈprəʊnaʊn] Objektpronomen OT 1
obligation [ˌɒblɪˈgeɪʃn] Verpflichtung OT 2
obliged [əˈblaɪdʒd] verpflichtet OT 5
oblivious [əˈblɪviəs] ahnungslos; unbewusst **WS 3**, 96
observation [ˌɒbzəˈveɪʃn] Beobachtung OT 3
to **observe** [əbˈzɜ:v] beobachten OT 4
observer [əbˈzɜ:və] Beobachter(in) OT 5

obsessed [əb'sɛst] besessen **WS 2**, 64
obsession [əb'seʃn] Fixierung; Bessessenheit **WS 3**, 104
to **obtain** [əb'teɪn] erhalten; erlangen **WS 3**, 95
obvious ['ɒbviəs] offensichtlich OT 3
obviously ['ɒbviəsli] offenbar; offensichtlich OT 1
occasion [ə'keɪʒn] Gelegenheit **WS 1**, 32
occasionally [ə'keɪʒnəli] gelegentlich OT 2
occupation [ˌɒkju'peɪʃn] Tätigkeit; Beschäftigung OT 4
to **occupy** ['ɒkjupaɪ] einnehmen **WS 2**, 63
to **occur** [ə'kɜːr] passieren **WS 1**, 14
ocean ['əʊʃn] Ozean OT 3
October [ɒk'təʊbə] Oktober OT 1
octopus ['ɒktəpəs] Krake; Oktopus OT 1
odd [ɒd] eigenartig OT 2
odd one out [ɒd wʌn aʊt] Außenseiter(in); etw., was nicht in die Reihe passt OT 2
oddity ['ɒdəti] Kuriosität OT 4
odourless ['oʊdərləs] geruchslos **WS 3**, 99
of [əv] von OT 1
off [ɒf] von; aus; weg OT 1
offence [ə'fens] Straftat OT 5
to **offend** [ə'fend] beleidigen OT 3
offender [ə'fendə] Täter(in) OT 5
offensive [ə'fensɪv] beleidigend **WS 2**, 69
offer ['ɒfə] Angebot OT 1
to **offer** ['ɒfə] anbieten OT 2
office ['ɒfɪs] Büro OT 1
office park ['ɒfɪs pɑːk] Büropark OT 2
officer ['ɒfɪsə] Offizier(in) OT 2
official [ə'fɪʃl] Amtsperson OT 3; offiziell OT 4
offstage ['ɒfˌsteɪdʒ] aus dem Off OT 2
often ['ɒfn] oft OT 1
oil [ɔɪl] Öl OT 1
OK [əʊ'keɪ] in Ordnung OT 1
old [əʊld] alt OT 1
old-fashioned [ˌəʊld'fæʃnd] altmodisch OT 4
Olympic [ə'lɪmpɪk] olympisch OT 1
omelette ['ɒmlət] Omelett OT 2
to **omit** [oʊ'mɪt] auslassen **WS 2**, 58
omnivore ['ɒmnɪvɔːr] Allesesser **WS 1**, 32
on [ɒn] auf; an; in OT 1
once [wʌns] einmal OT 2
Once upon a time... ['wʌns əpɒn ə 'taɪm] Es war einmal... OT 1
one [wʌn] eins OT 1
onion ['ʌnjən] Zwiebel OT 2
onion ring ['ʌnjən rɪŋ] Zwiebelring OT 2
online [ˌɒn'laɪn] online OT 1
online forum [ˌɒn'laɪn 'fɔːrəm] Online-Forum OT 4
only ['əʊnli] nur OT 1
onscreen [ˌɒn 'skriːn] auf dem Bildschirm; auf der Leinwand OT 2
onto ['ɒntuː] auf OT 1
open ['əʊpən] offen OT 1
opening times ['əʊpnɪŋ ˌtaɪmz] Öffnungszeiten OT 1
to **open** ['əʊpən] aufmachen; öffnen OT 1
to **operate** ['ɒpəreɪt] bedienen; operieren OT 5
operation [ˌɒpə'reɪʃn] Operation OT 3
operator ['ɒpəreɪtə] Leitstellendisponent(in); Telefonist(in) OT 2
opinion [ə'pɪnjən] Meinung OT 3
opponent [ə'pəʊnənt] Gegner(in) OT 2
opportunity [ˌɒpə'tjuːnəti] Gelegenheit OT 2
to **oppose** [ə'pəʊz] kämpfen gegen **WS 3**, 100
opposing [ə'pəʊzɪŋ] gegnerisch OT 3
opposite ['ɒpəzɪt] Gegenteil OT 1
opposition [ˌɒpə'zɪʃn] Opposition; Gegner OT 5
to **oppress** [ə'pres] unterdrücken **WS 2**, 72
oppression [ə'preʃn] Unterdrückung OT 5
oppressor [ə'presə] Unterdrücker(in) **WS 2**, 83
optimistic [ˌɒptɪ'mɪstɪk] optimistisch OT 2
to **optimize** ['ɒptɪmaɪz] optimieren OT 5
option ['ɒpʃn] Wahl OT 2
optional ['ɒpʃənl] optional OT 2
or [ɔː] oder OT 1
orange ['ɒrɪndʒ] orange OT 1
orangejuice ['ɒrɪndʒ dʒuːs] Orangensaft OT 1
orang-utan [ˌɒræŋ'uːtæn] Orang-Utan **WS 1**, 21
orbit ['ɔːbɪt] Orbit; Umlaufbahn OT 4
orchestra ['ɔːkɪstrə] Orchester OT 1
order ['ɔːdə] Bestellung; Reihenfolge OT 1
to **order** ['ɔːdə] bestellen; befehlen OT 1
orderly ['ɔːrdərli] ordentlich **WS 1**, 16
ordinary ['ɔːdnri] normal OT 2
organ ['ɔːgən] Orgel; Organ OT 3
organic [ɔː'gænɪk] biologisch (angebaut) OT 2
organization [ˌɔːgənaɪ'zeɪʃn] Organisation OT 2
organizational [ˌɔːgənaɪ'zeɪʃənl] organisatorisch OT 4
to **organize** ['ɔːgənaɪz] organisieren OT 1
organizer ['ɔːgənaɪzə] Organisator(in) OT 3
oriental [ˌɔːri'entl] orientalisch OT 1
orientation [ˌɔːriən'teɪʃn] Orientierung OT 4
origin ['ɒrɪdʒɪn] Ursprung OT 3
original [ə'rɪdʒənl] ursprünglich; Original... OT 3
originally [ə'rɪdʒənəli] ursprünglich OT 2
to **originate** [ə'rɪdʒɪneɪt] entstehen OT 5
orphan ['ɔːfn] Waise **WS 2**, 67
orphaned ['ɔːrfənd] verwaist **WS 2**, 67
other ['ʌðə] andere(r, -s) OT 1
otherwise ['ʌðəwaɪz] sonst; ansonsten OT 5
Ouch! [aʊtʃ] Aua! OT 1
ought to ['ɔːt tə] sollte etw. tun OT 5
our ['aʊə] unser OT 1
ours [ɑːz] unsere(r, -s) OT 2
ourselves [ɑː'selvz,ˌaʊə'selvz] uns OT 3
out [aʊt] heraus; aus OT 1
outage ['aʊtɪdʒ] Ausfall **WS 3**, 101
outback ['aʊtbæk] Hinterland OT 4
outbreak ['aʊtbreɪk] Ausbruch **WS 3**, 98
outcome ['aʊtkʌm] Ergebnis; Resultat OT 5
outcry ['aʊtkraɪ] Aufschrei **WS 1**, 25
outdated [ˌaʊt'deɪtɪd] veraltet OT 5
outdoor ['aʊtdɔː] draußen OT 3
outdoors ['aʊtdɔːz] draußen OT 2
outer ['aʊtər] Außen... OT 5
outfit ['aʊtfɪt] Kleider; Outfit OT 5
to **outline** ['aʊtlaɪn] skizzieren OT 3
to **outnumber** [aʊt'nʌmbə] übersteigen **WS 3**, 108
outraged ['aʊtreɪdʒd] entsetzt **WS 1**, 21
outside [ˌaʊt'saɪd] draußen OT 1
outsider ['aʊtˌsaɪdə] Außenseiter(in) **WS 2**, 63
outstanding [aʊt'stændɪŋ] herausragend OT 3
outward ['aʊtwəd] äußerlich; äußere (r, -s) OT 5
outward journey ['aʊtwəd 'dʒɜːni] Hinfahrt OT 3
oven ['ʌvn] Ofen OT 4

over ['əʊvə] über OT 1
overall [ˌəʊvə'ɔ:l] allgemein **WS 1**, 21
overboard ['əʊvəbɔ:d] über Bord OT 3
to **overcome** [ˌəʊvə'kʌm] überwinden; bewältigen **WS 2**, 72
overcrowded [ˌəʊvə'kraʊdɪd] überfüllt **WS 1**, 32
to **overdo** [ˌəʊvə'du:] übertreiben OT 5
to **overflow** [ˌəʊvə'fləʊ] überfließen **WS 3**, 101
overgrown [ˌəʊvə'grəʊn] überwuchert; überwachsen OT 4
to **overhear** [ˌəʊvə'hɪə] hören; mithören OT 3
to **overlook** [ˌəʊvə'lʊk] übersehen OT 5
overly ['əʊvəli] übermäßig OT 5
overnight [ˌəʊvə'naɪt] über Nacht OT 2
overseas [ˌəʊvə'si:z] ausländisch OT 2
to **oversee** [ˌəʊvə'si:] überwachen; beaufsichtigen OT 4
to **overthrow** [ˌoʊvə'θroʊ] stürzen **WS 2**, 72
overtly [oʊ'vɜ:rtli] offen **WS 2**, 61
to **overuse** [ˌəʊvə'ju:s] zu oft verwenden OT 2
overview ['əʊvəvju:] Überblick; Übersicht OT 4
overweight [ˌəʊvə'weɪt] übergewichtig OT 5
to **overwhelm** [ˌoʊvə'wɛlm] überwältigen **WS 1**, 27
Ow! [aʊ] Au! OT 1
own [əʊn] eigene(r, -s) OT 1
on one's own [ɒn wʌnz 'əʊn] allein OT 2
to **own** [əʊn] besitzen OT 4
owner ['əʊnə] Besitzer(in) OT 2
oxygen ['ɒksɪdʒən] Sauerstoff **WS 3**, 99
ozone layer ['oʊzoʊn 'leɪə] Ozonschicht **WS 3**, 98

P

PA (public address) system [pi: 'eɪ ˌsɪstəm] Lautsprecheranlage OT 2
to **pack** [pæk] packen OT 2
package ['pækɪdʒ] Paket OT 3
packaged food ['pækɪdʒd fu:d] verpacktes Essen OT 4
packaging ['pækɪdʒɪŋ] Verpackung OT 3
packet ['pækɪt] Paket OT 2
pad [pæd] Notizblock OT 5
paddle ['pædl] Paddel OT 3
paddle-boarding ['pædlbɔ:dɪŋ] Paddle-Boarding OT 1
paddling ['pædlɪŋ] Paddeln OT 4
paediatrician [ˌpi:di'ætrɪʃən] Kinderarzt / -ärztin **WS 2**, 67
page [peɪdʒ] Seite OT 1
pagoda [pə'goʊdə] Pagode **WS 1**, 25
pain [peɪn] Schmerz OT 2
painful ['peɪnfl] schmerzhaft OT 2
painfully ['peɪnfəli] schmerzhaft OT 2
painkiller ['peɪnkɪlə] Schmerzmittel OT 2
paint [peɪnt] Farbe OT 2
to **paint** [peɪnt] malen OT 1
painted ['peɪntɪd] gestrichen OT 1
painting ['peɪntɪŋ] Malen; Gemälde OT 1
pair [peə] Paar OT 1
pajamas [pə'dʒɑ:mə] Schlafanzug; Pyjama OT 4
Pakistani [ˌpɑ:kɪ'stɑ:ni] Pakistaner(in); pakistanisch OT 4
palace ['pæləs] Palast OT 1
palm oil [pɑ:m 'ɔɪl] Palmöl **WS 1**, 21
pan [pæn] Pfanne OT 2
pancake ['pænkeɪk] Pfannkuchen OT 4
panda ['pændə] Pandabär OT 1
pandemic [pæn'demɪk] Pandemie OT 5
panel ['pænl] Paneel; Platte OT 5
to **panic** ['pænɪk] in Panik geraten OT 2
panoramic [ˌpænə'ræmɪk] Panorama... OT 3
panther ['pænθə] Panther OT 2
paper ['peɪpə] Papier OT 1
paperback ['pæpbæk] Taschenbuch **WS 3**, 96
paperwork ['peɪpəwɜ:k] Schreibarbeit OT 5
para-athlete ['pærəˌæθli:t] Para-Athlet(in) **WS 2**, 61
parade [pə'reɪd] Umzug; Parade OT 2
paradise ['pærədaɪs] Paradies OT 4
paragliding ['pærəglaɪdɪŋ] Gleitschirmfliegen OT 5
paragraph ['pærəgrɑ:f] Absatz OT 1
parallelism ['pærəlelɪzəm] Parallelismus OT 5
Paralympics [ˌpærə'lɪmpɪks] paralympische Spiele OT 3
to **paralyse** ['pærəlaɪz] lähmen **WS 2**, 61
paramedic [ˌpærə'medɪk] Rettungssanitäter(in) OT 1
to **paraphrase** ['pærəfreɪz] umschreiben OT 5
parasite ['pærəsaɪt] Parasit **WS 4**, 138
parcel ['pɑ:sl] Paket OT 4
pardon ['pɑ:dn] Verzeihung; Entschuldigung OT 5
parent ['peərənt] Elternteil OT 1
park [pɑ:k] Park OT 1
to **park** [pɑ:k] parken OT 1
park ranger ['pɑ:k ˌreɪndʒə] Forstbeamter / -beamtin OT 2
parking ticket ['pɑ:kɪŋ tɪkɪt] Parkzettel OT 1
parliament ['pɑ:ləmənt] Parlament OT 1
part [pɑ:t] Teil OT 1
part of speech [ˌpɑ:t əv 'spi:tʃ] Wortart OT 2
participant [pɑ:'tɪsɪpənt] Teilnehmer(in) **WS 2**, 57
to **participate** [pɑ:'tɪsɪpeɪt] teilnehmen OT 5
participation [pɑ:ˌtɪsɪ'peɪʃn] Beteiligung OT 5
participle [pɑ:'tɪsɪpl] Partizip OT 2
particular [pə'tɪkjələ] besondere(r, -s) OT 4
in particular [ɪn pə'tɪkjələr] insbesondere OT 5
particularly [pə'tɪkjələli] besonders OT 5
partition [pɑ:r'tɪʃən] Teilung **WS 1**, 12
to **partition** [pɑ:r'tɪʃən] teilen; aufteilen **WS 1**, 14
partly ['pɑ:tli] teilweise OT 3
partner ['pɑ:tnə] Partner(in) OT 1
partnership ['pɑ:tnəʃɪp] Partnerschaft; Kooperation OT 4
part-time [ˌpɑ:t 'taɪm] Teilzeit...; nebenberuflich OT 4
party ['pɑ:ti] Party; Feier OT 1
to **pass** [pɑ:s] zuspielen; an etw. vorbeifahren OT 3
to pass an exam [ˌpɑ:s ən ɪg'zæm] eine Prüfung bestehen OT 2
passage ['pæsɪdʒ] Abschnitt; Passage **WS 2**, 79
passenger ['pæsɪndʒə] Passagier(in); Fahrgast OT 2
passion ['pæʃn] Leidenschaft **WS 1**, 21
passionate ['pæʃənət] leidenschaftlich OT 4
passionately ['pæʃənətli] leidenschaftlich OT 5
passport ['pɑ:spɔ:t] Pass OT 2
passport control ['pɑ:spɔ:t kənˌtrəʊl] Passkontrolle OT 2
password ['pɑ:swɜ:d] Kennwort; Passwort OT 4
past [pɑ:st] nach OT 1
past participle [ˌpɑ:st pɑ:'tɪsɪpl] Partizip Perfekt OT 2

past progressive [pɑ:st prəˈgresɪv] Verlaufsform der Vergangenheit OT 2
pasta [ˈpæstə] Nudeln OT 1
to **paste** [peɪst] kleben; einfügen OT 2
pastor [ˈpɑ:stə] Pfarrer(in) OT 2
pastry [ˈpeɪstri] Gebäck; Teigwaren **WS 1**, 16
pasture [ˈpɑ:stʃə] Weide(land) **WS 1**, 32
pat [pæt] Klaps OT 3
pâté [ˈpæteɪ] Pastete OT 1
patent [ˈpætnt] Patent OT 4
to **patent** [ˈpætnt] patentieren OT 4
path [pɑ:θ] Weg OT 1
patient [ˈpeɪʃnt] Patient(in) OT 1
patriarchal [ˌpeɪtriˈɑ:rkl] patriarchalisch **WS 1**, 42
patriot [ˈpeɪtriət] Patriot(in) OT 2
patriotic [ˌpeɪtriˈɒtɪk] patriotisch **WS 1**, 43
to **patrol** [pəˈtroʊl] patroulieren **WS 2**, 67
patron [ˈpeɪtrən] Schirmherr(in) OT 5
patronizing [ˈpætrənaɪzɪŋ] herablassend **WS 2**, 61
pattern [ˈpætn] Muster OT 1
pause [pɔ:z] Pause OT 3
to **pause** [pɔ:z] eine Pause machen OT 3
pavement [ˈpeɪvmənt] Gehweg; Bürgersteig OT 1
to **pay** [ˈpeɪ] bezahlen OT 1
payday [ˈpeɪdeɪ] Zahltag OT 5
payment [ˈpeɪmənt] Bezahlung OT 2
PE (physical education) [ˌpi:ˈi:] Sportunterricht OT 1
pea [pi:] Erbse OT 1
peace [pi:s] Frieden OT 5
peaceful [ˈpi:sfl] friedlich; einträchtig OT 2
peak [pi:k] Gipfel; Spitzen... OT 5
pear [peə] Birne OT 1
pedal [ˈpedl] Pedal OT 4
to **pedal** [ˈpedl] in die Pedale treten OT 4
pedigree [ˈpedɪgri:] Rasse... OT 3
to **pee** [pi:] pinkeln **WS 3**, 96
peer [pɪə] Peer OT 5
pen [pen] Stift OT 1
penal [ˈpi:nl] strafrechtlich OT 5
penalty [ˈpenəlti] Strafe; Strafstoß OT 3
pencil [ˈpensl] Bleistift OT 1
pencil case [ˈpensl ˌkeɪs] Federtasche OT 1
pencil sharpener [ˈpensl ˌʃɑ:pnə] Anspitzer OT 1
penguin [ˈpeŋgwɪn] Pinguin OT 1
penicillin [ˌpenɪˈsɪlɪn] Penizillin OT 2
penny [ˈpeni] Penny OT 1
people [ˈpi:pl] Leute OT 1
pepper [ˈpepə] Paprika; Pfeffer OT 2
to **perceive** [pəˈsi:v] empfinden; erkennen OT 5
percent [pəˈsent] Prozent OT 4
percentage [pəˈsentɪdʒ] Prozent OT 3
perception [pəˈsepʃn] Wahrnehmung **WS 2**, 62
perfect [ˈpɜ:fɪkt] perfekt OT 1
to **perfect** [ˈpɜ:fɪkt] perfektionieren OT 4
to **perform** [pəˈfɔ:m] auftreten OT 2
performance [pəˈfɔ:məns] Aufführung OT 2
performer [pəˈfɔ:mə] Künstler(in); Darsteller(in); Interpret(in) OT 2
perhaps [pəˈhæps] vielleicht OT 3
perilous [ˈperɪləs] gefährlich **WS 2**, 65
period [ˈpɪəriəd] Zeit; Epoche OT 3
periodically [ˌpɪəriˈɒdɪkli] regelmäßig **WS 4**, 133
permanent [ˈpɜ:mənənt] permanent; dauerhaft OT 5
permission [pəˈmɪʃn] Erlaubnis OT 2
permit [pəˈmɪt] Erlaubnis OT 3
to **permit** [pəˈmɪt] erlauben OT 5
to **persecute** [ˈpɜ:sɪkju:t] verfolgen **WS 2**, 82
persecution [ˌpɜ:sɪˈkju:ʃn] Verfolgung OT 4
person [ˈpɜ:sn] Person; Mensch OT 1
personal [ˈpɜ:sənl] persönlich OT 2
personality [ˌpɜ:səˈnæləti] Persönlichkeit OT 4
to **personalize** [ˈpɜ:sənəlaɪz] personalisieren OT 5
personification [pəˌsɒnɪfɪˈkeɪʃn] Personifikation; Verkörperung OT 5
personnel [ˌpɜ:səˈnel] Personal; Mitarbeiter OT 5
perspective [pəˈspektɪv] Ansicht; Perspektive OT 4
to **persuade** [pəˈsweɪd] überreden; überzeugen OT 3
persuasive [pəˈsweɪsɪv] überzeugend OT 5
pessimistic [ˌpesɪˈmɪstɪk] pessimistisch OT 4
pest [pest] Schädling; Plage; Plagegeist OT 2
pesticide [ˈpestɪsaɪd] Pestizid OT 4
pet [pet] Haustier OT 1
petition [pəˈtɪʃn] Antrag OT 3
petrol [ˈpetrəl] Benzin OT 4
pharmacist [ˈfɑ:məsɪst] Apotheker(in) OT 2
pharmacy [ˈfɑ:məsi] Apotheke OT 2
to **phase out** [feɪz aʊt] abschaffen **WS 3**, 111
PhD (Doctor of Philosophy) [ˌpi: eɪtʃ ˈdi:] Doktortitel; Doktor der Philosophie OT 5
phenomenon [fəˈnɒmɪnən] Phänomen OT 5
philanthropist [fɪˈlænθrəpɪst] Philanthrop(in); Wohltäter(in) **WS 3**, 100
philosophical [ˌfɪləˈsɒfɪkl] philosophisch **WS 2**, 68
philosophy [fəˈlɒsəfi] Philosophie OT 4
phone [fəʊn] Telefon OT 1
to **phone** [fəʊn] telefonieren OT 2
phone call [ˈfəʊn kɔ:l] Telefonat OT 2
phonograph [ˈfəʊnəgrɑ:f] Phonograph OT 4
photo [ˈfəʊtəʊ] Foto OT 1
to **photocopy** [ˈfəʊtəʊkɒpi] fotokopieren OT 4
photograph [ˈfəʊtəgrɑ:f] Foto OT 1
photographer [fəˈtɒgrəfə] Fotograf(in) OT 3
photography [fəˈtɒgrəfi] Fotografie OT 4
phrase [freɪz] Wendung OT 1
physical [ˈfɪzɪkl] körperlich OT 2
physics [ˈfɪzɪks] Physik OT 4
pianist [ˈpɪənɪst] Pianist(in) OT 2
piano [piˈænəʊ] Klavier OT 1
to **pick** [pɪk] pflücken; auswählen OT 1
to **pick up** [pɪk ʌp] aufheben OT 2
picker [ˈpɪkə] Sammler(in) OT 3
pickle [ˈpɪkl] Gurke; Gewürzgurke OT 1
pickpocket [ˈpɪkpɒkɪt] Taschendieb(in) OT 4
picnic [ˈpɪknɪk] Picknick OT 1
picture [ˈpɪktʃə] Bild OT 1
pie [paɪ] (gedeckter) Obstkuchen OT 1
piece [pi:s] Stück; Teil OT 1
in one piece [ɪn ˌwʌn ˈpi:s] heil OT 2
pier [pɪər] Kai OT 5
pierced [pɪəst] durchstochen OT 3
pig [pɪg] Schwein OT 1
pigeon [ˈpɪdʒɪn] Taube **WS 1**, 39
pile [paɪl] Haufen; Stapel OT 5
pilgrimage [ˈpɪlgrɪmɪdʒ] Pilgerfahrt OT 3
pill [pɪl] Pille OT 1
pillar [ˈpɪlə] Säule **WS 1**, 44
pillow [ˈpɪləʊ] Kopfkissen OT 2
pilot [ˈpaɪlət] Pilot(in) OT 3

to pilot ['paɪlət] steuern OT 4
pin [pɪn] Stecknadel OT 1
to pin [pɪn] heften OT 1
pineapple ['paɪnæpl] Ananas OT 3
ping-pong ['pɪŋ pɒŋ] Tischtennis OT 1
pink [pɪŋk] rosa OT 1
pioneer [ˌpaɪə'nɪə] Pionier(in) OT 4
to pipe [paɪp] pumpen **WS 1**, 24
pipeline ['paɪplaɪn] Pipeline OT 4
pirate ['paɪrət] Pirat(in) OT 3
pitch [pɪtʃ] Spielfeld OT 3
pizza ['pi:tsə] Pizza OT 1
pizza deliverer ['pi:tsə dɪ'lɪvərə] Pizzalieferant(in) OT 4
place [pleɪs] Ort OT 1
to place [pleɪs] plazieren; vermitteln **WS 2**, 55
place mat ['pleɪs mæt] Platzdeckchen OT 2
plagiarism ['pleɪdʒərɪzəm] Plagiat OT 2
to plagiarize ['pleɪdʒəraɪz] plagiieren OT 2
plain [pleɪn] nicht Besonders; gutbürgerlich OT 4
plains [pleɪnz] Prärie; Flachland OT 5
to plan [plæn] planen OT 1
plane [pleɪn] Flugzeug OT 1
planet ['plænɪt] Planet OT 2
planetarium [ˌplænɪ'teəriəm] Planetarium OT 1
planetary science ['plænətri 'saɪəns] planetarische Wissenschaft; Planetenforschung OT 4
planner ['plænə] Planer(in) OT 3
plant [plɑ:nt] Pflanze OT 2
plaster ['plɑ:stə] Verputz; Gips; Pflaster OT 1
plastic ['plæstɪk] Kunststoff OT 2
plate [pleɪt] Teller OT 1
platform ['plætfɔ:m] Bahnsteig OT 1
platypus ['plætɪpəs] Schnabeltier OT 5
plausible ['plɔ:zəbl] einleuchtend **WS 4**, 141
play [pleɪ] Theaterstück OT 1
to play [pleɪ] spielen OT 1
player ['pleɪə] Spieler(in) OT 1
playground ['pleɪgraʊnd] Spielplatz; Schulhof OT 1
playlist ['pleɪlɪst] Playlist; Wiedergabeliste OT 4
playwright ['pleɪraɪt] Dramatiker(in) OT 5
to plead [pli:d] sich bekennen; plädieren OT 5
pleasant ['pleznt] angenehm OT 5
please [pli:z] bitte OT 1
pleased [pli:zd] zufrieden OT 1
pleasure ['pleʒə] Freude OT 1
plenty ['plenti] reichlich; viel OT 2
plight [plaɪt] Notlage **WS 1**, 21
plot [plɒt] Handlung OT 4
plough [plaʊ] Pflug **WS 1**, 32
to pluck [plʌk] ziehen **WS 1**, 27
plum [plʌm] Pflaume OT 1
plural ['plʊərəl] Plural; Mehrzahl OT 1
poacher ['pəʊtʃə] Wilderer / Wilderin OT 3
poaching ['pəʊtʃɪŋ] Wilderei OT 3
pocket ['pɒkɪt] Tasche OT 2
pocketknife ['pɒkɪtnaɪf] Taschenmesser OT 2
pocket money ['pɒkɪt mʌni] Taschengeld OT 2
podcast ['pɒdkɑ:st] Podcast OT 1
podium ['pəʊdiəm] Podium OT 3
poem ['pəʊɪm] Gedicht OT 1
poet ['pəʊɪt] Dichter(in) OT 3
poetry ['pəʊətri] Poesie; Dichtung OT 1
poignant ['pɔɪnjənt] ergreifend; schmerzlich **WS 2**, 57
point [pɔɪnt] Punkt OT 1
to point [pɔɪnt] zeigen OT 1
pointless ['pɔɪntləs] sinnlos; zwecklos OT 4
pointy ['pɔɪnti] spitz; spitz zulaufend **WS 3**, 97
poison ['pɔɪzən] Gift OT 1
to poison [ˌpɔɪzn] vergiften **WS 4**, 136
poisonous ['pɔɪzənəs] giftig OT 5
polar bear ['pəʊlə beə] Eisbär **WS 3**, 98
to polarize ['pəʊləˌraɪz] polarisieren; spalten **WS 1**, 21
pole [pəʊl] Stange; Pol OT 3
police [pə'li:s] Polizei OT 1
police officer [pə'li:s ɒfɪsə] Polizist(in) OT 1
policy ['pɒləsi] Politik; Regel OT 3
Polish ['pəʊlɪʃ] polnisch OT 2
polite [pə'laɪt] höflich OT 1
political [pə'lɪtɪkl] politisch OT 4
politician [ˌpɒlə'tɪʃn] Politiker(in) OT 3
to politicize [pə'lɪtɪˌsaɪz] politisieren; auf Politik beziehen **WS 1**, 21
politics ['pɒlətɪks] Politik **WS 1**, 19
poll [pəʊl] Umfrage OT 5
pollen ['pɒlən] Pollen **WS 4**, 138
to pollinate ['pɒləneɪt] bestäuben **WS 4**, 133
to pollute [pə'lu:t] verschmutzen; verseuchen OT 5
pollution [pə'lu:ʃn] Umweltverschmutzung OT 2
polo ['pəʊləʊ] Polo OT 3
polyp ['pɒlɪp] Polyp OT 5
polyurethane [ˌpɒli'jʊərəθeɪn] Polyurethan (Kunststoff) OT 4
pond [pɒnd] Teich OT 4
pony ['pəʊni] Pony OT 3
poo [pu:] Kot **WS 2**, 67
pool [pu:l] Lache; Schwimmbecken OT 1
poor [pʊə] arm OT 1
pop [pɒp] Pop OT 2
popcorn ['pɒpkɔ:n] Popcorn OT 2
Pope [pəʊp] Papst OT 3
popular ['pɒpjələ] beliebt OT 1
to populate ['pɒpjuleɪt] bevölkern **WS 1**, 12
population [ˌpɒpjə'leɪʃən] Bevölkerung OT 3
to pop up [pɒp 'ʌp] auftauchen; erscheinen **WS 2**, 68
porch [pɔ:tʃ] Veranda OT 4
pork [pɔ:k] Schweinefleisch OT 2
porridge ['pɒrɪdʒ] Haferbrei OT 3
port [pɔ:t] Hafen OT 2
portable ['pɔ:təbl] tragbar OT 4
portal ['pɔ:tl] Portalseite OT 5
portfolio [pɔ:t'fəʊliəʊ] Mappe; Portfolio OT 4
portion ['pɔ:ʃn] Portion; Menge OT 4
to portray [pɔ:'treɪ] darstellen **WS 2**, 57
to pose [pəʊz] stellen; darstellen **WS 2**, 81
to pose a threat [pəʊz ə θret] eine Bedrohung darstellen OT 5
position [pə'zɪʃn] Position OT 3
to position [pə'zɪʃn] positionieren **WS 2**, 57
positive ['pɒzətɪv] Positiv OT 1
possession [pə'zeʃn] Besitz OT 5
possessive [pə'zesɪv] besitzanzeigend; Possessiv... OT 1
possessive determiner [pəˌzesɪv dɪ'tɜ:mɪnə] Possessivbegleiter OT 1
possibility [ˌpɒsə'bɪləti] Möglichkeit OT 2
possible ['pɒsəbl] möglich OT 2
post [pəʊst] Post OT 1
to post [pəʊst] posten OT 3
post-apocalyptic [pəʊst əˌpɒkə'lɪptɪk] postapokalyptisch; nach der Apokalypse **WS 3**, 104
post box ['pəʊst bɒks] Briefkasten OT 1
postcard ['pəʊstkɑ:d] Postkarte OT 1
postcode ['pəʊstkəʊd] Postleitzahl OT 1
poster ['pəʊstə] Plakat OT 1

postgraduate [ˌpəʊstˈgrædʒuət] Graduierten- **WS 3**, 112
potato [pəˈteɪtəʊ] Kartoffel OT 1
jacket potato [ˌdʒækɪt pəˈteɪtəʊ] Ofenkartoffel OT 1
mashed potato [ˌmæʃt pəˈteɪtəʊ] Kartoffelbrei OT 1
sweet potato [ˌswiːt pəˈteɪtəʊ] Süßkartoffel OT 4
potent [ˈpoʊtənt] mächtig **WS 1**, 19
potential [pəˈtenʃl] Potenzial OT 5
potion [ˈpoʊʃən] Trank **WS 2**, 62
poultry [ˈpəʊltri] Geflügel OT 2
pound [paʊnd] Pfund OT 1
to **pour** [pɔː] gießen OT 1
poverty [ˈpɒvəti] Armut OT 3
powder [ˈpaʊdər] Pulver **WS 1**, 12
power [ˈpaʊə] Kraft; Macht OT 5
powered [ˈpaʊəd] angetrieben OT 4
powerful [ˈpaʊəfl] mächtig; kräftig OT 5
powerhouse [ˈpaʊəhaʊs] Kraftzentrum **WS 1**, 25
powerless [ˈpaʊələs] kraftlos; machtlos OT 4
powwow [ˈpaʊwaʊ] Powwow **WS 3**, 95
practical [ˈpræktɪkl] praktisch OT 3
practice [ˈpræktɪs] Praxis; Übung OT 2
to **practise** [ˈpræktɪs] üben OT 1
practitioner [prækˈtɪʃənə] Fachkraft **WS 3**, 123
praise [preɪz] Lob **WS 1**, 26
to **praise** [preɪz] loben **WS 1**, 30
to **pray** [preɪ] beten OT 5
prayer [preə] Gebet OT 4
preacher [ˈpriːtʃə] Prediger(in) **WS 2**, 72
precept [ˈpriːsɛpt] Prinzip **WS 3**, 94
precise [prɪˈsaɪs] genau; konkret OT 5
preconception [ˌpriːkənˈsepʃn] Vorurteil **WS 2**, 71
predator [ˈpredətər] Raubtier; Räuber OT 5
to **predict** [prɪˈdɪkt] vorhersagen OT 4
predictable [prɪˈdɪktəbl] vorhersehbar OT 5
prediction [prɪˈdɪkʃn] Vorhersage OT 2
to **pre-empt** [priːˈɛmpt] zuvorkommen **WS 3**, 107
to **prefer** [prɪˈfɜː] vorziehen OT 1
preferable [ˈprɛfərəbl] vorziehbar **WS 2**, 78
preference [ˈprefrəns] Vorliebe OT 3
pregnant [ˈpregnənt] schwanger OT 4
prejudice [ˈpredʒədɪs] Nachteil; Vorurteil OT 5
premier [ˈpremiə] erste OT 2
preparation [ˌprepəˈreɪʃn] Vorbereitung OT 2
to **prepare** [prɪˈpeə] vorbereiten OT 1
preposition [ˌprepəˈzɪʃn] Präposition; Verhältniswort OT 2
preschool [ˈpriːskuːl] Kindergarten; Vorschule OT 5
to **prescribe** [prɪˈskraɪb] verschreiben **WS 1**, 39
presence [ˈprezns] Anwesenheit **WS 3**, 96
present [ˈpreznt] Geschenk; Gegenwart OT 1
to **present** [prɪˈzent] präsentieren; vorstellen OT 1
presentation [ˌpreznˈteɪʃn] Präsentation OT 1
presenter [prɪˈzentə] Moderator(in) OT 5
present perfect [ˌpreznt ˈpɜːfɪkt] vollendete Gegenwart OT 2
present progressive [ˈpreznt prəˌgresɪv] Verlaufsform des Präsens OT 1
to **preserve** [prɪˈzɜːv] erhalten OT 3
to **preside** [prɪˈzaɪd] den Vorsitz führen **WS 3**, 94
president [ˈprezɪdənt] Präsident(in) OT 4
to **press** [pres] drücken OT 1
pressure [ˈpreʃə] Druck OT 3
pressured [ˈpreʃəd] unter Druck gesetzt OT 5
prestige [prɛˈstiːʒ] Prestige **WS 3**, 107
prestigious [preˈstɪdʒəs] renommiert **WS 1**, 16
to **presume** [prɪˈzjuːm] annehmen **WS 3**, 106
to **pretend** [prɪˈtend] vorgeben; so tun, als ob OT 2
pretty [ˈprɪti] hübsch OT 1
to **prevent** [prɪˈvent] verhindern; abhalten OT 4
preventable [prɪˈventəbl] vermeidbar OT 5
prevention [prɪˈvenʃn] Vermeidung OT 2
previous [ˈpriːviəs] bisherig; vorherig OT 4
previously [ˈpriːviəsli] früher OT 3
price [praɪs] Preis OT 1
pride [praɪd] Stolz OT 4
primary [ˈpraɪməri] Haupt...; Grund... OT 1
prince [prɪns] Prinz OT 1
principal [ˈprɪnsəpl] Rektor(in) OT 2
principle [ˈprɪnsəpl] Prinzip **WS 1**, 18
principled [ˈprɪnsɪpəld] prinzipientreu **WS 1**, 18
to **print** [prɪnt] (aus)drucken OT 2
printer [ˈprɪntər] Drucker OT 5
prior [ˈpraɪə] vorherige **WS 1**, 38
to **prioritize** [praɪˈɒrətaɪz] priorisieren **WS 1**, 25
priority [praɪˈɒrəti] Priorität **WS 1**, 44
prison [ˈprɪzn] Gefängnis OT 1
prisoner [ˈprɪznər] Gefangene; Häftling OT 5
privacy [ˈprɪvəsi] Privatsphäre OT 3
private [ˈpraɪvət] privat OT 3
privateer [ˌpraɪvəˈtɪə] Freibeuter(in) OT 3
privilege [ˈprɪvəlɪdʒ] Privileg; Recht OT 5
privileged [ˈprɪvəlɪdʒd] privilegiert OT 5
prize [praɪz] Preis; Gewinn OT 1
probability [ˌprɒbəˈbɪləti] Wahrscheinlichkeit **WS 2**, 84
probably [ˈprɒbəbli] wahrscheinlich OT 2
probation [prəˈbeɪʃn] Bewährung OT 5
problem [ˈprɒbləm] Problem OT 1
problematic [ˌprɒbləˈmætɪk] problematisch **WS 2**, 57
problem-solver [ˈprɒbləm sɒlvə] Problemlöser(in) OT 4
problem-solving [ˈprɒbləm sɒlvɪŋ] problemlösend OT 4
pro bono [ˌprəʊ ˈbəʊnəʊ] ehrenamtlich; kostenlos OT 5
procedure [prəˈsiːdʒə] Prozedur; Verfahren OT 5
to **proceed** [prəˈsiːd] fortfahren **WS 1**, 39
process [ˈprəʊses] Prozess OT 4
to **process** [prəʊses] verarbeiten OT 4
procession [prəˈseʃn] Umzug OT 2
to **produce** [prəˈdjuːs] erzeugen OT 3
producer [prəˈdjuːsər] Erzeuger(in); Hersteller(in) OT 5
product [ˈprɒdʌkt] Produkt OT 2
production [prəˈdʌkʃn] Produktion; Herstellung OT 4
product placement [ˌprɒdʌkt ˈpleɪsmənt] Produktplatzierung OT 5
profession [prəˈfeʃn] Beruf; Profession OT 5
professional [prəˈfeʃənl] professionell OT 2
professor [prəˈfesə] Professor(in) OT 4
proficiency [prəˈfɪʃnsi] Kenntnisse **WS 3**, 111
profile [ˈprəʊfaɪl] Steckbrief; Profil OT 3

to **profile** ['prəʊfaɪl] ein Profil erstellen **WS 2**, 55
profit ['prɒfɪt] Profit; Gewinn OT 4
profound [prə'faʊnd] profund; tief OT 5
program ['prəʊgræm] Programm; Kurs OT 3
programme ['prəʊgræm] Programm; Sendung OT 2
to **programme** ['prəʊgræm] programmieren OT 2
programmer ['prəʊgræmə] Programmierer(in) OT 3
programming ['prəʊgræmɪŋ] Programmieren OT 1
progress ['prəʊgres] Fortschritt OT 4
progressive [prə'gresɪv] fortschrittlich; progressiv OT 1
project ['prɒdʒekt] Projekt OT 1
projector [prə'dʒektə] Projektor; Beamer OT 1
prolonged [prə'lɒŋd] anhaltend; verlängert OT 5
prom [prɒm] Schulball OT 3
prominent ['prɒmɪnənt] hervorstehend **WS 1**, 22
promise ['prɒmɪs] Versprechen OT 2
to **promise** ['prɒmɪs] versprechen OT 2
to **promote** [prə'məʊt] fördern OT 5
prompt [prɒmpt] Stichwort; Aufforderung OT 4
to **prompt** [prɒmpt] auslösen; veranlassen **WS 2**, 81
pronoun ['prəʊnaʊn] Pronomen; Fürwort OT 1
to **pronounce** [prə'naʊns] aussprechen OT 3
pronunciation [prəˌnʌnsi'eɪʃn] Aussprache OT 2
proof [pru:f] Beweis OT 4
prop [prɒp] Stütze; Requisite OT 1
proper ['prɒpə] richtig; anständig OT 3
properly ['prɒpəli] ordentlich; in richtiger Art und Weise OT 2
property ['prɒpəti] Eigentum; Immobilie OT 5
proportion [prə'pɔ:ʃn] Anteil OT 5
to **propose** [prə'pəʊz] einen Heiratsantrag machen OT 5
proposition [ˌprɒpə'zɪʃn] Vorschlag **WS 4**, 132
pro [prəʊ] Vorteil OT 2
to **prosecute** ['prɒsɪkju:t] bestrafen; verfolgen OT 5
prosecutor ['prɒsɪkju:tə] Staatsanwalt / -anwältin OT 5
prospective [prə'spektɪv] möglich **WS 3**, 103
prosperity [prɒ'sperəti] Wohlstand **WS 1**, 24
prosperous ['prɒspərəs] wohlhabend **WS 3**, 94
protagonist [prə'tægənɪst] Protagonist(in) OT 5
to **protect** [prə'tekt] schützen OT 2
protein ['prəʊti:n] Protein; Eiweiß OT 4
protest ['prəʊtest] Protest OT 3
to **protest** [prəʊ'test] protestieren OT 3
protester [prə'testə] Demonstrant(in); Protestierer(in) OT 5
protocol ['prəʊtəkɒl] Protokoll OT 5
prototype ['prəʊtətaɪp] Prototyp OT 4
proud [praʊd] stolz OT 2
to **prove** [pru:v] beweisen OT 3
proverb ['prɒvɜ:b] Sprichwort OT 5
to **provide** [prə'vaɪd] zur Verfügung stellen; versorgen (mit) OT 4
province ['prɒvɪns] Provinz OT 5
to **provoke** [prə'vəʊk] verursachen; hervorrufen OT 5
psycho ['saɪkəʊ] Psychopath(in) OT 4
psychologist [saɪ'kɒlədʒɪst] Psychologe / -login OT 5
psychology [saɪ'kɒlədʒi] Psychologie OT 5
pub [pʌb] Kneipe OT 2
puberty ['pju:bəti] Pubertät OT 5
public transport [ˌpʌblɪk 'trænspɔ:t] öffentliche Verkehrsmittel OT 2
public ['pʌblɪk] öffentlich OT 2
publication [ˌpʌblɪ'keɪʃn] Veröffentlichung OT 5
publicity [pʌb'lɪsəti] Publizität OT 5
to **publicize** ['pʌblɪˌsaɪz] veröffentlichen **WS 1**, 33
to **publish** ['pʌblɪʃ] veröffentlichen OT 2
publisher ['pʌblɪʃə] Verleger(in) OT 5
pueblo ['pwebləʊ] Pueblo OT 3
to **pull** [pʊl] ziehen OT 1
pulse [pʌls] Hülsenfrucht OT 4
to **pump** [pʌmp] pumpen OT 4
pumpkin ['pʌmpkɪn] Kürbis OT 2
pun [pʌn] Wortspiel **WS 3**, 119
punchy ['pʌntʃi] markant **WS 2**, 72
punctual ['pʌŋktʃuəl] pünktlich OT 4
to **punctuate** ['pʌŋktʃueɪt] mit Satzzeichen versehen OT 3
punctuation [ˌpʌŋktʃu'eɪʃn] Zeichensetzung OT 1
to **punish** ['pʌnɪʃ] bestrafen OT 3
punishment ['pʌnɪʃmənt] Strafe OT 5
puppet ['pʌpɪt] Marionette **WS 1**, 27
puppy ['pʌpi] Welpe OT 2
purchase ['pɜ:tʃəs] Kauf; Ankauf OT 4
to **purchase** ['pɜ:tʃəs] kaufen; erwerben **WS 3**, 98
pure [pjʊə] rein **WS 1**, 39
purple ['pɜ:pl] lila OT 1
purpose ['pɜ:pəs] Zweck OT 4
purposeful ['pɜ:pəsfl] zweckgerichtet **WS 3**, 112
to **pursue** [pə'sju:] verfolgen OT 4
pursuit [pə'sju:t] Suche; Verfolgung **WS 1**, 21
to **push** [pʊʃ] stoßen OT 2
pushy ['pʊʃi] aufdringlich; penetrant OT 4
to **put** [pʊt ʌp] tun; stellen OT 1
to **put away** [pʊt' əweɪ] wegräumen OT 2
to **put on** ['pʊt ɒn] aufführen; veranstalten OT 2
to **put out** [pʊt aʊt] löschen OT 2
to **put up** [pʊt] heben; errichten OT 1
puzzle ['pʌzl] Puzzle; Rätsel OT 2
pyjamas [pə'dʒɑ:məz] Schlafanzug OT 3

Q

quack! [kwæk] Quak! (Ente) OT 2
quad biking [kwɒd 'baɪkɪŋ] Vierradfahrzeug fahren OT 2
qualification [ˌkwɒlɪfɪ'keɪʃn] Qualifikation; Eignung OT 5
qualified ['kwɒlɪfaɪd] qualifiziert OT 5
to **qualify** ['kwɒlɪˌfaɪ] (sich) qualifizieren **WS 2**, 59
quality ['kwɒləti] Eigenschaft; Qualität OT 3
to **quantify** ['kwɒntɪfaɪ] quantifizieren **WS 4**, 142
quantity ['kwɒləti] Anzahl; Menge OT 4
quarantine ['kwɔ:rənˌti:n] Quarantäne **WS 2**, 67
quarry ['kwɒri] Steinbruch OT 1
quarter ['kwɔ:tə] Viertel; Quartier OT 1
quarter to ['kwɔ:tə tə] viertel vor OT 1
quarterback ['kwɔ:təbæk] Quarterback OT 2
queen [kwi:n] Königin OT 1
queer [kwɪər] schwul; queer OT 5
quesadilla [ˌkeɪsə'di:ə] Quesadilla OT 4
quest [kwɛst] Bestreben; Suche **WS 3**, 98
question ['kwestʃən] Frage OT 1
to **question** ['kwestʃən] (be)fragen; in Frage stellen **WS 1**, 15
questionnaire [ˌkwestʃə'neə] Fragebogen OT 1

queue [kjuː] Schlange; Warteschlange OT 1
to **queue** [kjuː] anstehen; Schlange stehen OT 4
quick [kwɪk] schnell OT 2
quickly ['kwɪkli] schnell OT 2
quiet ['kwaɪət] still; ruhig OT 1
quilt [kwɪlt] Steppdecke OT 4
to **quit** [kwɪt] kündigen; verlassen OT 4
quite [kwaɪt] ziemlich OT 2
quiz [kwɪz] Quiz OT 2
quotation mark [kwəʊ'teɪʃn mɑːk] Anführungszeichen OT 2
to **quote** [kwəʊt] zitieren OT 2

R

rabbit ['ræbɪt] Kaninchen OT 1
race [reɪs] Rennen OT 2
racial ['reɪʃl] Rassen- **WS 1**, 21
racing ['reɪsɪŋ] Rennsport OT 2
racism ['reɪsɪzəm] Rassismus OT 5
racist ['reɪsɪst] rassistisch OT 4
racket ['rækɪt] Schläger OT 2
radiation [ˌreɪdi'eɪʃən] Strahlung **WS 3**, 98
radical ['rædɪkl] radikal; grundlegend OT 4
to **radicalize** ['rædɪkəˌlaɪz] radikalisieren **WS 1**, 14
radio ['reɪdiəʊ] Radio OT 1
radio station ['reɪdiəʊ ˌsteɪʃn] Radiosender OT 2
radius ['reɪdiəs] Radius OT 2
rafting: white water rafting [waɪt 'wɔːtə 'rɑːftɪŋ] Wildwasser fahren OT 3
to **rage** [reɪdʒ] wüten OT 5
raid [reɪd] Razzia OT 5
rail [reɪl] Schiene; Eisenbahn OT 2
railway ['reɪlweɪ] Bahn; Eisenbahn OT 1
railway line ['reɪlweɪ laɪn] Eisenbahnlinie OT 2
to **rain** [reɪn] regnen OT 1
rainbow ['reɪnbəʊ] Regenbogen OT 1
raincoat ['reɪnkəʊt] Regenmantel OT 3
rainfall ['reɪnfɔːl] Regen; Niederschlag OT 5
rainforest ['reɪnfɒrɪst] Regenwald OT 2
rainstorm ['reɪnstɔːm] Regenschauer; Gewitter OT 5
rainwater ['reɪnwɔːtə] Regenwasser OT 4
to **raise** [reɪz] heben; erheben OT 2
rally ['ræli] Treffen; Kundgebung OT 4
ramp [ræmp] Rampe OT 2
random ['rændəm] zufällig; willkürlich OT 5
to **range** [reɪndʒ] umfassen; reichen von … bis OT 4
ranger ['reɪndʒə] Aufseher(in); Förster(in) OT 3
to **rank** ['ræŋk] in eine Rangfolge bringen OT 4
ranking ['ræŋkɪŋ] Rangfolge OT 4
rap [ræp] Rap OT 1
rape [reɪp] Vergewaltigung **WS 1**, 14
rapid ['ræpɪd] schnell **WS 3**, 98
rapping ['ræpɪŋ] Rappen OT 1
rare [reə] selten OT 2
raspberry ['rɑːzbəri] Himbeere OT 1
to **rate** [reɪt] bewerten OT 2
rather ['rɑːðə] ziemlich OT 3
to **ration** ['ræʃən] rationieren; einschränken **WS 1**, 24
raw [rɔː] roh OT 3
ray [reɪ] Strahl **WS 2**, 65
razor ['reɪzə] Rasierer **WS 2**, 79
to **reach** [riːtʃ] erreichen OT 3
to **react** [ri'ækt] reagieren OT 3
reaction [ri'ækʃn] Reaktion OT 4
to **read** [riːd] lesen OT 1
reader ['riːdə] Leser(in) OT 3
reading ['riːdɪŋ] Lesen OT 1
ready ['redi] bereit OT 1
real [rɪəl] echt OT 1
realistic [ˌriːə'lɪstɪk] realistisch OT 4
realistically [ˌriːə'lɪstɪkli] realistisch OT 5
reality [ri'æləti] Realität OT 4
to **realize** ['riːəlaɪz] erkennen OT 2
really ['riːəli] wirklich; sehr OT 1
reason ['riːzn] Grund OT 1
reasoned ['riːzənd] begründet **WS 3**, 112
to **reassess** [ˌriːə'ses] einschätzen OT 5
to **reassure** [ˌriːə'ʃʊr] versichern **WS 1**, 27
to **rebell** ['rebl] rebellieren OT 4
rebellion [rɪ'beljən] Aufstand OT 4
to **recall** [rɪ'kɔːl] erinnern an OT 5
to **receive** [rɪ'siːv] erhalten OT 2
recent ['riːsnt] neueste(r); jüngst OT 4
recently ['riːsntli] neulich OT 3
reception [rɪ'sepʃn] Rezeption; Empfang OT 1
receptionist [rɪ'sepʃənɪst] Empfangschef(in); Rezeptionist(in) OT 1
recess ['riːses] Pause **WS 2**, 63
recipe ['resəpi] Rezept OT 2
to **recite** [rɪ'saɪt] rezitieren; auswendig aufsagen OT 4
recognition [ˌrekəg'nɪʃn] Anerkennung OT 5
to **recognize** ['rekəgnaɪz] erkennen OT 2
to **recommend** [ˌrekə'mend] empfehlen OT 2
recommendation [ˌrekəmen'deɪʃn] Empfehlung OT 5
reconciliation [ˌrekənsɪli'eɪʃn] Versöhnung OT 5
to **record** [rɪ'kɔːd] aufnehmen OT 1
to **recount** [rɪ'kaʊnt] berichten von **WS 2**, 78
to **recover** [rɪ'kʌvə] sich erholen OT 4
re-creation [ˌriːkri'eɪʃn] Nachstellung; Neugestaltung OT 4
recreational [ˌrekri'eɪʃənl] Freizeit... OT 3
rectangular [rek'tæŋgjələ] rechteckig OT 2
to **recycle** [ˌriː'saɪkl] wiederverwerten OT 2
recycler [ˌriː'saɪklə] Wiederverwerter(in) OT 3
recycling [ˌriː'saɪklɪŋ] Recycling OT 2
red [red] rot OT 1
to **redevelop** [ˌriːdɪ'vɛləp] sanieren **WS 1**, 39
to **reduce** [rɪ'djuːs] reduzieren; verringern OT 2
reef [riːf] Riff OT 5
reel [riːl] Sammlung von Videos **WS 4**, 142
to **reel** [riːl] erschüttert sein **WS 3**, 97
re-enactment [ɪ'næktmənt] Nachstellung OT 4
to **refer** [rɪ'fɜː] sich beziehen OT 3
referee [ˌrefə'ri] Schiedsrichter(in) OT 3
reference ['refrəns] Orientierung; Verweis OT 4
referendum [ˌrefə'rendəm] Abstimmung; Referendum **WS 1**, 14
to **refine** [rɪ'faɪn] verfeinern OT 4
to **reflect** [rɪ'flekt] spiegeln OT 5
reformation [ˌrefə'meɪʃn] Reformation OT 4
refrain [rɪ'freɪn] Refrain **WW**, 11
refreshment [rɪ'freʃmənt] Erfrischungsgetränk OT 2
refrigerator [rɪ'frɪdʒəreɪtə] Kühlschrank OT 4
refugee [ˌrefju'dʒiː] Flüchtling OT 4
refugee camp [ˌrefju'dʒiː kæmp] Flüchtlingslager OT 4
refuse ['refjuːs] Müll OT 2
to **refuse** [rɪ'fjuːz] sich weigern OT 4

refuse collector ['refju:s ˌkəlektə] Müllmann / -frau OT 2
regard: with regard to [wɪð rɪ'gɑ:rd tu:] unter Berücksichtigung **WS 1**, 43
to **regard** [rɪ'gɑ:d] ansehen **WS 1**, 14
regarding [rɪ'gɑ:dɪŋ] bezüglich OT 5
reggae ['regeɪ] Reggae OT 2
regime [reɪ'ʒi:m] Regime **WS 2**, 73
region ['ri:dʒən] Region OT 4
regional ['ri:dʒənl] regional OT 5
to **register** ['redʒɪstə] (sich) anmelden; registrieren OT 4
to **regret** [rɪ'gret] bereuen OT 2
regular ['regjələ] regelmäßig OT 1
regularly ['regjələli] regelmäßig OT 2
regulation [ˌregju'leɪʃn] Vorschrift; Regulation OT 5
rehearsal [rɪ'hɜ:sl] Probe OT 2
to **rehearse** [rɪ'hɜ:s] proben OT 3
reign [reɪn] Herrschaft OT 3
to **reign** [reɪn] herrschen OT 3
to **reincarnate** [ˌri:ɪn'kɑ:rneɪt] wiedergeboren werden **WS 1**, 32
reindeer ['reɪndɪə] Rentier OT 2
to **reinforce** [ˌri:ɪn'fɔ:s] verstärken; bekräftigen OT 5
to **reinvent** [ˌri:ɪn'vent] wieder erfinden OT 4
to **reiterate** [ri:'ɪtəreɪt] wiederholen **WS 1**, 19
to **reject** [rɪ'dʒekt] zurückweisen **WS 3**, 103
to **relate** [rɪ'leɪt] sich beziehen auf OT 3
related to [rɪ'leɪtɪd tə] in Bezug auf OT 4
relation [rɪ'leɪʃn] Verwandte(r) OT 2
relationship [rɪ'leɪʃnʃɪp] Beziehung OT 3
relative ['relətɪv] Verwandte; Angehörige OT 1
relative ['relətɪv] relativ OT 2
relatively ['relətɪvli] relativ; ziemlich OT 5
relative pronoun [ˌrelətɪv 'prəʊnaʊn] Relativpronomen OT 2
to **relax** [rɪ'læks] sich entspannen; loslassen OT 2
relaxation [ˌri:læk'seɪʃn] Erholung OT 3
relaxing [rɪ'læksɪŋ] erholsam OT 2
to **release** [rɪ'li:s] veröffentlichen; auf den Markt bringen OT 4
relevance ['reləvəns] Bedeutung **WS 1**, 17
relevant ['reləvənt] wichtig; relevant OT 4
reliable [rɪ'laɪəbl] verlässlich OT 4
reliant [rɪ'laɪənt] abhängig **WS 3**, 110

relief [rɪ'li:f] Erleichterung; Hilfe OT 4
to **relieve** [rɪ'li:v] erleichtern; entlasten OT 5
relieved [rɪ'li:vd] erleichtert OT 2
religion [rɪ'lɪdʒən] Religion OT 3
religious [rɪ'lɪdʒəs] religiös OT 1
religious studies [rɪ'lɪdʒəs 'stʌdiz] Religionsunterricht OT 1
to **relish** ['relɪʃ] genießen **WS 2**, 79
to **relive** [ri:'lɪv] wieder erleben OT 4
to **relocate** [ˌri:ləʊ'keɪt] umziehen **WS 1**, 22
to **rely** [rɪ'laɪ] sich verlassen auf OT 5
to **remain** [rɪ'meɪn] bleiben OT 4
remaining [rɪ'meɪnɪŋ] restlich; übrig OT 5
remains [rɪ'meɪnz] Überreste OT 3
remark [rɪ'mɑ:k] Bemerkung OT 5
remarriage [ˌri:'mærɪdʒ] Wiederverheiratung OT 5
to **remarry** [ˌri:'mæri] wieder heiraten OT 5
to **remember** [rɪ'membə] (sich) erinnern an OT 1
to **remind** [rɪ'maɪnd] erinnern OT 2
reminder [rɪ'maɪndə] Erinnerung **WS 1**, 39
to **reminisce** [ˌrɛmɪ'nɪs] sich erinnern **WS 1**, 19
remorse [rɪ'mɔ:s] Reue OT 5
remote [rɪ'məʊt] entfernt; abgelegen OT 5
remotely [rɪ'məʊtli] aus der Ferne OT 4
remote control [rɪˌməʊt kən'trəʊl] Fernbedienung OT 4
removal [rɪ'mu:vl] Entfernung OT 5
removal van [rɪ'mu:vəl væn] Umzugswagen OT 2
to **remove** [rɪ'mu:v] entfernen OT 2
to **render** ['rendə] machen **WS 4**, 136
rendition [rɪn'dɪʃən] Wiedergabe **WS 1**, 43
to **renew** [rɪ'nju:] erneuern **WS 1**, 24
renewable [rɪ'nju:əbl] erneuerbar OT 5
renovation [ˌrenə'veɪʃn] Sanierung **WS 1**, 22
to **rent** [rent] mieten OT 4
rental ['rentl] Miet… OT 4
to **repaint** [ˌri:'peɪnt] übermalen OT 4
to **repair** [rɪ'peə] reparieren OT 2
to **repay** [rɪ'peɪ] vergüten; zurückzahlen OT 5
to **repeat** [rɪ'pi:t] wiederholen OT 1
repercussions [ˌri:pə'kʌʃənz] Auswirkungen **WS 1**, 18

repetition [ˌrepə'tɪʃn] Wiederholung OT 4
to **rephrase** [ˌri:'freɪz] neu formulieren; umformulieren OT 4
to **replace** [rɪ'pleɪs] ersetzen OT 3
replica ['replɪkə] Kopie OT 4
to **reply** [rɪ'plaɪ] antworten OT 1
report [rɪ'pɔ:t] Bericht OT 2
to **report** [rɪ'pɔ:t] berichten OT 1
reporter [rɪ'pɔ:tə] Reporter(in) OT 1
to **represent** [ˌreprɪ'zent] vertreten **WS 1**, 14
representation [ˌreprɪzen'teɪʃn] Darstellung **WS 4**, 139
representative [ˌreprɪ'zentətɪv] repräsentativ **WS 2**, 55
to **repress** [rɪ'prɛs] unterdrücken **WS 2**, 78
to **reproduce** [ˌri:prə'dju:s] reproduzieren **WS 4**, 133
reproduction [ˌri:prə'dʌkʃən] Fortpflanzung **WS 3**, 104
reptile ['reptaɪl] Reptil OT 2
republic [rɪ'pʌblɪk] Republik OT 4
reputation [ˌrepju'teɪʃn] Ruf; Reputation **WS 1**, 24
request [rɪ'kwest] Bitte OT 2
to **require** [rɪ'kwaɪə] verlangen; fordern OT 4
requirement [rɪ'kwaɪəmənt] Voraussetzung OT 5
rescue ['reskju:] Rettung OT 2
to **rescue** ['reskju:] retten OT 4
research [rɪ'sɜ:tʃ] Forschung OT 2
to **research** [rɪ'sɜ:tʃ] forschen OT 2
researcher [rɪ'sɜ:tʃə] Forscher(in) OT 2
to **resemble** [rɪ'zembl] aussehen wie **WS 1**, 22
reservation [ˌrezə'veɪʃn] Reservierung; Reservat OT 1
to **reserve** [rɪ'zɜ:v] reservieren OT 3
reserved [rɪ'zɜ:vd] reserviert OT 2
resettlement [ˌri:'setlmənt] Umsiedlung OT 4
residency ['rɛzɪdənsi] Aufenthaltsgenehmigung **WS 3**, 95
resident ['rezɪdənt] Bewohner(in) OT 3
residential [ˌrezɪ'denʃl] Wohn- **WS 1**, 25
to **resign** [rɪ'zaɪn] zurücktreten OT 5
to **resist** [rɪ'zɪst] widerstehen OT 5
resistance [rɪ'zɪstəns] Widerstand; Resistenz OT 5
resistant [rɪ'zɪstənt] widerstandsfähig; resistent OT 5
resolution [ˌrezə'lu:ʃn] Beschluss **WS 2**, 63

to resolve [rɪ'zɒlv] entscheiden OT 5
resort [rɪ'zɔ:t] Urlaubsort; Zuflucht OT 2
resource [rɪ'sɔ:s] Ressource; Mittel OT 4
resourceful [rɪ'sɔ:sfl] erfinderisch OT 4
respect [rɪ'spekt] Respekt **WS 1**, 15
to respect [rɪ'spekt] achten OT 3
respectful [rɪ'spektfl] respektvoll OT 3
to respond [rɪ'spɒnd] reagieren; antworten OT 3
respondent [rɪ'spɒndənt] Befragte(r) OT 5
response [rɪ'spɒns] Reaktion; Antwort OT 5
responsibility [rɪˌspɒnsə'bɪləti] Verantwortung OT 3
responsible [rɪ'spɒnsəbl] verantwortlich OT 3
rest [rest] übrige; restliche OT 1
to rest [rest] ausruhen OT 1
restaurant ['restrɒnt] Restaurant OT 1
to restore [rɪ'stɔ:] wiederherstellen OT 4
to restrict [rɪ'strɪkt] einschränken; beschränken **WS 2**, 78
restriction [rɪ'strɪkʃn] Einschränkung OT 5
result [rɪ'zʌlt] Ergebnis OT 2
to result [rɪ'zʌlt] zur Folge haben **WS 2**, 68
to resume [rɪ'zju:m] übernehmen; wieder annehmen OT 5
retailer ['ri:teɪlə] Händler(in); Einzelhändler(in) OT 4
to retain [rɪ'teɪn] behalten **WS 3**, 99
to retaliate [rɪ'tælieɪt] sich rächen **WS 1**, 29
to retell [ˌri:'tel] nacherzählen OT 4
retirement home [rɪ'taɪəmənt həʊm] Seniorenheim OT 3
retreat [rɪ'tri:t] Rückzug **WS 1**, 14
to retrieve [rɪ'tri:v] zurückholen **WS 1**, 25
to return [rɪ'tɜ:n] zurückkehren OT 2
reusable [ˌri:'ju:zəbl] wiederverwendbar OT 3
to reuse [ˌri:'ju:s] wiederverwenden OT 2
to reveal [rɪ'vi:l] verraten OT 5
to revere [rɪ'vɪərd] verehren **WS 1**, 32
to reverse [rɪ'vɜ:s] umdrehen **WS 3**, 98
review [rɪ'vju:] Rückblick OT 1
to revise [rɪ'vaɪz] revidieren; überarbeiten OT 2
to revive [rɪ'vaɪv] wiederbeleben **WS 3**, 98
revolting [rɪ'vəʊltɪŋ] abstoßend OT 2
revolution [ˌrevə'lu:ʃn] Revolution OT 2
to revolutionize [ˌrevə'lu:ʃənaɪz] revolutionieren OT 4
reward [rɪ'wɔ:d] Belohnung **WS 4**, 133
to reward [rɪ'wɔ:d] belohnen **WS 2**, 68
rewarding [rɪ'wɔ:dɪŋ] lohnend OT 4
to rewrite [ˌri:'raɪt] neu schreiben; umschreiben OT 1
rhetorical [rɪ'tɒrɪkl] rhetorisch OT 5
rhino ['raɪnoʊ] Nashorn **WS 2**, 64
rhinoceros [raɪ'nɒsərəs] Nashorn OT 2
rhyme ['raɪm] Reim OT 1
rhythm ['rɪðəm] Rhythmus **WS 2**, 72
ribbon ['rɪbən] Band; Franse **WS 3**, 95
rice [raɪs] Reis OT 1
rich [rɪtʃ] reich OT 1
rickshaw ['rɪkʃɔ:] Rikscha **WS 1**, 16
ride [raɪd] Fahrt OT 1
to ride [raɪd] fahren; reiten OT 1
rider ['raɪdə] Fahrer(in); Reiter(in) OT 1
rifle ['raɪfl] Gewehr OT 4
rift [rɪft] Spalte; Riss **WS 1**, 14
to right [raɪt] aufrichten OT 5
right [raɪt] rechte(r, -s); richtig OT 1
rights [raɪt] Rechte OT 3
rim [rɪm] Rand OT 3
to ring [rɪŋ] klingeln OT 1
riot ['raɪət] Aufstand; Protest **WS 1**, 14
ripe [raɪp] reif OT 4
ripped [rɪpt] gerissen OT 4
to rise [raɪz] aufsteigen OT 3
risk [rɪsk] Risiko; Gefahr OT 3
to risk [rɪsk] riskieren **WS 1**, 15
risky ['rɪski] gefährlich OT 3
ritual ['rɪtʃuəl] Ritual OT 5
rivalry ['raɪvlri] Konkurrenz OT 5
river ['rɪvə] Fluss OT 1
riverbank ['rɪvərbæŋk] Ufer **WS 1**, 27
road [rəʊd] Straße OT 1
roadside ['roʊdsaɪd] Straßenrand **WS 1**, 24
to roam around [rəʊm ə'raʊnd] durch stromern; herumwandern OT 5
roast [rəʊst] gebraten OT 1
robot ['rəʊbɒt] Roboter OT 4
robust [rəʊ'bʌst] belastbar; robust **WS 3**, 112
rock [rɒk] Stein; Rockmusik OT 2
rock and roll [ˌrɒk ən 'rəʊl] Rock and Roll OT 2
to rock [rɒk] schaukeln OT 3
rock climbing ['rɒk klaɪmɪŋ] Felsklettern OT 2
rocket ['rɒkɪt] Rakete OT 4
role [rəʊl] Rolle OT 1
roll [rəʊl] Rolle; Filmrolle OT 2
roller skate ['rəʊlə skeɪt] Rollschuh OT 4
Roman ['rəʊmən] römisch OT 2
roof ['ru:f] Dach OT 1
room ['ru:m] Raum OT 1
roommate ['rumˌmeɪt] Mitbewohner(in) OT 5
rooster ['ru:stə] Hahn **WS 1**, 17
root [ru:t] Wurzel OT 3
rope [rəʊp] Seil OT 1
rose [rəʊz] Rose OT 4
to rot ['rəʊtə] verfaulen OT 5
rough [rʌf] rau OT 4
round [raʊnd] rund; um ... herum OT 1
route [ru:t] Strecke OT 2
routine [ru:'ti:n] Routine; Tagesablauf OT 4
rover ['rəʊvə] Forschungsfahrzeug OT 4
row [rəʊ] Reihe OT 1
rowing boat ['rəʊɪŋ bəʊt] Ruderboot OT 1
royal ['rɔɪəl] königlich OT 1
royalty ['rɔɪəlti] Tantiemen **WS 2**, 68
to rub [rʌb] reiben OT 3
rubber ['rʌbə] Gummi; Radiergummi OT 1
rubbish ['rʌbɪʃ] Müll OT 2
rubbish bin ['rʌbɪʃˌbɪn] Mülleimer OT 2
rubbish collection ['rʌbɪʃ kəˌlekʃn] Müllabfuhr OT 2
rucksack ['rʌksæk] Rucksack OT 1
rude [ru:d] unhöflich OT 1
rugby ['rʌgbi] Rugby OT 1
ruin ['ru:ɪn] Ruine OT 2
to ruin ['ru:ɪn] zerstören **WS 1**, 14
rule [ru:l] Regel OT 1
rulebook ['ru:l bʊk] Regelwerk OT 2
ruler ['ru:lə] Lineal OT 1
rummy ['rʌmi] Rommee OT 2
rumour ['ru:mər] Gerücht OT 5
run [rʌn] Punkte OT 1
to run [rʌn] laufen; rennen OT 1
to run out [rʌn' aʊt] zur Neige gehen; zu Ende gehen OT 2
runaway ['rʌnəweɪ] Ausreißer(in) OT 5
runner ['rʌnə] Läufer(in) OT 2
rupee ['ru:pi] Rupie **WS 1**, 25
rural ['rʊərəl] ländlich OT 4
to rush [rʌʃ] eilen OT 2
to rush off [rʌʃ ɒf] losstürzen; wegrennen OT 2
rush hour ['rʌʃ aʊə] Hauptverkehrszeit OT 1
Russian ['rʌʃn] russisch OT 2

S

sack [sæk] Sack OT 2
to **sack** [sæk] entlassen **WS 2**, 85
sacred ['seɪkrɪd] heilig OT 4
sacrifice ['sækrɪfaɪs] Opfer **WS 3**, 120
sad [sæd] traurig OT 1
saddened ['sædnd] betrübt OT 5
saddle ['sædl] Sattel OT 3
safari [sə'fɑ:ri] Safari OT 2
safe [seɪf] sicher OT 1
safety ['seɪfti] Sicherheit OT 2
safety equipment [ˌseɪfti ɪ'kwɪpmənt] Sicherheitsausrüstung OT 2
to **sail** [seɪl] mit dem Schiff fahren; segeln OT 2
sailing ['seɪlɪŋ] Segeln OT 1
sailor ['seɪlə] Matrose OT 1
salad ['sæləd] Salat OT 1
salary ['sæləri] Gehalt; Lohn OT 5
sale [seɪl] Sale; Ausverkauf OT 4
salmon ['sæmən] Lachs OT 1
salt [sɔ:lt] Salz OT 3
salutation [ˌsælju'teɪʃən] Grußformel **WS 2**, 79
same [seɪm] gleich OT 1
sameness ['seɪmnəs] Gleichheit **WS 2**, 57
sample ['sɑ:mpl] Probe OT 4
sanction ['sæŋkʃn] Sanktion **WS 2**, 68
sanctuary ['sæŋktʃuəri] Schutzgebiet **WS 2**, 85
sand [sænd] Sand OT 1
sandal ['sændl] Sandale OT 4
sandwich ['sænwɪtʃ] Sandwich OT 1
sandy ['sændi] sandig OT 1
sassafras ['sæsəfræs] Sassafras OT 3
satellite ['sætəlaɪt] Satellit OT 4
satellite connection ['sætəlaɪt kə'nekʃn] Satellitenverbindung OT 4
satisfaction [ˌsætɪs'fækʃən] Genugtuung; Befriedigung **WS 2**, 79
satisfied ['sætɪsfaɪd] zufrieden **WS 3**, 92
satisfying ['sætɪsfaɪɪŋ] zufriedenstellend; befriedigend OT 5
Saturday ['sætədeɪ] Samstag OT 1
sauce [sɔ:s] Soße OT 1
sausage ['sɒsɪdʒ] Wurst OT 1
sauté ['səʊteɪ] geröstet OT 3
savage ['sævɪdʒ] Wilde(r) **WS 3**, 94
to **save** [seɪv] retten; sparen OT 2
savings ['seɪvɪŋz] Erspartes OT 3
savoury ['seɪvəri] pikant OT 3
savvy ['sævi] klug; schlau OT 5
saxophone ['sæksəfəʊn] Saxofon OT 2
to **say** [seɪ] sagen OT 1
scale [skeɪl] Skala; Waage **WS 1**, 30
to **scalp** [skælp] skalpieren **WS 3**, 94
to **scan** [skæn] überfliegen; scannen OT 3
scar [skɑ:r] Narbe **WS 1**, 15
to **scare** [skeə] Angst machen OT 2
scared [skeəd] verängstigt OT 1
scarf [skɑ:f] Schal OT 2
scary ['skeəri] unheimlich OT 1
to **scavenge** ['skævɪndʒ] nach etw. suchen OT 5
scenario [sə'nɑ:riəʊ] Szenario **WS 3**, 92
scene [si:n] Szene OT 2
scenery ['si:nəri] Landschaft OT 2
scenic ['si:nɪk] malerisch OT 5
sceptic ['skeptɪk] Skeptiker(in) **WS 1**, 33
schedule ['ʃedju:l] Stundenplan OT 2
to **schedule** ['ʃedju:l] festlegen; vereinbaren OT 5
scheme [ski:m] Schema OT 5
scholar ['skɒlə] Gelehrte(r) **WS 3**, 108
scholarship ['skɒləʃɪp] Stipendium **WS 2**, 55
school [sku:l] Schule OT 1
school bag ['sku:l bæg] Schultasche OT 1
school day [sku:l deɪ] Schultag OT 1
schooling ['sku:lɪŋ] Schulausbildung OT 4
school leaver ['sku:l li:vər] Schulabgänger(in) OT 5
schoolmate ['sku:lmeɪt] Schulkamerad(in) OT 4
science ['saɪəns] Wissen; Naturwissenschaften OT 1
science fiction [ˌsaɪəns 'fɪkʃn] Science-Fiction OT 2
scientific [ˌsaɪən'tɪfɪk] wissenschaftlich OT 3
scientist ['saɪəntɪst] Naturwissenschaftler(in) OT 1
scissors ['sɪzəz] Schere OT 1
scone [skəʊn] brötchenartiges, süßes Gebäck OT 3
to **score** [skɔ:] punkten OT 1
scoring ['skɔ:rɪŋ] Treffen; Erzielen OT 1
Scottish ['skɒtɪʃ] schottisch OT 3
scout [skaʊt] Pfadfinder(in) OT 3
scrap [skræp] Abfall OT 4
scrapple [skræpl] Scrapple OT 3
to **scratch** [skrætʃ] kratzen OT 2
to **scream** [skri:m] schreien; kreischen OT 3
screen [skri:n] Bildschirm; Leinwand OT 1
screenplay ['skri:npleɪ] Drehbuch **WS 3**, 104
script [skrɪpt] Drehbuch OT 1
sculpting ['skʌlptɪŋ] Körpermodellierung **WS 3**, 113
sculptor ['skʌlptə] Bildhauer(in) **WS 1**, 19
sculpture ['skʌlptʃə] Skulptur OT 2
sea [si:] Meer; See OT 1
seabed ['si:bed] Meeresboden OT 3
seabird ['si:bɜ:d] Seevogel OT 5
seafood ['si:fu:d] Meeresfrüchte OT 3
seal [si:l] Robbe OT 1
sealskin ['si:lskɪn] Seehundfell **WS 3**, 95
search [sɜ:tʃ] Suche OT 2
to **search** [sɜ:tʃ] suchen OT 2
searchlight ['sɜ:rtʃlaɪt] Suchscheinwerfer **WW**, 11
seaside ['si:saɪd] Küste OT 1
season ['si:zn] Jahreszeit OT 3
seasoning ['si:zənɪŋ] Gewürz OT 2
seat [si:t] Sitzplatz OT 1
seating ['si:tɪŋ] Sitzplätze OT 2
to **secede** [sɪ'si:d] sich abspalten **WS 1**, 14
second ['sekənd] Sekunde; zweite(r, -s) OT 1
secondary ['sekəndri] weiterführend; sekundär OT 1
secondary school ['sekəndri ˌsku:l] Sekundarschule; weiterführende Schule OT 1
secondly ['sekəndli] zweitens OT 2
secret ['si:krət] Geheimnis OT 2
secretary ['sekrətri] Sekretär(in) OT 1
section ['sekʃn] Teil OT 2
sector ['sektə] Sektor **WS 1**, 24
secure [sɪ'kjʊə] sicher OT 5
security [sɪ'kjʊərəti] Sicherheit OT 3
to **see** [si:] sehen OT 1
to **seek** [si:k] suchen OT 5
to **seem** [si:m] scheinen OT 2
segment ['segmənt] Segment; Abschnitt OT 5
to **segregate** ['segrɪgeɪt] trennen (durch Gesetzt) **WS 2**, 52
segregation [ˌsegrɪ'geɪʃn] Rassentrennung **WS 2**, 59
seldom ['seldəm] selten OT 5
to **select** [sɪ'lekt] wählen; auswählen OT 4
self: by one's self [baɪ wʌnz 'self] allein OT 2
self-catering [ˌself 'keɪtərɪŋ] mit Selbstversorgung OT 3
self-checkout [ˌself 'tʃekaʊt] Selbstzahlerkasse OT 4

self-employed [ˌself ɪm'plɔɪd] selbständig OT 5
selfie ['selfiː] Selfie OT 1
selfish ['selfɪʃ] egoistisch OT 3
self-motivated [ˌself 'məʊtɪveɪtɪd] motiviert OT 4
self-sufficient [ˌself sə'fɪʃnt] unabhängig; autark OT 4
to **sell** [sel] verkaufen OT 1
semester [sɪ'mestə] Halbjahr; Semester OT 3
semi- ['semi] halb- OT 5
to **send** [send] schicken OT 1
sender ['sendə] Absender(in) OT 3
senior ['siːniə] Oberstufenschüler(in); Senior(in) OT 4
senior citizen [ˌsiːniə 'sɪtɪzn] Senior(in) OT 3
sensation [sen'seɪʃn] Gefühl OT 4
sense [sens] Sinn OT 2
to **sense** [sens] fühlen **WS 3**, 97
sensible ['sensəbl] vernünftig OT 3
sensitive ['sensətɪv] empfindlich **WS 2**, 61
sensor ['sensə] Sensor OT 4
sentence ['sentəns] Satz OT 1
to **sentence** ['sentəns] verurteilen OT 5
sentencing ['sentənsɪŋ] Verurteilung OT 5
to **separate** ['seprət] (sich) trennen OT 4
separate ['seprət] getrennt OT 2
September [sep'tembə] September OT 1
sequel ['siːkwl] Fortsetzung **WS 3**, 127
sequence ['siːkwəns] Ablauf; Folge OT 4
to **sequence** ['siːkwəns] in eine Reihenfolge bringen OT 3
sequencing ['siːkwənsɪŋ] Sequenzierung; Reihenfolge OT 3
sequentially [sɪ'kwenʃəli] folgend; nacheinander OT 4
series ['sɪəriːz] Serie OT 1
serious ['sɪəriəs] ernst OT 2
seriously ['sɪəriəsli] ernst; im Ernst OT 2
seriousness ['sɪəriəsnəs] Ernsthaftigkeit OT 5
serpent ['sɜːpənt] Schlange OT 5
to **serve** [sɜːv] servieren; bedienen OT 1
server ['sɜːvə] Kellner(in) OT 4
service ['sɜːvɪs] Dienst OT 2
session ['seʃn] Sitzung; Session; Einheit OT 2
set [set] Satz OT 3
to **set the stage** [set ðə steɪdʒ] die Bühne vorbereiten OT 2
setting ['setɪŋ] Einstellung OT 3
to **settle** ['setl] sich ansiedeln OT 4
to **settle down** [ˌsetl 'daʊn] (sich) beruhigen OT 2
settlement ['setlmənt] Siedlung OT 4
settler ['setlə] Siedler(in) OT 3
seven ['sevn] sieben OT 1
seventeen [ˌsevn'tiːn] siebzehn OT 1
seventy ['sevnti] siebzig OT 1
several ['sevrəl] mehrere; einige OT 2
severe [sɪ'vɪə] schwer; stark OT 5
sewing machine ['səʊɪŋ məʃiːn] Nähmaschine OT 3
to **sew** [səʊ] nähen **WS 3**, 95
sewage ['suːɪdʒ] Abwasser **WS 3**, 98
sex [seks] Geschlecht; Sex OT 5
sexual ['sɛkʃul] sexuel **WS 1**, 14
shack [ʃæk] Hütte **WS 2**, 53
shade [ʃeɪd] Schatten; Schattierung OT 5
to **shadow** ['ʃædəʊ] auf Schritt und Tritt begleiten; beschatten OT 5
to **shake** [ʃeɪk] schütteln OT 2
to **shake hands** [ʃeɪk' hændz] jdm. die Hand geben OT 2
shaky ['ʃeɪki] wackelig OT 3
shall [ʃæl] werden OT 2
shame: That's a shame. [ðæts ə 'ʃeɪm] Das ist schade. OT 2
shampoo [ʃæm'puː] Shampoo OT 3
shape [ʃeɪp] Form OT 1
to **shape** [ʃeɪp] formen OT 3
shaped [ʃeɪpt] geformt OT 4
to **share** [ʃeə] teilen OT 1
shark [ʃɑːk] Hai OT 5
sharp [ʃɑːp] scharf **WS 2**, 58
she [ʃi] sie OT 1
shebang [ʃɪ'bæŋ] Ganze; Kram **WS 1**, 15
shed [ʃed] Schuppen OT 1
sheep [ʃiːp] Schaf OT 1
sheepdog ['ʃiːpdɒg] Hütehund OT 2
sheet [ʃiːt] Blatt OT 1
shelf [ʃelf] Regal OT 1
shelter ['ʃeltə] Unterschlupf OT 2
to **shelter** ['ʃeltə] beschützen **WS 3**, 97
shepherd ['ʃepəd] Schäfer(in) OT 2
shield [ʃiːld] Scheibe; Schild **WS 2**, 56
shift [ʃɪft] Schicht OT 4
to **shift** [ʃɪft] (sich) verschieben **WS 1**, 14
to **shine** [ʃaɪn] scheinen OT 1
ship [ʃɪp] Schiff OT 2
tall ship [ˌtɔːl 'ʃɪp] Großsegler OT 2
shipbuilding ['ʃɪpbɪldɪŋ] Schiffbau OT 3
shirt [ʃɜːt] Hemd OT 1
shock [ʃɒk] Überraschung OT 5
shocked [ʃɒkt] schockiert OT 4
shoe [ʃuː] Schuh OT 1
shoebox ['ʃuːbɒks] Schuhschachtel OT 3
to **shoot** [ʃuːt] schießen OT 3
shop [ʃɒp] Laden OT 1
to **shop** [ʃɒp] kaufen; einkaufen OT 1
shoplifting ['ʃɒplɪftɪŋ] Ladendiebstahl OT 5
shopper ['ʃɒpə] Käufer(in) OT 4
shopping ['ʃɒpɪŋ] Einkaufen OT 1
shopping rota ['ʃɒpɪŋ 'rəʊtə] Einkaufsdienst OT 5
shore [ʃɔː] Küste OT 2
short [ʃɔːt] kurz OT 1
shortage ['ʃɔːtɪdʒ] Mangel OT 5
to **shorten** ['ʃɔːtn] kürzen; abkürzen OT 5
shortlist ['ʃɔːtlɪst] Auswahlliste OT 2
shorts [ʃɔːts] kurze Hose; Shorts OT 1
shot [ʃɒt] Schuss; Schnappschuss OT 4
should [ʃəd] sollte(n) OT 1
shoulder ['ʃəʊldə] Schulter OT 1
shoulder pad ['ʃəʊldə pæd] Schulterpolster OT 2
to **shout** [ʃaʊt] laut rufen OT 1
shovel ['ʃʌvl] Schaufel OT 2
show [ʃəʊ] Vorstellung; Ausstellung OT 1
to **show** [ʃəʊ] zeigen OT 1
show-and-tell [ˌʃəʊ ən 'tel] Kurzvortrag über einen mitgebrachten Gegenstand OT 1
shower ['ʃaʊə] Dusche OT 2
showground ['ʃəʊgraʊnd] Ausstellungsgelände OT 2
showtime ['ʃəʊtaɪm] Vorstellungsbeginn OT 4
shredded ['ʃredɪd] gerieben; geschnetzelt OT 2
to **shrug** [ʃrʌg] Achseln zucken OT 5
to **shuffle** ['ʃʌfl] mischen **WS 4**, 139
to **shut** [ʃʌt] zumachen; schließen OT 2
shy [ʃaɪ] schüchtern OT 2
sibling ['sɪblɪŋ] Geschwister(kind); Bruder; Schwester OT 5
sick [sɪk] krank OT 1
side [saɪd] Seite OT 1
sidewalk ['saɪdwɔːk] Bürgersteig OT 4
sigh [saɪ] Seufzer OT 2
to **sigh** [saɪ] seufzen OT 3
sight [saɪt] Sehvermögen; Sehenswürdigkeit OT 1
sightseeing ['saɪtsiːɪŋ] Besichtigungen OT 1

sign [saɪn] Schild OT 1
to **sign** [saɪn] unterschreiben OT 2
signal ['sɪgnəl] Signal OT 2
to **signal** ['sɪgnl] signalisieren **WS 2**, 69
significance [sɪg'nɪfɪkəns] Bedeutung; Wichtigkeit OT 5
significant [sɪg'nɪfɪkənt] wichtig; signifikant **WS 1**, 15
signpost ['saɪnpəʊst] Wegweiser; Schild OT 5
signposting ['saɪnpəʊstɪŋ] Beschilderung; Wegweisung OT 5
sign-up sheet ['saɪn ʌp ˌʃi:t] Anmeldeliste OT 2
silence ['saɪləns] Stille OT 2
silent ['saɪlənt] stumm **WS 1**, 22
silly ['sɪli] dumm; albern OT 1
silver ['sɪlvə] Silber...; silbern OT 1
similar ['sɪmələ] ähnlich OT 2
similarity [ˌsɪmə'lærəti] Ähnlichkeit OT 3
simile ['sɪmɪli] Vergleich **WS 2**, 62
to **simmer** ['sɪmə] köcheln OT 2
simple ['sɪmpl] einfach OT 1
simple present [ˌsɪmpl 'preznt] einfaches Präsens; einfache Gegenwart OT 1
simplification [ˌsɪmplɪfɪ'keɪʃən] Vereinfachung **WS 1**, 14
simplified ['sɪmplɪfaɪ] vereinfacht OT 5
simplistic [sɪm'plɪstɪk] einfach **WS 2**, 62
since [sɪns] seit OT 3
sincere [sɪn'sɪə] ernsthaft **WS 2**, 69
sincerely [sɪn'sɪəli] aufrichtig; mit freundlichen Grüßen OT 4
to **sing** [sɪŋ] singen OT 1
singer ['sɪŋə] Sänger(in) OT 1
single ['sɪŋgl] Einzel... OT 3
singular ['sɪŋgjələ] Einzahl; Singular OT 1
sinister ['sɪnɪstə] bösartig **WS 2**, 61
sink [sɪŋk] Spülbecken OT 3
to **sink** [sɪŋk] sinken OT 3
sir [sɜ:] Herr OT 1
siren ['saɪrən] Sirene OT 3
sissy ['sɪsi] Weichei **WS 3**, 96
sister ['sɪstə] Schwester OT 1
to **sit** [sɪt] sitzen OT 1
to **sit down** [sɪt daʊn] hinsetzen OT 1
site [saɪt] Platz OT 2
sitter: to **miss a sitter** [mɪs ə 'sɪtə] eine Chance vergeben **WS 1**, 28
situated ['sɪtʃueɪtɪd] gelegen **WS 1**, 23
situation [ˌsɪtʃu'eɪʃn] Lage; Situation OT 1
six [sɪks] sechs OT 1
sixteen [ˌsɪks'ti:n] sechzehn OT 1
sixty ['sɪksti] sechzig OT 1
size [saɪz] Größe OT 1
to **sizzle** ['sɪzl] knistern OT 5
to **skate** [skeɪt] Schlittschuh laufen OT 2
skateboard ['skeɪtbɔ:d] Skateboard OT 4
to **skateboard** ['skeɪtbɔ:d] Skateboardfahren gehen OT 4
skeleton ['skelɪtn] Skelett OT 1
sketch [sketʃ] Skizze; Sketch OT 4
to **sketch** [sketʃ] skizzieren; zeichnen OT 4
to **ski** [ski:] Ski laufen OT 3
skier ['ski:ə] Skiläufer(in) OT 3
skiing ['ski:ɪŋ] Skifahren OT 2
skilful ['skɪlfl] geschickt OT 3
skill [skɪl] Geschick; Fähigkeit OT 2
skilled [skɪld] geschickt; ausgebildet OT 4
to **skim** [skɪm] querlesen; überfliegen OT 3
skimpy ['skɪmpi] knapp **WS 3**, 94
skin [skɪn] Haut OT 2
skinny ['skɪni] dünn **WS 2**, 60
skirt [skɜ:rt] Rock OT 1
skit [skɪt] Sketch OT 2
skunk [skʌŋk] Stinktier **WS 2**, 55
sky [skaɪ] Himmel OT 1
skyline ['skaɪlaɪn] Skyline OT 5
skyscraper ['skaɪskreɪpə] Wolkenkratzer OT 3
slang [slæŋ] Slang OT 5
to **slap on** [slæp ɒn] aufsetzen OT 5
slate: a clean slate [ə kli:n sleɪt] ein unbeschriebenes Blatt **WS 1**, 27
slave [sleɪv] Sklave; Sklavin OT 4
slavery ['sleɪvəri] Sklaverei OT 4
to **sleep** [sli:p] schlafen OT 1
sleeping bag ['sli:pɪŋ bæg] Schlafsack OT 2
sleepover ['sli:poʊvə] Pyjama-Party OT 1
sleeve [sli:v] Ärmel OT 3
sleeveless ['sli:vləs] ärmellos OT 4
slice [slaɪs] Scheibe OT 1
slide ['slaɪd] Folie OT 1
slideshow ['slaɪdʃəʊ] Präsentation; Diashow OT 3
slight [slaɪt] gering; leicht OT 5
slim [slɪm] schlank **WS 2**, 70
to **slip on** [slɪp] rasch anziehen OT 5
to **slither** ['slɪðə] sich schlängeln **WS 1**, 21
slogan ['sləʊgən] Slogan OT 2
slope [sləʊp] Piste OT 3
to **slop on** [slɒp ɒn] auftragen OT 5
slot-machine ['slɒt məʃi:n] Spielautomat **WS 4**, 133
slow [sləʊ] langsam OT 2
slowly ['sləʊli] langsam OT 2
to **slow down** [sləʊ'daʊn] (sich) verlangsamen OT 4
slum [slʌm] Slum OT 3
to **slump** [slʌmp] zusammensacken OT 4
small [smɔ:l] klein OT 1
smallpox ['smɔ:lpɒks] Pocken OT 4
small-scale ['smɔ:lˌskeɪl] Klein... **WS 1**, 25
smart [smɑ:t] intelligent; schlau OT 4
smartphone ['smɑ:tfəʊn] Smartphone OT 3
to **smell** [smel] riechen OT 1
to **smile** [smaɪl] lächeln OT 1
to **smirk** [smɜ:rk] grinsen **WS 2**, 62
smoke [sməʊk] Rauch OT 2
smooth [smu:ð] glatt OT 3
smoothly ['smu:ðli] glatt OT 3
snack [snæk] Snack OT 1
snake [sneɪk] Schlange OT 1
snakes and ladders [ˌsneɪks ən 'lædəz] Leiterspiel OT 2
snare [sneə] Falle **WS 2**, 67
to **snare** [sneə] Fallen stellen **WS 2**, 67
to **sneak** [sni:k] schleichen **WS 2**, 70
sneaker ['sni:kər] Turnschuh OT 4
sneaky ['sni:ki] heimtückisch; hinterhältig OT 5
snitch [snɪtʃ] Verräter(in) OT 5
snore [snɔ:] Schnarcher OT 1
snow [snəʊ] Schnee OT 1
snowboarding ['snəʊbɔ:dɪŋ] Snowboard fahren OT 3
snowy ['snəʊi] verschneit OT 3
so [səʊ] also OT 1
soaked [səʊkd] durchnässt OT 3
soap [səʊp] Seife OT 2
to **soar** [sɔ:] schweben OT 3
soccer ['sɒkə] Fußball OT 2
social ['səʊʃl] sozial OT 2
socialization [ˌsəʊʃəlaɪ'zeɪʃn] Sozialisation **WS 2**, 55
to **socialize** ['səʊʃəlaɪz] Kontakte pflegen; unter die Leute kommen OT 4
society [sə'saɪəti] Gesellschaft OT 4
sociolinguistic [ˌsoʊsioʊ'lɪŋgwɪstɪk] soziolinguistisch **WS 3**, 108
sociologist [ˌsoʊsi'ɒlədʒɪst] Soziologe / Soziologin **WS 3**, 92
sociology [ˌsəʊsi'ɒlədʒi] Soziologie OT 5

sock [sɒk] Socke OT 2
soda ['səʊdə] Limo; Sprudel OT 5
sofa ['səʊfə] Sofa OT 1
soft [sɒft] weich OT 3
software ['sɒftweə] Software OT 1
soil [sɔɪl] Erdboden; Erde; Erdreich OT 2
solar ['səʊlə] Sonnen... OT 3
solar panel [ˌsəʊlə 'pænl] Sonnenkollektor OT 3
solar power [ˌsəʊlə 'paʊə] Solarenergie; Sonnenenergie OT 4
solar system ['səʊlə sɪstəm] Sonnensystem OT 1
soldier ['səʊldʒə] Soldat(in) OT 1
sole [səʊl] alleinig **WS 2**, 68
solidarity [ˌsɒlɪ'dærɪti] Solidarität **WS 2**, 68
soliloquy [sə'lɪləkwi] Monolog; Soliloquium OT 5
solitary ['sɒlətri] einsam **WS 1**, 39
solo ['səʊləʊ] solo OT2; Solo OT 4
solution [sə'lu:ʃn] Lösung OT 2
to **solve** [sɒlv] lösen OT 3
some [sʌm] etwas; einige OT 1
somebody ['sʌmbədi] jemand OT 1
somehow ['sʌmhaʊ] irgendwie OT 5
someone ['sʌmwʌn] jemand OT 1
something ['sʌmθɪŋ] etwas OT 1
sometimes ['sʌmtaɪmz] manchmal OT 1
somewhere ['sʌmweər] irgendwo OT 1
son [sʌn] Sohn OT 1
song [sɒŋ] Lied OT 1
songwriter ['sɒŋraɪtə] Songwriter(in) OT 2
soon [su:n] bald OT 1
sophisticated [sə'fɪstɪkeɪtɪd] ausgefeilt **WS 4**, 133
sore [sɔ:] schmerzend OT 2
sorrow ['sɒrəʊ] Trauer; Kummer OT 5
sorry ['sɒri] Entschuldigung OT 1
sort [sɔ:t] Art OT 2
to **sort (out)** [sɔ:rt] (aus)sortieren **WS 1**, 28
soul [səʊl] Seele; Geist **WS 1**, 18
sound [saʊnd] Geräusch OT 1
to **sound** [saʊnd] klingen; ertönen OT 2
soup [su:p] Suppe OT 1
source [sɔ:s] Quelle OT 2
south [saʊθ] Süd- OT 1
southern ['sʌðən] südlich OT 3
southwest [ˌsaʊθ'west] Südwesten OT 3
souvenir [su:və'nɪə] Reiseandenken OT 1
sovereign ['sɒvrɪn] souverän **WS 1**, 14
sovereignty ['sɒvrɪnti] Souveränität **WS 1**, 14
to **sow** [soʊ] säen **WS 1**, 14
soy [sɔɪ] Soja **WS 4**, 133
spa [spɑ:] Heilbad OT 3
space [speɪs] Platz; Feld; Weltraum OT 2
spacecraft ['speɪskrɑ:ft] Raumfahrzeug OT 4
space exploration ['speɪsˌeksplə'reɪʃn] Weltraumforschung OT 4
spaceship ['speɪsʃɪp] Raumschiff OT 4
spacesuit ['speɪssu:t] Raumanzug OT 4
spaghetti [spə'geti] Spaghetti OT 1
to **span** [spæn] umspannen **WS 1**, 15
spaniel ['spænjəl] Spaniel OT 2
Spanish ['spænɪʃ] spanisch OT 1
to **spare** [speə] verschonen **WS 1**, 27
spark [spɑ:k] Funke OT 2
to **spark** [spɑ:k] entzünden OT 4
sparkling ['spɑ:klɪŋ] sprudelnd OT 1
to **speak** [spi:k] sprechen OT 1
speaker ['spi:kə] Sprecher(in) OT 1
speaking ['spi:kɪŋ] Sprechen OT 1
to **spear** [spɪər] aufspießen OT 5
special ['speʃl] Tagesgericht OT 1
special ['speʃl] besondere(r, -s) OT 1
specialist ['speʃəlɪst] speziell OT 5
to **specialize** ['speʃəlaɪz] sich spezialisieren OT 4
species ['spi:ʃi:z] Spezies; Art OT 5
specific [spə'sɪfɪk] bestimmt; konkret; spezifisch OT 3
spectacular [spek'tækjələ] spektakulär OT 2
spectator [spek'teɪtə] Zuschauer(in) OT 3
to **speculate** ['spekjuleɪt] spekulieren; nachdenken OT 4
speech [spi:tʃ] Rede OT 1
speech bubble ['spi:tʃ bʌbl] Sprechblase OT 2
speed [spi:d] Geschwindigkeit OT 2
to **spell** [spel] buchstabieren OT 1
spelling ['spelɪŋ] Rechtschreibung; Schreibweise OT 1
to **spend** [spend] ausgeben; verbringen OT 1
spice [spaɪs] Gewürz OT 3
spiced [spaɪst] gewürzt OT 4
spider ['spaɪdə] Spinne OT 1
spiky ['spaɪki] stachelig; spitz OT 5
to **spill** [spɪl] verschütten OT 2
spiral ['spaɪrəl] Spirale; Wendel OT 5
to **spiral** ['spaɪrl] wirbeln **WS 1**, 22
spirit ['spɪrɪt] Geist OT 2
spiritual ['spɪrɪtʃul] geistig **WS 2**, 71
to **spit** [spɪt] spucken OT 4
spite: in spite of [ɪn spaɪt əv] trotz OT 5
splash [splæʃ] Platschen **WS 1**, 27
split [splɪt] Riss OT 3
to **split up** [ˌsplɪt'ʌp] sich trennen OT 5
to **splutter** ['splʌtə] prusten **WS 1**, 27
to **spoil** [spɔɪl] verderben OT 2
spoilage ['spɔɪlɪdʒ] Verderben; Abfall OT 4
spokesperson ['spoʊksˌpɜ:rsən] Sprecher(in) **WS 2**, 67
spokeswoman ['spəʊkswʊmən] Sprecherin OT 2
sponsor ['spɒnsə] Sponsor(in); Geldgeber(in) OT 2
to **sponsor** ['spɒnsə] finanziell unterstützen OT 2
sponsored ['spɒnsəd] gesponsert; gestiftet OT 2
sponsorship ['spɒnsəʃɪp] finanzielle Unterstützung OT 2
spontaneous [spɒn'teɪniəs] spontan OT 5
spoon [spu:n] Löffel OT 2
spoonful ['spu:nfʊl] Löffel (Maßangabe) OT 2
sport [spɔ:t] Sport OT 1
to **be a good sport** [bi ə gʊd spɔ:t] kein(e) Spielverderber(in) sein OT 2
sporting ['spɔ:tɪŋ] sportlich; Sport... OT 5
sportsman ['spɔ:tsmən] Sportler OT 3
sportspeople ['spɔ:ts pi:pl] Sportler(innen) OT 3
sportsperson ['spɔ:rtsˌpɜ:rsən] Sportler(in) **WS 2**, 58
sportswoman ['spɔ:tswʊmən] Sportlerin OT 2
sporty ['spɔ:ti] sportlich **WS 2**, 54
to **spot** [spɒt] erspähen OT 1
spotlight ['spɒtlaɪt] Mittelpunkt des Interesses OT 4
to **sprain** [spreɪn] verstauchen OT 2
to **spray** [spreɪ] sprühen OT 5
to **spread (out)** [spred] verbreiten OT 4
spring [sprɪŋ] Frühling; Quelle OT 2
hot spring ['hɒt sprɪŋ] Thermalquelle OT 2
spring clean [ˌsprɪŋ 'kli:n] Frühjahrsputz OT 2
to **sprinkle** ['sprɪŋkl] streuen OT 2
sprint [sprɪnt] Sprint OT 3
sprinter ['sprɪntə] Sprinter(in) OT 3
squad [skwɒd] Truppe **WS 1**, 28

square [skweə] Quadrat; Feld; Platz OT 1
squash [skwɒʃ] Kürbis OT 4
squirrel ['skwɪrəl] Eichhörnchen OT 1
stability [stə'bɪləti] Stabilität OT 5
stable ['steɪbl] stabil; sicher OT 5
to **stack** [stæk] stapeln OT 4
stadium ['steɪdiəm] Stadion OT 1
staff [stɑ:f] Personal OT 3
stage [steɪdʒ] Phase; Bühne OT 2
stage directions ['steɪdʒ dərekʃnz] Bühnenanweisungen OT 2
staggering ['stægərɪŋ] erschütternd **WS 3**, 103
stairs ['steəz] Treppe, Treppenstufen OT 1
stalactite ['stæləktaɪt] Stalaktit OT 1
stalagmite ['stæləgmaɪt] Stalagmit OT 1
stall [stɔ:l] Bude; Stall OT 2
to **stand** [stænd] stehen OT 1
to **stand up** ['stænd ʌp] aufstehen OT 1
standard ['stændəd] normal; Standard... OT 3
stanza ['stænzə] Stanze; Strophe OT 5
stapler ['steɪplə] Tacker OT 2
star [stɑ:] Stern; Star OT 1
to **star** [stɑ:] eine Hauptrolle spielen **WS 3**, 126
to **stare** [steə] starren OT 2
start [stɑ:t] Anfang OT 1
to **start** [stɑ:t] anfangen; beginnen OT 1
starter ['stɑ:tə] Vorspeise OT 1
to **starve** [stɑ:v] hungern (lassen); verhungern (lassen) OT 1
state [steɪt] Staat OT 1
princely state ['prɪnsli steɪt] Fürstenstaat **WS 1**, 14
to **state** [steɪt] erklären; festlegen OT 5
statement ['steɪtmənt] Aussage OT 1
station ['steɪʃn] Station; Bahnhof OT 1
stationery ['steɪʃənri] Schreibwaren OT 5
statistic [stə'tɪstɪk] Statistik OT 3
statue ['stætʃu:] Statue OT 1
status ['steɪtəs] Status; Stand OT 4
status quo ['steɪtəs 'kwoʊ] Status quo **WS 2**, 55
to **stave off** [steɪv ɒf] aufhalten **WS 3**, 98
to **stay** [steɪ] bleiben OT 1
steady ['stedi] ruhig; stabil OT 3
steak [steɪk] Steak OT 1
to **steal** [sti:l] klauen OT 2
steam [sti:m] Dampf OT 2
steam train ['sti:m treɪn] Dampfzug OT 2
steel [sti:l] Stahl OT 2
steep [sti:p] steil OT 2
to **steer** [stɪə] steuern OT 3
stegosaurus [ˌstegə'sɔ:rəs] Stegosaurus OT 1
STEM (science, technology, engineering, mathematics) [stem] MINT (Mathematik, Informatik, Naturwissenschaft und Technik) OT 5
step [step] Schritt; Stufe OT 1
to **step** [step] treten OT 4
to **step in** [step 'ɪn] eintreten OT 4
stereotype ['steriətaɪp] Stereotype; Klischee OT 5
to **stereotype** ['steriətaɪp] stereotypisieren OT 5
stereotypical [ˌsteriə'tɪpɪkl] stereotypisch OT 5
stern [stɜ:rn] streng **WS 3**, 94
steroid ['sterɔɪd] Steroid OT 5
stew [stju:] Eintopf OT 2
steward ['stju:əd] Verwalter OT 4
to **stick** [stɪk] kleben OT 1
sticky ['stɪki] klebrig; selbstklebend OT 1
stigma ['stɪgmə] Stigma OT 5
still [stɪl] immer noch OT 1
still [stɪl] ruhig OT 4
to **stimulate** ['stɪmjʊleɪt] anregen **WS 3**, 110
sting [stɪŋ] Stich OT 2
to **sting** [stɪŋ] stechen OT 2
stingray ['stɪŋreɪ] Stachelrochen OT 5
stipend ['staɪpɛnd] Stipendium **WS 3**, 111
to **stir** [stɜ:] rühren OT 2
stock [stɒk] Viehbestand; Bestand OT 2
stockroom ['stɒkru:m] Lagerraum OT 5
stomach ['stʌmək] Magen OT 2
stone [stəʊn] Stein OT 1
stop [stɒp] Halt; Haltestelle OT 2
to **stop** [stɒp] anhalten; aufhören OT 1
storage ['stɔ:rɪdʒ] Lagerung; Aufbewahrung OT 3
store [stɔ:] Laden OT 1
to **store** [stɔ:] lagern **WS 3**, 99
storeroom ['stɔ:ru:m] Lagerraum; Abstellraum OT 5
storm [stɔ:m] Sturm OT 2
stormy ['stɔ:rmi] stürmisch **WS 2**, 60
story ['stɔ:ri] Geschichte OT 1
storyboard ['stɔ:ribɔ:d] Storyboard; Szenenbuch OT 4
storybook ['stɔ:ribʊk] Geschichtenbuch OT 2
storyline ['stɔ:riˌlaɪn] Handlungsstrang **WS 1**, 38
stove [stəʊv] Ofen OT 3
straight [streɪt] gerade; direkt OT 3
straight away [streɪt ə'weɪ] sofort; gleich OT 2
strain [streɪn] Belastung **WS 1**, 14
strange [streɪndʒ] seltsam OT 1
strategic [strə'ti:dʒɪk] strategisch OT 4
strategy ['strætədʒi] Strategie OT 4
straw [strɔ:] Trinkhalm; Strohhalm; Stroh OT 4
strawberry ['strɔ:bəri] Erdbeere OT 1
stream [stri:m] Bach OT 2
streamer ['stri:mə] Luftschlangen OT 4
street [stri:t] Straße OT 1
street collection ['stri:t kəlekʃn] Straßensammlung OT 2
strength [streŋθ] Stärke OT 2
to **strengthen** ['streŋkθn] stärker werden; stärker machen OT 5
stress [stres] Stress; Betonung OT 1
stressed [strest] gestresst; angestrengt OT 2
stressful ['stresfl] stressig OT 4
stressor ['stresə] Stressfaktor **WS 4**, 142
to **stretch** [stretʃ] dehnen OT 2
strewn [stru:n] übersät **WS 1**, 15
strict [strɪkt] streng OT 2
strike [straɪk] Streik OT 4
to **strike** [straɪk] schlagen; zuschlagen; streiken OT 1
to **strike a chord** [straɪk ə kɔ:rd] berühren **WS 2**, 72
striker ['straɪkə] Stürmer(in) OT 3
string [strɪŋ] Schnur; Saite OT 2
strip [strɪp] Band; Streifen OT 5
stroke [strəʊk] Schlag OT 3
strong [strɒŋ] stark OT 2
to **structure** ['strʌktʃə] strukturieren; aufbauen OT 5
structure ['strʌktʃə] Struktur OT 1
to **struggle** ['strʌgl] sich anstrengen; sich bemühen OT 5
stubborn ['stʌbərn] dickköpfig **WS 1**, 39
student ['stju:dnt] Student(in); Schüler(in) OT 1
student council ['stju:dnt 'kaʊnsl] Schülerrat OT 2
studies [stʌdiz] Studium; Wissenschaft OT 1
studio ['stju:diəʊ] Studio OT 5
to **study** ['stʌdi] studieren OT 1
stuff [stʌf] Zeug OT 2

to **stump** [stʌmp] ins Stocken bringen **WS 2**, 58
stun [stʌn] betäubend **WS 1**, 18
stunning ['stʌnɪŋ] toll; atemberaubend OT 5
stupid ['stju:pɪd] dumm OT 2
stupidly ['stju:pɪdli] dumm OT 2
style [staɪl] Stil OT 2
stylish ['staɪlɪʃ] schick OT 4
stylistic [staɪ'lɪstɪk] stilistisch OT 5
to **stylize** ['staɪlaɪz] stilisieren **WS 1**, 12
subcontinent [ˌsʌbkɒntɪ'nɛnt] Subkontinent **WS 1**, 12
sub-heading ['sʌb ˌhedɪŋ] Unterüberschrift OT 2
subject ['sʌbdʒɪkt] Thema; Fach; Subjekt OT 1
to **subject** ['sʌbdʒɪkt] unterwerfen OT 4
subjection [səb'dʒɛkʃən] Unterwerfung **WS 2**, 72
subject pronoun [ˌsʌbdʒekt 'prəʊnaʊn] Subjektpronomen OT 1
submarine [ˌsʌbmə'ri:n] U-Boot OT 3
submissive [səb'mɪsɪv] unterwürfig **WS 2**, 71
to **submit** [səb'mɪt] abliefern **WS 1**, 25
to **subscribe** [səb'skraɪb] abonnieren OT 5
subsequently ['sʌbsɪkwəntli] später **WS 1**, 23
substitute ['sʌbstɪtju:t] Ersatz OT 3
substitution [ˌsʌbstɪ'tju:ʃn] Ersatz OT 3
subtle ['sʌtl] subtil **WS 1**, 27
subtlety ['sʌtlti] Feinheit **WS 3**, 94
suburb ['sʌbɜ:rb] Außenbezirk **WS 2**, 52
subway ['sʌbweɪ] U-Bahn OT 1
to **succeed** [sək'si:d] erfolgreich sein OT 2
success [sək'ses] Erfolg OT 3
successful [sək'sesfl] erfolgreich OT 2
successive [sək'sesɪv] aufeinanderfolgend; fortlaufend OT 5
such [sʌtʃ] so OT 2
sudden ['sʌdn] plötzlich OT 2
suddenly ['sʌdənli] plötzlich OT 1
to **suffer** ['sʌfə] leiden OT 5
sufficient [sə'fɪʃnt] ausreichend; genug OT 5
sugar ['ʃʊgə] Zucker OT 3
to **suggest** [sə'dʒest] vorschlagen OT 1
suggestion [sə'dʒestʃən] Vorschlag OT 1
suicide ['su:ɪsaɪd] Selbstmord OT 5
suit [su:t] Anzug OT 1
to **suit** [su:t] jdm. stehen OT 1
suitable ['su:təbl] geeignet OT 4
suitcase ['su:tkeɪs] Koffer OT 2
to **sulk** [sʌlk] schmollen OT 3
to **sum up** [sʌm ʌp] zusammenfassen OT 4
to **summarize** ['sʌməraɪz] zusammenfassen OT 2
summary ['sʌməri] Zusammenfassung OT 3
summer ['sʌmə] Sommer OT 1
sun [sʌn] Sonne OT 1
sunburn ['sʌnbɜ:n] Sonnenbrand OT 2
sunburnt ['sʌnbɜ:nt] sonnenverbrannt OT 5
Sunday ['sʌndeɪ] Sonntag OT 1
sunglasses ['sʌnglɑ:sɪz] Sonnenbrille OT 2
sunny ['sʌni] sonnig OT 1
sunscreen ['sʌnskri:n] Sonnenschutzmittel OT 2
sunset ['sʌnset] Sonnenuntergang OT 3
sunshine ['sʌnʃaɪn] Sonnenschein OT 3
sunstroke ['sʌnstrəʊk] Sonnenstich OT 2
superhero ['su:pəhɪərəʊ] Superheld OT 5
superlative [su'pɜ:lətɪv] Superlativ OT 2
supermarket ['su:pəmɑ:kɪt] Supermarkt OT 1
to **supervise** ['su:pəvaɪz] beaufsichtigen OT 3
supervision [ˌsu:pə'vɪʒn] Überwachung; Aufsicht OT 5
supervisor ['su:pəvaɪzə] Leiter(in) OT 4
supplement ['sʌplɪmənt] Nahrungsergänzung OT 5
supply [sə'plaɪ] Vorrat OT 3
to **support** [sə'pɔ:t] unterstützen OT 1
supporter [sə'pɔ:tə] Befürworter(in); Fan OT 2
supportive [sə'pɔ:tɪv] unterstützend OT 5
to **suppose** [sə'pəʊz] vermuten; annehmen OT 1
sure [ʃʊə] sicher OT 1
to **make sure** [meɪk 'ʃʊə] sichergehen; sicherstellen OT 2
surely ['ʃʊəli] sicherlich OT 4
surface ['sɜ:fɪs] Oberfläche OT 3
surfer ['sɜ:fə] Surfer OT 4
surfing ['sɜ:fɪŋ] Surfen OT 1
surgeon ['sɜ:dʒən] Chirurg(in) OT 3
surgery ['sɜ:dʒəri] Sprechstunde; Praxis OT 5
surprise [sə'praɪz] Überraschung OT 1
surprised [sə'praɪzd] überrascht OT 1
surprising [sə'praɪzɪŋ] überraschend OT 2
to **surrender** [sə'rendə] sich ergeben **WS 1**, 39
to **surround** [sə'raʊnd] umgeben **WS 2**, 60
surveillance [sə'veɪləns] Überwachung **WS 3**, 104
survey ['sɜ:veɪ] Umfrage OT 1
to **survey** ['sɜ:veɪ] befragen OT 5
survival [sə'vaɪvl] Überleben OT 2
to **survive** [sə'vaɪv] überleben OT 3
sushi ['su:ʃi] Sushi OT 1
to **suspect** [sə'spekt] vermuten **WS 1**, 26
suspicious [sə'spɪʃəs] verdächtig **WS 2**, 67
sustainability [səˌsteɪnə'bɪləti] Nachhaltigkeit OT 3
sustainable [sə'steɪnəbl] nachhaltig OT 4
to **swallow** ['swɒləʊ] schlucken; hinunterschlucken OT 4
swamp [swɒmp] Sumpf OT 2
to **swap** [swɒp] tauschen OT 1
to **swear** [sweə] schwören OT 4
to **sweat** ['swet] schwitzen OT 2
sweatshirt ['swetʃɜ:t] Sweatshirt OT 1
sweaty ['sweti] verschwitzt OT 5
Swedish ['swi:dɪʃ] schwedisch OT 4
to **sweep** [swi:p] fegen OT 4
sweet [swi:t] Bonbon OT 2
sweet corn ['swi:t kɔ:n] Zuckermais OT 1
sweetheart ['swi:thɑ:t] Liebste(r); Liebes OT 5
swelling ['swelɪŋ] Schwellung OT 2
swift ['swɪft] zügig **WS 2**, 62
to **swim** [swɪm] schwimmen OT 1
swimmer ['swɪmə] Schwimmer(in) OT 2
swimming ['swɪmɪŋ] Schwimmen OT 1
to **swing** [swɪŋ] verändern **WS 2**, 72
switch [swɪtʃ] Schalter OT 3
to **switch on** [swɪtʃ ɒn] anschalten OT 1
swollen ['swəʊln] geschwollen OT 2
sword [sɔ:d] Schwert OT 1
syllable ['sɪləbəl] Silbe OT 2
symbol ['sɪmbl] Symbol OT 1
to **symbolize** ['sɪmbəlaɪz] symbolisieren **WS 2**, 62
sympathetic [ˌsɪmpə'θetɪk] mitfühlend OT 3
to **sympathize** ['sɪmpəθaɪz] mit jdm. mitleiden; mitfühlen OT 5
sympathy ['sɪmpəθi] Mitgefühl **WS 1**, 18
symptom ['sɪmptəm] Symptom; Anzeichen **WS 3**, 106

synaesthesia [ˌsɪnəsˈθiːziə] Synästhesie OT 2
synagogue [ˈsɪnəɡɒɡ] Synagoge OT 1
syndrome [ˈsɪndrəʊm] Syndrom; Krankheitsbild **WS 1**, 30
synonym [ˈsɪnənɪm] Synonym OT 2
to **synthesize** [ˈsɪnθəsaɪz] synthetisieren **WS 3**, 112
synthetic [sɪnˈθetɪk] synthetisch OT 4
syrup [ˈsɪrəp] Sirup OT 3
system [ˈsɪstəm] System OT 1
systematic [ˌsɪstəˈmætɪk] systematisch; methodisch **WS 3**, 121
systematically [ˌsɪstəˈmætɪkli] systematisch OT 5
systemic [sɪˈstiːmɪk] systembedingt **WS 2**, 57

T

tab [tæb] Tab OT 3
table [ˈteɪbl] Tisch OT 1
tablespoon [ˈteɪblspuːn] Esslöffel OT 2
tablet [ˈtæblət] Tablette OT 2
taboo [təˈbuː] Tabu **WS 1**, 33
to **tackle** [ˈtækl] angreifen OT 3
taco [ˈtækəʊ] Taco OT 1
tactic [ˈtæktɪk] Taktik OT 2
tag [tæɡ] Etikett; kurze Schnur, die gelochte Blätter zusammenhält OT 2
tail [teɪl] Schwanz OT 2
Taiwanese [taɪˈwɑːnˈniːz] taiwanisch OT 4
to **take** [teɪk] nehmen OT 1
to **take a joke** [teɪk ə dʒəʊk] Spaß verstehen OT 2
to **take a photo** [ˌteɪk ə ˈfəʊtəʊ] ein Foto machen OT 1
to **take charge** [teɪk tʃɑːdʒ] die Leitung übernehmen OT 2
to **take for granted** [teɪk fə ˈɡrɑːntɪd] für selbstverständlich halten OT 4
to **take into account** [teɪk ˈɪntə əˈkaʊnt] berücksichtigen; beachten OT 5
to **take out** [ˈteɪk aʊt] rausbringen OT 4
to **take part** [teɪk ˈpɑːt] teilnehmen OT 2
to **take turns** [teɪk tɜːnz] (sich) abwechseln OT 1
to **take up** [teɪk ʌp] mit etw. anfangen; aufnehmen OT 1
takeout [ˈteɪkaʊt] Essen zum Mitnehmen OT 4
tale [teɪl] Geschichte OT 2
talent [ˈtælənt] Talent; Begabung OT 2
talented [ˈtæləntɪd] talentiert OT 3
talk [tɔːk] Vortrag; Rede OT 2
to **talk** [tɔːk] reden OT 1
tall [tɔːl] groß; hoch OT 1
tally [ˈtæli] Gesamtliste OT 4
tank [tæŋk] Tank OT 3
to **tap** [tæp] tippen; klopfen OT 2
tape [teɪp] Klebeband OT 1
target [ˈtɑːɡɪt] Ziel OT 2
to **target** [ˈtɑːɡɪt] zielen auf OT 5
task [tɑːsk] Aufgabe OT 1
taste [teɪst] Geschmack OT 4
to **taste** [teɪst] schmecken OT 1
tasty [ˈteɪsti] schmackhaft OT 2
tatters [ˈtætərz] Fetzen **WS 2**, 79
tattoo [təˈtuː] Tätowierung OT 3
tax [tæks] Steuer OT 4
taxi [ˈtæksi] Taxi OT 1
tax-payer [ˈtækspeɪər] Steuerzahler(in) OT 5
tea [tiː] Tee OT 1
to **teach** [tiːtʃ] unterrichten OT 1
teacher [ˈtiːtʃə] Lehrer(in) OT 1
tea light [ˈtiː laɪt] Teelicht OT 2
team [tiːm] Mannschaft OT 1
teammate [ˈtiːmmeɪt] Mitspieler(in) OT 2
teamwork [ˈtiːmwɜːk] Teamwork; Gruppenarbeit OT 4
tear [tɪə] Träne OT 2
to **tear** [teə] reißen OT 2
to **tease** [tiːz] ärgern OT 1
tech [tek] technisch OT 2
tech-orientated [tekɔːrientɪd] techorientiert OT 5
technical [ˈteknɪkl] technisch OT 4
technique [tekˈniːk] Technik; Methode OT 4
technological [ˌteknəˈlɒdʒɪkl] technisch; technologisch OT 4
technology [tekˈnɒlədʒi] Technologie OT 1
teen [tiːn] Teenager OT 2
teenage [ˈtiːneɪdʒ] Teenager... OT 4
teenager [ˈtiːneɪdʒə] Teenager; Jugendliche(r) OT 2
tooth [tuːθ] Zahn OT 2
telecast [ˈtelɪkæst] Sendezeit **WS 1**, 39
teleconference [ˈtelikɒnfrəns] Telefonkonferenz OT 3
telegraph [ˈtelɪɡrɑːf] Telegraf OT 4
telescope [ˈtelɪskəʊp] Teleskop **WS 3**, 103
television [ˈtelɪvɪʒn] Fernseher OT 2
to **tell** [tel] erzählen OT 1
temperature [ˈtemprətʃə] Temperatur OT 2
template [ˈtempleɪt] Vorlage OT 4
temple [ˈtempl] Tempel OT 1
temporary [ˈtemprəri] vorübergehend **WS 1**, 14
to **tempt** [tempt] versuchen; locken OT 5
ten [ten] zehn OT 1
to **tend to** [tend] zu etw. neigen; zu etw. tendieren OT 5
to **tend** [tɛnd] sich kümmern um **WS 1**, 16
tennis [ˈtenɪs] Tennis OT 1
tense [tens] Zeitform; Tempus OT 1
tension [ˈtenʃn] Anspannung OT 4
tent [tent] Zelt OT 1
term [tɜːm] Semester OT 2
terrible [ˈterəbl] schrecklich OT 1
terrier [ˈteriə] Terrier OT 2
terrified [ˈterɪfaɪd] verängstigt OT 3
to **terrify** [ˈterɪˌfaɪ] erschrecken **WS 3**, 104
territorial [ˌterɪˈtɔːril] Gebiets- **WS 1**, 40
territory [ˈterətri] Gebiet OT 5
test [test] Test OT 1
text [tekst] SMS; Text OT 1
to **text** [tekst] texten OT 1
textile [ˈtekstaɪl] Textil- **WS 3**, 102
than [ðən] als OT 1
to **thank** [θæŋk] danken OT 1
thankful [ˈθæŋkfl] dankbar **WS 1**, 15
thanks [θæŋks] danke OT 1
Thanksgiving [ˌθæŋksˈɡɪvɪŋ] amerikanisches Erntedankfest OT 2
that [ðæt] diese(r, -s); jene(r, -s) OT 1
That'll be ... [ðætl bi] Das macht... OT 2
the [ðiː] der; die; das OT 1
theatre [ˈθɪətə] Theater OT 1
theft [θeft] Diebstahl OT 5
their [ðeə] ihr OT 1
theirs [ðeəz] ihre(r, -s) OT 2
them [ðem] sie; ihnen OT 1
theme [θiːm] Thema OT 4
themselves [ðəmˈselvz] sich (selbst) OT 3
then [ðen] dann OT 1
theoretical [ˌθɪəˈretɪkl] theoretisch OT 4
theoretically [ˌθɪəˈretɪkli] theoretisch OT 5
theory [ˈθɪəri] Theorie OT 1
there [ðeə] da; dort OT 1
there is / are [ðeə ɪz / ɑ] es gibt OT 1
thereafter [ˌðɛrˈæftə] danach **WS 1**, 39

therefore ['ðeəfɔː] deshalb OT 3
thermostat ['θɜːməstæt] Thermostat; Temperaturregler OT 5
these [ðiːz] diese OT 1
they [ðeɪ] sie OT 1
thick [θɪk] dick OT 1
thievery ['θiːvəri] Diebstahl **WS 2**, 71
thigh [θaɪ] Oberschenkel OT 1
thin [θɪn] dünn OT 1
thing [θɪŋ] Ding OT 1
to **think** [θɪŋk] denken OT 1
to **think about** ['θɪŋk əbaʊt] denken an; nachdenken über OT 1
to **think of** ['θɪŋk əv] denken an; sich erinnern an OT 1
third [θɜːd] Dritte(r, -s) OT 1
thirsty ['θɜːsti] durstig OT 1
thirteen [ˌθɜː'tiːn] dreizehn OT 1
thirty ['θɜːti] dreißig OT 1
this [ðɪs] diese(r, -s) OT 1
thorn [θɔːn] Stachel OT 2
thoroughly ['θʌrəli] völlig; durchaus OT 5
those [ðəʊz] diese; jene dort OT 1
though [ðəʊ] obwohl; jedoch OT 2
thought [θɔːt] Gedanke OT 4
thoughtful ['θɔːtfl] nachdenklich; rücksichtsvoll OT 3
thoughtless ['θɔːtləs] gedankenlos; rücksichtslos OT 2
thought-provoking ['θɔːt prəvəʊkɪŋ] zum Nachdenken anregend OT 5
thousand ['θaʊznd] tausend OT 1
threat [θret] Gefahr OT 5
to **threaten** ['θretn] gefährden OT 5
three [θri] drei OT 1
thrifting [θrɪftɪŋ] Secondhand shoppen OT 4
thrift store ['θrɪft stɔː] Secondhandladen OT 4
thrilling ['θrɪlɪŋ] spannend **WS 1**, 22
throat [θrəʊt] Hals OT 2
throne [θrəʊn] Thron OT 5
throng [θrɒŋ] Menchenmenge OT 2
through [θruː] durch OT 1
throughout [θruː'aʊt] während; durchweg OT 3
to **throw** [θrəʊ] werfen OT 1
to **throw away** [ˌθrəʊ ə'weɪ] wegwerfen OT 2
to **throw up** [θrəʊ ʌp] (sich) übergeben OT 2
thumb [θʌm] Daumen OT 4
thunderstorm ['θʌndəstɔːm] Gewitter OT 2
Thursday ['θɜːzdeɪ] Donnerstag OT 1

thus [ðʌs] dadurch; daher OT 5
tick [tɪk] Haken; Häkchen OT 2
ticket ['tɪkɪt] Eintrittskarte; Fahrkarte OT 1
ticket office ['tɪkɪt ˌɒfɪs] Fahrkartenschalter OT 2
tide [taɪd] Strömung; Gezeiten **WS 1**, 27
tidings ['taɪdɪŋz] Nachrichten **WS 2**, 78
to **tidy** ['taɪdi] aufräumen OT 1
tidy ['taɪdi] aufgeräumt OT 2
tie [taɪ] Krawatte OT 1
to **tie** [taɪ] binden; anbinden OT 2
tiger ['taɪgə] Tiger OT 1
tight [taɪt] eng; dicht **WS 1**, 15
till [tɪl] bis OT 2
to **tilt** [tɪlt] sich neigen OT 3
time [taɪm] Zeit OT 1
all the time [ɔːl ðiː taɪm] die ganze Zeit OT 2
time-consuming ['taɪm kən'sjuːmɪŋ] zeitraubend **WS 3**, 101
timeline ['taɪmlaɪn] Zeitachse OT 2
timely ['taɪmli] rechtzeitig; passend OT 3
timer ['taɪmər] Timer; Zeituhr OT 5
timetable ['taɪmteɪbl] Fahrplan; Stundenplan OT 1
timid ['tɪmɪd] zaghaft **WS 3**, 96
timing ['taɪmɪŋ] Zeitpunkt OT 3
tin [tɪn] Zinn; Dose OT 2
tinder ['tɪndə] Zunder OT 2
to **tingle** ['tɪŋgl] kribbeln **WS 1**, 30
tinned [tɪnd] in Dosen OT 2
tiny ['taɪni] winzig OT 1
tip [tɪp] Spitze; Hinweis OT 1
to **tip over** [tɪp 'əʊvə] umkippen OT 5
tipping point ['tɪpɪŋ pɔɪnt] Kipppunkt; Trendwende OT 5
tired ['taɪəd] müde OT 1
tireless ['taɪərləs] unermüdlich **WS 4**, 142
tissue ['tɪʃuː] Taschentuch OT 5
title ['taɪtl] Titel OT 1
to [tuː] zu OT 1
toad [təʊd] Kröte OT 2
toast [təʊst] Toast OT 2
tobacco [tə'bækəʊ] Tabak OT 3
today [tə'deɪ] heute OT 1
toe [təʊ] Zeh OT 1
tippy toes ['tɪpi toʊz] Zehenspitzen **WS 3**, 96
together [tə'geðə] zusammen OT 1
toilet ['tɔɪlət] Toilette OT 2
composting toilet ['kɒmpɒstɪŋ 'tɔɪlət] Biotoilette OT 3

toiletries ['tɔɪlɪtriːz] Toilettenartikel **WS 1**, 23
token ['təʊkən] Zeichen; Geste OT 5
tolerance ['tɒlərəns] Toleranz OT 5
tolerant ['tɒlərənt] tolerant OT 4
to **tolerate** ['tɒləˌreɪt] tolerieren **WS 3**, 122
tomato [tə'mɑːtəʊ] Tomate OT 1
tomboy ['tɒmbɔɪ] burschikoses Mädchen; Wildfang OT 5
tomorrow [tə'mɒrəʊ] morgen OT 1
ton [tʌn] Tonne OT 2
tone [təʊn] Ton OT 5
toned [toʊnd] straff **WS 4**, 142
toner cartridge ['təʊnə 'kɑːtrɪdʒ] Tonerkartusche OT 5
tongue [tʌŋ] Zunge OT 3
tonight [tə'naɪt] heute Abend OT 1
too [tuː] zu; auch OT 1
tool [tuːl] Werkzeug OT 2
toothbrush ['tuːθbrʌʃ] Zahnbürste OT 4
toothpaste ['tuːθpeɪst] Zahnpasta OT 4
top [tɒp] obere(r, -s); Spitze OT 1
to **top** [tɒp] belegen OT 3
topic ['tɒpɪk] Thema OT 1
torch [tɔːtʃ] Taschenlampe OT 1
torchlight ['tɔːtʃlaɪt] Licht der Taschenlampe OT 1
tortoise ['tɔːtəs] Schildkröte OT 1
to **toss** [tɒs] werfen OT 3
total ['təʊtl] gesamt OT 1
totalitarian [toʊˌtælɪ'tɛəriən] totalitär **WS 3**, 104
to **touch** [tʌtʃ] berühren; anfassen OT 1
touchdown ['tʌtʃdaʊn] Touchdown OT 2
touchscreen ['tʌtʃskriːn] Berührungsbildschirm OT 4
tough [tʌf] hart OT 4
tour [tʊə] Reise; Rundgang OT 1
to **tour** [tʊə] besuchen; besichten OT 5
tourism ['tʊərɪzəm] Tourismus OT 2
tourist ['tʊərɪst] Tourist(in) OT 1
tournament ['tɔːnəmənt] Turnier OT 3
towards [tə'wɔːdz] in Richtung OT 2
towel ['taʊəl] Handtuch OT 2
tower ['taʊə] Turm OT 1
to **tower** ['taʊə] überragen **WS 1**, 19
town [taʊn] Stadt OT 1
township ['taʊnʃɪp] Gemeinde OT 4
townspeople ['taʊnzpiːpl] Stadtbewohner(innen) OT 4
towpath ['təʊpɑːθ] Treidelpfad OT 3
toxic ['tɒksɪk] toxisch; giftig OT 4
toy [tɔɪ] Spielzeug OT 2

to **trace back** [treɪs bæk] zurückführen **WS 2**, 83
track [træk] Weg OT 1
tract [trækt] Gebiet **WS 4**, 136
tractor ['træktə] Traktor OT 2
trade [treɪd] Handel; Geschäft OT 5
to **trade** [treɪd] handeln **WS 1**, 14
trade off [treɪd ɒf] Kompromiss **WS 3**, 98
tradition [trə'dɪʃn] Tradition OT 2
traditional [trə'dɪʃənl] traditionell OT 1
traffic ['træfɪk] Verkehr OT 1
to **traffic** ['træfɪkt] verschleppen; illegalen Handel treiben OT 4
traffic jam ['træfɪk dʒæm] Stau OT 2
trafficker ['træfɪktə] Schlepper OT 4
tragedy ['trædʒədi] Tragödie OT 5
tragic ['trædʒɪk] tragisch **WS 1**, 38
trail [treɪl] Pfad; Spur OT 2
trailer ['treɪlə] Trailer OT 4
train [treɪn] Zug OT 1
to **train** [treɪn] trainieren OT 2
trainer ['treɪnər] Turnschuh; Trainer(in) OT 4
training ['treɪnɪŋ] Ausbildung OT 2
training course ['treɪnɪŋ kɔ:s] Ausbildungslehrgang; Weiterbildungslehrgang OT 2
trait [treɪt] Eigenschaft **WS 4**, 142
tram ['træm] Straßenbahn OT 1
trans [trænz] trans... OT 5
transaction [træn'zækʃn] Transaktion **WS 4**, 142
transatlantic [ˌtrænzət'læntɪk] transatlantisch OT 3
to **transcribe** [træn'skraɪb] abschreiben; transkribieren OT 5
transcriber [træn'skraɪbə] Transkribierer(in) OT 5
transcript ['trænskrɪpt] Abschrift; Niederschrift OT 5
to **transfer** [træns'fɜ:] transferieren; übertragen OT 4
transferable [træns'fɜ:rəbl] übertragbar **WS 3**, 110
to **transform** [træns'fɔ:m] verändern OT 4
transformation [ˌtrænsfə'meɪʃn] Veränderung; Verwandlung OT 4
transgender [trænz'dʒendər] transsexuell OT 5
transition [træn'zɪʃn] Wechsel; Übergang OT 5
to **translate** [træns'leɪt] übersetzen OT 1
transmission [træns'mɪʃən] Übertragung **WS 3**, 101
transphobia [træns'foʊbiə] Transphobie **WS 3**, 92
transplant [træns'plɑ:nt] Transplantation OT 3
to **transport** [træn'spɔ:t] transportieren **WS 3**, 99
transport ['trænspɔ:t] Verkehr; Verkehrsmittel OT 2
transportation [ˌtrænspɔ:r'teɪʃən] Verkehr **WS 2**, 55
to **trap** [træp] fangen OT 5
trash [træʃ] Abfall OT 2
trash can ['træʃ kæn] Mülleimer OT 2
trauma ['trɔ:mə] Trauma OT 5
traumatic [trɔ:'mætɪk] traumatisch **WS 1**, 15
travel ['trævl] Reisen OT 1
to **travel** ['trævl] reisen OT 1
travel agent ['trævl eɪdʒənt] Reisekauffrau / -kaufmann OT 3
traveller ['trævələ] Reisende(r) OT 3
tray [treɪ] Tablett OT 2
treadmill ['tredmɪl] Laufband OT 4
treasure ['treʒə] Schatz OT 3
to **treasure** ['treʒə] schätzen **WS 2**, 67
to **treat** [tri:t] behandeln OT 4
treatment ['tri:tmənt] Behandlung OT 5
tree [tri:] Baum OT 1
to **trek** [trek] trecken OT 2
to **tremble** ['trembl] zittern OT 2
trend [trend] Trend OT 4
trespasser ['trespəsər] Unbefugte(r) OT 5
trial ['traɪəl] Prozess OT 2
triangle ['traɪæŋgl] Dreieck; Triangel OT 2
triangular [traɪ'æŋgjələ] dreieckig OT 3
tribal ['traɪbl] Stammes... OT 3
tribe [traɪb] Stamm OT 3
tribute ['trɪbju:t] Tribut **WS 2**, 72
trick [trɪk] Trick OT 5
trickle ['trɪkl] Tropfen **WS 3**, 101
tricky ['trɪki] kompliziert OT 4
to **trigger** ['trɪgə] auslösen **WS 2**, 83
trillion ['trɪljən] Billion **WS 4**, 142
trilogy ['trɪlədʒi] Trilogie OT 5
trip [trɪp] Reise; Ausflug OT 1
to **trip** [trɪp] stolpern OT 2
triple ['trɪpl] Dreier **WS 4**, 137
triumph ['traɪʌmf] Triumph **WS 2**, 79
to **trivialize** ['trɪvɪəˌlaɪz] banalisieren **WS 2**, 69
trolley ['trɒli] Wagen OT 1
trophy ['trəʊfi] Pokal OT 2
tropical ['trɒpɪkl] tropisch OT 4
to **trot** [trɒt] traben OT 2
trouble ['trʌbl] Schwierigkeit; Ärger OT 2
troublemaker ['trʌblˌmeɪkə] Unruhestifter(in) **WS 2**, 78
trousers ['traʊzəz] Hose OT 1
truck [trʌk] Laster; Lastkraftwagen OT 1
true [tru:] wahr; richtig OT 1
truly ['tru:li] wirklich OT 5
trumpet ['trʌmpɪt] Trompete OT 2
trunk [trʌŋk] Kofferraum OT 2
to **trust** [trʌst] vertrauen OT 3
truth [tru:θ] Wahrheit OT 3
to **try** [traɪ] versuchen OT 1
to **try out** [traɪ aʊt] ausprobieren OT 2
tub [tʌb] Wanne **WS 3**, 101
tube [tju:b] Schlauch; Londoner U-Bahn OT 1
tuckshop ['tʌkʃɒp] Kiosk **WS 2**, 78
Tuesday ['tju:zdeɪ] Dienstag OT 1
tuition [tju'ɪʃn] Studiengebühr(en) OT 5
tuna ['tju:nə] Thunfisch OT 1
tune [tju:n] Melodie **WS 2**, 72
tunnel ['tʌnl] Tunnel OT 3
turban ['tɜ:rbən] Turban **WS 2**, 69
turbine ['tɜ:baɪn] Turbine OT 4
turkey ['tɜ:ki] Truthahn OT 1
turn: It's your turn. [ˌɪts 'jɔ: tɜ:n] Du bist dran. OT 1
to **turn** [tɜ:n] drehen OT 2
to **turn off** [tɜ:n' ɒf] ausschalten OT 2
turntable ['tɜ:nteɪbl] Drehscheibe OT 2
turtle ['tɜ:tl] Schildkröte OT 2
leatherback turtle ['leðəbæk ˌtɜ:tl] Lederrückenschildkröte OT 2
tusk [tʌsk] Stoßzahn OT 3
tutor ['tju:tə] Tutor(in) OT 4
to **tutor** ['tju:tə] Nachhilfeunterricht geben OT 4
TV [ˌti:'vi:] Fernsehen OT 1
tweezers ['twi:zəz] Pinzette OT 2
twelve [twelv] zwölf OT 1
twenty ['twenti] zwanzig OT 1
twice [twaɪs] zweimal OT 2
twig [twɪg] Zweig OT 2
twin [twɪn] Zwilling OT 1
to **twinkle** ['twɪŋkl] glitzern OT 4
twisted ['twɪstɪd] verdreht OT 1
two [tu:] zwei OT 1
type [taɪp] Art OT 2
typewriter ['taɪpraɪtə] Schreibmaschine OT 5

typical ['tɪpɪkl] typisch OT 2
typist ['taɪpɪst] Schreibkraft OT 5
tyrannosaurus rex [tɪˌrænə'sɔ:rəs reks] Tyrannosaurus rex OT 1

U
ugly ['ʌgli] hässlich OT 1
ulterior [ʌl'tɪəriə] verborgen **WS 3**, 112
umbrella [ʌm'brelə] Regenschirm OT 1
unable: to **be unable** [bi ʌn'eɪbl] nicht in der Lage sein **WS 2**, 69
unacceptable [ˌʌnək'septəbl] inakzeptabel OT 5
unaccompanied minor [ʌˌnəkʌmpənid 'maɪnə] alleinreisendes Kind OT 2
unaware [ˌʌnə'weər] in Unkenntnis; unwissend OT 5
unbelievable [ˌʌnbɪ'li:vəbl] unglaublich OT 2
unborn [ˌʌn'bɔ:n] Ungeborene(r) **WS 1**, 39
unbroken [ʌn'broʊkən] ungebrochen **WS 2**, 54
uncertain [ʌn'sɜ:rtən] ungewiss **WS 3**, 110
uncertainty [ʌn'sɜ:tnti] Ungewissheit **WS 3**, 104
unchaperoned [ʌn'ʃæpərəʊnd] unbeaufsichtigt **WS 4**, 133
uncle ['ʌŋkl] Onkel OT 1
uncomfortable [ʌn'kʌmftəbl] unbequem OT 3
unconquerable [ʌn'kɒŋkərəbl] unbesiegbar **WS 2**, 59
uncountable [ʌn'kaʊntəbl] unzählbar OT 1
to **uncover** [ʌn'kʌvə] freilegen OT 3
undecided [ˌʌndɪ'saɪdɪd] unentschieden; unentschlossen OT 5
under ['ʌndə] unter OT 1
underbelly ['ʌndərbɛli] Schattenseite **WS 1**, 16
underdog ['ʌndədɒg] Außenseiter(in); Underdog OT 5
to **undergo** [ˌʌndə'gəʊ] durchmachen OT 5
underground ['ʌndəgraʊnd] U-Bahn OT 1
to **underline** [ˌʌndə'laɪn] unterstreichen OT 1
underneath [ˌʌndə'ni:θ] darunter OT 3
under-resourced ['ʌndə rɪ'sɔ:rst] unterversorgt **WS 2**, 80
to **understand** [ˌʌndə'stænd] verstehen OT 1
to **understate** [ˌʌndə'steɪt] unterbewerten; untertreiben OT 5
to **undertake** [ˌʌndə'teɪk] durchführen **WS 1**, 21
underwater [ˌʌndə'wɔ:tə] Unterwasser-; unter Wasser OT 2
underworld ['ʌndəwɜ:ld] Unterwelt OT 5
undocumented [ˌʌn'dɒkjumentɪd] nicht erfasst OT 4
undoubtedly [ʌn'daʊtɪdli] zweifellos **WS 1**, 27
undrained [ˌʌn'dreɪnd] nicht abgetropft OT 2
undrinkable [ʌn'drɪŋkəbl] untrinkbar OT 5
unemployed [ˌʌnɪm'plɔɪd] arbeitslos OT 5
unemployment [ˌʌnɪm'plɔɪmənt] Arbeitslosigkeit OT 3
unexpected [ˌʌnɪk'spektɪd] unerwartet OT 5
unexpectedly [ˌʌnɪk'spektɪdli] unerwarteterweise OT 3
unfair [ˌʌn'feə] nicht fair OT 2
unfairness [ˌʌn'feənəs] Ungerechtigkeit; Unfairness OT 4
to **unfold** [ʌn'fəʊld] entfalten **WS 1**, 15
unforgettable [ˌʌnfə'getəbl] unvergesslich OT 5
unfortunately [ʌn'fɔ:tʃənətli] leider OT 3
unfriendly [ʌn'frendli] unfreundlich OT 4
unhappy [ʌn'hæpi] unglücklich OT 1
unhealthy [ʌn'helθi] ungesund OT 1
uni ['ju:ni] Uni OT 3
uniform ['ju:nɪfɔ:m] Uniform OT 1
to **unify** ['ju:nɪfaɪ] vereinigen OT 5
uninhabitable [ˌʌnɪn'hæbɪtəbl] unbewohnbar **WS 3**, 104
union ['ju:niən] Union; Bund OT 5
unique [ju'ni:k] einzigartig OT 2
unisex ['ju:nɪseks] Unisex-; nicht geschlechtsspezifisch OT 5
unit ['ju:nɪt] Einheit OT 5
to **unite** [ju'naɪt] sich vereinigen OT 5
unity ['ju:nəti] Einheit OT 5
universal [ˌju:nɪ'vɜ:sl] allgemein; universal OT 5
university [ˌju:nɪ'vɜ:səti] Universität OT 1
unknown [ˌʌn'nəʊn] unbekannt OT 3
unless [ən'les] außer wenn OT 4
unlike [ˌʌn'laɪk] anders als OT 3
unlikely [ʌn'laɪkli] unwahrscheinlich OT 4
to **unlock** [ˌʌn'lɒk] aufschließen; entriegeln OT 1
unlucky [ʌn'lʌki] glücklos OT 2
unnecessary [ʌn'nesəsəri] unnötig; überflüssig OT 4
to **unpack** [ˌʌn'pæk] auspacken OT 2
unpaid [ˌʌn'peɪd] unbezahlt OT 5
unpredictability [ˌʌnprɪˌdɪktə'bɪləti] Unberechenbarkeit OT 2
unreal [ˌʌn'rɪl] irreal **WS 1**, 29
unrecognizable [ʌn'rɛkəgnaɪzəbl] nicht wiedererkennbar **WS 1**, 15
unresolved [ˌʌnrɪ'zɒlvd] ungelöst **WS 2**, 68
unsafe [ʌn'seɪf] gefährlich OT 3
unshakable [ʌn'ʃeɪkəbl] unerschütterlich **WS 1**, 27
unspoilt [ˌʌn'spɔɪlt] unberührt OT 3
unsure [ʌn'ʃʊə] unsicher **WS 2**, 58
unsurprisingly [ˌʌnsə'praɪzɪŋlɪ] erwartungsgemäß OT 3
untended [ʌn'tɛndɪd] unbeachtet **WS 1**, 39
until [ʌn'tɪl] bis OT 3
untold [ˌʌn'təʊld] unermesslich **WS 4**, 136
untouchable [ʌn'tʌʧəbl] Unberührbare(r) **WS 1**, 16
unusual [ʌn'ju:ʒuəl] ungewöhnlich OT 2
to **unveil** [ʌn'veɪl] enthüllen **WS 1**, 19
unwell [ʌn'wel] krank OT 2
up [ʌp] hinauf; nach oben OT 1
upbeat ['ʌpbi:t] fröhlich **WS 2**, 72
upbringing ['ʌpbrɪŋɪŋ] Erziehung OT 5
upcoming [ˌʌp'kʌmɪŋ] aufstrebend; bevorstehend **WS 1**, 30
to **update** ['ʌpdeɪt] aktualisieren OT 3
to **uplift** [ʌp'lɪft] ermutigen **WW**, 11
to **upload** ['ʌpləʊd] hochladen OT 3
upmarket ['ʌpˌmɑ:rkɪt] exklusiv; reich **WS 2**, 53
uprising ['ʌpˌraɪzɪŋ] Aufstand **WS 2**, 83
uproar ['ʌpˌrɔ:r] Aufruhr **WS 2**, 58
to **upset** ['ʌpset] verärgern; enttäuschen **WS 1**, 21
upset [ʌp'set] verärgert; traurig OT 2
upside ['ʌpsaɪd] Vorteil OT 4
upstairs [ˌʌp'steəz] oben; im oberen Stockwerk OT 1
uptight [ˌʌp'taɪt] verklemmt OT 5
upwards ['ʊpwədz] aufwärts; nach oben OT 3
urban ['ɜ:bən] städtisch; urban OT 4

to urge [3:d3] dringend bitten; drängen OT 4
urgent ['3:d3ənt] dringend **WS 4**, 135
urgently ['3:d3əntli] dringend OT 5
us [ʌs] uns OT 1
usage ['ju:sɪd3] Nutzung **WS 4**, 133
to use [ju:z] benutzen OT 1
useful ['ju:sfl] nützlich OT 1
user ['ju:zə] Benutzer(in) OT 2
usher ['ʌʃə] Platzanweiser(in) OT 4
usual ['ju:3uəl] üblich OT 2
usually ['ju:3uəli] normalerweise OT 1
utmost ['ʌtmoʊst] größte(r) **WS 1**, 15
utopia [ju:'təʊpiə] Utopie **WS 3**, 92

V

vacation [veɪ'keɪʃn] Urlaub OT 2
vaccine ['væksi:n] Impfstoff **WS 3**, 101
vacuum ['vækju:m] Vakuum **WS 1**, 14
to vacuum ['vækju:m] staubsaugen OT 4
vacuum cleaner ['vækju:m kli:nə] Staubsauger OT 4
vague [veɪg] unbestimmt; vage OT 5
validity [və'lɪdəti] Glaubhaftigkeit **WS 3**, 112
valley ['væli] Tal OT 1
valuable ['væljuəbl] wertvoll OT 2
value ['vælju:] Wert OT 4
vampire ['væmpaɪə] Vampir(in) OT 2
van [væn] Transporter; Lieferwagen OT 4
to vandalize ['vændəlaɪz] zerstören; verwüsten OT 5
vanilla [və'nɪlə] Vanille OT 1
variation [,veəri'eɪʃn] Variante; Variation OT 5
variety [və'raɪəti] Vielfalt; Auswahl OT 5
various ['veəriəs] verschiedene OT 5
varnish ['vɑ:nɪʃ] Lack OT 5
to vary ['veəri] variieren OT 5
vast [vɑ:st] enorm; groß OT 5
vegan ['vi:gən] Veganer(in); vegan OT 1
vegetable ['ved3təbl] Gemüse OT 1
vegetarian [,ved3ə'teəriən] Vegetarier(in); vegetarisch OT 1
veggie ['ved3i] vegetarisch OT 2
vehicle [,vi:əkl] Fahrzeug OT 1
off-road vehicle ['ɒf rəʊd ,vi:əkl] Geländefahrzeug OT 1
vein [veɪn] Vene; Ader OT 5
velvety ['velvəti] samtartig OT 2
vending machine ['vendɪŋ məʃi:n] Automat OT 1
venom ['venəm] Gift OT 5
venue ['venju:] Veranstaltungsort OT 3
verb [v3:b] Verb; Zeitwort OT 1
verbal ['v3:bl] verbal; mündlich OT 5
to verify ['verɪfaɪ] verifizieren **WS 1**, 25
versatile ['v3:sətaɪl] vielseitig OT 3
verse [v3:s] Strophe OT 1
version ['v3:3n] Version OT 3
versus ['v3:səs] versus OT 4
vertical ['v3:tɪkl] senkrecht; vertikal OT 4
very ['veri] sehr OT 1
vest [vest] Weste; Unterhemd OT 2
vested ['vɛstɪd] Eigen-; persönlich **WS 3**, 99
vet [vet] Tierarzt / -ärztin OT 4
veterinarian [,vetərɪ'neəriən] Tierarzt / -ärztin OT 4
via ['vi:ə] über OT 2
vibe [vaɪb] Gefühl; Flair **WS 1**, 15
vibrant ['vaɪbrənt] dynamisch; lebhaft OT 5
to vibrate [vaɪ'breɪt] vibrieren; pulsieren OT 4
viceroy ['vaɪsrɔɪ] Vizekönig **WS 1**, 14
victim ['vɪktɪm] Opfer OT 4
victory ['vɪktəri] Sieg **WS 1**, 26
video ['vɪdiəʊ] Videokassette; Video OT 1
video clip ['vɪdiəʊ klɪp] Videoclip OT 2
video game ['vɪdiəʊ geɪm] Videospiel OT 2
view [vju:] Sicht; Aussicht OT 1
viewer ['vju:ə] Zuschauer(in) OT 3
viewing gallery ['vju:ɪŋ 'gæləri] Aussichtsgalerie OT 1
viewpoint ['vju:pɔɪnt] Aussichtspunkt OT 3
village ['vɪlɪd3] Dorf OT 1
villager ['vɪlɪd3ə] Dorfbewohner(in) OT 4
vindication [,vɪndɪ'keɪʃn] Rechtfertigung **WS 3**, 103
vintage ['vɪntɪd3] alt; klassisch OT 5
violation [,vaɪə'leɪʃn] Verletzung **WS 1**, 25
violence ['vaɪələns] Gewalt OT 4
non-violence [,nɒn 'vaɪələns] Gewaltlosigkeit OT 3
violent ['vaɪələnt] gewalttätig OT 5
violet ['vaɪələt] violett OT 1
violin [,vaɪə'lɪn] Geige OT 1
viral ['vaɪrl] viral **WS 2**, 69
virtual ['v3:tʃuəl] virtuell OT 4
virus ['vaɪrəs] Virus **WS 2**, 61
visa ['vi:zə] Visum OT 4
visible ['vɪzəbl] sichtbar **WS 1**, 21
vision ['vɪ3n] Vision OT 4
to visit ['vɪzɪt] besuchen OT 1
visitor ['vɪzɪtə] Besucher(in) OT 1
visual ['vɪ3uəl] visuell OT 2; Bildmaterial OT 4
visually ['vɪ3uəli] optisch; visuell OT 5
visual aid [,vɪ3uəl 'eɪd] Anschauungsmaterial OT 4
visual art ['vɪ3uəl 'ɑ:t] bildende Kunst OT 2
visualization [,vɪ3uəlaɪ'zeɪʃn] Visualisierung OT 3
to visualize ['vɪ3uəlaɪz] darstellen; visualisieren **WS 2**, 57
vital ['vaɪtl] lebenswichtig OT 4
vivid ['vɪvɪd] lebhaft **WS 1**, 43
vlog ['vlɒg] Vlog; Video-Blog OT 3
vlogger ['vlɒgə] Vlogger(in) OT 3
vocals ['vəʊklz] Gesang OT 2
vocational [vəʊ'keɪʃənl] beruflich OT 5
voice [vɔɪs] Stimme OT 2
tone of voice [təʊn əv vɔɪs] Tonfall; Artikulierung OT 4
to voice [vɔɪs] äußern; zum Ausdruck bringen OT 4
void [vɔɪd] nichtig **WS 1**, 39
volleyball ['vɒlibɔ:l] Volleyball OT 3
volunteer [,vɒlən'tɪə] Freiwillige(r); Ehrenamtliche(r) OT 2
to volunteer [,vɒlən'tɪə] (sich) freiwillig melden; ein Ehrenamt haben OT 2
voluntourism [vɒlən'tʊərɪzəm] Voluntourismus **WS 2**, 66
to vote [vəʊt] wählen OT 1
to vow [vaʊ] schwören **WS 1**, 27
vowel ['vaʊəl] Vokal; Selbstlaut OT 1
voyage ['vɔɪɪd3] Reise OT 3
vulnerable ['vʌlnərəbl] verletzlich; verwundbar **WS 1**, 40

W

wacky ['wæki] verrückt; verdreht OT 4
waffle ['wɒfl] Waffel OT 3
wage [weɪd3] Gehalt OT 4
wagon ['wægən] Wagen OT 4
wagon train ['wægən treɪn] Treck; Wagenzug OT 4
to wait [weɪt] warten OT 1
waiter ['weɪtə] Kellner(in) OT 1
to wake up ['weɪk ʌp] aufwachen OT 1
walk [wɔ:k] Spaziergang; Wanderung OT 2
to walk [wɔ:k] laufen; gehen (zu Fuß) OT 1

walker ['wɔ:kə] Wanderer / Wanderin OT 3
wall [wɔ:l] Wand OT 1
wall display [wɔ:l dɪ'spleɪ] Wandzeitung OT 2
wallet ['wɒlɪt] Brieftasche OT 1
to **want** [wɒnt] wollen OT 1
war [wɔ:] Krieg OT 2
to **war** [wɔ:] Krieg führen **WS 1**, 14
warder ['wɔ:rdə] Wärter(in) **WS 2**, 78
wardrobe ['wɔ:drəʊb] Kleiderschrank OT 1
warm [wɔ:m] warm OT 2
warm-up ['wɔ:m ʌp] Aufwärmübung OT 2
to **warm up** [wɔ:m ʌp] aufwärmen OT 2
to **warn** [wɔ:n] warnen OT 3
warrior ['wɒriə] Krieger(in) OT 2
warship ['wɔ:ʃɪp] Kriegsschiff OT 3
to **wash** [wɒʃ] waschen OT 2
washing up [ˌwɒʃɪŋ 'ʌp] Geschirrspülen OT 2
washroom ['wɒʃru:m] Waschraum **WS 3**, 96
wasp [wɒsp] Wespe OT 3
waste [weɪst] Abfall OT 3
to **waste** [weɪst] verschwenden OT 3
to **watch** [wɒtʃ] beobachten OT 1
watchman ['wɒtʃmən] Wächter OT 5
water ['wɔ:tə] Wasser OT 1
waterbus ['wɔ:tə bʌs] Wasserbus OT 3
waterfall ['wɔ:təfɔ:l] Wasserfall OT 1
waterhole ['wɔ:təhəʊl] Wasserloch OT 5
watering hole ['wɔ:tərɪŋ həʊl] Wasserstelle OT 5
waterproof ['wɔ:təpru:f] wasserdicht OT 2
waterproofs ['wɔ:təpru:fs] wasserdichte Kleidung OT 3
wave [weɪv] Welle OT 1
to **wave** [weɪv] winken OT 2
way [weɪ] Weg OT 1
waypoint ['weɪpɔɪnt] Zwischenstation OT 2
we [wi] wir OT 1
weak [wi:k] schwach OT 3
weakness ['wi:knəs] Schwäche OT 4
wealth [welθ] Reichtum; Vermögen OT 4
wealthy ['welθi] reich **WS 1**, 12
weapon ['wepən] Waffe OT 3
to **wear** [weə] tragen OT 1
weather ['weðə] Wetter OT 1
webinar ['webɪnɑ:] Webinar OT 4
website ['websaɪt] Webseite OT 1
to **wed** ['wedɪd] heiraten OT 3
wedding ['wedɪŋ] Hochzeit OT 3
Wednesday ['wenzdeɪ] Mittwoch OT 1
weed [wi:d] Unkraut OT 5
week [wi:k] Woche OT 1
weekday ['wi:kdeɪ] Wochentag OT 3
weekend ['wi:kend] Wochenende OT 1
weekly ['wi:kli] wöchentlich OT 3
to **weigh** [weɪ] wiegen OT 3
weight [weɪt] Gewicht OT 4
weightlessness ['weɪtləsnəs] Schwerelosigkeit OT 4
weightlifting ['weɪtlɪftɪŋ] Gewichtheben OT 4
weird [wɪəd] seltsam OT 1
welcome ['welkəm] willkommen OT 1
well [wel] Brunnen **WS 1**, 25
well [wel] gut OT 1
well done [wel 'dʌn] gut gemacht OT 1
wellness ['welnəs] Wellness; Wohlbefinden OT 4
Welsh [welʃ] walisisch OT 1
west [west] West- OT 1
westward ['westwəd] westwärts OT 4
wet [wet] nass OT 2
wetsuit ['wetsu:t] Taucheranzug; Neoprenanzug OT 1
whale [weɪl] Wal OT 1
whaling ['weɪlɪŋ] Walfang OT 2
what [wɒt] was OT 1
whatever [wɒ'tevə] was auch immer; egal welche OT 3
wheat [wi:t] Weizen OT 5
wheel [wi:l] Rad OT 1
wheelbarrow ['wi:lbærəʊ] Schubkarre **WS 1**, 21
wheelchair ['wi:ltʃeə] Rollstuhl OT 2
wheelchair user ['wi:ltʃeə ˌju:zə] Rollstuhlfahrer(in) OT 2
when [wen] wann OT 1
whenever [wen'evə] wann auch immer OT 4
where [weə] wo OT 1
whereas [ˌweər'æz] während OT 5
wherever [weər'evə] wo (auch) immer OT 3
whether ['weðə(r)] ob; falls; wann OT 1
which [wɪtʃ] welche(r, -s) OT 1
while [waɪl] während OT 1
whilst [waɪlst] während **WS 2**, 62
to **whisper** ['wɪspə] flüstern **WS 1**, 26
whistle [wɪsl] Pfeife OT 2
to **whistle** [wɪsl] pfeifen OT 2
white [waɪt] weiß OT 1
to **whizz** [wɪz] zischen OT 2
who [hu:] wer / wen / wem OT 1
whoever [hu:'evə] wer auch immer OT 4
whole [həʊl] ganz OT 1
whose [hu:z] wessen; dessen / deren OT 2
why [waɪ] warum OT 1
wicket ['wɪkɪt] Wicket; Törchen OT 1
wide [waɪd] weit OT 2
widespread ['waɪdspred] weitverbreitet **WS 1**, 18
to **wield** [wi:ld] als Waffe einsetzen **WS 2**, 78
wife [waɪf] Frau; Ehefrau OT 1
wig [wɪg] Perücke **WS 2**, 69
wild [waɪld] wild OT 2
wilderness ['wɪldənəs] Wildnis OT 2
wildfire ['waɪldfaɪə] Waldbrand OT 2
wildlife ['waɪldlaɪf] Tierwelt; Pflanzenwelt OT 2
willing: to **be willing** [bi 'wɪlɪŋ] bereit sein OT 4
wimp [wɪmp] Feigling; Schwachmat OT 5
to **win** [wɪn] gewinnen OT 1
wind [wɪnd] Wind OT 2
to **wind** ['waɪnd] sich schlängeln; winden OT 5
windlass ['wɪndləs] Winsch OT 3
window ['wɪndəʊ] Fenster OT 1
to **windsurf** ['wɪndsɜ:f] windsurfen OT 1
windsurfer ['wɪndsɜ:fə] Windsurfer(in) OT 1
windsurfing ['wɪndsɜ:fɪŋ] Windsurfen OT 1
windy ['wɪndi] windig OT 2
wine [waɪn] Wein OT 1
wing [wɪŋ] Flügel OT 1
winner ['wɪnə] Gewinner(in); Sieger(in) OT 1
winning ['wɪnɪŋ] gewinnend OT 5
winter ['wɪntə] Winter OT 1
wipe [waɪp] Wischtuch OT 4
to **wipe** [waɪp] (ab)wischen **WS 1**, 16
wisdom tooth ['wɪzdəm] Weisheitszahn OT 5
wisdom ['wɪzdəm] Weisheit **WS 1**, 19
to **wish** [wɪʃ] wünschen OT 3
witch [wɪtʃ] Hexe OT 2
with [wɪð] mit OT 1
withdrawal [wɪð'drɔ:l] Entzug **WS 4**, 142
to **withhold** [wɪð'hoʊld] zurückhalten **WS 2**, 78
within [wɪ'ðɪn] innerhalb OT 4
without [wɪ'ðaʊt] ohne OT 2

to witness ['wɪtnəs] Zeug / Zeugin einer Sache sein; beobachten OT 5
witty ['wɪti] witzig; clever **WS 1**, 17
woman ['wʊmən] Frau OT 1
wombat ['wɒmbæt] Wombat OT 5
to wonder ['wʌndə] sich fragen OT 3
wonderful ['wʌndəfl] wunderbar OT 1
wood [wʊd] Holz OT 2
wood-burning ['wʊd'bɜːnɪŋ] holzverbrennend OT 4
wooden ['wʊdn] hölzern OT 1
wool [wʊl] Wolle OT 2
woolly ['wʊli] wollig; aus Wolle OT 2
word [wɜːd] Wort OT 1
to work [wɜːk] arbeiten OT 1
to work out [wɜːk aʊt] herausfinden OT 2
workbook ['wɜːkbʊk] Arbeitsheft OT 1
worker ['wɜːkə] Arbeiter(in) OT 2
workforce ['wɜːkfɔːs] Arbeitskräfte OT 5
workload ['wɜːkləʊd] Arbeitsbelastung; Arbeitslast OT 5
workman ['wɜːkmən] Arbeiter OT 3
workout ['wɜːkaʊt] Fitnesstraining OT 5
workplace ['wɜːkpleɪs] Arbeitsplatz OT 2
work placement ['wɜːk pleɪsmənt] Praktikum OT 5
workshop ['wɜːkʃɒp] Werkstatt OT 1
workspace ['wɜːkspeɪs] Arbeitsbereich OT 5
world [wɜːld] Welt OT 1
worldview ['wɜːrld,vjuː] Weltsicht **WS 2**, 57
worldwide [,wɜːld'waɪd] weltweit OT 3
worm [wɜːm] Wurm OT 1
worried ['wʌrid] besorgt OT 1
to worry ['wʌri] (sich) Sorgen machen OT 1
No worries. [nəʊ 'wʌriz] Keine Sorge. OT 2
to worsen ['wɜːsn] verschlechtern; verschlimmern OT 5
to worship ['wɜːʃɪp] eine Religion ausüben; anbeten OT 4
worth [wɜːθ] lohnenswert OT 4
to be worth it [wɜːθ ɪt] (sich) lohnen OT 1
worthwhile [,wɜːθ'waɪl] lohnend OT 2
Wow! [waʊ] Toll! OT 1
wowed [waʊd] entzückt; begeistert OT 4
to wrap [ræp] einwickeln OT 2
wreath [riːθ] Kranz OT 3
wreck [rek] Wrack OT 3
to wrench [rentʃd] reissen; ziehen **WS 1**, 27
wrestling ['reslɪŋ] Ringen OT 2
to wriggle ['rɪgl] schlängeln OT 2
wrist [rɪst] Handgelenk OT 1
wristband ['rɪstbænd] Armband OT 4
to write [raɪt] schreiben OT 1
to write down [,raɪt 'daʊn] aufschreiben OT 2
writer ['raɪtə] Autor(in); Schriftsteller(in) OT 2
writing ['raɪtɪŋ] Schreiben OT 1
wrong [rɒŋ] falsch OT 1
What's wrong? [wɒts' rɒŋ] Was ist los? OT 2

X

X-ray ['eks reɪ] Röntgen OT 1

Y

yacht [jɒt] Jacht OT 2
yard [jɑːd] Garten OT 2
yeah [jeə] ja OT 1
year [jɪə] Jahr OT 1
to yearn [jɜːrn] sich sehnen **WS 2**, 79
yellow ['jeləʊ] gelb OT 1
yes [jes] ja OT 1
yesterday ['jestədeɪ] gestern OT 1
yet [jet] noch; schon OT 2
to yield [jiːld] liefern; nach sich ziehen **WS 3**, 98
yoga ['jəʊgə] Yoga OT 5
yoghurt ['jɒgət] Joghurt OT 1
yolk [jəʊk] Eigelb; Dotter **WS 1**, 22
you [ju] du / Sie; man OT 1
young [jʌŋ] jung OT 1
youngster ['jʌŋstə] Jugendliche(r) **WS 1**, 25
your [jɔː] dein / Ihr; euer / Ihr OT 1
yours [jɔːz] deine(r, -s); eure(r, -s); ihre(r, -s) OT 2
yourself [,jə'self] dich / sich (selbst) OT 1
youth [juːθ] Jugend OT 1
youth hostel ['juːθ hɒstl] Jugendherberge OT 2
yuck [jʌk] Igitt! OT 3

Z

zebra ['zebrə] Zebra OT 1
zebra crossing [,zebrə 'krɒsɪŋ] Zebrastreifen OT 1
zero ['zɪərəʊ] null OT 1
zip [zɪp] Reißverschluss OT 1
zip line ['zɪp laɪn] Seilrutsche OT 1
zombie ['zɒmbi] Zombie OT 2
zone [zəʊn] Zone OT 2
zoo [zuː] Zoo OT 1
zucchini [zu'kiːni] Zucchini OT 3

Dictionary: German – English

A

Aal eel OT 4
Abbild effigy **WS 1**, 43
abbilden to depict **WS 2**, 72
abdecken to cover OT 2
Abdeckung cover OT 1
Abend evening OT 1
Abendessen dinner OT 1
Abenteuer adventure OT 1
abenteuerlustig adventurous OT 2
aber but OT 1
Abfahrt exit; departure OT 2
Abfall garbage; trash OT 2; waste OT 3; spoilage; scrap OT 4
herumliegende Abfälle litter OT 2
Abflug departure OT 2
Abfluggate departure gate OT 2
Abflugschalter check-in desk OT 2
abgefüllt bottled OT 3
abgelegen remote OT 5
Abgeordnete MP (Members of Parliament) OT 5
abgetropft drained OT 2
nicht abgetropft undrained OT 2
abgießen to drain OT 2
abhalten to prevent OT 4
abhängen to hang out OT 1
abhängen (von) to depend OT 2
abhängig addicted OT 3; reliant **WS 3**, 110; dependent **WS 4**, 133
abhärten to harden **WS 2**, 56
abholen to fetch OT 4
abholzen to deforest **WS 1**, 21
Abholzung deforestation OT 5
Abklärung clarification OT 4
abkürzen to shorten OT 5
Abkürzung abbreviation OT 5
Ablauf sequence OT 4
ablegen to ditch **WS 3**, 122
(sich) ableiten to derive **WS 2**, 61
abliefern to submit **WS 1**, 25
Abmessung dimension OT 2
abnagen to gnaw OT 2
abonnieren to subscribe OT 5
abreißen to demolish OT 5
abrupt abrupt **WS 2**, 65
absagen to cancel OT 4
Absatz paragraph OT 1; heel **WS 1**, 28
abschaffen to abolish **WS 2**, 54; to phase out **WS 3**, 111
abschalten to disconnect **WS 1**, 44
abschätzen to measure OT 4
abschließen to finish OT 1; to lock OT 2; to finalize OT 5
Abschluss degree OT 4
Abschnitt segment OT 5; passage **WS 2**, 79
Abschreckung deterrent **WS 3**, 99
Abschreckungsmittel deterrent **WS 3**, 99
abschreiben to transcribe OT 5
Abschrift transcript OT 5
abseilen to abseil OT 2
Absender(in) sender OT 3
Absicht aim OT 4; intention **WS 3**, 99
absichtlich deliberate OT 5
absolut absolute OT 3
Absolvent(in) alumnus OT 4
absondern to isolate **WS 2**, 83
absorbieren to absorb **WS 3**, 108
sich abspalten to secede **WS 1**, 14
absprengen to blast OT 5
abstammen von to descend from OT 5
Abstammung descent OT 5; ancestry **WS 2**, 55
abstauben to dust off OT 5
absteigend downward OT 5
Abstellraum storeroom OT 5
Abstimmung referendum **WS 1**, 14
abstoßend revolting OT 2
abstrakt abstract OT 5
Abstufung gradation **WS 2**, 78
Abteilung department OT 5
abwärts downward OT 5
Abwasch: den Abwasch machen to do the dishes OT 2
Abwasser sewage **WS 3**, 98
abwechseln to take turns OT 1
abweichen to differ OT 5
Abweichung anomaly **WS 2**, 63
abweisend dismissive **WS 2**, 82
Abwesenheit absence **WS 2**, 65
abwischen to dust off OT 5
Abzeichen badge OT 1; insignia **WS 3**, 95
Achse axis OT 4
Achseln zucken to shrug OT 5
acht eight OT 1
achten to respect OT 3
achtzehn eighteen OT 1
achtzig eighty OT 1
Ackerland farmland OT 4
Adel aristocracy **WS 2**, 64
Ader vein OT 5
Adjektiv adjective OT 1
Adler eagle OT 2
Adrenalinstoß adrenaline rush OT 1
Adresse address OT 1
adressieren to address **WS 1**, 20
Adverb adverb OT 1
Affäre affair **WS 1**, 38
Affe monkey OT 2; ape **WS 1**, 21
afrikanisch African OT 2
Agakröte cane toad OT 5
Agentur agency OT 4
aggressiv aggressive OT 3
Aggressivität hostility **WS 1**, 21
ähnlich similar OT 2
Ähnlichkeit similarity OT 3
ahnungslos oblivious **WS 3**, 96
Ahorn maple OT 3
Akademie academy **WS 2**, 84
akademisch academic OT 5; academical **WS 2**, 55
einen akademischen Grad erlangen to graduate OT 3
Akkordeon accordion OT 2
akquirieren acquire **WS 1**, 32
Akrostichon acrostic OT 5
Aktion action OT 1; campaign OT 3
aktiv energetic OT 2; active OT 4
aktivieren to activate OT 4
Aktivismus activism OT 4
Aktivist(in) activist OT 5; campaigner **WS 1**, 21
Aktivität activity OT 1
aktualisieren to update OT 3
aktuell current OT 4
akustisch acoustic OT 2
Akzent accent OT 1
akzeptabel acceptable OT 5
Alarm alarm OT 2
alarmieren to alert OT 2
alaskisch Alaskan OT 2
albern silly OT 1
Albtraum nightmare OT 4
Album album OT 3
Algorithmus algorithm OT 5
Alkohol alcohol OT 3
alkoholisch alcoholic OT 3
alle all; everybody OT 1
Allee avenue OT 1
allein on one's own OT 2
alleinreisendes Kind unaccompanied minor OT 2
alleinig sole **WS 2**, 68
Allergie allergy OT 1

allergisch allergic OT 2
alles all; everything OT 1
Allesesser omnivore **WS 1**, 32
Allesfresser omnivore **WS 1**, 32
allgemein general OT 3; universal OT 5; overall **WS 1**, 21
im Allgemeinen generally OT 4
Allianz alliance **WS 1**, 33
Alliteration alliteration OT 5
allmählich gradual **WS 2**, 83
alltäglich everyday OT 3
Alpaka alpaca OT 2
Alphabet alphabet OT 1
alphabetisch alphabetical OT 2
als as; than OT 1
also like; so; well OT 1
alt old OT 1; vintage OT 5
alt werden to age **WS 1**, 39
Alter age OT 1
im Alter von aged OT 1
älter elderly OT 4
altern to age **WS 1**, 39
Alternative alternative OT 2
Älteste(r) elder OT 5
altmodisch old-fashioned OT 4
altruistisch altruistic **WS 2**, 68
Ambition ambition OT 4; aspiration **WS 2**, 59
ambitioniert aspirational **WS 1**, 32
Ameise ant **WS 1**, 39
amerikanisch American OT 1
Amphitheater amphitheatre OT 3
amputieren to amputate **WS 2**, 84
Amtsperson official OT 3
amüsant entertaining OT 3; amusing OT 5
amüsiert amused OT 3
an at; on OT 1
analphabetisch illiterate OT 4
Analyse analysis OT 5
analysieren to analyse OT 3
Ananas pineapple OT 3
anbauen to grow OT 1; to cultivate OT 4
anbeten to worship OT 4
anbieten to offer OT 2
anbinden to tie OT 2
Andachtshaus meetinghouse OT 4
andauern to continue OT 1; to last OT 2
andere(r, -s) other OT 1
anders als unlike OT 3
ändern to change OT 1; to modify **WS 3**, 104
Änderung change OT 1
andeuten to hint **WS 2**, 73
Android android **WS 3**, 104
Aneignung appropriation OT 5
Anekdote anecdote OT 4
anerkannt certified OT 5
anerkennen to acknowledge; to appreciate OT 5
Anerkennung recognition OT 5; acclaim **WS 2**, 80
Anfang start OT 1
anfangen to start; to take up; to begin OT 1; to commence OT 4
anfangs initially OT 5
Anfangs... introductory OT 5
anfassen to feel; to touch OT 1
anfechten to dispute **WS 1**, 14
anfragen to enquire **WS 3**, 111
anfreunden to make friends OT 2
anführen to cite OT 2
Anführung (einer Quelle) citation OT 2
Anführungszeichen quotation mark OT 2
angeben to indicate OT 5
Angebot offer OT 1
Angehörige relative OT 1
Angelegenheit issue; matter OT 2; affair **WS 1**, 38
Angeln fishing OT 2
angemessen appropriately OT 3; appropriate OT 4; adequate OT 5
angenehm enjoyable OT 2; pleasant OT 5
anschalten to switch on OT 1
angeschlossen hyper-connected OT 4
angesehen werden to be deemed **WS 2**, 78
Angestellte(r) employee OT 4
angestrengt stressed OT 2
angetrieben powered OT 4
angreifen to attack; to tackle OT 3
angrenzend adjoining OT 3
Angriff assault OT 5
Angst fear OT 3
Angst machen to scare OT 2
ängstlich afraid OT 2
Ängstlichkeit anxiety **WS 4**, 144
anhalten to stop OT 1
anhaltend prolonged OT 5; chronic **WS 1**, 23
Anhänger(in) follower OT 3
anheben to lift OT 3
Animationen animations **WS 4**, 133
animieren to animate **WS 3**, 103
Ankauf purchase OT 4
ankern to anchor OT 4
anklagen to charge OT 5; to accuse **WS 1**, 20
anklicken to click on OT 3
ankommen to arrive OT 1
Ankunft arrival OT 2
geschätzte Ankunftszeit ETA (estimated time of arrival) OT 2
ankurbeln to boost **WS 3**, 110
Anlage facility OT 4
anlegen to moor OT 3
Anlegeplatz mooring OT 3
Anliegen cause OT 2
Anmeldeliste sign-up sheet OT 2
anmelden to register OT 4; to enrol **WS 3**, 103
annehmen to suppose OT 1; to accept OT 3; to adopt OT 5; to presume **WS 3**, 106
wieder annehmen to resume OT 5
Annehmlichkeit amenity **WS 2**, 79
annotieren to annotate **WS 2**, 63
Anomalie anomaly **WS 2**, 63
anordnen to mandate OT 5
anpassen to conform OT 5; to assimilate **WS 3**, 95
(sich) anpassen to adjust **WS 1**, 24
Anpassung assimilation OT 4
anpassungsfähig flexible; adaptable OT 4
anregen to stimulate **WS 3**, 110
anregend motivating OT 5; evocative **WS 2**, 55
Anruf call OT 1
einen Anruf entgegennehmen to take a call OT 2
anrufen to call OT 1
Anrufer(in) caller OT 2
Ansage announcement OT 2
ansagen to announce OT 2
Ansammlung cluster **WS 4**, 140
Ansatz approach **WS 1**, 21
anschauen to look at OT 1
Anschauungsmaterial visual aid OT 4
anscheinend apparently OT 4
Anschlagbrett noticeboard OT 1
Anschlagtafel bulletin board OT 4
anschließen to fasten OT 1
ansehen to look at OT 1; to regard **WS 1**, 14
Ansicht attitude OT 3
ansiedeln to settle OT 4
Ansiedler(in) colonizer OT 5
ansonsten otherwise OT 5
Anspannung tension OT 4
Anspielung allusion **WS 2**, 62
Anspitzer pencil sharpener OT 1
ansprechen to appeal **WS 1**, 22; to address **WS 1**, 20
anständig proper OT 3; decent **WS 2**, 54
anstehen to queue OT 4

Anstellung appointment **WS 2**, 81
anstoßen to bump into OT 2
anstrengen to exert **WS 3**, 103
  sich anstrengen to struggle OT 5
Anstrengung effort OT 5
Anteil proportion OT 5
Antenne antenna OT 2
anthropozentrisch anthropocentric **WS 1**, 21
antibiotisch antibiotic OT 5
antik ancient OT 2
Antilope antelope **WS 2**, 59
antiseptisch antiseptic OT 2
Antrag petition OT 3; application OT 4
Antwort answer OT 1; response OT 5
antworten to reply OT 1
anwachsen to increase OT 3
Anwalt / Anwältin counsel OT 5; advocate **WS 3**, 95
Anweisung instruction OT 1; direction OT 3
Anwesenheit presence **WS 3**, 96
Anzahl quantity OT 4
Anzeichen symptom **WS 3**, 106
anziehen to attract OT 4
  rasch anziehen to slip on OT 5
anziehend attractive OT 4
Anzug suit OT 1 62
anzünden to light OT 5; to ignite **WS 2**, 62
Apartheid apartheid **WS 2**, 52
Apfel apple OT 1
Apotheke chemist's shop; drugstore; pharmacy OT 2
Apotheker(in) chemist; pharmacist OT 2
App app OT 4
Appetit appetite **WS 3**, 104
appetitlich appetizing OT 3
applaudieren to applaud OT 2
Applaus applause OT 2
April April OT 1
Aquädukt aqueduct OT 3
aquatisch aquatic OT 4
Äquator equator OT 5
Ära era OT 4
Arbeit labour OT 4; employment OT 5
  gute Arbeit leisten to do a good / great job OT 2
arbeiten to work OT 1; to labour **WS 1**, 18
Arbeiter workman OT 3
Arbeiter(in) worker OT 2
Arbeitgeber(in) employer OT 3
Arbeitsbelastung workload OT 5
Arbeitsbereich workspace OT 5
Arbeitsheft workbook OT 1
Arbeitskraft labor OT 4
  Arbeitskräfte workforce OT 5
Arbeitslast workload OT 5
arbeitslos jobless; unemployed OT 5
Arbeitslosigkeit unemployment OT 3
Arbeitsplatz workplace OT 2
Archäologe / Archäologin archeologist OT 4
Architekt(in) architect OT 5
Architektur architecture OT 2
archivieren to archive OT 4
Arena arena OT 1; amphitheatre OT 3
Ärger trouble OT 2; anger OT 3
  Ärger bekommen to be in trouble OT 2
ärgerlich annoying; angrily OT 2; irksome **WS 2**, 78
ärgern to tease OT 1; to annoy OT 3
argumentativ argumentative OT 5
argumentieren to argue OT 2
Aristokratie aristocracy **WS 2**, 64
Arktis Arctic OT 4
arktisch Arctic OT 4
Arm arm OT 1
arm poor OT 1
Armband wristband OT 4
Armee army OT 3
Ärmel sleeve OT 3
ärmellos sleeveless OT 4
Armut poverty OT 3
Art kind OT 1; type; sort OT 2; species OT 5; mode **WS 3**, 99
Artikel article OT 1
Artikulierung tone of voice OT 4
Artwork artwork OT 5
Arzt / Ärztin doctor OT 1
asexuell asexual OT 5
asiatisch Asian OT 4
Aspekt aspect OT 4
Assimilation assimilation OT 4
assimilieren to assimilate **WS 3**, 95
Assistent(in) assistant OT 1
Assistenzhund service dog OT 2
assoziieren to associate OT 4
Ast branch OT 2
Asterisk asterisk OT 4
Astronaut(in) astronaut OT 4
Astronom(in) astronomer **WS 3**, 103
Astronomie astronomy OT 1
Asylbewerber(in) asylum seeker OT 4
Atem(zug) breath OT 2
  außer Atem out of breath OT 2
atemberaubend breathtaking OT 3; stunning OT 5
atemlos breathless OT 3
athletisch athletic OT 4
atmen to breathe OT 2
Atmosphäre atmosphere OT 3
Atom... nuclear OT 3
Attentat assassination **WS 1**, 18
Attentäter(in) assassin **WS 1**, 18
attraktiv attractive OT 4
ätzend gross OT 3
Au-pair au pair OT 5
Au! Ow! OT 1
Aua! Ouch! OT 1
Aubergine eggplant OT 2
auch too; also; as well OT 1
  auch nicht either OT 1; neither OT 2
Audiodatei audio file OT 2
Audiotagebuch audio diary OT 2
auf on; onto OT 1
aufbauen to structure OT 5
aufbewahren to keep OT 2
Aufbewahrung storage OT 3
aufbrechen to head out OT 4
aufdrängen to inflict OT 5
aufdringlich pushy OT 4
aufeinanderfolgend successive OT 5
Aufenthaltsgenehmigung residency **WS 3**, 95
Aufenthaltsraum breakout area OT 5; lounge **WS 1**, 23
auffällig flashy **WS 2**, 53
Aufforderung invitation OT 1; prompt OT 4
aufführen to put on OT 2
Aufführung performance OT 2
Aufgabe task; job OT 1; assignment OT 4
aufgeben to give up OT 2
aufgeputscht lathered up **WS 3**, 94
aufgeräumt tidy OT 2
aufgeregt excited OT 1; frantic OT 3
Aufgliederung breakdown **WS 3**, 103
aufgrund von due to OT 5
aufhalten to stave off **WS 3**, 98
aufheben to pick up OT 2
aufhören to finish; to stop OT 1; to cease **WS 3**, 120
aufkeimend budding **WS 3**, 96
aufklären to enlighten **WS 1**, 21
aufladen to charge OT 4; to load up OT 5
auflisten to list OT 3
aufmachen to open OT 1
Aufmerksamkeit attention OT 2
aufmuntern cheer up OT 1
Aufmunterung encouragement OT 5
aufnehmen to take up; to record OT 1; to absorb **WS 3**, 108
aufpassen to pay attention OT 2
  aufpassen auf to look after OT 1
aufräumen to tidy OT 1

aufregend exciting OT 1
Aufregung excitement OT 3; fuss OT 4
aufrichten to right OT 5
aufrichtig sincerely OT 4
Aufruf appeal OT 2
Aufruhr uproar **WS 2**, 58
Aufsatz essay OT 2
Aufschläger(in) server OT 3
aufschließen to unlock OT 1
Aufschrei outcry **WS 1**, 25
aufschreiben to write down OT 2
Aufschwung boom **WS 1**, 14
Aufseher(in) attendant; ranger OT 3
aufsetzen to slap on OT 5
Aufsicht supervision OT 5
aufspießen to spear OT 5
Aufstand rebellion OT 4; riot **WS 1**, 14; uprising **WS2**, 83
aufstehen to stand up; to get up OT 1
aufsteigen to rise OT 3
aufstrebend upcoming **WS 1**, 30
aufsuchen to frequent OT 5
auftauchen to appear OT 3; to pop up **WS 2**, 68
aufteilen to partition **WS 1**, 14
auftragen to slop on OT 5
Auftragnehmer(in) contractor OT 5
auftreten to perform OT 2
Auftritt gig OT 5
aufwachen to wake up OT 1
aufwärmen to warm up OT 2
Aufwärmübung warm-up OT 2
aufwärts upwards OT 3
aufzeichnen to chronicle **WS 2**, 78
Auge eye OT 1
  im Auge behalten to bear in mind **WS 4**, 138
Augenbraue eyebrow OT 4
Augenlid eyelid OT 2
Augenöffner eye-opener **WS 2**, 82
August August OT 1
Aula assembly hall OT 1
aus from; out; off OT 1
ausbeuten to exploit OT 3
ausbeuterisch exploitative **WS 2**, 67
Ausbeutung exploitation OT 4
Ausbildung training OT 2; education OT 3; appenticeship OT 5
Ausbildungslehrgang training course OT 2
ausbrechen to erupt **WS 1**, 15
Ausbruch outbreak **WS 3**, 98
ausbrüten to breed **WS 1**, 24
ausbuhen to boo **WS 2**, 60
ausdehnen to extend **WS 3**, 95
Ausdehnung expansion **WS 3**, 108
ausdenken to devise **WS 2**, 57
Ausdruck expression OT 1
  zum Ausdruck bringen to voice OT 4
ausdrucken to print OT 2
ausdrücken to express OT 3
auseinander apart **WS 1**, 15
auseinanderfallen to fall apart OT 4
Auseinandersetzung argument OT 1
Ausfall outage **WS 3**, 101
Ausflug trip OT 1
ausführen to elaborate **WS 2**, 55
Ausführung delivery OT 3
Ausgabe issue OT 2
Ausgang exit OT 2
Ausgangssperre curfew OT 3
ausgeben to spend OT 1; to dispense **WS 3**, 94
ausgebildet skilled OT 4
ausgefeilt sophisticated **WS 4**, 133
ausgeglichen evenly OT 4
  nicht ausgeglichen imbalanced **WS 2**, 82
ausgehen to go out OT 1
  mit jdm. ausgehen to date OT 5
ausgeprägt distinctive OT 5
ausgesetzt sein to be exposed to **WS 2**, 56
ausgestorben extinct OT 2
ausgezeichnet excellent OT 3; distinguished **WS 1**, 68
ausgrenzen to marginalize **WS 2**, 69
Ausgrenzung discrimination OT 5
aushalten to endure **WS 2**, 72
aushandeln to negotiate **WS 1**, 21
Ausland abroad OT 4
ausländisch foreign OT 1; overseas OT 2
auslassen to omit **WS 2**, 58
auslöschen to excise **WS 2**, 79
auslösen to prompt **WS 2**, 81; to trigger **WS 2**, 83
ausmachen to determine OT 5
  etw. macht jdm. etw. aus to mind OT 4
Ausmaß extent OT 5
ausmerzen to eradicate OT 4
ausmessen to measure OT 4
ausnutzen to capitalize **WS 2**, 57
auspacken to unpack OT 2
ausprobieren to try out OT 2
ausrangieren to discard **WS 3**, 98
ausreichend sufficient; adequate OT 5
Ausreißer(in) runaway OT 5
ausrichten to host OT 3
ausrotten to eradicate OT 4
Ausrottung decimation **WS 1**, 21
ausrufen to declare OT 4
ausruhen to rest OT 1
ausrüsten to equip **WS 1**, 23
Ausrüstung kit; equipment OT 2
Aussage statement OT 1
ausschalten to turn off OT 2
Ausschau lookout **WS 1**, 28
Ausschlag blip **WS 3**, 98
ausschließen to exclude OT 5; to disqualify **WS 2**, 58
ausschließlich exclusively OT 5
Ausschluss exclusion **WS 4**, 133
Ausschnitt clip OT 1; excerpt OT 5
Ausschuss committee OT 2
Aussehen appearance OT 3
aussehen wie to resemble **WS 1**, 22
Außen... outer OT 5
Außenbezirk suburb **WS 2**, 52
Außenseiter(in) odd one out OT 2; misfit OT 4; underdog OT 5; outsider **WS 2**, 63
außer except OT 2; apart from OT 3
  außer wenn unless OT 4
außerdem moreover; besides; furthermore; in addition OT 5
äußere (r, -s) outward OT 5
außergewöhnlich exceptional **WS 1**, 23
Außerirdische(r) alien OT 2
äußerlich outward OT 5
außermusikalisch extra-musical OT 2
äußern to voice OT 4
Aussicht view OT 1; perspective OT 4
Aussichtsgalerie viewing gallery OT 1
Aussichtspunkt viewpoint OT 3
aussieben to filter out **WS 3**, 127
aussortieren to sort out **WS 1**, 28
Aussprache pronunciation OT 2
aussprechen to pronounce OT 3
ausstehen: nicht ausstehen können to loathe OT 5
aussteigen to get off OT 2
ausstellen to exhibit OT 2
Aussteller(in) exhibitor **WS 4**, 138
Ausstellung show; exhibition OT 1; display OT 3
Ausstellungsgelände showground OT 2
Aussterben extinction OT 5
Ausstoss emission OT 3
ausstoßen to emit **WS 3**, 102
ausstreichen to cross out OT 1
Austausch exchange OT 1
Austreten leakage **WS 3**, 104
Ausverkauf sale OT 4
Auswahl variety OT 5
auswählen to choose OT 1
Auswahlfach elective OT 4
Auswahlliste shortlist OT 2

Auswanderer / Auswanderin emigrant OT 3
auswandern to emigrate OT 4
ausweisen to deport OT 4
auswendig by heart OT 2
auswendig aufsagen to recite OT 4
auswirken: sich auswirken auf to affect OT 3
Auswirkung impact OT 3
Auswirkungen repercussions **WS 1**, 18
auszeichnen to label **WS 2**, 58
Auszeichnung award OT 2
Auszubildende(r) apprentice OT 5
Auszug extract OT 4; excerpt OT 5
autark self-sufficient OT 4
authentisch authentic OT 5
Authentizität authenticity **WS 1**, 23
Auto car OT 1
Autobiografie autobiography **WS 2**, 62
autobiografisch autobiographical **WS 2**, 62
autokrank carsick OT 2
Automat vending machine OT 1
automatisch automatic **WS 2**, 78
automatisieren to automate OT 4
Automobil automobile OT 4
autonom autonomous OT 4
Autor(in) author OT 1; writer OT 2
Autorenschaft authorship **WS 4**, 140
autorisiert authorized OT 5
autoritär authoritarian **WS 3**, 92
Autorität authority OT 4
Avatar avatar OT 3

B

Baby baby OT 1
babysitten to babysit OT 4
Babysitter(in) babysitter OT 4
Bach stream OT 2; creek OT 3
Backe cheek **WS 1**, 22
backen to bake OT 1
Bäcker(in) baker OT 3
Bäckerei bakery OT 4
Background-Sänger(in) backing artist **WS 2**, 68
Backup backup OT 4
Bad bath OT 2
Badewanne bath OT 2; bathtub **WS 3**, 101
Badezimmer bathroom OT 1
Badminton badminton OT 1
Bagel bagel OT 1
Bahn railway OT 1
Bahnhof station OT 1
Bahnsteig platform OT 1
Bakterie bacteria OT 5
Balance balanced **WS 2**, 82
bald soon OT 1
Balken beam OT 3
Balkendiagramm bar chart OT 4
Ball ball OT 1
Ballett ballet OT 3
Ballon balloon OT 3
banalisieren to trivialize **WS 2**, 69
Banane banana OT 1
Band: das strip; ribbon **WS 3**, 95
Band: die band OT 1
Bande gang OT 5
Bank bench; bank OT 3
Banking banking OT 5
Bankwesen banking OT 5
Bar bar OT 1
Bär bear OT 1
Barbar(in) barbarian **WS 1**, 14
barbarisch barbaric **WS 1**, 21
Barbierladen barbershop **WS 3**, 97
barfuß barefoot **WS 2**, 60
Bargeld cash OT 1
Barriere barrier OT 3
barrierefrei accessible OT 2
Baseball baseball OT 1
basieren to base on OT 4
Basis base OT 4; basis OT 5
Basketball basketball OT 1
Batik- batik **WS 2**, 71
Batterie battery OT 2
Bau construction OT 4
Bauarbeiter(in) builder OT 2
Bauch belly **WS 1**, 16
bauen to build OT 1
Bauer / Bäuerin farmer OT 2
Bauernhaus farmhouse OT 3
Bauernhof farm OT 1
Baum tree OT 1
Baumstamm caber OT 3
Baumwolle cotton OT 4
bayerisch Bavarian OT 2
beabsichtigen to aim OT 4; to intend OT 5
beachten to take into account OT 5; to bear in mind **WS 4**, 138
Beamer projector OT 1
beanspruchen to claim OT 5
beantworten to answer OT 1
bearbeiten to alter **WS 3**, 113
beaufsichtigen to supervise OT 3; to oversee OT 4
beauftragen to delegate OT 4
bebauen to cultivate OT 4
Becher mug OT 3
Becken basin OT 3
Bedenken concern OT 5
bedenklich concerning **WS 4**, 133
bedeuten to mean OT 1
bedeutend major OT 2; considerable **WS 2**, 58
Bedeutung meaning OT 1; importance OT 2; significance OT 5; relevance **WS 1**, 17
bedienen to serve OT 1; to operate OT 5
bedingt causal **WS 4**, 140
Bedingung condition OT 3
Bedrohung threat OT 5
eine Bedrohung darstellen to pose a threat OT 5
beeilen: sich beeilen to hurry OT 1
beeindrucken to impress OT 5
beeindruckt awestruck **WS 1**, 14
beeinflussen to influence OT 4
Beeinträchtigung impairment **WS 2**, 61
beenden to conclude OT 4
beengt cramped OT 3
Beerdigung funeral OT 5
Beere berry OT 4
Beet bed OT 1
Befähigung empowerment **WS 3**, 98
befehlen to order OT 1
Befehlsform imperative OT 1
befehlshabend commanding OT 2
befestigen to attach OT 4
befragen to survey OT 5; to question **WS 1**, 15
Befragte(r) respondent OT 5
Befragung census OT 5
befreit freed OT 4
Befreiung liberation **WS 2**, 68
befriedigend satisfying OT 5
Befriedigung satisfaction **WS 2**, 79
Befund finding OT 4
Befürworter(in) supporter OT 2
Begabung talent OT 2; genius **WS 1**, 26
begegnen to face OT 4; to encounter **WS 2**, 67
Begegnung encounter **WS 2**, 67
begehen to commit OT 4
begehren to desire **WS 2**, 78
begeisternd inspirational **WS 1**, 21
begeistert excited OT 1; enthusiastic OT 3; wowed OT 4
Begeisterung eagerness **WS 2**, 79
Beginn advent OT 5
beginnen to start; to begin OT 1; to embark **WS 1**, 15
beglaubigt certified OT 5
Begleiter(in) escort OT 3
begleitet accompanied OT 3
begrenzen to limit OT 3
Begriff concept OT 4

begründen to found; to establish OT 4
begründet reasoned **WS 3**, 112
Begründung motivation OT 5
behalten to keep OT 2; to retain **WS 3**, 99
Behälter bin; container OT 2
behandeln to treat OT 4
Behandlung treatment OT 5
behaupten to claim OT 5; to assert **WS 1**, 14; to allege **WS 1**, 18
behindert disabled **WS 2**, 61
Behinderung disability OT 2
bei at OT 1; by OT 1
beide both OT 1
Beifall acclaim **WS 2**, 80
Beiklang connotation **WS 1**, 21
Bein leg OT 1
  wieder auf die Beine kommen to bounce back OT 5
beindruckt impressed OT 4
beinhalten to contain OT 3
Beispiel example OT 1
  zum Beispiel for instance OT 5
beispielsweise for instance OT 5
Beitrag contribution; input OT 4
Beiträger(in) contributor **WS 3**, 92
bekämpfen to combat **WS 3**, 99
bekannt well known; familiar OT 2
  bekannt geben to announce OT 2
Bekanntgabe announcement OT 2
bekennen: sich bekennen to plead OT 5
bekommen to get OT 1
bekräftigen to reinforce OT 5
Belag fuzz OT 4
belanglos insignificant **WS 1**, 21
belastbar robust **WS 3**, 112
Belästigung harassment **WS 3**, 106
Belastung strain **WS 1**, 14
beleben to energize **WW**, 11
belegen to top OT 3
beleidigen to offend OT 3; to insult **WS 2**, 60
  jdn. beleidigen to cause offense **WS 3**, 107
beleidigend offensive **WS 2**, 69
beleidigt insulted OT 5
Beleuchtung lighting OT 4
beliebt popular OT 1
  sich beliebt machen to endear **WS 2**, 63
bellen to bark OT 2
belohnen to reward **WS 2**, 68
Belohnung reward **WS 4**, 133
bemannt crewed OT 4
bemerken to notice OT 1
bemerkenswert notable **WS 2**, 65
Bemerkung remark OT 5
bemühen: sich bemühen to struggle OT 5
Benachrichtigung notification **WS 4**, 133
benachteiligt disadvantaged; discriminated OT 5
Benchmark benchmark **WS 2**, 62
Benehmen behaviour OT 2
benehmen: sich benehmen to behave OT 2
beneiden to envy OT 5
benennen to name OT 4
benutzen to use OT 1
Benutzer(in) user OT 2
Benutzeroberfläche desktop OT 4
Benzin gas OT 3; petrol OT 4
beobachten to watch OT 1; to observe OT 4; to witness OT 5
Beobachter(in) observer OT 5
Beobachtung observation OT 3
bequem comfortable OT 1
Bequemlichkeit convenience OT 4
Berater(in) counsellor OT 2; advisor; consultant OT 5
Beratung counselling OT 5
berauben to deprive **WS 2**, 81
berechnen to calculate **WS 3**, 124
Berechnung calculation **WS 2**, 59
berechtigt authorized OT 5; eligible **WS 2**, 61
Bereich domain **WS 1**, 40
bereichern to enrich **WS 3**, 110
bereit ready OT 1; all set OT 2
  bereit sein to be willing OT 4
bereits already OT 2
bereuen to regret OT 2
Berg mountain OT 1
bergab downhill OT 5
Bergarbeiter(in) miner OT 4
Bergbau... mining OT 3
Bergkette mountain range OT 4
Bergsteigen climbing OT 1
Bergwerk mine OT 2
Bericht report OT 2; account **WS 1**, 14
berichten to report OT 1
  berichten von to recount **WS 2**, 78
berücksichtigen to take into account OT 5
Berücksichtigung: unter Berücksichtigung with regard to **WS 1**, 43
Beruf profession OT 5
beruflich vocational OT 5
beruhigen to settle down OT 2
berühmt famous OT 1
berühren to touch OT 1; to strike a chord **WS 2**, 72
beschädigen to damage OT 2
beschäftigen to engage OT 4; to employ **WS 4**, 133
beschäftigt busy OT 1
Beschäftigung occupation OT 4; employment OT 5; engagement **WS 1**, 13
Beschäftigungsfähigkeit employability **WS 3**, 110
beschämt ashamed OT 3
beschatten to shadow OT 5
bescheiden humble **WS 2**, 80
Beschilderung signposting OT 5
beschleunigen to expedite **WS 1**, 14; to accelerate **WS 3,** 99
Beschluss resolution **WS 2**, 63
beschränken to restrict **WS 2**, 78
beschreiben to describe OT 1
beschreibend descriptive OT 5
Beschreibung description OT 2
beschriften to label **WS 2**, 58
beschuldigen to accuse **WS 1**, 20
beschützen to shelter **WS 3**, 97
Beschwerde complaint OT 2
beschweren: sich beschweren to complain OT 3
beseitigen to eliminate **WS 3**, 107
Besen broom **WS 1**, 39
besessen obsessed **WS 2**, 64
besichten to tour OT 5
Besichtigungen sightseeing OT 1
besiegen to beat OT 2; to defeat **WS 3**, 98
Besitz possession OT 5
besitzanzeigend possessive OT 1
besitzen to own OT 4
Besitzer(in) owner OT 2
besondere(r, -s) special OT 1
besonders especially OT 2; in particular OT 4; particularly OT 5
besorgt worried OT 1; anxious OT 2; concerned OT 5
besorgt worried OT 1; anxious OT 2; concerned OT 5
  besorgt sein to care OT 1
besprechen to discuss OT 1
Besprechung discussion; meeting OT 1
besser better OT 1
Bessessenheit obsession **WS 3**, 104
Bestand stock OT 2
Bestandteil element OT 2
bestätigen to confirm OT 4; to acknowledge OT 5
Bestätigung confirmation **WS 3**, 112

bestäuben to pollinate **WS 4**, 133
beste(r, -s) best OT 1
bestechen to bribe **WS 2**, 58
bestechlich corrupt **WS 2**, 78
Besteck cutlery OT 3
bestehen: aus etw. bestehen to consist of OT 5
bestehen auf to insist **WS 2**, 62
Bestellung order OT 1
Bestie beast OT 5
bestimmen to define OT 4; to dictate; to detemine OT 5
bestimmt definite OT 1; assertive; specific OT 3
bestimmter Artikel definite article OT 1
Bestimmungswort determiner OT 1
bestrafen to punish; to prosecute OT 5
Bestreben quest **WS 3**, 98
bestreiten to dispute **WS 1**, 14
Bestreiter(in) denier **WS 1**, 21
besuchen to attend; to visit OT 2; to tour OT 5
Besucher(in) visitor OT 1
betäuben to drug **WS 3**, 104
betäubend stun **WS 1**, 18
Bete: Rote Bete beetroot OT 4
Beteiligung participation OT 5
beten to pray OT 5
betonen to emphasize OT 5
Betonung stress OT 1; emphasis OT 5
Betreuer(in) guardian OT 2; carer OT 5
betrübt saddened OT 5
Bett bed OT 1
betteln to beg OT 5
beugen: sich beugen to bow **WS 4**, 133
Beule dent **WS 3**, 102
beunruhigt alarmed OT 3
beurteilen to judge OT 2; to assess OT 5
Beurteilung judging OT 2
bevölkern to populate **WS 1**, 12
Bevölkerung population OT 3
Bevölkerungsstatistik demographics **WS 3**, 108
Bevölkerungszählung census OT 5
bevorstehend upcoming **WS 1**, 30; impending **WS 3**, 96; imminent **WS 3**, 124
bewachen to guard **WS 2**, 83
bewaffnet armed OT 5
bewahren to conserve **WS 2**, 64
Bewährung probation OT 5
bewältigen to overcome **WS 2**, 72
bewegen to move OT 1
beweglich agile OT 3
Beweglichkeit mobility **WS 3**, 108
Bewegung movement OT 5
Beweis proof OT 4; evidence **WS 1**, 33
beweisen to prove OT 3
bewerben to apply OT 3
Bewerber(in) applicant OT 4
Bewerbung application OT 4
bewerten to rate OT 2; to evaluate OT 4
Bewertung evaluation OT 5; assessment **WS 3**, 97
bewohnbar liveable; livable OT 4
Bewohnbarkeit habitation OT 4
bewohnen to inhabit OT 5
Bewohner(in) resident OT 3; dweller OT 4
bewölkt cloudy OT 4
bewundern to admire **WS 1**, 31
Bewunderung admiration **WS 2**, 64
bewusst aware; deliberately OT 5; conscious **WS 3**, 102
Bewusstsein awareness OT 5
bezahlbar affordable OT 4
bezahlen to pay OT 1
Bezahlung payment OT 2
beziehen to refer OT 3
sich auf etw. beziehen to relate to OT 3; to centre around OT 5
Beziehung relationship OT 3
Bezirk district OT 1
Bezug: in Bezug auf related to OT 4
bezüglich regarding OT 5
Bibliothek library OT 1
Bibliothekar(in) librarian OT 4
Biene bee OT 1
Bier beer OT 3
Bild picture; image OT 1
bilden to form OT 4; to craft **WS 3**, 94
Bilder imagery **WS 2**, 62
Bildhauer(in) sculptor **WS 1**, 19
Bildmaterial visual OT 4
Bildschirm screen OT 1
Bildsprache imagery **WS 2**, 62
Bildtext caption OT 1
Bildungs... educational OT 3
Bildunterschrift caption OT 1
bilingual bilingual OT 2
billig cheap OT 2; inexpensive OT 4
Billion trillion **WS 4**, 142
binden to tie OT 2; to bind **WS 3**, 94
Bingo bingo OT 1
Binnenland interior OT 5
Biodiversität biodiversity OT 4
Biografie biography OT 4
biografisch biographical OT 5
Biologe / Biologin biologist OT 4
Biologie biology OT 2
biologisch biological OT 5
biologisch angebaut organic OT 2
Biotoilette composting toilet OT 3
Birne pear OT 1
bis till OT 2; until OT 3
bisexuell bisexual OT 5
bisher so far OT 2
bisherig previous OT 4
Biss bite OT 2
Bitte request OT 2
bitte please OT 1
bitten to ask OT 1; urge OT 4
bitterlich bitterly OT 5
Blase bubble OT 1; blister OT 2
blasen to blow OT 2
Blaskapelle marching band OT 4
Blatt sheet OT 1; leaf OT 4
ein unbeschriebenes Blatt a clean slate **WS 1**, 27
blau blue OT 1
Blazer blazer OT 1
bleiben to stay OT 1; to keep OT 2; to remain OT 4
Bleistift pencil OT 1
Blick glimpse OT 5
Blickwinkel angle OT 5
blind blind OT 2
Blindenführhund guide dog OT 2
Blocker blocker OT 5
blockieren to block OT 3
blöd dumb; foolish OT 5
Blog blog OT 1
Blogeintrag blogpost OT 4
Blogger(in) blogger OT 3
blond blonde OT 1; blond-haired **WS 3**, 96
blondhaarig blond-haired **WS 3**, 96
bloß mere **WS 1**, 14
Blues blues OT 1
blühen to bloom **WS 2**, 79
Blume flower OT 1
Blut blood OT 2
blutig bloody **WS 1**, 14
blutrünstig bloodthirsty **WS 3**, 94
blutunterlaufen bloodshot **WS 1**, 28
Blutvergießen bloodshed OT 5
BMX-Rad fahren BMXing OT 5
Boden ground; bottom; floor OT 1
am Boden zerstört devastated OT 5
Bodenstation ground control OT 4
Bogen bow OT 2
Bogenschütze / -schützin archer **WS 2**, 62
Bohne bean OT 1

Bohnen in Tomatensoße baked beans OT 1
bohren to drill OT 4
bombardieren to bombard **WS 2**, 85
Bonbon sweet OT 2
Bonus bonus OT 5
Boom boom **WS 1**, 14
boomed to boom **WS 1**, 24
Boot boat OT 1
Boot fahren to cruise OT 3
Bord aboard OT 4
an Bord gehen to board OT 4
Bordstein curb OT 5
bösartig sinister **WS 2**, 61
Böse evil OT 5
böse angry OT 1; mad OT 2
Botschafter(in) ambassador **WS 1**, 21
Bouquet bouquet OT 3
Boygroup boyband OT 2
Boykott boycott **WS 2**, 68
boykottieren to boycott **WS 2**, 68
brainstormen to brainstorm OT 2
Brandbekämpfung firefighting OT 2
branden to brand **WS 2**, 55
brandmarken to brand **WS 2**, 55
brandneu brand-new OT 2
brasilianisch Brazilian OT 2
braten to fry OT 2
Bratensoße gravy OT 1
brauchen to need OT 1
braun brown OT 1
brechen to break OT 1
brennbar flammable OT 2
brennen to burn OT 2
brennend blazing OT 5
Brennholz firewood OT 4
Brennstoff fuel OT 2
Brett board OT 1
Brief letter OT 1
Briefkasten post box OT 1; mailbox OT 4
Brieftasche wallet OT 1
Briefumschlag envelope OT 2
Brille glasses OT 1
bringen to bring OT 1
Brise breeze OT 3
britisch British OT 1
Broccoli broccoli OT 1
Brombeere blackberry OT 1
Broschüre brochure OT 1; booklet OT 2
Brot bread OT 1
Brotkrumen breadcrumbs OT 3
Brotverdiener(in) breadwinner OT 5
Browser browser OT 4
brüchig brittle **WS 2**, 62
Brücke bridge OT 1
Bruder brother OT 1
Brunnen well **WS 1**, 25
Brust chest **WS 1**, 15
Brustpanzer breast plate **WS 3**, 94
Brustplatte breast plate **WS 3**, 94
brutal brutal OT 5
Brutalität brutality OT 5
Buch book OT 1
buchen to book OT 2
Bücherregal bookcase OT 1
Buchstabe letter OT 1
buchstabieren to spell OT 1
buchstäblich literally **WS 3**, 100
Bucht bay OT 1
Buchung booking OT 2
Bude stall OT 2
Büffel buffalo OT 4
Buffet buffet OT 3
Bühne stage OT 2
Bühnenanweisungen stage directions OT 2
Bund federation OT 5
Bündel bundle **WS 3**, 102
Bundesregierung federal government OT 5
Bündnis alliance **WS 1**, 33
Bungee-Jumping bungee jumping OT 3
bunt coloured OT 1
Burg castle OT 1
Bürger... civil **WS 1**, 18
bürgerlich civil **WS 1**, 18
Bürgermeister(in) mayor OT 3
Bürgersteig pavement OT 1; sidewalk OT 4
Bürgerwehr militia **WS 1**, 14
Büro office OT 1
Bürokratie bureaucracy **WS 3**, 104
Büropark office park OT 2
Bürste brush OT 2
Bus bus OT 1
Busch bush OT 2
Buschfeuer bushfire OT 5
Buschland bushland OT 5
Bushaltestelle bus stop OT 1
Busladung busload OT 5
Bussard buzzard OT 2

C

Café café OT 1
Cafeteria cafeteria OT 2
Camp camp OT 1
Camper(in) camper OT 2
Camping camping OT 1
Campingplatz campsite OT 1
Campus campus OT 2
Canyon canyon OT 3
Cartoon cartoon OT 4
Catwalk catwalk **WS 2**, 69
CCTV cctv **WS 3**, 104
Cellist(in) cellist OT 2
Cello cello OT 2
Celsius centigrade OT 4
Cent cent OT 1
Champignon mushroom OT 1
Champion champion **WS 1**, 18
Chaos: ein Chaos anrichten to make a mess OT 2
chaotisch disorganized; messy OT 2; chaotic OT 5
Charakter character OT 1
charakterisieren to characterize **WS 4**, 134
Charakterisierung characterization OT 5
charmant charming OT 3
Chart chart OT 4
Chauffeur(in) chauffeur **WS 2**, 62
Checkliste checklist OT 1
Cheerleader(in) cheerleader OT 3
Chef(in) boss OT 2
Chemikalie chemical OT 3
Chemiker(in) chemist OT 2
Chili chili OT 2
chillen to chill OT 5
chinesisch Chinese OT 1
Chip crisp OT 1
Chirurg(in) surgeon OT 3
Cholera cholera OT 4
Chor choir OT 1; chorus **WS 1**, 31
Chorizo chorizo OT 2
chronisch chronic **WS 1**, 30
clever witty **WS 1**, 17
Coaching coaching OT 4
Cola cola OT 1
Comicheft comic OT 1
Commonwealth commonwealth OT 5
Computer computer OT 1
computerbasiert computerized OT 4
computergesteuert computerized OT 4
Computerraum computer lab OT 2
Computing computing OT 5
Container container OT 2
cool cool OT 1
Cornflakes cereal OT 1
Cornrow cornrow **WS 2**, 69
Countdown countdown OT 4
Cousin(e) cousin OT 1
Couture couture **WS 2**, 71
Cracker cracker OT 3
Cranberry cranberry OT 4
Credit credit **WS 2**, 68
cremefarben creamy-skinned **WS 1**, 16
Curriculum curriculum **WS 3**, 124

Curry(gericht) curry OT 1
  mit Curry gewürzt curried OT 1
cybermobben to cyberbully OT 5
Cybermobbing cyber bullying OT 4
Cybersicherheit cyber security OT 4

D
da there OT 1
Dach roof OT 1
Dachboden attic OT 3
dadurch thus OT 5
daher thus OT 5
Dame lady OT 1
Damespiel checkers; draughts OT 1
Damm dam **WS 3**, 99
Dämon demon OT 5
Dampf steam OT 2
Dampfzug steam train OT 2
danach afterwards OT 3; thereafter **WS 1**, 39
dankbar grateful OT 5; thankful **WS 1**, 15
danke thanks OT 1
danken to thank OT 1
dann then OT 1
Darlehen loan OT 5
darstellen to illustrate OT 3; to portray **WS 2**, 57; to visualize **WS 2**, 57; to depict **WS 2**, 72; to pose **WS 2**, 81
  falsch darstellen to misrepresent **WS 2**, 66
Darsteller(in) performer OT 2
Darstellung representation **WS 4**, 139
darunter underneath OT 3; beneath OT 5
das the OT 1
Datei file OT 3
Daten data OT 3
Datum date OT 2
dauerhaft permanent OT 5
Daumen thumb OT 4
  Daumen gedrückt fingers crossed OT 1
Deal deal OT 4
Debatte debate OT 3
Debattierklub debating club OT 4
Decke blanket OT 2; ceiling OT 4
Deckel lid OT 2
defekt faulty OT 2
definieren to define OT 4
Definition definition OT 1
definitiv definitely OT 1
Degradierung degradation OT 5
dehnen to stretch OT 2
dehydriert dehydrated OT 2
dein your OT 1
  deine(r, -s) yours OT 2
Dekade decade OT 5
Dekorateur(in) decorator OT 3
dekorieren to decorate OT 4
delegieren to delegate OT 4
delegitimieren to delegitimize **WS 3**, 108
Delfin dolphin OT 1
Delikatesse delicacy OT 3
Delle dent **WS 3**, 102
Demografie demographics **WS 3**, 108
Demokratie democracy **WS 1**, 12
demokratisch democratic OT 4
Demonstrant(in) protester OT 5
Demonstration demonstration OT 4
Demonstrativbegleiter demonstrative OT 1
demütig humble **WS 2**, 80
demütigen to humiliate **WS 1**, 27
Demütigung indignity OT 5
demzufolge consequently **WS 2**, 85
Denim denim OT 4
denken to think OT 1
  denken an to think about; to think of OT 1
Denkmal monument OT 1
dennoch nevertheless **WS 1**, 16
deportieren to deport OT 4
Depression depression OT 4
deprimierend depressing OT 4
deprimiert depressed OT 4
der the OT 1
deren whose OT 2
derzeit currently OT 5
deshalb therefore OT 3
Design design OT 1
Designer(in) designer OT 3
designieren to designate OT 5
desinteressiert disengaged **WS 1**, 21
Desktop desktop OT 4
dessen whose OT 2
Detail detail OT 2
detailliert detailed OT 3
deutlich clearly OT 3; considerably OT 5
deutsch German OT 1
Dezember December OT 1
Dezimierung decimation **WS 1**, 21
Dhoti (indisches Kleidungsstück) dhoti **WS 1**, 19
Diabetes diabetes OT 5
diagnostizieren to diagnose OT 4
Diagramm diagram OT 3; chart OT 4; graph OT 5
Dialekt dialect OT 5
Dialog dialogue OT 1
Diashow slideshow OT 3
Diät diet OT 3
Diäten dieting OT 5
diätetisch dietary OT 5
dich yourself OT 1
dicht tight **WS 1**, 15
Dichte density OT 4; closeness OT 5
Dichter(in) poet OT 3
Dichtung poetry OT 1
dick thick OT 1; clumpy **WS 2**, 70
dickköpfig stubborn **WS 1**, 39
didaktisch didactic **WS 3**, 104
die the OT 1
Diebstahl theft OT 5; thievery **WS 2**, 71
Diele hall OT 1
Diener(in) attendant OT 3
Dienst service OT 2
Dienstag Tuesday OT 1
diese these; those OT 1
diese(r, -s) this; that OT 1
Diesel diesel OT 3
digital digital OT 3
Digitalisierung digitalization OT 5
Diktator(in) dictator **WS 3**, 104
Diktatur dictatorship **WS 3**, 92
Dilemma dilemma OT 4
Ding thing OT 1
Dingo dingo OT 5
Dinosaurier dinosaur OT 1
Dioxid dioxide **WS 3**, 98
Diplom diploma OT 5
Diplomatie diplomacy **WS 3**, 108
direkt straight; direct OT 3
diskriminieren to discriminate OT 5
Diskriminierung discrimination OT 5
Diskussion discussion OT 1
Disput dispute **WS 1**, 40
disqualifizieren to disqualify **WS 2**, 58
Disziplin discipline **WS 3**, 112
ditto ditto OT 4
diversifizieren to diversify **WS 3**, 100
Doktortitel PhD OT 5
Dokument document OT 4
Dokumentation documentary OT 2
Dollar dollar OT 1
Dolmetscher(in) interpreter OT 4
Domäne domain **WS 1**, 40
Dominanz dominance **WS 3**, 109
Donnerstag Thursday OT 1
Dopamin dopamine **WS 4**, 133
Doppel (Tennis) doubles OT 3
Doppel... double OT 1
doppelt double OT 1
Doppelung duplication **WS 4**, 139
Dorf village OT 1
Dorfbewohner(in) villager OT 4
dort there OT 1
Dose can; tin OT 2

in Dosen tinned; canned OT 2
Dotter yolk WS 1, 22
Drache dragon OT 1
Drachen kite WS 1, 43
Drama drama OT 1
Dramatiker(in) playwright OT 5
dramatisch dramatic OT 5
drängen to urge OT 4
drastisch drastic OT 5
draußen outside OT 1; outdoor(s) OT 2
Dreck dirt OT 4; mud WS 1, 16
dreckig grubby OT 2; filthy OT 4
Drehbuch script OT 1; screenplay WS 3, 104
drehen to turn OT 2
Drehscheibe turntable OT 2
drei three OT 1
Dreieck triangle OT 2
dreieckig triangular OT 3
Dreier triple WS 4, 137
dreißig thirty OT 1
dreiundzwanzig twenty-three OT 1
dreizehn thirteen OT 1
Dresscode dress code OT 4
dringend urgent OT 5
drinnen indoors OT 3
Dritte(r, -s) third OT 1
Droge drug OT 3; junk WS 3, 97
Drogerie drugstore OT 2
drohend impending WS 3, 96
Drohne drone OT 3
Druck pressure OT 3
unter Druck setzen to pressure OT 5
drücken to press OT 1
Drucker printer OT 5
Drüse gland OT 5
Dschungel jungle OT 4
du you OT 1
Dudelsack bagpipe OT 3
dumm silly OT 1; stupid OT 2; dumb OT 5
Dung manure OT 3; dung WS 1, 36
Dünger fertilizer OT 3
dunkel dark OT 1
Dunkelheit darkness OT 5
dünn thin OT 1; skinny WS 2, 60
durch through OT 1
durchaus absolutely OT 2
durcheinander jumbled; mixed up OT 2
durcheinanderbringen to mix up OT 2
durchführen to conduct OT 3; to undertake WS 1, 21; to implement WS 3, 124
durchmachen to undergo OT 5
durchnässt soaked OT 3
durchschnittlich average OT 4
durchsetzen to enforce OT 4; to assert WS 1, 14; to impose WS 2, 55
durchstochen pierced OT 3
durchstromern to roam around OT 5
durchweg throughout OT 3
dürfen to be allowed to OT 2
dürr arid OT 5
Dürre drought OT 5
durstig thirsty OT 1
Dusche shower OT 2
düster bleak WW, 11; grim WS 2, 78
Dutzend dozen OT 4
Dynamik dynamic OT 5
dynamisch vibrant OT 5
Dynastie dynasty WS 1, 14
Dystopie dystopia WS 3, 104
dystopisch dystopian OT 5

E

ebenfalls ditto OT 4
ebenso alike OT 5
echt real OT 1; genuine; authentic OT 5
Echtheit authenticity WS 1, 23
Ecke corner OT 1
E-Commerce e-commerce OT 4
edel noble WS 3, 94
effizient efficient OT 4
Effizienz efficiency WS 3, 99
egal welche whatever OT 3
egoistisch selfish OT 3
Ehe marriage OT 5
Ehefrau wife OT 1
ehemalig former OT 4
Ehemalige(r) alumnus OT 4
Ehemann husband OT 2
Ehre glory WS 2, 62
ehren to honour OT 5
Ehrenamt: ein Ehrenamt haben to volunteer OT 2
ehrenamtlich pro bono OT 5
Ehrenamtliche(r) volunteer OT 2
ehrfürchtig awestruck WS 1, 14
ehrgeizig ambitious OT 4
ehrlich honest OT 3; frank WS 3, 105
Ei egg OT 1
Eichhörnchen squirrel OT 1
Eifer eagerness WS 2, 79
eifersüchtig jealous WS 2, 64
eifrig eager OT 2
Eigelb yolk WS 1, 22
Eigen- vested WS 3, 99
eigenartig odd OT 2
eigene(r, -s) own OT 1
Eigenschaft feature OT 1; quality OT 3; trait WS 4, 144
eigenständig distinct OT 5
eigentlich actually OT 2
Eigentum property OT 5
Eignung qualification OT 5
Eiland isle OT 5
eilen to rush OT 2
Eimer bin OT 2
ein(e) a OT 1
ein(e) andere(r, -s) another OT 1
einbauen to incorporate WS 3, 112
einbeziehen to involve OT 4
Einbildung imagination OT 4
Einblick exposure WS 3, 109
eindeutig definite OT 1; distinct OT 5
Eindruck impression OT 5
einfach easy OT 1; simplistic WS 2, 62
einfallsreich fancy OT 2
einfangen to capture OT 4
einfetten to grease WS 1, 22
Einfluss influence OT 4
politischer Einfluss political clout OT 4
einflussreich influential WS 3, 108
einfügen to paste OT 2
einführen to import OT 3
Einführung introduction OT 2; advent; induction OT 5
Einführungs... introductory OT 4
Eingang entrance OT 1
Eingangsbereich entrance hall OT 1
Eingangshalle entrance hall OT 1
Eingebung inspiration OT 4
eingestehen to admit WS 1, 26
eingravieren to engrave OT 4
Eingriff invasion OT 5
einheimisch local OT 2; native OT 3; indigenous OT 5
Einheimische(r) local OT 2; native OT 3
Einheit session OT 2
einig: sich einig sein to agree OT 1
einige some OT 1; several OT 2
Einkaufen shopping OT 1
einkaufen to shop OT 1
Einkaufsdienst shopping rota OT 5
Einkaufszentrum mall OT 3
Einkommen income OT 4
einkommensschwach low-income OT 4
einladen to invite OT 2
mit einladen to invite along OT 2
Einladung invitation OT 1
einleuchtend plausible WS 4, 141
einloggen to log on OT 3
einmal once OT 2
Es war einmal... Once upon a time ... OT 1
einmarschieren to invade OT 3
einnehmen to occupy WS 2, 63

einordnen to categorize **WS 1**, 14

einpendeln to level off OT 5

einräumen to concede **WS 3**, 107

einreichen to hand in OT 2

einrichten to furnish **WS 1**, 39

Einrichtung institution OT 4

eins one OT 1

einsam lonely OT 3; solitary **WS 1**, 39

Einsatz dedication **WS 1**, 21

  im Einsatz in action OT 2

einschätzen to judge OT 2; to reassess OT 5

Einschätzung assessment **WS 3**, 97

einschlafen to go to sleep OT 1; to fall asleep OT 2

einschließen to include OT 1

einschränken to limit OT 3; to ration **WS 1**, 24; to restrict **WS 2**, 78

  sich einschränken to downsize OT 3

Einschränkung restriction OT 5

einschreiben to enrol **WS 3**, 103

Einsendung entry OT 2

einsetzen to employ **WS 4**, 133

  sich einsetzen to advocate **WS 1**, 25

Einsicht insight OT 5

einsperren to imprison **WS 1**, 18; to confine **WS 2**, 61

einsprachig monolingual OT 5

Einstand deuce OT 3

einstellen to cease **WS 3**, 120

Einstellung setting; attitude OT 3

einstufen to classify **WS 2**, 58

Einstufung classification **WS 2**, 78

eintippen to key in OT 2

Eintopf stew OT 2

einträchtig peaceful OT 2

Eintrag entry OT 2

eintragen to enter OT 2

einträufeln to instil **WS 2**, 82

eintreten to enter OT 2; to step in OT 4

  eintreten in to join OT 1

Eintritt admission OT 5

Eintrittskarte ticket OT 1

einundzwanzig twenty-one OT 1

Einwand objection OT 3

Einwanderer / Einwanderin immigrant OT 3

einwandern to immigrate OT 5

Einwanderungskontrolle immigration OT 2

Einweckglas jar OT 2

Einweihung dedication **WS 1**, 21

einweisen to instruct OT 5

einwickeln to wrap OT 2

Einwohner(in) citizen OT 3

Einzahl singular OT 1

Einzel... single OT 3

Einzelhändler(in) retailer OT 4

einzeln individually OT 4

Einzelne(r) individual OT 4

einzigartig unique OT 2

Eis ice; ice cream OT 1

  Eis am Stiel ice lolly OT 1

Eisbär polar bear **WS 3**, 98

Eisberg iceberg OT 3

Eiscreme ice cream OT 1

Eisen iron **WS 1**, 32

Eisenbahn rail OT 2

Eisenbahnlinie railway line OT 2

eisig icy OT 5

Eiweiß protein OT 4

ekelhaft disgusting; gross OT 3

ekeln to disgust OT 5

Elefant elephant OT 1

Elefantenführer mahout **WS 1**, 21

Elefantenhaken bull hook **WS 1**, 21

Elektrifizierung electrification **WS 3**, 99

elektrisch electric OT 1; electrical OT 4

Elektrolyseur electrolyser **WS 3**, 99

Elektronik electronics OT 2

elektronisch electronical OT 4; electronic OT 5

elementar elementary OT 2

Elend hardship **WS 2**, 61

elf eleven OT 1

Elfenbein ivory OT 3

Elite elite **WS 2**, 59

Ellbogen elbow OT 1

Elternteil parent OT 1

E-Mail email OT 1

  E-Mail schreiben to email OT 2

Emblem emblem **WS 2**, 59

Embryo embryo **WS 3**, 126

Emission emission OT 3

emittieren to emit **WS 3**, 102

Emoji emoji OT 3

Emoticon emoticon OT 5

emotional emotional OT 5; emotive **WS 1**, 20

Empathie empathy **WS 3**, 112

empathisieren to empathize **WS 2**, 67

Empfang reception OT 1

Empfangschef(in) receptionist OT 1

empfehlen to recommend OT 2

Empfehlung recommendation OT 5

empfinden to perceive OT 5

empfindlich sensitive **WS 2**, 61

empören to disgust OT 5

Ende end OT 1; ending OT 2

enden to end OT 1

endgültig final OT 1

endlos endless OT 4

Endung ending OT 2

Endzone end zone OT 2

Energie energy OT 2

  Energie geben to energize **WW**, 11

energisch energetic OT 2

eng narrow OT 2; close OT 3; tight **WS 1**, 15

Engagement engagement **WS 1**, 13

engagiert dedicated OT 5

Engel angel OT 3

englisch English OT 1

Enkel grandson OT 1

Enkelin granddaughter OT 3

Enkelkind grandchild OT 3

enorm vast OT 5

entdecken to discover OT 3; to happen upon OT 4

Entdeckung discovery OT 4

Ente duck OT 2

entfalten to unfold **WS 1**, 15

Entfärbung bleaching OT 5

entfernen to remove OT 2

entfernt remote OT 5

  weit entfernt distant **WS 3**, 104

Entfernung distance OT 2; removal OT 5

entführen to abduct OT 4

Entführer(in) kidnapper OT 2; captor **WS 1**, 14

enthalten to contain OT 3

enthaupten to behead OT 3

enthüllen to unveil **WS 1**, 19

Enthusiasmus enthusiasm **WS 1**, 32

entkommen to escape OT 2

entlang along OT 1

entlassen to dismiss; to fire OT 5; to sack **WS 2**, 85

entlasten to relieve OT 5

entleeren to empty OT 4

entleert deflated **WS 1**, 21

entlegitimieren to delegitimize **WS 3**, 108

entmachten to disempower **WS 3**, 104

entmenschlichen to dehumanize **WS 2**, 55

entmutigen to discourage OT 5

entmutigt deflated **WS 1**, 21

entriegeln to unlock OT 1

entschädigen to make amends OT 5

Entschädigung compensation OT 5

entscheiden to decide; to resolve OT 1

entscheidend decisive OT 5; crucial **WS 3**, 99

Entscheidung decision OT 1

entschlossen determined OT 3

Entschlossenheit determination OT 5

entschuldigen to excuse OT 1; to apologize OT 2
Entschuldigung apology OT 2; pardon OT 5
Entschuldigung! sorry OT 1
entsetzlich appalling **WS 1**, 38; dire **WS 4**, 138
entsetzt appalled **WS 1**, 18; outraged **WS 1**, 18
entspannen: (sich) entspannen to relax OT 2; to chill (out) OT 4
entspannt relaxed; laid-back OT 4
entsprechend equivalent OT 4; corresponding OT 5
entstehen to originate OT 5; to arise **WS 1**, 29
Entstellung mutilation **WS 1**, 14
enttäuschen to upset **WS 1**, 21; to disappoint **WS 2**, 83
enttäuschend disappointingly OT 3
enttäuscht disappointed OT 2
Enttäuschung disappointment OT 5
Entvölkerung depopulation **WS 3**, 104
entwalden to deforest **WS 1**, 21
entwerfen to design OT 3; to draft OT 5
entwickeln to develop OT 2; to devise **WS 2**, 57
sich entwickeln to evolve OT 4
Entwickler(in) developer OT 5
Entwicklung development OT 4; evolution OT 5
Entwurf design OT 1; draft OT 2
entziehen to deprive **WS 2**, 81
entzückt delighted OT 3; wowed OT 4
Entzug withdrawal **WS 4**, 144
Entzugsprogramm detox OT 2
entzünden to spark OT 4; to ignite **WS 2**, 62
Entzündung infection OT 2
Epidemie epidemic OT 4
Epoche period OT 3
er he OT 1
Erbe heritage OT 5; legacy **WS 1**, 14
Erbe / Erbin heir OT 5
erben to inherit **WS 1**, 16
Erbgut gene **WS 1**, 15
Erbse pea OT 1
Erdanziehungskraft gravity OT 4
Erdbeben earthquake OT 2
Erdbeere strawberry OT 1
Erdboden soil OT 2
Erde ground OT 1; earth OT 2
Erderwärmung global warming OT 3
Erdferkel aardvark **WS 2**, 53
Erdkugel globe OT 5
Erdkunde geography OT 1

Ereignis event OT 1; incident OT 5
erfahren experienced OT 3
Erfahrung experience OT 2
erfasst: nicht erfasst undocumented OT 4
erfinden to invent OT 2
Erfinder(in) inventor OT 2
erfinderisch resourceful OT 4
Erfindung invention OT 4
Erfolg success OT 3
erfolgreich successful OT 2
erfolgreich sein to succeed OT 2
erforderlich to require OT 4
erforschen to explore OT 1
erfreut delighted OT 3
Erfrischungsgetränk refreshment OT 2
erfüllen to fulfil OT 4
erfunden fictional OT 2
ergeben: sich ergeben to surrender **WS 1**, 39
Ergebnis result OT 2; finding OT 4; outcome OT 5
ergreifend poignant **WS 2**, 57
erhalten to receive OT 2; to preserve OT 3; to obtain **WS 3**, 95
erhältlich available OT 3
Erhaltung conservation OT 2
erheben to raise OT 2
erheblich considerable **WS 2**, 58
erhöhen to raise OT 2; to increase OT 3
erholen to recover OT 4
erholsam relaxing OT 2
Erholung relaxation OT 3
erinnern to remind OT 2
erinnern an to recall OT 5; to commemorate **WS 2**, 83
sich erinnern an to remember; to think of OT 1; to reminisce **WS 1**, 19
Erinnerung memoir OT 5; reminder **WS 1**, 39
Erkältung cold OT 5
erkennbar apparent **WS 1**, 25
erkennen to realize; to recognize OT 2; to perceive OT 5
erklären to explain OT 1; to state OT 5
erklärend explanatory **WS 4**, 136
Erklärung explanation OT 1; declaration OT 4
erkunden to explore OT 1
erkundigen: sich erkundigen to enquire **WS 3**, 111
erlangen to gain OT 1; to obtain **WS 3**, 95
erlauben to allow OT 3; to permit OT 5
Erlaubnis permission OT 2; permit; licence OT 3
erlaubt allowed OT 3

erleben to relive OT 4
erleichtern to relieve OT 5
Erleichterung relief OT 4
erleuchten to enlighten **WS 1**, 21
ermächtigen to empower OT 5
Ermächtigung empowerment **WS 3**, 98
Ermittler(in) investigator OT 4
ermöglichen to enable **WS 1**, 16
ermorden to murder OT 4; to assassinate **WS 1**, 18
Ermordung assassination **WS 1**, 18
ermutigen to encourage OT 2
ermutigen to uplift **WW**, 11
Ernährer(in) breadwinner OT 5
Ernährung nutrition OT 4
ernennen to designate; to appoint OT 5
Ernennung nomination OT 4
erneuerbar renewable OT 5
erneuern to renew **WS 1**, 24
erniedrigen to humiliate **WS 1**, 27
erniedrigend demeaning **WS 2**, 78
ernst serious OT 2
ernsthaft intense OT 5; sincere **WS 2**, 69; intent **WS 3**, 97
Ernsthaftigkeit seriousness OT 5
Ernte crop; harvest OT 4
Erntedankfest Thanksgiving OT 2
Erntehelfer(in) farmhand OT 4
ernten to harvest OT 4
E-Roller e-scooter OT 5
erreichen to reach OT 3; to achieve OT 4
errichten to put up OT 1
Ersatz substitution; substitute OT 3
erscheinen to appear OT 3
erschöpft exhausted OT 2
Erschöpfung fatigue **WS 4**, 138
erschrecken to frighten OT 3; to terrify **WS 3**, 104
erschreckend frightening OT 1
erschütternd harrowing **WS 1**, 21; staggering **WS 3**, 103
erschüttert devastated OT 5
erschüttert sein to reel **WS 3**, 97
ersetzen to replace OT 3
erspähen to spot OT 1
Erspartes savings OT 3
erstaunen to amaze OT 5
erstaunlich amazing OT 1; astonishing OT 5; miraculous **WS 1**, 27
erstaunlicherweise astonishingly OT 3
erstaunt amazed OT 3; astonished **WS 1**, 27
erste(r, -s) first OT 1; premier OT 2; maiden **WS 2**, 55
Erste Hilfe first aid OT 2
ersticken to choke **WS 1**, 39

erstrebenswert aspirational **WS 1**, 32
ertönen to sound OT 2
ertragen to bear **WS 1**, 14; to endure **WS 2**, 72
ertrinken to drown OT 3
erwachsen to mature **WS 2**, 83
Erwachsene(r) adult OT 1
erwähnen to mention OT 3
erwarten to expect OT 2
Erwartung expectation OT 5
erwartungsgemäß unsurprisingly OT 3
erweitern to expand OT 4
erweitern to broaden **WS 3**, 110; to diversify **WS 3**, 100
erweitert extended OT 5
erwerben acquire **WS 1**, 32; to purchase **WS 3**, 98
erzählen to tell OT 1; to narrate **WS 1**, 16
Erzähler(in) narrator OT 5
Erzählung narrative **WS 1**, 26; narration **WS 2**, 79
Erzbischof archbishop **WS 2**, 72
erzeugen to produce OT 3; to generate OT 4
Erzeuger(in) producer OT 5
erziehen to educate OT 5
Erziehung upbringing OT 5
Erzielen scoring OT 1
es it OT 1
  es gibt there is / are OT 1
essbar edible **WS 4**, 140
Essen food OT 1
  Essen zum Mitnehmen takeout OT 4
Esslöffel tablespoon OT 2
Essstäbchen chopstick OT 1
Esszimmer dining room OT 1
etablieren to institutionalize **WS 2**, 55
Etagenbett bunk bed OT 3
ethisch ethical OT 3
ethnisch ethnical OT 5
Ethnizität ethnicity **WS 3**, 92
Etikett label OT 1; tag OT 2
Etikette etiquette OT 3
etikettieren to label **WS 2**, 58
etwa approximately OT 5
etwas some; something OT 1
euch (selbst) yourselves OT 3
euer your OT 1
eure(r, -s) yours OT 2
evokativ evocative **WS 2**, 55
Evolution evolution OT 5
ewig eternal OT 4; everlasting **WS 4**, 144
Ewigkeit eternity **WS 2**, 62
exekutieren to execute OT 3
Existenz existence OT 5
existieren to exist OT 3
exklusiv upmarket **WS 2**, 53
Exodus exodus **WS 1**, 40
exotisch exotic OT 2
expandieren to expand OT 4
Expansion expansion **WS 3**, 108
Expedition expedition OT 2
Experiment experiment OT 1
experimentieren to experiment OT 4
Experte / Expertin expert OT 3
explizit explicitly OT 5
explodieren to explode OT 5
Explosion explosion **WS 1**, 15
Exporteur(in) exporter OT 5
exportieren export OT 5
Extra... extra OT 1
extravagant extravagant **WS 2**, 71
Extrem extreme OT 5
extrem extreme OT 3; drastic OT 5
Extremist(in) extremist **WS 1**, 18
extrovertiert extroverted OT 5

F

fabelhaft fabulous OT 2
Fabrik factory OT 4
Fach subject OT 1
Fachkraft practitioner **WS 3**, 123
Fachrichtung discipline **WS 3**, 112
Fachzeitschrift journal OT 5
fähig capable OT 4; competent OT 5
Fähigkeit skill; ability OT 2; capacity **WS 3**, 108
Fahne flag OT 1
Fahranfänger(in) learner OT 3
Fähre ferry OT 2
fahren to go; to drive; to ride OT 1; to motor OT 3
Fahrer(in) rider; driver OT 1; chauffeur **WS 2**, 62
Fahrerkabine cab OT 4
Fahrerlaubnis driver's license OT 4
Fahrgast passenger OT 2
Fahrkarte ticket OT 1
Fahrkartenschalter booking office; ticket office OT 2
Fahrplan timetable OT 1
Fahrpreis fare OT 5
Fahrrad bike OT 1; bicycle OT 2
  Fahrrad fahren to cycle OT 1
Fahrspur lane OT 2
Fahrt journey; ride OT 1
Fahrzeug vehicle OT 1
fair unfair OT 2
Fäkalien faeces **WS 1**, 16
Fakt fact OT 1
Faktor factor OT 5
Falle snare **WS 2**, 67
  Fallen stellen to snare **WS 2**, 67
fallen to fall OT 1; to decrease OT 5
  fallen lassen to drop OT 1
falls whether; if OT 1
falsch false; wrong OT 1; fake OT 5
  falscher Freund false friend OT 2
fälschlich mistakenly OT 5
falten to fold OT 2
Familie family OT 1; kin OT 5
Fan fan OT 1; supporter OT 2
Fanatiker(in) fanatic **WS 1**, 18
fangen to catch OT 1; to trap OT 5
Fantasie fantasy OT 2; imagination OT 4
fantasievoll imaginative OT 4
fantastisch fantastic OT 1
Fantasy fantasy OT 2
Farbe colour OT 1; paint OT 2; dye OT 4
Färbemittel dye OT 4
farbenfroh colourful OT 3
farbig coloured OT 1
Färbung colouring **WS 3**, 94
Farmarbeiter(in) farmworker OT 4
Faschismus fascism **WS 3**, 104
Fassade facade **WS 1**, 24
fast nearly OT 1; almost OT 2
Faszination fascination OT 4
faszinieren to fascinate **WS 1**, 17
faszinierend fascinating OT 3
Faust fist OT 5
Februar February OT 1
Feder feather OT 2
Federtasche pencil case OT 1
Fee fairy OT 2
Feedback feedback OT 1
fegen to sweep OT 4
fehlen to be missing OT 1
Fehler fault; mistake OT 2; error **WS 1**, 18
fehlerhaft blemished OT 5; flawed **WS 2**, 62
fehlgeleitet errant **WS 3**, 94
Fehlverhalten malpractice **WS 3**, 98
Feier party OT 1; celebration; ceremony OT 2
feierlich ceremonial OT 3
feiern to celebrate OT 1; to feast OT 4
Feigling wimp OT 5
Feind(in) enemy OT 1
feindlich hostile **WS 1**, 20
feindselig hostile **WS 1**, 20
Feindseligkeit hostility **WS 1**, 21
Feinheit subtlety **WS 3**, 94; nuance **WS 3**, 107
Feinkostladen deli OT 5
Feld field; square OT 1; space OT 2
Fels rock OT 2
Felsen cliff OT 5

Fenster window OT 1
Ferienlager camp OT 1
fern far-off OT 2; faraway OT 4
Fernbedienung remote control OT 4
fernbleiben to keep away OT 2
Ferne: aus der Ferne remotely OT 4
Fernglas binoculars OT 2
fernhalten to keep away OT 2
Fernsehen TV OT 1; television OT 2
fertigstellen to finalize OT 5
Fertilität fertility **WS 1**, 43
fesseln an to confine **WS 2**, 61
Fest festival OT 1; feast OT 4
fest firm **WS 1**, 40
festhalten to grasp **WS 1**, 27
an etw. festhalten to cling to OT 2; to adhere to **WS 3**, 124
Festival festival OT 1
Festland mainland OT 3
festlegen to schedule; to state OT 5
festlich festive **WS 1**, 43
Festlichkeit festivity OT 4
festmachen to fasten OT 1
Festmahl feast OT 4
festnehmen to capture OT 4
Festnetz landline OT 4
Festung fort OT 2; fortress OT 3
Fett fat OT 2
fettgedruckt bold OT 1
Fetzen tatters **WS 2**, 79
Feuer fire OT 2
Feuerwache fire station OT 2
Feuerwehrmann / -frau firefighter OT 2
Feuerwerk fireworks OT 3; firework display OT 4
Figur figure OT 3; figurine **WS 1**, 27
figurativ figurative OT 5
Fiktion fiction OT 2
fiktiv imaginary OT 4
Film film; movie OT 1; motion picture OT 4
Filmemacher(in) filmmaker OT 5
Filmmaterial footage **WS 1**, 21
Filmrolle roll OT 2
filtern to filter **WS 3**, 98
Filzstift marker OT 1
Finalist(in) finalist OT 5
finanziell financial OT 5
finanziell unterstützen to sponsor OT 2
finanzieren to fund OT 3
Finanzwirtschaft finance OT 5
finden to find OT 1; to locate **WS 4**, 14
Finger finger OT 1
Fingernagel fingernail OT 2
Firma company OT 1; firm OT 5
Fisch fish OT 1
Fischstäbchen fish finger OT 1
Fischsuppe chowder OT 3
Fitness fitness OT 2
körperliche Fitness able-bodiedness **WS 2**, 57
Fitnesscenter gym OT 3
Fitnesstraining workout OT 5
Fixierung obsession **WS 3**, 104
Flachland plains OT 5
Flaggschiff flagship OT 3
Flair vibe **WS 1**, 15
Flamingo flamingo OT 2
Flamme flame **WS 1**, 43
Flasche bottle OT 1
Flashback flashback **WS 3**, 106
flattern to flutter **WS 3**, 96
flauschig fluffy OT 2
flechten to braid **WS 2**, 69
Fleisch meat OT 1; flesh OT 2
Fleischer(in) butcher OT 4
Fleischfresser(in) carnivore **WS 2**, 64
Fleischklößchen meatball OT 1
flexibel flexible OT 4
Flexibilität flexibility OT 5
flicken to cobble **WS 3**, 94
Fliege bow-tie OT 2
fliegen to fly OT 1
fliehen to flee **WS 1**, 14
fließend fluent OT 3; flowing OT 5
flimmern to flutter **WS 3**, 96
Flohmarkt flea market OT 5
Fluch curse **WS 1**, 21
fluchen to curse **WS 1**, 39
Flucht exodus **WS 1**, 40
flüchten to flee **WS 1**, 14
Flüchtling refugee OT 4
Flüchtlingslager refugee camp OT 4
Flug flight OT 2
Flugblatt handout OT 4
Flügel wing OT 1
Flughafen airport OT 1
Flugpersonal flight crew OT 2
Flugzeug plane OT 1; airplane; aeroplane OT 4
Fluss river OT 1; flow **WS 3**, 101
flüssig liquid OT 2
flüstern to whisper **WS 1**, 26
Flut flood OT 2
Fluten flooding OT 4
Flyer flyer OT 4
Fokus focus OT 1
fokussieren to focus OT 4
Folge consequence; sequence OT 4; episode OT 5
zur Folge haben to result **WS 2**, 68
folgen to follow OT 2
folgend sequentially OT 4
folgerichtig logical OT 5
folglich consequently **WS 2**, 85
Folie slide OT 1
Folklore folklore OT 5
fordern to require; to demand OT 4
fördern to promote OT 5
Förderung grant OT 5
Form form; shape OT 1
in Form fit OT 2
Format format OT 5
Formation formation OT 5
formell formal OT 5
formen to shape OT 3; to craft **WS 3**, 94
förmlich formal OT 5
formulieren to formulate OT 4
neu formulieren to rephrase OT 4
forschen to research OT 2
Forscher(in) researcher OT 2; explorer OT 3
Forschung research OT 2
Forstbeamter / -beamtin park ranger OT 2
Förster(in) ranger OT 3
fortfahren to proceed **WS 1**, 39
fortgeschritten advanced OT 4
fortlaufend successive OT 5
Fortpflanzung reproduction **WS 3**, 104
Fortschritt advance; progress OT 4
fortschrittlich progressive OT 1
Fortsetzung sequel **WS 3**, 127
Forum forum OT 5
fossil fossil OT 3
Foto photo; photograph OT 1
ein Foto machen to take a photo OT 1
Fotoapparat camera OT 1
Fotograf(in) photographer OT 3
Fotografie photography OT 4
fotokopieren to photocopy OT 4
foulen to foul OT 3
fracken to frack OT 5
Fracking fracking OT 5
Frage question OT 1
in Frage stellen to question **WS 1**, 15
Fragebogen questionnaire OT 1
fragen to ask OT 1
sich fragen to wonder OT 3
Franse ribbon **WS 3**, 95
französisch French OT 1
Frau Mrs; woman; wife OT 1
Frauenfeind misogynist **WS 1**, 31
Frauenhasser misogynist **WS 1**, 31
Freak freak OT 4
frech cheeky OT 1
frei free OT 1

Freiberufler(in) freelancer OT 5
freiberuflich freelance OT 5
Freibeuter(in) privateer OT 3
Freigebigkeit generosity **WS 1**, 25
Freiheit liberty OT 1; freedom OT 3
freilegen to uncover OT 3
Freitag Friday OT 1
freiwillig: sich freiwilig melden to volunteer OT 2
Freiwillige(r) volunteer OT 2
Freizeit leisure OT 3
Freizeit... recreational OT 3
fremd foreign OT 1
Fremde(r) foreigner OT 3
Freude pleasure OT 1
freuen: sich auf etw. freuen to look forward to OT 1
Freund(in) friend OT 1
freundlich friendly; kind OT 1
Freundlichkeit kindness **WS 1**, 25
Freundschaft friendship OT 3
Frieden peace OT 5
friedlich peaceful OT 2
Frisbee frisbee OT 1
frisch fresh OT 2
Friseursalon barbershop **WS 3**, 97
Frisur hairstyle OT 5
Fritte chip OT 1
frittieren to fry OT 2
froh glad OT 1
fröhlich cheerful; gay OT 5; gleeful **WS 1**, 39; upbeat **WS 2**, 72; joyful **WS 2**, 72
Frosch frog OT 5
Fruchtbarkeit fertility **WS 1**, 43
früh early OT 1
früher previously OT 3
Frühling spring OT 2
Frühjahrsputz spring clean OT 2
Frühstück breakfast OT 1
Frühstücksflocken cereal OT 1
frustrierend frustrating OT 5
frustriert frustrated OT 3
Fuchs fox OT 1
fügsam docile **WS 2**, 78
fühlen to feel OT 1; to sense **WS 3**, 97
führen to lead OT 3
Führer(in) guide OT 1
Führerhaus cab OT 4
führerlos driverless OT 4
Führerschein driving licence OT 2; driver's license OT 4
Führung leadership OT 4
Führungskraft executive OT 5
füllen to fill OT 2
Fundament foundation OT 5
fünf five OT 1
fünfte(r, -s) fifth OT 1
fünfzehn fifteen OT 1
fünfzig fifty OT 1
Funke spark OT 2
Funktion function OT 4
funktionieren to function **WS 3**, 94
für for OT 1; in favour **WS 1**, 14
Furcht fear OT 3
furchtbar horrible OT 2; dire **WS 4**, 138
fürchten to dread **WS 3**, 105
fürchterlich awful OT 1
Fürstenstaat princely state **WS 1**, 14
Fürwort pronoun OT 1
Fusion fusion **WS 1**, 30
Fuß foot OT 1
Fußabdruck footprint OT 3
Fußball football OT 1; soccer OT 2
Fussel fuzz OT 4
Fußknöchel ankle OT 1
Fußpfad footpath OT 1
Fußstapfen footsteps **WS 1**, 41
Füttern feeding OT 2
füttern to feed OT 2

G

Gabel fork OT 2
Gabelstapler forklift OT 5
gaffen to gongoozle OT 3
Gaffer gongoozler OT 3
Galaxie galaxy OT 1
Galerie gallery OT 1
Galionsfigur figurehead **WS 2**, 55
Gallone gallon OT 3
Galopp to gallop **WS 3**, 94
galoppieren to gallop **WS 3**, 94
Gamer(in) gamer OT 4
Gang course OT 1
Gans goose OT 4
ganz whole OT 1; completely OT 2
ganze(r, -s) entire OT 3
Garage garage OT 4
garantieren to guarantee OT 5
Garten garden OT 1; yard OT 2
Garten hinterm Haus backyard OT 2
Gartenarbeit gardening OT 1
Gärtner(in) gardener OT 4
Gas gas OT 3
Gasse lane OT 2
Gast guest OT 2
Gastfreundschaft hospitality OT 2
Gasthaus lodge; inn OT 2
Gauner(in) crook **WS 2**, 56
Gebäck pastry **WS 1**, 16
Gebäude building OT 1
geben to give OT 1
Gebet prayer OT 4
Gebetshaus meetinghouse OT 4
Gebiet area OT 1; territory OT 5; tract **WS 4**, 136
Gebiets... territorial **WS 1**, 40
gebildet cultured OT 4
Gebirgszug mountain range OT 4
geboren sein to be born OT 2
gebraten roast OT 1
gebrochen broken OT 1
Gebühr fee OT 3
gebunden sein to be bound to **WS 3**, 96
Geburt birth OT 2
Geburtsdatum date of birth OT 2
Geburtsort birthplace OT 4
Geburtstag birthday OT 1
Gedächtnis memory OT 1
Gedanke thought OT 4
gedankenlos thoughtless OT 2
Gedicht poem OT 1
geeignet fit OT 2; suitable OT 4
Geek geek OT 5
geerdet grounded **WS 1**, 29
Gefahr danger; hazard OT 2; risk OT 3; threat OT 5
in Gefahr bringen to jeopardize **WS 3**, 124
gefährden to threaten; to endanger OT 5; to jeopardize **WS 3**, 124
gefährdet endangered OT 2
gefährlich dangerous OT 1; risky; unsafe OT 3; perilous **WS 2**, 65
gefangen nehmen to arrest OT 5
Gefangene(r) prisoner OT 5
Gefangenschaft captivity **WS 1**, 32; imprisonment **WS 2**, 78
Gefängnis prison OT 1; jail OT 5
Geflügel poultry OT 2
geformt shaped OT 4
gefriergetrocknet freeze-dried OT 4
Gefrierschrank freezer OT 3
gefroren frozen OT 4
Gefühl feeling OT 2; emotion OT 3; sensation OT 4; vibe **WS 1**, 15
gefühlvoll emotive **WS 1**, 20
gegen against OT 1
Gegenargument counterargument **WS 1**, 13
Gegend area; district OT 1
gegensätzlich contrasting OT 4
gegenseitig mutual **WS 1**, 33
Gegenstand object OT 1; item OT 2
Gegenteil opposite OT 1; contrast OT 3
im Gegenteil on the contrary **WS 3**, 104
Gegenwart present OT 1

Gegner(in) opponent OT 2; opposition OT 5
gegnerisch opposing OT 3
gegrillt barbecued OT 4
gehackt chopped OT 2
Gehalt wage OT 4; salary OT 5
Gehege enclosure **WS 2**, 64
Geheimnis secret OT 2
geheimnisvoll mysterious **WS 1**, 26; enigmatic **WS 3**, 104
gehen to go OT 1
zu Fuß gehen to walk OT 1
Geheul howl OT 5
Gehirn brain OT 2
Gehirnwäsche: einer Gehirnwäsche unterziehen to brainwash OT 5
gehorchen to obey **WS 3**, 104
nicht gehorchen to disobey OT 5
gehören to belong OT 2
Gehörlose deaf OT 5
gehorsam docile **WS 2**, 78
Gehweg pavement OT 1
Geige violin OT 1
Geiselnehmer(in) captor **WS 1**, 14
Geisha geisha **WS 2**, 69
Geist spirit; ghost OT 2; soul **WS 1**, 18
Geisteshaltung mentality **WS 3**, 106
Geisteswissenschaften humanities **WS 3**, 112
geistig mental OT 4; spiritual **WS 2**, 71; intellectual **WS 3**, 112
gekocht boiled OT 1
Gel gel OT 1
Geländearbeit fieldwork OT 4
Geländefahrzeug off-road vehicle OT 1
gelangweilt bored OT 1
gelassen leisurely **WS 2**, 79
gelb yellow OT 1
gelb-orange amber **WS 3**, 118
Geld money OT 1
Geldgeber(in) sponsor OT 2; investor OT 4
gelegen located OT 5; situated **WS 1**, 23
Gelegenheit opportunity OT 2; occasion **WS 1**, 31
gelegentlich occasionally OT 2
Gelehrte(r) scholar **WS 3**, 108
Geleitzug convoy **WS 1**, 15
gelockt curly OT 3
gelten to be deemed **WS 2**, 78
Gemälde painting OT 1
gemäß according to OT 3
gemein mean OT 2
Gemeinde township OT 4
gemeinnützig non-profit OT 4
Gemeinplatz cliché **WS 3**, 94
gemeinsam mutual **WS 1**, 33
Gemeinschaft community OT 2
gemeinschaftlich collaborative **WS 3**, 109
gemischt blended OT 5
gemischtgeschlechtlich co-ed; co-educational OT 2
Gemüse vegetable OT 1
gemütlich cozy OT 3; comfy OT 4
Gen gene **WS 1**, 15
genau just OT 1; exact OT 2; detailed OT 3; accurate OT 4; precise OT 5
Genauigkeit accuracy **WS 3**, 113
genehmigen to approve OT 3
Generation generation OT 4
die Generation der Jahrtausendwende millennial OT 4
Generator generator **WS 3**, 99
genervt annoyed OT 2
genetisch genetically **WS 3**, 104
genial brilliant OT 1
Genie genius **WS 1**, 26
genießen to enjoy OT 1; to relish **WS 2**, 79
Genre genre OT 4
Gentleman gentleman OT 3
genug enough OT 1; sufficient OT 5
Genugtuung satisfaction **WS 2**, 79
Geocache geocache OT 2
Geografie geography OT 1
geografisch geographical OT 4
Geologie geology OT 2
Gepäck baggage OT 2; luggage OT 4
Gepäckausgabe baggage claim OT 2
gerade straight OT 3; currently OT 5
Gerät appliance; device OT 3; gadget OT 4
Geräusch sound; noise OT 1
gerecht fair OT 2
Gerechtigkeit justice OT 4
Gericht dish OT 2; court OT 5
jüngstes Gericht Judgement Day OT 4
gering minor; slight OT 5; minimal **WS 1**, 14
geringschätzig dismissive **WS 2**, 82
gerinnen to curdle **WS 1**, 39
gerissen ripped OT 4; cunning **WS 1**, 16
gernhaben to like OT 1; to care about OT 2
hätte(n) gern would like / love OT 1
geröstet sauté OT 3
gerötet bloodshot **WS 1**, 28
geruchslos odourless **WS 3**, 99
Gerücht rumour OT 5
gesamt total OT 1
Gesamtliste tally OT 4
Gesandte(r) ambassador **WS 1**, 21
Gesang vocals OT 2
Geschäft business OT 3; deal OT 4; trade OT 5
Geschäftsfrau businesswoman OT 4
Geschäftsführer(in) manager OT 1
Geschäftsführung management OT 5
Geschäftsmann businessman OT 4
geschehen to happen OT 1
Geschenk present; gift OT 1
Geschenkgutschein gift voucher OT 1
Geschichte history; story OT 1; tale OT 2; narrative **WS 1**, 26
Geschichtenbuch storybook OT 2
geschichtlich historical OT 2
Geschick skill OT 2
geschickt skilful OT 3; skilled OT 4
Geschirr dishes OT 2
Geschirrspülen washing up OT 2
Geschirrspülmaschine dishwasher OT 4
Geschlecht gender OT 4; sex OT 5
geschlechtslos genderless OT 5
geschlechtsspezifisch gendered OT 5
Geschlechtswort article OT 1
geschlossen closed OT 1
Geschmack flavour OT 2; taste OT 4
geschnetzelt shredded OT 2
Geschwindigkeit speed OT 2
Geschwister(kind) sibling OT 5
geschwollen swollen OT 2
Gesellschaft society OT 4
Gesetz law OT 3; act OT 5
Gesicht face OT 1
Gesichtsausdruck facial expression OT 4
Gesichtszüge facial features **WW**, 11
gespannt curious OT 4; intent **WS 3**, 97
gesponsert sponsored OT 2
Gespräch conversation OT 1; negotiation **WS 1**, 18
Gesprächs... conversational OT 5
gesprächig chatty OT 3
Geständnis confession **WS 1**, 26
Geste gesture OT 4; token OT 5
gestern yesterday OT 1
gestiftet sponsored OT 2
gestikulieren to gesticulate **WS 4**, 144
gestresst stressed OT 2; distressed **WS 1**, 21
gestrichen painted OT 1
gesund healthy OT 2
Gesundheit health OT 2
Gesundheitswesen healthcare OT 4
Getränk drink OT 1

Getreide crop OT 4
getrennt divided; separate OT 2
Gewalt violence OT 4
Gewaltlosigkeit non-violence OT 3
gewalttätig violent OT 5; abusive **WS 1**, 29
Gewehr rifle OT 4
Gewicht weight OT 4
Gewichtheben weightlifting OT 4
Gewinn prize OT 1; profit OT 4
gewinnen to win OT 1
Gewinner(in) winner OT 1
Gewissheit certainty **WS 2**, 58
Gewitter thunderstorm OT 2; rainstorm OT 5
Gewohnheit habit OT 4
gewöhnlich normally OT 1; common OT 4
gewohnt accustomed **WS 2**, 56
Gewürz seasoning OT 2; spice OT 3
Gewürzgurke pickle OT 1
gewürzt spiced OT 4
Gezeiten tide **WS 1**, 27
gießen to pour OT 1
Gift poison OT 1; venom OT 5
giftig toxic OT 4; poisonous OT 5
Gig gig OT 5
gigantisch ginormous OT 2
Gipfel peak OT 5
Gips plaster OT 1
Giraffe giraffe OT 1
Gitarre guitar OT 1
Gitarrist(in) guitarist OT 1
Gladiator(in) gladiator OT 3
Glamour glamour **WS 2**, 64
glamourös glamorous OT 4
Glanz glamour **WS 2**, 64
Glas glass OT 1
glatt smooth OT 3
Glaube belief OT 4; faith **WS 1**, 15
glauben to believe OT 2
Glaubhaftigkeit validity **WS 3**, 112
gleich same OT 1
gleichartig fellow OT 5
gleichberechtigt equal OT 4
Gleichberechtigung equality OT 5
gleichgesinnt like-minded **WS 1**, 41
Gleichgewicht balance OT 3
Gleichheit sameness **WS 2**, 57
Gleitschirmfliegen paragliding OT 5
Glitzern glimmer **WS 2**, 65
glitzern to glitter OT 2; to twinkle OT 4
global global OT 4
Globus globe OT 5
Glocke bell OT 1
Glück luck OT 1; fortune OT 3
glückbringend lucky OT 2
glücklich happy OT 1; lucky OT 2; fortunate **WS 1**, 15
glücklicherweise fortunately OT 5
glücklos unlucky OT 2
Glückwünsche congratulations OT 2
Glühbirne lightbulb OT 3
Gold gold OT 2
golden golden OT 3
Goldrausch gold rush OT 4
Goldschmied(in) goldsmith **WS 1**, 16
Gospel gospel OT 2
Gosse gutter **WS 1**, 31
Gott God OT 4
Grab grave OT 5
graben to dig OT 1
Grad degree OT 4
Gradation gradation **WS 2**, 78
Graduierten- postgraduate **WS 3**, 112
Graffiti graffiti OT 5
Grafik graphic OT 3
Gramm gram OT 2
Grammatik grammar OT 1
Grammofon gramophone OT 4
grandios grand OT 5
Graph graph OT 5
Gras grass OT 1
Gräte fishbone **WS 4**, 140
gratulieren to congratulate OT 2
grau grey OT 1
Grauen horror OT 2
grausam ferocious **WS 1**, 16; cruel **WS 1**, 21
Grausamkeit cruelty OT 5
gravieren to engrave OT 4
greifen to grab OT 3; to grasp **WS 1**, 27
Grenze border OT 3; boundary OT 5
Grenzland frontier OT 4
griechisch Greek OT 2
Griff handle OT 2
Grill grill OT 5
Grillen barbecue OT 2
grimmig grim **WS 2**, 78
grinsen to grin OT 2; to smirk **WS 2**, 62
Grippe influenza OT 5
grooven to groove **WS 1**, 15
groß tall; big; great OT 1; large OT 2; vast OT 5
großartig awesome OT 2; grand OT 5
Großaufnahme close-up OT 4
Großbuchstabe capital letter OT 1
Größe size OT 1
Großeltern grandparents OT 1
Großmutter grandmother OT 1
Großsegler tall ship OT 2
Großstadt metropolis **WS 1**, 12
größte(r) utmost **WS 1**, 15
Großvater grandfather OT 2
großzügig generous OT 3
Großzügigkeit generosity **WS 1**, 25
grün green OT 1
Grund reason OT 1; cause OT 2
Grund... primary OT 1; elementary OT 2; basic OT 4; fundamental **WS 2**, 68
Grundbesitzer landlord **WS 1**, 16
gründen to found; to form OT 4
Gründer(in) founder OT 5
Grundlage foundation; basis OT 5
  Grundlagen basics **WS 2**, 55
grundlegend radical OT 4
gründlich in-depth **WS 4**, 133
grundsätzlich basic OT 4
Grundschule elementary school OT 2
Grunzen grunt **WS 3**, 94
Gruppe group OT 1
Gruppenarbeit teamwork OT 4
gruselig creepy OT 5
Gruß greeting OT 5
  mit freundlichen Grüßen sincerely OT 4
grüßen to greet OT 5
Grußformel salutation **WS 2**, 79
günstig convenient OT 4
Gurke pickle OT 1
Gurt harness OT 1
Gürtel belt OT 2
gut fine; good; all right OT 1
  gut aussehend handsome OT 1
Gutacher(in) assessor OT 5
gutbürgerlich plain OT 4
Güte kindness **WS 1**, 25; goodness **WS 1**, 27
Güter goods OT 4
gutgläubig naive **WS 3**, 98
Gutschein coupon OT 2
guttun to benefit OT 2
Gymnastik gymnastics OT 1

H

Haare hair OT 1
Haarschnitt haircut OT 2
Habe belongings OT 3
haben feature OT 1
Habitat habitat OT 4
Hackbraten meatloaf OT 3
Hackfleischbällchen meatball OT 1
Hafen port; harbour OT 2
Haferbrei porridge OT 3
Haferflocken oats OT 3
haften to adhere **WS 3**, 124
Häftling prisoner OT 5
Hahn rooster **WS 1**, 17

Hähnchen chicken OT 1
Hai shark OT 5
Häkchen tick OT 2
Haken tick OT 2
haken to hook OT 4
halal halal OT 3
halb half OT 1; halfway OT 3
  eine halbe Stunde nach half past OT 1
  halb... semi- OT 5
halbieren to halve **WS 4**, 134
Halbjahr semester OT 3
Halbmarathon half marathon OT 2
halbwegs halfway OT 3
Halbzeit half-time OT 2
Halle hall OT 1
hallo hello; hi OT 1
Halloween Halloween OT 2
Hals neck OT 1; throat OT 2
  Hals über Kopf head over heels **WS 1**, 28
Halsband collar OT 2
  Halsband aus Knochen bone choker **WS 3**, 94
Halskette necklace **WS 2**, 71
Halt stop OT 2
halten to hold OT 1
Halter holder OT 5
Haltestelle stop; halt OT 2
Haltung attitude OT 3
Hamburger burger OT 1; hamburger OT 2
Hamster hamster OT 1
Hand hand OT 1
  jdm. die Hand geben to shake hands OT 2
  mit der Hand schreiben to handwrite OT 5
Handbuch handbook OT 3; manual **WS 1**, 22
Handel trade; commerce OT 5
  illegalen Handel treiben to traffic OT 4
handeln to trade **WS 1**, 14
Handgelenk wrist OT 1
Händler(in) retailer OT 4
Handlung plot OT 4
Handlungsstrang storyline **WS 1**, 38
Handout handout OT 4
Handschrift handwriting OT 2
handschriftlich handwritten OT 5
Handschuh glove OT 1
Handtasche handbag OT 3
Handtuch towel OT 2
Handy mobile phone OT 1; cell phone OT 2
hängen to hang **WS 1**, 28
Harfe harp OT 1
Harfenist(in) harpist OT 3
harmlos harmless OT 5
hart hard OT 1; tough OT 4
härten to harden **WS 2**, 56
Hashtag hashtag OT 5
Hass hatred **WS 2**, 62
hassen to hate OT 1; to loathe OT 5
hässlich ugly OT 1
Haufen heap OT 4; pile OT 5; bunch **WW**, 11
häufig frequently OT 3; many times OT 4; frequent OT 5
Häufigkeit frequency OT 1
Haupt... primary; main OT 1; core OT 4
Hauptgang main course OT 1
Hauptgedanke keynote **WS 4**, 139
Hauptlast: die Hauptlast tragen to bear the brunt **WS 1**, 14
Hauptrolle: eine Hauptrolle spielen to star **WS 3**, 126
hauptsächlich mainly OT 2; generally OT 4
Hauptsitz headquarter OT 4
Hauptstadt capital OT 1
Hauptverkehrszeit rush hour OT 1
Hauptwort noun OT 1
Haus house OT 1
Hausarbeit housework OT 1; chore OT 4
Hausarrest: jdm. Hausarrest erteilen to ground OT 5
Hausaufgaben homework OT 1
Hausboot narrowboat; houseboat OT 3
Häuschen cottage OT 3
Hausfrau housewife OT 5
Haushälter(in) housekeeper OT 3
Haushalts... household OT 4
Haushaltsgerät appliance OT 3
häuslich household OT 4; domestic **WS 2**, 65
Hausmeister(in) caretaker OT 1
Haustier pet OT 1
Haut skin OT 2
  helle Haut creamy-skinned **WS 1**, 16
Headquarter headquarter OT 4
Headset headset OT 4
heben to raise OT 2; to lift OT 3
Hecke hedge OT 5
heften to pin OT 1
heftig fierce **WS 2**, 62
hegen to cherish **WS 2**, 79
heil in one piece OT 2
Heilbad spa OT 3
heilen to cure OT 4; to heal **WS 3**, 113
heilig sacred OT 4
Heilkunde medical science OT 4
Heilung healing OT 5
Heimat homeland OT 4
heimatlos homeless OT 3
Heimatstadt hometown OT 4
heimtückisch sneaky OT 5
Heimweh homesickness OT 4
heiraten to marry OT 1; to wed OT 3
Heiratsantrag: einen Heiratsantrag machen to propose OT 5
heiß hot OT 1
heizen to heat OT 3
Heizung heater OT 2; heating OT 3
Hektar hectare OT 5
hektisch frantic OT 3; hectic OT 4
Held(in) hero OT 3
helfen to help OT 1
Helfer(in) helper OT 3
Helm helmet OT 1
Hemd shirt OT 1
Hemisphäre hemisphere OT 5
Henne hen OT 2
herablassend patronizing **WS 2**, 61
herabsetzen to lower **WS 1**, 27
herabsetzend demeaning **WS 2**, 78
heraufhusten to hack up **WS 1**, 27
heraus out OT 1
herausbilden: sich herausbilden to crystallize **WS 4**, 139
herausfiltern to filter out **WS 3**, 127
herausfinden to find out OT 1; to work out OT 2
Herausforderer / -forderin challenger **WS 2**, 84
herausfordern to challenge OT 5
Herausforderung challenge OT 2
Herausgeber(in) editor OT 2
herausragend outstanding OT 3; exceptional **WS 1**, 23
Herbst autumn OT 2
Herd cooker OT 3
Herde herd OT 4
herleiten to derive **WS 2**, 61
Herr Mr; Sir OT 1; gentleman OT 3
herrisch bossy OT 2
Herrschaft reign OT 3
herrschen to reign OT 3
Herrscher(in) monarch OT 5
Herrscherhaus dynasty **WS 1**, 14
Hersteller(in) manufacturer OT 4; producer OT 5
Herstellung production; manufacture OT 4; manufacturing OT 5
Herumblödeln to muck around OT 5
herumhängen to hang out OT 1
herumwandern to roam around OT 5

herumziehend migrant OT 4
hervorheben to highlight OT 3
hervorragend distinguished **WS 2**, 68
hervorrufen to provoke OT 5; to evoke **WS 2**, 72
hervorstehend prominent **WS 1**, 22
Herz heart OT 2
herzhaft hearty OT 2; fruity **WS 3**, 97
Heteronormativität heteronormativity **WS 2**, 57
heterosexuell heterosexual OT 5
Heureka-Erlebnis eureka moment OT 4
heute today OT 1
  heute Abend tonight OT 1
heutzutage nowadays OT 3
Hexe witch OT 2
hier here OT 1; locally OT 3
Hierarchie hierarchy **WS 3**, 108
Highway highway OT 3
Hijab hijab **WS 1**, 21
Hilfe relief OT 4
hilflos helpless; hopeless OT 4
hilfreich helpful OT 1
Himbeere raspberry OT 1
Himmel sky OT 1; heaven OT 5
hinauf up OT 1
hindeuten: auf etw. hindeuten to denote OT 5
hinduistisch Hindu OT 1
Hinfahrt outward journey OT 3
hinfallen to fall over OT 2
hinsetzen to sit down OT 1
hinsichtlich concerning **WS 4**, 133
hinter behind OT 1
Hintergrund background OT 3
hinterhältig sneaky OT 5
Hinterland outback OT 4
hinterlassen to leave behind OT 2
hinüber across OT 1
hinunter down OT 1
hinunterkommen to get down OT 2
hinunterschlucken to swallow OT 4
Hinweis tip; clue OT 1
hinzufügen to add OT 1
Hip-Hop hip hop OT 1
hispanisch Hispanic OT 3
hissen to hoist **WS 1**, 43
Historiker(in) historian OT 3
historisch historic OT 3
Hitzewelle heatwave OT 5
Hobby hobby OT 1
hoch high; tall OT 1
hochheben to lift OT 3
hochladen to upload OT 3
Hochschule college OT 2
Hochwasser flood OT 2
Hochzeit wedding OT 3
Hockey hockey OT 1
Hof court; courtyard OT 3
hoffen to hope OT 1
hoffentlich hopefully OT 4
hoffnungslos hopeless OT 4
hoffnungsvoll hopeful OT 5
höflich polite OT 1
Höhe height OT 1; altitude **WS 2**, 60
Höhepunkt climax OT 5
Höhle cave OT 1
holen to fetch OT 4
Hölle hell OT 5
holprig bumpy OT 4
Holz wood OT 2
hölzern wooden OT 1
Holzscheit log OT 3
homophob homophobic **WS 3**, 107
Honig honey OT 2
hören to hear OT 1
Hörer(in) listener OT 1
Horizont horizon OT 5
horizontal horizontal OT 4
Hormon hormone OT 5
Horn horn OT 2
Horror horror OT 2
Hose trousers OT 1
  kurze Hose shorts OT 1
Hostel hostel OT 2
Hotdog hot dog OT 2
Hotel hotel OT 1
Hotline helpline OT 2
hübsch lovely; pretty OT 1
Hubschrauber helicopter OT 2
Hüfte hip OT 3
Hügel hill OT 1
hügelig hilly OT 2
Huhn chicken OT 1
Hühnerstall coop OT 4
Hülle cover OT 1
Hülsenfrucht pulse OT 4
humanisieren to humanize **WS 1**, 25
humanitär humanitarian OT 5
Humor humour OT 3
humorvoll humorous OT 5
Hund dog OT 1
Hundedreck dog mess OT 2
hundert hundred OT 1
Hunger hunger OT 4
hungern (lassen) to starve OT 1
Hungersnot famine OT 4
hungrig hungry OT 1
Hurrikan hurricane OT 5
husten to cough OT 2
Hut hat OT 1
Hütehund sheepdog OT 2
Hüter(in) keeper OT 4
Hütte shack **WS 2**, 53
hydratisieren to hydrate OT 4
Hydro- hydro **WS 3**, 99
Hygiene hygiene OT 4
Hymne anthem OT 5; hymn **WS 1**, 26
Hype hype OT 5
Hyperlink hyperlink OT 3

I

ich I OT 1
  ich selbst myself OT 3
ideal ideal OT 2
  idealerweise ideally OT 5
idealisieren to idolize **WS 2**, 60
idealistisch idealistic **WS 2**, 79
Idee idea OT 1
identifizieren to identify OT 3
identisch identical OT 5
Identität identity OT 3
Idol idol OT 5
Igel hedgehog OT 1
Igitt! yuck OT 3
ignorant ignorant **WS 1**, 21
Ignoranz ignorance **WS 1**, 21
ignorieren to ignore OT 4
ihm him OT 1
ihn him OT 1
ihnen them OT 1
ihr / Ihr their; her; your OT 1
ihre(r, -s) hers; theirs; yours OT 2
Ikone icon OT 5
ikonisch iconic OT 3
illegal illegal OT 3
Illustration illustration OT 2
illustrieren to illustrate OT 3
imaginär imaginary OT 4
Imitation imitation **WS 2**, 69
immateriell intangible **WS 1**, 15
immer always OT 1
  für immer forever OT 2
  immer noch still OT 1
Immobilie property OT 5
Imperativ imperative OT 1
imperial imperial **WS 1**, 40
Impfstoff vaccine **WS 3**, 101
importieren to import OT 3
Improvisation improvisation OT 2
improvisieren to improvise OT 2
in at; on; into; inside OT 1
inakzeptabel unacceptable OT 5
Inbegriff epitome **WS 1**, 21
Index index OT 4
Indexer(in) indexer OT 4
indisch Indian OT 2
individuell individual OT 3

Industrie industry OT 2
Industrie... industrial OT 2
Industrieller magnate **WS 3**, 100
Infinitiv infinitive OT 2
Influencer(in) influencer OT 5
Influenza influenza OT 5
Infografik infographic OT 3
Information information OT 1
informativ informative OT 3
informell informal OT 5
informieren to inform OT 4
Ingenieur(in) engineer OT 3
Ingenieurwesen engineering OT 1
Inhaftierung imprisonment **WS 2**, 78
Inhalt content OT 2
inhuman inhumane OT 4
Initiative initiative OT 4
Inklusion inclusion OT 5
inklusive including; include OT 1
Inklusivität inclusivity **WS 2**, 57
Inkubator incubator OT 5
inländisch domestic **WS 2**, 65
inmitten von amidst **WS 2**, 65
innen indoor(s) OT 2
Innenhof courtyard OT 3
Innenstadt downtown; inner city OT 4
Innere: das Innere interior OT 5
Innereien insides OT 3
innerer inner OT 5
innerhalb inside OT 1; within OT 4
Innovation innovation OT 4
innovativ innovative OT 4
Innovator(in) innovator OT 4
insbesondere in particular OT 5
Insekt insect OT 1
Insektenhaus bughouse OT 1
Insel island OT 2
kleine Insel isle OT 5
Inserat advert OT 1
Insignien insignia **WS 3**, 95
Inspiration inspiration OT 4
inspirieren to inspire OT 3
installieren to install OT 4
instruktiv informative OT 3; instructive OT 5
Instrument instrument OT 1
Insulaner(in) islander OT 5
intakt intact **WS 1**, 39
integrativ inclusive OT 4
integrieren to integrate **WS 2**, 68; to incorporate **WS 3**, 112
integriert integrated OT 5
intellektuell intellectual **WS 3**, 112
intelligent clever OT 1; intelligent OT 2; smart OT 4

Intelligenz: künstliche Intelligenz AI (artificial intelligence) OT 5
Intensität intensity **WS 1**, 39
interagieren to interact OT 4
Interaktion interaction OT 4
interaktiv interactive OT 5
interessant interesting OT 1
Interesse interest OT 1
im Interesse von on behalf of OT 5
interessieren: sich interessieren to care about OT 2
interessiert interested OT 1
Interferenz interference **WS 4**, 138
interkulturell intercultural OT 5
intermittierend intermittent **WS 3**, 101
intern internal OT 5
Internat boarding school **WS 3**, 95
international international OT 1
Internet internet OT 1
Internethandel e-commerce OT 4
Interpret(in) performer OT 2
Interpretation interpretation OT 5
interpretieren to interpret OT 4
Intersex intersex OT 5
Interview interview OT 1
interviewen to interview OT 1
Interviewer(in) interviewer OT 1
Interviewte(r) interviewee **WS 2**, 67
Intonation intonation OT 4
Invasion invasion OT 5
invasiv invasive OT 5
Inversion inversion OT 5
investieren to invest OT 3
Investition investment OT 3
Investor(in) investor OT 4
involviert involved OT 3
inzwischen meanwhile OT 5
iranisch Iranian OT 4
irgendein(e) any OT 1
irgendetwas anything OT 1
irgendjemand anybody OT 1; anyone OT 2
irgendwie like OT 1; somehow OT 5
irgendwo somewhere OT 1; anywhere OT 2
irisch Irish OT 1
Ironie irony OT 5
irrational irrational **WS 3**, 106
Irre madman OT 4
irreal unreal **WS 1**, 29
irreführend misleading OT 3
irrend errant **WS 3**, 94
Irrtum error **WS 1**, 18
irrtümlicherweise mistakenly OT 5
islamisch Islamic OT 5
Islamophobie Islamophobia **WS 1**, 21

isolieren to isolate **WS 2**, 83
israelisch Israeli OT 2
italienisch Italian OT 2
italienisches Eiscafé gelateria OT 5
Itinerar itinerary **WS 2**, 64

J

ja yes; yeah OT 1
Jacht yacht OT 2
Jacke jacket OT 1
jagen to chase OT 1; to hunt OT 2
Jäger(in) hunter OT 5
Jahr year OT 1
Jahrestag anniversary **WS 1**, 19
Jahreszeit season OT 3
Jahrhundert century OT 2
jährlich annual OT 5
Jahrmarkt fairground OT 2; fair OT 4
Jahrzehnt decade OT 5
jamaikanisch Jamaican OT 1
Januar January OT 1
japanisch Japanese OT 1
Jazz jazz OT 2
je ever OT 1
Jeans(hose) jeans OT 1
Jeansstoff denim OT 4
jede(r, -s) everybody; every; each; everyone OT 1
jederzeit anytime OT 3
jedoch though; however OT 2
jemand someone; somebody OT 1
jene(r, -s) that OT 1
jene dort those OT 1
jenseits beyond OT 5
jetzt now OT 1
Job job OT 1
joggen to jog OT 2
Joghurt yoghurt OT 1
Journal journal OT 5
Journalismus journalism OT 5
Journalist(in) journalist OT 2
jubeln to cheer OT 2
juckend itchy OT 2
Judo judo OT 1
Jugend youth OT 1
Jugendbetreuer(in) counsellor OT 2
Jugendherberge youth hostel OT 2
Jugendliche(r) teenager OT 2; youngster **WS 1**, 25
Juli July OT 1
jung young OT 1
Junge boy OT 1
jüngst recent OT 4
Juni June OT 1
Junior(in) junior OT 2
Juwel jewel OT 1

K
Kabel cable OT 5
Kabine cabin OT 2
Kabinett cabinet OT 5
Kaffee coffee OT 1
Käfig cage OT 4
Kai pier OT 5
kaiserlich imperial **WS 1**, 40
Kajakfahren kayaking OT 2
Kalender calendar OT 1
Kalkulation calculation **WS 2**, 59
kalkulieren to calculate **WS 3**, 124
Kalorie calorie OT 5
kalt cold OT 1; freezing OT 2
Kamel camel OT 5
Kamera camera OT 1
Kamerad(in) comrade **WS 2**, 83
Kameramann cameraman OT 5
Kamin fireplace OT 1
Kamm comb OT 2
Kammer chamber OT 2
  kleine Kammer closet OT 2
Kampagne campaign OT 3; initiative OT 4
Kampf fight OT 1
kämpfen to fight OT 1; to grapple **WS 2**, 65
  kämpfen gegen to oppose **WS 3**, 100
Kanal canal OT 3
Kanalboot narrowboat OT 3
Kandidat(in) candidate OT 4
Känguru kangaroo OT 5
Kaninchen rabbit OT 1
Kantine canteen OT 1
Kanu canoe OT 1
Kanufahren canoeing OT 1
Kanzlei firm OT 5
kapitalisieren to capitalize **WS 2**, 57
Kapitalismus capitalism **WS 3**, 94
Kapitän(in) sein to captain **WS 2**, 59
Kapitel chapter OT 1
Kapsel capsule OT 4
Kapuzenpullover hoodie OT 1
Karamelle caramel OT 3
Karate karate OT 1
Karbon carbon OT 3
karg barren **WS 2**, 78
Karma karma **WS 1**, 32
Karotte carrot OT 1
Karren cart **WS 1**, 32
Karriere career OT 3
Karte card OT 1
Karteikarte cue card OT 4
Kartoffel potato OT 1
Kartoffelbrei mashed potato OT 1
Karton carton OT 2
Kartrennen kart racing OT 3
Käse cheese OT 1
Kasino casino **WS 1**, 29
kaskadieren to cascade **WS 4**, 136
Kasse cash register OT 2; check-out OT 4
Kassierer(in) cashier; bank teller OT 4
Kästchen box OT 1
Kaste caste **WS 1**, 13
katastrophal catastrophic OT 4
Katastrophe disaster OT 2; cataclysm **WS 3**, 92; catastrophe **WS 4**, 142
Katastrophengebiet disaster area OT 2
Kategorie category OT 3
kategorisieren to categorize **WS 1**, 14
Kathedrale cathedral OT 1
Katholik(in) Catholic OT 3
katholisch catholic OT 3
Katze cat OT 1
Kauf purchase OT 4
kaufen to buy; to shop OT 1; to purchase **WS 3**, 98
Käufer(in) shopper OT 4
Kaugummi bubblegum **WS 2**, 68
kaum hardly OT 3
Kavallerie cavalry **WS 3**, 94
keimtötend antiseptic OT 2
keine(r, -s) none OT 2
Keks biscuit OT 1; cookie OT 3
Keller cellar OT 4
Kellner(in) waiter OT 1
kenntnisreich knowledgeable OT 3
Kenntnisse proficiency **WS 3**, 111
Kennwort password OT 4
kennzeichnen to characterize **WS 4**, 134
Kerl guy OT 2
Kern core OT 4
Kernland heartland OT 4
Kerze candle OT 2
Kerzenlicht candlelight OT 4
Kessel kettle OT 2
Ketchup ketchup OT 1
Kette chain OT 2
keuchen to gasp OT 2
Keulen cull OT 5
keulen to cull OT 5
Keyboard keyboard OT 1
Kickball kickball OT 4
Kidneybohne kidney bean OT 2
Kilometer kilometre OT 1
Kind child; kid OT 1
Kinderarzt / -ärztin paediatrician **WS 2**, 67
Kinderbetreuung childcare **WS 2**, 67
Kindergarten preschool OT 5; nursery **WS 3**, 80
Kindheit childhood OT 3
Kino cinema OT 1
Kiosk tuckshop **WS 2**, 78
kippen to dump OT 5
Kipppunkt tipping point OT 5
Kirche church OT 1
Kirchenlied hymn **WS 1**, 26
Kissen cushion OT 1
Kiste box OT 1; crate OT 4
Kitesurfen kite-surfing OT 5
Kiwi kiwi OT 1
Klammer clip OT 1; bracket OT 2
klammern to cling OT 2
Klan clan OT 3
Klang (einer Glocke) bong OT 1
Klaps pat OT 3
klar clear OT 2; evident OT 5
klären to clarify OT 4
Klarinette clarinet OT 2
Klasse class OT 1
Klassenkamerad(in) classmate OT 3
Klassenstufe grade OT 2
Klassenzimmer classroom OT 1
Klassiker classics **WS 3**, 97
klassisch classic; classical OT 2; vintage OT 5
klatschen to clap OT 1
klauen to steal OT 2
Klavier piano OT 1
Klebeband tape OT 1
kleben to stick OT 1; to paste OT 2; to glue **WS 1**, 26
klebend sticky OT 4
klebrig sticky OT 1
Klebstoff glue OT 1
Kleid dress OT 3
  Kleider clothes OT 1; outfit OT 5
Kleiderordnung dress code OT 4
Kleiderschrank wardrobe OT 1
Kleidung clothes OT 1; clothing OT 3; gear **WS 1**, 15
klein small; little OT 1; minor OT 5
  sehr klein miniature OT 3
Klein... small-scale **WS 1**, 25
Kleinbus minibus OT 2
Kleingeld cash OT 1
Kleinigkeiten incidentals **WS 2**, 78
Kletterer(in) climber OT 2
klettern to climb OT 1
klicken to click OT 5
Klima climate OT 2
Klimaerwärmung global warming OT 3
Klingel doorbell OT 2
klingeln to ring OT 1
klingen to sound OT 2
Klinik clinic OT 5
klinisch clinical OT 5

Klippe cliff OT 5
klirren to clash OT 2
Klischee stereotype OT 5; cliché **WS 3**, 94
Klo loo OT 2
Klopfen knock OT 2
klopfen to tap OT 2
Kloß dumpling OT 4
Kloster monastery OT 3; cloister **WS 1**, 23
Klub club OT 1
klug savvy OT 5
klumpig clumpy **WS 2**, 70
knacken to crack **WS 2**, 62
knapp skimpy **WS 3**, 94
Kneipe pub OT 2
Knete dough OT 2
Knie knee OT 1
knien to kneel OT 1
knistern to sizzle OT 5; to crackle **WS 1**, 22
Knochen bone OT 1
Knödel dumpling OT 4
Knopf button OT 1
knospend budding **WS 3**, 96
knuddelig cuddly OT 1
koagulieren to curdle **WS 1**, 39
Koala koala OT 5
Koch / Köchin chef OT 1
köcheln to simmer OT 2
kochen to make; to cook OT 1; to boil OT 2
  kochend heiß boiling OT 1
Kochfeld hob OT 3
Kochnische kitchenette **WS 1**, 23
Koffein caffeine OT 5
Koffer case OT 1; suitcase OT 2
Kofferraum trunk OT 2
kohärent coherent **WS 4**, 139
Kohl cabbage OT 1
Kohle coal OT 2
  glühende Kohle ember OT 5
Kohlendioxid carbon dioxide OT 5
Kohlenhydrat carbohydrate; carb OT 5
kohlensäurehaltig fizzy OT 2
Kojote coyote OT 5
Kollaboration collaboration **WS 3**, 109
Kollege / Kollegin colleague OT 4
Kollektiv collective **WS 2**, 71
kolonial colonial OT 4
Kolonialisierung colonization OT 5
Kolonialismus colonialism **WW**, 10
Kolonie colony OT 4
kolonisieren to colonize OT 5
Kolonist(in) colonist OT 3
Kombination combination OT 3
kombinieren to combine OT 4
Komiker(in) comedian **WS 2**, 62
Komitee committee OT 2
Komma comma OT 3
Kommandant(in) captain; commander OT 4
kommen to come OT 1
  näher kommen to approach OT 4
Kommentar comment OT 1
kommentieren to comment OT 3; to annotate **WS 2**, 63
Kommerz commerce OT 5
kommerziell commercial OT 4
Kommode dresser **WS 1**, 27
kommunizieren to communicate OT 4
Komödie comedy OT 5
Komparativ comparative OT 2
Kompass compass OT 2
kompatibel compatible **WS 1**, 28
kompetent competent OT 5
Kompetenz competence OT 5
kompilieren to compile **WS 2**, 60
komplex complex OT 5
Kompliment compliment OT 5
kompliziert complicated OT 2; tricky OT 4
komponieren to compose OT 3
Komponist(in) composer OT 2
Kompost compost OT 3
kompromettieren to compromise **WS 1**, 21
Kompromiss compromise OT 5; trade off **WS 3**, 98
Kondor condor OT 3
Konferenz conference OT 4
Konflikt conflict OT 2
Kongress convention OT 4
König king OT 1
Königin queen OT 1
königlich royal OT 1
Königreich kingdom OT 4
konkret specific OT 3; precise OT 5
Konkurrent(in) competitor OT 4
Konkurrenz competition OT 1; rivalry OT 5
konkurrenzorientiert competitive OT 3
konkurrieren to compete OT 2
Können ability OT 2
können can OT 1; to be able to; to be allowed to OT 2
  könnte might; may OT 1
Konnotation connotation **WS 1**, 21
konsequent consistent **WS 3**, 99
Konsequenz consequence OT 4
konservieren to conserve **WS 2**, 64
Konstellation constellation OT 5
konstruktiv constructive OT 5
Kontakt contact OT 1
  in Kontakt bleiben to keep in touch OT 2
  Kontakte pflegen to socialize OT 4
Kontamination contamination **WS 3**, 100
kontaminieren to contaminate **WS 3**, 100
Kontext context OT 4
Kontinent continent OT 3
Kontrabass double bass OT 2
Kontrast contrast OT 3
Kontrolle control OT 3
kontrollieren to control OT 4; to monitor **WS 2**, 83
Kontroverse controversy **WS 2**, 58
konturieren to contour **WS 2**, 70
Konvention convention OT 4
konvertieren to convert **WS 1**, 25
Konvoi convoy **WS 1**, 15
Konzentration concentration OT 4
konzentrieren to concentrate OT 3
  sich auf etw. konzentrieren to centre around OT 5
konzentrisch concentric **WS 3**, 108
Konzept concept OT 4
Konzert concert OT 1
Kookaburra kookaburra OT 5
Kooperation partnership OT 4
Kopf head OT 1
  Kopf hoch! cheer up OT 1
Kopfband headband OT 3
Kopfbedeckung headdress **WS 2**, 69
Kopfkissen pillow OT 2
Kopfsalat lettuce OT 2
Kopfschmerzen headache OT 1
Kopftuch hijab **WS 1**, 21
Kopie replica OT 4
kopieren to copy OT 1
Koralle coral OT 5
Korb basket OT 3
Kordel lanyard OT 5; cord **WS 2**, 62
koreanisch Korean OT 1
Korn grain OT 5
Körper body OT 1
körperlich physical OT 2
Körpermodellierung sculpting **WS 3**, 113
Korporations... corporate OT 5
Korrektur correction OT 4
Korridor corridor OT 2
korrigieren to correct OT 1; to fix; to mark OT 2
korrupt corrupt **WS 2**, 78
Korruption corruption **WS 1**, 17

kosmopolitisch cosmopolitan OT 5
Kosten cost OT 1
kosten to cost OT 1
kostenlos free OT 1; pro bono OT 5
kostspielig costly **WS 3**, 101
Kostüm costume; fancy dress OT 2
Kot faeces **WS 1**, 16; poo **WS 2**, 97
krabbeln to crawl OT 5
Krabbeltier creepy-crawly OT 2
krachen to crash OT 3
Kraft force OT 1; power OT 5
kräftig powerful OT 5
kraftlos powerless OT 4
Kraftzentrum powerhouse **WS 1**, 25
Krähe crow **WS 1**, 21
Krake octopus OT 1
Kram shebang **WS 1**, 15
Krampf cramp OT 2
Kran crane OT 4
krank sick OT 1; unwell; ill OT 2
Krankenhaus hospital OT 1
Krankenpfleger(in) nurse OT 1
Krankenschwester nurse OT 1
Krankenwagen ambulance OT 1
Krankheit disease; illness OT 2
Krankheitsbild syndrome **WS 1**, 30
Kranz wreath OT 3
Krapfen doughnut OT 2
kratzen to scratch OT 2
kraus frizzy OT 3
Kraut herb OT 3
Krawatte tie OT 1
kreativ creative OT 2
Kreativität creativity OT 4
Krebs cancer OT 4
Kreditkarte credit card OT 1
kreieren to create OT 2
Kreis circle OT 1
kreischen to scream OT 3
Kreisdiagramm pie chart OT 4
kreuzen to cross OT 1
Kreuzfahrt cruise OT 2
  eine Kreuzfahrt machen to cruise OT 3
Kreuzgang cloister **WS 1**, 23
Kreuzung crossroads OT 1
kribbeln to tingle **WS 1**, 30
Kricket cricket OT 1
kriechen to crawl OT 5
Krieg war OT 2
  Krieg führen to war **WS 1**, 14
Krieger(in) warrior OT 2
Kriegsschiff warship OT 3
Kriminelle(r) criminal OT 3
Krise crisis OT 3
Kritik criticism OT 5
Kritiker(in) critic **WS 1**, 18
kritisch critical OT 5
kritisieren to criticize OT 3
Krokodil crocodile OT 5
Krone crown OT 1
krönen to crown OT 1
Kröte toad OT 2
Krücke crutch OT 2
Küche kitchen OT 1; cuisine OT 3
  kleine Küche kitchenette **WS 1**, 23
Kuchen cake OT 1
Küchenchef(in) chef OT 1
Kugel bullet **WS 2**, 67
Kugelschreiber ballpoint pen OT 1
Kuh cow OT 1
Kuhhirt(in) cowherd **WS 1**, 16
kühl cool OT 1
kühlen to cool OT 3
Kühlschrank fridge OT 1; refrigerator OT 4
Kult... iconic OT 3
kultiviert cultured OT 4
Kultur culture OT 1
kulturell cultural OT 3
Kummer sorrow OT 5
kümmern: sich kümmern um to tend **WS 1**, 16
Kumpel buddy OT 2; mate OT 5
Kunde / Kundin customer OT 3; client OT 5
Kundgebung rally OT 4
kündigen to quit OT 4
Kunst art OT 1
  bildende Kunst visual art OT 2
Kunstfehler malpractice **WS 3**, 98
Künstler(in) performer OT 2; entertainer; artist OT 3
künstlerisch artistic **WS 2**, 68
künstlich man-made OT 1; artifical OT 3
Kunststoff plastic OT 2
Kunstwerk artwork OT 5
Kunstwissenschaft fine art OT 2
Kupfer copper OT 1
Kuppel cupola OT 4
Kürbis pumpkin OT 2; squash OT 4
Kürbislaterne jack-o-lantern OT 2
Kuriosität oddity OT 4
Kurs course OT 1; program OT 3; approach **WS 1**, 21
kursieren to circulate OT 4
kurz short OT 1; brief OT 5
kürzen to shorten OT 5
kuschelig cuddly OT 1
Kuss kiss OT 3
Küste seaside; coast OT 1; shore OT 2; coastline OT 5
Küsten... coastal OT 1
Küstenlinie coastline OT 5
Küstenwache coastguard OT 2
Kutsche buggy OT 4
Kutschfahrten carriage driving OT 2

L

Labor lab OT 2; laboratory OT 4
Lache pool OT 1
lächeln to smile OT 1
lachen to laugh OT 1
  Lachender Hans kookaburra OT 5
Lachs salmon OT 1
Lack varnish OT 5
Laden shop; store OT 1
Ladendiebstahl shoplifting OT 5
Ladung cargo OT 3; load OT 5
Lage situation OT 1; circumstance OT 5
  nicht in der Lage sein to be unable **WS 2**, 69
Lagerfeuer campfire OT 2; bonfire **WS 1**, 43
lagern to store **WS 3**, 99
Lagerraum stockroom; storeroom OT 5
Lagerung storage OT 3
lähmen to paralyse **WS 2**, 61
Lähmung: zerebrale Lähmung cerebal palsy **WS 2**, 61
Lamm lamb OT 1
Lampe lamp OT 1
Land countryside OT 1
  an Land ashore OT 4
  im ganzen Land countrywide **WS 2**, 83
Landarbeiter(in) farmhand; farmworker OT 4
landen to land OT 1
landesweit countrywide **WS 2**, 83
Landkarte map OT 1
ländlich rural OT 4
Landschaft landscape; scenery OT 2
Landstrasse highway OT 3
Landwirtschaft farming; agriculture OT 2
landwirtschaftlich agricultural OT 4; agrarian OT 5
lang long OT 1
Länge length OT 2
langsam slow OT 2
langweilig boring OT 1; dull OT 5
Lappen cloth OT 2
Laptop laptop OT 1
Lärm noise OT 1
Lasagne lasagna OT 1
Laser laser OT 3
lassen to let OT 1

lässig casual OT 5
Laster truck OT 1
lästig irksome **WS 2**, 78
Lastkraftwagen truck OT 1; lorry **WS 3**, 99
Latein Latin OT 1
lateinamerikanisch Latino OT 2
Laterne lantern OT 2
lauern to lurk **WS 2**, 62
Laufband treadmill OT 4
laufen to walk; to run OT 1
Läufer(in) runner OT 2
Laufsteg catwalk **WS 2**, 69
laut loud; noisy OT 1; aloud OT 2
Lautsprecher loudspeaker OT 2
Lautsprecheranlage PA (public address) system OT 2
Lava lava OT 5
leasen to lease OT 4
Leben life OT 1; lifetime OT 2
Leben nach dem Tod afterlife OT 5
leben to live OT 1
lebendig alive OT 4
lebensbedrohlich life-threatening OT 2
lebenslang lifelong **WS 2**, 67
Lebenslauf Curriculum Vitae OT 5
Lebensmittel groceries OT 4
Lebensmittelladen grocery store OT 4
Lebensmittelverarbeitung food processing OT 4
Lebensmittelvergiftung food poisoning OT 2
Lebensraum habitat OT 4
Lebenssaft lifeblood **WS 2**, 78
Lebensstil lifestyle OT 4
lebenswichtig vital OT 4
Lebenszeit lifetime OT 2
Leber liver OT 5
Lebewesen creature OT 4
lebhaft lively; vibrant OT 5; vivid **WS 1**, 43
Leckage leakage **WS 3**, 104
lecken to lick OT 3
lecker delicious OT 1
LED Birne LED bulb OT 3
Leder leather OT 3
lediglich mere **WS 1**, 14
leer empty OT 1; blank OT 4
leeren to empty OT 4
legal legal OT 4
legalisieren to legalize OT 5
legendär legendary **WS 2**, 84
Legende legend OT 2; myth OT 5
legitim legitimate **WS 3**, 107
lehnen to lean OT 3
Lehrer(in) teacher OT 1; instructor OT 3
lehrhaft didactic **WS 3**, 104
Lehrling apprentice OT 5
Lehrmeister(in) mentor OT 4
Lehrplan curriculum **WS 3**, 124
lehrreich instructive OT 5
Lehrstelle apprenticeship OT 5
Leibwächter(in) bodyguard **WS 2**, 59
Leiche corpse OT 5
leicht easy OT 2; light OT 3; slight OT 5
Leichtathletik athletics OT 1
Leichtigkeit ease **WS 1**, 28
leichtsinnig carelessly OT 2
leiden to suffer OT 5
Leidenschaft passion **WS 1**, 21
leidenschaftlich passionate OT 4
leider unfortunately OT 3
leihen to lend; to borrow OT 2
Leihgabe loan OT 5
Leinwand screen OT 1
auf der Leinwand onscreen OT 2
leisten to afford OT 2
Leistung achievement OT 2
Leitartikel editorial **WS 1**, 25
leiten to manage OT 1
Leiter ladder OT 2
Leitmotiv keynote **WS 4**, 139
Leitung: die Leitung übernehmen to take charge OT 2
Lendenschurz loincloth **WS 3**, 94
Leopard leopard OT 2
lernen to learn OT 1
auswendig lernen to memorize OT 4
Lernende(r) learner OT 3
lesbisch lesbian OT 5
Lesen reading OT 1
lesen to read OT 1
Leser(in) reader OT 3
Lesezeichen marker OT 1
letzte(r, -s) last OT 1
leuchtend bright OT 1
leugnen to deny OT 5
Leugner(in) denier **WS 1**, 21
Leugnung denial **WS 3**, 103
Leute people OT 1; folks; guys OT 2
unter die Leute kommen to socialize OT 4
Licht light OT 1
ans Licht kommen to emerge **WS 1**, 14
Lidschatten eyeshadow **WS 2**, 70
liebe(r, -s) dear OT 1
lieben to love OT 1
liebenswert endearing **WS 1**, 21
Liebes sweetheart OT 5
Liebhaber(in) lover OT 3
Lieblings... favourite OT 1
Liebste(r) sweetheart OT 5
Lied song OT 1
Liedtext lyrics OT 2
liefern to deliver OT 4; to yield **WS 3**, 98
Lieferung delivery OT 3
Lieferwagen van OT 4
liegen to lie OT 1
Lifestyle lifestyle OT 4
Liga league OT 2
lila purple OT 1
Limo soda OT 5
Lineal ruler OT 1
Lingua Franca lingua franca **WS 3**, 108
Linguist(in) linguist OT 5
Linguistik linguistics **WS 3**, 108
Linie line OT 1
linke(r, -s) left OT 1
Linse lens OT 4
Lippe lip OT 2
lispeln to lisp **WS 3**, 96
Liste list OT 1
Liter litre; liter OT 4
literarisch literary OT 5
Literatur literature OT 4
LKW lorry **WS 3**, 99
Lob praise **WS 1**, 26
loben to praise **WS 1**, 30
Loch hole OT 1
Locher hole punch OT 5
locken to tempt OT 5
locker laid-back OT 4; casual OT 5
Löffel spoon OT 2
logisch logical OT 5
Logo logo OT 1
Lohn salary OT 5
lohnen to be worth it OT 1
lohnend worthwhile OT 2; rewarding OT 4
lohnenswert worth OT 4
Lokführer(in) engineer OT 3
Lokomotive engine OT 2
löschen to put out OT 2; to delete OT 4
Löscher extinguisher OT 5
lösen to solve OT 3
losfahren to head out OT 4
loslassen to relax OT 2
losstürzen to rush off OT 2
Lösung solution OT 2
loswerden to get rid of OT 3
Lotterie lottery OT 3
Löwe lion OT 1
Löwin lioness **WS 2**, 64
Loyalität loyalty **WS 1**, 40
Luchs lynx OT 2
Lücke gap OT 3
Luft air OT 1
luftig breezy **WS 3**, 97

Luftschlangen streamer OT 4
Lunge lung OT 3
Lust lust OT 5
auf etw. Lust haben to be keen on sth. OT 4
lustig funny OT 1; amusing OT 5
luxuriös luxurious OT 2
Luxus luxury OT 5
Lynchjustiz lynch mob **WS 3**, 106

M

machen to make; to do OT 1; to render **WS 4**, 136
Das macht ... That'll be ... OT 2
Macher(in) maker OT 3
Macht power OT 5
mächtig mighty OT 3; powerful OT 5; potent **WS 1**, 19
machtlos powerless OT 4
Mädchen girl OT 1
burschikoses Mädchen tomboy OT 5
Magen stomach OT 2
magisch magical OT 2
Magnat magnate **WS 3**, 100
Magnet magnet OT 1
magnetisch magnetic OT 2
mähen to mow OT 5
Mahlzeit meal OT 1
Mai May OT 1
Mailbox mailbox OT 4
Mais corn OT 3
Maisbrot cornbread OT 4
malen to paint OT 1
malerisch scenic OT 5
Mama mum OT 1
man you OT 1
Management management OT 5
managen to manage OT 1
Manager(in) manager OT 1
manchmal sometimes OT 1
Mandant(in) client OT 5
Mandel almond **WS 1**, 22
Mangel lack OT 3; shortage OT 5; deficit **WS 3**, 103
mangelhaft junky OT 4; flawed **WS 2**, 62
manipulieren to manipulate **WS 2**, 67
Mann man OT 1; husband OT 2
männlich male OT 2
Männlichkeit masculinity **WS 2**, 57
Mannschaft team OT 1; crew OT 2
Mantel coat OT 1
Mappe portfolio OT 4
Marathon marathon OT 2
Märchen fairy tale OT 1
marginalisieren to marginalize **WS 2**, 69
Marine navy OT 3
Marine... maritime OT 3
Marionette puppet **WS 1**, 27
markant punchy **WS 2**, 72
Marke brand OT 4
Marketing marketing OT 4
markieren to bookmark OT 4
Markise marquee OT 2
Markt market OT 1; marketplace OT 5
auf den Markt bringen to launch; to release OT 4
Marktsegment market segment OT 5
Marmelade jam OT 2
Marsch march OT 3
März March OT 1
Maschine machine OT 1
Maschinen machinery OT 2
Masern measles OT 5
Maske mask OT 3
Maß measurement OT 2
Massaker massacre OT 3
Masse: Masse zusetzen to bulk up OT 5
Maßeinheit measurement OT 2
Massen... mass OT 4
Massensport mass sport OT 3
Maßstab benchmark **WS 2**, 62
Material material OT 3
Mathe maths; math OT 1; mathematics OT 3
Mathematik maths; math OT 1; mathematics OT 3
Mathematiker(in) mathematician OT 3
Matrose sailor OT 1
Maultier mule OT 3
Maus mouse OT 2
Mauszeiger cursor OT 3
Maximum maximum OT 2
Mayonnaise mayonnaise OT 1
mechanisch mechanical OT 5
meckern to nag OT 5
Medaille medal OT 2
Medaillengewinner(in) medallist **WS 2**, 61
Mediation mediation OT 1
Medien media OT 2
Medikament medicine OT 2
Medikation medication OT 5
Medizin medicine OT 2; medical science OT 4
medizinisch medical OT 1
Meer sea OT 1
Meeres... marine OT 4
Meeresboden seabed OT 3
Meeresfrüchte seafood OT 3
Mehl flour OT 3
mehr more OT 1; anymore OT 2
mehrere several OT 2
Mehrheit majority OT 4
Mehrzahl plural OT 1
Meile mile OT 1
Meilenstein milestone **WS 3**, 103
mein my OT 1
meine(r, -s) mine OT 2
Meinung opinion OT 3
anderer Meinung sein to disagree OT 2
Meinungsverschiedenheit disagreement OT 2
meiste most OT 1
Meister(in) master OT 4
Melodie melody OT 2
Melodie tune **WS 2**, 72
Memoiren memoir OT 5
Menge crowd OT 1; amount OT 2; portion; quantity OT 4
eine Menge loads of OT 3
Mensch person OT 1; human OT 5
Menschenaffe ape **WS 1**, 21
menschengemacht man-made OT 1
Menschenmenge crowd OT 1; throng OT 2
menschenunwürdig inhumane OT 4
menschenzentriert anthropocentric **WS 1**, 21
Menschheit humanity **WS 4**, 136
menschlich human OT 3
mental mental OT 4
Mentalität mindset **WS 3**, 103
Mentor(in) mentor OT 4
merken: sich merken to memorize OT 4
Merkmal feature OT 1
merkwürdig funny OT 1
messen to measure OT 4
Messer knife OT 2
Messing brass **WS 1**, 27
Metall metal OT 1
Metapher metaphor OT 5
Meter metre OT 1
Methode method OT 1; technique OT 4
methodisch systematic **WS 3**, 121
Metropole metropolis **WS 1**, 12
Metzger(in) butcher OT 4
Meute mob OT 5
mexikanisch Mexican OT 4
mich me OT 1
Miet... rental OT 4
mieten to hire OT 3; to rent OT 4
Migrant(in) migrant OT 4
Migration migration OT 3
migrieren to migrate OT 3
Mikrobe microbe OT 4
Mikrodrama microdrama **WS 3**, 119
Mikrofon microphone OT 4

Mikroskop microscope OT 4
Mikrowelle microwave OT 5
Milch milk OT 1
Milchprodukte dairy **WS 4**, 133
militant militant **WS 2**, 79
Militär military OT 4
Miliz militia **WS 1**, 14
Milliarde billion OT 2
Million million OT 1
Minderheit minority OT 5
minderwertig inferior **WS 2**, 71
Mindest… minimum OT 1
Mindmap mind map OT 1
Mine mine OT 2
minimal minimal **WS 1**, 14
Minister(in) minister **WS 1**, 12
MINT (Mathematik, Informatik, Naturwissenschaft und Technik) STEM (science, technology, engineering, mathematics) OT 5
Minute minute OT 1
Minze mint OT 2
mir me OT 1
mischen to mix OT 2; to combine OT 4; to blend **WS 1**, 15; to shuffle **WS 4**, 139
Mischung mixture OT 3
missachten to despise **WS 2**, 78
Missbrauch abuse OT 4
missbrauchen to abuse **WS 2**, 78
Misserfolg failure OT 4
Misshandlung mistreatment OT 5
Mission mission OT 4
Missionar(in) missionary **WS 3**, 95
Misstrauen distrust **WS 1**, 14
Missverständnis misunderstanding OT 4
missverstehen to misunderstand OT 5
Mist dung **WS 1**, 32
mit with OT 1
Mitarbeiter(in) colleague OT 4
Mitarbeiter personnel OT 5
mitbegründen to co-found OT 4
Mitbewerber(in) competitor OT 4
Mitbewohner(in) roommate OT 5
mitfühlen to sympathize OT 5; to empathize **WS 2**, 67
mitfühlend sympathetic OT 3; compassionate **WS 1**, 32
Mitgefühl sympathy **WS 1**, 18
Mitglied member OT 1
Mitglied werden in to join OT 1
mithören to overhear OT 3
mitleiden to sympathize OT 5
Mitspieler(in) teammate OT 2
Mittag noon; midday OT 4
Mittagessen lunch OT 1
Mittagspause lunch break OT 1
Mittagszeit lunchtime OT 1
Mitte centre; middle OT 1; midst **WS 2**, 65
in der Mitte mid OT 4
Mitteilungsblatt newsletter OT 4
Mittel resource OT 4
Mittelfeldspieler(in) midfielder OT 3
mittelgroß medium OT 1; medium-sized OT 2
Mittelschule middle school OT 2
Mitternacht midnight OT 1
mittlerweile meanwhile OT 5
Mittwoch Wednesday OT 1
mitwirken to contribute OT 4
Mitwirkende(r) contributor **WS 3**, 92
Mitwirkung contribution OT 4
mobben to bully OT 5
Mobbing bullying OT 2
Möbel furniture OT 1
mobil mobile OT 1
Mobilität mobility **WS 3**, 108
Mobilteil handset OT 2
Mobiltelefon cellphone **WS 1**, 39
möblieren to furnish **WS 1**, 39
möchte(n) would like / love OT 1
Modalverb modal OT 2
Mode fashion OT 1
Modell model OT 1
Moderator(in) presenter OT 5
modern modern OT 1
Modetrend fashion fad **WS 2**, 69
Modewort buzz word **WS 2**, 69
modifizieren to modify **WS 3**, 104
Modul module OT 4
Modus mode **WS 3**, 99
mogeln to cheat **WS 1**, 16
mögen to like OT 1; to be fond of OT 4
nicht mögen to dislike OT 3
möglich possible OT 2; prospective **WS 3**, 103
Möglichkeit chance; possibility OT 2
Moment moment OT 1
momentan at the moment OT 2
Monarch(in) monarch OT 5
Monat month OT 1
Mönch monk OT 3
Mond moon OT 4
Monolog monologue; soliloquy OT 5
monoton monotone OT 4
Monster monster OT 1
Monsun monsoon **WS 1**, 39
Montag Monday OT 1
Moosberre cranberry OT 4
Moral moral **WS 3**, 113
moralisch ethical OT 3
Morgen morning OT 1; acre OT 4
morgen tomorrow OT 1
Morgendämmerung dawn OT 4
Moschee mosque OT 1
mosern to grumble OT 2
Motel motel OT 3
Motiv motif OT 5
Motivation motivation OT 5
motivieren to motivate OT 4
motiviert self-motivated OT 4; motivated OT 5
Motor engine OT 2
Motto motto **WS 2**, 67
Mountainbiken mountain biking OT 2
Mücke midge OT 3
müde tired OT 1
Muffin muffin OT 1
Mühe effort OT 5
Müll rubbish; refuse OT 2
Müllabfuhr rubbish collection OT 2
Müllarbeiter(in) garbage collector OT 4
Mülldeponie landfill OT 3
Mülleimer rubbish bin; trash can OT 2
Müllmann / -frau refuse collector OT 2
multikulturell multicultural OT 5
Multilog multilogue OT 5
multiplizieren to multiply **WS 4**, 134
Mumie mummy OT 2
Mund mouth OT 1
mündig mature OT 5
mündlich verbal OT 5
Mundschutz mouthguard OT 2
Mundwasser mouthwash OT 4
Munition ammunition **WS 2**, 83
Münze coin OT 1
murmeln to mutter **WS 3**, 103
Murmelspiel marbles OT 4
murren to grumble OT 2
mürrisch crossly OT 3
Muschel mussel OT 4
Museum museum OT 1
Musik music OT 1
musikalisch musical OT 2
Musiker(in) musician OT 2
Musikinstrument musical instrument OT 2
Muskel muscle OT 4
Muskeln aufbauen to bulk up OT 5
Muslim(in) Muslim OT 3
müssen must; to have to OT 1
Muster pattern OT 1
Mut courage **WS 1**, 25; bravery **WS 1**, 25
mutig bold OT 1
Mutter mother OT 1
Mutti mum OT 1
Mütze hat; cap OT 1

Mysterium mystery OT 2
Mythos myth OT 5

N
nach after; past OT 1; according to OT 3
nach hinten backwards OT 3
nach oben up OT 1; upwards OT 3
nach Christus AD (Anno Domini) OT 2
Nachahmung imitation **WS 2**, 69
Nachbar(in) neighbour OT 2
Nachbarschaft neighbourhood OT 4
nachdenken to speculate OT 4; to consider OT 5
zum Nachdenken anregend thoughtprovoking OT 5
nachdenken über to think about OT 1
nachdenklich thoughtful OT 3
nacheinander sequentially OT 4
nacherzählen to retell OT 4
Nachfrage demand OT 4
nachgeben to cave **WS 1**, 14
nachhallen to echo OT 5
nachhaltig sustainable OT 4
Nachhaltigkeit sustainability OT 3
nachher afterwards OT 3
Nachhilfe: Nachhile geben to tutor OT 4
nachklingen to echo OT 5
Nachkomme descendant OT 4
Nachmittag afternoon OT 1
Nachname last name OT 2
Nachricht message OT 1; notification **WS 4**, 133
Nachrichten tidings **WS 2**, 78
Nachruf obituary **WS 2**, 79
nächste(r, -s) next OT 1
Nachstellung re-creation; re-enactment OT 4
Nacht night OT 1
Nachteil con OT 2; disadvantage; downside OT 3; drawback OT 5
Nachtisch dessert OT 1
Nachwirkungen aftermath **WS 1**, 14
Nagel nail OT 5
nah near OT 1; close OT 4
nahe near OT 1; close OT 4
Nähe closeness OT 5
in der Nähe nearby OT 3
nähen to sew **WS 3**, 95
nähern to approach OT 4
Nähmaschine sewing machine OT 3
nahrhaft nutritious OT 4
Nahrungsergänzung supplement OT 5
naiv naive **WS 3**, 98
Name name OT 1
mit dem Namen called OT 1
namens called OT 1
Narbe scar **WS 1**, 15
Narration narration **WS 2**, 79
Nase nose OT 2
Nasenbluten nosebleed OT 5
Nashorn rhinoceros OT 2; rhino **WS 2**, 64
nass wet OT 2
Nation nation OT 2
national national OT 1
Nationalhymne anthem OT 5
Natur nature OT 2
natürlich of course; natural OT 1
Naturschützer(in) conservationist **WS 2**, 67
Naturwissenschaften science OT 1
Naturwissenschaftler(in) scientist OT 1
Navigation navigating OT 4
Nebel fog **WS 4**, 140
neben by; next to OT 1; beside OT 2; in addition to OT 4; alongside **WS 1**, 21
nebenberuflich part-time OT 4
Negativ negative OT 1
nehmen to take OT 1
Neige: zur Neige gehen to run out OT 2
neigen to tilt OT 3
zu etw. neigen to tend to OT 5
nein no OT 1
nennen to call OT 1
Neoprenanzug wetsuit OT 1
Nerv nerve OT 3
nervig annoying OT 2
nervös nervous OT 2
Nest nest OT 3
Netbook netbook OT 4
nett nice; kind OT 1
Netz net OT 3; grid **WS 2**, 57
vom Netz off the grid OT 4
Netzball netball OT 1
Netzsicherheit cyber security OT 4
Netzwerk network OT 5
neu new OT 1
neueste(r) recent OT 4
Neugestaltung re-creation OT 4
Neugier curiosity OT 4
neugierig curious OT 4
Neuheit innovation OT 4
Neuigkeit(en) news OT 1
neulich recently OT 3
neun nine OT 1
neunzehn nineteen OT 1
neunzig ninety OT 1
neutral neutral OT 3
Neutronenbombe nuclear bomb OT 3
Newsletter newsletter OT 4
nicht not OT 1
nichtig void **WS 1**, 39
nichts nothing OT 1
nichtsdestoweniger nonetheless **WS 2**, 65
nicken to nod OT 2
Nickerchen nap OT 5
nie never OT 1
Niedergang demise **WS 4**, 138
Niederschlag rainfall OT 5
Niederschrift transcript OT 5
niedlich cute OT 1
niemand nobody OT 1
Nilpferd hippopotamus OT 2
nirgendwo nowhere OT 2
Niveau level OT 2
noch yet OT 2; nor OT 4
noch ein(e) another OT 1
nomadisch nomadic OT 5
Nomen noun OT 1
nominieren to nominate OT 4
Nominierung nomination OT 4
Nonne nun OT 4
nonverbal non-verbal OT 4
Nord... north OT 1
nördlich northern OT 2
nörgeln to nag OT 5
normal normal OT 1; ordinary OT 2; standard OT 3; common OT 4
Not hardship **WS 2**, 61
Notaufnahme Accident and Emergency OT 1
Notfall emergency OT 1
Notiz note OT 1
Notizblock pad OT 5
Notizbuch notebook OT 2
Notlage plight **WS 1**, 21
notwendig necessary OT 3
Notwendigkeit necessity OT 5
Novelle novella **WS 3**, 96
November November OT 1
Nuance nuance **WS 3**, 107
Nudeln pasta OT 1
Nuklear... nuclear OT 3
null zero OT 1
Nummer number OT 1
nur just; only OT 1
Nuss nut OT 4
Nutzen benefit OT 2
nützlich useful OT 1; beneficial; handy OT 2
Nutzung usage **WS 4**, 133

O
ob whether OT 1
obdachlos homeless OT 3
Obdachlosigkeit homelessness OT 4
oben upstairs OT 1; above OT 3

obere(r, -s) top OT 1
im oberen Stockwerk upstairs OT 1
Oberfläche surface OT 3
oberhalb above OT 3
Oberkörper: mit nacktem Oberkörper bare-chested **WS 1**, 19
Oberschenkel thigh OT 1
Oberschicht elite **WS 2**, 59
Oberstufenschüler(in) senior OT 4
Objekt object OT 1
Obst fruit OT 1
Obstkuchen pie OT 1
obwohl although; though OT 2; despite **WS 1**, 17
oder or OT 1
Ofen stove OT 3; oven OT 4
Ofenkartoffel jacket potato OT 1
Off: aus dem Off offstage OT 2
offen open OT 1; overtly **WS 2**, 76
offenbar obviously OT 1
offensichtlich obvious OT 1; evident OT 5; apparent **WS 1**, 25
öffentlich public OT 2
öffentliche Verkehrsmittel public transport OT 2
offiziell official OT 4
Offizier(in) officer OT 2
öffnen to open OT 1
Öffnungszeiten opening times OT 1
oft often OT 1
oftmals many times OT 4
ohne without OT 2
ohnmächtig werden to faint OT 2
Ohr ear OT 1
Öko-Aktivismus eco-activism **WS 1**, 21
ökologisch environmental OT 2; eco-friendly OT 3; ecological OT 5
Ökonomie economy OT 3
Ökosystem ecosystem **WS 1**, 21
Ökotourismus ecotourism OT 3
Oktober October OT 1
Oktopus octopus OT 1
Öl oil OT 1
olympisch Olympic OT 1
Oma grandma OT 1
Omelett omelette OT 2
Onkel uncle OT 1
online online OT 1
Opa grandpa; granddad OT 1
Operation operation OT 3
operieren to operate OT 5
Opfer victim OT 4; sacrifice **WS 3**, 120
Opposition opposition OT 5
optimieren to optimize OT 5
optimistisch optimistic OT 2
optional optional OT 2
optisch visually OT 5
Orang-Utan orang-utan **WS 1**, 21
orange orange OT 1
Orangensaft orange juice OT 1
Orbit orbit OT 4
Orchester orchestra OT 1
ordentlich properly OT 2; neat OT 4; orderly **WS 1**, 16
Ordnung: in Ordnung OK; all right OT 1
Organ organ OT 3
Organisation organization OT 2; agency OT 4
Organisator(in) organizer OT 3
organisatorisch organizational OT 4
organisieren to organize OT 1
Orgel organ OT 3
orientalisch oriental OT 1
Orientierung reference; orientation OT 4
Original original OT 3
Orkan hurricane OT 5
Ort place OT 1
am Ort locally OT 3
direkt vor Ort on the doorstep OT 4
orten to locate **WS 4**, 138
Osten east OT 1
Ostern Easter OT 1
Österreicher(in) Austrian OT 4
östlich eastern OT 2
Outfit outfit OT 5
Ozean ocean OT 3
Ozonschicht ozone layer **WS 3**, 98

P

Paar pair OT 1; couple OT 2
packen to pack OT 2
packend catchy **WW**, 11
Pädagoge / Pädagogin educator OT 4
Paddel paddle OT 3
Paddle-Boarding paddle-boarding OT 1
paddeln to paddle OT 4
Pagode pagoda **WS 1**, 25
Paket packet OT 2; package OT 3; parcel OT 4
pakistanisch Pakistani OT 4
Palast palace OT 1
Palmöl palm oil **WS 1**, 21
Pandabär panda OT 1
Pandemie pandemic OT 5
Paneel panel OT 5
Paniermehl breadcrumbs OT 3
Panik: in Panik geraten to panic OT 2
Panorama... panoramic OT 3
Panther panther OT 2
pantomimisch darstellen to mime OT 2
Papa dad OT 1
Papier paper OT 1
Paprika pepper OT 2
Papst Pope OT 3
Para-Athlet(in) para-athlete **WS 2**, 61
Parade parade OT 2
Parade-Wagen float OT 4
Paradies paradise OT 4
Parallelismus parallelism OT 5
paralympische Spiele Paralympics OT 3
Parasit parasite **WS 4**, 138
Park park OT 1
parken to park OT 1
Parkplatz car park OT 1
Parkzettel parking ticket OT 1
Parlament parliament OT 1
parteiisch biased OT 4
Partizip participle OT 2
Partizip Perfekt past participle OT 2
Partner(in) partner OT 1
Partnerschaft partnership OT 4
Party party OT 1
Pass passport OT 2
Passage passage **WS 2**, 79
Passagier(in) passenger OT 2
passen to fit OT 1
passend timely; appropriately OT 3
passieren to happen OT 1; to occur **WS 1**, 14
Passkontrolle passport control OT 2
Passwort password OT 4
Pastete pâté OT 1
Patent patent OT 4
Patentante godmother OT 5
patentieren to patent OT 4
Patient(in) patient OT 1
patriarchalisch patriarchal **WS 1**, 42
Patriot(in) patriot OT 2
patriotisch patriotic **WS 1**, 43
patroulieren to patrol **WS 2**, 67
Pause break OT 1; pause OT 3; recess **WS 2**, 63
Pause machen to pause OT 3
Pavian baboon **WS 2**, 67
Pedal pedal OT 4
in die Pedale treten to pedal OT 4
Peer peer OT 5
peinlich embarrassing OT 2
Peinlichkeit awkwardness **WS 1**, 28
pendeln to commute OT 5
Pendler(in) commuter OT 2
penetrant pushy OT 4
Penizillin penicillin OT 2
Penny penny OT 1
Pensionat boarding school **WS 3**, 95
perfekt perfect OT 1
perfektionieren to perfect OT 4

periodisch intermittent **WS 3**, 101
Perlenarbeit beadwork **WS 3**, 95
Perlenkette beaded necklace **WS 2**, 71
Perlenkunst beadwork **WS 3**, 95
permanent permanent OT 5
Personal crew OT 2; staff OT 3; personnel OT 5
personalisieren to personalize OT 5
Personifikation personification OT 5
persönlich personal OT 2
persönliche Sachen belongings OT 3
Persönlichkeit personality OT 4
Perspektive perspective OT 4
Perücke wig **WS 2**, 69
pessimistisch pessimistic OT 4
Pestizid pesticide OT 4
Pfad trail OT 2
Pfadfinder(in) scout OT 3
Pfanne pan OT 2
Pfannkuchen pancake OT 4
Pfarrer(in) pastor OT 2
Pfeffer pepper OT 2
Pfeife whistle OT 2
pfeifen to blow; to whistle OT 2
Pfeil arrow OT 3
Pferd horse OT 1
pferdebespannt horse-drawn OT 1
Pferdewagen buggy OT 4
Pflanze plant OT 2
Pflanzenwelt wildlife OT 2
Pflaster plaster OT 1
Pflaume plum OT 1
pflegen to maintain OT 4
Pflicht duty OT 5
pflücken to pick OT 1
Pflug plough **WS 1**, 32
Pfund pound OT 1
Phänomen phenomenon OT 5
Phase stage OT 2
Philanthrop(in) philanthropist **WS 3**, 100
Philosophie philosophy OT 4
philosophisch philosophical **WS 2**, 68
Phonograph phonograph OT 4
Physik physics OT 4
Pianist(in) pianist OT 2
Picknick picnic OT 1
piepen to beep **WS 1**, 39
pikant savoury OT 3
Pilgerfahrt pilgrimage OT 3
Pille pill OT 1
Pilot(in) pilot OT 3
Pilz mushroom OT 1; fungus **WS 4**, 138
pingelig fussy OT 2
Pinguin penguin OT 1
pinkeln to pee **WS 3**, 96
Pinsel brush OT 2
Pinwand bulletin board OT 4
Pinzette tweezers OT 2
Pionier(in) pioneer OT 4
Pipeline pipeline OT 4
Pirat(in) pirate OT 3
Piste slope OT 3
Pizza pizza OT 1
plädieren to plead OT 5
Plage pest OT 2
Plagegeist pest OT 2
Plagiat plagiarism OT 2
plagiieren to plagiarize OT 2
Plakat poster OT 1
planen to plan OT 1; to arrange OT 2; to design OT 5
Planer(in) planner OT 3
Planet planet OT 2
planetarisch planetary OT 4
Planetarium planetarium OT 1
Planetenforschung planetary science OT 4
planieren to bulldoze OT 5
Platschen splash **WS 1**, 27
Platte panel OT 5
Platz square; ground OT 1; site; space OT 2; court OT 3
auf die Plätze, fertig, los! Ready, set, go! OT 1
einen ... Platz belegen to come ... OT 2
Platzanweiser(in) usher OT 4
Platzdeckchen place mat OT 2
platzieren to place **WS 2**, 55
plaudern to chatter OT 2
Playlist playlist OT 4
plötzlich suddenly OT 1; sudden OT 2; abrupt **WS 2**, 65
Plural plural OT 1
Pocken smallpox OT 4
Podcast podcast OT 1
Podium podium OT 3
Poesie poetry OT 1
Pokal trophy OT 2
Pol pole OT 3
polarisieren to polarize **WS 1**, 21
Politik policy OT 3; politics **WS 1**, 19
Politiker(in) politician OT 3
politisch political OT 4
politisieren to politicize **WS 1**, 21
Polizei police OT 1
Polizist(in) police officer OT 1
Pollen pollen **WS 4**, 138
polnisch Polish OT 2
Polo polo OT 3
Polyp polyp OT 5
Polyurethan (Kunststoff) polyurethane OT 4
Pommes frites (French) fries OT 2
Pony pony OT 3
Pop pop OT 2
Popcorn popcorn OT 2
Portalseite portal OT 5
Portfolio portfolio OT 4
Portion portion OT 4
Portraitfoto headshot OT 5
Position position OT 3
positionieren to position **WS 2**, 57
Possessivbegleiter possessive determiner OT 1
Post post; mail OT 1
postapokalyptisch post-apocalyptic **WS 3**, 104
Postbote / -botin mail carrier OT 4
posten to post OT 3
Postkarte postcard OT 1
Postleitzahl postcode OT 1
Potenzial potential OT 5
Powwow powwow **WS 3**, 95
prägen to coin **WS 2**, 64
Praktikant(in) intern OT 4
Praktikum internship OT 4; work placement OT 5
praktisch handy OT 2; practical OT 3; convenient OT 4
Präposition preposition OT 2
Prärie plains OT 5
Präsentation presentation OT 1; slideshow OT 3
präsentieren to present OT 1; to feature OT 4
Präsident(in) president OT 4
prasseln to crackle **WS 1**, 22
Praxis practice OT 2; surgery OT 5
präzise accurate OT 4
Prediger(in) preacher **WS 2**, 72
Preis prize; price OT 1
preisgekrönt award-winning OT 4
Preisrichter(in) judge OT 2
preiswert inexpensive OT 4
Prestige prestige **WS 3**, 107
prima fine OT 1
Prinz prince OT 1
Prinzip principle **WS 1**, 18; precepts **WS 1**, 18
prinzipientreu principled **WS 1**, 18
priorisieren to prioritize **WS 1**, 25
Priorität priority **WS 1**, 44
privat private OT 3
Privatsphäre privacy OT 3
Privileg privilege OT 5
privilegiert privileged OT 5

Probe rehearsal OT 2; sample OT 4
proben to rehearse OT 3
Problem problem OT 1; matter OT 2
problematisch problematic **WS 2**, 57
Problemlöser(in) problem-solver OT 4
Produkt product OT 2
Produktion production; manufacture OT 4; manufacturing OT 5
Produktplatzierung product placement OT 5
Profession profession OT 5
professionell professional OT 2
Professor(in) professor OT 4
Profil profile OT 3
ein Profil erstellen to profile **WS 2**, 55
Profit profit OT 4
profitieren to benefit OT 2
profund profound OT 5
Prognose forecast OT 3
Programm programme; channel OT 2; program OT 3
programmieren to programme OT 2
Programmierer(in) programmer OT 3
progressiv progressive OT 1
Projekt project OT 1
Projektor projector OT 1
Prominente(r) celebrity OT 3
Pronomen pronoun OT 1
Protagonist(in) protagonist OT 5
Protein protein OT 4
Protest protest OT 3; riot **WS 1**, 14
protestieren to protest OT 3
Protestierer(in) protester OT 5
Protokoll protocol OT 5
Prototyp prototype OT 4
Provinz province OT 5
Prozedur procedure OT 5
Prozent percentage OT 3; percent OT 4
Prozess trial OT 2; process OT 4
Prüfer(in) checker OT 3
Prüfung exam OT 1
prusten to splutter **WS 1**, 27
Psychologe / -login psychologist OT 5
Psychologie psychology OT 5
psychologische(r) Betreuer(in) counsellor OT 2
Psychopath(in) psycho OT 4
Pubertät puberty OT 5
Publikum audience OT 2
Publizität publicity OT 5
Pullover jumper OT 1
pulsieren to vibrate OT 4
Pulver powder **WS 1**, 12
pumpen to pump OT 4; to pipe **WS 1**, 24
Punkt point OT 1
punkten to score OT 1
pünktlich punctual OT 4
Puppe doll OT 3
Püree mash **WS 4**, 139
putzen to brush OT 4; to clean OT 5
Puzzle puzzle OT 2
Pyjama pajamas OT 4
Pyjama-Party sleepover OT 1

Q

Quadrat square OT 1
Quadratfuß square foot OT 2
quälen: sich quälen to labour **WS 1**, 18
quälend harrowing **WS 1**, 21
Quälerei cruelty OT 5
Qualifikation qualification OT 5
(sich) qualifizieren to qualify **WS 2**, 59
qualifiziert qualified OT 5
Qualität quality OT 3
quantifizieren to quantify **WS 4**, 144
Quarantäne quarantine **WS 2**, 67
Quarterback quarterback OT 2
Quartier quarter OT 1
queer queer OT 5
Quelle spring; source OT 2
querfeldein cross-country OT 2
Querflöte flute OT 2
querlesen to skim OT 3
Quintessenz epitome **WS 1**, 21
Quiz quiz OT 2

R

rächen: sich rächen to retaliate **WS 1**, 29
Rad wheel OT 1
Rad fahren to bike OT 3
Radfahrer(in) cyclist OT 3
Radiergummi rubber OT 1
radikal radical OT 4
Radikale(r) extremist **WS 1**, 18
radikalisieren to radicalize **WS 1**, 14
Radio radio OT 1
Radiosender radio station OT 2
Radius radius OT 2
Radweg bike lane OT 4
Rahmen frame OT 4; framework **WS 4**, 134
Rakete rocket OT 4
Rampe ramp OT 2
Rand edge; rim OT 3; margin OT 5
Rangfolge ranking OT 4
in eine Rangfolge bringen to rank OT 4
Rap rap OT 1
Rasen lawn OT 5
Rasierer razor **WS 2**, 79
Rasse... pedigree OT 3; racial **WS 1**, 21
Rassentrennung segregation **WS 2**, 59
Rassismus racism OT 5
rassistisch racist OT 4
Rat advice OT 1; council OT 3
raten to guess OT 1; to advise OT 4
rationieren to ration **WS 1**, 24
Rätsel puzzle; mystery OT 2
rätselhaft mysterious **WS 1**, 26; enigmatic **WS 3**, 104
Rätselraten guessing game OT 1
rau rough OT 4; harsh OT 5
Räuber predator OT 5
Raubtier predator OT 5
Rauch smoke OT 2
Raum room OT 1
Raumanzug spacesuit OT 4
räumen to clear OT 4
Raumfahrzeug spacecraft OT 4
Raumkapsel capsule OT 4
Raumschiff spaceship OT 4
rausbringen to take out OT 4
Razzia raid OT 5
reagieren to react; to respond OT 3
Reaktion reaction OT 4; response OT 5
realistisch realistic OT 4
Realität reality OT 4
rebellieren to rebell OT 4
Rechenschaft: zur Rechenschaft ziehen to hold accountable OT 5
Rechner computer OT 1
Rechnung bill OT 3
Recht privilege OT 5
Rechte rights OT 3
das Recht haben to be entitled **WS 2**, 78
rechte(r, -s) right OT 1
rechteckig rectangular OT 2
rechtfertigen to justify OT 5
Rechtfertigung vindication **WS 3**, 103
rechtlich legal OT 4
rechtmäßig legitimate **WS 3**, 107
Rechtsanwalt / -anwältin lawyer OT 4; barrister OT 5
Rechtschreibung spelling OT 1
Rechtshilfe legal aid OT 5
Rechtsvorschriften legislation OT 5
rechtzeitig timely OT 3
Recycling recycling OT 2
Redakteur(in) editor OT 2
Rede speech OT 1; talk OT 2
reden to talk OT 1
redigieren to edit OT 3
reduzieren to reduce OT 2; to downsize OT 3
referendum referendum **WS 1**, 14
Reformation reformation OT 4
Refrain refrain **WW**, 11; chorus **WS 1**, 31

Regal shelf OT 1
Regel rule OT 1; guideline; policy OT 3; norm OT 5
regelmäßig regular OT 1; periodically **WS 4**, 133
Regelung arrangement OT 3
Regelwerk rulebook OT 2
Regen rainfall OT 5
saurer Regen acid rain **WS 3**, 98
Regenbogen rainbow OT 1
Regenmantel raincoat OT 3
Regenschauer rainstorm OT 5
Regenschirm umbrella OT 1
Regenwald rainforest OT 2
Regenwasser rainwater OT 4
Reggae reggae OT 2
Regie führen to direct **WS 2**, 67
regieren to govern OT 3
Regierung government OT 3
Regime regime **WS 2**, 73
Region region OT 4
regional regional OT 5
Regisseur(in) film director OT 2
Register index OT 4
regnen to rain OT 1
Regulation regulation OT 5
reiben to rub OT 3
Reich empire **WS 1**, 14
reich rich OT 1; wealthy **WS 1**, 12; upmarket **WS 2**, 53
reichen to range OT 4; to hand OT 5
reichlich plenty OT 2
Reichtum fortune OT 3; wealth OT 4
reif ripe OT 4; mature OT 5
reifen to mature **WS 2**, 83
Reihe row OT 1
Reihenfolge order OT 1; sequencing OT 3
in eine Reihenfolge bringen to sequence OT 3
Reim rhyme OT 1
rein pure **WS 1**, 39
reinigen to clean OT 5
Reinigungsmittel cleaner OT 3
Reinigungstuch cleaning wipe OT 2
Reis rice OT 1
Reise journey; trip; tour OT 1; voyage OT 3
Reiseandenken souvenir OT 1
Reisebus coach OT 1
Reiseführer guidebook OT 1
Reisekauffrau / -kaufmann travel agent OT 3
reisen to travel OT 1
Reisende(r) traveller OT 3
Reiseroute itinerary **WS 2**, 64
Reiseziel destination OT 4
reissen to wrench **WS 1**, 27
reißen to tear OT 2
Reißverschluss zip OT 1
reiten to ride OT 1
Reiter(in) rider OT 1
reizbar irritable OT 3
reizend endearing **WS 1**, 21
reizvoll attractive OT 4
Reklamezettel leaflet OT 2
Rektor(in) principal OT 2
relativ relatively OT 5
Relativpronomen relative pronoun OT 2
Relativsatz relative clause OT 2
relevant relevant OT 4
Religion religion OT 3
eine Religion ausüben to worship OT 4
Religionsunterricht religious studies OT 1
religiös religious OT 1
Rennen race OT 2
rennen to run OT 1
Rennsport racing OT 2
renommiert prestigious **WS 1**, 16
Rentier reindeer OT 2
reparieren to repair OT 2
Reporter(in) reporter OT 1
repräsentativ representative **WS 2**, 55
reproduzieren to reproduce **WS 4**, 133
Reptil reptile OT 2
Republik republic OT 4
Reputation reputation **WS 1**, 24
Requisite prop OT 1
Reservat reservation OT 1
reservieren to reserve OT 3
Reservierung reservation OT 1
resistent resistant OT 5
Resistenz resistance OT 5
Respekt respect **WS 1**, 15
respektlos disrespectful OT 3
respektvoll respectful OT 3
Ressource resource OT 4
Restaurant restaurant OT 1
restlich remaining OT 5
restliche rest OT 1
Resultat outcome OT 5
retten to save OT 2; to rescue OT 4
Rettung rescue OT 2
Rettungsdienste emergency services OT 2
Rettungssanitäter(in) paramedic OT 1
Rettungsschwimmer(in) lifeguard OT 4
Reue remorse OT 5
revidieren to revise OT 2
Revolution revolution OT 2
revolutionieren to revolutionize OT 4
Rezept recipe OT 2
Rezeption reception OT 1
Rezeptionist(in) receptionist OT 1
rezitieren to recite OT 4
rhetorisch rhetorical OT 5
Rhythmus rhythm **WS 2**, 72
Richter(in) judge OT 2
richtig correct; right; true OT 1; proper OT 3; actual OT 5
Richtlinie guideline OT 3
Richtung direction OT 3
in Richtung towards OT 2
riechen to smell OT 1
Riesenrad ferris wheel OT 4
riesig enormous OT 1; huge; giant OT 2; massive OT 3
Riff reef OT 5
Rikscha rickshaw **WS 1**, 16
Rinder cattle OT 5
Rinderbrust beef brisket OT 4
Rindfleisch beef OT 2
Ringen wrestling OT 2
ringen to grapple **WS 2**, 65
Risiko hazard OT 2; risk OT 3
riskieren to risk **WS 1**, 15
Riss split OT 3; rift **WS 1**, 14
Ritual ritual OT 5
Robbe seal OT 1
Roboter robot OT 4; android **WS 3**, 104
robust robust **WS 3**, 112
Rock skirt OT 1
Rockmusik rock OT 2
roh raw OT 3
Rolle role OT 1; roll OT 2
Rollschuh roller skate OT 4
Rollstuhl wheelchair OT 2
Rollstuhlfahrer(in) wheelchair user OT 2
Roman novel OT 2
Romanautor(in) novelist **WS 3**, 104
römisch Roman OT 2
Rommee rummy OT 2
Röntgen X-ray OT 1
rosa pink OT 1
Rose rose OT 4
rot red OT 1
Routine routine OT 4
Routinearbeit chore OT 5
Rückblende flashback **WS 3**, 106
Rückblick review OT 1
Rücken back OT 1
Rückgang decline OT 5
Rückgrat backbone OT 2
Rückhand backhand OT 3

Rucksack rucksack OT 1; backpack OT 2
mit Rucksack reisen to backpack OT 3
Rücksicht consideration OT 5
rücksichtslos thoughtless OT 2
rücksichtsvoll thoughtful OT 3
Rückspiegel rearview mirror **WS 3**, 92
rückwärts backwards OT 3
Rückzug retreat **WS 1**, 14
Ruderboot rowing boat OT 1
Ruf fame OT 3
rufen to shout OT 1
Rugby rugby OT 1
ruhig quiet OT 1; calm OT 2; steady OT 3; still OT 4
Ruhm fame OT 3
rühmen: sich rühmen to boast **WS 1**, 23
rühren to stir OT 2
Ruine ruin OT 2
rumhängen to hang out OT 1
rund round OT 1
Rundgang tour OT 1
Rupie rupee **WS 1**, 25
russisch Russian OT 2

S
sachlich factual OT 4
Sack sack OT 2
säen to sow **WS 1**, 14
Safari safari OT 2
Saft juice OT 1
sagen to say OT 1
Sahne cream OT 1
Saite string OT 2
Salat salad OT 1
Salz salt OT 3
sammeln to collect OT 1; to collate **WS 4**, 139
Sammler(in) picker OT 3; gatherer OT 5
Sammlung collection OT 2
Samstag Saturday OT 1
samtig velvety OT 2
Sand sand OT 1
Sandale sandal OT 4
sandig sandy OT 1
Sandwich sandwich OT 1
sanft gently OT 3
Sänger(in) singer OT 1
sanieren to redevelop **WS 1**, 39
Sanierung renovation **WS 1**, 22
Sanktion sanction **WS 2**, 68
Satellit satellite OT 4
Sattel saddle OT 3
Satz sentence OT 1; set OT 3
Satzteil clause OT 2
sauber clean OT 1
sauer acidic OT 5
Sauerstoff oxygen **WS 3**, 99
Säugetier mammal OT 2
Säugling baby OT 1
Säule column OT 1; pillar **WS 1**, 44
Saxofon saxophone OT 2
scannen to scan OT 3
Schach chess OT 1
Schachbrett chessboard OT 1
schade: Das ist schade. That's a shame. OT 2
schaden to harm; to damage OT 2
Schädigung impairment **WS 2**, 61
schädlich harmful OT 3; destructive OT 5
Schädling pest OT 2
Schaf sheep OT 1
Schäfer(in) shepherd OT 2
schaffen to create OT 2; to achieve OT 4
Schal scarf OT 2
Schale dish OT 2
Schalter switch OT 3
Schaltkreis circuit OT 4
Schande disgrace **WS 2**, 59
scharf hot OT 1; sharp **WS 2**, 58
auf etw. scharf sein to be keen on sth. OT 4
Schatten shade OT 5
Schattenseite underbelly **WS 1**, 16
Schattierung shade **WS 3**, 112
Schatz treasure OT 3
Schatz (als Kosename) honey OT 2
schätzen to guess OT 1; to estimate; to appreciate OT 5; to treasure **WS 2**, 67; to cherish **WS 2**, 79
Schaubild diagram OT 3
Schaufel shovel OT 2
schaukeln to rock OT 3
Schauspieler(in) actor OT 1
Scheibe slice OT 1; shield **WS 2**, 70
scheiden: sich scheiden lassen to divorce OT 3
Scheidung divorce OT 3
Schein note OT 1
scheinen to shine OT 1; to seem OT 2; to appear OT 3
scheitern to fail OT 2
schelmisch mischievous **WS 1**, 43
Schema scheme OT 5
Schere scissors OT 1
scheuen to dread **WS 3**, 105
Scheune barn OT 2
Schicht shift OT 4; layer **WS 3**, 98
schick fancy OT 2; stylish OT 4
schicken to send OT 1
Schicksal destiny **WS 1**, 16; fate **WS 1**, 29
Schiedsrichter(in) referee OT 3
Schiene rail OT 2
schießen to shoot OT 3
Schiff ship OT 2
mit dem Schiff fahren to sail OT 2
Schiffbau shipbuilding OT 3
Schikane harassment **WS 3**, 106
Schild sign OT 1; signpost OT 5; shield **WS 2**, 56
Schildkröte tortoise OT 1; turtle OT 2
Schimmer glimmer **WS 2**, 65
schimpfen to grumble OT 2
Schinken ham OT 3
Schirmherr(in) patron OT 5
Schlacht battle OT 1
Schlachten cull OT 5
schlachten to cull OT 5
Schlafanzug pyjamas OT 3; pajamas OT 4
schlafen to sleep OT 1
schlafend asleep **WS 1**, 15
schlaff limp OT 4
Schlafsaal dorm **WS 2**, 67
Schlafsack sleeping bag OT 2
Schlafzimmer bedroom OT 1
Schlag stroke OT 3
schlagen to bash **WS 3**, 94
Schläger bat OT 1; racket OT 2
Schlagwort catchphrase OT 5; buzz word **WS 2**, 69
Schlagzeile headline OT 2
Schlagzeug drums OT 1
Schlamm mud **WS 1**, 16
Schlange queue; snake OT 1; serpent OT 5
Schlange stehen to queue OT 4
schlängeln: sich schlängeln to wriggle OT 2; to wind OT 5; to slither **WS 1**, 21
schlank slim **WS 2**, 70
Schlankheitskuren dieting OT 5
schlau smart OT 4; savvy OT 5; cunning **WS 1**, 16
Schlauch tube OT 1
schlecht bad OT 1; junky OT 4
schleichen to sneak **WS 2**, 70
Schleife loop **WS 4**, 140
schlemmen to feast OT 4
Schlepper(in) trafficker OT 4; coyote OT 5
schließen to close OT 1; to shut OT 2
schließen (aus etw.) to conclude OT 4
Schließfach locker OT 2
schließlich finally OT 1; eventually OT 3
Schlittschuh laufen to skate OT 2
Schloss lock OT 2
Schlucht canyon OT 3

Schluckauf hiccup OT 2
schlucken to swallow OT 4
Schluss conclusion OT 3
Schlüssel key OT 1
schlüssig coherent **WS 4**, 139
schmackhaft tasty OT 2
schmecken to taste OT 1
Schmeichelei flattery **WS 2**, 69
schmelzen to melt OT 4
Schmelztiegel melting pot **WS 2**, 72
Schmerz pain OT 2
schmerzen to hurt OT 1; to ache OT 3
schmerzend sore OT 2
schmerzhaft painful OT 2
schmerzlich poignant **WS 2**, 57
Schmerzmittel painkiller OT 2
Schmetterling butterfly OT 2
Schminke face paint OT 2
schmollen to sulk OT 3
Schmuck jewelry OT 2
schmücken to decorate OT 4
Schmutz dirt OT 4
schmutzig dirty OT 1
Schnabel beak **WS 1**, 32
Schnabeltier platypus OT 5
Schnäppchen bargain OT 4
Schnappschuss shot OT 4
Schneckenpost snail mail OT 4
Schnee snow OT 1
Schneide blade **WS 1**, 22
schneiden to cut OT 2; to chop OT 3
schnell fast OT 1; quick OT 2; rapid **WS 3**, 98
schnitzen to carve OT 2
Schnur cord **WS 2**, 62
schockiert shocked OT 4
Schokolade chocolate OT 1
schon already; yet OT 2
schön beautiful; nice; lovely OT 1
Schönheit beauty OT 3; glory **WS 2**, 62
Schöpfung creation **WS 2**, 62
schottisch Scottish OT 3
Schrank cupboard OT 1; cabinet OT 5
schrecklich terrible; awful OT 1; horrendous **WS 1**, 25
Schreibarbeit paperwork OT 5
Schreiben writing OT 1
schreiben to write OT 1
  neu schreiben to rewrite OT 1
Schreibkraft typist OT 5
Schreibmaschine typewriter OT 5
Schreibtisch desk OT 1
Schreibwaren stationery OT 5
Schreibweise spelling OT 1
schreien to scream OT 3
Schriftsteller(in) writer OT 2
Schriftverkehr correspondence OT 4
schrill flashy **WS 2**, 53
Schritt step OT 1
  auf Schritt und Tritt begleiten to shadow OT 5
schrittweise gradual **WS 2**, 83
Schubkarre wheelbarrow **WS 1**, 21
Schublade drawer OT 3
schüchtern shy OT 2
Schuh shoe OT 1
Schuhschachtel shoebox OT 3
Schulabgänger(in) school leaver OT 5
Schulausbildung schooling OT 4
Schulball prom OT 3
Schuld debt OT 4; guilt **WS 1**, 26
Schuldgefühl guilt **WS 1**, 26
schuldig guilty OT 5
Schuldige(r) culprit **WS 3**, 101
Schuldknecht bonded laborer OT 4
Schule school OT 1
Schüler(in) student OT 1
Schülerrat student council OT 2
Schulhof playground OT 1
Schulkamerad(in) schoolmate OT 4
Schulleiter(in) head teacher OT 1
Schultag school day OT 1
Schultasche school bag OT 1
Schulter shoulder OT 1
Schulterpolster shoulder pad OT 2
schummeln to cheat **WS 1**, 16
Schuppen shed OT 1
Schurz loincloth **WS 3**, 94
Schuss shot OT 4
Schüssel bowl OT 1
Schusswaffe gun OT 4
schütteln to shake OT 2
Schutz conservation OT 2; custody OT 5
Schütze gunman OT 4
schützen to protect OT 2
Schutzgebiet sanctuary **WS 2**, 85
schwach weak OT 3; dim OT 4
Schwäche weakness OT 4
schwächen to disempower **WS 3**, 104
schwanger pregnant OT 4
Schwanz tail OT 2
schwarz black OT 1
Schwätzer(in) (umgangssprachlich) batuni **WS 1**, 25
schweben to float; to soar OT 3
schwedisch Swedish OT 4
Schwein pig OT 1
Schweinefleisch pork OT 2
Schwellung swelling OT 2
schwer difficult; heavy OT 1; severe OT 5
Schwerelosigkeit weightlessness OT 4
Schwerkraft gravity OT 4
Schwert sword OT 1
Schwester sister OT 1; sibling OT 5
schwierig difficult; challenging OT 1
Schwierigkeit trouble OT 2; difficulty OT 4
Schwimmbecken pool OT 1
schwimmen to swim OT 1
Schwimmer(in) swimmer OT 2
schwindelerregend dizzying **WS 1**, 43
Schwindler(in) crook **WS 2**, 56
schwindlig faint OT 2
schwirren to buzz **WS 2**, 138
schwitzen to sweat OT 2
schwören to swear OT 4; to vow **WS 1**, 27
schwul gay; queer OT 5
Science-Fiction science fiction OT 2
sechs six OT 1
sechzehn sixteen OT 1
sechzig sixty OT 1
Secondhandladen thrift store OT 4
See: der lake; loch OT 1
See: die sea OT 1
Seehundfell sealskin **WS 3**, 95
Seele soul **WS 1**, 18
Seeufer lakefront; lakeside OT 4
Seevogel seabird OT 5
segeln to sail OT 2
Segment segment OT 5
segnen to bless **WS 1**, 19
sehen to look; to see OT 1
Sehenswürdigkeit sight OT 1; attraction OT 2
sehnen: sich sehnen to yearn **WS 2**, 79
sehr very; really; a lot OT 1; mighty OT 3
  sehr gut brill OT 1
Sehvermögen sight OT 1
Seife soap OT 2
Seil line; rope OT 1
Seilrutsche zip line OT 1
seine(r, -s) his; its OT 1
sein to be OT 1
seit since OT 3
Seite page; side OT 1
  an der Seite von alongside **WS 1**, 21
  auf der anderen Seite across OT 1
Sekretär(in) secretary OT 1
Sektor sector **WS 1**, 24
sekundär secondary OT 1
Sekundarschule secondary school OT 1
Sekunde second OT 1
selbst: (sich) selbst himself OT 1; themselves; herself; itself OT 3
  selbst gemacht homemade OT 3
selbständig self-employed OT 5
selbstbewusst confident OT 2
Selbstlaut vowel OT 1

selbstlos altruistic **WS 2**, 68
Selbstmord suicide OT 5
selbstständig independent OT 3
Selbstversorgung self-catering OT 3
selbstverständlich: für selbstverständlich halten to take for granted OT 4
Selbstvertrauen confidence OT 5
Selbstzahlerkasse self-checkout OT 4
Selfie selfie OT 1
selten rare OT 2; seldom OT 5
seltsam strange; weird OT 1
Semester term OT 2; semester OT 3
senden to broadcast **WS 1**, 33
Sendezeit telecast **WS 1**, 39
Sendung programme OT 2
Senf mustard OT 2
Senior(in) senior citizen OT 3; senior OT 4
Seniorenheim retirement home OT 3
senken to lower **WS 1**, 27
senkrecht vertical OT 4
Sensor sensor OT 4
September September OT 1
Sequenzierung sequencing OT 3
Serie series OT 1
servieren to serve OT 1
Sessel armchair OT 1
Session session OT 2
seufzen to sigh OT 3
Seufzer sigh OT 2
Sex sex OT 5
sexuel sexual **WS 1**, 14
Shampoo shampoo OT 3
Shorts shorts OT 1
sich yourself OT 1
Sichel crescent OT 2
sicher sure OT 1; safe OT 1; certainly OT 1; certain OT 3; stable OT 5; secure OT 5
sichergehen to make sure OT 2
Sicherheit safety OT 2; security OT 3
Sicherheitsausrüstung safety equipment OT 2
Sicherheitsgurt harness OT 1
sicherlich certainly OT 1; surely OT 4
sicherstellen to make sure OT 2; to ensure OT 4
Sicht view OT 1
sichtbar visible **WS 1**, 21
Sichtbarkeit exposure **WS 3**, 109
sie / Sie they; her; them; she; you OT 1
sieben seven OT 1
Siebenkampf heptathlon OT 2
siebzehn seventeen OT 1
siebzig seventy OT 1
Siedler(in) settler OT 3
Siedler(in) homesteader **WS 3**, 94
Siedlung settlement OT 4
Sieg victory **WS 1**, 26
Sieger(in) winner OT 1
Signal signal OT 2
signalisieren to beep **WS 1**, 39; to signal **WS 2**, 69
signifikant significant **WS 1**, 15
Silbe syllable OT 2
Silber... silver OT 1
singen to sing OT 1
Singular singular OT 1
sinken to sink OT 3
Sinn meaning OT 1; sense OT 2
sinneserweiternd mind-expanding OT 2
sinnlos pointless OT 4; futile **WS 3**, 98
sinnvoll meaningful OT 5
Sirene siren OT 3
Sirup syrup OT 3
Situation situation OT 1
sitzen to sit OT 1
Sitzplatz seat OT 1
Sitzung session OT 2
Skala scale **WS 1**, 30
skalpieren to scalp **WS 3**, 94
Skateboard skateboard OT 4
Skelett skeleton OT 1
Skeptiker(in) sceptic **WS 1**, 33
skeptisch cynical **WS 1**, 17
Sketch skit OT 2; sketch OT 4
Ski laufen to ski OT 3
Skiläufer(in) skier OT 3
Skizze sketch OT 4
skizzieren to outline OT 3; to sketch OT 4
Sklave / Sklavin slave OT 4
Sklaverei slavery OT 4
Skulptur sculpture OT 2
Skyline skyline OT 5
Slang slang OT 5
Slogan slogan OT 2
Slum slum OT 3
Smartphone smartphone OT 3
SMS text OT 1
Snack snack OT 1
Snowboard fahren snowboarding OT 3
so such OT 2
Socke sock OT 2
Sofa sofa OT 1
sofort immediately OT 1; straight away OT 2; in an instant **WS 2**, 63
Software software OT 1
sogar even OT 1; actually OT 2
Sohn son OT 1
Soja soy **WS 4**, 133
Solarenergie solar power OT 4
Soldat(in) soldier OT 1
Solidarität solidarity **WS 2**, 68
sollte(n) should OT 1; ought to OT 5
Solo solo OT 4
solo solo OT 2
Sommer summer OT 1
Sommersprose freckle OT 2
Songtext lyrics OT 2
Songwriter(in) songwriter OT 2
Sonne sun OT 1
Sonnen... solar OT 3
Sonnenbrand sunburn OT 2
Sonnenbrille sunglasses OT 2
Sonnenenergie solar power OT 4
Sonnenkollektor solar panel OT 3
Sonnenschein sunshine OT 3
Sonnenschutzmittel sunscreen OT 2
Sonnenstich sunstroke OT 2
Sonnensystem solar system OT 1
Sonnenuntergang sunset OT 3
sonnenverbrannt sunburnt OT 5
sonnig sunny OT 1
Sonntag Sunday OT 1
sonst otherwise OT 5
sonst noch else OT 1
Sorge concern OT 5; anxiety **WS 4**, 144
keine Sorge no worries OT 2
sich Sorgen machen to worry OT 1
sorgfältig careful OT 1
sorglos careless OT 2
sortieren to sort **WS 1**, 28
Soße sauce OT 1
souverän sovereign **WS 1**, 14
Souveränität sovereignty **WS 1**, 14
sozial social OT 2
Sozialisation socialization **WS 2**, 55
soziolinguistisch sociolinguistic **WS 3**, 108
Soziologe / Soziologin sociologist **WS 3**, 92
Soziologie sociology OT 5
Spaghetti spaghetti OT 1
Spalte column OT 1; rift **WS 1**, 14
spalten to polarize **WS 1**, 21
spaltend divisive **WS 2**, 57
Spaniel spaniel OT 2
spanisch Spanish OT 1
spannend thrilling **WS 1**, 22
sparen to save OT 2
Spaß fun OT 1
Spaß verstehen to take a joke OT 2
spät late OT 1
später subsequently **WS 1**, 23
Spaziergang walk OT 2
Speck bacon OT 1

Speisekarte menu OT 1
spektakulär spectacular OT 2
spekulieren to speculate OT 4
Spende donation OT 2
spenden to make a donation; to donate OT 2
Spendensammler(in) fundraiser OT 2
Spendensammlung fundraising OT 2
Spender dispenser OT 5
spezialisieren to specialize OT 4
Spezialist(in) geek OT 5
speziell specialist OT 5
Spezies species OT 5
spezifisch specific OT 3
Spiegel mirror OT 1
spiegeln to reflect OT 5
Spiel game; match OT 1
Spielautomat slot-machine **WS 4**, 133
Spielbank casino **WS 1**, 29
Spielekonsole game console OT 4
spielen to play OT 1
Spieler(in) player OT 1; gamer OT 4
Spielfeld pitch OT 3
  in der Mitte des Spielfeldes midfield **WS 1**, 28
Spielfilm motion picture OT 4
Spielführer(in) captain OT 4
Spielplatz playground OT 1
Spielverderber: kein Spielverderber sein to be a good sport OT 2
Spielzeug toy OT 2
Spind locker OT 2
Spinne spider OT 1
Spirale spiral OT 5
spitz spiky OT 5; pointy **WS 3**, 97
Spitze tip; top OT 1
Spitzen... peak OT 5
Spitzensport elite sports OT 3
Spitzname nickname OT 4
  Spitzname geben to nickname OT 5
Sponsor(in) sponsor OT 2
spontan spontaneous OT 5
Sport sport; athletics OT 1
Sport... sporting OT 5
Sporthalle gymnasium OT 4
Sportjacke blazer OT 1
Sportler(in) jock; sportsman, sportswoman OT 3; sportsperson **WS 2**, 58
  Sportler(innen) sportspeople OT 3
sportlich athletic OT 4; sporting OT 5; sporty **WS 2**, 54
Sportlichkeit athleticism **WW**, 11
Sportunterricht PE (physical education) OT 1
Sprachbeherrschung fluency OT 5
Sprache language OT 1
Sprachfehler lisp **WS 3**, 96
Sprachwissenschaftler(in) linguist OT 5
Sprechblase speech bubble OT 2
Sprechen speaking OT 1
sprechen to speak OT 1
Sprecher(in) speaker OT 1; spokesman; spokeswoman OT 2; spokesperson **WS 2**, 67
Sprechstunde surgery OT 5
Sprichwort proverb OT 5
Springbrunnen fountain OT 1
springen to jump OT 2
Sprint sprint OT 3
Sprinter(in) sprinter OT 3
Spritztour (mit einem gestohlenen Auto) joyride OT 5
spröde brittle **WS 2**, 62
Sprudel soda OT 5
sprudelnd sparkling OT 1
sprühen to spray OT 5
Sprung leap OT 5
spucken to spit OT 4
Spülbecken sink OT 3
Spur trail OT 2
Spürhund hound OT 2
Staat state OT 1
Staatsangehörigkeit nationality OT 2
Staatsanwalt / -anwältin prosecutor OT 5
Staatsbürger(in) national **WS 2**, 85
Staatsbürgerschaft citizenship **WS 2**, 85
stabil steady OT 3; stable OT 5
Stabilität stability OT 5
Stachel thorn OT 2
stachelig spiky OT 5
Stachelrochen stingray OT 5
Stadion stadium OT 1
Stadt town; city OT 1
Stadtbewohner(innen) townspeople OT 4
städtisch urban OT 4
Stahl steel OT 2
Stalagmit stalagmite OT 1
Stalaktit stalactite OT 1
Stall stall OT 2
Stamm tribe OT 3
Stammes... tribal OT 3
Stand status OT 4; caste **WS 1**, 13
Standard level OT 2; default OT 3; norm OT 5
ständig constant **WS 3**, 104
Standort location OT 2
Stange pole OT 3
Stanze stanza OT 5
Stapel pile OT 5
stapeln to stack OT 4
Star star OT 1
stark strong OT 2; intense; severe OT 5
  stärker machen to strengthen OT 5
  stärker werden to strengthen OT 5
Stärke strength OT 2; intensity **WS 1**, 39
stärken to empower OT 5
starren to stare OT 2; to glare **WS 1**, 28
starten to launch OT 4
Startseite homepage OT 1
Station station OT 1
Statistik statistic OT 3
stattdessen instead OT 2
Statue statue OT 1
Statuette figurine **WS 1**, 27
Status status OT 4
Status quo status quo **WS 2**, 55
Stau traffic jam OT 2
Staub dust **WS 1**, 39
staubsaugen to vacuum OT 4
Staubsauger vacuum cleaner OT 4
Staudamm dam **WS 3**, 99
Steak steak OT 1
stechen to sting OT 2
Stechmücke mosquito OT 2
Steckbrief profile OT 3
Stecknadel pin OT 1
Stegosaurus stegosaurus OT 1
stehen to stand OT 1
  jdm. stehen to suit sb. OT 1
steigen to climb OT 1
steigern to boost **WS 3**, 110
steil steep OT 2
Stein stone OT 1; rock OT 2
Steinbruch quarry OT 1
Stelle job OT 1
stellen to put OT 1; to pose **WS 2**, 81
stellvertretend deputy OT 5
Steppdecke quilt OT 4
sterben to die OT 1
Stereotype stereotype OT 5
stereotypisch stereotypical OT 5
stereotypisieren to stereotype OT 5
Stern star OT 1
Sternchen asterisk OT 4
Steroid steroid OT 5
Steuer tax OT 4
steuern to steer OT 3; to pilot OT 4
Steuerzahler(in) tax-payer OT 5
Stich sting OT 2
  im Stich lassen to abandon **WS 2**, 56; to desert **WS 2**, 65
Stichwort headword OT 2; keyword; prompt OT 4

Stickerei embroidery **WS 1**, 25
Stiefel boot OT 1
Stift pen OT 1
Stigma stigma OT 5
Stil style OT 2
stilisieren to stylize **WS 1**, 12
stilistisch stylistic OT 5
still quiet OT 1
Stille silence OT 2
Stimme voice OT 2
  mit lauter Stimme aloud OT 2
Stimmung mood OT 5
Stinktier skunk **WS 2**, 55
Stipendium scholarship **WS 2**, 55; stipend **WS 3**, 111
Stirn: die Stirn runzeln (über) to frown (upon) **WS 2**, 69
Stirnband headband OT 3
Stockbett bunk bed OT 3
Stocken: ins Stocken bringen to stump **WS 2**, 58
Stockwerk floor OT 1
  im unteren Stockwerk downstairs OT 1
Stoff material OT 3; fabric **WS 1**, 27
stolpern to trip OT 2
Stolz pride OT 4
stolz proud OT 2
stören to bother OT 4; to disturb OT 5; to disrupt **WS 2**, 65
Störung disruption **WS 1**, 21; disturbance **WS 2**, 65; blip **WS 3**, 98; interference **WS 4**, 138
Storyboard storyboard OT 4
stoßen to bump; to push OT 2
Stoßzahn tusk OT 3
Strafe penalty OT 3; punishment OT 5
straff toned **WS 4**, 144
Sträfling convict **WS 2**, 83
strafrechtlich penal OT 5
Strafstoß penalty OT 3
Straftat offence OT 5
Strahl ray **WS 2**, 65
Strahlung radiation **WS 3**, 98
Strand beach OT 1
Strandsegeln land yachting OT 3
Sträßchen laneway OT 5
Straße road; street OT 1
Straßenbahn tram OT 1
Straßenmusiker(in) busker OT 5
Straßenrand roadside **WS 1**, 24
Straßensammlung street collection OT 2
Strategie strategy OT 4
strategisch strategic OT 4
Strauß bouquet OT 3
Strecke route OT 2
Streifen strip OT 5
Streik strike OT 4
streiken to strike OT 1
Streit argument OT 1
streiten to argue OT 2
Streitgespräch dispute **WS 1**, 40
streng strict OT 2; stern **WS 3**, 94
Stress stress OT 1
Stressfaktor stressor **WS 4**, 144
stressig stressful OT 4
streuen to sprinkle OT 2
Stroh straw OT 4
Strohhalm straw OT 4
Strom electricity OT 2; flow **WS 3**, 101
strömen to flock **WS 1**, 15
Stromerzeuger generator **WS 3**, 99
Strömung tide **WS 1**, 27
Strophe verse OT 1; stanza OT 5
Struktur structure OT 1
strukturieren to structure OT 5
Stück piece; bit OT 1
Student(in) student OT 1
  Student im ersten Jahr freshman OT 4
Studentenwohnheim dorm **WS 2**, 67
Studienanfänger(in) freshman OT 4
Studiengebühr(en) tuition OT 5
studieren to study OT 1
Studio studio OT 5
Studium studies OT 1
Stufe step OT 1; level OT 2
Stuhl chair OT 1
stumm silent **WS 1**, 22
Stunde hour OT 1
Stunden... hourly OT 5
Stundenplan timetable OT 1; schedule OT 2
stündlich hourly OT 5
Sturm storm OT 2
Stürmer(in) striker OT 3
stürmisch stormy **WS 2**, 60
stürzen to fall OT 1; to overthrow **WS 2**, 72
Stütze prop OT 1
Subjekt subject OT 1
Subjektpronomen subject pronoun OT 1
Subkontinent subcontinent **WS 1**, 12
Substantiv noun OT 1
subtil subtle **WS 1**, 27
Suche search OT 2; pursuit **WS 1**, 21; quest **WS 3**, 98
suchen to search OT 2; to seek OT 5
  nach etw. suchen to scavenge for OT 5
Suchscheinwerfer searchlight **WW**, 11
süchtig addicted OT 3
  süchtig machend addictive **WS 4**, 132
Süd... south OT 1
südlich southern OT 3
Südwesten southwest OT 3
Sumpf swamp OT 2
Superheld superhero OT 5
Superlativ superlative OT 2
Supermarkt supermarket OT 1
Suppe soup OT 1
Surfen surfing OT 1
Surfer(in) surfer OT 4
Sushi sushi OT 1
Süßigkeit candy OT 4
Süßkartoffel sweet potato OT 4
Süßwasser freshwater **WS 3**, 100
Sweatshirt sweatshirt OT 1
Symbol symbol OT 1; icon OT 5; emblem **WS 2**, 59
Symbolfigur figurehead **WS 2**, 55
symbolisieren to symbolize **WS 2**, 62
Symptom symptom **WS 3**, 106
Synagoge synagogue OT 1
Synästhesie synaesthesia OT 2
Syndrom syndrome **WS 1**, 30
Synonym synonym OT 2
synthetisch synthetic OT 4
synthetisieren to synthesize **WS 3**, 112
System system OT 1
systematisch systematic OT 5
systembedingt systemic **WS 2**, 57
Szenario scenario **WS 3**, 92
Szene scene OT 2
Szenenbuch storyboard OT 4

T
Tab tab OT 3
Tabak tobacco OT 3
Tablett tray OT 2
Tablette tablet OT 2
Tabu taboo **WS 1**, 33
Tacker stapler OT 2
Tafel board OT 1
Tag day OT 1
Tagebuch diary OT 1
Tagesablauf routine OT 4
Tagesausflug day trip; day out OT 2
Tagesgericht special OT 1
Tagesordnung agenda OT 3
Tageszeit daytime OT 1
täglich daily OT 2
taiwanisch Taiwanese OT 4
Takt beat OT 1
Taktik tactic OT 2
Tal valley OT 1

Talent talent OT 2
talentiert talented OT 3
Tank tank OT 3
Tante aunt OT 1
Tantiemen royalty **WS 2**, 68
Tanz dance OT 1
tanzen to dance OT 1
Tänzer(in) dancer OT 3
tapfer brave OT 1
Tasche case; bag OT 1; pocket OT 2
Taschenbuch paperback **WS 3**, 96
Taschendieb(in) pickpocket OT 4
Taschengeld pocket money OT 2; allowance OT 3
Taschenlampe torch OT 1; flashlight OT 2
Taschenmesser pocketknife OT 2
Taschentuch tissue OT 5
Tasse cup OT 1; mug OT 3
Tastatur keyboard OT 1
Tat deed OT 5
Täter(in) offender OT 5
Tätigkeit occupation OT 4
Tätowierung tattoo OT 3
Tatsache fact OT 1
tatsächlich actually OT 2; indeed **WS 2**, 64
Taube pigeon **WS 1**, 39
tauchen to dive OT 1; to dip OT 4
Taucheranzug wetsuit OT 1
tauschen to swap OT 1
täuschen to fool **WS 1**, 32; to bluff **WS 4**, 141
Täuschung bluff **WS 4**, 141
tausend thousand OT 1
Taxi taxi OT 1; cab OT 4
Teamwork teamwork OT 4
Technik technique OT 4
technisch tech OT 2; technological; technical OT 4
  technische Spielerei gadget OT 4
Technologie technology OT 1
technologisch technological OT 4
techorientiert tech-orientated OT 5
Tee tea OT 1
Teelicht tea light OT 2
Teenager teenager; teen OT 2
Teich pond OT 4
Teig dough OT 2
Teigwaren pastry **WS 1**, 16
Teil piece; part OT 1; section OT 2
teilen to share OT 1; to divide OT 2; to partition **WS 1**, 14
teilnehmen to take part OT 2; to participate OT 5
Teilnehmer(in) participant **WS 2**, 57
Teilung division OT 5; partition **WS 1**, 12
teilweise partly OT 3
Teilzeit... part-time OT 4
Telefon phone OT 1
Telefonat phone call OT 2
telefonieren to phone OT 2
Telefonist(in) operator OT 2
Telefonkonferenz teleconference OT 3
Telegraf telegraph OT 4
Teleskop telescope **WS 3**, 103
Teller plate OT 1
Tempel temple OT 1
Temperatur temperature OT 2
Temperaturregler thermostat OT 5
Tempus tense OT 1
tendieren zu to tend to OT 5
Tennis tennis OT 1
Teppich carpet OT 4
Termin appointment **WS 2**, 81
Terminkalender diary OT 1
Terrier terrier OT 2
Test test OT 1
teuer expensive OT 1; costly **WS 3**, 101
Teufel devil OT 5
Text text OT 1
  Text (eines Schauspielers) line OT 1
texten to message OT 3
Textil- textile **WS 3**, 102
Theater theatre OT 1
  Theater spielen to act OT 1
Theaterstück play OT 1
Theke counter OT 3
Thema subject OT 1
theoretisch theoretical OT 4
Theorie theory OT 1
Thermalquelle hot spring OT 2
Thermosflasche flask OT 3
Thermostat thermostat OT 5
Thron throne OT 5
Thunfisch tuna OT 1
tief low; deep OT 1; profound OT 5
tiefgreifend in-depth **WS 4**, 133
Tier animal OT 1; beast OT 5
Tierarzt / -ärztin veterinarian; vet OT 4
Tierwelt wildlife OT 2
Tiger tiger OT 1
Timer timer OT 5
Tinte ink **WS 2**, 79
tippen to tap OT 2
Tisch table OT 1
Tischtennis ping-pong OT 1
Titel title OT 1
  mit dem Titel entitled **WS 1**, 25
Toast toast OT 2
Tochter daughter OT 1
Tod death OT 2
Todesanzeige obituary **WS 2**, 79
Todesdatum date of death OT 2
tödlich fatal **WS 2**, 81
Toilette toilet OT 2
Toilettenartikel toiletries **WS 1**, 23
tolerant tolerant OT 4
Toleranz tolerance OT 5
tolerieren to tolerate **WS 3**, 122
toll great OT 1; awesome OT 2; stunning OT 5
  Toll! Wow! OT 1
Tomate tomato OT 1
Ton clay OT 4; tone OT 5
Tonerkartusche toner cartridge OT 5
Tonne ton OT 2
Tor goal; gate OT 1
Tortendiagramm pie chart OT 4
Torwart(in) goalkeeper OT 3
tot dead OT 1
total absolutely OT 2
totalitär totalitarian **WS 3**, 104
töten to kill OT 1; to execute OT 3
Touchdown touchdown OT 2
Tourismus tourism OT 2
Tourist(in) tourist OT 1
toxisch toxic OT 4
traben to trot OT 2
Tradition tradition OT 2; heritage OT 5
traditionell traditional OT 1
tragbar portable OT 4
tragen to wear; to carry OT 1
Tragetasche carrier bag OT 2
tragisch tragic **WS 1**, 38
Tragödie tragedy OT 5
Trailer trailer OT 4
Trainer(in) coach OT 1
trainieren to train OT 2
Traktor tractor OT 2
Träne tear OT 2
Trank potion **WS 2**, 62
trans... trans OT 5
Transaktion transaction **WS 4**, 144
transatlantisch transatlantic OT 3
transferieren to transfer OT 4
transkribieren to transcribe OT 5
Transkribierer(in) transcriber OT 5
Transphobie transphobia **WS 3**, 92
Transplantation transplant OT 3
transportieren to transport **WS 3**, 99
transsexuell transgender OT 5
trauen: sich trauen to dare OT 2
Trauer grief; sorrow OT 5
Traum dream OT 1
Trauma trauma OT 5
traumatisch traumatic **WS 1**, 15
träumen to dream OT 4

Träumer(in) dreamer OT 2
Traumzeit dreamtime OT 5
traurig sad OT 1; upset OT 2
Treck wagon train OT 4
trecken to trek OT 2
Treffen meeting; scoring OT 1; rally OT 4
treffen to meet OT 1
treiben to herd OT 2; to float OT 3
Treibhaus greenhouse OT 1
Treidelpfad towpath OT 3
Trend fashion OT 1; trend OT 4
Trendwende tipping point OT 5
trennen to separate OT 4; to split up OT 5; to disconnect **WS 2**, 52
  durch Gesetz trennen to segregate **WS 2**, 52
trennend divisive **WS 2**, 57
Trennung division OT 5
Treppe stairs OT 1
Treppenstufen stairs OT 1
treten to kick OT 1; to step OT 4
treu loyal OT 5
Treue loyalty **WS 1**, 40
Treuebruch betrayal **WS 3**, 96
Triangel triangle OT 2
Tribut tribute **WS 2**, 72
Trick trick OT 5
Trikot jersey **WS 2**, 59
Trilogie trilogy OT 5
trinken to drink OT 1
Trinkhalm straw OT 4
Triumph triumph **WS 2**, 79
trocken dry OT 2; arid OT 5
Trödelmarkt flea market OT 5
Trompete trumpet OT 2
tropisch tropical OT 4
Tropfen trickle **WS 3**, 101
tropfen to drip OT 3
trösten to comfort OT 5
trotz in spite of OT 5; despite **WS 1**, 17
trotzdem anyway OT 1; nevertheless **WS 1**, 16; nonetheless **WS 2**, 65
trotzen to defy **WS 1**, 29
trüb cloudy; murky; dim OT 4
Truhe chest **WS 1**, 15
Truppe squad **WS 1**, 28
Truthahn turkey OT 1
Tschüss! bye OT 1
tun to put; to do OT 1
  so tun, als ob to pretend OT 2
Tunnel tunnel OT 3
Tür door OT 1
Turban turban **WS 2**, 69
Turbine turbine OT 4
Turm tower OT 1
Turnhalle gym OT 3
Turnier tournament OT 3
Turnschuh trainer OT 1
Tüte bag OT 1
Tutor(in) tutor OT 4
typisch typical OT 2
Tyrannosaurus rex tyrannosaurus rex OT 1

U
U-Bahn metro; subway; underground OT 1
Übel evil OT 5
üben to practise OT 1
über about; over OT 1; via OT 2
  über Bord overboard OT 3
  über Nacht overnight OT 2
überall everywhere OT 1; all over OT 2
überarbeiten to revise OT 2; to edit OT 3
Überblick overview OT 4
übereinstimmen to correspond **WS 2**, 62
Überfall assault OT 5
überfliegen to scan OT 3
überfließen to overflow **WS 3**, 101
überflüssig unnecessary OT 4
Überflutung flooding OT 4
überfüllt crowded OT 2; overcrowded **WS 1**, 32
Übergang transition OT 5
übergeben to throw up OT 2
übergenau fussy OT 2
übergewichtig overweight OT 5
Überleben survival OT 2
überleben to survive OT 3
übermalen to repaint OT 4
übermäßig overly OT 5; excess **WS 3**, 101
übernehmen to resume OT 5
überprüfen to check OT 1
überqueren to cross OT 1
überragen to tower **WS 1**, 19
überraschend surprising OT 2
überrascht surprised OT 1; amazed OT 3
Überraschung surprise OT 1; shock OT 5
überreden to persuade OT 3; to convince OT 4
Überreste remains OT 3
übersät strewn **WS 1**, 15
überschlagen: sich überschlageb to cascade **WS 4**, 136
Überschrift heading OT 1
überschüssig excess **WS 3**, 101
übersehen to overlook OT 5
übersetzen to translate OT 1
Übersetzungsfalle false friend OT 2
Übersicht overview OT 4
übersteigen to outnumber **WS 3**, 108
übertragbar transferable **WS 3**, 110
übertragen to transfer OT 4
Übertragung transmission **WS 3**, 101
übertreiben to exaggerate OT 4; to overdo OT 5
Übertreibung hyperbole **WS 2**, 62
überwachen to oversee OT 4
überwachsen overgrown OT 4
Überwachung supervision OT 5; surveillance **WS 3**, 104
Überwachungskamera cctv **WS 3**, 104
überwältigen to overwhelm **WS 1**, 27
überwiegend dominant OT 5
überwinden to overcome **WS 2**, 72
überwintern to hibernate **WS 3**, 98
überwuchert overgrown OT 4
überzeugen to persuade OT 3; to convince OT 4
überzeugend persuasive OT 5
Übetragung transmission **WS 3**, 101
üblich usual OT 2
U-Boot submarine OT 3
übrig remaining OT 5
übrige rest OT 1
Übung exercise OT 1; practice OT 2
Übungsheft exercise book OT 1
Ufer bank OT 3; riverbank **WS 1**, 27
Uhr clock OT 1
  um around OT 1
  um ... herum about; round OT 1
  um ... Uhr at ... o'clock OT 1
umarmen to hug OT 4; to embrace OT 5
Umarmung hug OT 1
umdrehen to flip OT 4; to reverse **WS 3**, 98
umfallen to fall over OT 2
umfangreich considerably OT 5
umfassen to involve; to range OT 4
umfassend comprehensive **WS 3**, 103
Umfeld environment OT 2
umformulieren to rephrase OT 4
Umfrage survey OT 1; poll OT 5
umgeben to surround **WS 2**, 60
umgehen to deal with OT 2
umgehend immediate OT 5
umgesiedelt displaced **WS 1**, 14
Umhang cloak OT 1
umkehren to invert OT 5
umkippen to tip over OT 5
Umkleide changing room OT 1
Umlaufbahn orbit OT 4
umschreiben to rewrite OT 1; to paraphrase OT 5
umsetzen to implement **WS 3**, 124
Umsiedlung resettlement OT 4
umspannen to span **WS 1**, 15

Umstand circumstance OT 5
Umstandswort adverb OT 1
umstellen to invert OT 5
umstoßen to knock over OT 2
umstritten controversial OT 5; debatable **WS 2**, 59
umwandeln to convert **WS 1**, 25
Umwelt environment OT 2
Umwelt... environmental OT 2
Umweltbewegung environmentalism **WS 1**, 21
Umweltschutz environmentalism **WS 1**, 21
Umweltschützer(in) environmentalist OT 3
Umweltverschmutzung pollution OT 2
Umweltwissen environmental literacy **WS 3**, 98
umziehen to move OT 1; to relocate **WS 1**, 22
Umzug procession; parade OT 2
Umzugswagen moving van; removal van OT 2
unabdingbar inalienable **WS 2**, 55
unabhängig autonomous OT 4
Unabhängigkeit independence OT 2
unangenehm nasty OT 2; disagreeable **WS 2**, 78; inconvenient **WS 3**, 94
unartig mischievous **WS 1**, 43
unausgeglichen imbalanced **WS 2**, 82
Unausgereiftheit immaturity **WS 1**, 20
unbeachted untended **WS 1**, 39
unbeaufsichtigt unchaperoned **WS 4**, 133
unbedenklich harmless OT 5
unbedeutend insignificant **WS 1**, 21
Unbefugte(r) trespasser OT 5
unbeholfen awkward OT 5
Unbeholfenheit awkwardness **WS 1**, 28
unbekannt unknown OT 3
unbekümmert breezy **WS 3**, 97
unbequem uncomfortable OT 3; inconvenient **WS 3**, 94
Unberechenbarkeit unpredictability OT 2
Unberührbare(r) untouchable **WS 1**, 16
unberührt unspoilt OT 3
unbesiegbar invincible **WS 1**, 21; unconquerable **WS 2**, 59
Unbeständigkeit intermittency **WS 3**, 101
unbestimmt indefinite OT 1; vague OT 5
unbestritten indisputable **WS 3**, 112
unbewohnbar uninhabitable **WS 3**, 104
unbewusst oblivious **WS 3**, 96
unbezahlbar invaluable **WS 2**, 62
unbezahlt unpaid OT 5
unbezwingbar invincible **WS 1**, 21
und and OT 1
  und so weiter etc. (et cetera) OT 1
Underdog underdog OT 5
uneben bumpy OT 4
unecht fake OT 5
unendlich endless; infinite OT 4
unentschieden undecided OT 5
unentschlossen undecided OT 5
Unentschlossenheit indecision OT 5
unerfahren inexperienced OT 5
unermesslich untold **WS 4**, 136
unermüdlich tireless **WS 4**, 144
unerschütterlich unshakable **WS 1**, 27
unerwartet unexpected OT 5
unerwarteterweise unexpectedly OT 3
Unfairness unfairness OT 4
Unfall accident OT 1
unfassbar intangible **WS 1**, 15
unfreundlich unfriendly OT 4
unfruchtbar barren **WS 2**, 78
ungarisch Hungarian OT 2
Ungeborene(r) unborn **WS 1**, 39
ungebrochen unbroken **WS 2**, 54
ungeduldig impatient OT 3
ungefähr about OT 1; approximately OT 5
Ungehorsam disobedience **WS 1**, 18
ungelöst unresolved **WS 2**, 68
Ungerechtigkeit injustice; unfairness OT 4
ungeschickt clumsy OT 2; awkward OT 5
ungesund unhealthy OT 1
  ungesundes Essen junk food OT 5
ungewiss uncertain **WS 3**, 110
Ungewissheit uncertainty **WS 3**, 104
ungewöhnlich unusual OT 2; extraordinary **WS 1**, 25
unglaublich incredible; unbelievable OT 2
Ungleichheit inequality **WS 1**, 31
unglücklich unhappy OT 1
unheimlich scary OT 1
unhöflich rude OT 1
Uni uni OT 3
Uniform uniform OT 1
uninteressant dull OT 5
Union union OT 5
Unisex- unisex OT 5
universal universal OT 5
Universität university OT 1
Unkenntnis: in Unkenntnis unaware OT 5
unklug foolish OT 5
Unkraut weed OT 5
unmittelbar immediate OT 5; imminent **WS 3**, 124
unmöglich impossible OT 2
unnötig unnecessary OT 4
unordentlich messy OT 2
Unordnung mess OT 3
unpassend inappropriate OT 5
unpraktisch impractical OT 4
unregelmäßig irregular OT 1
Unreife immaturity **WS 1**, 20
Unruhe disturbance **WS 2**, 65
Unruhestifter(in) troublemaker **WS 2**, 78
uns us OT 1; ourselves OT 3
unsere(r, -s) our OT 1; ours OT 2
unschätzbar invaluable **WS 2**, 62
unschuldig innocent OT 5
unsicher unsure **WS 2**, 58
Unsicherheit insecurity **WS 4**, 144
unsichtbar invisible **WS 1**, 21
Unstetigkeit intermittency **WS 3**, 101
unsympathisch disagreeable **WS 2**, 78
unter under OT 1; below OT 2; among OT 3
unterbewerten to understate OT 5
unterbrechen to interrupt OT 2; to disrupt **WS 2**, 65
Unterbrechung disruption **WS 1**, 21
unterdrücken to oppress **WS 2**, 72; to repress **WS 2**, 72
Unterdrücker(in) oppressor **WS 2**, 83
Unterdrückung oppression OT 5
unterhalten to entertain OT 4
Unterhalter(in) entertainer OT 3
unterhaltsam entertaining OT 3
Unterhaltung chat OT 1; entertainment OT 3; amusement **WS 1**, 21
Unterhemd vest OT 2
Unterkühlung hypothermia OT 2
Unterkunft housing OT 3
unterlegen inferior **WS 2**, 71
Unterleib belly **WS 1**, 16
Unternehmen company OT 1; corporation OT 4
unternehmensweit corporate OT 5
Unternehmer(in) businessman; businesswoman OT 4; entrepreneur OT 5
Unterricht class; lesson OT 1
unterrichten to teach OT 1
untersagt forbidden **WS 2**, 79
unterscheiden to differentiate OT 5
  zwischen etw. unterscheiden to distinguish between OT 5
Unterschied difference OT 1
unterschiedlich different OT 1

unterschiedlich behandeln to discriminate OT 5
Unterschlupf shelter OT 2
unterschreiben to sign OT 2
unterstreichen to underline OT 1
unterstützen to support OT 1; to assist OT 5; to endorse **WS 3**, 100
unterstützend supportive OT 5
Unterstützer von Start-ups incubator OT 5
Unterstützung backup OT 4
finanzielle Unterstützung sponsorship OT 2
Unterstützungs(Künstler(in)) backing artist **WS 2**, 68
untersuchen to examine **WS 1**, 38; to investigate **WS 4**, 140
Untersuchung analysis OT 5
unterteilt divided OT 2
Untertitel caption OT 1
untertreiben to understate OT 5
Unterüberschrift sub-heading OT 2
unterversorgt under-resourced **WS 2**, 80
Unterwelt underworld OT 5
unterwerfen to subject OT 4
Unterwerfung subjection **WS 2**, 72
unterwürfig submissive **WS 2**, 71
untrinkbar undrinkable OT 5
unverantwortlich irresponsible **WS 1**, 21
unveräußerlich inalienable **WS 2**, 55
unvergesslich memorable OT 3; unforgettable OT 5
unversehrt intact **WS 1**, 39
unverwechselbar distinctive OT 5
unvorsichtig careless OT 2
unwahrscheinlich unlikely OT 4
unwiderstehlich irresistible **WS 2**, 60
unwissend unaware OT 5; ignorant **WS 1**, 21
Unwissenheit ignorance **WS 1**, 21
unzählbar uncountable OT 1
unzivilisiert barbaric **WS 1**, 21
unzugänglich inaccessible OT 3
uralt ancient OT 2
urban urban OT 4
Urheberschaft authorship **WS 4**, 140
Urkunde diploma OT 5
Urlaub holiday OT 1; vacation OT 2
Urlauber(in) holidaymaker OT 3
Urlaubsort resort OT 2
ursächlich causal **WS 4**, 140
Ursprung origin OT 3
ursprünglich originally OT 2; original OT 3
usw. etc. (et cetera) OT 1
Utopie utopia **WS 3**, 92

V

vage vague OT 5
Vakuum vacuum **WS 1**, 14
Vampir(in) vampire OT 2
Vanille vanilla OT 1
Vanillesoße custard OT 1
Variante variation OT 5
Variation variation OT 5
variieren to vary OT 5
Vater father OT 1
vegan vegan OT 1
Veganer(in) vegan OT 1
Vegetarier(in) vegetarian OT 1
vegetarisch vegetarian OT 1; veggie OT 2
Vene vein OT 5
verachten to despise **WS 2**, 78
veraltet outdated OT 5
Veranda porch OT 4
verändern to transform OT 4; to swing **WS 2**, 72; to alter **WS 3**, 113
Veränderung transformation OT 4
verängstigt scared; frightened OT 1; terrified OT 3
veranlassen to prompt **WS 2**, 81
veranstalten to put on OT 2
Veranstaltungsort venue OT 3
verantwortlich responsible OT 3
verantwortlich sein to be in charge of OT 3
Verantwortung responsibility OT 3
verärgern to upset **WS 1**, 21; to anger **WS 2**, 68
verärgert upset; irritated OT 2
Verb verb OT 1
verbal verbal OT 5
Verband association; bandage OT 2
Verbandkasten first aid kit OT 2
verbergen to conceal OT 5
verbessern to improve OT 2; to enrich **WS 3**, 110
Verbesserung improvement OT 3
verbieten to ban OT 3
verbinden to connect OT 2
Verbindung connection; link OT 2; combination OT 3; bond **WS 1**, 15
Verbindungswort linking word OT 4
verblassen to fade OT 2
verblüfft astonished **WS 1**, 27
verborgen ulterior **WS 3**, 112
verboten forbidden **WS 2**, 79
Verbrauch consumption **WS 3**, 102
Verbraucher(in) consumer OT 5
Verbrechen crime OT 4
verbreiten to spread (out) OT 4
verbreitern to broaden **WS 3**, 110
Verbrennungs... internal combustion OT 4
verbringen to spend OT 1
verbunden connected OT 1
verdächtig suspicious **WS 2**, 67
verdammt damn **WS 2**, 59; damned **WS 3**, 103
Verderben spoilage OT 4
verderben to spoil OT 2
verdienen to deserve OT 2; to earn OT 3
verdreht twisted OT 1; wacky OT 4
verdünnen to dilute **WS 2**, 55
verehren to revere **WS 1**, 32
Verein club OT 1; association OT 2
vereinbaren to arrange OT 2; to schedule OT 5
Vereinbarung arrangement; agreement OT 3
vereinfacht simplified OT 5
Vereinfachung simplification **WS 1**, 14
vereinigen to unite; to unify OT 5
Verfahren procedure OT 5
verfallen to decline OT 5
Verfallsdatum expiry date **WS 1**, 39
verfälschen to misrepresent **WS 2**, 66
Verfassung constitution OT 5
verfaulen to rot OT 5
verfeinern to refine OT 4
verfluchen to curse **WS 1**, 39
verfolgen to pursue OT 4; to persecute **WS 2**, 82
Verfolgung persecution OT 4; pursuit **WS 1**, 21
verfügbar available OT 3
Verfügbarkeit availability **WS 3**, 99
Verfügung: zur Verfügung stellen to provide OT 4
vergeben to forgive OT 2; to award OT 4
vergeblich futile **WS 3**, 98
vergeigen to mess up OT 2
vergessen to forget OT 1
Vergewaltigung rape **WS 1**, 14
vergiften to poison **WS 4**, 136
Vergleich comparison OT 2; simile **WS 2**, 62
vergleichen to compare OT 1
Vergnügen amusement **WS 1**, 21
vergnügt gleeful **WS 1**, 39
vergöttern to idolize **WS 2**, 60
vergüten to repay OT 5
verhaften to arrest OT 5
verhalten to act OT 1
Verhaltensregeln code of conduct OT 5
Verhältniswort preposition OT 2
verhandeln to negotiate **WS 1**, 21

Verhandlung negotiation **WS 1**, 18
verhängen to impose **WS 2**, 55; to issue **WS 2**, 68
verheerend disastrous **WS 4**, 134
verhindern to prevent OT 4
verhungern (lassen) to starve OT 1
verifizieren to verify **WS 1**, 25
verkannt misunderstood OT 4
verkaufen to sell OT 1
Verkehr traffic OT 1; transport OT 2; transportation **WS 2**, 55
Verkehrsmittel transport OT 2
Verkehrssprache lingua franca **WS 3**, 108
verkleiden to dress up OT 2
Verkleidung disguise **WS 1**, 31
verklemmt uptight OT 5
verknallt: in jdn. verknallt sein to have a crush on OT 4
Verkörperung personification OT 5
verkünden to declare OT 4
Verkuppeln matchmaking **WS 1**, 28
Verlangen appetite **WS 3**, 104
verlangen to demand OT 4; to long **WS 2**, 55
verlängert prolonged OT 5
verlangsamen to slow down OT 4
verlassen to leave OT 1
  sich verlassen auf to depend on OT 2; to rely on OT 5
verlässlich reliable OT 4
verlegen embarrassed OT 3
Verleger(in) publisher OT 5
verleihen to award OT 4
verletzen to harm OT 2; to insult **WS 2**, 60
verletzend hurtful **WS 3**, 107
verletzlich vulnerable **WS 1**, 40
Verletzung injury OT 2; violation **WS 1**, 25
verlieren to lose OT 1
Verlierer(in) loser OT 5
verloben: sich verloben to get engaged **WS 1**, 29
Verlust loss OT 5
Vermächtnis legacy **WS 1**, 14
vermarktbar marketable OT 4
Vermarktung marketing OT 4
vermeidbar preventable OT 5
vermeiden to avoid OT 4
Vermeidung prevention OT 2
vermenschlichen to humanize **WS 1**, 25
vermischen to mix up OT 2
vermissen to miss OT 2
vermitteln to impart; to communicate OT 4; to convey OT 5; to place **WS 2**, 55
Vermittlung mediation OT 1
Vermögen wealth OT 4
vermuten to suppose OT 1; to suspect **WS 1**, 26
vernachlässigen to neglect **WS 2**, 53
Verneinung negative OT 1
Vernetzung connectivity **WS 4**, 133
vernichten to destruct **WS 1**, 21; to annihilate **WS 4**, 136
vernünftig sensible OT 3
veröffentlichen to publish OT 2; to release OT 4; to publicize **WS 1**, 33
Veröffentlichung publication OT 5
Verordnung act OT 5
Verpächter landlord **WS 1**, 16
Verpackung packaging OT 3
Verpflegungsservice catering service OT 4
verpflichten to bind **WS 3**, 94
verpflichtet obliged OT 5
Verpflichtung obligation OT 2; commitment **WS 2**, 67
Verputz plaster OT 1
Verrat betrayal **WS 3**, 96
verraten to reveal OT 5
Verräter(in) snitch OT 5
verringern to reduce OT 2
verrückt crazy OT 2; wacky OT 4; insane OT 5
Verrückter madman OT 4
Versammlung assembly OT 1
verschieben to shift **WS 1**, 14
verschieden diverse OT 4
  verschiedene various OT 5
verschlechtern to worsen OT 5
verschlimmern to worsen OT 5; to compound **WS 4**, 133
Verschlüsselung code OT 1
Verschmelzung fusion **WS 1**, 30
verschmutzen to pollute OT 5
verschneit snowy OT 3
verschonen to spare **WS 1**, 27
verschreiben to prescribe **WS 1**, 39
verschütten to spill OT 2
verschwenden to waste OT 3
verschwimmen to blur OT 5
verschwinden to disappear OT 3
verschwitzt sweaty OT 5
versehentlich by accident; by mistake OT 2; accidentally OT 3
verseuchen to pollute OT 5
versichern to reassure **WS 1**, 27; to assure **WS 2**, 55
Version version OT 3
Versöhnung reconciliation OT 5
versorgen (mit) to provide OT 4
Versprechen promise OT 2
versprechen to promise OT 2
Verstand mind OT 1
verstärken to reinforce OT 5; to amplify **WS 1**, 14; to enhance **WS 3**, 110
verstärken to amplify **WS 1**, 14
Verstärker amplifier OT 2
verstaubt dusty **WW**, 11
verstauchen to sprain OT 2
verstecken to hide OT 3
verstehen to understand OT 1
Verstümmelung mutilation **WS 1**, 14
Versuch attempt OT 2
  einen Versuch machen to have a go OT 2
versuchen to try OT 1
  jdn. versuchen to tempt OT 5
versus versus OT 4
vertäuen to moor OT 3
verteidigen to defend OT 3
Verteidiger(in) defender OT 3
Verteidigung defence OT 5
verteilen to distribute OT 4; to dispense **WS 3**, 94
Verteilung distribution **WS 3**, 101
vertikal vertical OT 4
Vertrauen faith **WS 1**, 15
vertrauen to trust OT 3
vertraut familiar OT 2; accustomed **WS 2**, 56
vertreten to represent **WS 1**, 14
Vertreter(in) champion **WS 1**, 18
vertrieben displaced **WS 1**, 14
verunreinigen to contaminate **WS 3**, 100
Verunreinigung contamination **WS 3**, 100
verursachen to cause OT 2
verurteilen to sentence; to convict OT 5
Verurteilte(r) convict OT 5
Verurteilung sentencing OT 5
vervielfachen to multiply **WS 4**, 134
vervollständigen to complete OT 1
Verwahrung custody OT 5
verwaist orphaned **WS 2**, 67
Verwalter(in) steward OT 4
Verwaltung bureaucracy **WS 3**, 104
Verwandlung transformation OT 4
Verwandte(r) relative OT 1; relation OT 2
Verwandtschaft kin OT 5
Verweigerung denial **WS 3**, 103
verweilen to dwell **WS 1**, 15
Verweis reference OT 4
verwelken to fade OT 2
verwirklichen to fulfil OT 4
verwirrend confusing OT 2

verwirrt confused OT 2
verwundbar vulnerable **WS 1**, 40
verwundern to amaze OT 5
verwüsten to vandalize OT 5; to devastate **WS 1**, 128
Verzeihung pardon OT 5
verzögern to delay **WS 1**, 22
verzweifelt desperate OT 3; distressed **WS 1**, 21
vibrieren to vibrate OT 4
Video video OT 1
  Sammlung von Videos reel **WS 4**, 144
Video-Blog vlog OT 3
Videoclip video clip OT 2
Videokassette video OT 1
Videokonferenztechnik video conferencing OT 4
Videospiel video game OT 2
Vieh livestock OT 5
Viehbestand stock OT 2; livestock OT 5
Viehhaltung cattle ranching OT 5
Viehhirt(in) cowherd **WS 1**, 16
viel lots; a lot; much OT 1; plenty OT 2
  viele many OT 1; numerous OT 5
Vielfalt variety OT 5; array **WS 1**, 43
vielfältig diverse OT 4
Vielfältigkeit diversity OT 4
vielleicht maybe OT 1; perhaps OT 3
vielseitig versatile OT 3
vier four OT 1
Viertel quarter OT 1
  viertel vor quarter to OT 1
vierundzwanzig twenty-four OT 1
vierzehn fourteen OT 1
vierzig forty OT 1
violett violet OT 1
viral viral **WS 2**, 69
virtuell virtual OT 4
Virus virus **WS 2**, 61
Vision vision OT 4
visualisieren to visualize **WS 2**, 57
Visualisierung visualization OT 3
visuell visual OT 2
Visum visa OT 4
Vita Curriculum Vitae OT 5
Vizekönig viceroy **WS 1**, 14
Vlog vlog OT 3
Vlogger(in) vlogger OT 3
Vogel bird OT 1
Vokal vowel OT 1
Volks... folk OT 2
Volksheld folk hero OT 4
Volkstanz country dancing OT 1
voll full OT 1
Volleyball volleyball OT 3
völlig thoroughly OT 5
Vollstreckung enforcement OT 5
Volontär(in) intern OT 4
Voluntourismus voluntourism **WS 2**, 66
von of; from; by; off OT 1
vor ago; before; in front of OT 1
Voraus: im Voraus beforehand OT 5
voraus ahead OT 3
Voraussetzung requirement OT 5
vorbeifahren to pass OT 3
vorbereiten to prepare; to get ready OT 1
Vorbereitung preparation OT 2
Vordergrund foreground OT 3
Vorderseite front OT 1
Vorderteil front OT 1
Voreingenommenheit bias OT 5
Vorfahr(in) ancestor OT 3
Vorfall incident OT 5
Vorfreude anticipation **WS 2**, 78
vorführen to act out OT 1; to demonstrate OT 4
vorgeben to pretend OT 2
Vorhand forehand OT 3
Vorhang curtain OT 2
vorherig previous OT 4
vorherige prior **WS 1**, 38
Vorherrschaft dominance **WS 3**, 109
Vorhersage prediction OT 2
vorhersagen to predict OT 4
vorhersehbar predictable OT 5
vorhersehen to foresee **WS 2**, 56
vorknöpfen: sich vorknöpfen to button-hole **WS 1**, 28
Vorlage template OT 4
Vorliebe preference OT 3
vormundschaftlich custodial OT 5
Vorname first name OT 2
Vorrat supply OT 3
Vorschlag suggestion OT 1; proposition **WS 4**, 132
vorschlagen to suggest OT 1
Vorschrift regulation OT 5
Vorschule preschool OT 5
vorsichtig careful OT 1; cautious **WS 3**, 103
  vorsichtig sein to beware **WS 3**, 112
Vorsitz: den Vorsitz führen to preside **WS 3**, 94
Vorspeise starter OT 1
Vorsprung headstart **WS 2**, 56
vorstellen to imagine; to present OT 1; to introduce OT 2
Vorstellung show OT 1; introduction OT 2
Vorstellungsbeginn showtime OT 4
Vorstellungsgespräch interview OT 1
  ein Vorstellungsgespräch führen to interview OT 1
Vorteil benefit; pro OT 2; advantage OT 3
Vortrag talk OT 2
vorübergehend temporary **WS 1**, 14
Vorurteil prejudice OT 5; preconception **WS 2**, 71
vorwärts forward **WS 1**, 15
vorwerfen to allege **WS 1**, 18
Vorwurf: jdm. Vorwürfe machen to blame OT 5
vorziehbar preferable **WS 1**, 78
vorziehen to prefer OT 1

W

Waage scale **WS 1**, 30
wach awake OT 2
Wachsamkeit guard **WS 1**, 27
wachsen to grow OT 1
Wachstum growth OT 5
Wächter watchman OT 5
Wächter(in) guard **WS 1**, 27
wackelig shaky OT 3
Waffe weapon OT 3
  als Waffe einsetzen to wield **WS 2**, 78
Waffel waffle OT 3
Wagen trolley; carriage OT 1; wagon OT 4; cart **WS 1**, 32
wagen to dare OT 2
Wagenzug wagon train OT 4
Wahl choice OT 1; option OT 2; election OT 3
wählen to vote OT 1; to dial OT 2; to select; to elect OT 4
wählerisch fussy OT 2
wahnsinnig insane OT 5
wahr true OT 1
während while OT 1; during OT 2; throughout OT 3; whereas OT 5; whilst **WS 2**, 62
Wahrheit truth OT 3
Wahrnehmung perception **WS 2**, 62
wahrscheinlich probably OT 2; likely OT 3
Wahrscheinlichkeit probability **WS 2**, 84
Währung currency **WS 1**, 12
Wahrzeichen landmark OT 4
Waise orphan **WS 2**, 67
Wal whale OT 1
Wald forest OT 1
Waldbrand wildfire OT 2
Waldhorn French horn OT 1
Walfang whaling OT 2
walisisch Welsh OT 1

Walspeck blubber OT 2
Wand wall OT 1
Wanderer / Wanderin hiker OT 2; walker OT 3
Wandern hiking OT 1
wandern to hike OT 1
Wanderstiefel hiking boot OT 2
Wanderung walk; hike OT 2
Wandgemälde mural OT 2
Wandschrank closet OT 2
Wandzeitung wall display OT 2
wann when OT 1
wann auch immer whenever OT 4
Wanne tub **WS 3**, 101
warm warm OT 2
warnen to warn OT 3
warten to wait OT 1; to hang on OT 2
Wärter(in) warder **WS 2**, 78
Warteschlange queue OT 1
Wartung maintenance OT 3
warum why OT 1
was what OT 1
was auch immer whatever OT 3
Wäsche laundry OT 4
waschen to wash OT 2
Waschraum washroom **WS 3**, 96
Wasser water OT 1
unter Wasser underwater OT 2
Wasser... aquatic OT 4; hydro **WS 3**, 99
Wasserbus waterbus OT 3
wasserdicht waterproof OT 2
Wasserfall falls; waterfall OT 1
Wasserhahn faucet OT 4
Wasserkocher kettle OT 2
Wasserloch waterhole OT 5
Wasserstelle watering hole OT 5
Wasserstoff hydrogen **WS 3**, 99
Webinar webinar OT 4
Webkonferenz web conference OT 4
Webseite website OT 1
Wechsel transition OT 5
Wechselgeld change OT 1
wechseln to change OT 1
Wecker alarm; alarm clock OT 2
weder neither OT 2
weder noch nor OT 4
Weg track; way; path OT 1
weg off; away OT 1
Wegbereiter(in) groundbreaker **WS 4**, 138
wegen due to OT 5
wegräumen to put away OT 2
wegrennen to rush off OT 2
wegschicken to dismiss OT 5
Wegweiser signpost OT 5
wegwerfen to throw away OT 2; to discard **WS 3**, 98
wehen to blow OT 2
wehtun to hurt OT 1; to ache OT 3
weiblich female OT 2; feminine **WS 2**, 70
weich soft OT 3
Weichei sissy **WS 3**, 96
Weide(land) pasture **WS 1**, 32
weigern: sich weigern to refuse OT 4
Weihnachten Christmas OT 1
Weihnachtsmarkt Christmas market OT 2
weil because OT 1
Wein wine OT 1
weinen to cry OT 1
Weise manner OT 2
Weisheit wisdom **WS 1**, 19
Weisheitszahn wisdom tooth OT 5
weiß white OT 1
weit far OT 1; wide OT 2
weiter anymore OT 2; further OT 4
Weiterbildungslehrgang training course OT 2
weiterführende Schule secondary school OT 1
weitergehen to move on OT 4
weiterhin furthermore OT 5
weitermachen to continue OT 1; to go ahead OT 4
weitverbreitet widespread **WS 1**, 18
Weizen wheat OT 5
welche(r, -s) which OT 1
Welle wave OT 1
Wellensittich budgie OT 1
Wellness wellness OT 4
Welpe puppy OT 2
Welt world OT 1
aus aller Welt from around the world OT 1
weltoffen cosmopolitan OT 5
Weltraum space OT 2
Weltraumforschung space exploration OT 4
Weltsicht worldview **WS 2**, 57
weltweit worldwide OT 3; global OT 4
Wendel spiral OT 5
Wendung phrase OT 1
wenige few OT 1
wer who OT 1
wer auch immer whoever OT 4
Werbeagentur advertiser OT 3
Werbebanner banner ad OT 5
Werber advertiser OT 3
Werbung advertisement OT 1; ad; advertising OT 2
Werbung machen für to advertise OT 2
werden to become; shall; will OT 2
werfen to throw OT 1; to toss OT 3
Werft dockyard OT 3
Werkstatt workshop OT 1; garage OT 4
Werkzeug tool OT 2
Wert value OT 4
wertvoll valuable OT 2
Wesen creature OT 4; essence **WS 3**, 96
wesentlich essential OT 4; crucial **WS 3**, 96
Wesentliche essence **WS 3**, 96
Wespe wasp OT 3
wessen whose OT 2
Weste vest OT 2
Westen west OT 1
mittlerer Westen midwest; midwestern OT 4
westwärts westward OT 4
Wettbewerb competition OT 1
wetteifernd competitively OT 4
wetten to bet OT 1
Wetter weather OT 1
Wettkampf match OT 1
wichtig important OT 1; relevant; essential OT 4; critical; dominant OT 5; significant **WS 1**, 15
Wichtigkeit importance OT 2; significance OT 5
widersetzen: sich widersetzen to defy **WS 1**, 29
widersprechen to contradict **WS 1**, 38
Widerspruch contradiction **WS 2**, 53
Widerstand resistance OT 5; disobedience **WS 1**, 18
widerstandsfähig resistant OT 5
widerstehen to resist OT 5
wie how; as OT 1
wieder again OT 1
wiederbeleben to revive **WS 3**, 98
Wiedergabe rendition **WS 1**, 43
Wiedergabeliste playlist OT 4
wiedergeboren werden to reincarnate **WS 1**, 32
Wiedergutmachung:
Wiedergutmachung leisten to make amends OT 5
wiederherstellen to restore OT 4
wiederholen to repeat OT 1; to reiterate **WS 1**, 19
wiederholter Stellenwechsel job hopping OT 5
Wiederholung repetition OT 4
Wiedersehen! goodbye OT 1
Wiederverheiratung remarriage OT 5

wiederverwendbar reusable OT 3
wiederverwenden to reuse OT 2
wiederverwerten to recycle OT 2
Wiederverwerter(in) recycler OT 3
wiegen to weigh OT 3
Wiese meadow OT 2
wild wild OT 2; feral OT 5; ferocious **WS 1**, 16; fierce **WS 2**, 62
Wilde(r) savage **WS 3**, 94
Wilder barbarian **WS 1**, 14
Wilderei poaching OT 3
Wilderer / Wilderin poacher OT 3
Wildfang tomboy OT 5
Wildnis wilderness OT 2
Wildwasser fahren white water rafting OT 3
willkommen welcome OT 1
willkürlich random OT 5
Wimper eyelash **WS 2**, 70
Wind wind OT 2
Windel nappy OT 3
winden to wind OT 5
windig windy OT 2
windsurfen to windsurf OT 1
Windsurfer(in) windsurfer OT 1
winken to wave OT 2
Winsch windlass OT 3
Winter winter OT 1
Winterschlaf: Winterschlaf halten to hibernate **WS 3**, 98
winzig tiny OT 1
wir we OT 1
wirbeln to spiral **WS 1**, 22
wirklich really OT 1; truly; actual OT 5
wirksam effective OT 4
Wirksamkeit effectiveness OT 5; efficiency **WS 3**, 144
Wirkung effect OT 3
Wirtschaft economy OT 3
wirtschaftlich economic OT 4
Wirtschaftswissenschaften economics OT 5
Wirtschaftswissenschaftler(in) economist **WS 4**, 142
wischen to wipe **WS 1**, 16
Wischtuch wipe OT 4
Wissen science OT 1; knowledge OT 4
wissen to know OT 1
Wissenschaft studies OT 1
wissenschaftlich scientific OT 3
Witz joke OT 2
witzig witty **WS 1**, 17
wo where OT 1
  wo (auch) immer wherever OT 3
woanders elsewhere OT 5
Woche week OT 1
Wochenende weekend OT 1
Wochentag weekday OT 3
wöchentlich weekly OT 3
Wohlbefinden wellness OT 4
Wohlfahrtsorganisation charity OT 2
wohlhabend prosperous **WS 3**, 94
Wohlstand prosperity **WS 1**, 24
Wohltäter(in) philanthropist **WS 3**, 100
Wohltätigkeits... charitable **WS 1**, 44
Wohlwollen goodness **WS 1**, 27
Wohn... residential **WS 1**, 25
wohnen to live OT 1
Wohnmobil camper van OT 4
Wohnraum housing OT 3
Wohnung flat; apartment OT 1
Wohnwagen caravan OT 1
Wohnzimmer living room OT 1
Wolke cloud OT 1
Wolkenkratzer skyscraper OT 3
wolkig cloudy OT 4
Wolle wool OT 2
  aus Wolle woolly OT 2
wollen to want OT 1
wollig woolly OT 2
Wombat wombat OT 5
Wort word OT 1
Wortart part of speech OT 2
Wörterbuch dictionary OT 1
wörtlich literal OT 5
Wortspiel pun **WS 3**, 119
Wrack wreck OT 3
wunderbar wonderful OT 1; miraculous **WS 1**, 27
wunderschön gorgeous **WS 2**, 61
wünschen to wish OT 3
wünschenswert desirable **WS 1**, 21
Würde dignity **WS 2**, 55
Wurm worm OT 1
Wurst sausage OT 1
Wurzel root OT 3
wuseln to bustle **WS 2**, 65
Wüste desert OT 3
Wüstenbildung desertification **WS 4**, 136
Wut anger OT 3
wüten to rage OT 5
wütend furious **WS 2**, 58

Y
Yoga yoga OT 5

Z
zaghaft timid **WS 3**, 96
Zahl number OT 1; figure OT 3
zählbar countable OT 1
zählen to count OT 1
zahlreich numerous OT 5
Zahltag payday OT 5
Zahn tooth OT 2
Zahnarzt / -ärztin dentist OT 5
Zahnbürste toothbrush OT 4
Zahnpasta toothpaste OT 4
Zauber magic OT 1
Zauberer / Zauberin magician OT 1
Zaun fence OT 5
Zebra zebra OT 1
Zebrastreifen zebra crossing OT 1
Zeh toe OT 1
Zehenspitzen tippy toes **WS 3**, 96
zehn ten OT 1
Zeichen drawing OT 1; token OT 5
Zeichensetzung punctuation OT 1
Zeichentrickfilm cartoon OT 4
zeichnen to draw OT 1; to sketch OT 4
Zeichnung drawing OT 1
zeigen to show OT 1; to indicate OT 5
Zeit time OT 1; period OT 3
Zeitachse timeline OT 2
Zeitform tense OT 1
zeitgenössisch contemporary OT 3
Zeitpunkt timing OT 3
zeitraubend time-consuming **WS 3**, 101
Zeitrechnung: unserer Zeitrechnung AD (Anno Domini) OT 2
Zeitschrift magazine OT 1
Zeituhr timer OT 5
Zeitung newspaper OT 1
Zeitwort verb OT 1
Zelle cell OT 1; booth OT 4
Zelt tent OT 1; marquee OT 2
zelten to camp OT 1
Zeltplatz campsite OT 1; campground OT 2
zensieren to censor **WS 2**, 79
Zensierung censorship **WS 2**, 79
Zensor(in) censor **WS 2**, 79
Zensur censorship **WS 2**, 79
Zentimeter centimetre (cm) OT 2
Zentral- central OT 1
Zentrum centre OT 1
zerbröckeln to crumble **WS 2**, 62
zeremoniell ceremonial OT 3
zerfallen to crumble **WS 2**, 62
zerkleinert shredded OT 2
zerschlagen to crush **WS 1**, 25
zerstören to destroy OT 2; to vandalize OT 5; to ruin **WS 1**, 14; to destruct **WS 1**, 21; to devastate **WS 1**, 41
zerstörend destructive OT 5
Zerstörung destruction **WS 1**, 21
Zertifikat certificate OT 1
Zeug stuff OT 2; gear **WS 1**, 15

Zeuge / Zeugin in einer Sache sein to witness OT 5
Zeugnis certificate OT 1
Ziege goat OT 4
ziehen to draw; to pull OT 1; to pluck **WS 1**, 27; to wrench **WS 1**, 27
nach sich ziehen to yield **WS 3**, 98
Ziel target OT 2; aim; ambition; objective OT 4
zielen to aim OT 4
zielen auf to target OT 5
ziemlich quite OT 2; rather OT 3; relatively OT 5
Ziffer digit OT 2
Zinn tin OT 2
zirkulieren to circulate OT 4
Zirkus circus **WS 2**, 65
zischen to whizz OT 2
Zitadelle fortress OT 3
zitieren to quote; to cite OT 2
Zitronenlimonade lemonade OT 1
zittern to tremble OT 2
Zivilisation civilization **WS 1**, 12
zögern to hesitate OT 3
Zoll customs OT 2
Zoll (2,54 cm) inch OT 2
zollfrei duty free OT 2
Zombie zombie OT 2
Zone zone OT 2
Zoo zoo OT 1
Zopf: dünner Zopf cornrow **WS 2**, 69
Zöpfe braids **WS 2**, 69
zornig angrily OT 2
zu too; to OT 1
Zubehör accessory OT 3
Zucchini zucchini OT 3
züchten to breed **WS 1**, 24
Zucker sugar OT 3
Zuckerguß icing **WS 2**, 59
Zuckermais sweet corn OT 1
Zufall chance OT 2
zufällig accidentally OT 3; random OT 5
Zufälligkeiten incidentals **WS 2**, 78
Zuflucht resort OT 2
zufrieden pleased OT 1; satisfied **WS 2**, 93
zufriedenstellend satisfying OT 5
Zug train OT 1
Zugang access OT 4
zugänglich accessible OT 2
zugeben to admit OT 4
zugestehen to concede **WS 3**, 107
zügig swift **WS 2**, 62
zugreifen auf to access OT 4
Zugriff access OT 4
zugunsten in favour **WS 1**, 14
Zuhause home OT 1
zuhören to listen OT 1
Zuhörer(in) listener OT 1
Zukunft future OT 2
zumachen to shut OT 2
zunächst initially OT 5
Zunahme increase OT 3
Zunder tinder OT 2
Zündung ignition OT 4
zunehmend increasingly OT 5
Zuneigung affection OT 5
Zunge tongue OT 3
zurechtkommen to cope OT 5
zurück back OT 1
zurückführen to trace back **WS 2**, 83
zurückgehen to decrease OT 5; to backtrack **WS 4**, 133
zurückhalten to withhold **WS 2**, 78
zurückholen to retrieve **WS 1**, 25
zurückkehren to return OT 2; to head back OT 5
zurückrudern to backtrack **WS 4**, 133
zurücktreten to resign OT 5
zurückweisen to reject **WS 3**, 103
zurückzahlen to repay OT 5
zusammen together OT 1; jointly **WS 2**, 54
Zusammenarbeit cooperation **WS 3**, 98; collaboration **WS 3**, 109
zusammenarbeiten to collaborate **WS 1**, 41
Zusammenbruch breakdown **WS 3**, 103
zusammenfassen to summarize OT 2; to sum up OT 4
Zusammenfassung summary OT 3
Zusammenhang context OT 4
zusammenkommen to bond **WS 1**, 15
zusammenpassen:
nicht zusammenpassen to clash OT 2
zusammenpassend:
nicht zusammenpassend mismatched OT 4
zusammensacken to slump OT 4
zusammenstellen to compile **WS 2**, 60
zusammenstoßen to bump into OT 2
zusammentragen to collate **WS 4**, 139
zusammenziehen to contract **WS 4**, 136
zusätzlich in addition to OT 4; additional **WS 4**, 136
Zuschauer(in) spectator; viewer OT 3; bystander **WS 4**, 136
zuschlagen to strike OT 1
zuschreiben to credit **WS 1**, 31; to attribute **WS 2**, 81
Zuschreibung credit **WS 2**, 68
Zuschuss grant OT 5
zuspielen to pass OT 3
zuständig in charge OT 1
zusteigen to get on OT 2
zustimmen to approve OT 3
Zutat ingredient OT 2
zuversichtlich confident; confidently OT 2
zuvorderst foremost OT 5
zuvorkommen to pre-empt **WS 3**, 107
Zwangsarbeiter(in) bonded laborer OT 4
zwanzig twenty OT 1
Zweck purpose OT 4
zweckgerichtet purposeful **WS 3**, 112
zwecklos pointless OT 4
zweckmäßig: zweckmäßiges Gerät convenience OT 4
zwei two OT 1
zwei Wochen fortnight OT 2
Zweifel doubt OT 4; distrust **WS 1**, 14
zweifellos undoubtedly **WS 1**, 27; arguably **WS 1**, 30
Zweig twig OT 2
zweimal twice OT 2
zweisprachig bilingual OT 2
zweite(r, -s) second OT 1
zweitens secondly OT 2
zweiundzwanzig twenty-two OT 1
Zwiebel onion OT 2
Zwiebelring onion ring OT 2
Zwilling twin OT 1
zwingen to force OT 2
zwischen between OT 1; among OT 3
Zwischenstation waypoint OT 2
zwölf twelve OT 1
zynisch cynical **WS 1**, 17

Dictionary: Names

A

African National Congress (ANC) ['æfrɪkən 'næʃənəl 'kɒŋgres] a political group established to fight for the rights of black people in South Africa **WS 2,** 54

Afrikaans [æfrɪ'kɑ:ns] a language of South Africa **WS 2,** 52

Aldous Huxley ['hʌksli, 'ɔ:ldəs] British writer, author of *Brave New World* **WS 3,** 104

All-India Muslim League [ɔ:l-'ɪndiə 'mʊslɪm li:g] political party founded in British India in 1904 to advocate for Muslim interests in the region **WS 1,** 37

Angie Thomas ['ændʒi 'tɒməs] American writer, most famous for her book *The Hate U Give* **WS 3,** 97

Aravind Adiga [ə'rævɪnd ə'di:gə] Indian writer and journalist who wrote *The White Tiger* **WS 1,** 16

Autumn Peltier ['ɔ:təm 'pɛltiər] a water-rights advocate and global youth environmental activist **WS 3,** 95

B

Balaknama ['bələkˌnɑ:mə] an Indian newspaper which is run by children living in the slums of Delhi **WS 1,** 25

Bangalore ['bæŋgəlɔ:r] the capital and largest city of the southern Indian state of Karnataka **WS 1,** 16

Basil D'Oliveira ['bæzəl dɒlɪ'vɪərə] an international cricketer of South African Cape Coloured background **WS 2,** 58

Bella Lack [''belə læk] a young environmental campaigner from England **WS 1,** 21

Bengal [ˌben'gɔ:l] an area of South Asia that includes Bangladesh and the Indian state of West Bengal **WS 1,** 14

Bhangra ['bʌŋgrə] a type of music that is a mixture of Punjabi traditional music and western popular music **WS 1,** 15

Bombay [ˌbɒm'beɪ] the largest city in India, on the west coast of the country; it is now called Mumbai **WS 1,** 31

Buddhism ['bʊdɪzəm] a religion of East and Central Asia, based on the teaching of Gautama Buddha **WS 1,** 32

C

Calcutta [kæl'kʌtə] the former name of Kolkata, a city and port in Eastern India on the Hooghly River and capital of West Bengal state **WS 1,** 14

Cape Town [keɪp taʊn] a large city in South Africa near the Cape of Good Hope **WS 2,** 64

Chad le Clos [tʃæd lə 'kloʊ] a South African swimmer **WS 2,** 80

Charl du Toit [ʃɑ:rl du: 'tɔɪt] a South African former paralympic sprinter **WS 2,** 61

D

Desmond Tutu ['dezmənd 'tu:tu:] a South African priest in the Anglican religion, who was Archbishop of Cape Town **WS 2,** 83

Dhaka ['dækə] the capital and the most important industrial city of Bangladesh **WS 1,** 14

Diwali [dɪ'wɑ:li] a Hindu festival that is celebrated in autumn **WS 1,** 12

Donald Wood ['dɒnəld wʊd] a South African journalist and anti-apartheid activist **WS 2,** 76

Durban ['dɜ:rbən] the third most populous city in South Africa after Johannesburg and Cape Town **WS 2,** 53

E

Earthshot [ɜ:θʃɒt] a prize awarded to five winners each year for their contributions to environmentalism **WS 3,** 101

Eddy Grant ['ɛdi gɹ'ænt] Guyanese-British singer, songwriter and multi-instrumentalist **WS 2,** 72

Edmonton ['edməntən] the capital city of Alberta, West Canada, on the North Saskatchewan River **WS 3,** 114

Enoch Sontonga ['i:nɒk sɒn'tɒŋgə] a South African composer, who is best known for writing the Xhosa hymn *Nkosi Sikelel' iAfrika* **WS 2,** 68

Extinction Rebellion [ɪks'tɪŋkʃən rɪ'bɛliən] a UK-founded global environmental movement **WS 1,** 21

F

Fahrenheit 451 [færənhaɪt] a 1953 dystopian novel by American writer Ray Bradbury **WS 3,** 104

Falgun [f'ælgʌn] the 12th month of the Hindu calendar **WS 1,** 40

Frederik Willem de Klerk [də 'klɜ:k] president of South Africa from 1989 to 1994 **WS 2,** 54

G

George Orwell [dʒɔ:dʒ 'ɔ:wel] the pen name of Eric Blair, a British writer best known for his novels *Animal Farm* and *Nineteen Eighty-Four* **WS 3,** 104

Greenland ['gri:nlənd] a large island in the North Atlantic Ocean, near Northeast Canada **WS 3,** 95

Gully Boy Divine ['gʌli bɔɪ dɪ'vaɪn] an Indian rapper of Goan descent **WS 1,** 31

H

Hector Pieterson ['hektə 'pi:təsən] a South African schoolboy who was shot and killed at the age of 12 during the Soweto uprising **WS 2,** 79

Himalaya [ˌhɪmə'leɪəz] a long range of mountains in Southern Asia which includes the highest mountain in the world, Mount Everest **WS 1,** 12

Hindi ['hɪndi] an official language in India **WS 1,** 12

Hinduism ['hɪndu-ɪzəm] the main religion in India, which includes the belief in reincarnation **WS 1,** 12

HIV [ˌeɪtʃ aɪ 'vi:] a type of virus that enters the body through blood or sexual activity, and can develop into AIDS **WS 2,** 67

Holi ['ho:li:] a popular and significant Hindu festival celebrated as the Festival of Colours, Love, and Spring **WS 1,** 12

Hong Kong [ˌhɒn ˈkɒŋ] an area on the south coast of China **WS 3,** 108

I

India [ˈɪndiə] a large country in Southern Asia **WW,** 10

Indian Ocean [ˈɪndiən ˈəʊʃən] the third largest ocean in the world, which lies between Africa and Australia **WS 1,** 12

Inuit [ˈɪnjuɪt] someone who belongs to a race of people who live in the very cold areas of North America **WS 3,** 95

Invictus [ɪnvˈɪktəs] a 2009 biographical sports film directed by Clint Eastwood and starring Morgan Freeman and Matt Damon **WS 2,** 59

isiXhosa [ˌɪsɪkshˈkɔːsə] the Bantu language spoken by the Xhosa people, which is known for including sounds called 'clicks' **WS 2,** 52

isiZulu [ˌɪsɪkshzuːluː] the language used by the Zulu people **WS 2,** 52

J

Joburg [ˈdʒəʊbɜːg] an informal name for Johannesburg **WS 2,** 72

Johannesburg [dʒəʊˈhænəsbɜːg] the largest city in South Africa, and a centre for business and industry **WS 2,** 52

K

Karachi [kəˈrɑːtʃi] a city in southern Pakistan, formerly the capital and still the main port and industrial centre **WS 1,** 14

Kashmir [ˌkæʃˈmɪə] an area of Northwest India and Northeast Pakistan; part of it belongs to India, and part to Pakistan **WS 1,** 14

Kenya [ˈkenjə] a country in East Africa which became independent from Britain in 1963, and is a member of the British Commonwealth **WS 1,** 21

Kruger National Park [ˈkryjər ˈnæʃənəl pɑːk] a South African National Park and one of the largest game reserves in Africa **WS 2,** 53

Kwela [ˈkweɪlə] a pennywhistle-based street music from South Africa with jazzy underpinnings and a distinctive, skiffle-like beat **WS 2,** 68

L

Labrador [ˈlæbrədɔː] a geographic and cultural region within the Canadian province of Newfoundland and Labrador **WS 3,** 95

Lahore [ləˈhɔːr] the second largest city of Pakistan and the provincial capital of Punjab; located near the Indian border on Ravi river **WS 1,** 14

Lake Huron [ˈhjʊərən] the second largest of the Great Lakes, on the border between the US and Canada **WS 3,** 100

M

Mahatma Gandhi [məˈhætmə ˈgɑndi] an Indian lawyer and politician who led the fight for India's independence from the British **WS 1,** 14

Malala Yousafzai [məˈlaːlə jusəf ˈzəj] a Pakistani female education activist **WS 1,** 38

Marabi [mæɹˈɑːbi] a style of music that evolved in South Africa over the 20th century **WS 2,** 68

Margaret Atwood [ˈmɑːgərət ˈætwʊd] a Canadian writer of short stories, poems, and novels, usually about the lives and relationships of women **WS 3,** 92

Mbube [ˈɛmbjˈuːb] a form of South African vocal music, made famous by the South African group Ladysmith Black Mambazo **WS 2,** 68

Muhammad Ali Jinnah [məʊˈhæməd ˈæli ˈdʒɪnə] the first governor-general of Pakistan, from 1947 until his death; Jinnah was the leader of the Muslim League in India for many years **WS 1,** 14

Mumbai [ˌmʊmˈbaɪ] the name of the city formerly known as Bombay; it is the largest city in India, on the west coast of the country **WS 1,** 12

N

Natalie du Toit [nˈærɛli dˈuː dʊˈtɔɪ] a South African swimmer **WS 2,** 80

Nelson Mandela [ˈnɛlsən mænˈdelə] the leader of South Africa's ANC party from 1994 to 1997, and the first black president of South Africa, from 1994 to 1999 **WS 2,** 52

New Delhi [njuː ˈdɛli] the capital city of India, built to the south of the old city of Delhi by the British in 1912 **WS 1,** 12

O

Olympics [əˈlɪmpɪks] an international sports event held every four years in different countries **WS 2,** 60

Ontario [ɒnˈteəriəʊ] a province in the east of central Canada, containing the country's largest city, Toronto, and over a third of its population **WS 3,** 92

Ottawa [ˈɒtəwə] the capital city of Canada, in the Southeast of the country; one third of its people are French-speaking **WS 3,** 104

P

Pakistan [ˌpɑːkɪˈstɑːn,] a Muslim country in Asia, west of India and east of Afghanistan and Iran **WS 1,** 12

Paralympics [ˌpærəˈlɪmpɪks] an international sports event held every four years for disabled athletes **WS 2,** 61

Parsi [pɑːˈsiː] a member of an ancient Persian religious group in India **WS 1,** 14

Paul Simon [pɔːl ˈsaɪmən] a US singer and songwriter who made many successful records with Art Garfunkel in the 1960s **WS 2,** 68

Plains Cree [pleɪnz kɹˈiː] a specific community of North American Indigenous people **WS 3,** 95

Pretoria [prɪˈtɔːriə] a city in the northern part of South Africa, where the government departments are based **WS 2,** 59

Punjab [ˈpʌndʒɑːb] a large area in Eastern Pakistan and Northwestern India **WS 1,** 14

Punjabi [pʌnˈdʒɑːbi] someone from the Punjab **WS 1,** 15

Q

Quebec [kwɪˈbek] a province in Eastern Canada, whose capital city is also called Quebec, and whose largest city is Montreal **WS 3,** 111

R
Ray Bradbury [reɪ ˈbrædbəri] an American science-fiction writer whose best-known stories include *Fahrenheit 451* and *The Halloween Tree* **WS 3,** 104
Richard Attenborough [ˌrɪtʃəd ˈætnbrə] an English film actor and director **WS 2,** 76

S
Sanskrit [ˈsænskrɪt] an ancient language of India **WS 1,** 18
Sikh [siːk] a member of an Indian religious group that developed from Hinduism in the 16th century **WS 1,** 12
Soweto [səˈwetəʊ] a large township that was established near Johannesburg in South Africa for black people to live in during the time of apartheid **WS 2,** 52

T
Table Mountain [ˈteɪbəl ˈmaʊntɪn] a high mountain in South Africa **WS 2,** 53
Taj Mahal [ˌtɑːdʒ məˈhɑːl] a beautiful building made of white marble in Agra, Northern India **WS 1,** 23
Thomas King [ˈtɒməs kɪŋ] a Canadian writer and broadcast presenter who most often writes about First Nations people **WS 3,** 94
Trevor Noah [ˈtrɛvə ˈnəʊə] a South African comedian, writer, producer, political commentator, actor, and former television host **WS 2,** 62
Tsotsi [tsˈɑːtsi] a 2005 crime drama film written and directed by Gavin Hood and produced by Peter Fudakowski **WS 2,** 56

U
Urdu [ˈʊəduː] the official language of Pakistan, also used in India **WS 3,** 119

V
Vasco da Gama [ˈvæskəʊ də ˈgɑːmə] a Portuguese sailor and explorer **WS 2,** 52

W
Winnipeg [ˈwɪnɪpeg] the capital city of Manitoba, in Canada **WS 3,** 95

X
Xhosa [ˈkɔːsə] a member of a group of Bantu people of South Africa **WS 2,** 63

Y
Yamuna [jəmʊnɑː] the second-largest tributary river of the Ganges by discharge and the longest tributary in India **WS 1,** 23

Z
Zambia [ˈzæmbiə] a country in South Central Africa, between Zimbabwe and the Democratic Republic of the Congo **WS 2,** 65
Zimbabwe [zɪmˈbɑːbweɪ] a country in South Central Africa, south of Zambia and north of South Africa **WS 2,** 76
Zulu [zuːluː] a member of a people in South Africa **WS 2,** 54

Acknowledgements

Text credits
Individual text credits can be found under or next to the respective texts on the page.

Picture credits
|akg-images GmbH, Berlin: Africa Media Online / Motlhalefi Mahlabe / South Photos 68.3; African Pictures 68.1. |Alamy Stock Photo, Abingdon/Oxfordshire: Action Foto Sport 53.2; Arnold, Rob 115.1; Asianet-Pakistan 24.3; Avpics 21.1; Bellinger, Jamie 106.2; Bethge, Thomas 96.1; Brlek, Dalibor 13.3; Bulley, Stephen 30.1; Burdiak, Volodymyr 64.1; Canetti 106.3; Cecil, Charles O. 15.1; Chin, Robert K. 106.4; Chris Howes/Wild Places Photography 109.4; Ciccolella, Marco 20.1; Crandall, Rob 52.5; CTK 109.1; Cukrov, Steve 23.2; Daemmrich, Bob 68.2; Deep, Vlad 69.1; Dinodia Photos 43.2; edpics 109.3; Figel, Adam Jan 66.1; Furian, Peter Hermes 52.1; gajendra bhati 34.1; Goddard Archive 2 72.1; Gorlov, Kyryl 109.5; Graham, Jeremy 41.1; Greatstock 54.2; Grimm, Michele and Tom 52.4; Harms, Frank 122.1; Horree, Peter 13.1; IanDagnall Computing 18.2; ibreakmedia 126.1; imageBROKER 13.2; insta_photos 69.2; Jeffrey Isaac Greenberg 12+ 12.1; Lacheev, Roman 57.1; Laming, Alistair 12.2; Lecocq, Sebastien 53.1; LEE SNIDER 28.1; Lund, Jacob 33.1; Majority World CIC 71.1; Marinic, Borislav 17.1; May, Steven 104.2; mohit khatri 24.2; NurPhoto SRL 67.1; Orkidia 56.1; Otis, Dimitri 52.2; PA Images 61.1, 61.2, 72.2, 100.2; Palivoda, Arsenii 45.1; Pendzich, Erik 62.1; Pham, Jamie 53.3; Pixel-shot 32.1; Prisma by Dukas Presseagentur GmbH 23.1; Prott, Andreas 93.3; PSL Images RF 52.3; public domain sourced / access rights from Hernan Caputo 93.2; public domain sourced / access rights from History and Art Collection 10.3; public domain sourced / access rights from Matteo Omied 40.1; Scammell, Gordon 115.2; Shotshop GmbH 12.3; Singh, Raj 24.1; SOPA Images Limited 70.2; Spitzbart, Wolfgang 109.2; Stevanovic, Igor 110.1; Sunshine Seeds 66.2; Tanomsup, Peachaya 92.3; Temps, Dietmar 15.2; Universal Images Group North America LLC 60.1; Wheatley, Michael 10.2; Willcocks, Helga 47.1; Wilson, Alan 102.1; Zoonar GmbH 12.5, 42.1; ZUMA Press, Inc. 54.1. |Alamy Stock Photo (RMB), Abingdon/Oxfordshire: Berkut, Anna 134.1; Daemmrich, Bob 143.1; Evans, Robert 134.2; Fernandez, Antonio Guillem

137.1; Hyderabad 140.3; Lou-Foto 132.2; Patti McConville/Stockimo 141.2; PjrNews 118.1; robertharding 136.1; Sourav Mitra 12.4; Stirling, Charles 118.2; Zefrog 106.1; ZUMA Press, Inc. 121.1. |CartoonStock.com, Bath: Baloo 2.2; Flanagan, Mike 2.1. |Creative Listening, Newick: 142.1. |Digital Learning Associates, London: 70.3. |Domke, Franz-Josef, Wunstorf: 259.1. |Donnelly, Karen, Brighton: 120.1, 139.1, 139.2, 140.1, 140.2, 143.2, 144.1. |fotolia.com, New York: rupbilde 133.1. |Getty Images, München: Gallo Images 70.1; Lee, Christopher 84.2; Media24/Gallo Images 84.1; Mondadori Portfolio/Scala, Giorgio 84.3; Natkin, Paul 86.1. |Getty Images (RF), München: VEAM Visuals 85.1; xavierarnau 46.1. |iStockphoto.com, Calgary: AaronAmat 123.1; Artis 777 67.2, 67.7, 77.1, 77.6; CarlFourie 87.1; Chainarong Prasertthai 73.1; champpixs 108.1, 117.1; dohtar 99.1; FG Trade 82.1; riya-takahashi 39.1; shank_ali 75.1; Stadtratte 95.1; Tirachard 111.3; Virtaa 67.4, 67.5, 67.6, 77.3, 77.4, 77.5. |Picture-Alliance GmbH, Frankfurt a.M.: AP Photo/Drew, Richard 100.1; dpa/Kumar, Siddhartha 25.1, 25.2; Jordan, Hanne 68.4. |Shutterstock.com, New York: A. Mertens 111.2; asiandelight 92.2; Baker, Darren 105.4; CarlosDavid 10.1; Cineberg 110.2; Dan, Comaniciu 105.2; DisobeyArt 124.1; Duval, Fred 11.1; FARBAI 96.2; fireFX 111.1; Gomez, John 21.2; Jan S. 45.2; KKFilms 10.4; McCann, Josh 138.1; Megarupa 43.1; Monkey Business Images 92.1; N. Steele 93.1; PhotographerIncognito 132.1; Rawpixel.com 94.1; Stock 4you 105.3; Vivida Photo PC 105.1. |Shutterstock.com (RM), New York: 26.2; Anglo Enterprise/Vineyard/Kobal 104.1; Celador Films/Pathe International/Kobal 26.1; ErikaDoss/20th Century Fox/Kobal 97.1; Moviestore 59.1. |stock.adobe.com, Dublin: Andy 67.3, 77.2; donatas1205 141.1; Olga 18.1. |United Nations, New York, NY: https://www.un.org/sustainabledevelopment/ “The content of this publication has not been approved by the United Nations and does not reflect the views of the United Nations or its officials or Member States.” 135.1. |Williamson, Pete, Kent, Southorough, Tunbridge Wells: 48.1, 49.1, 50.1, 50.2, 50.3, 51.1, 88.1, 89.1, 89.2, 90.1, 90.2, 91.1, 91.2, 128.1, 129.1, 130.1, 131.1, 131.2.

Audio credits

Dialogues and words and phrases produced by Anne Rosenfeld for RBA Productions (rbaproductions.co.uk). Recording engineer Mark Smith.

Video credits

Video 3, 4, 7, 10, 14, 16, 21, 24: produced by Wildfang Video- und Audioproduktion, Berlin
Video 6: Born Free Foundation, Born Free Podcast #3 | Bella Lack, 13.09.2019
Video 18: produced by Digital Learning Associates (DLA), London
Video 23: Duke Fuqua Insights: How Environmentally Literate Are You?, Duke University – The Fuqua School of Business, 23.04.2019
Video 28: What we found on the Antarctic seafloor, Greenpeace UK, 23.02.2018
Video 30: produced by Creative Listening (https://www.creativelistening.co.uk). Producers Rachel Booth, Jackaby Barsby.

Classroom phrases

What your teacher can say
Can anyone remember … from our last session?
Who would like to explain?
What did you find out?
Don't interrupt each other.
Remember the advice about …
Can you think of any other tips?
Check your spelling in the dictionary.
Read and comment on each other's texts.
Compare your answers / solutions with a partner.
Make some notes about key points.
Give reasons for your opinion.
Read the text about … and be ready to talk about it in the next lesson.
Practise your talk at home or in front of your friends.

Working with a partner / in a group / in class
Would you like to join us?
Let's go through our notes.
I'd like to make a suggestion.
Do you have a spare pen?
Can I borrow your book for a second?
Is there anything you would like to add?
I disagree. / I don't agree.
I agree (but …).
I see what you mean, but …
How do you fel about …?
That's a good point.
It's my turn / your turn.
You have a point, but …
Could I just say …
Sorry to interrupt …
Go ahead.
I'm sorry, what did you say?
When you say …, what exactly do you mean?
So what you're saying is …
What I mean is …
Just let me explain …
Whose turn is it?

What you can say
What page are we on?
Can you write it on the board, please?
What does … mean?
What do you mean by …?
What's this in German / English?
Can you spell it, please?
Can you repeat the task, please?
I haven't finished the task yet.
I've already finished the task.
I've got something different.
Are we allowed to use our phones?
Can we do research on the internet?
Can we work with a partner / group?

Giving feedback
You did a great job.
I liked the part where you …
I had a feeling you really knew …
The visual aids were helpful.
The sound quality of your video is really clear.
I like the way you added …
What I really liked about your talk was that …
My favourite part was … because …
I think your presentation is good / interesting / funny because …
I like the way you used …
It really impressed me when you …
Can you say more about …, please?
My tip for you is to …
It would be better if you …
How about …?
Next time you should speak more clearly / loudly / slowly …
One suggestion would be …
Perhaps you should add …
Maybe you could include more information about …
You could also talk about …
I would like more descriptions of … / more information about … / more conversations between …

Media use	
Let's make a new document / slide.	Type the website address into the browser.
Copy / Insert the photo / text …	We need to refine our search.
Mark the text and copy it …	Let's read the information on the website …
Delete / Save the file.	Can you scroll up / down?
Let's share / post our blog / vlog online.	Click on the link.
We can drag and drop the files …	Let's watch the video.
Let's search for information online.	We should check the terms and conditions.
Let's go to the website.	We should bookmark our sources.

Useful phrases and operators

Add more words.	Füge weitere Wörter hinzu.
Analyse ...	Analysiere ...
Brainstorm ...	Brainstorme ...
Check ...	Überprüfe ...
Collect. ..	Sammle ...
Compare ...	Vergleiche ...
Complete ...	Vervollständige ...
Copy ...	Übertrage ...
Decide ...	Entscheide ...
Describe ...	Beschreibe ...
Discuss ...	Diskutiere ...
Do some research ...	Recherchiere ...
Draw a conclusion ...	Zieh eine Schlussfolgerung.
Exchange ...	Tauscht euch aus ...
Expand ...	Erweitere ...
Explain ...	Erkläre ...
Fill in ...	Fülle ... aus.
Form groups.	Bildet Gruppen.
Give reasons for your answer.	Begründe deine Antwort.
Give feedback.	Gib Feedback.
Listen to ...	Hör dir ... an.
Make a mind map / notes / poster / ...	Erstelle eine Mindmap / Notizen / ein Poster / ...
Match ...	Füge ... zusammen.
Outline ...	Skizziere ... / Erläutere ...
Point out ...	Stelle ... heraus.
Practise the dialogue.	Übt den Dialog ein.
Present ...	Präsentiere ... / Stelle ... vor.
Read the text.	Lies den Text.
Record ...	Nehmt ... auf...
Rehearse your dialogue.	Probt euren Dialog.
Report ...	Berichte ...
Scan the text for details.	Suche den Text nach Details ab.
Skim the text.	Überfliege den Text.
State ...	Führe aus ... / Gib an ...
Structure your text.	Strukturiere deinen Text.
Summarize ...	Fasse zusammen ...
Take notes.	Mach dir Notizen.
Take turns.	Wechselt euch ab.
Tell your partner about ...	Berichte deinem Partner / deiner Parterin von ...
Think of other examples.	Überlege dir weitere Beispiele.
Use the prompts / words from the box.	Verwende die Stichwörter / Wörter aus dem Kasten.
Write a dialogue / a report / a short summary.	Schreib einen Dialog / einen Bericht / eine kurze Zusammenfassung.

8016KX © Westermann
Canada
The United States of America
Mexico
Pacific Ocean
Atlantic Ocean
Gulf of Mexico
Rocky Mountains
Newfoundland and Labrador
Quebec
Ontario
Manitoba
Saskatchewan
Alberta
British Columbia
New Brunswick
Nova Scotia
Prince Edward Island
Edmonton
Calgary
Vancouver
Victoria
Regina
Winnipeg
Ottawa
Montreal
Quebec
Toronto
Fredericton
Halifax
Washington
Oregon
California
Nevada
Idaho
Montana
Wyoming
Utah
Colorado
Arizona
New Mexico
Texas
Oklahoma
Kansas
Nebraska
South Dakota
North Dakota
Minnesota
Iowa
Missouri
Wisconsin
Illinois
Michigan
Indiana
Ohio
Kentucky
Tennessee
Arkansas
Louisiana
Mississippi
Alabama
Georgia
Florida
South Carolina
North Carolina
Virginia
West Virginia
Pennsylvania
New York
Maine
Vermont
New Hampshire
Massachusetts
Rhode Island
Connecticut
New Jersey
Delaware
Maryland
Alaska
Hawaii
Seattle
Portland
San Francisco
San José
Fresno
Los Angeles
San Diego
Las Vegas
Phoenix
Tucson
Santa Fé
Albuquerque
El Paso
Denver
Oklahoma City
Dallas
Fort Worth
San Antonio
Houston
New Orleans
Memphis
Nashville
Atlanta
Charlotte
Charleston
Jacksonville
Miami
Louisville
Indianapolis
Columbus
Chicago
Milwaukee
Detroit
Cedar Rapids
Rochester
New York City
Philadelphia
Baltimore
Washington, D.C.
Boston
Lexington
Plymouth
Grand Canyon National Park
Colorado River
Monument Valley
Mount Rushmore
Independence Rock
Route 66
New England
The Mid-Atlantic
The South
The Midwest
The Southwest
The West
Capital cities of the U.S. and Canada
0
500 miles